I0864625

Time Out

London

timeout.com/london

Time Out Guides Ltd
Universal House
251 Tottenham Court Road
London W1T 7AB
United Kingdom
Tel: +44 (0)20 7813 3000
Fax: +44 (0)20 7813 6001
Email: guides@timeout.com
www.timeout.com

Published by Time Out Guides Ltd, a wholly owned subsidiary of Time Out Group Ltd.
Time Out and the Time Out logo are trademarks of Time Out Group Ltd.

10 9 8 7 6 5 4 3 2 1

This edition first published in Great Britain in 2010 by Ebury Publishing.
A Random House Group Company
20 Vauxhall Bridge Road, London SW1V 2SA

Random House Australia Pty Ltd 20 Alfred Street, Milsons Point, Sydney, New South Wales 2061, Australia

Random House New Zealand Ltd 18 Poland Road, Glenfield, Auckland 10, New Zealand

Random House South Africa (Pty) Ltd Isle of Houghton, Corner Boundary Road & Carse O'Gowrie, Houghton 2198, South Africa

Random House UK Limited Reg. No. 954009

For further distribution details, see www.timeout.com.

ISBN: 978-1-84670-165-8

A CIP catalogue record for this book is available from the British Library.

Printed and bound by Firmengruppe APPL, aprinta druck, Wemding, Germany.

The Random House Group Limited supports The Forest Stewardship Council (FSC), the leading international forest certification organisation. All our titles that are printed on Greenpeace approved FSC certified paper carry the FSC logo. Our paper procurement policy can be found at http://www.rbooks.co.uk/environment.

Time Out carbon-offsets its flights with Trees for Cities (www.treesforcities.org).

Contents

In Context   13

History	14
London Today	30
Architecture	34
Credit Crunch Culture	42

Sights   45

The South Bank & Bankside	46
The City	59
Holborn & Clerkenwell	75
Bloomsbury & Fitzrovia	78
Covent Garden & the Strand	84
Soho & Leicester Square	91
Oxford Street & Marylebone	97
Paddington & Notting Hill	103
Piccadilly Circus & Mayfair	105
Westminster & St James's	110
Chelsea	120
Knightsbridge & South Kensington	123
North London	128
East London	135
South-east London	143
South-west London	151
West London	158

Consume   165

Hotels	166
Restaurants & Cafés	198
Pubs & Bars	227
Shops & Services	242

Arts & Entertainment   269

Calendar	270
Children	278
Comedy	284
Dance	287
Film	290
Galleries	294
Gay & Lesbian	301
Music	308
Nightlife	321
Sport & Fitness	329
Theatre	337

Escapes & Excursions   347

Escapes & Excursions	348
Map: Escapes & Excursions	349

Directory   361

Getting Around	362
Resources A-Z	367
Further Reference	377
Index	379
Advertisers' Index	388

Maps   389

Overview Maps	390
Street Maps	394
London Underground	416

Introduction

Whatever you expect from this city, London is going to give you something different. You're looking for tradition? Shoreditch is full of tomorrow's music and art from the day after that, traditional pubs transformed into hip clubs, reckless hats and all manner of posing. You want a contemporary city? Less than a mile south of Shoreditch, gruff, scarlet-coated residents of a small 11th-century castle still guard the Crown Jewels. In between Shoreditch and the Tower of London, City bankers pocket the bonuses that accrue to the beneficiaries of modern international banking, yet turn out in thousands for the annual inauguration of the Square Mile's own Lord Mayor, paraded in a 250-year-old gold carriage through the original walled City that was the foundation of today's London.

The 2009 instalment of the Lord Mayor's Show wasn't a total success. For the first time in more than two decades, the traditional Thames firework display that follows the pageant had to be cancelled due to horrendous winds and rain. In light of the year's bitter recession, might this be an ill omen? Definitely not if you're coming to London on holiday: hotel prices have begun to fall, and the shops seem to be running an endless sale. Yes, a number of prized restaurants have closed, but the range of options and the displays of culinary skill that have survived the downturn still dazzle. And the capital's cultural riches – half a dozen world-class museums that charge nothing for entry, extraordinarily lively music, art, dance, theatre and nightclubs – seem untouchable. There are other cities in the world that rival London, but not many.

Perhaps you're returning to London? Much has changed. You could plug into the secret dining scene, for example, or find out what molecular gastronomy has done to cocktails. You could sleep in the designer's house in scruffy east London that's attracted artists and movie stars. Perhaps you're visiting London for the first time? Your only problem is working out what you can afford to miss. Which World Heritage Site gets crossed off the must-see list? Do you do the V&A or the British Museum? Where's best to sample modern British cooking? This book was put together to help you decide. Every word was written by locals who love their city, in the hope it might guide you to excellent adventures. *Simon Coppock, Editor*

London in Brief

IN CONTEXT

Recession is only the latest trauma to afflict London, a city that's survived more than 2,000 years of turbulence. From art squats to old buildings adapted for modern needs, the capital is meeting new challenges with renewed creativity, as we suggest in this series of features. We also consider how politics in London might prefigure wider changes, especially in relation to the funding of museums.
► *For more, see pp13-44.*

SIGHTS

Some of London's attractions write their own headlines: the world-renowned British Museum or the marvellous art at the riverside Tates. But such major sights come nowhere near accounting for the city's wealth of attractions: within these pages, you'll also find everything from ancient palaces to shiny new developments, quirky museums to expansive parks.
► *For more, see pp45-164.*

CONSUME

The British reputation for lousy cooking is no longer justified, as a visit to St John and its followers will prove, but whether you're eating, drinking or shopping, variety is the keynote. Smoothly elegant cocktail bars jostle with generations-old pubs, a traditional umbrella shop plies its trade not far from bleeding-edge boutiques, and the deluxe hotels and humble B&Bs are getting spruced up.
► *For more, see pp165-267.*

ARTS & ENTERTAINMENT

London's music scene is famously lively, with new venues such as Kings Place enhancing already stellar options. Head to Shoreditch for clubs and the best gay nights, and to pretty much anywhere in town for contemporary art. Add compelling theatre (both fringe and mainstream), viciously exciting comedy and uniquely hybrid dance shows, and you have a cultural scene that's second to none.
► *For more, see pp269-346.*

ESCAPES & EXCURSIONS

When trying to get round the innumerable attractions of London has started to feel too much like hard work, take a break. Breezy Brighton is an easy train ride from the city and nothing but cheery seaside fun; other escapes covered here range from austere Dungeness to the discreet joys of Cambridge, from medieval Canterbury to 100 casks of Sussex cider.
► *For more, see pp347-360.*

London in 48 Hours
Day 1 Trafalgar, Tradition and the Thames

10AM Start the day in **Trafalgar Square** (*see p110*). The centre of London is an impressive sight, especially when it's not too full of tourists snapping themselves with the lions. The masterpieces of the **National Gallery** (*see p110*) are on the square's pedestrianised northern side.

10.45AM Head south down Whitehall, keeping an eye out for the cavalryman on sentry duty. You should arrive in time to see Horse Guards with shiny swords and helmets go through the daily **Changing of the Guard** (*see p276* **Standing on Ceremony**; it's an hour earlier on Sunday). The **Household Cavalry Museum** (*see p118*) is just off the parade ground if you want to learn more; otherwise, head into **St James's Park** (*see p117*) to feed the ducks and admire **Buckingham Palace** (*see p117*) at the end of the lake. **Inn the Park** (*see p216*) is a convenient early stop-off if you're already peckish or flagging.

NOON Just out of the park's southern corner is Parliament Square. Admire the tobacco-yellow stone of **Westminster Abbey**, **Parliament** and **Big Ben** (*see pp113-115*), then cross Westminster Bridge for County Hall and the **London Eye** (*see p50*). This walk is modern London's biggest tourist cliché, but it's wonderful to stroll along the South Bank. Busy places to eat surround the **Southbank Centre** (*see p51*).

3PM Go with the flow past **BFI Southbank** (*see p292*) and the **National Theatre** (*see p339*) to **Tate Modern** (*see p55*) and **Shakespeare's Globe** (*see p54*), and finish your afternoon by crossing the Millennium Bridge for the slow climb up to **St Paul's Cathedral** (*see p63*), handily close to St Paul's tube station.

7PM Enough history and culture. Head north into Clerkenwell for brilliant food: modern British at **St John** (*see p203*) or Antipodean fusion at the **Modern Pantry** (*see p201*). If you're here at the weekend and you've still got some energy, join the queue for London's coolest superclub, **Fabric** (*see p323*).

NAVIGATING THE CITY
London is a wonderful place to visit, but its size can be overwhelming. Don't worry: with a little understanding of the geography and transport, not to mention reliable street maps (*see pp390-407*), it becomes much easier to navigate.

The tube is the most straightforward way to get around town – you're rarely far from a station in central London. Mix your tube journeys with bus rides to get a handle on London's topography; free bus maps are available at many tube stations and from the Britain & London Visitor Centre (*see p375*). And don't forget the river: commuter and tourist boats run all day on the Thames. For more on travel, *see pp362-366*; for our selection of guided tours, *see p366*.

SEEING THE SIGHTS
To escape queues and overcrowding, try to avoid visiting major attractions at the weekend – and using any form of public

Day 2 Culture and Clubbing from West to East

10AM Start at one of the world's finest museums – early enough to avoid the crowds. The **British Museum** (*see p79*) is so full of treasures you may not know where to begin, but turn left out of the spectacular central courtyard and the monumental antiquities won't disappoint.

NOON Wander south to the boutiques dotted around Seven Dials until lunch. **Great Queen Street** (*see p205*) is a good option if you didn't try St John last night; **Wahaca** (*see p207*) and **Food for Thought** (*see p205*) are handy on a budget. Covent Garden market is here, but the excellent **London Transport Museum** and the inspiringly opulent **Royal Opera House** (for both, *see p87*) are the principal reasons to linger.

3PM Covent Garden station puts you on the right tube line for South Kensington's trio of superb museums: at this time of day, the magnificent **Victoria & Albert Museum** (*see p127*) is quietest, but parents should let themselves be bullied into the **Natural History Museum** (*see p124*) or **Science Museum** (*see p125*). If there's still some walking left in you after yesterday, head to Hyde Park for the **Albert Memorial** (*see p124*) and Kensington Gardens for the understated **Serpentine Gallery** (*see p126*).

7PM By now, you'll need food. Take on a sturdy refuel at **Madsen** (*see p219*) or, if you're in the park, head to **Le Café Anglais** (*see p220*) or the cheaper **Kiasu** (*see p221*).

9PM Not quite ready to head back to the hotel? Grown-ups head a little further west: **Notting Hill Gate** is the place for civilised cocktailing (*see p233*). Hip kids and the young at heart should get to a tube station and take the Central (red) underground line east: Liverpool Street station is the gateway to bleakly nondescript **Shoreditch**. Yes, the edgiest and artiest are migrating north and east, but you'll still find enough exciting concept bars (*see p239*), trend-setting clubs (*see pp325-328*) and wispily mustachioed youths to give you a feel for what all the fuss has been about over the last decade.

transport during rush hour (8-9.30am and 4.30-7pm, Monday to Friday). Many attractions, including all the big museums, offer free admission, so if you're on a budget you can tick off large numbers of places on your must-see list just for the price of getting there.

We've given last-entry times where they precede an attraction's closing time by more than an hour. Some smaller venues may close early when they're quiet, and many places close all day on certain public holidays (notably Christmas). Call ahead before making a special trip.

PACKAGE DEALS

The **London Pass** (www.londonpass.com) gives pre-paid access to more than 50 sights and attractions. Unless you're prepared to visit several sights a day for four or five days, you're unlikely to get your money's worth. However, you will be able to jump the queues at such ultra-popular sights as the Tower of London.

London in Profile

THE SOUTH BANK & BANKSIDE
Running along the Thames from the London Eye to Gabriel's Wharf, the **South Bank** is the centre of the nation's arts scene. Directly east is **Bankside**, which has risen to prominence thanks to Tate Modern and Borough Market.
▶ *For more, see pp46-57.*

THE CITY
Reminders of London's long, ramshackle and occasionally great history jostle with latter-day citadels of high finance in the City, the fascinating 'square mile' (it's actually slightly over a mile) that essentially *was* London for centuries.
▶ *For more, see pp59-74.*

HOLBORN & CLERKENWELL
Just west of the City lie two different, distinct locales. Quietly historic **Clerkenwell** boasts some of London's best bars and restaurants. Adjacent **Holborn**, meanwhile, is the city's legal quarter, and sits on the fringes of London's West End.
▶ *For more, see pp75-77.*

BLOOMSBURY & FITZROVIA
North-west of Holborn, literary **Bloomsbury** draws millions to the British Museum, but the nearby, restaurant-packed area of **Fitzrovia** concerns itself only with its media-industry locals. North of Bloomsbury is fast-improving **King's Cross**.
▶ *For more, see pp78-83.*

COVENT GARDEN & THE STRAND
Covent Garden, just south of Bloomsbury, is a genuine visitor-magnet: tourists adore its open-plan piazza and wearingly cheery street entertainers. Between here and the Thames lies the traffic-choked, theatre-lined **Strand**.
▶ *For more, see pp84-90.*

SOHO & LEICESTER SQUARE
The hub of the West End, **Soho** is London's most notorious district. These days, it's far more civilised than its naughty reputation suggests, but is still fun to wander. Just south sit bustling **Chinatown** and touristy **Leicester Square**.
▶ *For more, see pp91-96.*

OXFORD STREET & MARYLEBONE
London's shoppers get to choose from countless different shopping areas, but chain-heavy **Oxford Street** is where most of the money is spent. Oxford Street separates Soho and Mayfair from Fitzrovia and **Marylebone**, an agreeably villagey district dotted with boutiques and restaurants.
▶ *For more, see pp97-102.*

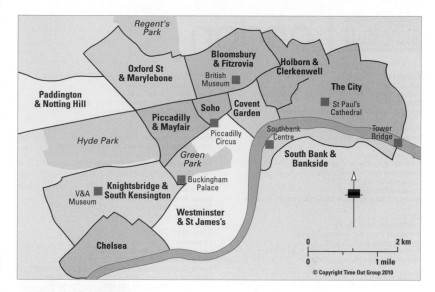

© Copyright Time Out Group 2010

PADDINGTON & NOTTING HILL
Millions have been spent improving north-westerly **Paddington** in recent years, but the area still lacks focus. It's better to head west to the market, bars and boutiques of **Notting Hill**.
▶ *For more, see pp103-104.*

PICCADILLY & MAYFAIR
The flashing neon beguiles small-town tourists, but **Piccadilly Circus** is little more than a charmless traffic island nowadays. Instead of lingering there, stroll west into **Mayfair**, home to London's most upmarket shops and prestigious hotels.
▶ *For more, see pp105-109.*

WESTMINSTER & ST JAMES'S
With the northern edge of Trafalgar Square pedestrianised, the centre of London is a pleasant place to be. Just south is historic **Westminster**, the home of government; go south-west and you'll reach immaculate, aristocratic **St James's**.
▶ *For more, see pp110-119.*

CHELSEA
Chelsea starts in earnest at Sloane Square, before stretching west and ebbing outwards off the shop-lined King's Road. Its southern border is the Thames.
▶ *For more, see pp120-122.*

KNIGHTSBRIDGE & SOUTH KENSINGTON
Knightsbridge draws devotees with a welter of high-class, high-priced shops. Adjoining **South Kensington** is where the throngs pile into London's three palatial Victorian museums.
▶ *For more, see pp123-127.*

Time Out London

Editorial

Editor Simon Coppock
Deputy Editors Will Fulford-Jones, Anna Norman
Copy Editor Patrick Welch
Listings Editors William Crow, Toby Pearce, Kohinoor Sahota
Proofreader Patrick Mulkern
Indexer Anna Norman

Managing Director Peter Fiennes
Editorial Director Ruth Jarvis
Series Editor Will Fulford-Jones
Business Manager Dan Allen
Editorial Manager Holly Pick
Assistant Management Accountant Ija Krasnikova

Design

Art Director Scott Moore
Art Editor Pinelope Kourmouzoglou
Senior Designer Henry Elphick
Graphic Designers Kei Ishimaru, Nicola Wilson
Advertising Designer Jodi Sher

Picture Desk

Picture Editor Jael Marschner
Deputy Picture Editor Lynn Chambers
Picture Researcher Gemma Walters
Picture Desk Assistant Ben Rowe
Picture Librarian Christina Theisen

Advertising

Commercial Director Mark Phillips
Sales Manager Alison Wallen
Advertising Sales Ben Holt, Jason Trotman
Copy Controller Alison Bourke

Marketing

Marketing Manager Yvonne Poon
Sales & Marketing Director, North America & Latin America Lisa Levinson
Senior Publishing Brand Manager Luthfa Begum
Art Director Anthony Huggins

Production

Group Production Director Mark Lamond
Production Manager Brendan McKeown
Production Controller Damian Bennett

Time Out Group

Chairman Tony Elliott
Chief Executive Officer David King
Group Financial Director Paul Rakkar
Group General Manager/Director Nichola Coulthard
Time Out Communications Ltd MD David Pepper
Time Out International Ltd MD Cathy Runciman
Time Out Magazine Ltd Publisher/MD Mark Elliott
Group IT Director Simon Chappell
Marketing & Circulation Director Catherine Demajo

Contributors

Introduction Simon Coppock. **History** Simon Coppock (*Time Machine* Museum of London; *Plaque Attack* Peter Watts). **London Today** Peter Watts. **Architecture** Simon Coppock (*Spotter's Guide* Simon Coppock, Peter Watts). **Credit Crunch Culture** Peter Watts. **Sights** Simon Coppock, Charlie Godfrey-Faussett, Chris Hunt, Peter Watts (*Profile: London Eye* Ronnie Haydon; *Profile: Museum of London, Walk: The 21st-Century City, Walk: Lit Stops, The Art of Memory, Profile: V&A Museum* Peter Watts; *Garden City, Police Tactics, Snapshot* Simon Coppock; *Glad to Be Gay* Patrick Welch; *Walk: Back to the Back Streets* Helen Walasek; *Shakespeare in Shoreditch, Snapshot* Sally Harrild; *Overground to the Underground* Nuala Calvi). **Hotels** Simon Coppock, Peterjon Cresswell, Charlie Godfrey-Faussett, Ronnie Haydon, Anna Norman, Patrick Welch (*Pushing the Boundary, Playing House* Simon Coppock). **Restaurants & Cafés** contributors to *Time Out Eating & Drinking* (*Eating In… and Eating Out, Do You Want to Know a Secret?, The Art of Cooking* Charmaine Mok). **Pubs & Bars** contributors to *Time Out Bars, Pubs & Clubs* (*In the Mix* Charlie Godfrey-Faussett; *Profile: Sambrook's Brewery* Guy Dimond). **Shops & Services** Anna Norman (*Top of the Shops* Patrick Welch). **Calendar** Sally Harrild, Anna Norman (*Standing on Ceremony* Charlie Godfrey-Faussett; *Small is Beautiful* Anna Norman). **Children** Anna Norman. **Comedy** Patrick Welch (*Stand Up to Be Counted* Tim Arthur). **Dance** Lyndsey Winship. **Film** John Watson. **Galleries** Martin Coomer. **Gay & Lesbian** Patrick Welch (*Dressing Up, Getting Out* Simone Baird). **Music** Chris Parkin. **Nightlife** Simone Baird. **Sport & Fitness** Simon Coppock, Patrick Welch (*Ride: Cycle the Sights* Simone Baird). **Theatre** Nuala Calvi. **Escapes & Excursions** Anna Norman & contributors to *Time Out Great Days Out* (*Country Flavours* Maisie Tomlinson). **Directory** Simon Coppock, Anna Norman, Peter Watts.

The Editor would like to thank all contributors to previous editions of *Time Out London* and *Time Out* magazine, whose work forms the basis for parts of this booK.

Maps john@jsgraphics.co.uk.

Photography Michelle Grant, except: pages 3, 9 (bottom), 361 Olivia Rutherford; pages 4, 8 (bottom), 9, 128, 132, 165, 199, 234, 252, 259, 280, 341, 347, 348, 357 Britta Jaschinski; pages 5 (top), 8 (second top right), 9 (top), 77, 92, 93, 96, 107, 114, 136, 129, 171 (top), 182, 284, 285, 290, 295, 308, 324, 350, 353 Jonathan Perugia; pages 5 (bottom), 8 (top right), 30, 31, 54, 79, 82, 85, 205, 207, 208, 229, 231, 233, 238, 286, 350 (top right), 329 Rob Greig; pages 6, 8 (top and bottom left), 40, 50 (bottom), 88 (left), 104, 111, 158 Andrew Brackenbury; pages 7, 66, 133, 279, 301, 305 Heloise Bergman; pages 13, 34, 35, 36, 61, 102, 195 Ben Rowe; page 14 The Bridgeman Art Library; page 19 Rob Greig/Peter Watts; page 23 Mary Evans Picture Library; pages 25, 293, 333 Getty Images; page 42 Craig Deane; pages 44, 150, 278, 281 Elisabeth Blanchet; pages 47, 223 Ming Tang-Evans; page 50 (top) Matt Writtle; page 55 Simon Leigh; page 56 Abigail Lelliott; pages 76, 274 Nick Ballon; page 81 Trustees of the British Museum; pages 88 (right), 156 Susie Rea; page 90 Simon Leigh; page 112 Christina Theisen; page 115 Leon Chew; pages 118, 119, 271 Martyn J Brooks; pages 121, 174, 242, 248, 249 Emma Wood; pages 124, 237 (top) Michael Franke; pages 135, 197, 221, 230, 232, 303 (right) Alys Tomlinson; page 146 Tove K Breitstein; pages 149, 358 Nerida Howard; page 152 Andreas Schmidt; page 171 (bottom) Heike Bohnstengel; page 198 Steven Atkinson; page 200 Jitka Hynkova; page 217 Matthew Booth; pages 243, 254 Damian O'Hara; page 269 John Persson; page 270 Marzena Zoladz; page 273 Alex de Mora; page 283 Gary Mulcahey; page 287 Bill Cooper; page 298 Henry Elphick; page 304 Efie Tsitsopoulou; page 315 Adrian Panucci; page 318 James Quinton; page 341 Tristram Kenton. The following images were provided by the featured establishments/artists: pages 267, 277, 306, 314, 317, 345.

About the Guide

GETTING AROUND
The back of the book contains street maps of London, as well as overview maps of the city and its surroundings. The maps start on page 389; on them are marked the locations of hotels (**❶**), restaurants and cafés (**❶**), and pubs and bars (**❶**). The majority of businesses listed in this guide are located in the areas we've mapped; the grid-square references in the listings refer to these maps.

THE ESSENTIALS
For practical information, including visas, disabled access, emergency numbers, lost property, useful websites and local transport, please see the Directory. It begins on page 362.

THE LISTINGS
Addresses, phone numbers, websites, transport information, hours and prices are all included in our listings, as are selected other facilities. All were checked and correct at press time. However, business owners can alter their arrangements at any time, and fluctuating economic conditions can cause prices to change rapidly.

The very best venues in the city, the must-sees and must-dos in every category, have been marked with a red star (★). In the Sights chapters, we've also marked venues with free admission with a **FREE** symbol.

PHONE NUMBERS
The area code for London is 020. You don't need to use the code when calling from within London: simply dial the eight-digit number as listed in this guide.

From outside the UK, dial your country's international access code (011 from the US) or a plus symbol, followed by the UK country code (44), 20 for London (dropping the initial zero) and the eight-digit number as listed in the guide. So, to reach the British Museum, dial +44 20 7323 8000. For more on phones, including information on calling abroad from the UK and details of local mobile-phone access, *see p374*.

FEEDBACK
We welcome feedback on this guide, both on the venues we've included and on any other locations that you'd like to see featured in future editions. Please email us at guides@timeout.com.

Time Out Guides

Founded in 1968, Time Out has grown from humble beginnings into the leading resource for anyone wanting to know what's happening in the world's greatest cities. Alongside our influential weeklies in London, New York and Chicago, we publish more than 20 magazines in cities as varied as Beijing and Beirut; a range of travel books, with the City Guides now joined by the newer Shortlist series; and an information-packed website. The company remains proudly independent, still owned by Tony Elliott four decades after he launched *Time Out London*.

Written by local experts and illustrated with original photography, our books also retain their independence. No business has been featured because it has advertised, and all restaurants and bars are visited and reviewed anonymously.

ABOUT THE EDITOR
Based in east London, **Simon Coppock** has edited a variety of books about London for Time Out, and has also written travel pieces on his favourite city for the *Sunday Times* and the *Sunday Telegraph*.

A full list of the book's contributors can be found opposite. However, we've also included details of our writers in selected chapters through the guide.

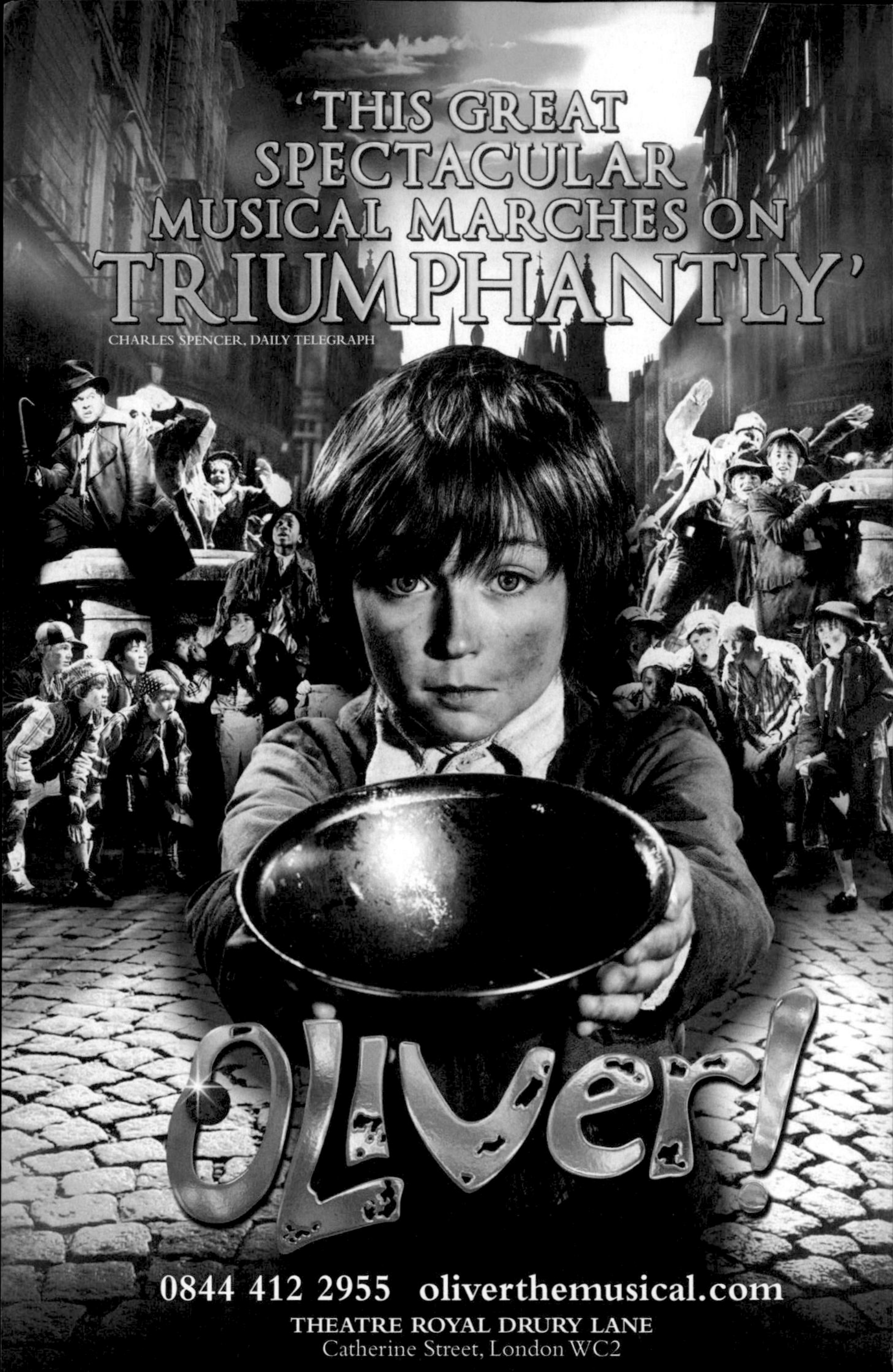
'THIS GREAT SPECTACULAR MUSICAL MARCHES ON TRIUMPHANTLY'
CHARLES SPENCER, DAILY TELEGRAPH
Oliver!
0844 412 2955 oliverthemusical.com
THEATRE ROYAL DRURY LANE
Catherine Street, London WC2

In Context

St Pancras International. *See p39.*

History	14
Time Machine AD 290s	15
Time Machine 1210s	17
Time Machine 1480s	18
Plaque Attack	19
Time Machine 1830s	24
Time Machine 1910s	27
Key Events	29

London Today	**30**

Architecture	**34**
Spotter's Guide to Tudor Windows	35
Spotter's Guide to Baroque Spires	36
Spotter's Guide to Art Deco	39
Spotter's Guide to City Skyscrapers	40

Credit Crunch Culture	**42**

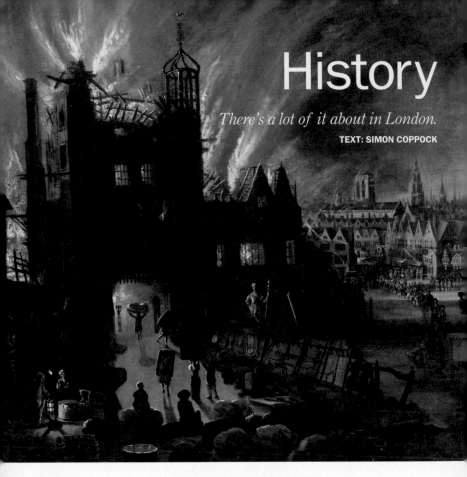

History

There's a lot of it about in London.

TEXT: SIMON COPPOCK

Over the last 2,000 years, London has faced plagues and invasions, fires and wars, religious turbulence and financial turmoil. It hasn't always emerged smiling from its troubles, but the city's inhabitants pride themselves on the fact that somehow it has always emerged.

Looking back, London's history seems fundamentally cyclical. Wars and acts of terrorism are borne with stoicism, then peace is welcomed in a frenzy of commerce. Once-beloved leaders are cruelly dismissed, then their departure lamented. Booms beget depressions beget booms. More than anything, this city's past is a tale of resilience, of locals grinning while bearing their burdens of disaster.

From Blitz-blackened Wren churches in the City, built out of the ruins of the Great Fire, to a fragment of glass deeply embedded in a wall at the Old Bailey, evidence of centuries of strife is everywhere. There's surely more to come, but don't bet against this city handling it with aplomb.

LATIN LESSONS

The city's origins are hardly grand. Celtic tribes lived in scattered communities along the banks of the Thames before the Romans arrived in Britain, but there's no evidence of a settlement on the site of the future metropolis before the invasion of the Emperor Claudius in AD 43. During the Roman conquest, they forded the Thames at its shallowest point (probably near today's London Bridge) and, later, built a timber bridge there. A settlement developed on the north side of this crossing.

Over the next two centuries, the Romans built roads, towns and forts in the area. Progress was halted in AD 61 when Boudicca, the widow of an East Anglian chieftain, rebelled against the imperial forces who had seized her land, flogged her and raped her daughters. She led the Iceni in a revolt, destroying the Roman colony at Colchester before marching on London. The Romans were massacred and their settlement razed.

After order was restored, the town was rebuilt; around AD 200, a two-mile, 18-foot wall was put up around it. Chunks of the wall survive today; the early names of the original gates – Ludgate, Newgate, Bishopsgate and Aldgate – are preserved on the map of the modern city, with the street known as London Wall tracing part of its original course. But through to the fourth century, racked by invasions and internal strife, the Roman Empire was clearly in decline (*see below* **Time Machine**). In 410, the last troops were withdrawn, and London became a ghost town.

INTO THE DARK

During the fifth and sixth centuries, history gives way to legend. The Saxons crossed the North Sea; apparently avoiding the ruins of London, they built farmsteads and trading posts outside the city walls. Pope Gregory sent Augustine to convert the English to Christianity in 596; Mellitus, one of his missionaries, was appointed the first Bishop of London, founding a cathedral dedicated to St Paul inside the old city walls in 604.

From this period, the history of London is one of expansion. Writing in 731, the Venerable Bede described 'Lundenwic' as 'the mart of many nations resorting to it by land and sea' Yet the city faced a new danger during the ninth century: the Vikings. The city was ransacked in 841 and again in 851, when Danish raiders returned with 350 ships. It was not until 886 that King Alfred of Wessex, Alfred the Great, regained the city, re-establishing London as a major trading centre.

Throughout the tenth century the city prospered. Churches were built, parishes established and markets set up. However, the 11th century brought more harassment from the Vikings, and the English were forced to accept a Danish king, Cnut (Canute, 1016-35), during whose reign London replaced Winchester as the capital of England.

Time Machine AD 290s

By Jenny Hall, Roman curator at the Museum of London.

Who's in control? Carausius declares Home Rule for Britain in AD 293 and makes London his base; Constantius Chlorus, junior emperor of the Roman Empire, is charged with returning Britain to Roman control

Average wage Unskilled labourer, 25 to 50 silver denarii a day

Life expectancy 26 to 45

Key concerns How long could this unofficial empire last? What would happen to Londoners who sided with Carausius and Allectus if the Roman Empire won back Britain?

Local legislation Coins are minted in London for the first time after a period of rampant inflation

Flash point Allectus assassinates Carausius, giving Constantius the opportunity to make a two-pronged attack from the sea and save London from Allectus's rebel army in AD 296

TIME TO VISIT GREENWICH
THREE MUSEUMS FOR FREE
ONE BREATHTAKING VIEW
Just 20 minutes from central London

Museums open daily

 Cutty Sark Zone 2    Greenwich Zone 2    Greenwich Pier

Maritime GREENWICH
A WORLD HERITAGE SITE

MNATIONAL
MARITIME
MUSEUM

OROYAL
OBSERVATORY
GREENWICH

QTHE
QUEEN'S HOUSE
GREENWICH

nmm.ac.uk

After a brief spell under Danish rule, the country reverted to English control in 1042 under Edward the Confessor, who devoted himself to building England's grandest church two miles west of the City on an island in the river marshes at Thorney: 'the West Minster' (Westminster Abbey, *see p115*). Just a week after the consecration, he died. London now had two hubs: Westminster, centre of the royal court, government and law; and the City of London, centre of commerce.

On Edward's death, foreigners took over. Duke William of Normandy was crowned king on Christmas Day 1066, having defeated Edward's brother-in-law Harold at the Battle of Hastings. The pragmatic Norman resolved to win over the City merchants by negotiation rather than force, and in 1067 granted the burgesses and the Bishop of London a charter – still available to researchers in the London Metropolitan Archives – that acknowledged their rights and independence in return for taxes. He also ordered strongholds to be built at the city wall 'against the fickleness of the vast and fierce population', including the White Tower (the tallest building in the Tower of London; *see p74*) and the now-lost Baynard's Castle that stood at Blackfriars.

PARLIAMENT AND RIGHTS

In 1295, the Model Parliament, held at Westminster Hall by Edward I and attended by barons, clergy and representatives of knights and burgesses, agreed the principles of English government. The first step towards establishing personal rights and political liberty, not to mention curbing the power of the king, had already been taken in 1215 with the signing of the Magna Carta by King John (*see below* **Time Machine**). Then, in the 14th century, subsequent assemblies gave rise to the House of Lords and the House of Commons. During the 12th and 13th centuries, the king and his court travelled the kingdom, but the Palace of Westminster was now the permanent seat of law and government; noblemen and bishops began to build palatial houses along the Strand from the City to Westminster, with gardens stretching down to the river.

Relations between the monarch and the City were never easy. Londoners guarded their privileges, and resisted attempts by kings to squeeze money out of them to finance wars and construction projects. Subsequent kings were forced to turn to Jewish and Lombard moneylenders, but the City merchants were as intolerant of foreigners as of the royals. Rioting, persecution and lynching were common in medieval London.

The self-regulation privileges granted to the City merchants under Norman kings were extended by the monarchs who followed – in return for finance. In 1191, the City of London was recognised by Richard I as a self-governing community; six years later, it won control of the Thames. King John had in 1215 confirmed the city's right 'to elect every year a mayor', a position of authority with power over the Sheriff and the Bishop of London. A month later, the mayor joined the rebel barons in signing the Magna Carta.

Over the next two centuries, the power and influence of the trade and craft guilds (later known as the City Livery Companies) increased as dealings with Europe grew. The City's markets drew produce from miles around: livestock at Smithfield, fish at

IN CONTEXT

Time Machine 1210s

By Jackie Keily, medieval curator at the Museum of London.

Who's in control? Nominally King John
Average wage Unskilled labourer, 2d a day; skilled craftsman, 3d to 5d a day
Key concerns Fire, fighting, Frenchmen
Local legislation After a Southwark fire in 1212, straw roofs are banned

Flash point In 1215, Londoners side with the barons against King John; and in 1216, they support Prince Louis of France when he arrives in the city. Never crowned king, Louis is defeated at the battle of Lincoln in 1217

Billingsgate, poultry at Leadenhall. The street markets ('cheaps') around Westcheap (now Cheapside) and Eastcheap were crammed with a variety of goods. As commerce increased, foreign traders and craftsmen settled around the port; the population within the city walls grew from about 18,000 in 1100 to well over 50,000 in the 1340s.

WAKE UP AND SMELL THE ISSUE

Lack of hygiene became a serious problem. Water was provided in cisterns, but the supply, more or less direct from the Thames, was limited and polluted. The street of Houndsditch was so named because Londoners threw their dead animals into the furrow there; in the streets around Smithfield (the Shambles), butchers dumped entrails into the gutters. These conditions helped foster the greatest catastrophe of the Middle Ages: the Black Death of 1348 and 1349, which killed about 30 per cent of England's population. The plague came to London from Europe, carried by rats on ships, and was to recur in London several times during the next three centuries.

Disease left the harvests short-handed, causing unrest among the peasants whose labour was in such demand. The imposition of a poll tax of a shilling a head proved the final straw, leading to the Peasants' Revolt of 1381. Thousands marched on London, led by Jack Straw from Essex and Wat Tyler from Kent; the Archbishop of Canterbury was murdered and hundreds of prisoners were set free. After meeting the Essexmen near Mile End, the 14-year-old Richard II rode out to the rioters at Smithfield and spoke with Tyler. During their discussion, Tyler was fatally stabbed by the Lord Mayor; the revolt collapsed and the ringleaders were hanged. But no more poll taxes were imposed.

ROSES, WIVES AND BLOODY MARY

Its growth spurred by the discovery of America and the opening of ocean routes to Africa and the Orient, London became one of Europe's largest cities under the Tudors (1485-1603). The first Tudor monarch, Henry VII, had ended the Wars of the Roses by might, defeating Richard III at the Battle of Bosworth, and policy, marrying Elizabeth of York, a daughter of his rivals (*see below* **Time Machine**). By the time his son took the throne, the Tudor dynasty was firmly established. But progress under Henry VIII was not without its hiccups. His first marriage to Catherine of Aragon failed to produce an heir, so in 1527 he determined the union should be annulled. When the Pope refused to co-operate, Henry defied the Catholic Church, demanding to be recognised as Supreme Head of the Church in England and ordering the execution of anyone who

IN CONTEXT

Time Machine 1480s

By Jackie Keily, medieval curator at the Museum of London.

Who's in control? Complicated! Four kings in three years: Edward IV and his son, Edward V, both die in 1483 and are succeeded by Edward IV's brother Richard III, who in turn is defeated and killed at the Battle of Bosworth in 1485 by Henry Tudor, who becomes Henry VII
Average wage Unskilled labourer, 4d a day
Unusual imports In 1480-81, Portuguese ships bring 300,000 oranges; a single Venetian galley brings a mixed cargo including coral beads, pepper, sponges, ginger, satin, silk, Corinth raisons and two apes
Key concerns Avoiding major unrest
Local legislation In 1484, statutes are passed to stop the importation of certain foreign manufactured goods, so as to protect local jobs
Flash point In June 1483, London supports Richard III as king instead of the imprisoned 12-year-old Edward V. The young prince, one of the 'Princes in the Tower', never leaves the Tower of London (*see p74*)

Plaque Attack

London's walls commemorate notables who once lived within them.

The first blue plaque celebrating a notable Londoner was erected in 1867, when the Royal Society of Arts put up a memorial at the (now-demolished) birthplace of Lord Byron. The low-key scheme found increased popularity under the auspices of the London County Council (1901-65) and the Greater London Council (1965-85); when the GLC was shut, the scheme passed to English Heritage (www.english-heritage.org.uk). To be eligible for consideration for a blue plaque, a person must have been dead for 20 years or born more than a century ago (so, for instance, nothing yet celebrating Paul McCartney), and a building associated with them must survive (which is why there's no blue plaque honouring Shakespeare).

The popularity of the scheme has been such that it's spawned imitators. Some are operated by councils: Westminster City Council has a green plaque scheme, while Camden prefers brown and Southwark favours a rich, dark blue. And they aren't all round: the City of London goes for square plaques, while Croydon has a nice green oval. Other schemes are run by groups such as Equity and the British Film Institute, and some companies have got in on the act: HMV unveiled one after they left their old Oxford Street store, while Bentley erected one for the first car they produced (near Baker Street). There's even a black plaque: on Porchester Square, for Szmul Zygielbojm, a Polish trade unionist who killed himself 'nearby' in 1943 in despair at the world's indifference to Jewish suffering.

Many plaques look official but aren't: check out the perfect tones and font of the blue plaque to 'film-maker Monty Python' above the comic troupe's old HQ in Neal's Yard. There are even plaques to fictional characters, such as Great Russell Street's tribute to Charles Kitterbell from Charles Dickens' *Sketches by Boz*. Dickens, incidentally, is London's most plaqued resident: there are ten devoted to him, erected by the LCC, the Dickens Fellowship, Southwark Council and Haringey Council. Some have even been privately erected, either by local enthusiasts or by businesses hoping to improve the value and prestige of their property.

IN CONTEXT

opposed the plan (including Sir Thomas More, his otherwise loyal chancellor). The subsequent dissolution of the monasteries transformed the face of the medieval city.

When not transforming the politico-religious landscape, Henry found time to develop a professional navy, founding the Royal Dockyards at Woolwich in 1512. He also established palaces at Hampton Court (*see p157*) and Whitehall, and built a residence at St James's Palace. Much of the land he annexed for hunting became today's Royal Parks, among them Greenwich Park, Hyde Park and Regent's Park.

RENAISSANCE MEANS REBIRTH

Elizabeth I's reign (1558-1603) saw the founding of the Royal Exchange in 1566, which enabled London to emerge as Europe's commercial hub. Merchant venturers and the first joint-stock companies established new trading enterprises, as pioneering seafarers Francis Drake, Walter Raleigh and Richard Hawkins sailed to the New World. As trade

'For all its devastation, the Great Fire of 1666 at least allowed planners the chance to rebuild London as a modern city.'

grew, so did London: it was home to some 200,000 people in 1600, many living in dirty, overcrowded conditions. The most complete picture of Tudor London is given in John Stow's *Survey of London* (1598), a fascinating first-hand account by a diligent Londoner whose monument stands in the church of St Andrew Undershaft.

These were the glory days of English drama. The Rose (1587) and the Globe (1599, now recreated; *see p54*) were erected at Bankside, providing homes for the works of popular playwrights Christopher Marlowe and William Shakespeare. Deemed officially 'a naughty place' by royal proclamation, 16th-century Bankside was a vibrant mix of entertainment and 'sport' (bear-baiting, cock-fighting), drinking and whoring – and all within easy reach of the City, which had outlawed theatres in 1575.

In 1605, two years after the Tudor dynasty ended with Elizabeth's death, her Stuart successor, James I, escaped assassination on 5 November, when Guy Fawkes was found underneath the Palace of Westminster. Commemorated with fireworks each year as Bonfire Night, the Gunpowder Plot was hatched in protest at the failure to improve conditions for the persecuted Catholics, but only resulted in an intensification of anti-papist sentiment. James I is more positively remembered for hiring Inigo Jones to design court masques (musical dramas) and London's first influential examples of the classical Renaissance architectural style: the Queen's House (1616; *see p148*), the Banqueting House (1619; *see p113*) and St Paul's Covent Garden (1631; *see p87*).

ROYALISTS AND ROUNDHEADS
Charles I succeeded his father in 1625, but gradually fell out of favour with the City of London and an increasingly independent-minded Parliament over taxation. The country slid into civil war (1642-49), the supporters of Parliament (the Roundheads, led by Puritan Oliver Cromwell) opposing the supporters of the king (the Royalists).

Both sides knew that control of the country's major city and port was vital for victory, and London's sympathies were with the Parliamentarians. In 1642, 24,000 citizens assembled at Turnham Green to face Charles's army, but the king withdrew. The move proved fatal: Charles never threatened the capital again, and was eventually found guilty of treason. Taken to the Banqueting House in Whitehall on 30 January 1649, he declared himself a 'martyr of the people' and was beheaded. A commemorative wreath is still laid at the site of the execution on the last Sunday in January each year.

For the next decade, the country was ruled as a Commonwealth by Cromwell. But his son Richard's subsequent rule was brief: due to the Puritans closing theatres and banning Christmas (a Catholic superstition), the Restoration of the exiled Charles II in 1660 was greeted with great rejoicing. The Stuart king had Cromwell exhumed from Westminster Abbey, and his body was hung in chains at Tyburn (near modern-day Marble Arch). His severed head was displayed on a pole outside the abbey until 1685.

PLAGUE, FIRE AND REVOLUTION
The year 1665 saw the most serious outbreak of bubonic plague since the Black Death, killing nearly 100,000. Then, on 2 September 1666, a second disaster struck. The fire that spread from a carelessly tended oven in Thomas Farriner's baking shop on Pudding Lane raged for three days and consumed four-fifths of the City.

The Great Fire at least allowed planners the chance to rebuild London as a modern city. Many blueprints were considered, but Londoners were so impatient to get on with

IN CONTEXT

business that the City was reconstructed largely on its medieval street plan (albeit in brick and stone rather than wood). The prolific Sir Christopher Wren oversaw work on 51 of the 54 rebuilt churches. Among them was his masterpiece: the new St Paul's (see p63), completed in 1710 and effectively the world's first Protestant cathedral.

In the wake of the Great Fire, many well-to-do City dwellers moved to new residential developments west of the old quarters, an area subsequently known as the West End. In the City, the Royal Exchange was rebuilt, but merchants increasingly used the new coffeehouses to exchange news. With the expansion of the joint-stock companies and the chance to invest capital, the City emerged as a centre not of manufacturing but of finance. Even at this early stage, economic instability was common: the 1720 financial disaster known as the South Sea Bubble ruined even Sir Isaac Newton.

Anti-Catholic feeling still ran high. The accession in 1685 of Catholic James II aroused such fears of a return to papistry that a Dutch Protestant, William of Orange, was invited to take the throne with his wife, Mary Stuart (James's daughter). James fled to France in 1688 in what became known (by its beneficiaries) as the 'Glorious Revolution'. It was during William's reign that the Bank of England was founded, initially to finance the king's religious wars with France.

CREATION OF THE PRIME MINISTER

In 1714, the throne passed to George, the Hanover-born great-grandson of James I. The German-speaking king (he never learned English) became the first of four long-reigning Georges in the Hanoverian line.

During George I's reign (1714-27), and for several years after, Sir Robert Walpole's Whig party monopolised Parliament. Their opponents, the Tories, supported the Stuarts and had opposed the exclusion of the Catholic James II. On the king's behalf, Walpole chaired a group of ministers (the forerunner of today's Cabinet), becoming, in effect, Britain's first prime minister. Walpole was presented with 10 Downing Street (built by Sir George Downing) as a residence; it remains the official prime-ministerial home.

During the 18th century, London grew with astonishing speed. New squares and terraced streets spread across Soho, Bloomsbury, Mayfair and Marylebone, as wealthy landowners and speculative developers cashed in on the new demand for leasehold properties. South London also became more accessible with the opening of the first new bridges for centuries: Westminster Bridge (opened 1750) and Blackfriars Bridge (completed 1769) joined London Bridge, previously the only Thames crossing.

GIN-SOAKED POOR, NASTY RICH

In London's older districts, people were lived in terrible squalor. Some of the most notorious slums were located around Fleet Street and St Giles's (north of Covent Garden), only a short distance from fashionable residences. To make matters worse, gin ('mother's ruin') was readily available at low prices; many poor Londoners drank excessive amounts in an attempt to escape the horrors of daily life. The well-off seemed complacent, amusing themselves at the popular Ranelagh and Vauxhall Pleasure Gardens or with trips to mock the patients at the Bedlam lunatic asylum. Public executions at Tyburn were popular events in the social calendar; it's said that 200,000 people gathered to see the execution (after he had escaped from prison four times) of the folk-hero thief Jack Sheppard in 1724.

The outrageous imbalance in the distribution of wealth encouraged crime, and there were daring daytime robberies in the West End. Reformers were few, though there were exceptions. Henry Fielding, author of the picaresque novel Tom Jones, was also an enlightened magistrate at Bow Street Court. In 1751, he and his blind half-brother John set up a volunteer force of 'thief-takers' to back up the often ineffective efforts of the parish constables and watchmen who were, until then, the city's only law-keepers. This crime-busting group of early cops, known as the Bow Street Runners, were the forerunners of today's Metropolitan Police (established in 1829).

Theatregoers at the **Globe**. *See p21.*

Meanwhile, five major new hospitals were founded by private philanthropists. St Thomas's and St Bartholomew's were long-established monastic institutions for the care of the sick, but Westminster (1720), Guy's (1725), St George's (1734), London (1740) and the Middlesex (1745) went on to become world-famous teaching hospitals. Thomas Coram's Foundling Hospital (*see p81*) was another remarkable achievement.

INDUSTRY AND CAPITAL GROWTH

It wasn't just the indigenous population of London that was on the rise. Country folk, whose common land had been replaced by sheep enclosures, were faced with a choice between starvation wages or unemployment, and so drifted into the towns. Just outside the old city walls, the East End drew many poor immigrant labourers to build the docks towards the end of the 18th century. London's total population had grown to one million by 1801, the largest of any city in Europe. By 1837, when Queen Victoria came to the throne (*see p24* **Time Machine**), five more bridges and the capital's first passenger railway (from Greenwich to London Bridge) gave hints of huge expansion.

As well as being the administrative and financial capital of the British Empire, London was its chief port and the world's largest manufacturing centre. On one hand, it had splendid buildings, fine shops, theatres and museums; on the other, it was a city of poverty, pollution and disease. Residential areas were polarised into districts of fine terraces maintained by squads of servants and overcrowded, insanitary slums.

The growth of the metropolis in the century before Victoria came to the throne had been spectacular, but during her reign (1837-1901), thousands more acres were covered with roads, houses and railway lines. If you visit a street within five miles of central London, its houses will be mostly Victorian. By the end of the 19th century, the city's population had swelled to more than six million, an incredible growth of five million in just 100 years.

Despite social problems, memorably depicted in the writings of Charles Dickens, steps were being taken to improve conditions for the majority of Londoners by the turn of the century. The Metropolitan Board of Works installed an efficient sewerage system, street lighting and better roads. The worst slums were replaced by low-cost building schemes funded by philanthropists such as the American George Peabody, whose Peabody Donation Fund continues to provide subsidised housing to the working classes). The London County Council (created in 1888) also helped to house the poor.

The Victorian expansion would not have been possible without an efficient public transport network with which to speed workers into and out of the city from the new suburbs. The horse-drawn bus appeared on London's streets in 1829, but it was the opening of the first passenger railway seven years later that heralded the commuters of the future. The first underground line, which ran between Paddington and Farringdon Road, opened in 1863 and proved an instant success, attracting 30,000 travellers on the first day. The world's first electric track in a deep tunnel – the 'tube' – opened in 1890 between the City and Stockwell, later becoming part of the Northern line.

THE CRYSTAL PALACE

If any single event symbolised this period of industry, science, discovery and invention, it was the Great Exhibition of 1851. Prince Albert, the Queen's Consort, helped organise the triumphant showcase, for which the Crystal Palace, a vast building of iron and glass was erected in Hyde Park. It looked like a giant greenhouse; hardly surprising as it was designed not by a professional architect but by the Duke of Devonshire's gardener, Joseph Paxton. Condemned by art critic John Ruskin as the model of dehumanisation in design, the Palace came to be presented as the prototype of modern architecture. During the five months it was open, the Exhibition drew six million visitors. The profits were used by the Prince Consort to establish a permanent centre for the study of the applied arts and sciences; the enterprise survives today in the South Kensington museums of natural history, science, and decorative and applied arts (*see pp124-6*), and in three colleges (of art, music and science). After the Exhibition, the Palace was moved to Sydenham and used as an exhibition centre until it burned down in 1936.

ZEPPELINS ATTACK FROM THE SKIES

London entered the 20th century as the capital of the largest empire in history. Its wealth and power were there for all to see in grandstanding monuments such as Tower Bridge (*see p74*) and the Midland Grand Hotel at St Pancras Station (*see p83*), both of which married the retro stylings of High Gothic with modern iron and steel technology. During the brief reign of Edward VII (1901-10), London regained some of the gaiety and glamour it had lacked in the later years of Victoria's reign. Parisian chic came to London with the opening of the Ritz (*see p109*); Regent Street's Café Royal hit the heights as a meeting place for artists and writers; gentlemen's clubs proliferated; and 'luxury catering for the little man' was provided at the new Lyons Corner Houses (the Coventry Street branch held 4,500 people).

Road transport, too, was revolutionised. By 1911, horse-drawn buses were abandoned, replaced by the motor cars, which put-putted around the city's streets, and the motor bus, introduced in 1904. Disruption came in the form of devastating air raids

---

Time Machine 1830s

By Alex Werner, head of history at the Museum of London.

Who's in control? In 1837, 18-year-old Queen Victoria arrives on the throne. Prime Minister Lord Melbourne holds together a divided cabinet and mentors the young queen, who turned a blind eye to past indiscretions (and his wife's infamous affair with Lord Byron)
Population About two million

Average wage Tailor, 5s a day; about half the female labour force are servants
Key concerns Stopping cholera: many die in epidemics during the 1830s
Local legislation The London to Birmingham Railway opens in 1837, but the line yet ready; early riders can only get as far as Hemel Hempstead

The Blitz. *See p27.*

during World War I (1914-18). Around 650 people lost their lives in Zeppelin raids, but the greater impact was psychological – the mighty city had experienced helplessness.

CHANGE, CRISIS AND SHEER ENTERTAINMENT

Political change happened quickly after the war. At Buckingham Palace (*see p117*), the suffragettes had fiercely pressed the case for women's rights before hostilities began (*see p27* **Time Machine**) and David Lloyd George's government averted revolution in 1918-19 by promising 'homes for heroes' (the returning soldiers). They didn't deliver, and in 1924 the Labour Party, led by Ramsay MacDonald, formed its first government.

A live-for-today attitude prevailed in the Roaring '20s among the young upper classes, who flitted from parties in Mayfair to dances at the Ritz. But this meant little to the mass of Londoners, who were suffering in the post-war slump. Civil disturbances, brought on by the high cost of living and rising unemployment, resulted in the nationwide General Strike of 1926, when the working classes downed tools en masse in support of striking miners. Prime Minister Baldwin encouraged volunteers to take over the public services and the streets teemed with army-escorted food convoys, aristocrats running soup kitchens and students driving buses. After nine days of chaos, the strike was called off.

The economic situation only worsened in the early 1930s following the New York Stock Exchange crash of 1929. By 1931, more than three million Britons were jobless. During these years, the London County Council (LCC) began to have a greater impact on the city, clearing slums and building new houses, creating parks and taking control of public services. All the while, London's population increased, peaking at nearly 8.7 million in 1939. To accommodate the influx, the suburbs expanded, particularly to the north-west with the extension of the Metropolitan line to an area that became known as 'Metroland'. Identical gabled houses sprang up in their thousands.

At least Londoners were able to entertain themselves with film and radio. Not long after London's first radio broadcast was beamed from the roof of Marconi House in the Strand in 1922, families were gathering around huge Bakelite wireless sets to hear the

BBC (the British Broadcasting Company; from 1927 the British Broadcasting Corporation). TV broadcasts started on 26 August 1936, when the first telecast went out from Alexandra Palace, but few Londoners could afford televisions until the 1950s.

BLITZKRIEG

Abroad, events had taken on a frightening impetus. Neville Chamberlain's policy of appeasement towards Hitler's Germany collapsed when the Germans invaded Poland. Britain duly declared war on 3 September 1939. The government implemented precautionary measures against air raids, including the evacuation of 600,000 children and pregnant mothers, but the expected bombing raids didn't happen during the autumn and winter of 1939-40 (the so-called 'Phoney War'). Then, in September 1940, hundreds of German bombers dumped explosives on east London and the docks, destroying entire streets and killing or injuring more than 2,000 in what was merely an opening salvo. The Blitz had begun. Raids on London continued for 57 consecutive nights, then intermittently for a further six months. Londoners reacted with stoicism, famously asserting 'business as usual'. After a final raid on 10 May 1941, the Nazis had left a third of the City and the East End in ruins.

From 1942 onwards, the tide began to turn, but Londoners had a new terror to face: the V1 or 'doodlebug'. Dozens of these deadly, explosive-packed, pilotless planes descended on the city in 1944, causing widespread destruction. Later in the year, the more powerful V2 rocket was launched. The last fell on 27 March 1945 in Orpington, Kent, around six weeks before Victory in Europe (VE Day) was declared on 8 May 1945.

'NEVER HAD IT SO GOOD'

World War II left Britain almost as shattered as Germany. Soon after VE Day, a general election was held and Winston Churchill was defeated by the Labour Party under Clement Attlee. The new government established the National Health Service in 1948, and began a massive nationalisation programme that included public transport, electricity, gas, postal and telephone services. For most people, however, life remained regimented and austere. In war-ravaged London, local authorities struggled with a critical shortage of housing. Prefabricated bungalows provided a temporary solution for some (60 years later, six prefabs on the Excalibur estate in Catford, south-east London, were given protection as buildings of historic interest), but the huge new high-rise housing estates that the planners devised proved unpopular with their residents.

IN CONTEXT

Time Machine 1910s

By Jenny Hall, curator of social history at the Museum of London.

Who's in control? In 1910, the London County Council assumes greater responsibility for governing London, particularly in areas such as education, health and housing

Life expectancy Men, 52; women, 55

Average wage 31s 6d

Prices The maximum retail price of a 4lb loaf in 1912 is 6d

Key concerns The death of a whole generation of young men during World War I: about 60,000 Londoners die in the trenches

Local legislation In 1918, the Representation of the People's Act gives eight million women over 30 the right to vote in parliamentary elections for the first time, and also enfranchises all adult males over the age of 21 who are resident householders

Flash point In May 1914, police stop suffragettes entering Buckingham Palace (*see p117*) in a bid to present a 'Votes for Women' petition to the king; 66 women are arrested, including Emmeline Pankhurst

There were bright spots. London hosted the Olympics in 1948; three years later came the Festival of Britain, resulting in the first full redevelopment of the riverside site into the South Bank (now Southbank) Centre (*see p51*). As the 1950s progressed, life and prosperity returned, leading Prime Minister Harold Macmillan in 1957 to proclaim that 'most of our people have never had it so good'. However, many Londoners were leaving. The population dropped by half a million in the late 1950s, causing a labour shortage that prompted huge recruitment drives in Britain's former colonies. London Transport and the National Health Service were both particularly active in encouraging West Indians to emigrate to Britain. Unfortunately, as the Notting Hill race riots of 1958 illustrated, the welcome these new immigrants received was rarely friendly. Still, there were several areas of tolerance: Soho, for instance, which became famous for its mix of cultures and the café and club life they brought with them.

THE SWINGING '60S

By the mid 1960s, London had started to swing. The innovative fashions of Mary Quant and others broke the stranglehold Paris had on couture: boutiques blossomed along the King's Road, while Biba set the pace in Kensington. Carnaby Street (*see p95*) became a byword for hipness as the city basked in its new-found reputation as music and fashion capital of the world – made official, it seemed, when *Time* magazine devoted its front cover to 'swinging London' in 1966. The year of student unrest in Europe, 1968, saw the first issue of *Time Out* hit the streets in August; it was a fold-up sheet, sold for 5d. The decade ended with the Rolling Stones playing a free gig in Hyde Park that drew around 500,000 people.

Then the bubble burst. Many Londoners remember the 1970s as a decade of economic strife, the decade in which the IRA began its bombing campaign on mainland Britain. After the Conservatives won the general election in 1979, Margaret Thatcher instituted a monetarist economic policy that depended on cuts to public services that widened the gap between rich and poor. Riots in Brixton (1981) and Tottenham (1985) were linked to unemployment and heavy-handed policing, keenly felt in London's black communities. The Greater London Council (GLC), led by Ken Livingstone, mounted vigorous opposition to the government with a series of populist measures, but it was abolished in 1986.

The replacement of Thatcher by John Major in October 1990 signalled a short-lived upsurge of hope among Londoners. A riot in Trafalgar Square had helped to see off both Maggie and her inequitable Poll Tax, yet the early 1990s were scarred by continuing recession and more IRA terrorist attacks.

THINGS CAN ONLY GET BETTER?

In May 1997, the British people ousted the Tories and gave Tony Blair's Labour Party the first of three election victories, but enthusiasm waned. The government hoped the Millennium Dome (now the O2; *see p147*) would be a 21st-century rival to the 1851 Great Exhibition. It wasn't, and ate £1 billion on the way to becoming a national joke.

The new millennium saw Ken Livingstone return to power as London's first directly elected mayor and head of the new Greater London Assembly (GLA). Livingstone was re-elected in 2004 for a second term, a thumbs-up for first-term policies that included a congestion charge that sought to ease traffic gridlock by forcing drivers to pay £5 (now more) to enter the city centre. Summer 2005 brought the elation, as London won the bid to host the 2012 Olympics, and devastation, as bombs on tube trains and a bus killed 52 people and injured 700.

Aided by support from the suburbs that Livingstone had neglected, thatch-haired Conservative Boris Johnson took over as Mayor in 2008, but has so far achieved little. In the light of the economic recession, the run-up to the Olympics in 2012 may prove a stern test of Johnson's mettle, and that of the city in general. But in the last two millennia, London has lived through plenty worse.

Key Events

London in brief.

43 The Romans invade; Londinium is founded.
61 Boudicca burns Londinium; the city is rebuilt and made provincial capital.
200 A city wall is built.
410 Roman troops evacuate Britain.
c600 Saxon London is built to the west.
841 The Norse raid for the first time.
c871 The Danes occupy London.
886 Alfred the Great takes London.
1013 The Danes take back London.
1042 Edward the Confessor builds a palace and 'West Minster' upstream.
1066 William I is crowned in Westminster Abbey.
1078 The Tower of London begun.
1123 St Bart's Hospital is founded.
1197 Henry Fitzalwin is the first mayor.
1215 The mayor signs the Magna Carta.
1240 First Parliament at Westminster.
1290 Jews are expelled from London.
1348 The Black Death arrives.
1381 The Peasants' Revolt.
1397 Richard Whittington is Lord Mayor.
1476 William Caxton sets up the first printing press at Westminster.
1534 Henry VIII cuts off the Catholic Church.
1555 Martyrs burned at Smithfield.
1565 Sir Thomas Gresham proposes the Royal Exchange.
1572 First known map of London.
1599 The Globe Theatre opens.
1605 Guy Fawkes's plot to blow up James I fails.
1642 The start of the Civil War.
1649 Charles I is executed; Cromwell establishes Commonwealth.
1664 Beginning of the Great Plague.
1666 The Great Fire.
1675 Building starts on the new St Paul's Cathedral.
1694 The Bank of England is set up.
1710 St Paul's is completed.
1766 The city wall is demolished.
1769 Blackfriars Bridge opens.
1773 The Stock Exchange is founded.
1820 The Regent's Canal opens.

1824 The National Gallery is founded.
1827 Regent's Park Zoo opens.
1829 The Metropolitan Police Act is passed.
1833 The London Fire Brigade is set up.
1835 Madame Tussauds opens.
1836 The first passenger railway opens; Charles Dickens publishes *The Pickwick Papers*, his first novel.
1843 Trafalgar Square is laid out.
1851 The Great Exhibition takes place.
1853 Harrods opens its doors.
1858 The Great Stink: pollution in the Thames reaches hideous levels.
1863 The Metropolitan line opens as the world's first underground railway.
1866 London's last major cholera outbreak; the Sanitation Act is passed.
1868 The last public execution is held at Newgate prison (now the Old Bailey).
1884 Greenwich Mean Time is established.
1888 Jack the Ripper prowls the East End; London County Council is created.
1890 The Housing Act enables the LCC to clear the slums; the first electric underground railway opens.
1897 Motorised buses introduced.
1908 London hosts the Olympic.
1915 Zeppelins begin three years of bombing raids on London.
1940 The Blitz begins.
1948 London again hosts the Olympics.
1951 The Festival of Britain is held.
1952 The last 'pea-souper' smog.
1953 Queen Elizabeth II is crowned.
1981 Riots in Brixton.
1982 The last London docks close.
1986 The GLC is abolished.
1990 Poll Tax protesters riot.
1992 One Canada Square tower opens on Canary Wharf.
2000 Ken Livingstone is elected mayor; Tate Modern and the London Eye open.
2005 London wins bid to host 2012 Olympics; suicide bombers kill 52.
2008 Boris Johnson becomes mayor.
2009 The G-20 meet in London.

IN CONTEXT

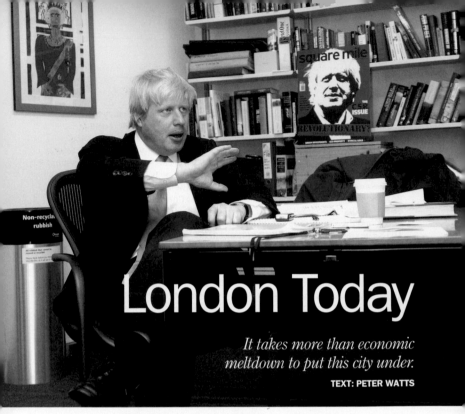

London Today

It takes more than economic meltdown to put this city under.

TEXT: PETER WATTS

'KEEP CALM AND CARRY ON.'

Conceived by the Ministry of Information in August 1939, the simple slogan above was designed to secure the nation's morale in the event of a Nazi invasion. It was never used at the time, but 2009 saw it plastered all over London: on mags and bags, posters and T-shirts. Unusually for the UK, such pilfering from the past was not entirely ironic.

When, in 2008, the UK began to brace itself for recession, economists at various think tanks predicted that London was going to get the worst of it. Their reasoning was simple: the recession was caused by bubbles in the financial industry and the housing market, and London was the bellows that had been doing most of the inflating.

But London is like the Terminator, a predator that has learnt to heal itself. By summer 2009, experts had begun to argue that the city would bounce back from the brink quicker than any other region in the UK, largely because it was so much less dependent on the sort of public spending (39 per cent against 61.6 per cent in the north-east of England) that may soon be in short supply. Things were looking up.

Peter Watts is the features writer for Time Out *magazine.*

WHAT'S THE DAMAGE?

No one would argue London emerged from 2009 unscathed. Unemployment is higher than the national average, house prices are down, home repossessions have steadily increased and thousands of businesses have been forced to close. But the decline in the UK economy as a whole has been to the city's advantage.

As the pound plummeted against the dollar and euro, London became a financially attractive holiday destination for the first time in years. Having spent most of the 2000s as one of the world's most expensive cities, according to the Economist Intelligence Unit's annual cost-of-living survey, London plummeted to 27th place on the list in 2009 – below Caracas, some delightedly pointed out – and tourist spending rose accordingly. London also did well from domestic visits (or 'staycations', as holidays taken at home were unfortunately dubbed). Despite the twin threats of recession and swine flu, as well as the ever-present dread of terrorism, the city marched on.

The increase in visitors was welcome news for the arts world, which has already lost funding to the 2012 Olympics and is bracing itself for an incoming Conservative government committed to swingeing cuts. (There will be a General Election in 2010, and the Conservatives are favourites to win it.) In 2001, the Labour government scrapped admission prices to 11 of the country's leading museums. As a result, attendance rose by 83 per cent over the next five years; of the ten most visited free museums in the UK during 2008, eight are in London. But although the Tories maintained their commitment to free admission in 2007, many museum directors are privately wary.

Such fears were stoked in September when Mayor Boris Johnson returned to London from a trip to New York and proposed voluntary admission charges at museums and galleries based on a US model, arguing that the effect of free admission was that 'cynical young people think they're seeing something that isn't prized' (which is surely better than them *not* seeing something that *is* prized). Proposed extensions to the British Museum and Tate Modern are already in doubt, as a golden age for galleries and museums comes to a close.

LIFE UNDER BORIS

Perhaps we shouldn't be too concerned. London has had a dose of Toryconomics under Mayor Boris Johnson, and the roof hasn't fallen in. Johnson has made cuts, but not to the extent many feared, and has occasionally allowed common sense to overrule ideology. The budget for London's tourist agency, Visit London, had initially been cut by £1.5 million, but the mayor later halved the cut when the depth of the recession became apparent.

Johnson's strangest extravagance has been in the realm of public transport. After boldly stating in his manifesto that he was going to phase out the articulated 18-metre 'bendy buses' that replaced some of London's beloved double-decker Routemasters, Johnson has been forced to splash out on an expensive new fleet of totally unnecessary buses. These new buses will carry fewer passengers than the bendies, but should prove more popular with drivers and cyclists. Class warriors were quick to note a Tory inclination to favour middle-class car-owners and cyclists over the poorer Londoners who actually use buses and quite liked bendies. It was also intriguing to see those on the right defend Johnson's decision on grounds of aesthetics, while those on the left criticised it on grounds of profligacy. Buses are never far from the London agenda; plans for a new-generation Routemaster continue to chug along.

Otherwise, Johnson's first term has thus far been notable only for its lack of noteworthiness. He continues to shed deputies at the rate of about one every three months and occasionally says something amusing or silly to the press, often directly contradicting Conservative leader David Cameron. But Johnson's administration seems

afflicted by a curious absence of purpose, a lack of vision. The occasional innovation is announced, such as the wholly admirable but ultimately rather pointless Story of London festival celebrating London's history, which then flounder as soon as the mayor's considerable energy but limited attention span is directed elsewhere.

And one compelling question remains: what will happen to the fiercely ambitious Johnson should the Tories win the General Election? Cameron may secretly be pleased at Johnson's relative lack of success in London: it means the Conservative leader won't be forced into giving his popular rival a seat in the Cabinet, where the blond bombshell could really do some damage. And then there's the question of whether Johnson would even want to leave City Hall before 2012, when a mayoral election will be swiftly followed by an Olympics that would put London at the centre of the world's attention. Assuming Johnson secures a second term, it's an opportunity he wouldn't want to miss.

THE VIEW FROM MOUNT OLYMPICS

Construction on the Olympic site in Stratford continues apace, with the main stadium rising at a speed that has silenced sceptics who believed that there was no chance any project of this size would be completed on time. Indeed, given the cost of the recession to the rest of the construction industry, this sometimes seems to be the only active building site in town. The City's love of iconic tall buildings has not entirely abated (*see p70* **Walk**), but the forest of cranes that marked much of the past decade has certainly thinned out a bit.

Despite all this, London remains quietly optimistic. For some, recession brings opportunity: art squats, pop-up shops, front-room restaurants and related happenings have all helped give London's underground scene a real zip (*see pp42-44* **Credit Crunch Culture**), and social networking sites such as Twitter have brought these events to wider audiences than ever before. At the other end of the scale, there's a surfeit of well-endowed bankers looking to invest their humongous redundancy packages: one ex-City banker has opened a gin distillery in Kensington, while another jacked in the suit and tie to become a fisherman on the south coast, returning to north London at weekends to sell his catch at farmers' markets. Expect many more such stories to emerge in 2010 as ambitious plans come to fruition and, all around, Londoners simply keep calm and carry on.

IN CONTEXT

Architecture

*Planning controversies and
a tradition of mischief.*

TEXT: SIMON COPPOCK

During the 2000s, it seemed that every street in central London was obliged by law to engage a cluster of cranes. But with the recession making loans expensive, property returns unpredictable and investors wary, the city's mania for redevelopment may be drawing to a close. Various grand plans remain on the drawing board, but it's anyone's guess how many of them will make it any further.

At the same time, arguments rage over who's in charge of our built landscape. Prince Charles angered architects by using his influence to stop a Richard Rogers redevelopment of Chelsea Barracks in 2009, at the same time that Mayor Boris Johnson overruled the local council and granted planning permission for a 63-storey skyscraper in Docklands.

Despite attempts to polarise architectural debate, pitching 'traditional' against 'progressive', London's buildings remain a happy mix. Even in the 17th and 18th centuries, architects were adapting continental sources, from Palladians Inigo Jones to baroque star Sir Christopher Wren. More recently, Lords Rogers and Foster have become ubiquitous creators of statement buildings here without losing their global reach.

THE NEW CITY

Modern London sprang into being after the Great Fire of 1666. It was well named: the fire destroyed five-sixths of the City of London, burning some 13,200 houses and 89 churches. The devastation was commemorated by Sir Christopher Wren's 202-foot **Monument** (*see p72*), recently renovated, but many of the finest buildings in the City still stand as testament to the talents of Wren, the architect of the great remodelling, and his successors.

London was a densely populated place built largely of wood, and fire control was primitive. It was only after the three-day inferno that the authorities insisted on a few basic regulations. Brick and stone became the construction materials of choice, and key streets were widened to act as firebreaks. But despite of grand proposals from architects, Wren among them, who hoped to reconfigure the city along classical lines, London reshaped itself around its old street pattern, with buildings that had survived the Fire standing as monuments to earlier ages. Chief of these was the Norman **Tower of London** (*see p74*), begun soon after William's 1066 conquest and extended over the next 300 years; the Navy cheated the advancing flames of the Great Fire by blowing up the surrounding houses before the inferno could get to it.

Another longstanding building, **Westminster Abbey** (*see p115*) was begun in 1245 when the site lay far outside London's walls; it was completed in 1745 by Nicholas Hawksmoor's west towers. Although the abbey is the most French of England's Gothic churches in spirit, the chapel added by Henry VII (and completed under Henry VIII in 1512) is pure Tudor. Centuries later, Washington Irving gushed: 'Stone seems, by the winning labour of the chisel, to have been robbed of its weight and density, suspended aloft, as if by magic.' (For more on Tudor architecture, *see below* **Spotter's Guide**.)

A LATE FLOWERING

The European Renaissance came late to Britain, making its London debut with Inigo Jones's 1622 **Banqueting House** (*see p137*). The sumptuously decorated ceiling,

---

Spotter's Guide to Tudor Windows

An ancient architectural style made new friends in the 19th century.

Reputedly built so he could keep tabs on his monks praying at the altar without having to leave his quarters, Prior Bolton's oriel window at **St Bartholomew-the-Great** (*see p65*) is a classic example of the characteristic Renaissance design. The bay window bears the Prior's rebus (an arrow from a crossbow piercing a wine barrel; bolt + tun = bolton), and shows a parabolic arch (the top curves distinguishing it from the more steeply curving Gothic arch) with a plain trefoil design at the top of the upper panes. The form found popularity with Victorian architects, as they sought a style sufficiently British to support their imperial aims; this is why oriel windows are so common in London's institutional buildings.

Spotter's Guide to Baroque Spires

How Hawksmoor reinvented the English church.

Under the Fifty New Churches Act of 1711, which used a coal tax to fund the building of 'churches of stone… with Towers and Steeples', Nicholas Hawksmoor designed, in whole or part, eight new places of worship. Like Wren, Hawksmoor was in love with the classical temple, a style at odds with the Act's Anglican insistence on spires. **St Mary Woolnoth**, **St Anne Limehouse** and **St George-in-the-East** all offer unorthodox resolutions of this contradiction, but the 'spire' of **St George's Bloomsbury** (*see p81; pictured*) is the barmiest.

Aping the Mausoleum of Halicarnassus, Hawksmoor created a peculiar stepped pyramid design, plopped a giant statue of George I in a toga on top and then added unicorns and lions.

Hawksmoor's ruinous overspends (**St Anne's** was so costly no money was left for the rector's salary) was one reason why just a dozen of the proposed 50 churches were built. Still, the four corner towers of Thomas Archer's **St John's, Smith Square** (*see p310*) and the spire 'portholes' of **St Martin-in-the-Fields** (*see p112*) today provide further delightful evidence of baroque invention.

IN CONTEXT

added in 1635 by Rubens, celebrated the Stuart monarchy's Divine Right to rule, although 14 years later King Charles I provided an greater spectacle as he was led from the room and beheaded on a stage outside. Tourists also have Jones to thank for **St Paul's Covent Garden** (*see p87*) and the immaculate **Queen's House** (*see p148*), but they're not his only legacies. He mastered the art of piazzas (such as the one at Covent Garden), porticos and pilasters, changing British architecture for ever. His work influenced the careers of succeeding generations of architects and introduced a habit of venerating the past that it would take 300 years to kick.

Nothing cheers a builder like a natural disaster, and one can only guess at the relish with which Christopher Wren and co began rebuilding after the Fire. They brandished classicism like a new broom: the pointed arches of English Gothic were rounded off, Corinthian columns made an appearance and church spires became as multi-layered as a wedding cake.

Wren blazed the trail with his daring plans for **St Paul's Cathedral** (*see p63*), spending an enormous (for the time) £500 on the oak model of his proposal. But the scheme, incorporating a Catholic dome rather than a Protestant steeple, was too Roman for the establishment and the design was rejected. Wren quickly produced a redesign and gained planning permission by incorporating a spire, only to set about a series of mischievous U-turns to give us the building, domed and heavily suggestive of an ancient temple, that's survived to this day.

Wren's baton was picked up by Nicholas Hawksmoor and James Gibbs, who benefited from a 1711 decree that 50 extra churches should be built (*see above* **Spotter's Guide**). Gibbs became busy around Trafalgar Square with the steepled Roman temple of **St Martin-in-the-Fields** (*see p112*), as well as the baroque **St Mary-le-Strand** and the tower of **St Clement Danes** (for both, *see p89*). His work was well received, but the more experimental Hawksmoor had a rougher ride. For one thing, not everyone admired his stylistic innovations; for another, even fewer approved of his financial planning, or lack of it. **St George's Bloomsbury** (*see p81*), for instance, cost three times its £10,000 budget and took 15 years to build.

'With the Houses of Parliament, Pugin created a Victorian fantasy that would later be condemned as the Disneyfication of history.'

One of a large family of Scottish architects, Robert Adam found himself at the forefront of a movement that came to see Italian baroque as a corruption of the real thing, with architectural exuberance dropped in favour of a simpler interpretation of ancient forms. The best surviving work of Adam and his brothers James, John and William can be found in London's great suburban houses **Osterley Park**, **Syon House** (*see p164*) and **Kenwood House** (*see p132*), but the project for which they're most famous no longer stands: the cripplingly expensive Adelphi housing estate off the Strand. Most of the complex was pulled down in the 1930s and replaced by an office block, and only a small part of the original development survives; it's now the **Royal Society of Arts** (8 John Adam Street, Covent Garden, WC2N 6EZ).

SOANE AND NASH

Just as the first residents were moving into the Adelphi, a young unknown called John Soane was embarking on a domestic commission in Ireland. It was never completed, but Soane eventually returned to London and went on to build the **Bank of England** (*see p68*) and **Dulwich Picture Gallery** (*see p145*). The Bank was demolished between the wars, leaving only the perimeter walls and depriving London of Soane's masterpiece, though his gracious Stock Office has been reconstructed in the museum. A more authentic glimpse of what those bankers might have enjoyed can be gleaned from a visit to Soane's house, now the quirky **Sir John Soane's Museum** (*see p76*), an extraordinary and exquisite architectural experiment.

A near-contemporary of Soane's, John Nash was a less talented architect, but his contributions – among them the inner courtyard of **Buckingham Palace** (*see p117*), the **Theatre Royal Haymarket** (Haymarket, SW1Y 4HT) and **Regent Street** (W1) – have proved comparable to those of Wren. Regent Street began as a proposal to link the West End to the planned park further north, as well as a device to separate the toffs of Mayfair from the riff-raff of Soho; in Nash's own words, a 'complete separation between the Streets occupied by the Nobility and Gentry, and the narrow Streets and meaner houses occupied by mechanics and the trading part of the community'.

By the 1830s, the classical form of building had been established in England for some 200 years, but this didn't prevent a handful of upstarts from pressing for change. In 1834, the **Houses of Parliament** (*see p113*) burned down, leading to the construction of Sir Charles Barry's Gothic masterpiece. Barry sought out Augustus Welby Northmore Pugin. Working alongside Barry, if not always in agreement with him (of Barry's symmetrical layout, he famously remarked, 'All Grecian, sir. Tudor details on a classic body'), Pugin created a Victorian fantasy that would later be condemned as the Disneyfication of history.

GETTING GOTHIC

This was the beginning of the Gothic Revival, a move to replace what was considered foreign and pagan with something that was native and Christian. Architects would often decide that buildings weren't Gothic enough; as with the **Guildhall**'s 15th-century Great Hall (*see p69*), which gained its corner turrets and central spire only in 1862. The argument between Classicists and Goths erupted in 1857, when the government hired Sir George Gilbert Scott, a leading light of the Gothic movement, to design a new home for the Foreign Office. Scott's design incensed anti-Goth Lord Palmerston, then

Make the most of London life

prime minister, whose diktats prevailed. But Scott exacted his revenge by building an office in which everyone hated working, and by going on to construct Gothic edifices all over town, among them the **Albert Memorial** (*see p124*) and the impressive frontage of what is now **St Pancras International** train station (*see p83*), due to be returned to its original function as a hotel by late 2010.

St Pancras was completed in 1873, after the Midland Railway commissioned Scott to build a London terminus that would dwarf that of its rivals next door at King's Cross. Using the project as an opportunity to show his mastery of the Gothic form, Scott built an asymmetrical castle that obliterated views of the train shed behind, itself an engineering marvel completed earlier by William Barlow. Other charming and imposing neo-Gothic buildings around the city include the **Royal Courts of Justice** (*see p60*), the **Natural History Museum** (*see p124*) and **Tower Bridge** (*see p74*). Under the influence of the Arts and Crafts movement, medievalism morphed into such mock Tudor buildings as the wonderful half-timbered **Liberty** department store (*see p244*).

BEING MODERN

World War I and the coming of modernism led to a spirit of renewal and a starker aesthetic. **Freemasons' Hall** (*see p88*) and the BBC's **Broadcasting House** (*see p99*) are good examples of the pared-down style of the 1920s and '30s, but perhaps the finest example of between-the-wars modernism can be found at **London Zoo** (*see p102*). Built by Russian émigré Bertold Lubetkin and the Tecton group, the spiral ramps of the Penguin Pool were a showcase for the possibilities of concrete. The material was also put to good use on the London Underground, enabling the quick, cheap building of cavernous spaces with sleek lines and curves. While there was nothing quick or cheap about the art deco **Daily Express** building (*see below* **Spotter's Guide**), the same taste for the simple, perfect curve is evident.

Spotter's Guide to Art Deco

London didn't go curveless in the roaring '20s.

Dating from the mid-1920s, the art deco architectural style favoured streamlined geometrical simplicity, in keeping with the Jazz Age's wide-eyed belief in a bright and beautiful future. From tube stations to cinemas, London has some prime examples of the style, but one of the best art deco buildings here is the old **Daily Express Building** (121-128 Fleet Street, City). Built in 1931, it's an early example of 'curtain wall' construction, its radical black vitrolite and glass façade (by Sir Owen Williams) hung on an internal frame, and demonstrates the modernist belief that form should reflect function. There's no public access (except during Open House events; *see p275*), but you can stick your head around the door and glimpse the Robert Atkinson interior of plaster reliefs, oval staircase

and lots of silver and gilt. No wonder the *Architects' Journal* called it a 'defining monument of 1930s London'.

The bombs of World War II left large areas of London ruined, providing another opportunity for builders to cash in. Lamentably, the city was little improved by the rebuild; in many cases, it was left worse off. The destruction left the capital with a dire housing shortage, so architects were given a chance to demonstrate the grim efficiency with which they could house large numbers of families in tower blocks.

There were post-war successes, however, including the **Royal Festival Hall** (see p51) on the South Bank. The sole survivor of the 1951 Festival of Britain, the RFH was built to celebrate the end of the war and the centenary of the Great Exhibition, held in 1851 and responsible for the foundation in South Kensington of the Natural History Museum, the Science Museum and the V&A. Next door to the RFH, the **Hayward** gallery (see p51) is an exemplar of the 1960s vogue for Brutalist architecture, a style more thoroughly explored at the **Barbican** (see p65), loved by many but never fully rehabilitated from the vilification it received in the years after it opened in 1982.

HERE COME THE STARCHITECTS

The 1970s and '80s offered up a pair of alternatives to concrete: post-modernism and high-tech. The former is represented by César Pelli's blandly monumental **One Canada Square** (see p140) in Docklands, an oversized obelisk that's perhaps the archetypal expression of late '80s architecture. Richard Rogers' high-tech **Lloyd's of London** building (see p71) is much more widely admired. A clever combination of commercial and industrial aesthetics that adds up to one of the most significant British buildings since the war, it was mocked on completion in 1986, but outclasses newer projects.

Apart from Rogers, the city's most visible contemporary architect has been Norman Foster, whose **City Hall** (see p56) and **30 St Mary Axe** (aka 'the Gherkin') have caught up with Big Ben and black taxis as movie shorthand for 'Welcome to London!'. His prolific practice set new standards in sports design with the soaring arch of the new **Wembley Stadium** (see p331); the exercise in complexity that is the £100 million Great Court at the **British Museum** (see p79) did the same for London's cultural gem. The Great Court is the largest covered square in Europe, but every one of its 3,300 triangular glass panels is unique.

Spotter's Guide to City Skyscrapers

A tale of two towers.

When some wag dubbed Lord Foster's 40-storey Swiss Re Tower, now **30 St Mary Axe**, 'the Erotic Gherkin' in 2004, it wasn't with fondness. Yet the name became such a badge of honour that Foster now gives every new skyscraper a nickname: the Walkie-Talkie, the Helter Skelter, Darth Vader's Helmet. Lord Rogers' **Lloyd's of London**, just nearby, fails to command the levels of affection shown the Gherkin, despite Londoners having had more than two decades to get used to the brilliant inside-out 'high tech' design. Perhaps his 48-storey **122 Leadenhall Street** ('the Cheese Grater'), under way right opposite, will do the trick for him too.

Much new architecture is to be found cunningly inserted into old buildings. Herzog & de Meuron's fabulous transformation of a Bankside power station into **Tate Modern** (see p54) is perhaps the most famous example. Equally ground-breaking was Future Systems' NatWest Media Centre at **Lord's Cricket Ground** (see p331). Built from aluminium in a boatyard and perched high above the pitch, it's one of London's most daring constructions to date, especially given the traditional setting.

LOCAL COLOUR AND OLYMPIC FEATS

Architecture hasn't all been about headline projects and eye-troubling commercial developments. Will Alsop's multicoloured **Peckham Library** (122 Peckham Hill Street, SE15 5JR) has helped redefine community architecture, as did David Adjaye's later **Idea Stores** (www.ideastore.co.uk) in Poplar (1 Vesey Path, East India Dock Road, E14 6BT) and Whitechapel (321 Whitechapel Road, E1 1BU); the crisp aesthetic of these buildings is a world away from the traditional Victorian library. Adjaye's inspiration in shop design is even more explicit in the **Rivington Place** gallery (Rivington Place, Shoreditch, EC2A 3BA), with the main entrance tucked to the side so that passers-by are drawn into the main gallery by a display window – just like the display window of a department store. The subtle Robbrecht en Daem expansion of **Whitechapel Gallery** (see p138) into the stylistically very different former library next door reversed the process, giving a new democratic openness to a pair of landmark Victorian buildings.

PLANNING THE FUTURE

With so much going on in so many parts of town, it's difficult to get a grip on the whole picture. The magnificent **Open House** festival (see p275) and the biennial **London Festival of Architecture** (www.lfa2010.org) do a terrific job of getting locals engaged with their built environment, but for an overview of what the city might look like in a few years' time, get off the tube at Goodge Street and visit **New London Architecture** (see p300 **Inside Track**). The centre's impressive centrepiece is a 39-foot-long scale model of London, stretching from Battersea Power Station in the south, north up to King's Cross and out to Docklands and Stratford in the east. Currently, the dozens of unbuilt schemes on the model include **One Blackfriars Road**, a spectacular 560-foot hotel and residential building (topped off with a public viewing platform) that will appear beside Tate Modern, probably by 2012.

It's clear that 2012 is going to be an important year for London. In addition to the new buildings directly related to Olympics, many property owners are seeking to get involved (the Pan Peninsula Towers in Docklands this year reached an agreement to broadcast a countdown to the games, then provide live results during the competition) or using the event as a fund-raising focus: both Tate Modern and the British Museum have announced hugely ambitious expansion plans with 2012 completion dates. Periodic tours are already being run around the new buildings in the formerly disregarded corner of east London where the games will be staged. Walking north along the riverbank of the Lee Navigation, the exterior structure of the main stadium already looks complete, and work on the 17,500-seat **London Aquatics Centre**, Zaha Hadid's first permanent structure to be built in her adopted country, is well under way: all 2,800 tonnes of distinctive, swooping roof were gingerly lowered into place in early November 2009.

London is big enough to accommodate more than one colossal building site, of course, and the transformation of King's Cross is continuing apace. St Pancras International and **Kings Place** (see p309) – the first of a series of cultural edifices, to be followed in 2011 by the University of the Arts London in a huge Victorian granary – are just the vanguard of the 67-acre brownfield redevelopment known as King's Cross Central. As well as the arts and education, two dozen new streets are being built to service 2,000 new homes. The property speculators may have taken a hit over the last year, but there's little sign of the city's builders hanging up their trowels.

IN CONTEXT

Credit Crunch Culture

Down so long it looks like up to us.

TEXT: PETER WATTS

This will come as no consolation to those who lost jobs, businesses or even homes in the recent economic crisis, but downturns have their upsides. Here in London, the recessions of the late 1970s and early 1990s both produced cultural movements of artistic and financial value. From the '70s came punk; from the '90s emerged the Young British Artist movement led by Damien Hirst and Tracey Emin.

It's not yet apparent whether a similar cultural revolution might emerge from the recent recession, but *Time Out* first noted the stirrings of a new scene when, in October 2008, we reported on a group of young, unpretentious artists who'd taken over a deserted six-storey mansion on Grosvenor Street in Mayfair and turned it into a space for shows and happenings. Founder Simon McAndrew told us that he was aiming for 'some kind of artistic, bohemian microcosm'. But did he find it, and why does it matter to London?

'Perhaps some of us dream of dropping out to form our own art-squat community, with free love and free paintbrushes for all.'

ART TAKEOVER

McAndrew's Mayfair enterprise was not the first art squat in London – the concept goes back at least to the 1960s. What's more, the DA! Collective, as the Mayfair group were called, had been in existence since 2005, previously squatting at properties in Knightsbridge, Soho and Tottenham Court Road. However, the Grosvenor Square squat attracted huge media attention because of the nature of the building (it was worth an estimated £6 million), the state of the country's finances and the recently established news cycle, which uses Twitter and Facebook to respond quickly to emerging trends. Within days of *Time Out*'s story, the Mayfair squat was all over the tabloid newspapers.

The squatters at MADA!, as the site became known, were evicted in December 2008, but not before they'd attracted enough attention to inspire a new breed of squatter. Take 'Lucky Jim', who wrote on *Time Out*'s blog: 'I'm 31 years old and have lived in London for 13 years, but only started squatting in November [2008]. I was a cycle courier, a rootless and impoverished master of the city, and could hardly afford to pay rent. Before that I'd been a legal secretary, a terrible poker player and a PhD student. At no point was I in a position to consider buying a property to be life's ultimate goal. I remembered a passage in *The Ragged Trousered Philanthropists* that equated tramps with aristocrats. Envying the unspeakably rich, I wondered if I might find similar freedom through being unspeakably poor. Could I find a way to live without the need for money?'

MOVING IN

On gaining acceptance ('Squats,' says Jim, 'particularly art squats, are not lawless places, and new arrivals can be rigorously policed'), Jim hung out in Mayfair and Camberwell. In time, he hooked up with Dan Simon of the Oubliette Collective, which attracted considerable attention by squatting a disused language school near Waterloo Station in May 2009 and turning it into a multi-platform performance space before the group's inevitable eviction. Simon told the *Evening Standard*: 'In two weeks, we have built two galleries, a cinema, a theatre and more in what was a rotting, derelict space. Before we arrived, there was fungus everywhere and the place was falling apart. We have damaged nothing and are trying to create an ambitious space for art that will benefit London.'

Simon and Jim then teamed up at another empty language school on Oxford Street, where they created the 24-hour 'Fifth Plinth' performance art project; it was a homage of sorts to sculptor Antony Gormley's headline-grabbing *One & Other* (2009), which saw members of the public apply to spend an hour apiece on the vacant fourth plinth in Trafalgar Square. The pair were around the corner from yet another squatted language school (sensing a theme?) at which a group of kids who had met at the Mayfair squats opened the VHS Basement Cinema, screening free films every night for anybody who was interested. Around the same time, a group of eco-squatters momentarily liberated Raven's Ait, an entire Thames island near Hampton Court, and turned it into an 'eco haven' for a few weeks before the police arrived to turf them out.

SQUATS GOING ON

So what's prompted this flurry of artistic-minded squatting? The simplest answer is the recession. As Simon explains, 'There are a lot more empty properties. It is a tragedy and more of them should be used for projects like this.' Many language

IN CONTEXT

schools have been forced to close by stringent new regulations, while other buildings across the city have been left empty by failing businesses or by developers who are unable or unwilling to meet the cost of renovation.

Equally important is the new spirit created by the economic downturn. Rising unemployment among 18- to 25-year-olds has meant that young people have been forced to seek alternatives to work, and the public as a whole has proven open to new and unusual ideas that might alleviate the grind of day-to-day existence. Perhaps some of us even dream of dropping out to form our own art-squat community, with free love and free paintbrushes for all. A vocal minority react angrily to such transgressions – how dare anybody occupy a property that they don't own! – but more Londoners have responded with sympathy, supportive of anyone making creative and public use of a building that would otherwise be left to fester until the good times return.

Given that there'll be less money to spend on arts funding in the next few years, and that the bubble in the commercial market has burst, the art-squat movement could be a key avenue for ambitious young artists hoping to make a splash. Its colourful come-and-have-a-go ethos offers a welcome counterpoint to more conventional, state-funded artistic movements, and chimes with a trend detectable in other participatory events in 2009. Gormley's *One & Other* was the officially sanctioned epitome of this, but it could also be seen in carefree events such as Luke Jarram's *Play Me I'm Yours*, which placed 30 old pianos in various locations around the City and West End and invited Londoners to bang out a few tunes; perhaps surprisingly, they did. Of similar ilk was *Tales from a Park Bench*, which placed a bench in an empty-shop-turned-gallery on Chalk Farm Road for a week and invited passers-by to perform on it.

In the case of *Tales from a Park Bench*, the shop was willingly offered up by landlords happy to see it used, something that also happened in Herne Hill when a group of artists took over an old video shop and turned it into a performance space for an event that they called Live at the Apollo. Some of the shops that had been part of Woolworths, the countrywide retail chain that went into administration in 2008, were used in a similar way, by squatters in Camden and under invitation in Walthamstow. Credit crunch, recession, depression – call it what you will, but in some ways, London has never been so affordable.

Play Me I'm Yours.

Sightseeing

St Paul's Cathedral. *See p63.*

The South Bank & Bankside	**46**
Profile London Eye	50
The City	**59**
Profile Museum of London	66
Walk The 21st-Century City	70
Holborn & Clerkenwell	**75**
Bloomsbury & Fitzrovia	**78**
Walk Lit Stops	80
Covent Garden & the Strand	**84**
Garden City	85
Soho & Leicester Square	**91**
Glad to Be Gay	93
Hard Times Square	96
Oxford Street & Marylebone	**97**
Walk Back to the Back Streets	98
Paddington & Notting Hill	**103**

Piccadilly Circus & Mayfair	**105**
The Art of Memory	109
Westminster & St James's	**110**
A Transport of Delight	112
Chelsea	**120**
Knightsbridge & South Kensington	**123**
Profile V&A Museum	127
North London	**128**
East London	**135**
Shakespeare in Shoreditch	137
South-east London	**143**
Overground to the Underground	144
South-west London	**151**
West London	**158**
Police Tactics	162

The South Bank & Bankside

Central London's riverside has never looked better.

An estimated 14 million people come this way each year, and it's easy to see why. Between the **London Eye** and **Tower Bridge**, the south bank of the Thames offers a two-mile procession of diverting, largely state-funded arts and entertainment venues, while also affording breezy, traffic-free views of a succession of city landmarks (Big Ben, St Paul's, the Tower of London) that lie on the other side of the water.

The area's modern-day life began in 1951 with the Festival of Britain, staged in a bid to boost morale in the wake of World War II. The **Royal Festival Hall** stands testament to the inclusive spirit of the project; it was later expanded into the Southbank Centre, alongside **BFI Southbank** and the concrete ziggurat of the **National Theatre**. However, it wasn't until the new millennium that the riverside really took off, with the threefold arrival of the **London Eye**, **Tate Modern** and the **Millennium Bridge**. Ever since, the area has been top of most tourists' itineraries.

Map p401, pp404-405	Restaurants & cafés p197
Hotels p167	Pubs & bars p227

THE SOUTH BANK

Lambeth Bridge to Hungerford Bridge

Embankment or Westminster tube, or Waterloo tube/rail.

Thanks to the sharp turn the Thames makes around Waterloo, **Lambeth Bridge** lands you east of the river, not south, opposite the Tudor gatehouse of **Lambeth Palace**. Since the 12th century, it's been the official residence of the Archbishops of Canterbury. The palace is not normally open to the public, except on holidays. The church next door, St Mary at Lambeth, is now the **Garden Museum** (*see right*).

The benches along the river here are great for viewing the Houses of Parliament opposite, before things get crowded after **Westminster Bridge**, where London's major riverside tourist zone begins. Next to the bridge is **County Hall**, once the residence of London's city government, now home to the revamped **Sea Life London Aquarium** (*see p49*), **Dalí Universe** (*see below*) and newcomer attraction **Moviem** (*see p49*). The massive wheel of the **London Eye** (*see right*) rotates in front of you.

Dalí Universe

County Hall Gallery, County Hall, Riverside Building, Queen's Walk, SE1 7PB (7620 2720, www.thedaliuniverse.com). Westminster tube or Waterloo tube/rail. **Open** 9.30am-7pm daily. **Admission** £14; £12 reductions; £38 family. **Credit** AmEx, DC, MC, V. **Map** p401 M9.

This reverential, rather lugubrious but far from droopy celebration of the famous surrealist's work, features trademark attractions, such as the *Mae West Lips* sofa and the *Spellbound* painting, as well as sculptures, watercolours (including flamboyant tarot cards), rare etchings and lithographs.

Garden Museum.

Downstairs, you can print your own Dalí T-shirt for £15 in the workshop area. A café serves organic fare amid large portraits of the mustachioed master.
▶ *Peter Moore, the City of Westminster's Town Crier, quite a surreal sight in himself, rings his bell and hollers outside three days a week.*

Florence Nightingale Museum
St Thomas's Hospital, 2 Lambeth Palace Road, SE1 7EW (7620 0374, www.florence-nightingale. co.uk). Westminster tube or Waterloo tube/rail. **Open** 10am-5pm daily. **Admission** £5.80; £4.80 reductions; £16 family; free under-5s. **Credit** AmEx, MC, V. **Map** p401 M9.
The nursing skills and campaigning zeal that made Nightingale a Victorian legend are honoured here. Due to reopen after refurbishment for the centenary of her death in spring 2010, the museum is a chronological tour through a remarkable life under three key themes: family life, the Crimean War, health reformer. Among the period mementoes – clothing, furniture, books, letters and portraits – we hope there's still space for her stuffed pet owl, Athena.

Garden Museum
Lambeth Palace Road, SE1 7LB (7401 8865, www.gardenmuseum.org.uk). Lambeth North tube or Waterloo tube/rail. **Open** 10.30am-5pm daily. **Admission** £6, £5 reductions; free under-16s. **Credit** AmEx, MC, V. **Map** p401 L10.
Recently renamed and renovated, the world's first horticulture museum (formerly the Museum of Garden History) now fits more neatly into the old church of St Mary's. A new 'belvedere' gallery, constructed of eco-friendly Eurban wood sheeting, contains the permanent collection of artworks, antique gardening tools and horticultural memorabilia. The ground floor has been freed up for temporary exhibitions; until 17 Mar 2010, they're celebrating The Good Life, Britain's healthy perennial interest in grow-your-own, a show that should be followed by a look at the late Christopher Lloyd's garden at Great Dixter. In the small garden at the back, the replica of a 17th-century knot garden was created in honour of John Tradescant, intrepid plant hunter and gardener to Charles I, who's buried here. A magnificent stone sarcophagus contains the remains of William Bligh, the captain of the mutinous HMS *Bounty*.
▶ *The breadfruit that ruined Bligh's expedition can be seen at Kew Gardens; see p155.*

★ London Eye
Jubilee Gardens, SE1 7PB (0870 500 0600, www.londoneye.com). Westminster tube or Waterloo tube/rail. **Open** *Oct-May* 10am-8pm daily. *June-Sept* 10am-9pm daily. **Admission** £17.50; £8.75-£14 reductions (only applicable Mon-Fri Sept-June); free under-4s. **Credit** AmEx, MC, V. **Map** p401 M8.
See p50 **Profile.**

SIGHTS

Sea Life London Aquarium.

Movieum

County Hall, Riverside Building, SE1 7PB (7202 7040, www.themovieum.com). Westminster tube or Waterloo tube/rail. **Open** 10am-5pm Mon-Fri; 10am-6pm Sat, Sun. **Admission** £17; £12 reductions. **Credit** MC, V. **Map** p401 M8.

Dedicated to British film since the 1950s (films *made* in Britain, that is, so unexpected blockbusters like *Star Wars* can sneak in), the Movieum was opened in 2008 in the heart of the old County Hall. The quondam corridors of power are dedicated to telling the stories of great studios such as Pinewood and Ealing, discussing David Lean and other great directors, and detailing different types of movie that have emanated from these islands. The box-like offices lining these corridors contain sets and displays on individual films or themes; the Rotunda room is largely taken up by Harry Potter. Among thousands of original artefacts, you can see the Rank gong; techniques from the *Superman* films allow visitors to take part in one of more than 200 films.

Sea Life London Aquarium

County Hall, Riverside Building, Westminster Bridge Road, SE1 7PB (0871 663 1678, Tours 7967 8007, www.sealife.co.uk). Westminster tube or Waterloo tube/rail. **Open** 10am-6pm daily. **Admission** £16; £14 reductions; £11 child reductions; £50 family; free under-3s. **Credit** MC, V. **Map** p401 M8.

Recently given a thorough overhaul, with new themed displays and more dramatic lighting, this is one of Europe's largest aquariums and a huge hit with kids. The inhabitants are grouped according to geographical origin beginning with the Atlantic, where blacktail bream seem to swim alongside the

Thames Embankment. The Ray Lagoon is still popular, though touching the friendly flatfish is now not allowed (it's bad for their health). Starfish, crabs and anemones can be handled in special open rock pools instead, and the clown fish still draw crowds. There's a mesmerising Seahorse Temple and a tank full of turtles, with one gallery given over to conservation. Temperate freshwater fish from the rivers of Europe and North America can be found on the ground floor. The centrepieces, though, are the two massive Pacific and Indian Ocean tanks, with menacing sharks quietly circling fallen Easter Island statues and dinosaur bones. Be prepared for long queues for the loos.

Topolski Century

Hungerford Bridge Arch 158, Concert Hall Approach, behind the Royal Festival Hall, SE1 8XU (7620 1275, www.topolskicentury.org.uk). Waterloo tube/rail. **Open** 11am-7pm Mon-Sat; noon-6pm Sun. **Admission** £2; £1 reductions. **Credit** MC, V. **Map** p401 M8.

Underneath the arches near Waterloo, this extensive mural depicts an extraordinary procession of 20th-century events and faces, from Bob Dylan to Winston Churchill via Chairman Mao and Malcolm

INSIDE TRACK BINGO!

With terraces overlooking the Thames, the Royal National Theatre's **Green Room Bar** (7452 3555) stays open until 1am on Fridays and also Saturdays, when it's been staging popular musical bingo nights.

Profile London Eye

The city's wheel of fortune gets a makeover.

At the hub of the South Bank's millennial makeover rolls the **London Eye** (*listings p47*), here only since 2000 but already up there with Tower Bridge and the Houses of Parliament as the capital's most postcard-friendly tourist asset. Assuming you choose a clear day, a 30-minute circuit on the Eye affords predictably great views of the city. Take a few snaps from the comfort of your pod and that's your sightseeing done.

The London Eye was the vision of husband-and-wife architect team Julia Barfield and David Marks, who entered a 1992 competition to design a structure auspicious enough to mark the millennium. The Marks' giant wheel idea came second in the contest; the winning entry is currently conspicuous by its absence. The Eye was planned as a temporary structure but its removal now seems unthinkable. Indeed, the wheel's popularity is

such that its owners, Merlin Entertainments, have seen fit to future-proof their investment with a three-year renovation in time for the Olympics.

Before summer 2012, each of the wheel's 32 pods (one for every London borough) will be unpinned from its cantilevered moorings in turn. The first ten-tonne pod was detached in May 2009, placed on to a pontoon and floated down the Thames on the tide to Tilbury Docks, from where it was loaded on to a truck and escorted by road to a Worcester workshop. So the wheel can keep its balance, dummy capsules are put in place of those that are missing. The renovation has been a knotty problem for Merlin; a spokesman says that more than 20 companies have been involved in the project.

So what can we expect from the shiny new Eye pods? They will be, said a press spokesman, more high tech with improved climate control. Some will be given screens, so business folk can hire them for high-level presentations. So while it's not exactly a case of Pimp my Eye (the attraction won't look any different), we're promised a snappier, happier ride.

THREE MORE VIEWS

The Monument
Over the City.
See p72.

Wolfe Monument, Greenwich Park
The Thames and beyond.
See p147.

Richmond Park
Sprawl to the east, 'burbs to the west.
See p155.

X. It's the work of Feliks Topolski, a Polish-born artist who travelled the world from 1933 until his death in 1989, popping up at just about every major event from the liberation of Bergen-Belsen to the coronation of Queen Elizabeth II. The museum has recently re-opened, losing some of its bombed-out atmosphere but now much better annotated and considerably easier to decipher.

Hungerford Bridge to Blackfriars Bridge

Embankment or Temple tube, Blackfriars rail or Waterloo tube/rail.

When the **Southbank Centre** (*see p311*) was built in the 1950s, the big concrete boxes that together contain the Royal Festival Hall (RFH), the Queen Elizabeth Hall (QEH) and the Purcell Room were hailed as a daring statement of modern architecture. Along with the Royal National Theatre and the Hayward, they comprise one of the largest and most popular arts centres in the world.

The centrepiece is Sir Leslie Martin's **Royal Festival Hall** (1951), recently given a £75 million overhaul. The main auditorium has had its acoustics enhanced and seating refurbished; the upper floors include an improved Poetry Library, and event rooms in which readings are delivered against the backdrop of the Eye and, on the far side of the river, Big Ben. Behind the hall on Belvedere Road, **Festival**

Square now hosts off-beat but crowd-pulling events, markets and exhibitions.

Next door, just across from the building housing the QEH and the Purcell Room, the **Hayward** (*see p53*) is a landmark of brutalist architecture. *Waterloo Sunset*, the gallery's elliptical glass pavilion, was designed in collaboration with light artist Dan Graham. Tucked under Waterloo Bridge is **BFI Southbank** (*see p292*); the UK's premier arthouse cinema, it's run by the British Film Institute. At the front is a second-hand book market. **Waterloo Bridge** itself, designed by Sir Giles Gilbert Scott in 1942, provides some of the finest views of the City, especially at dusk.

East of the bridge is Denys Lasdun's terraced **National Theatre** (*see p339*), a brutalist concrete structure that divides opinion like few other buildings in the city. There are popular free outdoor performances outside in the summer and free chamber music within during winter. Shaded by LED-dotted trees (their trunks were wrapped in shocking pink polka dot by 80-year-old Japanese artist Yayoi Kusama in summer 2009), the river path then leads past a rare sandy patch of the river bed, often busy with sand sculptors in the summer months, to **Gabriel's Wharf**, a collection of small independent shops that range from stylish to kitschy.

Next door, the deco tower of **Oxo Tower Wharf** was designed to circumvent advertising regulations for the stock-cube company that

SIGHTS

Topolski travelled to China during the Second World War, and went back in 1966. He returned to London with hundreds of drawings and devoted a whole year of his *Chronicle* to China.

In a juxtaposition characteristic of Topolski, the next section of the *Century* contrasts revolutionary China with the pomp and ceremony of the coronation of Queen Elizabeth II.

Topolski Century. *See p49.*

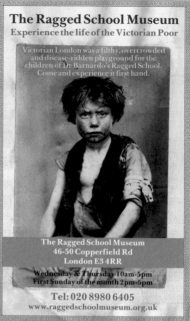

INSIDE TRACK
PAGAN SOUTHWARK

In the corridor of **Southwark Cathedral**'s **Millennium Buildings** (see p56), there's a small statue of a Roman hunter god from the early fourth century AD, discovered at the bottom of a well in the crypt in 1977. Beside the statue, a 'window on the past' reveals archaeological evidence including a Roman road and a 13th-century stone coffin, dotted now with well-wishers' coins.

used to own the building. Saved by local action group Coin Street Community Builders, it now provides affordable housing, interesting designer shops and galleries, two restaurants on the second floor, and a rooftop restaurant and bistro with more wonderful views. Behind, **Bernie Spain Gardens** is great for a break from the crowds.

Hayward
Southbank Centre, Belvedere Road, SE1 8XX (0871 663 2519, www.southbankcentre.co.uk). Embankment tube or Waterloo tube/rail. **Open** 10am-6pm Mon-Thur, Sat, Sun; 10am-10pm Fri. **Admission** varies, check website for details. **Credit** AmEx, MC, V. **Map** p401 M8.
Led by curator-director Ralph Rugoff, who arrived on the South Bank in 2006 having made his name at San Francisco's Wattis Institute, this versatile gallery continues its excellent programme of contemporary exhibitions, loaned from around the world. Shows for 2010 include Brazilian artist Ernesto Neto (17 June-5 Sept) and a dissection of the links between art and dance since the 1960s (Oct-Jan). Casual visitors to the Hayward can hang out in the industrial-look café downstairs (it's a bar at night), aptly called Concrete, before visiting the free contemporary exhibitions at the inspired Hayward Project Space; take the stairs to the first floor from the glass foyer extension.

Around Waterloo

Waterloo tube/rail.

Surprisingly, perhaps, there's plenty of interest around the stone-meets-glass rail terminus of London Waterloo. The most obvious attraction is the massive **BFI IMAX** (see p292), located in the middle of a roundabout at the southern end of Waterloo Bridge. The £20 million cinema makes imaginative use of a desolate space that, in the 1990s, was notorious for its 'Cardboard City' population of homeless residents.

South, on the corner of Waterloo Road and the Cut, is the restored Victorian façade of the

Old Vic Theatre (see p340), now overseen by Kevin Spacey. Further down the Cut is the renovated home of the **Young Vic** (see p346), a hotbed of theatrical talent with a stylish balcony bar. Both bring a touch of West End glamour across the river. To the north of the Cut, off Cornwall Road, are a number of atmospheric terraces made up of mid 19th-century artisans' houses.

BANKSIDE
Borough or Southwark tube, or London Bridge tube/rail.

In Shakespeare's day, the area known as Bankside was the centre of bawdy Southwark, neatly located just beyond the jurisdiction of the City fathers. As well as playhouses such as the Globe and the Rose, there were the famous 'stewes' (brothels) presided over by the Bishops of Winchester, who made a tidy income from the fines they levied on the area's 'Winchester Geese' (or, in common parlance, prostitutes). There's less drinking, carousing and mischief-making here these days, but the area's cultural heritage remains alive thanks to the reconstructed **Shakespeare's Globe** (see p54) and, pretty much next door to it, **Tate Modern** (see p55), a former power station that's now a gallery.

Spanning the river in front of the Tate, the **Millennium Bridge** opened in 2000, when it became the first new Thames crossing in London since Tower Bridge (1894). Its early days were fraught with troubles; after just two days, the bridge was closed because of a pronounced wobble, and didn't reopen until 2002. Still, its troubles long behind it, the bridge is now an extremely elegant structure; a 'ribbon of steel' in the words of its conceptualists, architect Lord Foster and sculptor Anthony Caro. Cross it and you'll find yourself at the foot of the stairs leading up to **St Paul's Cathedral** (see p63).

Continuing past the Globe and Southwark Bridge, you'll reach the **Anchor Bankside** pub (34 Park Street, 7407 1577). Built in 1775 on the site of an even older inn, the Anchor has, at various points, been a brothel, a chapel and a ship's chandlers. The outside terrace, across the pathway, offers fine river views.

All that's left of the Palace of Winchester, home of successive bishops, is the ruined rose window of the Great Hall on Clink Street. It stands next to the site of the bishop's former Clink prison, where thieves, prostitutes and debtors all served their sentences; it's now the **Clink Prison Museum** (1 Clink Street, SE1 9DG, 7403 0900, www.clink.co.uk). Around the corner is the entrance to the wine showcase

SIGHTS

SIGHTS

Snapshot
Post-war London

Where to see how London lived.

After the Blitz, vast tracts of land were left desolate and thousands of London residents needed rehousing. The city's saviour was surprising and divisive: concrete. Cheap, quick and strong enough to create extraordinary geometric buildings, it was loved by architects and hated by pretty much everyone else. The saw-tooth towers of the huge Barbican Centre are the most frequently debated example; just as visible, though, is the still-divisive **National Theatre**, right on the South Bank.

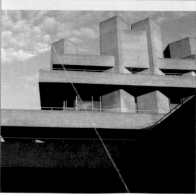

Vinopolis (*see right*). At the other end of Clink Street, St Mary Overie's dock contains a terrific full-scale replica of Sir Francis Drake's ship, the **Golden Hinde** (*see below*).

FREE Bankside Gallery
48 Hopton Street, SE1 9JH (7928 7521, www.banksidegallery.com). Southwark or London Bridge tube/rail. **Open** 11am-6pm daily. **Admission** free; donations appreciated. **Credit** MC, V. **Map** p404 O7.
In the shadow of Tate Modern, this tiny gallery is the home of the Royal Watercolour Society and the Royal Society of Painter-Printmakers. The gallery runs a frequently changing programme of delightful print and watercolour exhibitions throughout the year; many of the works on show are for sale. Both societies hold frequent events here, including talks and demonstrations.

Golden Hinde
St Mary Overie Dock, Cathedral Street, SE1 9DE (7403 0123, www.goldenhinde.com). London Bridge tube/rail. **Open** 10am-5pm daily. **Admission** £6; £4.50 reductions; £18 family. **Credit** MC, V. **Map** p404 P8.
This meticulous replica of Sir Francis Drake's 16th-century flagship is thoroughly seaworthy: the ship has even reprised the privateer's circumnavigatory voyage. 'Living History Experiences' (some overnight) allow participants to dress in period clothes, eat Tudor fare and learn the skills of the Elizabethan seafarer; book well in advance. On weekends, it swarms with children dressed up as pirates for birthday dos.

★ Shakespeare's Globe
21 New Globe Walk, SE1 9DT (7401 9919, www.shakespeares-globe.org). Southwark tube or London Bridge tube/rail. **Open** *Exhibition & tours* 10am-5pm daily. *Tours* every 15mins. **Admission** £10.50; £8.50 reductions; £6.50 children; £28 family. **Credit** AmEx, MC, V. **Map** p404 O7.
The original Globe Theatre, where many of William Shakespeare's plays were first staged and which he co-owned, burned to the ground in 1613 during a performance of *Henry VIII*. Nearly 400 years later, it was rebuilt not far from its original site, using construction methods and materials as close to the originals as possible, and is now open to the public for 90-minute tours throughout the year. During matinées, the tours go to the site of the Rose (21 New Globe Walk, SE1 9DT, 7261 9565, www.rosetheatre.org.uk), built by Philip Henslowe in 1587 as the first theatre on Bankside; red lights show the position of the original theatre. Funds are being sought to continue excavations and preserve the site.

Under the adventurous artistic directorship of Dominic Dromgoole, the Globe is also a fully operational theatre. In 2010, from 23 April, the bard's birthday, into early October, four of Shakespeare's plays and one new drama will be performed in repertory. For more on the theatre, *see p340*.

★ FREE Tate Modern

*Bankside, SE1 9TG (7887 8888, www.tate.
org.uk). Southwark tube or London Bridge
tube/rail.* **Open** 10am-6pm Mon-Thur, Sun;
10am-10pm Fri, Sat. *Tours* 11am, noon, 2pm, 3pm
daily. **Admission** free. *Temporary exhibitions*
vary. **Credit** AmEx, MC, V. **Map** p404 O7.
Thanks to its industrial architecture, this power-house of modern art is awe-inspiring even before you enter. Built after World War II as Bankside Power Station, it was designed by Sir Giles Gilbert Scott, architect of Battersea Power Station (*see p152*). The power station shut in 1981; nearly 20 years later, it opened as an art museum, and has enjoyed spectacular popularity ever since. The gallery attracts five million visitors a year to a building intended for half that number; work on a £165-million addition called TM2, a pyramid-like annexe, should start in 2010.

Inside, the original cavernous turbine hall is used to jaw-dropping effect as the home of large-scale, temporary installations (Miroslaw Balka's *How It Is* will be here until 5 April 2010). Beyond, the permanent collection draws from the Tate's collections of modern art (international works from 1900) and features heavy hitters such as Matisse, Rothko and Beuys. If you don't know where to start, take one of the tours (ask at the information desk). The galleries group artworks according to movement (Surrealism, Minimalism, Post-war abstraction) rather than theme. Most recently, in 2009, the east side of Level 5 was given over to the 1960s Italian movement Arte Povera. Temporary exhibitions in 2010 will include a photography show entitled *Exposed: Voyeurism, Surveillance and the Camera* (28 May 19 Sept) and a Gauguin retrospective (30 Sept 2010-16 Jan 2011).
▶ *The Tate-to-Tate boat links with Tate Britain (see p116) and runs every 20 minutes, stopping along the way at the London Eye (see p47). Tickets are available at both Tates, on board, online or by phone (7887 8888, £5 adult).*

Vinopolis

*1 Bank End, SE1 9BU (0870 241 4040,
www.vinopolis.co.uk). London Bridge tube/rail.*
Open noon-10pm Thur, Fri; 11am-10pm Sat;
noon-6pm Sun. **Admission** £25-£60. **Credit**
AmEx, MC, V. **Map** p404 P8.
Glossy Vinopolis is more of an introduction to wine-tasting than a resource for cognoscenti, but you do need to have some prior interest to get a kick out of it. Participants are furnished with a wine glass and an audio guide. Exhibits are set out by country, with five opportunities to taste wine or champagne from different regions. Gin crashes the party courtesy of a Bombay Sapphire cocktail, and you can also sample Caribbean rum, beer from the venue's microbrewery and even different types of absinthe.

Shakespeare's Globe.

BOROUGH

*Borough or Southwark tube, or London Bridge
tube/rail.*

At Clink Street, the route cuts inland, skirting the edge of the district of Borough. The landmark here is the Anglican **Southwark Cathedral** (*see p56*), formerly St Saviour's and before that the monastic church of St Mary Overie. Shakespeare's brother Edmund was buried in the graveyard; there's a monument to the playwright inside.

Just south of the cathedral you'll find the roof of **Borough Market**, a busy food market dating from the 13th century. It's wholesale only for most of the week, but hosts London's best public food market (*see p261*) on Thursdays, Fridays and Saturdays (when it can get very crowded) and is surrounded by good places to eat and drink. Not far away, at 77 Borough High Street, is the quaint **George** (7407 2056), London's last surviving galleried coaching inn.

Around London Bridge station, tourist attractions clamour for attention. One of the grisliest, with its displays of body parts and surgical implements, is the **Old Operating Theatre, Museum & Herb Garret** (*see p56*), but it's the less scary **London Dungeon** (*see p56*) that draws the biggest queues. Competing with the blood-curdling shrieks emanating from its entrance are the dulcet tones of Vera Lynn, broadcast in an attempt to lure visitors into **Winston Churchill's Britain at War Experience** (*see below*). Underneath the arches, there's the **London Bridge Experience** (*see below*).

London Bridge Experience

2-4 Tooley Street, SE1 2SY (0800 043 4666, www.thelondonbridgeexperience.com). London Bridge tube/rail. **Open** 10am-6pm daily. **Admission** £19.95; £14.95 reductions. **Credit** MC, V. **Map** p405 Q8.

Billing itself as two shows for the price of one, this costumed whistle-stop tour comprises a family-friendly lesson on the history of London Bridge, as well as a scary walk through the haunted foundations of the bridge for over-11s only. Upstairs, it's all good, smoke-filled fun as actors ham it up in front of wobbly sets and a bewildered, rapidly bonding audience. A Viking warrior urges us to heave on hawsers to pull the bridge down; a chamber of gore is hosted by the chap in charge of putting chopped-off heads on poles. Downstairs, dark, pestilential corridors are peopled by crazed zombies, animatronic torture victims and a Hannibal Lecter-esque butcher wielding a chainsaw. The calmness of the exhibition of the late Peter Jackson's artefacts associated with London Bridge down the ages comes as a real relief.

London Dungeon

28-34 Tooley Street, SE1 2SZ (7403 7221, www.thedungeons.com). London Bridge tube/rail. **Open** *Jan* 10.30am-5pm daily. *Feb, Mar* 9.30am-6.30pm daily. *Apr, Aug* 9.30am-7pm daily. *May-July, Sept, Oct* 10am-5.30pm daily. *Nov, Dec* 10am-5pm daily. **Admission** £21.95; £15.95-£19.95 reductions. **Credit** AmEx, MC, V. **Map** p405 Q8.

Enter the Victorian railway arches of London Bridge for this jokey and rather expensive celebration of torture, death and disease. Visitors are led through a dry-ice fog past gravestones and hideously rotting corpses to experience nasty symptoms from the Great Plague exhibition: an actor-led medley of corpses, boils, projectile vomiting, worm-filled skulls and scuttling rats. The Great Fire and Judgement Day also get the treatment.

★ Old Operating Theatre, Museum & Herb Garret

9A St Thomas's Street, SE1 9RY (7188 2679, www.thegarret.org.uk). London Bridge tube/rail. **Open** 10.30am-5pm daily. **Admission** £5.60; £3.25-£4.60 reductions; £13.75 family. **No credit cards. Map** p405 Q8.

The tower that houses this salutary reminder of antique surgical practice used to be part of the chapel of St Thomas's Hospital. Visitors enter via a vertiginous spiral staircase to view a pre-anaesthetic operating theatre dating from 1822, with tiered viewing seats for students. Just as gruesome are the operating tools that look like torture implements.

Tate Modern.

FREE Southwark Cathedral

London Bridge, SE1 9DA (7367 6734, www.southwark.anglican.org). London Bridge tube/rail. **Open** 10am-5pm daily (closing times vary on religious holidays). *Services* 8am, 8.15am, 12.30pm, 12.45pm, 5.30pm Mon-Fri; 9am, 9.15am, 4pm Sat; 8.45am, 9am, 11am, 3pm, 6.30pm Sun. *Choral Evensong* 5.30pm Mon, Thur (girls); 5.30pm Tue (boys & men); Fri (men only). **Admission** free; suggested donation £4. **Credit** AmEx, MC, V. **Map** p404 P8.

The oldest bits of this building date back more than 800 years. The retro-choir was the setting for several Protestant martyr trials during the reign of Mary Tudor. The courtyard is one of the area's prettiest places for a rest, especially during the summer. Inside, there are memorials to Shakespeare, John Harvard (benefactor of the American university) and Sam Wanamaker (the force behind the reconstruction of the Globe); Chaucer features in the stained glass. The new Millennium Buildings, including a refectory, were designed by Ptolemy Dean and Richard Griffiths and opened in 2001.

Winston Churchill's Britain at War Experience

64-66 Tooley Street, SE1 2TF (7403 3171, www.britainatwar.co.uk). London Bridge tube/rail. **Open** *Apr-Oct* 10am-5pm daily. *Nov-Mar* 10am-4.30pm daily. **Admission** £11.45; £5.50-£6.50 reductions; £29 family. **Credit** AmEx, MC, V. **Map** p405 Q8.

SIGHTS

This old-fashioned exhibition recalls the privations endured by the British during World War II. Visitors descend from street level in an ancient lift to a reconstructed tube station shelter. The experience continues with displays about London during the Blitz, including bombs, rare documents, photos and reconstructed shopfronts. The displays on rationing, food production and Land Girls are fascinating, and the set-piece walk-through bombsite is quite disturbing.

LONDON BRIDGE TO TOWER BRIDGE

Bermondsey tube/London Bridge tube/rail.

Across the street from the Dungeon is **Hay's Galleria**. Once an enclosed dock, it's now dominated by a peculiar kinetic sculpture called *The Navigators*. Exiting on the riverside, you can walk east past the great grey hulk of **HMS Belfast** (*see right*) to Tower Bridge.

Beyond the battleship you pass the pristine, but rather soulless environs of **City Hall**, home of London's current government. Designed by Lord Foster, the eco-friendly rotund glass structure leans squiffily away from the river (to prevent it casting shade on the walkers below – very thoughtful). There's a pleasant outside 'amphitheatre' called the Scoop, used for lunch breaks, sunbathing and outdoor events. It's part of a massive corporate development with the rather asinine name of **More London**.

South of here, many of the historic houses on Bermondsey Street now host hip design studios. This is also where you'll find the **Fashion & Textile Museum** (*see right*). The redevelopment of Bermondsey Square has spared the eel and pie shop **M Manze** (*see p198*). The Friday antiques market here (4am-2pm) is still great for browsing, even though the best of the bargains have usually gone before breakfast.

Back on the riverfront, a board announces when **Tower Bridge** is next due to be raised, which happens about 900 times a year. (The schedule is also posted at www.towerbridge.org.uk.) The bridge is one of the lowest bridges over the Thames, hence the twin lifting sections or bascules. The original steam-driven machinery can still be seen at the **Tower Bridge Exhibition** (*see p74*), which also offers the visitor fantastic views from the top. Further east, the former warehouses of **Butler's Wharf** are now mainly given over to expensive riverside dining; one of them also now houses the **Design Museum** (*see below*).

Design Museum

Shad Thames, SE1 2YD (7403 6933, www. designmuseum.org). Tower Hill tube or London Bridge tube/rail. **Open** 10am-5.45pm daily.

Admission £8.50; £5-£6.50 reductions; free under-12s. **Credit** AmEx, MC, V. **Map** p405 S9.
Exhibitions in this white 1930s building, once a banana warehouse, focus on modern and contemporary design. The smart Blueprint Café has a fine balcony overlooking the Thames. You can buy designer books in the museum's shop, as well as items related to the exhibitions, which in 2010 include shows dedicated to sustainable design, David Adjaye's photographs of African cities (both shows: 31 Mar-5 Sept) and fashion drawings (23 June-31 Oct).
▶ *Fine exhibitions of contemporary design are also held at the V&A; see p126.*

Fashion & Textile Museum

83 Bermondsey Street, SE1 3XF (7407 8664, www.ftmlondon.org). London Bridge tube/rail. **Open** 11am-6pm Wed-Sun. **Admission** £6.50; free-£3.50 reductions. **Credit** AmEx, MC, V. **Map** p405 Q9.
As flamboyant as its founder, fashion designer Zandra Rhodes, this pink and orange museum reopened in 2008. It holds 3,000 of Rhodes' garments, some on permanent display, along with her archive of paper designs, sketchbooks, silk screens and show videos. A quirky shop sells ware by new designers. Featured shows in 2009 included an exhibition dedicated to the evolution of underwear.

HMS Belfast

Morgan's Lane, Tooley Street, SE1 2JH (7940 6300, www.iwm.org.uk). London Bridge tube/rail. **Open** Mar-Oct 10am-6pm daily. Nov-Feb 10am-5pm daily. **Admission** £10.70; £8.60 reductions; free under-16s (must be accompanied by an adult). **Credit** MC, V. **Map** p405 R8.
This 11,500-ton 'Edinburgh' class large light cruiser is the last surviving big gun World War II warship in Europe. A floating branch of the Imperial War Museum (see p142), it makes an unlikely playground for children, who tear easily around its cramped complex of gun turrets, bridge, decks, and engine room. The *Belfast* was built in 1938, provided cover for convoys to Russia, and was instrumental in the Normandy Landings. She also supported United Nations forces in Korea, before being decommissioned in 1965. Running until autumn 2010, a new interactive exhibition explores British shipbuilding techniques through the ages, from the days of sail to modern prefabrication.

INSIDE TRACK
MONKS AND MARTINIS

At **Del'aziz** (www.delaziz.co.uk) in Bermondsey Square, you can sip martinis while inspecting the foundations of the medieval Bermondsey Abbey beneath the glass floor.

SIGHTS

The City

London began here, and continues to be driven from its wealthy core.

The City's current status as the financial heart of London hardly does justice to the 2,000 years of history that pepper its streets. This was where the Romans founded the city they called Londinium, building a bridge west of today's **London Bridge**. Here were a forum-basilica, an amphitheatre, public baths and, eventually, the surrounding defensive wall that still more or less defines the area we now call the Square Mile (actually 1.21 square miles).

Although the City has only 9,000 residents, more than 750,000 arrive each day to work as bankers, brokers, lawyers and traders, taking over 85 million square feet of office space. Tourists come, too, to see **St Paul's Cathedral** and the **Tower of London**, but there's much else besides. No area of London offers quite so much to see in so small a space, from Roman ruins and medieval marvels to iconic 21st-century offices.

Map p402, pp404-405	**Restaurants & cafés** p200
Hotels p169	**Pubs & bars** p227

SIGHTS

INTRODUCING THE CITY

London has long been divided in two, with Westminster the centre of politics and the City the capital of commerce. Many of the City's administrative affairs are still run on a feudal basis under the auspices of the City of London, Britain's richest local authority. The wealth of the area has always been hard to comprehend; this is, after all, an area that was able to bounce back after losing half its population to the Black Death and half its buildings first to the Great Fire and, later, to Nazi bombs during the Blitz.

To understand the City properly, visit on a weekday when the great economic machine is running at full tilt. At weekends, many of the streets fall quiet, although key areas – around St Paul's (*see p63*), say – are busy all week.

FREE City of London Information Centre
St Paul's Churchyard, EC4M 8BX (7332 1456, www.cityoflondon.gov.uk). St Paul's tube. **Open** 9.30am-5.30pm Mon-Sat; 10am-4pm Sun. **Credit** (shop) MC, V. **Map** p404 O6.
Run by the City of London, this new tourist office near St Paul's opened in 2008. As well as information and brochures on sights, events, walks and talks, it offers tours with specialist guides.

FLEET STREET

Temple tube or Blackfriars rail.

Without Fleet Street, the daily newspaper might never have been invented. Named after the vanished River Fleet, Fleet Street was a major artery for the delivery of goods into the City, including the first printing press, which was installed behind **St Bride's Church** (*see p60*) in 1500 by William Caxton's assistant, Wynkyn de Worde, who also set up a bookstall in the churchyard of St Paul's. In 1702, London's first daily newspaper, the *Daily Courant*, rolled off the presses; in 1712, Fleet Street saw the first of many libel cases when the *Courant* leaked the details of a private parliamentary debate.

By the end of World War II, half a dozen offices were churning out scoops and scandals between the Strand and Farringdon Road. Most of the newspapers moved away after Rupert Murdoch won his war with the print unions in the 1980s; the last of the news agencies, Reuters, finally followed suit in 2005. Until recently, the only periodical published on Fleet Street was a comic, the much-loved *Beano*. However, in 2009, left-wing weekly the *New Statesman* moved into offices around the corner from Fleet Street on Carmelite Street. And some interesting relics from the media days remain: the Portland-stone **Reuters building** (no.85), the Egyptian-influenced **Daily Telegraph building** (no.135) and the sleek, black **Daily Express building** (nos.121-128), designed by Owen Williams in the 1930s and arguably the only art deco building of note in London.

Tucked away on an alley behind St Bride's Church is the **St Bride Foundation Institute** (7353 3331, www.stbridefoundation.org), with a library (7353 4660, www.stbride.org; noon-5.30pm Tue, Thur; noon-9pm Wed) dedicated to printing and typography. Recently refurbished, the library mounts temporary exhibitions showing off its collections, which include rare works by Eric Gill and maquettes for Kinnear and Calvert's distinctive road signs.

Back on Fleet Street sits the church of **St Dunstan-in-the-West** (7405 1929, www.stdunstaninthewest.org; free tours 11am-3pm Tue), where the poet John Donne was rector in the 17th century. The church was rebuilt in the 1830s, but the eye-catching clock with chimes beaten by clockwork giants dates to 1671. It's now designated the Diocese of London's Church for Europe. Next door, no.186 is the house where Sweeney Todd, the 'demon barber of Fleet Street', reputedly murdered his customers before selling their bodies to a local pie shop. The legend, sadly, is a porky pie: Todd was invented by the editors of a Victorian penny dreadful in 1846 and propelled to fame rather later by a stage play.

Fleet Street has always been known for its pubs; half the newspaper editorials in London were once composed over liquid lunches. Much earlier, **Ye Olde Cheshire Cheese** (no.145, 7353 6170) was a favourite of Dickens and, later Yeats; in its heyday, it hosted the bibulous literary salons of Dr Samuel Johnson, who lived nearby at 17 Gough Square (*see right*). It also had a famous drinking parrot, the death of whom prompted obituaries in hundreds of newspapers. At no.66, the **Tipperary** (7583 6470) is the oldest Irish pub outside Ireland: it opened in the 1700s and sold the first pint of Guinness on the British mainland shortly after.

Dr Johnson's House

17 Gough Square, off Fleet Street, EC4A 3DE (7353 3745, www.drjohnsonshouse.org). Chancery Lane tube or Blackfriars rail. **Open** *May-Sept* 11am-5.30pm Mon-Sat. *Oct-Apr* 11am-5pm Mon-Sat. *Tours* by arrangement, groups of 10 or more only. **Admission** £4.50; £1.50-£3.50 reductions; £10 family; free under-5s. *Tours* free. **No credit cards. Map** p404 N6.

Famed as the author of one of the first – as well as being surely the most significant and certainly the wittiest – dictionary of the English language, Dr Samuel Johnson (1709-84) also wrote poems, a novel and one of the earliest travelogues, an acerbic account of a tour of the Western Isles with his indefatigable biographer James Boswell. You can tour the stately Georgian townhouse off Fleet Street where Johnson came up with his inspired definitions – 'to make dictionaries is dull work,' was his definition of the word 'dull'. A neat statue of Johnson's cat Hodge adorns the square outside.

FREE St Bride's Church

Fleet Street, EC4Y 8AU (7427 0133, www.stbrides.com). Temple tube. **Open** 8.30am-5.30pm Mon-Fri; 11am-3pm Sat; 11am-noon, 6.30-7.30pm Sun. Times vary Mon-Sat, so phone ahead to check. **Admission** free. **No credit cards. Map** p404 N6.

Hidden away down an alley south of Fleet Street, St Bride's is still popularly known as the journalists' church. In the north aisle, there's a shrine dedicated to journos killed in action. Down in the crypt a very fine museum displays a number of fragments of the churches that have existed on this site since the sixth century. The Wren-designed spire is said to have inspired the traditional tiered wedding cake.

TEMPLE

Temple tube or Blackfriars rail.

At its western end, Fleet Street becomes the Strand at **Temple Bar**, the City's ancient western boundary and once the site of Wren's great gateway (now relocated to Paternoster Square beside St Paul's; *see right*). The area has long been linked to the law, and here, on the edge of Holborn (*see p75*), stands the splendid neo-Gothic **Royal Courts of Justice** (7947 6000, www.hmcourts-service.gov.uk). Two of the highest civil courts in the land sit here – the High Court and the Appeals Court, justice at its most bewigged and ermine-robed – and visitors are welcome to observe the process of law in any of the 88 courtrooms. Across the road are the courtyards of the **Middle Temple** (7427 4800,www.middletemple.org.uk) and **Inner Temple** (7797 8250, www.innertemple.org.uk), two of the Inns of Court that provided training and lodging for London's medieval lawyers.

Anybody may visit the grounds, but access to buildings is usually reserved for lawyers and barristers. Tours of the Inner Temple can be arranged for £10 per person (minimum five people; book on 7797 8241).

The site was formerly the headquarters of the Knights Templar, an order of warrior monks founded in the 12th century to protect pilgrims travelling to the Holy Land. The Templars built the original **Temple Church** (*see below*) in 1185, but they fell foul of Catholic orthodoxy during the Crusades and the order was disbanded for heresy. Dan Brown used the Temple Church as a setting for his bestselling conspiracy novel *The Da Vinci Code* (2003). Robin Griffith-Jones, the master of Temple Church, has produced a robust response to his claims at www.beliefnet.com/templechurch.

FREE Temple Church
Fleet Street, EC4Y 7BB (7353 8559, www. templechurch.com). Chancery Lane or Temple tube. **Open** 2-4pm Tue-Fri; phone or check website for details. *Services* 1.15pm Thur; 8.30am, 11.15am Sun. **Admission** free. **No credit cards. Map** p404 N6.

Inspired by Jerusalem's Church of the Holy Sepulchre, the Temple Church was the private chapel of the mystical Knights Templar. The rounded apse contains the worn gravestones of several Crusader knights, but the church was refurbished by Wren and the Victorians, and was damaged in the Blitz. Not that it puts off the wild speculations of all those avid *Da Vinci Code* fans. There are organ recitals most Wednesdays (phone for details).
▶ *There's a Crusader altar in All Hallows by the Tower; see p73. For the Hospitallers, try the Museum of the Order of St John; see p77.*

ST PAUL'S & AROUND

St Paul's tube.

After Big Ben, the towering dome of **St Paul's Cathedral** (*see p63*) is probably the definitive symbol of London, an architectural two fingers to the Great Fire and later, in a famous photograph, to the German bombers that tried to destroy the city. Immediately north of the cathedral is the redeveloped **Paternoster Square**, a modern plaza incorporating a sundial that only rarely tells the time. The

Royal Courts of Justice.

SIGHTS

name harks to the days when priests from St Paul's walked the streets chanting the Lord's Prayer (which begins *Pater noster*, 'Our Father').

Also of interest is Wren's statue-covered **Temple Bar**. It once stood at the intersection of Fleet Street and the Strand, marking the boundary between the City of London and neighbouring Westminster; during the Middle Ages, the monarch was only allowed to pass through the Temple Bar into the City with the approval of the Lord Mayor of London. The archway was dismantled as part of a Victorian road-widening programme in 1878 and became a garden ornament for a country estate in Hertfordshire, before being installed in its current location, as the gateway between St Paul's and Paternoster Square, in 2004. The gold-topped pillar in the centre of the square looks as if it commemorates something important, but's just an air vent for the underground. Victorians would admire such spirited decoration of the mundane.

South of St Paul's, a cascade of steps runs down to the **Millennium Bridge**, which spans the river to **Tate Modern** (*see p54*) and now offers the main gateway to the City for tourists. The stairs take you close to the 17th-century **College of Arms** (*see right*), the official seat of heraldry in Great Britain. East of the cathedral is narrow Bow Lane. At one end sits **St Mary-le-Bow** (7248 5139, www.stmaryle bow.co.uk, 7am-6pm Mon-Wed; 7am-6.30pm Wed; 7am-4pm Fri), constructed by Wren between 1671 and 1680; its peals once defined anyone born within earshot as a true Cockney. At the other is **St Mary Aldermary** (7248 9902, www.stmaryaldermary.co.uk, 11am-3pm Mon Fri), its pin straight spire designed by Wren's office; it was the only Gothic church by Wren to survive World War II. Inside, there's a fabulous moulded plaster ceiling and original wooden sword rest (London parishioners carried arms until the late 19th century). Roman coins are sold here to fund renovation work.

There are more Wren creations south of St Paul's. On Garlick Hill, named for the medieval garlic market, is **St James Garlickhythe** (7236 1719, www.stjamesgarlickhythe.org.uk, 10.30am-4pm Mon-Fri). The official church of London's vintners and joiners, it was built by Wren in 1682 and contains the naturally mummified remains of a young man, Jimmy Garlick, discovered in the vaults in 1855 and now hidden from view in the tower. The church was hit by bombs in World Wars I and II, and partly ruined by a falling crane in 1991, but the interior has been convincingly restored. Off Victoria Street is **St Nicholas Cole Abbey**, the first church rebuilt after the Great Fire.

To the north-west of the cathedral is the **Old Bailey** (*see right*), built on the site of

infamous Newgate Prison. A remnant of the prison's east wall can be seen in nearby Amen Corner.

FREE College of Arms
130 Queen Victoria Street, EC4V 4BT (7248 2762, www.college-of-arms.gov.uk). St Paul's tube or Blackfriars rail. **Open** 10am-4pm Mon-Fri. *Tours* by arrangement. **Admission** free. **No credit cards. Map** p404 O7.

Originally created to identify competing knights at medieval jousting tournaments, coats of arms soon became an integral part of family identity for the landed gentry of Britain. Visitors interested in tracking down their family history can arrange tours. The building was hit by a fire in February 2009, but mercifully escaped more or less unscathed.

FREE Old Bailey (Central Criminal Court)
Corner of Newgate Street & Old Bailey, EC4M 7EH (7248 3277). St Paul's tube. **Open** *Public gallery* 10am-1pm, 2-4.30pm Mon-Fri. **Admission** free. No under-14s; 14-16s only if accompanied by adults. **No credit cards. Map** p404 O6.

A gilded statue of blind (meaning impartial) justice stands atop London's most famous criminal court. The current building was completed in 1907; the site itself has hosted some of the most famous trials in British history, including that of Oscar Wilde. Anyone is welcome to attend a trial, but bags, cameras, dictaphones, mobile phones and food are banned (and no storage facilities are provided).
▶ *A blocked-up door in St Sepulchre is the only visible remains of a priest tunnel into the court.*

★ St Paul's Cathedral
Ludgate Hill, EC4M 8AD (7236 4128, www.stpauls.co.uk). St Paul's tube. **Open** 8.30am-4pm Mon-Sat. *Galleries, crypt & ambulatory* 9.30am-4.15pm Mon-Sat. Special events may cause closure; check before visiting. *Tours of cathedral & crypt* 10.45am, 11.15am, 1.30pm, 2pm Mon-Sat. **Admission** *Cathedral, crypt & gallery* £11; £3.50-£10 reductions; £25 family; free under-6s. *Tours* £3; £1-£2.50 reductions. **Credit** AmEx, MC, V. **Map** p404 O6.

INSIDE TRACK
HALL OR NOTHING

The City is dotted with halls belonging to the powerful Livery Companies, originally established as Guilds but now largely charitable institutions. One of the most striking is the **Cutlers' Hall** on Warwick Lane, which boasts a fine stone frieze of cutlers at work.

SIGHTS

The first cathedral to St Paul was built on this site in 604, but fell to Viking marauders. Its Norman replacement, a magnificent Gothic structure with a 490-foot spire (taller than any London building until the 1960s), burned in the Great Fire. The current church was commissioned in 1673 from Sir Christopher Wren as the centrepiece of London's resurgence from the ashes. Modern buildings now encroach on the cathedral from all sides, but the passing of three centuries has done nothing to diminish the appeal of London's most famous cathedral.

Start with the exterior. Over the last decade, a £40m restoration project has painstakingly removed most of the Victorian grime from the walls and the extravagant main façade looks as brilliant today as it must have when the last stone was placed in 1708. On the south side of the cathedral, an austere park has been laid out, tracing the outline of the medieval chapter house whose remains lie 4ft under it.

The vast open spaces of the interior contain memorials to national heroes such as Wellington and Lawrence of Arabia. The statue of John Donne, metaphysical poet and former Dean of St Paul's, is frequently overlooked, but it's the only monument to have been saved from Old St Paul's. The Whispering Gallery, inside the dome, is reached by 259 shallow steps from the main hall; the acoustics here are so good that a whisper can be bounced clearly to the other side of the dome. Steps continue up to first the Stone Gallery (119 tighter, steeper steps), with its high external balustrades, then outside to the Golden Gallery (152 steps), with its giddying views. Come here to orient yourself before setting off in search of other City monuments.

Before leaving St Paul's, head down to the maze-like crypt (through a door whose frame is decorated with skull and crossbones), which contains a shop and café and memorials to such dignitaries as Alexander Fleming, William Blake and Admiral Lord Nelson, whose grand tomb (purloined from Wolsey by Henry VIII but never used by him) is right beneath the centre of the dome. To one side is the small, plain tombstone of Christopher Wren himself, inscribed by his son with the epitaph, 'Reader, if you seek a monument, look around you'; at their request, Millais and Turner were buried near him.

As well as tours of the main cathedral and self-guided audio tours (£4, £3.50 reductions), you can join special tours of the Triforium, visiting the library and Wren's 'Great Model', at 11.30am and 2pm on Monday and Tuesday and at 2pm on Friday (pre-book on 7246 8357, £16 incl admission).

NORTH TO SMITHFIELD

Barbican or St Paul's tube.

North of St Paul's Cathedral on Foster Lane is **St Vedast-alias-Foster** (7606 3998, 8am-6pm Mon-Fri), another finely proportioned Wren church, restored after World War II using spare trim from other churches in the area. Nearby, off Aldersgate Street, peaceful **Postman's Park** contains the Watts Memorial to Heroic Sacrifice: a wall of Victorian ceramic plaques, each of which commemorates an heroic but doomed act of bravery. Take the story of Sarah Smith, a pantomime artiste, who received

St Paul's Cathedral. *See p63*.

'terrible injuries when attempting in her inflammable dress to extinguish the flames which had engulfed her companion (1863)'.

Further west on Little Britain (named after the Duke of Brittany, not the TV show) is **St Bartholomew-the-Great** (*see below*), founded along with **St Bartholomew's Hospital** in the 12th century. Popularly known as St Bart's, the hospital treated air-raid casualties throughout World War II; shrapnel damage from German bombs is still visible on the outside walls. Scottish nationalists now come here to lay flowers at the monument to William Wallace, executed in front of the church on the orders of Edward I in 1305. Just beyond St Bart's is **Smithfield Market** (*see p77*).

FREE Museum of St Bartholomew's Hospital

St Bartholomew's Hospital, North Wing, West Smithfield, EC1A 7BE (7601 8152, www. bartsandthelondon.nhs.uk/museums). Barbican tube or Farringdon tube/rail. **Open** 10am-4pm Tue-Fri. **Admission** free; donations welcome. **No credit cards. Map** p402 O5.
Be glad you're living in the 21st century. Many of the displays in this small museum inside St Bart's Hospital relate to the days before anaesthetics, when surgery and carpentry were kindred occupations. Every Friday at 2pm, visitors can take a guided tour of the museum (£5, book ahead on 7837 0546) that takes in the Hogarth paintings in the Great Hall, the little church of St Bartholomew-the-Less, neighbouring St Bartholomew-the-Great and Smithfield.

St Bartholomew-the-Great

West Smithfield, EC1A 9DS (7606 5171, www. greatstbarts.com). Barbican tube or Farringdon tube/rail. **Open** 8.30am-5pm Mon-Fri (until 4pm Nov-Feb); 10.30am-4pm Sat; 8.30am-8pm Sun. *Services* 12.30pm Tue; 8.30am Thur 9am, 10am, 11am, 6.30pm Sun. **Admission** £4; £3 reductions; £10 family. **No credit cards. Map** p402 O5.
This atmospheric medieval church was built over the remains of the 12th-century priory hospital of St Bartholomew, founded by Prior Rahere, a former courtier of Henry I. The church was chopped about during Henry VIII's reign and the interior is now firmly Elizabethan, although it also contains donated works of modern art. You may recognise the main hall from *Shakespeare in Love* or *Four Weddings and a Funeral*.

NORTH OF LONDON WALL

Barbican tube or Moorgate tube/rail.

From St Bart's, the road known as London Wall runs east to Bishopsgate, following the approximate route of the old Roman walls.

INSIDE TRACK IN MEMORIAM

In 2009, the first new plaque for 70 years was added to **Postman's Park** (*see left*). It was dedicated to Leigh Pitt, who died in 2007 while saving a child from drowning in Thamesmead.

Tower blocks have sprung up here like daisies, but the odd lump of weathered stonework can still be seen poking up between the office blocks, marking the path of the old City wall. You can patrol the remaining stretches of the wall, with panels (some barely legible) pointing out highlights along a route of two miles. The walk starts near the **Museum of London** (*see p67*) and runs to the Tower of London.

The area north of London Wall was reduced to rubble by German bombs in World War II. In 1958, the City of London and London County Council clubbed together to buy the land for the construction of 'a genuine residential neighbourhood, with schools, shops, open spaces and amenities'. What Londoners got was the **Barbican**, a vast concrete estate of 2,000 flats that feels a bit like a university campus after the students have all gone home. Casual visitors may get the eerie feeling they have been miniaturised and transported into a giant architect's model, but design enthusiasts will recognise the Barbican as a prime example of 1970s brutalism, softened a little by time and rectangular ponds of friendly resident ducks.

The main attraction here is the Barbican arts complex, with its library, cinema, theatre and concert hall – each reviewed in the appropriate chapters – plus an art gallery (*see below*) and the **Barbican Conservatory** (noon-5pm Sun), a huge greenhouse full of exotic plants. Sadly, pedestrian access wasn't high on the architects' list of priorities: the Barbican is a maze of blank passages and dead-end walkways. Marooned amid the towers is the only pre-war building in the vicinity: the restored 16th-century church of **St Giles Cripplegate** (7638 1997, www. stgilescripplegate.com, 11am-4pm Mon-Fri), where Oliver Cromwell was married and John Milton buried.

North-east of the Barbican on City Road are **John Wesley's House** (*see p67*) and **Bunhill Fields**, the nonconformist cemetery where William Blake, the preacher John Bunyan and novelist Daniel Defoe are buried.

Barbican Art Gallery

Barbican Centre, Silk Street, EC2Y 8DS (7382 7006, www.barbican.org.uk). Barbican tube or Moorgate tube/rail. **Open** 11am-8pm Mon-Wed, Fri-Sun; 11am-8pm Thur. **Admission** £8; £4-£6

Profile Museum of London

The capital's story gets retold at this newly relaunched museum.

The **Museum of London** (*listings right*) shares the job of telling London's story with its sibling, the Museum of London Docklands (*see p141*). In the last five years, the museum has received a top-to-bottom £22-million refurbishment that's set to conclude in spring 2010 with the unveiling of a remodelled lower-ground-floor gallery covering the city from 1666 to the present day. Previously, the modern London gallery ended before the First World War, but the new space will feature everything from an unexploded World War II bomb to a multimedia display on the Brixton riots.

The biggest obstacle faced by the museum is its difficult location: the entrance is two floors above street level, hidden behind a roundabout. However, a new space has been created on the ground floor, which will allow key exhibits – the Lord Mayor's coach, for instance – to be seen from the street.

Upstairs, the chronological displays begin with 'London Before London': flint axes from 300,000 BC found near Piccadilly; bones from an aurochs and hippopotami; and the Bronze Age Dagenham idol, a fertility image carved from a single piece of Scots pine. 'Roman London' includes an impressive reconstructed dining room complete with mosaic floor. Windows overlook a sizeable fragment of the City wall, whose Roman foundations have clearly been built upon many times over the centuries. Sound effects and audio-visual displays illustrate the medieval city, with clothes, shoes and armour on display. From Elizabethan and Jacobean London, heyday of the Globe Theatre, comes the Cheapside Hoard, an astonishing cache of jewellery unearthed in 1912.

The downstairs galleries focus on how London's relationship with the world changed through trade, war and empire. There are displays on poverty, finance, shopping, 20th-century fashion, a recreation of a Victorian pleasure garden plus lots of audio-visual and interactive material. The website has details of temporary exhibitions and activities for children.

BACK IN TIME
There's more City history at the **Bank of England Museum** (*see p68*), **Dr Johnson's House** (*see p60*) and the **Monument** (*see p72*).

reductions; under-12s free. **Credit** AmEx, MC, V.
Map p402 P5.

The art gallery at the Barbican Centre on the third floor isn't quite as 'out there' as it would like you to think, but the exhibitions on design, architecture and pop culture are usually pretty diverting, as are their often attention-grabbing titles.

▶ *On the ground floor, the Curve is a long, thin gallery (yes, it's curved) that stages free exhibitions of specially commissioned art.*

FREE John Wesley's House & Museum of Methodism

Wesley's Chapel, 49 City Road, EC1Y 1AU (7253 2262, www.wesleyschapel.org.uk). Moorgate or Old Street tube/rail. **Open** 10am-4pm Mon-Sat; after the service until 1.45pm Sun. *Tours* arrangements on arrival; groups of 10 or more phone ahead. **Admission** free; donations welcome. **Credit** AmEx, MC, V. **Map** p403 Q4.

John Wesley (1703-91), the founder of Methodism, was a man of legendary self-discipline. You can see the minister's nightcap, preaching gown and personal experimental electric-shock machine on a tour of his austere home on City Road. The adjacent chapel has a small museum on the history of Methodism and fine memorials of dour, sideburn-sporting preachers. Downstairs (to the right) are some of the finest public toilets in London, built in 1899 with original fittings by Sir Thomas Crapper.

★ FREE Museum of London

150 London Wall, EC2Y 5HN (0870 444 3851, www.museumoflondon.org.uk). Barbican or St Paul's tube. **Open** 10am-6pm daily. **Admission** free; suggested donation £2. **Credit** AmEx, MC, V. **Map** p402 P5.

See left **Profile**.

BANK & AROUND

Mansion House tube or Bank tube/DLR.

Above Bank station, seven streets come together to mark the symbolic heart of the Square Mile, ringed by some of the most important buildings in the City. Constructed from steely Portland stone, the Bank of England, the Royal Exchange and Mansion House form a stirring monument to the power of money: most decisions about the British economy are still made within this small precinct. Few places in London have quite the same sense of pomp and circumstance.

Easily the most dramatic building here is the **Bank of England**, founded in 1694 to fund William III's war against the French. It's a fortress, with no accessible windows and just one public entrance (leading to the **Bank of England Museum**; *see p68*). The outer walls were constructed in 1788 by Sir John Soane, whose own museum can still be seen in Holborn

(*see p76*). Although millions have been stolen from its depots elsewhere in London, the bank itself has never been robbed. Today, it's responsible for printing the nation's banknotes and setting the country's base interest rate.

On the south side of the square is the Lord Mayor of London's official residence, **Mansion House** (7626 2500, group visits by written application to Diary Office, Mansion House, Walbrook, EC4N 8BH, or by phone), an imposing neoclassical building constructed by George Dance in 1753. It's the only private residence in the country to have its own court and prison cells for unruly guests. Just behind Mansion House is the superbly elegant church of **St Stephen Walbrook** (7626 9000, www.ststephenwalbrook.net, 11am-4pm Mon-Fri), built by Wren in 1672. Its gleaming domed, coffered ceiling was borrowed from Wren's original design for St Paul's; other features include an incongruous altar, sculpted by Sir Henry Moore and dubbed 'the camembert'. The Samaritans were founded here in the 1950s.

To the east of Mansion House is the **Royal Exchange**. It's the Parthenon-like former home of the London Stock Exchange, founded back in 1565 to facilitate the newly invented trade in stocks and shares with Antwerp. In 1972, the exchange shifted to offices on Threadneedle Street, thence to Paternoster Square; today, the Royal Exchange houses a posh champagne bar and some staggeringly expensive emporia. Flanking the Royal Exchange are statues of James Henry Greathead, who invented the machine that cut the tunnels for the London Underground, and Paul Reuter, who founded the Reuters news agency here in 1851.

The period grandeur is undermined by the monstrosity on the west side of the square, **No.1 Poultry**. The name fits: it's a turkey. A short walk down Queen Victoria Street will lead you to the eroded foundations of the **Temple of Mithras**, constructed by Roman soldiers in AD 240-250. Beliefs from the cult of Mithras were incorporated into Christianity when Rome abandoned paganism in the fourth century, but what remains of the site is rather unimpressive.

SIGHTS

Further south, on Cannon Street, you can see the **London Stone**. Depending who you talk to, it marks the Roman's measuring point for distances across Britain, it's a druidic altar or it's just a lump of rock. Whichever way, it's a small thing, easily missed and preserved behind a grille in the wall.

Nearby on College Hill is the late Wren church of **St Michael Paternoster Royal** (7248 5202, 9am-5pm Mon-Fri), the final resting place of Richard 'Dick' Whittington. Later transformed into a rags-to-riches pantomime hero, the real Dick Whittington was a wealthy merchant who was elected Lord Mayor four times between 1397 and 1420. The role of Dick Whittington's cat is less clear – many now believe that 'cat' was actually slang for a ship – but an excavation to find Whittington's tomb in 1949 did uncover the body of a mummified medieval moggy. The happy pair are depicted in the stained-glass windows.

Returning to Bank, stroll north along Prince's Street, beside the Bank of England's blind wall. Look right along Lothbury to find **St Margaret Lothbury** (7726 4878, www.stml.org.uk, 7am-5.15pm Mon-Fri). The grand screen dividing the choir from the nave was designed by Wren himself; other works here by his favourite woodcarver, Grinling Gibbons, were recovered from various churches damaged in World War II. Lothbury also features a beautiful neo-Venetian building, now apartments, built by 19th-century architect Augustus Pugin, who worked with Charles Barry on the Houses of Parliament.

South-east of Bank on Lombard Street is Hawksmoor's striking **St Mary Woolnoth**, squeezed in between the 17th-century banking houses. Only their gilded signboards now remain, a hanging heritage artfully maintained by the City's planners. The gilded grasshopper at 68 Lombard Street is the heraldic emblem of Sir Thomas Gresham, who founded the Royal Exchange and **Gresham College**.

Further east on Lombard Street is Wren's **St Edmund the King** (7621 1391, www.spiritualitycentre.org, 10am-6pm Mon-Fri), which now houses a centre for modern spirituality. Other significant churches in the area include Wren's handsome red-brick **St Mary Abchurch**, off Abchurch Lane, and **St Clement**, on Clement's Lane, immortalised in the nursery rhyme 'Oranges and Lemons'. Over on Cornhill are two more Wren churches; **St Peter-upon-Cornhill**, mentioned by Dickens in *Our Mutual Friend*, and **St Michael Cornhill**, which contains a bizarre statue of a pelican feeding its young with pieces of its own body; a medieval symbol for the Eucharist, it was sculpted by someone who had plainly never seen a pelican.

North-west of the Bank of England is the **Guildhall**, the City of London headquarters. 'Guildhall' can either describe the original banqueting hall (*see right*) or the cluster of buildings around it, of which the **Guildhall Art Gallery** (*see p71*), the **Clockmakers' Museum & Library** (*see below*) and the church of **St Lawrence Jewry** (7600 9478, 7am-1pm Mon-Fri), opposite the hall, are also open to the public. St Lawrence is another restored Wren, with an impressive gilt ceiling. Within, you can hear the renowned Klais organ used for lunchtime organ recitals, usually held from 1pm on Tuesdays.

Glance north along Wood Street to see the isolated tower of **St Alban**, built by Wren in 1685 but ruined in World War II and now an eccentric private home. At the end of the street is **St Anne & St Agnes** (7606 4986, 10.30am-5pm Mon-Fri, Sun), laid out in the form of a Greek cross. Recitals take place here on weekday lunchtimes.

FREE Bank of England Museum

Entrance on Bartholomew Lane, EC2R 8AH (7601 5545, www.bankofengland.co.uk/museum). Bank tube/DLR. **Open** 10am-5pm Mon-Fri. *Tours* by arrangement. **Admission** free. *Tours* free. **No credit cards. Map** p405 Q6.

Housed inside the former Stock Offices of the Bank of England, this engaging and surprisingly lively museum explores the history of the national bank. As well as ancient coins and original artwork for British banknotes, the museum offers a rare chance to manhandle a real 13kg gold bar (closely monitored by CCTV). One exhibit looks at the life of Kenneth Grahame, author of *The Wind in the Willows* and a long-term employee of the bank. Child-friendly temporary exhibitions take place in the museum lobby.

FREE Clockmakers' Museum & Guildhall Library

Aldermanbury, EC2V 7HH (Guildhall Library 7332 1868, www.clockmakers.org). St Paul's tube or Bank tube/DLR. **Open** 9.30am-5pm Mon-Sat. **Admission** free. **No credit cards. Map** p404 P6.

Hundreds of ticking, chiming clocks and watches are displayed in this single-room museum, from the egg-sized Elizabethan pocket watches to marine chronometers via a 'fuse for a nuclear device'. Highlights include Marine Chronometer H5, built by John Harrison (1693-1776) to solve the problem of longitude, and the plain Smith's Imperial wristwatch worn by Sir Edmund Hillary on the first (Rolex-sponsored) ascent of Everest. Just down the corridor, the library has books, manuscripts and prints relating to the history of London – original historic works can be requested for browsing (bring ID). The bookshop stocks loads of London books and maps.

FREE Guildhall

Gresham Street, EC2P 2EJ (7606 3030, tours 7606 1463, www.cityoflondon.gov.uk). St Paul's tube or Bank tube/DLR. **Open** *May-Sept* 10am-5pm daily. *Oct-Apr* 10am-5pm Mon-Sat. *Tours* by arrangement; groups of 10 or more only. **Admission** free. **No credit cards**. **Map** p404 P6.

The City of London and its progenitors have been holding grand ceremonial dinners in this hall for eight centuries. Memorials to national heroes line the walls, shields of the 100 livery companies grace the ceiling, and every Lord Mayor since 1189 gets a namecheck on the windows. Many famous trials have taken place here, including the treason trial of 16-year-old Lady Jane Grey, 'the nine days' queen', in 1553. Above the entrance to the Guildhall are statues of Gog and Magog. Born of the union of demons and exiled Roman princesses, these two mythical giants are said to protect the City of London. The current statues replaced 18th-century forebears that were destroyed in the Blitz.

Monument. *See p72.*

SIGHTS

SIGHTS

Walk The 21st-Century City

Peter Rees, the City Planning Officer, tells us about the area's best new buildings.

Along Gresham Street and Aldermanbury are three new buildings that blend in with the existing City. There's Lord Foster's at **10 Gresham Street**, dark metal with stone corners; the stone acts as buttresses to encase escape stairs, and the roof is thrown back to provide light for surrounding buildings. At **20 Gresham Street** is a building by Kohn Pedersen Fox in metal and stone that looks very modern; from afar, it looks like a basket. And the building at **30 Gresham Street**, designed by Sidell Gibson Architects, follows the curve of the street. The street curves because it was originally going round a Roman amphitheatre, the remains of which you can see in the **Guildhall Art Gallery** (*see right*).

Walk down Gresham Street towards the **Bank of England** (*see p68*). Most of these buildings have been refurbished: some have retained façades, others have been stretched. On your right, look out for the two buildings either side of **Ironmonger Lane**: one new and one old, they complement each other perfectly.

Along Throgmorton Street at the site of the old Stock Exchange, we've put an alleyway – **Threadneedle Walk** – between two new buildings at **125 Old Broad Street** and **60 Threadneedle Street**. It's on your right. Walk down it and look at the building opposite on the angle of Threadneedle Street and Old Broad Street. It has three new floors, but the average Joe would never notice. In fact, it fits in much better with the neighbours now. Planning means you can put right things that went wrong before.

Head along Threadneedle Street to **22-38 Bishopsgate**. Work is starting on Kohn Pederson Fox's Pinnacle, better known as the Helter Skelter. It will be the tallest building in the City when completed in 2011. Next door is **122 Leadenhall**, the proposed site of the wedge-shaped Cheesegrater. At the north end of Bishopsgate is the **Heron Tower**, which should be completed in 2010 or 2011.

Head south. At **20 Gracechurch Street** you can see something we got wrong in the past: this building has been described as

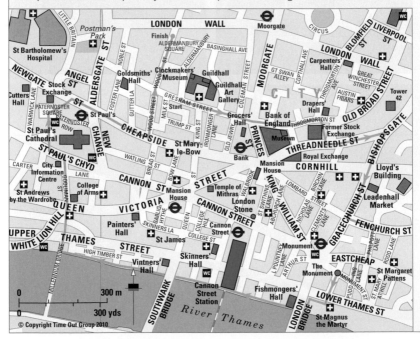

'mating jukeboxes'. We've put retail in the bottom and taken off some of the more ephemeral decoration, but there's not much you can do with it. Sometimes you get saddled with bad buildings.

Nearby, **10 Fenchurch Street** is by Denys Lasdun, the architect of the Royal National Theatre. It's a sympathetic restoration of a classic 1960s design. **20 Fenchurch Street** is the site of what will be the Walkie Talkie. Head down towards the Monument and cross Lower Thames Street; turn right past St Magnus the Martyr church (*see p72*) and left on to Riverside Walk.

Walk east by the Thames and you'll pass two adjacent new buildings, David Walker's **Riverbank House** and Fletcher Priest Architects' **Watermark Place**. The latter is on the site of Mondial House, the BT building Prince Charles described as like a 'giant word processor'. Go through the tunnel under Southwark Bridge and keep on the walk until you reach Arup and Foster's Millennium Bridge. Head up to St Paul's (*see p63*). Here's our exciting new **Visitor Centre**, designed by Ken Shuttleworth. It's amazing how quickly it has settled in.

Head north past St Paul's, under Temple Bar and into Paternoster Square. Turn right and make your way out on to Cheapside, where we're building **One New Change**, centrepiece of our new Cheapside strategy that will make it a seven-day-a-week retail destination. When Jean Nouvel came into my office, he produced an Airfix construction kit of a stealth bomber and said, 'We have to come under the radar of St Paul's.'

Proceed down Cheapside and turn left up Wood Street. Halfway along on your left, note the alleyway, **St Alban's Court**, created in the wall of no.100 by Norman Foster, with a glass walkway above. Next, **5 Aldermanbury Square** was designed by Eric Parry and nominated for the 2009 Stirling Prize. From its curved, shiny metal façade you can see the Foster and the Parry, a Farrell (the brown-striped towers of **125 London Wall**), a Rogers (**88 Wood Street**, with its primary-coloured funnels) and even a Wren: the church tower of **St Alban** remains in the centre of Wood Street at no.35.

★ Guildhall Art Gallery

Guildhall Yard, off Gresham Street, EC2P 2EJ (7332 3700, www.guildhall-art-gallery.org.uk). St Paul's tube or Bank tube/DLR. **Open** 10am-5pm Mon-Sat; noon-4pm Sun. **Admission** £2.50; £1 reductions; free under-16s. Free to all from 3.30pm daily, all day Fri. **Credit** MC, V. **Map** p404 P6.

The City of London's gallery contains numerous dull or unimpressive portraits of royalty and long-gone mayors, but also some wonderful surprises, including a brilliant Constable, some wonderfully camp Pre-Raphaelite works (Clytemnestra looks mighty riled) and a number of absorbing paintings of London, from moving depictions of war and melancholy working streets to the likes of the grandiloquent (and never-enacted) George Dance plan for a new London Bridge. The collection's centrepiece is the massive *Siege of Gibraltar* by John Copley, which spans two entire stories of the purpose-built gallery. A sub-basement contains the scant remains of London's 6,000-seater Roman amphitheatre, built around AD 70; Tron-like figures and crowd sound effects give a quaint inkling of scale.

MONUMENT & AROUND

Monument tube.

From Bank, King William Street runs south-east towards London Bridge, passing the small square containing the **Monument** (*see p72*). South on Lower Thames Street is the moody-looking church of **St Magnus the Martyr** (*see p72*); nearby are several relics from the days when this area was a busy port, including the old Customs House and **Billingsgate Market**, London's main fish market until 1982 (when it was relocated to east London).

North of the Monument along Gracechurch Street is the atmospheric **Leadenhall Market**, constructed in 1881 by Horace Jones (who also built the market at Smithfield; *see p77*). The vaulted roof was restored to its original Victorian finery in 1991 and city workers come here in droves to lunch at the pubs, cafés and restaurants, including the historic Lamb Tavern. Fantasy fans may recognise the market as Diagon Alley in *Harry Potter & the Philosopher's Stone*.

Behind the market is Lord Rogers' high-tech **Lloyd's of London** building, constructed in 1986, with all its ducts, vents, stairwells and lift shafts on the outside, like an oil rig dumped in the heart of the City. The original Lloyd's Register of Shipping, decorated with evocative bas-reliefs of sea monsters and nautical scenes, is on Fenchurch Street. South on Eastcheap (derived from the Old English 'ceap' meaning 'barter') is Wren's **St Margaret Pattens**, with an original 17th-century interior.

SIGHTS

SIGHTS

★ Monument

*Monument Street, EC3R 8AH (7626 2717,
www.themonument.info). Monument tube.*
Open 9.30am-5pm daily. **Admission** £3;
£2 reductions; free under-5s. **No credit cards**.
Map p407 Q7.

One of 17th-century London's most important landmarks, the Monument reopened in 2009 after an 18-
month refurbishment costing £4.5 million. It was
designed by Sir Christopher Wren and his (often
overlooked) associate Robert Hooke as a memorial
to the Great Fire of London, and is the world's tallest
free-standing stone column: it measures 202 feet
from the ground to the tip of the golden flame lick-
ing around the orb at its top, exactly the distance
east to Farriner's bakery in Pudding Lane, where the
fire is supposed to have begun on 2 September 1666.
A plaque on its base originally blamed on the fire on
'Popish frenzy' but this was removed in 1830.

The recent refurbishment has seen the column's
magnificent Portland stone cleaned and repaired,
and the golden orb at the top regilded with more
than 30,000 leaves of gold. New lighting has been
installed, and the cumbersome old iron bars of the
viewing platform have been replaced with a new,
lightweight mesh cage. For those reluctant or unable
to climb the Monument's 311 steps up the internal
spiral staircase (everybody who makes it to the top
gets a certificate), a live feed beams views from the
top to visitors on the ground floor. The surrounding
area has also been spruced up as part of the renewal,
with the addition of a stone and glass pavilion specially designed to reflect the Monument's gleaming
orb and gilded flames from its roof. All in all, it's
been given the care and attention that it deserves as
a memorial to the resurrection of London after the
most cataclysmic event in its history. *Photos p69.*

⬛ St Magnus the Martyr

*Lower Thames Street, EC3R 6DN (7626 4481,
www.stmagnusmartyr.org.uk). Monument tube.*
Open 10am-4pm Tue-Fri; 10am-1pm Sun. *Mass*
12.30pm Tue, Thur, Fri; 11am Sun. **Admission**
free; donations appreciated. **No credit cards**.
Map p405 Q7.

Downhill from the Monument, this looming Wren
church marked the entrance to the original London
Bridge. A cute scale model of the old bridge is
displayed inside the church, along with a statue of

INSIDE TRACK OUT OF ORBIT

The **Monument** (*see above*) was built to
act as a scientific instrument: the pillar
was intended to be used as a telescope,
viewed from the cellar, to be used to
study the Earth's movement round the
Sun. Sadly, vibrations from passing traffic
rendered it unusable.

---

axe-wielding St Magnus, the 12th-century Earl of
Orkney. The church is mentioned at one of the
climaxes of TS Eliot's *The Waste Land*: 'Where the
walls/Of Magnus Martyr hold/Inexplicable splendour
of Ionian white and gold.'

TOWER OF LONDON

Tower Hill tube or Tower Gateway DLR.

Marking the eastern edge of the City, the
Tower of London (*see p74*) was the palace
of the medieval kings and queens of England.
Home to the Crown Jewels and the Royal
Armoury, it's one of Britain's best-loved tourist
attractions and, accordingly, is mobbed by
visitors seven days a week.

At the south-east corner of the Tower is
Tower Bridge (*see p74*), built in 1894 and still
London's most distinctive bridge. Used as
a navigation aid by German bombers, it
escaped the firestorm of the Blitz. East across
Bridge Approach is **St Katharine's Docks**,
the first London docks to be formally closed
when the River Thames silted up in the 1960s.
The restaurants around the marina offer more
dignified dining than those around the Tower.

North of the Tower, **Trinity Square
Gardens** are a humbling memorial to the tens
of thousands of merchant seamen killed in the
two World Wars. Across the road is a small
square in which London's druids celebrate
each spring equinox with an elaborate
ceremony. Just beyond is one of the City's
finest Edwardian buildings: the former **Port
of London HQ** at 10 Trinity Square, with a
huge neoclassical façade and gigantic statues
symbolising Commerce, Navigation, Export,
Produce and Father Thames. It's now being
turned into a luxury hotel. Next door is **Trinity
House**, the home of the General Lighthouse
Authority, founded by Henry VIII for the
upkeep of shipping beacons along the river.

The surrounding streets and alleys have
evocative names: Crutched Friars, Savage
Gardens, Pepys Street and the like. The famous
diarist lived in nearby Seething Lane and
observed the Great Fire of London from
All Hallows by the Tower (*see right*).
Pepys is buried in the church of **St Olave** on
Hart Street, nicknamed 'St Ghastly Grim' by
Dickens for the leering skulls at the entrance.

North of the Tower are **St Botolph's-
without-Aldgate** (*see right*) and the tiny stone
church of **St Katharine Cree** (7283 5733,
10.30am-4pm Mon-Thur, 10.30am-1pm Fri) on
Leadenhall Street, one of only eight churches to
survive the Great Fire. Inside is a memorial to
Sir Nicholas Throckmorton, Queen Elizabeth I's
ambassador to France, who was imprisoned for
treason on numerous occasions, despite – or

Tower Bridge.

SIGHTS

perhaps because of – his friendship with the temperamental queen. Just north of St Katharine is Mitre Square, site of the fourth Jack the Ripper murder. Nearby on Bevis Marks is the superbly preserved **Bevis Marks Synagogue** (7626 1274, 10.30am-2pm Mon, Wed, Thur; 10.30am-1pm Tue, Fri; 10.30am-12.30pm Sun), founded in 1701 by Sephardic Jews fleeing the Spanish Inquisition. Services are still held in Portuguese as well as Hebrew. On neighbouring Heneage Lane is the classy kosher **Bevis Marks Restaurant** (no.4, 7283 2220, www.bevismarkstherestaurant.com).

Bevis Marks connects with St Mary Axe, named after a vanished church that is said to have contained an axe used by Attila the Hun to behead English virgins. Here you'll find Lord Foster's **30 St Mary Axe**, arguably London's finest modern building. It's known as 'the Gherkin' (and, occasionally, more suggestive nicknames) for reasons that will be obvious once you see it. On curved stone benches either side of 30 St Mary Axe are separately inscribed the 20 lines of Scottish poet Ian Hamilton Finlay's 'Arcadian Dream Garden', a curious counterpart to Lord Foster's hugely popular building. Nearby are two more medieval churches that survived the Great Fire: **St Helen's Bishopsgate** (*see p74*) and **St Andrew Undershaft**.

To the west of St Mary Axe is the ugly and rather dated **Tower 42** (25 Old Broad Street), the tallest building in Britain until the construction of **1 Canada Square** in Docklands in 1990. Behind, on Bishopsgate, is **Gibson Hall**, the ostentatious former offices of the National Provincial Bank of England. Currently under construction at no.110 is

Heron Tower, which will be the tallest building in the UK when completed in 2011.

One block north, St Mary Axe intersects with Houndsditch, where Londoners threw dead dogs and other rubbish in medieval times. The ditch ran outside the London Wall (*see p65*), dividing the City from the East End.

FREE All Hallows by the Tower
Byward Street, EC3R 5BJ (7481 2928, www.ahbtt.org.uk). Tower Hill tube or Tower Gateway DLR. **Open** 8.30am-6pm Mon-Fri; 10am-4pm Sat, Sun. *Tours* phone for details; donation requested. *Services* 6pm Wed; 11am Sun. **Admission** free; donations appreciated. **No credit cards. Map** p405 R7.
Often described as London's oldest church, All Hallows is built on the foundations of a seventh-century Saxon church. Much of what survives today was reconstructed after World War II, but several Saxon details can be seen in the main hall, where the Knights Templar were tried by Edward II in 1314. The undercroft contains a museum with Roman and Saxon relics and a Crusader altar. William Penn, the founder of Pennsylvania, was baptised here in 1644.

FREE St Botolph's-without-Aldgate
Aldgate High Street, EC3N 1AB (7283 1670, www.stbotolphs.org.uk). Aldgate tube. **Open** 10am-3pm Mon, Wed-Thur; 11am-3pm Tue; 10am-12.30pm Sun. *Eucharist* 10.30am Sun. **Admission** free; donations appreciated. **No credit cards. Map** p405 R6.
The oldest of three churches of St Botolph in the City, this handsome monument was built at the gates of Roman London as a homage to the patron saint of travellers. The building was reconstructed by George Dance in 1744 and a beautiful ornamental ceiling was

added in the 19th century by John Francis Bentley, who also created Westminster Cathedral.

FREE St Ethelburga Centre for Reconciliation & Peace

78 Bishopsgate, EC2N 4AG (7496 1610, www.stethelburgas.org). Bank tube/DLR or Liverpool Street tube/rail. **Open** 11am-3pm Wed, Fri. **Admission** free; donations appreciated. **No credit cards. Map** p405 R6.

Built around 1390, the tiny church of St Ethelburga was reduced to rubble by an IRA bomb in 1993 and rebuilt as a centre for peace and reconciliation. Behind the chapel is a Bedouin tent where events are held to promote dialogue between the faiths (phone or check the website for details), an increasingly heated issue in modern Britain. Meditation classes are held here on Tuesdays and Thursdays.

FREE St Helen's Bishopsgate

Great St Helen's, off Bishopsgate, EC3A 6AT (7283 2231, www.st-helens.org.uk). Bank tube/DLR or Liverpool Street tube/rail. **Open** 9.30am-5pm Mon-Fri. *Services* 10.30am, 4pm, 6.30pm Sun. *Lunchtime meetings* 1-2pm Tue, Thur. **Admission** free. **No credit cards. Map** p405 R6.

Founded in 1210, St Helen's Bishopsgate is actually two churches knocked into one, which explains its unusual shape. The church survived the Great Fire and the Blitz, but was partly wrecked by IRA bombs in 1992 and 1993. The hugely impressive 16th- and 17th-century memorials inside include the grave of Thomas Gresham, founder of the Royal Exchange (*see p67*).

Tower Bridge Exhibition

Tower Bridge, SE1 2UP (7403 3761, www.towerbridge.org.uk). Tower Hill tube or Tower Gateway DLR. **Open** *Apr-Sept* 10am-6.30pm daily. *Oct-Mar* 9.30am-6pm daily. **Admission** £7; £3-£5 reductions; £15.50 family; free under-5s. **Credit** AmEx, MC, V. **Map** p405 R8.

Opened in 1894, this is the 'London Bridge' that wasn't sold to America. Originally powered by steam, the drawbridge is now opened by electric rams when big ships need to venture upstream (check when the bridge is next due to be raised on the bridge's website or follow the feed on Twitter). An entertaining exhibition on the history of the bridge is displayed in the old steamrooms and the west walkway, which provides a crow's-nest view along the Thames.

★ Tower of London

Tower Hill, EC3N 4AB (0844 482 7777, www.hrp.org.uk). Tower Hill tube or Tower Gateway DLR. **Open** *Mar-Oct* 10am-5.30pm Mon, Sun; 9am-5.30pm Tue-Sat. *Nov-Feb* 10am-4.30pm Mon, Sun; 9am-4.30pm Tue-Sat. **Admission**

£17; £9.50-£14 reductions; £47 family; free under-5s. **Credit** AmEx, MC, V. **Map** p405 R8.

If you haven't been to the Tower of London before, go now. Despite exhausting crowds and long climbs up inaccessible stairways, this is one of Britain's finest historical attractions. Who would not be fascinated by a close-up look at the crown of Queen Victoria or the armour (and prodigious codpiece) of King Henry VIII? The buildings of the Tower span 900 years of history and the bastions and battlements house a series of interactive displays on the lives of British monarchs, and the often excruciatingly painful deaths of traitors. There's plenty here to fill a whole day, and it's worth joining one of the highly recommended and entertaining free tours led by the Yeoman Warders (or Beefeaters).

Make the Crown Jewels your first stop, and as early in the day as possible: if you wait until you've pottered around other things, the queues may be immense. Beyond satisfyingly solid vault doors, you get to glide along travelators (branded with the Queen's 'EIIR' badge) past such treasures of state as the Monarch's Sceptre, mounted with the Cullinan I diamond, and the Imperial State Crown, worn by the Queen each year for the opening of Parliament.

The other big draw to the tower is the Royal Armoury in the central White Tower, with its swords, armour, poleaxes, halberds, morning stars (spiky maces) and other gruesome tools for separating human beings from their body parts. Kids are entertained by swordsmanship games, coin-minting activities and even a child-sized long bow. The garderobes (medieval toilets) also seem to appeal.

Back outside, Tower Green – where executions of prisoners of noble birth were carried out, continuing until 1941 – is marked by a glass pillow, sculpted by poet and artist Brian Catling. Overlooking the green, Beauchamp Tower, dating to 1280, has an upper floor full of intriguing graffiti by the prisoners that were held here (including Anne Boleyn, Rudolf Hess and the Krays). Back towards the entrance, the 13th-century Bloody Tower is another must-see that gets overwhelmed by numbers later in the day. The ground floor is a reconstruction of Sir Walter Raleigh's study, the upper floor details the fate of the Princes in the Tower. In the riverside wall is the unexpectedly beautiful Medieval Palace, with its reconstructed bedroom and throne room, and spectacularly complex stained glass in the private chapel. The whole palace is deliciously cool if you've been struggling round on a hot summer's day.

INSIDE TRACK RIVER WALK

Much of the north bank of the Thames can now be accessed by the public. The **Riverside Walk** offers a splendid and tourist-free counterpoint to the more popular South Bank.

Holborn & Clerkenwell

Meat traders meet clubbers and lawyers in this unusual district.

Along Fleet Street and Holborn, the West End dives into the City of London and heads for St Paul's. The newspapers who once called Fleet Street home have long since jumped ship for Docklands and Kensington, but some of their grand old offices remain, flanked by the collegiate quiet of the barristers' ancient inns of court.

Meanwhile, across the Farringdon Road, the boom years have transmogrified **Clerkenwell** from an earnest and shabby suburb of Grub Street into a playground for afterwork City boys, bambi-eyed clubbers and design-led media businesses. And in a typically startling juxtaposition, the butchers of **Smithfield Market** still ply their bleeding trade right in the thick of the party.

Map p399 & p402	**Restaurants &**
Hotels p170	**cafés** p201
	Pubs & bars p228

HOLBORN

Holborn tube.

A sharp left out of Holborn tube and left again leads into the unexpectedly lovely **Lincoln's Inn Fields**. Surely London's largest square (indeed, it's more of a park), it's blessed with gnarled oaks casting dappled shade over a tired bandstand. In summer, book an outside seat for Caribbean-accented modern European food at

the **Terrace** (7430 1234, www.theterrace.info), an airy, eco-friendly building by the tennis courts. On the south side of the square, the neoclassical façade of the Royal College of Surgeons hides the **Hunterian Museum** (*see p76*); facing it from the north is the magical **Sir John Soane's Museum** (*see p76*).

East of the square lies **Lincoln's Inn** (7405 1393, www.lincolnsinn.org.uk), one of the city's four Inns of Court. Its grounds are open to the public, ogling an odd mix of Gothic, Tudor and Palladian buildings. On nearby Portsmouth Street lies the **Old Curiosity Shop**, its timbers apparently known to Dickens. And nearby, Gray's Inn Road runs north beside the second Inn of Court. The sculpted gardens at **Gray's Inn** (7458 7800, www.graysinn.org.uk), dating to 1606, are open on weekdays, 10am-2.30pm.

Opened in 1876 on Chancery Lane as a series of strongrooms in which the upper classes could secure their valuables, the **London Silver Vaults** (7242 3844, www.thesilvervaults.com) now have a hive of dealers buying, selling and repairing silverware. Equally liable to turn brown eyes green with envy are the glittering

**INSIDE TRACK
GRESHAM LECTURES**

Maintaining a 400-year-old tradition started by Sir Thomas Gresham, founder of the Stock Exchange, **Gresham College** lays on a series of free evening lectures on a wide variety of subjects throughout the year at Barnards Inn Hall, Holborn and elsewhere in the City. Check www.gresham.ac.uk for details.

Exmouth Market.

SIGHTS

window displays of **Hatton Gardens**, London's jewellery and diamond centre. It's a short walk but a million miles from the Cockney fruit stalls and sock merchants of the market on **Leather Lane** (10am-2.30pm Mon-Fri).

Further on is **Ely Place**, its postcode absent from the street sign as a result of it technically falling under the jurisdiction of Cambridgeshire. The church garden of ancient **St Etheldreda** (*see right*) produced strawberries so delicious that they made the pages of Shakespeare's *Richard III*; a celebratory Strawberrie Fayre is still held on the street each June. The 16th-century **Ye Old Mitre** (1 Ely Court, EC1N 6SJ, 7405 4751) remains an atmospheric pub.

FREE Hunterian Museum
Royal College of Surgeons, 35-43 Lincoln's Inn Fields, WC2A 3PE (7869 6560, www.rcseng.ac.uk/museums). Holborn tube. **Open** 10am-5pm Tue-Sat. **Admission** free. **No credit cards**. **Map** p399 M6.
The collection of medical specimens once held by John Hunter (1728-93), physician to King George III, can be viewed in this museum. The sparkling glass cabinets of the main room offset the goriness of the exhibits, which include Charles Babbage's brain and Winston Churchill's dentures, as well as shelf after shelf of diligently classified pickled body parts. The upper floor holds a brutal account of surgical techniques. Kids' activities include occasional demonstrations by a 'barber surgeon' (book on 7869 6560).

FREE St Etheldreda
14 Ely Place, EC1N 6RY (7405 1061, www.stetheldreda.com). Chancery Lane tube. **Open** 8am-5pm daily. **Admission** free; donations appreciated. **No credit cards**. **Map** p402 N5.
Dedicated to the saintly seventh-century Queen of Northumbria, this is Britain's oldest Catholic church, London's only surviving example of 13th-century Gothic architecture; it was saved from the Great Fire by a change in the wind. The crypt is darkly atmospheric, untouched by traffic noise, and the stained glass (actually from the 1960s) stunning.

★ FREE Sir John Soane's Museum
13 Lincoln's Inn Fields, WC2A 3BP (7405 2107, www.soane.org). Holborn tube. **Open** 10am-5pm Tue-Sat; 10am-5pm, 6-9pm 1st Tue of mth. *Tours* 11am Sat. **Admission** free; donations appreciated. *Tours* £5; free reductions. **Credit** AmEx, MC, V. **Map** p399 M5.
When he wasn't designing notable buildings, among them the original Bank of England, Sir John Soane (1753-1837) obsessively collected art, furniture and architectural ornamentation. In the 19th century, he turned his house into a museum to which, he said, 'amateurs and students' should have access. The result is this perfectly amazing place.

Much of the museum's appeal derives from the domestic setting. The modest rooms were modified by Soane with ingenious devices to channel and direct daylight, and to expand space, including walls that open out like cabinets to display some of his many paintings (Canaletto, Turner, Hogarth). The Breakfast Room has a beautiful domed ceiling, inset with convex mirrors. The extraordinary Monument Court contains a sarcophagus of alabaster, so fine that it's almost translucent, that was carved for the pharaoh Seti I (1291-78 BC) and discovered in his tomb in Egypt's Valley of the Kings. There are also numerous examples of Soane's eccentricity, not least the cell set aside for his imaginary monk 'Padre Giovanni'. The museum has launched an appeal that will eventually open Soane's top-floor 'private apartments', recreated from contemporary watercolours.

CLERKENWELL & FARRINGDON

Farringdon tube/rail.

Few places encapsulate London's capacity for reinvention quite like Clerkenwell, an erstwhile religious centre that takes its name from the parish clerks who once performed Biblical mystery plays on its streets. The most lasting holy legacy is that of the 11th-century knights of the **Order of St John**; the remains of their priory can still be seen at St John's Gate, a crenellated gatehouse that dates from 1504 and is home to the **Museum & Library of the Order of St John** (*see right*).

INSIDE TRACK FREE THE WORD

The *Guardian* newspaper moved from 60 Farringdon Road in 2008, but the building continues to espouse traditions of worthy wordiness in the form of the **Free Word Centre** (7324 2570, www.freewordonline. com). Housing a number of independent publishers and literacy and free speech advocates, it has its own café, and hosts performance, readings, seminars, workshops, exhibitions and debates.

By the 17th century, this was a fashionable locale, but the Industrial Revolution soon buried it under warehouses and factories. Printing houses were established, and the district gained a reputation as a safe haven for radicals, from 16th-century Lollards to 19th-century Chartists. In 1903, Lenin is believed to have met Stalin for a drink in what is now the **Crown Tavern** (43 Clerkenwell Green, 7253 4973), one year after moving the publication of *Iskra* to neighbouring 37A (now the **Marx Memorial Library**; 7253 1485, www.marx-memorial-library.org).

Industrial dereliction and decay were the theme until property development in the 1980s and '90s turned Clerkenwell into a desirable area. The process was aided by a slew of artfully distressed gastropubs (following the lead of the **Eagle**; *see p201*), and the food shops, fashion boutiques, restaurants and bars along the colourful strip of **Exmouth Market**.

FREE **Islington Museum**

245 St John Street, Finsbury, EC1V 4NB (7527 3235, www.islington.gov.uk). Angel tube. **Open** 10am-5pm Mon, Tue, Thur-Sat. **Admission** free. **No credit cards. Map** p402 O3.
Islington Museum opened in May 2008, so all the displays are still gleaming and new. Most deal with local history and the political and ethical credentials of the borough, exemplified by local residents such as reformist preacher John Wesley, playwright Joe Orton and eminent feminist Mary Wollstonecraft.

FREE **Museum & Library of the Order of St John**

St John's Gate, St John's Lane, Clerkenwell, EC1M 4DA (7324 4005, www.sja.org.uk/museum). Farringdon tube/rail. **Open** 10am-5pm Mon-Fri; 10am-4pm Sat. *Tours* 11am, 2.30pm Tue, Fri, Sat. **Admission** free. *Tours* free. Suggested donation £5; £4 reductions. **Credit** MC, V. **Map** p402 O4.
The Order of St John is best known for its ambulance service, but its roots lie in the Christian medical practices of the Crusades between the 11th and 13th centuries. A collection of artefacts related to the Order of Hospitaller Knights, from Jerusalem, Malta

and the Ottoman Empire, is displayed; there's a separate collection relating to the evolution of the modern ambulance service. Both are being given a £1.7-million refurbishment, adding a learning centre and new galleries and opening up the garden and 12th-century crypt; it's due to reopen in June 2010.

SMITHFIELD

Farringdon tube/rail.

Smithfield Market provides a colourful link to an age when the quality of British beef was a symbol of national virility and good humour. Meat has been traded here for a millennium or more; the current market, designed by Horace Jones, opened in 1868, though it's since been altered (in part out of necessity, thanks to World War II bombs). Meat trucks start arriving around 11pm; early risers will find traders setting up stalls at first light. The **Cock Tavern** (7248 2918) is licensed from 6am to serve beer and breakfast to meat handlers.

The meat traders are joined at night these days by revellers settling in for dinner at vast **Smiths of Smithfield** (67-77 Charterhouse Street, EC1M 6HJ, 7251 7950, www.smithsof smithfield.co.uk) or nearby **St John** (*see p203*), tucking into a glass or two at **Vinoteca** (*see p229*) or taking to the dancefloor at superclub **Fabric** (*see p323*). For a little peace and quiet, stroll by the **Charterhouse**. This Carthusian monastery, founded in 1370, is now Anglican almshouses that retain the original 14th-century chapel and a 17th-century library.

Sir John Soane's Museum.

SIGHTS

Bloomsbury & Fitzrovia

Culture still comes to the fore in these twin neighbourhoods.

London's twin neighbourhoods north of Oxford Street both carry traces of bookishness and bohemia. **Bloomsbury** is best known as the home of the **British Museum**, but the presence of University College London (UCL) also helps to lend the area a surprisingly youthful, if studious, tone. The unofficial heart of the area is the redeveloped **Brunswick Centre** and the network of surrounding streets.

To the north, the regeneration of **King's Cross** threatens to give the famously seedy area near the station a respectable tone; **St Pancras International**, the rail station, has become a destination spot in its own right. To the west, **Fitzrovia** is a media playground that centres around Charlotte Street and spills into a succession of excellent pubs and restaurants.

Map pp398-399	Restaurants &
Hotels p173	cafés p203
	Pubs & bars p229

BLOOMSBURY

Euston Square, Holborn, Russell Square or Tottenham Court Road tube.

Bloomsbury's florid name is, prosaically, taken from 'Blemondisberi' – the manor ('bury') of William Blemond, who acquired the area in the 13th century. It remained rural until the 1660s, when the fourth Earl of Southampton built Bloomsbury Square around his house. The Southamptons intermarried with the Russells, the Dukes of Bedford; together, they developed the area as one of London's first planned suburbs.

Over the next two centuries, the group built a series of grand squares. **Bedford Square** (1775-80) is London's only complete Georgian square (its garden is closed to the public); huge **Russell Square** has been restored as a public park with a popular café. To the east is the cantilevered post-war **Brunswick Centre**, boasting shops, flats and a cinema. The nearby streets, particularly **Marchmont Street**, are some of the most characterful in the West End.

Bloomsbury's charm is the sum of its parts, best experienced on a meander through its bookshops (many on **Great Russell Street**) and pubs. The blue plaques here are a who's-who of English literature: WB Yeats lived at 5 Upper Woburn Place, Edgar Allan Poe at 83 Southampton Row and TS Eliot at 28 Bedford Place; 6 Store Street was the birthplace of Anthony Trollope; and Dickens lived at 48 Doughty Street, now the **Charles Dickens Museum** (*see p81*). The Bloomsbury Group was based at 50 Gordon Square, where the likes of EM Forster, Lytton Strachey and Duncan Grant would discuss literature, art, politics and, above all, each other. Virginia Woolf lived at 52 Tavistock Square; Wyndham Lewis's Rebel Art Centre occupied 38 Great Ormond Street.

On Bloomsbury's western border, Malet Street, Gordon Street and Gower Street are dominated by the **University of London**. The most notable building is Gower Street's **University College**, founded in 1826. Inside is the 'autoicon' of utilitarian philosopher and founder of the university Jeremy Bentham: his preserved cadaver, fully clothed, sitting in a glass-fronted cabinet. The university's main library is housed in towering **Senate House** on Malet Street, one of the city's bulkiest and most imposing examples of monumental art deco. Monolithic and brooding, it was the model for Orwell's Ministry of Truth in *1984*.

South of the university sprawls the **British Museum** (*see below*). Running off Great Russell Street, where you'll find the museum's main entrance, are three attractive parallel streets (Coptic, Museum and Bury) and, nearby, the **Cartoon Museum** (*see p81*); also close by, Bloomsbury Way is home to Hawksmoor's restored **St George's Bloomsbury** (*see p81*). Across from here, **Sicilian Avenue** is an Italianate, pedestrian precinct of colonnaded shops that links with Southampton Row.

North-east of the British Museum is **Lamb's Conduit Street**, a convivial neighbourhood lined with interesting shops and, at the top of the street, **Coram's Fields** (*see p283*), a delightful children's park on the grounds of the former Thomas Coram's Foundling Hospital. Coram's legacy is commemorated in the beautiful **Foundling Museum** (*see p81*).

★ FREE British Museum

Great Russell Street, WC1B 3DG (7323 8299, www.britishmuseum.org). Russell Square or Tottenham Court Road tube. **Open** *Galleries* 10am-5.30pm Mon-Wed, Sat, Sun; 10am 8.30pm Thur, Fri. *Great Court* 9am-6pm Mon-Wed, Sun; 9am-11pm Thur-Sat. *Highlights tours* (90mins) 10.30am, 1pm, 3pm daily. *Eye opener tours* (50mins) phone for details. **Admission** free; donations appreciated. *Temporary exhibitions* prices vary. *Highlights tours* £8; £5 reductions. *Eye opener tours* free. **Credit** (shop) AmEx, DC, MC, V. **Map** p399 K5.

Officially the country's most popular tourist attraction, the British Museum opened to the public in 1759 in Montagu House, which then occupied this site. The current building is a neoclassical marvel built in 1847 by Robert Smirke, one of the pioneers of the Greek Revival style. The most high profile addition since then was Lord Foster's popular if rather murky glass-roofed Great Court, open since 2000 and now claimed to be 'the largest covered public square in Europe'. This £100m landmark surrounds the domed Reading Room (used by the British Library until its move to King's Cross; *see p82*), where Marx, Lenin, Dickens, Darwin, Hardy and Yeats once worked.

Star exhibits include ancient Egyptian artefacts – the Rosetta Stone on the ground floor (with a barely noticed, perfect replica in the King's Library), mummies upstairs – and Greek antiquities, including the marble friezes from the Parthenon known as the Elgin Marbles. The Celts gallery upstairs has Lindow Man, killed in 300 BC and preserved in peat, while the Wellcome Gallery of Ethnography holds an Easter Island statue and regalia from Captain Cook's travels. The King's Library, which opened in 2004, provides a calming home to a permanent exhibition entitled 'Enlightenment: Discovering the World in the 18th Century', a 5,000-piece collection devoted to the extraordinary formative period of the museum. The remit covers archaeology, science and the natural world; the objects displayed range from Indonesian puppets to a beautiful orrery.

You won't be able to see everything in one day, so buy a souvenir guide and pick out the showstoppers, or plan several visits. Highlights tours focus on specific aspects of the huge collection; Eye-Opener tours offer specific introductions to world cultures. There are also regular blockbuster exhibitions (such as 'Fra Angelico to Leonardo: Italian Renaissance Drawings', 22 Apr-25 July 2010), for which it may be necessary to book in advance.

▶ *The historic Museum Tavern (49 Great Russell Street, 7242 8987), by the front gate, is no mere tourist trap: it serves fine ales.*

Senate House.

INSIDE TRACK LIFE CLASSES

The **School of Life** (70 Marchmont Street, 7833 1010, www.theschooloflife.com) is one of the area's most idiosyncratic finds. Part bookshop, part further-education classroom, it's an enterprise unlike any other in London.

Walk Lit Stops

Explore the world of Faber & Faber, the city's most important poetry publisher.

One of Britain's most important publishing houses, **Faber & Faber** were founded in 1929 on the north-west corner of Russell Square (no.24), where this walk begins. The poet TS Eliot was appointed literary advisor, and pored over the work of authors and poets such as Ted Hughes and Sylvia Plath. Eliot romanced his secretary Valerie Fletcher for eight years at the **Russell Hotel** (nos.1-8), marrying her in 1957 to the astonishment of his fellow staff.

Head south along Southampton Row and turn left down Cosmo Place until you reach **Queen Square**. No.3 served as Faber's home from 1971 to 2008. And on the right is **St George-the-Martyr** (www. stgeorgesbloomsbury.org.uk), where Plath and Hughes married on 16 June 1956.

Over on **Mecklenburgh Street**, no.44 was home to Hilda Doolittle, an imagist poet whose work delighted Eliot. Doolittle's husband was the writer Richard Aldington; his mistress, Dorothy Yorke, lived in another part of the house. Yorke was friends with DH Lawrence, who came here in 1917 to write *Women in Love*.

Head through the alleyway that skirts around the Coram Trust, then weave your way through to **Woburn Walk**. From 1895 to 1919, no.5 (marked by a square metal plaque) was home to WB Yeats, who later became one of Faber's 11 Nobel laureates.

Down the road, Virginia Woolf lived for a time at 52 Tavistock Square (now the **Tavistock Hotel**). Woolf published Eliot's *Poems* in 1919. Close by, Woolf and her assorted Bloomsbury Group cohorts and scions gathered at **50 Gordon Square** in the 1920s; many were Faber authors.

Go past **Senate House**, then left behind the **British Museum** (*see p79*). From here, cross the corner of Russell Square to **28 Bedford Place**; Eliot briefly lived in this 'cheap boarding house' in 1914.

Finally, turn right on to Great Russell Street and stop outside nos.74-77: **Bloomsbury House**, the current home of Faber & Faber. Congratulations: you've just completed 80 years of literary history in an hour. Celebrate with cake, coffee and something to read at the **London Review Bookshop** (*see p247*).

SIGHTS

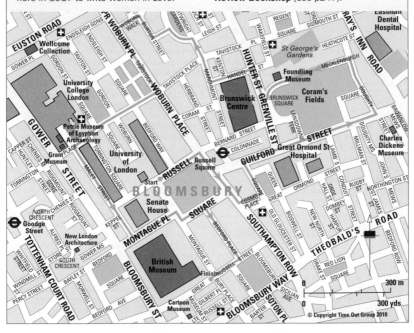

Cartoon Museum

*35 Little Russell Street, WC1A 2HH (7580 8155,
www.cartoonmuseum.org). Tottenham Court
Road tube.* **Open** 10.30am-5.30pm Tue-Sat;
noon-5.30pm Sun. **Admission** £5.50; free-£4
reductions. **Credit** (shop) MC, V. **Map** p407 Y1.
The best of British cartoon art is displayed on the
ground floor of this former dairy. The displays start
in the early 18th century, when high-society types
back from the Grand Tour introduced the Italian
practice of *caricatura* to polite company. From
Hogarth, it moves through Britain's cartooning
'golden age' (1770-1830) to examples of wartime cartoons, ending up with modern satirists such as
Gerald Scarfe and the wonderfully loopy Ralph
Steadman. Upstairs is a celebration of UK comic art,
with original 1921 *Rupert the Bear* artwork by Mary
Tourtel, Frank Hampson's Dan Dare, Leo
Baxendale's Bash Street Kids and a painted *Asterix*
cover by that well-known Briton, Albert Uderzo.
▶ *The nearby Political Cartoon Gallery (32 Store
Street, 7580 1114) may also be of interest.*

Charles Dickens Museum

*48 Doughty Street, WC1N 2LX (7405 2127,
www.dickensmuseum.com). Chancery Lane or
Russell Square tube.* **Open** 10am-5pm Mon-Sun.
Tours by arrangement. **Admission** £6; £3-£4.50
reductions; £15 family. **Credit** AmEx, DC, MC,
V. **Map** p399 M4.
London is scattered with plaques (*see p19* **Plaque
Attack**) marking addresses where Dickens lived,
but this is the only building still standing. He lived
here from 1837 to 1840, writing *Nicholas Nickleby* and
Oliver Twist while in residence. Ring the doorbell to
gain access to four floors of Dickensiana, collected
over the years from various former residences. Some
rooms are arranged as they might have been when
he lived here; others deal with different aspects of his
life, from struggling hack to famous performer.

Foundling Museum

*40 Brunswick Square, WC1N 1AZ (7841 3600,
www.foundlingmuseum.org.uk). Russell Square
tube.* **Open** 10am-5pm Tue-Sat; 11am-5pm Sun.
Admission £5; £4 reductions; free under-16s.
Credit MC, V. **Map** p399 L4.
The Foundling Museum recalls the social history of
the Foundling Hospital, set up in 1739 by shipwright
and sailor named Thomas Coram. Returning to
England from America in 1720, Coram was appalled
by the number of abandoned children on the streets.
Securing royal patronage, he persuaded Hogarth and
Handel to become governors; it was Hogarth who
decreed the building should become Britain's first
public art gallery, and works by artists as notable as
Gainsborough and Reynolds remain on display.
Among the pictures, manuscripts and objects on display, the most heart-rending is a tiny case of mementoes that were all mothers could leave the children
they abandoned here. There are monthly concerts.

Snapshot
Iron Age London

Where to see how London lived.

Although the Romans had yet to
transform a cluster of settlements into
the walled city of Londinium, the Iron
Age treasures displayed in the Britain and
Europe room of the **British Museum** (*see
p79*) are testimony to the flamboyance
and complexity of life here up to the
invasion of AD 43. In spite of its name,
the Battersea Shield –
unearthed from the
Thames in 1857 and
dating back as far
as 350 BC – is more
pretty than protective.
Too short and flimsy
to have been used
in battle, it was
more likely have been
thrown or placed
in the river as a
showy sacrifice, its
intricate design a
clear indication of
the sophistication
of tribal craftsmen.

SIGHTS

FREE **Petrie Museum of
Egyptian Archaeology**
*University College London, Malet Place,
WC1E 6BT (7679 2884, www.petrie.ucl.ac.uk).
Goodge Street or Warren Street tube.* **Open**
1-5pm Tue-Fri; 10am-1pm Sat. **Admission**
free; donations appreciated. **No credit cards**.
Map p399 K4.
Set up in 1892 by eccentric traveller and diarist
Amelia Edwards, the Petrie Museum is named after
Flinders Petrie, tireless excavator of ancient Egypt.
Where the British Museum's Egyptology collection
is strong on the big stuff, the Petrie is dim case after
dim case of minutiae: pottery shards, grooming
accessories, jewellery and the like. Highlights
include artefacts from the heretic pharaoh
Akhenaten's short-lived capital Tell el Amarna.
Wind-up torches illuminate the gloomy corners.

FREE **St George's Bloomsbury**
*Bloomsbury Way, WC1A 2HR (7242 1979,
www.stgeorgesbloomsbury.org.uk). Holborn or
Tottenham Court Road tube.* **Open** 11am-4pm
Mon-Fri; 11.30am-5pm Sat; 10.30am-5pm Sun.
Services 1.10pm Wed, Fri; 10.30am Sun.
Admission free. **No credit cards**.
Map p399 L5.

SIGHTS

INSIDE TRACK HIDDEN BONES

Just down the alley from the **Petrie Museum** (*see above*), past the security guards and into UCL, the **Grant Museum** (7679 2647) is an eccentric joy, an array of Victorian animal skeletons crammed into an atmospheric single room. It's open only on weekday afternoons.

Consecrated in 1730, St George's is a grand and disturbing Hawksmoor church, with an offset, stepped spire inspired by Pliny's account of the Mausoleum at Halicarnassus. Highlights of its recent renovation include the mahogany reredos and the sculptures of lions and unicorns clawing at the base of the steeple. The hours are erratic, but on Sundays, the church always remains open for visitors after the regular service. Check online for details of concerts.
▶ *Hawksmoor's Christ Church Spitalfields is another recently restored masterpiece; see p135.*

★ FREE Wellcome Collection
183 Euston Road, NW1 2BE (7611 2222, www.wellcomecollection.org). Euston Square tube or Euston tube/rail. **Open** 10am-6pm Tue, Wed, Fri, Sat; 10am-10pm Thur; 11am-6pm Sun. *Library* 10am-6pm Mon-Wed, Fri; 10am-8pm Thur; 10am-4pm Sat. **Admission** free. **Credit** MC, V. **Map** p399 K4.

St Pancras International.

Sir Henry Wellcome, a pioneering 19th-century pharmacist, amassed a vast and idiosyncratic collection of implements and curios relating to the medical trade, now displayed here. In addition to these fascinating and often grisly items – ivory carvings of pregnant women, used guillotine blades, Napoleon's toothbrush – there are several serious works of modern art, most on display in a smaller room to one side of the main chamber of curiosities. The temporary exhibitions are usually wonderfully interesting; check online for a 2010 programme.

KING'S CROSS & ST PANCRAS
King's Cross tube/rail.

North-east of Bloomsbury, King's Cross is becoming a major European transport hub, thanks to a £500-million makeover of the area and the opening of the renovated and restored **St Pancras International** (*see right*). The gaping badlands to the north are being transformed into a mixed-use nucleus called **King's Cross Central**. Until then, there are still a few places to explore: the **London Canal Museum** (*see below*), north of King's Cross Station by the **Kings Place** arts complex (*see p309* **Profile**); **Camley Street Natural Park** (*see p283*), a kids' favourite; and **St Pancras Old Church** (*see right*).

★ FREE British Library
96 Euston Road, Somers Town, NW1 2DB (7412 7332, www.bl.uk). Euston or King's Cross tube/rail. **Open** 9.30am-6pm Mon, Wed-Fri; 9.30am-8pm Tue; 9.30am-5pm Sat; 11am-5pm Sun. **Admission** free; donations appreciated. **Credit** (shop) AmEx, MC, V. **Map** p399 K3.

'One of the ugliest buildings in the world,' opined a Parliamentary committee on the opening of the new British Library in 1997. But don't judge a book by its cover: the interior is a model of cool, spacious functionality, the collection is unmatched (150 million items and counting), and the reading rooms (open only to cardholders) are so popular that regular users complain that they're too busy. The library's main treasures are displayed in the John Ritblat Gallery, from the Magna Carta and the Lindisfarne Gospels to original Beatles lyrics. The focal point of the building is the King's Library, a six-storey glass-walled tower housing George III's collection. The temporary shows are often superb.

London Canal Museum
12-13 New Wharf Road, off Wharfdale Road, N1 9RT (7713 0836, www.canalmuseum.org.uk). King's Cross tube/rail. **Open** 10am-4.30pm Tue-Sun. **Admission** £3; £2 reductions; £1.50 children; free under-8s. **No credit cards**. **Map** p399 M2.

Housed in a former 19th-century ice warehouse, the London Canal Museum includes an exhibit on the history of the ice trade. It's perhaps the most interesting part of the exhibition; the collection looking at the history of the waterways and those who worked on them is sparse by comparison. The canalside walk from here to Camden Town is pleasant.

FREE St Pancras International
Pancras Road, Somers Town, NW1 2QP (7843 4250, www.stpancras.com). King's Cross tube/rail. **Open** 3.45am-12.30am Mon-Fri; 5am-12.30am Sat; 6am-12.30am Sun. **Admission** free. **No credit cards. Map** p399 L3.
William Barlow's gorgeous Victorian glass-and-iron train shed welcomes high-speed Eurostar trains from Paris. The redeveloped station has become somewhere to linger, but for all the public art, 'the longest champagne bar in Europe', the high-end boutiques, the gastropubs, the restaurants and the farmers' market, St Pancras is really worth a diversion because of the beauty of the original structure. Also refurbished is Sir George Gilbert Scott's magnificent neo-Gothic hotel building at the front of the station.

FREE St Pancras Old Church & St Pancras Gardens
St Pancras Road, NW1 1UL (7387 4193). Mornington Crescent tube or King's Cross tube/rail. **Open** *Gardens* 7am-dusk daily. *Services* 9am Mon-Fri; 7pm Tue; 9.30am Sun. **Admission** free. **No credit cards. Map** p399 K2.
St Pancras Old Church has been ruined and rebuilt many times. The current structure is handsome, but it's the churchyard that delights. Among those buried here are writer William Godwin and his wife, Mary Wollstonecraft; over this grave, their daughter Mary Godwin (author of *Frankenstein*) declared her love for poet Percy Bysshe Shelley. The grave of Sir John Soane is one of only two Grade I-listed tombs (the other is Karl Marx's, in Highgate Cemetery; *see p133*); designed for his wife, its dome influenced Gilbert Scott's design for the red British phone box.

FITZROVIA
Goodge Street or Tottenham Court Road tube.

Squeezed in between Tottenham Court Road, Oxford Street, Great Portland Street and Euston Road, Fitzrovia isn't as famous as Bloomsbury, but its history is just as rich. The origins of the name are hazy: some believe it comes from **Fitzroy Square**, named after Henry Fitzroy (son of Charles II); others insist it's due to the famous **Fitzroy Tavern** (16 Charlotte Street, 7580 3714), ground zero for London bohemia of the 1930s and '40s and a favourite with the likes of Dylan Thomas and George Orwell. Fitzrovia also had its share of artists: James McNeill

Whistler lived at 8 Fitzroy Square, later taken over by British Impressionist Walter Sickert, while Roger Fry's Omega Workshops, blurring the distinction between fine and decorative arts, had its studio at no.33. However, this raffish image is largely a thing of the past, and the area is better known as a high-powered media hub.

The district's icon is the **BT Tower**, completed in 1964 as the Post Office Tower. Its revolving restaurant and observation deck featured in any film that wanted to prove how prodigiously London was swinging (*Bedazzled* is just one example). The restaurant is now reserved for corporate functions, but **Charlotte Street** and neighbouring byways remain a good destination for dining and drinking.

FREE All Saints
7 Margaret Street, W1W 8JG (7636 1788, www.allsaintsmargaretstreet.org.uk). Oxford Circus tube. **Open** 7am-7pm daily. *Services* 7.30am, 8am, 1.10pm, 6pm, 6.30pm Mon-Fri; 7.30am, 8am, 6pm, 6.30pm Sat; 8am, 10.20am, 11am, 5.15pm, 6pm Sun. **Admission** free. **No credit cards. Map** p406 U1.
Respite from the tumult of Oxford Street, this 1850s church was designed by William Butterfield, one of the great Gothic Revivalists. The church looks as if it has been lowered into its tiny site, so tight is the fit; its lofty spire is the second-highest in London. Behind the polychromatic brick façade, the shadowy, lavish interior is one of the capital's finest ecclesiastical triumphs, with luxurious marble, flamboyant tile work and glittering stones built into its pillars.

Pollock's Toy Museum
1 Scala Street, W1T 2HL (7636 3452, www.pollockstoymuseum.com). Goodge Street tube. **Open** 10am-5pm Mon-Sat. **Admission** £5; £2-£4 reductions; free under-3s. **Credit** AmEx, MC, V. **Map** p398 J5.
Housed in a creaky Georgian townhouse, Pollock's is named after Benjamin Pollock, the last of the Victorian toy theatre printers. By turns beguiling and creepy, it's a nostalgia-fest of old board games, tin trains, porcelain dolls and Robertson's gollies. It's fascinating for adults but less so for children, for whom the displays may seem a bit static; describing a pile of painted woodblocks stuffed in a cardboard box as a 'Build a skyscraper' kit may make them feel lucky to be going home to their Wii.

INSIDE TRACK OFF THE WALL

Many of Fitzrovia's more rakish characters appear in the 60-foot **Fitzrovia Mural**, next to Goodge Street tube on Tottenham Court Road. Painted in 1980, it features many local characters and familiar buildings.

SIGHTS

Covent Garden & the Strand

London's former fruit market now draws not traders but tourists.

From the Royal Opera House, still in place, to the capital's wholesale fruit and veg market, long since relocated to Vauxhall, **Covent Garden** has long been familiar with both the highs and the lows of London life. Where on that slippery scale you think the place now stands will probably depend on your tolerance to crowds, who descend daily on the restored 19th-century market and its encompassing cobbled 'piazza' to peruse the la-di-da shops and gawp at the street entertainment. And yet there's appeal here: at the revamped London Transport Museum, given a 21st-century overhaul; the Royal Opera House, which has survived in some considerable style; and, down by the river on the **Strand**, the superb Courtauld collection of fine art inside the reborn Somerset House.

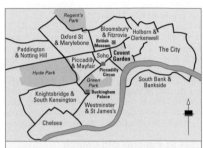

Map p405 & p407   **Restaurants &**
Hotels p175   **cafés** p204
    Pubs & bars p230

COVENT GARDEN

Covent Garden or Leicester Square tube.

Covent Garden was once the property of the medieval Abbey ('convent') of Westminster. Upon Henry VIII's dissolution of the monasteries, it passed to John Russell, first Earl of Bedford, in 1552; his family still owns land hereabouts. During the 16th and 17th centuries, they developed the area: the fourth Earl employed Inigo Jones to create the Italianate open square that remains the area's centrepiece.

Market activity in Covent Garden was first documented in 1640 on the south side of the square, with stalls selling fruit and vegetables. The market grew until it had become London's pre-eminent fruit and vegetable wholesaler, employing over 1,000 porters; its success led to the opening of coffeehouses, theatres, gambling dens and brothels. A flower market was added (where the **London Transport Museum** now stands; *see p87*); the main market building itself was redesigned in the 19th century by Charles Fowler.

In the second half of the 20th century, it became obvious that the congested streets of central London were unsuitable for such market traffic and the decision was taken to move the traders out; for a look at the market shortly before it closed, watch Alfred Hitchcock's 1972 thriller *Frenzy*. In 1974, with the market gone, the threat of property development loomed for the empty stalls and offices. It was only through demonstrations that the area was saved. It's now a pleasant place for a stroll if you catch it early enough on a fine morning.

Covent Garden Piazza

Centred on Covent Garden Piazza, the area now offers a combination of gentrified shops, restaurant and cafés, supplemented by street artists and busking musicians in the lower courtyard. The majority of the entertainment takes place under the portico of **St Paul's Covent Garden** (*see p87*).

Tourists favour the old covered market (7836 9136, www.coventgardenlondonuk.com), which combines upmarket chain stores such

SIGHTS

Garden City

Tourist trap or historic heartland? Both, says Peter Ackroyd.

Tourists adore Covent Garden, so why don't the locals? Peter Ackroyd, all-round expert on the capital and an inhabitant who must cross the nightmarish tract each day to get from office to home, knows all too well. 'Prices are inflated, café prices are too high, the pubs aren't very good,' he admits. 'It's just a tourist trap.' And yet Ackroyd has created a new walking map of the area for tourists and Londoners alike. So why the change of heart?

Although Ackroyd's relationship with Covent Garden may be partly pragmatic, he's adamant that if you go beyond the droves of chattering tourists, you'll find an exhilarating historical labyrinth, populated since the sixth century and subject to countless changes since. Standing outside the **Theatre Royal** (Catherine Street, WC2B 5JF, www.theatreroyaldrurylane.co.uk), you can envisage Nell Gwynne selling her oranges to Charles II. And just to the north at **26 Wellington Street**, an image of Victorian London is conjured by a plaque marking the location of Charles Dickens' offices (it's now a run-of-the-mill tea room).

All this history prompts our guide on a role call of other characters, real and imagined that have inhabited the area. Hitchcock had the murderer of his 1972 thriller *Frenzy* living at no.3 Henrietta Street, more than 150 years after Jane Austen lodged at no.10 (now the Rohan shop); Turner's birthplace is to the south of the market, at what's now Irish beer-haven the **Porterhouse** (nos.21-22, 7836 9931, www.porterhousebrewco.com). But for all of Ackroyd's fascination with the past, he doesn't begrudge the changes, cheerily explaining how Bow Street Magistrates' Court is being redeveloped as a hotel. 'The spirit remains the same,' he insists, 'even if the interior changes.'

Alongside the memorial of the first recorded performance of Punch and Judy in the UK, Ackroyd reveals that **St Paul's Covent Garden** (*see p87*) was built the wrong way round. It explains the baffling backside of a building that imposes on one side of the square and yet seems to serve little purpose other than as an impromptu stage for the unflagging efforts of the street entertainers. But Ackroyd's top tip for unearthing the Covent Garden beneath the stalls of tourist tat is the warren of alleyways that have largely escaped modernisation. In the claustrophobic passage by the **Nell Gwynne** (1-2 Bull Inn Court, WC2R 0NP, 7240 5579), it isn't hard to imagine grubby liaisons between King Charles and the orange-seller.

▶ *You can pick up the text and route map of Peter Ackroyd's Walking Tour from the Market Building information office or at www.coventgardenlondonuk.com.*

Bicester Village   Warwick Castle   Shakespeare's Birthplace, Stratford-upon-Avon

Get out of London for a day

There are lots of truly wonderful places that are easily and quickly reached from London when you take a Chiltern Railways train.

There's the historic market town and castle at Warwick.

Or fantastic bargains on designer labels at the Bicester Village shopping outlet.

And don't forget all that Stratford-upon-Avon, home of William Shakespeare, has to offer.

Plus you can enjoy some fantastic views of the beautiful English countryside along the way.

With a frequent train service from our central London terminus at Marylebone, and a wide range of fares for individuals, small groups and families, it's easy to make the most of your time in London and also see some of England on its doorstep by train.

And what's more, our website makes planning your day out even easier.

Take a look at **www.chilternrailways.co.uk/daysout** for some great inspiration.

London Marylebone | **Bicester North** | **Warwick** | **Stratford-upon-Avon**

www.chilternrailways.co.uk/daysout or call 08456 005 165

Chiltern Railways

as **Hobbs**, **Whistles** and **Crabtree & Evelyn** with a collection of small, sometimes quirky and often rather twee independent shops. The **Apple Market**, in the North Hall, has arts and crafts stalls every Tuesday to Sunday, and antiques on Monday. Across the road, the tackier **Jubilee Market** deals mostly in novelty T-shirts and other tat. The Piazza and market are best viewed from the Amphitheatre Café Bar's terrace loggia at the **Royal Opera House** (*see below*).

★ London Transport Museum

Covent Garden Piazza, WC2E 7BB (7379 6344, www.ltmuseum.co.uk). Covent Garden tube. **Open** 10am-6pm Mon-Thur, Sat, Sun; 11am-6pm Fri. **Admission** £10; £6-£8 reductions; free under-16s. **Credit** AmEx, DC, MC, V. **Map** p407 Z3.
Re-opened in 2007 after the most thorough refurbishment since its move to Covent Garden in 1980, the London Transport Museum traces the city's transport history from the horse age to the present day. As well as a remodelled interior, the museum has emerged with a much more confident focus on social history and design, illustrated by a superb array of preserved buses, trams and trains. Appropriately, it's now also much easier to get around.

The collections are in broadly chronological order, beginning with the Victorian gallery, where a replica of Shillibeer's first horse-drawn bus service in 1829 takes pride of place. Another gallery is dedicated to the museum's truly impressive collection of poster art. Under the leadership of Frank Pick, in the early

London Transport Museum.

20th century London Transport developed one of the most coherent brand identities in the world. The new museum also raises some interesting and important questions about the future of public transport in the city, with a display on ideas that are 'coming soon'.
▶ *For the museum's Acton depot, see p161* **Inside Track**.

Royal Opera House

Bow Street, WC2E 9DD (7304 4000, www.roh. org.uk). Covent Garden tube. **Open** 10am-3.30pm Mon-Sat. **Admission** free. *Stage tours* £10; £8 reductions. **Credit** AmEx, DC, MC, V. **Map** p407 Y3.
The Royal Opera House was founded in 1732 by John Rich on the profits of his production of John Gay's *Beggar's Opera*; the current building, constructed roughly 150 years ago but extensively remodelled since, is the third on the site. Visitors can explore the massive eight-floor building as part of an organised tour, including the main auditorium, the costume workshops and sometimes even a rehearsal. Certain parts of the building are also open to the general public, including the glass-roofed Floral Hall, the Crush Bar (so named because in Victorian times, the only thing served during intermissions was orange and lemon crush) and the Amphitheatre Café Bar. *Photos p88*.
▶ *For the Royal Opera House's primary function as a music venue, see p311.*

FREE St Paul's Covent Garden

Bedford Street, WC2E 9ED (7836 5221, www. actorschurch.org). Covent Garden or Leicester Square tube. **Open** 9am-4.30pm Mon-Fri; 9am-12.30pm Sun. *Services* 1.10pm Tue, Wed; 6am Thur; 11am Sun. *Choral Evensong* 4pm 2nd Sun of mth. **Admission** free; donations appreciated. **No credit cards. Map** p407 Y3.
Known as the Actors' Church for its long association with Covent Garden's theatres, this magnificently spare building was designed by Inigo Jones for the Earl of Bedford in 1631. A beautiful limewood wreath carved by the 17th-century master Grinling Gibbons hangs inside the front door as a reminder that he and his wife are interred in the crypt.

Thespians commemorated on its walls range from those destined for immortality (Charlie Chaplin, for

SIGHTS

one) to those lost in obscurity (step forward Percy Press, the Punch and Judy man). Perhaps most charming are the sublunary figures, such as William Henry Pratt: although his birth name is forgotten to all but devotees, he's famous as the real flesh behind unforgettable monsters under his pseudonym, Boris Karloff. Surely no more romantic tribute is paid anywhere in the city than here to Vivien Leigh, whose plaque is simply inscribed with words from Shakespeare's *Antony & Cleopatra*: 'Now boast thee, death, in thy possession lies a lass unparallel'd.'

Elsewhere in Covent Garden

Outside Covent Garden Piazza, the area offers a offers a mixed bag of entertainment, eateries and shops. Nearest the markets, most of the more unusual shops have been superseded by a homogeneous mass of cafés, while big fashion chains have all but domesticated Long Acre. There are more interesting stores north of here on Neal Street and Monmouth Street; Earlham Street is also home to the **Donmar Warehouse** (*see p345*), a former banana-ripening depot that's now an intimate and groundbreaking theatre. On tiny Shorts Gardens next door is the **Neal's Yard Dairy** (*see p263*), purveyor of pungent and exceptional UK cheeses; down a passageway one door along is Neal's Yard itself, known for its co-operative cafés, herbalists and head shops.

South of Long Acre and east of the Piazza, historical depravity is called to account at the

**INSIDE TRACK
TREASURE HUNT**

Monmouth and Earlham Streets meet Shorts Gardens at **Seven Dials**, named after the sundials incorporated into the central monument (the seventh is the pillar itself). The original pillar, an famous criminal rendezvous, was torn down in 1773 by a mob who believed there was treasure buried at its base. There wasn't.

former **Bow Street Magistrates Court**. Once home to the Bow Street Runners, the precursors of the Metropolitan Police, this was also where Oscar Wilde entered his plea when arrested for 'indecent acts' in 1895. It's currently being converted into a hotel. To the south, Wellington and Catherine Streets mix restaurants and theatres, including the grand **Theatre Royal**. Other diversions in and around Covent Garden include the museum at **Freemasons' Hall** (7831 9811, www. freemasonry.london.museum; call for details of tours), an impressive stone building where Long Acre becomes Great Queen Street; and, at opposite ends both of St Martin's Lane and the social spectrum, lap-dancing club **Stringfellows** (16-19 Upper St Martin's Lane, 7240 5534) and the **Coliseum** (*see p311*), home of the English National Opera.

Royal Opera House. *See p87.*

THE STRAND & EMBANKMENT

Embankment tube or Charing Cross tube/rail.

Until as recently as the 1860s, the Strand ran beside the Thames; indeed, it was originally the river's bridlepath. In the 14th century, it was lined with grand residences with gardens that ran down to the water. It wasn't until the 1870s that the Thames was pushed back with the creation of the Embankment and its adjacent gardens. By the time George Newnes's famed *Strand* magazine was introducing its readership to Sherlock Holmes (1891), the street after which the magazine was named boasted the Cecil Hotel (long since demolished), **Simpson's**, **King's College** and **Somerset House** (*see p90*). Prime Minister Benjamin Disraeli described it as 'perhaps the finest street in Europe'. Nobody would make such a claim today – there are too many overbearing office blocks and underwhelming restaurants – but there's still plenty to interest visitors.

In 1292, the body of Eleanor of Castile, consort to King Edward I, completed its funerary procession from Lincoln in the small hamlet of Charing, at the western end of what is now the Strand. The occasion was marked by the erection of the last of 12 elaborate crosses. A replica of the Eleanor Cross was placed in 1865 on the forecourt of **Charing Cross Station**; it remains there today, looking like the spire of a sunken cathedral. Across the road, behind **St Martin-in-the-Fields** (*see p112*), is Maggie Hambling's decidedly eccentric memorial to a more recent queen, *A Conversation with Oscar Wilde*.

The Embankment itself can be reached down Villiers Street. Pass through the tube station to the point at which boat tours with on-board entertainment depart. Just to the east stands **Cleopatra's Needle**, an obelisk presented to the British nation by the viceroy of Egypt, Mohammed Ali, in 1820 but not set in place by the river for a further 59 years. The obelisk was originally erected around 1500 BC by the pharaoh Tuthmosis III at a site near modern-day Cairo, before being moved to Alexandria, Cleopatra's capital, in 10 BC. By this time, however, the great queen was 20 years dead.

Back on the Strand, the majestic **Savoy Hotel** is currently undergoing extensive refurbishment, due to finish in spring 2010. It first opened in 1889, financed by the profits made from Richard D'Oyly Carte's productions of Gilbert and Sullivan's light operas at the neighbouring Savoy Theatre. Indeed, the theatre pre-dates the hotel by eight years, becoming the first theatre to use electric lights, and has remained open during the renovations.

Benjamin Franklin House

36 Craven Street, the Strand, WC2N 5NF (7925 1405, www.benjaminfranklinhouse.org). Charing Cross tube/rail or Embankment tube. **Open** pre-book tours by phone or online. **Box office** 10.30am-5pm Wed-Sun. **Admission** £7; £5 reductions; free under-16s. **Credit** AmEx, MC, V. **Map** p407 Y5.

Restoration of the house where Franklin – scientist, diplomat, philosopher, inventor and Founding Father of the US – lived between 1757 and 1775 was completed in 2006. The house is not a museum in the conventional sense, but it can be explored on well-run, pre-booked 'experiences' lasting a short but intense 45 minutes (noon, 1pm, 2pm, 3.15pm and 4.15pm, Wed-Sun). The tours are led by an actress playing Franklin's landlady Margaret Stevenson, using projections and sound to conjure up the world and times in which Franklin lived. From noon on Mondays, the house offers more straightforward, 20-minute tours given by house interns (£3.50).

THE ALDWYCH

Temple tube.

At the eastern end of the Strand is the Aldwych. This grand crescent dates only from 1905, but the name 'ald wic' (old settlement) has its origins in the 14th century. To the south is regal **Somerset House** (*see p90*); even if you aren't interested in the galleries, it's worth visiting the fountain courtyard. Almost in front of it is **St Mary-le-Strand** (7836 3126, open 11am-4pm Mon-Sat, 10am-3pm Sun), James Gibbs's first public building, built from 1714 to 1717. Original plans called for a statue of Queen Anne on a column beside it, but she died before it could be built and the plan was scrapped. On Strand Lane, reached via Surrey Street, is the so-called **'Roman' bath** where Dickens took the waters.

On a traffic island just east of the Aldwych is **St Clement Danes** (7242 2380). It's believed that a church was first built here by the Danish in the ninth century, but the current building is mainly Wren's handiwork. It's the principal church of the RAF. Just beyond the church are the **Royal Courts of Justice** (*see p90*) and the original site of Temple Bar, which once marked the boundary between Westminster and the City of London. The Temple Bar is now next to **St Paul's Cathedral** (*see p63*).

★ Courtauld Gallery

Strand, WC2R 1LA (7848 2526, www.courtauld.ac.uk/gallery). Temple tube or Charing Cross tube/rail. **Open** 10am-6pm daily. *Tours* phone for details. **Admission** £5; £4 reductions. Free 10am-2pm Mon; students & under-18s daily. **Credit** MC, V. **Map** p401 M7.

Located in the north wing of Somerset House (*see right*), the Courtauld has one of Britain's greatest collections of paintings, and contains several works of world importance. Although there are some outstanding works from earlier periods (the wonderful *Adam & Eve* by Lucas Cranach, for one), the collection's strongest suit is its holdings of Impressionist and post-Impressionist paintings. There are some popular masterpieces: Manet's astonishing *A Bar at the Folies-Bergère* is the centrepiece, alongside plenty of superb Monets and Cézannes, important Gauguins (including *Nevermore*) and some excellent Van Goghs and Seurats. On the top floor, there's a selection of gorgeous Fauvist works, a lovely room of Kandinskys and plenty more besides.

Hidden downstairs, the sweet little gallery café is frequently forgotten, but it feels delightfully separate from the rest of Somerset House. Make a free Monday-morning visit to the art collection and finish with a relaxed lunch. Note that bulky backpacks must be carried, not worn, through the collection; there are a few coin-operated lockers downstairs.
▶ *The Courtauld Gallery was the first home of the Royal Academy; see p108.*

FREE Royal Courts of Justice

Strand, WC2A 2LL (7947 6000, www.hmcourtsservice.gov.uk). Temple tube. **Open** 9am-5pm Mon-Fri. **Admission** free. **Credit** MC, V.
Map p399 M6.
The magnificent Royal Courts preside over the most serious civil cases in British law. Members of the public can attend most trials, but there are very few in August and September. Two-hour tours are given on the first and third Tuesday of each month (except late July and early August) at 11am and 2pm; costing £10, they can be booked by

phoning 7947 7684. Cameras and children under 14 are not allowed on the premises.

FREE Somerset House & the Embankment Galleries

Strand, WC2R 1LA (7845 4600, www.somersethouse.org.uk). Temple tube or Charing Cross tube/rail. **Open** 10am-6pm (last entry 5.15pm) daily. *Tours* phone for details.
Admission *Courtyard & terrace* free.
Embankment Galleries £8; £6 reductions. Free students & under-18s daily. *Tours* phone for details. **Credit** MC, V. **Map** p401 M7.
The original Somerset House was a Tudor palace commissioned by the Duke of Somerset. In 1775, it was demolished to make way for an new building, effectively the first purpose-built office block in the world. The architect Sir William Chambers spent the last 20 years of his life working on the neoclassical edifice overlooking the Thames, built to accommodate learned societies such as the Royal Academy. Various governmental offices also took up residence here, including the Inland Revenue.

The taxmen are still here, but the rest of the building is open to the public. Attractions include a formidable art gallery (the wonderful Courtauld; *see above*), the handsome fountain court, a terraced café and a classy restaurant. The Embankment Galleries explore connections between art, architecture and design with a series of temporary exhibitions, and at Christmas usually host an adventurous market; downstairs, a ceremonial Thames barge and information boards explain the place's history, to the accompaniment of Handel's *Water Music*. In summer, children never tire of running through the choreographed fountains; in winter, a hugely popular ice rink is erected on top of them.

Somerset House.

Soho & Leicester Square

London's bohemian core retains at least part of its unique appeal.

For more than two centuries, poseurs, spivs, tarts, toffs, drunks and divas have gathered in **Soho** to ply their trades. Many of the area's music, film and advertising businesses have moved on, but the gay scene still thrives, and now drives the non-stop party atmosphere.

Hemmed in by Oxford Street to the north, Charing Cross Road to the east, Shaftesbury Avenue to the south and Regent Street to the west, Soho is packed with a huge range of restaurants, clubs and bars, sharing the streets with a sizeable residential community. Just to the south, beyond tiny **Chinatown**, **Leicester Square** is many a drunken exhibitionist's favourite late-night stamping ground.

Map pp406-407
Hotels p175

Restaurants & cafés p207
Pubs & bars p231

SOHO SQUARE

Tottenham Court Road tube.

Forming the area's northern gateway, **Soho Square** was laid out in 1681. It was initially called King's Square; a weather-beaten statue of Charles II stands just north of centre. On warmer days, the grassy spaces are filled with courting couples as snacking workers occupy its benches; one of these benches is dedicated to singer Kirsty MacColl, in honour of her song named after the square. The denominations of the two churches on the square testify to the area's long-standing European credentials: as well as the French Protestant church, you'll find St Patrick's, one of the first Catholic churches built in England after the Reformation.

Two classic Soho streets run south from the square. **Greek Street**, its name a nod to a church that once stood here, is lined with restaurants and bars, among them 50-year-old Hungarian eaterie the **Gay Hussar** (no.2, 7437 0973) and the nearby **Pillars of Hercules** pub (no.7, 7437 1179), where the literati once enjoyed long liquid lunches. Just by the Pillars, an arch

leads to Manette Street and the Charing Cross Road, where you'll find **Foyles** (*see p247*). Back on Greek Street, no.49 was once Les Cousins, a folk venue (note the heldover mosaic featuring a musical note); Casanova lived briefly at no.46.

Parallel to Greek Street is **Frith Street**, once home to Mozart (1764-65, no.20) and John Constable (1810-11, no.49). Humanist essayist William Hazlitt died in 1830 at no.6, now a discreet hotel named in his memory (*see p177*). Further down is **Ronnie Scott's** (*see p320*), Britain's best-known jazz club. And across from Ronnie's is the similarly mythologised **Bar Italia** (no.22, 7437 4520). A large portrait of Rocky Marciano dominates the narrow, chrome bar, but it's the place's 24-hour opening that makes it likely you'll have to fight for a seat.

OLD COMPTON STREET & AROUND

Leicester Square or Tottenham Court Road tube.

Linking the Charing Cross Road to Wardour Street and crossed by Greek, Frith and Dean Streets, **Old Compton Street** is now London's

Soho Square. *See p91.*

gay superhighway. Tight T-shirts congregate around **Balans** (*see p302*), **Compton's** (nos.51-53) and the **Admiral Duncan** (no.54), among other venues. But the street has an interesting history that dates back long before rainbow flags were hung above its doors. Now the **Boulevard Bar & Dining Room**, 59 Old Compton Street was formerly the 2i's Coffee Bar, the skiffle venue where stars and svengalis mingled in the late 1950s and early 1960s at the dawn of the British rock 'n' roll scene. Around this time, the street drew a raffish collection of chancers, ne'er-do-wells and criminals, two of whom – Jack Spot and Albert Dimes – faced off in a famous knife fight at the intersection of Old Compton Street and Frith Street in 1955.

Visit Old Compton Street in the morning for a sense of the immigrant Soho of old. Cheeses and cooked meats from **Camisa** (no.61, 7437 7610) and roasting beans from the **Algerian Coffee Stores** (*see p259*) scent the air, as **Pâtisserie Valerie** (no.44, 7437 3466, www.patisserie-valerie.co.uk) does a brisk trade in buttery croissants and cakes. Its traditional French rival is the older **Maison Bertaux** (*see p209*), a lovely holdover from the 19th century that sits near the southern extremity of Greek Street.

Maison Bertaux is far from the only point of interest on the roads south of Old Compton Street. At the corner of Greek and Romilly Streets sits the the **Coach & Horses** (no.29, 7437 5920), where Soho flâneur Jeffrey Bernard held court for decades. It's almost opposite the members' club **Soho House** (no.40, 7734 5188), where a current crop of wannabes hopes to channel the same vibe. Two streets along, Dean

Street holds the **French House** (*see p231*); formerly the York Minster pub, it was De Gaulle's London base for French resistance in World War II and later became a favourite of painters Francis Bacon and Lucian Freud.

North of Old Compton Street on Dean Street sits the **Groucho Club** (no.45), a members-only media hangout founded in the mid '80s, named in honour of the old Groucho Marx quote about not wanting to join any club that would have him as a member. A few doors along, **Quo Vadis** (26-29 Dean Street, W1D 3LL, 7437 9585, www.quovadissoho.co.uk), has a costly, sophisticated grill room with a members-only bar upstairs. Karl Marx, who lived here in the garret at no.28 from 1850 to 1856, would probably not have approved. To the north is the **Soho Theatre** (*see p346*), which programmes new plays and comedy.

WARDOUR STREET & AROUND

Leicester Square or Tottenham Court Road tube.

Parallel to Dean Street, **Wardour Street** provides offices for film and TV production companies, but is also known for its rock history. What's now upscale tapas joint **Meza** (no.100, 7314 4002, www.mezabar.co.uk) was, for nearly three decades, the Marquee, where Led Zeppelin played their first London gig and Hendrix appeared four times. The latter's favourite Soho haunt was the nearby **Ship** pub (no.116, 7437 8446), still with a sprinkling of music-themed knick-knacks. There's more music history at Trident Studios on nearby

St Anne's Court: Lou Reed recorded *Transformer* here, and David Bowie cut both *Hunky Dory* and *The Rise and Fall of Ziggy Stardust and the Spiders from Mars* on the site.

Back when he was still known as David Jones, Bowie played a gig at the Jack of Clubs on Brewer Street, now **Madame JoJo's** (*see p323*). But this corner of Soho is most famous not for music but for its position at the heart of Soho's dwindling but still-notorious sex trade.

The **Raymond Revuebar** opened on the neon alleyway of Walker's Court in 1958, swiftly becoming London's most famous strip club. It closed in 2004, but numerous smaller, seedier establishments continue to tout for business close by on Brewer Street and Tisbury Court.

North of here, **Berwick Street** is a lovely mix of old-school London raffishness and new-Soho style. The former comes courtesy of the amiable street food market, with stalls offering

Glad to Be Gay

Strolling down luvvies lane, you'd hardly notice the scene has moved elsewhere.

Walk down **Old Compton Street** and it'll be obvious that you're in Europe's queerest quarter. Coffeeshops overflow with orange-hued queens, tag teams hand out flyers and drinks promos, and there's plenty of covert and not-so-covert checking-out. In short, it's fagtastic. So why, then, have London's boys and girls been emigrating en masse to Shoreditch and to Vauxhall?

Soho's perma-tanned princes and showtunes are seen as a little bridge-and-tunnel by your average Shoreditch fashion gay, while Vauxhall marys tend to baulk at Westminster Council's limited opening hours ('Closed by 1am? We haven't even snorted dessert yet'). But all the talk of Soho going the way of Earl's Court, the city's onetime queer quarter, is premature.

For one thing, out east and down south there's basically nothing to do and no one to look at during the day. Not so in Soho. Old Compton Street's coffeeshops (**Caffè Nero** at the corner with Frith Street, **Balans**

at no.60, **Costa** at no.39) are prime perches for eyeing up the motorway of moxes. The food is good and so are the drinks; check out the **Admiral Duncan** (no.54), **Freedom** (66 Wardour Street) or **Friendly Society** (79 Wardour Street). And when night falls, venues such as G-A-Y at **Heaven** (*see p304*) are scene institutions.

Soho's queer credentials remain strong because of its location. This is London's cosmopolitan heartland and it overflows with theatres, production companies and publishing houses, hornets' nests of homosexuality. There's a real mix of people, which means there's none of the scenester snootiness of the east or the crazed-eye sweatiness of the south. You get all sorts in Soho – tourists talking to recently-popped-out-the-closets, out-of-towners mixing with post-work drinkers – and that's the real attraction. And in a city as notoriously cold as London, Soho's gay venues are arguably its friendliest corners.

SIGHTS

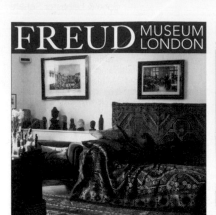
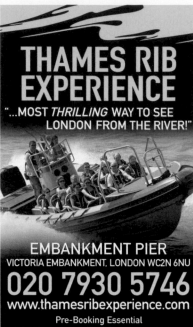

sweets, nuts, fruit, vegetables and even fresh fish (9am-6pm Mon-Sat), and the egalitarian, old-fashioned and unceasingly popular **Blue Posts** pub (no.22, 7437 5008), where builders, post-production editors, restaurateurs and market traders gabble and glug as one beneath a portrait of Berwick Street-born star of stage and radio Jessie Matthews (1907-81). It's quite a contrast with the **Endurance** (no.90, 7437 2944), the street's gastropub; **Flat White** (no.17, 7734 0370, www.flat-white.co.uk), a chic coffee bar; and **Yauatcha** (*see p211*), Alan Yau's design-led teahouse and pioneering all-day dim sum eaterie housed in a building by Lord Rogers with a Christian Liagre interior.

WEST SOHO

Piccadilly Circus tube.

West of Berwick Street, Soho has been branded 'West Soho' in a misplaced bid to give some kind of upmarket identity to its shops. That said, **Brewer Street** does have a handful of interesting places; among them is the **Vintage Magazine Store** (nos.39-43, 7439 8525), offering everything from retro robots to pre-war issues of *Vogue*. On Great Windmill Street is the **Windmill Theatre** (nos.17-19), which gained fame in the 1930s and 1940s for its 'revuedeville' shows with erotic 'tableaux' – naked girls who remained stationary in order to stay within the law. The place is now a lap-dancing joint. North of Brewer Street is **Golden Square**. Developed in the 1670s, it became the political and ambassadorial district of the late 17th and early 18th centuries, and remains home to some of the area's grandest residential buildings (many now home to media firms).

Just north of Golden Square is **Carnaby Street**, which became a fashion mecca shortly after John Stephen opened His Clothes here in 1956; Stephen, who went on to own more than a dozen fashion shops on the street is now commemorated with a plaque at the corner with Beak Street. After thriving during the Swingin' '60s, Carnaby Street went on to become a rather seamy commercialised backwater. However, along with nearby

Newburgh Street (*see p255* **Inside Track**) and Kingly Court, it's recently undergone a revival, with the tourist traps and chain stores now joined by a wealth of interesting independent stores. Kingly Street retains fashionable bars such as **Two Floors** (no.3; 7439 1007) and, secreted in Kingly Court, popular boho drinks club **Tatty Bogles** (no.11, 7734 4475).

CHINATOWN & LEICESTER SQUARE

Leicester Square tube.

Shaftesbury Avenue is the very heart of Theatreland. The Victorians built seven grand theatres here, six of which still stand. The most impressive is the gorgeous **Palace Theatre** on Cambridge Circus, which opened in 1891 as the Royal English Opera House; when grand opera flopped, the theatre reopened as a music hall two years later. Appropriately, it's most famous for the musicals staged here *The Sound of Music* (1961) and *Jesus Christ Superstar* (1972) had their London premières here, and *Les Misérables* racked up 7,602 performances between 1985 and 2004. The current resident is *Priscilla, Queen of the Desert*.

Just opposite the Palace Theatre, what's now the Med Kitchen occupies premises that were once home to Marks & Co, the shop made famous by Helene Hanff's *84 Charing Cross Road*. Second-hand bookshops still line Charing Cross Road to the south, heading towards Leicester Square. West of Charing Cross Road and south of Shaftesbury Avenue, meanwhile, and officially just outside Soho's boundaries, is the city's **Chinatown**.

The Chinese are relative latecomers to this part of town. London's original Chinatown was set around Limehouse in east London, but hysteria about Chinese opium dens and criminality led to 'slum clearances' in 1934 (interestingly, the surrounding slums were deemed to be in less urgent need of clearance).

SIGHTS

It wasn't until the 1950s that the Chinese put down roots here, attracted by the cheap rents along Gerrard and Lisle Streets.

The ersatz oriental gates, stone lions and pagoda-topped phone boxes around Gerrard Street suggest a Chinese theme park, but this remains a close-knit residential and working enclave, a genuine focal point for the Chinese community in London. The area is crammed with restaurants, Asian grocery stores and a host of small shops selling iced-grass jelly, speciality teas and cheap air tickets to Beijing.

South of Chinatown, **Leicester Square** was one of London's most exclusive addresses in the 17th century; in the 18th, it became home to the royal court of Prince George (later George II). How different it all is now (*see below* **Hard Times Square**). Satirical painter William Hogarth had a studio here (1733-64), as did 18th-century artist Sir Joshua Reynolds; both are commemorated by busts in the small

gardens that lie at the heart of the square, although it's the statue of a tottering Charlie Chaplin that gets all the attention. There's no particular reason for Chaplin to be here, other than the fact that Leicester Square is considered the home of British film thanks to its numerous cinemas. The monolithic **Odeon Leicester Square** (*see p291*) once boasted the UK's largest screen, and probably still has the UK's highest ticket prices. Like the neighbouring **Empire**, it's regularly used for movie premières.

The **Hippodrome**, on the corner of Cranbourn Street and Charing Cross Road beside the tube station, is an impressive red-brick edifice designed by the prolific theatre architect Frank Matcham. It became famous as the 'Talk of the Town' cabaret venue in the 1960s, featuring the likes of Shirley Bassey and Judy Garland. Currently being refurbished, it's scheduled to become a casino in 2010.

Hard Times Square

Central London's least appealing space gets a refit – but will it help?

Londoners tend to avoid the fast food, expensive cinemas and tacky pavement artists of **Leicester Square**. Apart from the **tkts** booth (*see p339* **The Cheap Seats**), selling cut-price, same-day theatre tickets, and Leicester Place's unlikely neighbours the **Prince Charles Cinema** (*see p292*) and the French Catholic church of **Notre Dame de France** (no.5, 7437 9363, www.notredamechurch.co.uk), with its Jean Cocteau murals, there's little reason to venture here. The green patch in

the centre is bearable on a sunny day, but don't head here after dark unless you enjoy being jostled by throngs of drunken idiots.

In 2008, plans were announced for a major redevelopment, with a new layout in the centre, improved lighting and modish 'ribbon' seating that's doubtless designed to prevent the homeless getting a good kip. Along the northern edge, expect a W hotel and an outpost of the brilliant St John restaurant (*see p203*). But until they arrive, there are better places to spend your time.

Oxford Street & Marylebone

Department stores, designer labels and endangered species.

Oxford Street continues its brave struggle to remain London's top retail destination. A revamped roundabout at Marble Arch, wider pavements, innovative pedestrian crossings and an all-new 'eastern gateway' development should, come the Olympics, combine to make sunset on London's High Street memorable for more of the right reasons. Until then, discerning, crowdphobic locals will continue to favour the luxury cafés and boutiques of **Marylebone**, the flowering green acres of **Regent's Park** and, on occasion, London Zoo.

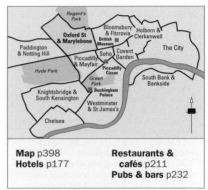

Map p398	Restaurants &
Hotels p177	cafés p211
	Pubs & bars p232

OXFORD STREET

Bond Street, Marble Arch, Oxford Circus or Tottenham Court Road tube.

Official estimates put the annual footfall at somewhere near 200 million people per year. But few Londoners love **Oxford Street**. A shopping district since the 19th century, it's unmanageably busy on weekends and in the run-up to Christmas. But even outside these times, it's never pretty, lined with over-familiar chain stores and choked with road traffic.

The street gets smarter as you walk from east to west. Just west of chaotic **Oxford Circus**, you'll find a string of big department stores, among them **John Lewis** (nos.278-306, 7629 7711), **Debenhams** (nos.334-348, 0844 561 6161) and **Selfridges** (no.400; *see p244*). Selfridges opened in 1909, but much of its building was completed in the art deco '20s. Opposite, the stalled Park House development is set to become a tented space for temporary events. Elsewhere on the street, architectural interest is largely limited to Oxford Circus's four identical convex corners, constructed between 1913 and 1928. The crowds and rush of traffic hamper investigations, a problem the council attempted to address in 2009 by widening pavements, removing street clutter and creating Tokyo Shibuya-style diagonal crossings.

Oxford Street gained notoriety as the route by which condemned men were conveyed from Newgate to the old Tyburn gallows, stopping only for a last pint at the **Angel** (61 St Giles High Street, 7240 2876). Thousands gathered to watch the countless executions that were held at Tyburn over six centuries; held in 1783, the final execution to be carried out here is marked by an X on a traffic island at the junction of the Edgware and Bayswater Roads.

Close by, at the western end of Oxford Street, stands **Marble Arch**, with its Carrara marble cladding and sculptures celebrating Nelson and Wellington. It was designed by John Nash in 1827 as the entrance to a rebuilt Buckingham

---

INSIDE TRACK I BELIEVE IN...

A young Paul McCartney woke up one morning in 1965 at **57 Wimpole Street**, the house of then-girlfriend Jane Asher's parents. He dashed to the piano to transcribe a tune that had been playing in his dreams: it became 'Yesterday', one of the most performed songs of all time.

Palace, but the arch was moved here in 1851, after – it is said – a fuming Queen Victoria found it to be too narrow for her coach. Now given a £2-million revamp, it's been joined by renovated water fountains and gardens that contain an ongoing series of public sculpture commissions. The current incumbent is Nic Fiddian-Green's giant *Horse at Water*, a vast horse's head poised on its lips amid the lawns.

North of Oxford Circus

Great Portland Street, Oxford Circus or Regent's Park tube.

North of Oxford Circus runs **Langham Place**, notable for the Bath stone façade of John Nash's **All Souls Church** (Langham Place, 2 All Souls Place, 7580 3522, www.allsouls.org).

Walk Back to the Back Streets

Avoid Oxford Street's horrors with a trail through the side streets.

When it comes to shopping on Oxford Street, the average Londoner doesn't. But if a visit is unavoidable, you can escape the crowds by diving into the streets that fringe the main drag. This walk introduces the hinterlands of Oxford Street, prized by locals; walk the whole thing or, just as easily, pick it up and leave it at any point.

Rathbone Place marks the lower reaches of Fitzrovia, where the worlds of media and design collide with the rag trade. The fun begins at **Hobgoblin** (no.24, 7323 9040), a folk music store where musicians test-drive zithers, banjos and ukuleles. Close by on Percy Street, **Contemporary Applied Arts** (*see p264*) sells outstanding British crafts, from jewellery to furniture.

Keep north up restaurant-lined Charlotte Street, buzzing with media types, then turn left beside the suave **Charlotte Street Hotel** (*see p171*) through Percy Passage. Cross the dog-leg of Rathbone Street, and head on via Dickensian Newman Passage

to emerge in Newman Street. Pause for a snap of the **BT Tower**, then go left and right on to Eastcastle Street. Detour up Margaret Street to **All Saints Church** (*see p83*).

Back on Eastcastle Street sits cutting-edge gallery **Stuart Shave/Modern Art** (*see p297*). Over the road, **Fever** (no.52, 7636 6326) mixes cute retro-inspired clothing and accessories with vintage, while the **Getty Images Gallery** (no.46, 7291 5380) holds great photography exhibitions. Market Place opens ahead, a mellow collection of sidewalk cafés yards from the frenzy of Oxford Street. Stop for refreshment and then head across Oxford Street down Argyll Street, aiming for the half-timbered **Liberty** building (*see p244*).

Next, cross Regent Street towards Conduit Street, where a visit to **Vivienne Westwood**'s flamboyant flagship store (no.44, 7439 1109, www.vivienne westwood.com) provides a taste of punky London couture. Continue to New Bond

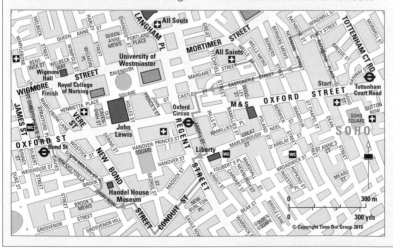

Its bold combination of a Gothic spire and classical rotunda wasn't always popular: in 1824, a year after it was opened, the church was condemned in the House of Commons as a 'deplorable and horrible object'.

Opposite the church you'll find the BBC's **Broadcasting House**, an oddly asymmetrical art deco building that's shipshape in more ways than one. Prominent among the carvings is a statue of Shakespeare's Prospero and Ariel, his spirit of the air – or, in this case, the airwaves. The statue caused controversy when it was unveiled due to the flattering size of the airy sprite's manhood; artist Eric Gill was recalled and asked to make it more modest. Major renovations are under way, due for completion in 2011. Over the road is the **Langham Hotel** (1C Portland Place, Regent Street, W1B 1JA, 7636 1000, http://london.langhamhotels.co.uk), opened in 1865 as Britain's first grand hotel and home at various points to Mark Twain, Napoleon III and Oscar Wilde.

North, Langham Place turns into **Portland Place**, designed by Robert and James Adam as the glory of 18th-century London. Its Georgian terraced houses are now mostly occupied by embassies and swanky offices. At no.66 is the **Royal Institute of British Architects** (RIBA; *see p300*). Running parallel to Portland Place are **Harley Street**, famous for its high-cost dentists and doctors, and **Wimpole Street**, erstwhile home to the poet Elizabeth Barrett Browning (no.50) and Sir Arthur Conan Doyle (2 Upper Wimpole Street).

MARYLEBONE

Baker Street, Bond Street, Marble Arch, Oxford Circus or Regent's Park tube.

North of Oxford Street, the fashionable district known to its boosters as 'Marylebone Village' has become a magnet for moneyed Londoners. Many visitors to the area head directly for the waxworks of **Madame Tussauds** (*see p101*); there's also a small and oft-overlooked museum at the neighbouring **Royal Academy of Music** (7873 7300, www.ram.ac.uk). However, the area's beating heart is **Marylebone High Street**, teeming with interesting shops.

St Marylebone Church stands in its fourth incarnation at the northern end of the street. The name of the neighbourhood is a contraction of the church's earlier name, St Mary by the Bourne; the 'bourne' in question, Tyburn stream, still filters into the Thames near Pimlico, but its entire length is now covered. The church's lovely garden hosts designer clothing and artisan food stalls at the **Cabbages & Frocks** market on Saturdays (www.cabbagesandfrocks.co.uk).

More lovely boutiques can be found on winding **Marylebone Lane**, along with the **Golden Eagle** (no.59, 7935 3228), which hosts regular singalongs around its piano. There's fine food here, too, with smart, often upmarket eateries snuggling alongside delicatessens such as **La Fromagerie** (2-6 Moxon Street, W1U 4EW, 7935 0341, www.lafromagerie.co.uk) and century-old lunchroom **Paul Rothe & Son** (35

Street into Grosvenor Street, then right up Avery Row. This is the land of Victorian London's great aristocratic estates, where narrow service alleys brought tradesmen to the rear entrances of the grand residences. The alleys still offer services to the gentry, but they're now exclusive little boutiques and restaurants that are hidden from the dazed tourists wandering nearby. Top marks on Avery Row go to French cobblers **Hardrige** (no.4, 7355 1504) and the **Paul Smith Sale Shop** (no.23, 7493 1287).

Adjoining Lancashire Court is home to restaurants and the **Handel House Museum** (*see p107*), which faces Brook Street and, close by, Italian design legend **Alessi** (no.22, 7518 9091). Move on to pedestrianised South Molton Street and its strong mix of chain stores, cafés and independents, among them glittery **Butler & Wilson** (no.20, 7409 2955). Take the passage to the left of fashion queen **Browns** (*see p251*) and pop out by the imposing terracotta structure of **Grays Antique Market** (*see p266*).

Cross Oxford Street again, battling your way to the freestanding clock signposting the narrow entrance to St Christopher's Place. This warren of little streets houses a traffic-free complex of cafés and shops, among them handbag specialists **Ollie & Nic** (no.5, 7935 2185) and Finnish designers **Marimekko** (nos.16-17, 7486 6454). There's also a fountain and a flower-decked Victorian WC.

Need a rest? Head north to Wigmore Street for one last stop at **Robert Clergerie Shoes** (no.67, 7935 3601), before heading a couple of doors down to **Comptoir Libanais** (no.65, 7935 1110, www.lecomptoir.co.uk). This colourful and inviting Lebanese eaterie is the perfect place to mull over your buys with a rosewater macaroon and a mint tea.

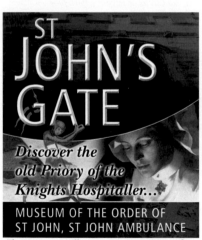

Marylebone Lane, 7935 6783). **Marylebone Farmers' Market** takes place in the Cramer Street car park every Sunday.

Further south, the soaring neo-Gothic interior of the 19th-century **St James's Roman Catholic Church** (22 George Street) is lit dramatically by stained-glass windows; Vivien Leigh (née Hartley) married barrister Herbert Leigh Hunt here in 1932. Other cultural diversions include the **Wallace Collection** (*see right*) and the **Wigmore Hall** (*see p311*).

Madame Tussauds

Marylebone Road, NW1 5LR (0870 400 3000, www.madametussauds.com/london). Baker Street tube. **Open** 9.30am-6pm daily. **Admission** £25; £21 reductions; £87 family (internet advance booking only). **Credit** MC, V. **Map** p398 G4.
Streams of humanity jostle excitedly here for the chance to take pictures of each other planting a smacker on the waxen visage of fame and fortune. Madame Tussaud brought her show to London in 1802, 32 years after it was founded in Paris, and it's been expanding ever since. There are 300 figures in the collection now, among them a suspiciously clear-complexioned Amy Winehouse; Angelina, Brad and Keira receive all the attention their A-lister status affords them. If you're not already over-heating, your palms will be sweating by the time you descend to the alarming Chamber of Horrors, the 'Live!' element of which only teens claim to enjoy. Much more pleasant is the kitsch Spirit of London ride, whisking you through 400 years of London life in a taxi pod. Get here before 10am to avoid the enormous queues, and book online in advance to make the steep admission price a little more palatable.

★ FREE Wallace Collection

Hertford House, Manchester Square, W1U 3BN (7935 0687, www.wallacecollection.org). Bond Street tube. **Open** 10am-5pm daily. **Admission** free. **Credit** (shop) AmEx, MC, V. **Map** p398 G5.
Built in 1776, this handsome house contains an exceptional collection of 18th-century French furniture, painting and objets d'art, as well as an amazing array of medieval armour and weaponry. It all belonged to Sir Richard Wallace, who, as the illegitimate offspring of the fourth Marquess of Hertford, inherited in 1870 the treasures his father had amassed in the last 30 years of his life. Room after grand room contains Louis XIV and XV furnishings and Sèvres porcelain; the galleries are hung with paintings by Gainsborough, Velázquez, Fragonard, Titian and Reynolds; Franz Hals's *Laughing Cavalier* (neither laughing nor a cavalier) is one of the best known, along with Fragonard's *The Swing*. There are also regular temporary exhibitions.
▶ *Oliver Peyton runs the museum restaurant, beautifully set in a glass-roofed courtyard.*

REGENT'S PARK

Baker Street or Regent's Park tube.

Regent's Park (open 5am-dusk daily) is one of London's most delightful open spaces. Originally a hunting ground for Henry VIII, it remained a royals-only retreat long after it was formally designed by John Nash in 1811; only in 1845 did it open to the public as a spectacular shared space. Attractions run from the animal noises and odours of **ZSL London Zoo** (*see p102*) to the enchanting **Open Air Theatre**

SIGHTS

Marble Arch.

INSIDE TRACK ANIMAL ANTICS

The brand new, state-of-the-art Children's Zoo at **ZSL London Zoo** (*see below*) is aimed at the three-to-six age group and features a series of different natural zones where children can play, learn about wildlife, and run a little wild themselves.

(*see p340*); rowing boat hire, spectacular rose gardens, ice-cream stands and the **Garden Café** (7935 5729, www.thegardencafe.co.uk) complete the postcard-pretty picture.

West of Regent's Park rises the golden dome of the **London Central Mosque** (www.iccuk. org) and the northern end of **Baker Street**, unsurprisingly heavy on nods to the world's favourite freelance detective. At the **Sherlock Holmes Museum** (no.221B, 7935 8866, www.sherlock-holmes.co.uk), Holmes stories are earnestly re-enacted, but serious fans may find more of interest among the books and photos of the **Sherlock Holmes Collection** at Marylebone Library (7641 1206, by appointment only); or, for that matter, at Arthur Conan Doyle's former home on Upper Wimpole Street and the Langham Hotel (for both, *see p99*), which features in several of the stories.

The Beatles painted 94 Baker Street with a psychedelic mural before opening it in December 1967 as the Apple Boutique, a clothing store run on such whimsical hippie principles that it had to close within six months due to financial losses. Fab Four pilgrims head to the **London Beatles Store** (no.231, 7935 4464, www.beatlesstorelondon.co.uk), where the ground-floor shop offers a predictable array of Beatles-branded accessories alongside genuine collectibles. Next door, **Elvisly Yours** (7486 2005) caters to the blue-suede-shoed fraternity.

★ ZSL London Zoo

Regent's Park, NW1 4RY (7722 3333, www. zsl.org/london-zoo). Baker Street or Camden Town tube then 274, C2 bus. **Open** 10am-5.30pm daily. **Admission** £18; £15-£17 reductions; free under-3s. **Credit** AmEx, MC, V. **Map** p398 G2.
London Zoo has been open in one form or another since 1826. Spread over 36 acres and containing more than 600 species, it cares for many of the endangered variety – part of the entry price (pretty steep at £17, if you include the voluntary donation) goes towards the ZSL's projects around the world. The emphasis is on upbeat education. Regular events include 'animals in action' and keeper talks; explanations are simple, short and lively. Exhibits are entertaining: look out, in particular, for the recreation of a kitchen overrun with large cockroaches. The 'Meet the Monkeys' attraction allows visitors to walk through an enclosure that recreates the natural habitat of black-capped Bolivian squirrel monkeys, while personal encounters of the avian kind can be had in the Blackburn Pavilion. The reptile house, as always, delights and horrifies in equal measure; likewise the Komodo dragons. Bring a picnic and you can spend a day here.
▶ *The children's zoo in Battersea Park is a winner, and half the price; see p281.*

ZSL London Zoo.

SIGHTS

Paddington & Notting Hill

Middle Eastern kitchens, mazy markets and media darlings.

Sprawled beneath the Westway flyover, with its railway terminus and dedicated branch of the Grand Union Canal, **Paddington** is where central London meets the west of England. It's not an immediately attractive area, but it does hold appeal thanks to the Arab influence around the Edgware Road, and, on the Marylebone side, the goodies on offer at Alfie's Antique Market. There's nothing hidden away about **Notting Hill**: the indefatigable **Portobello Market** is surrounded by some of the most desirable addresses in west London, one of which houses the inimitable **Museum of Brands, Packaging & Advertising**.

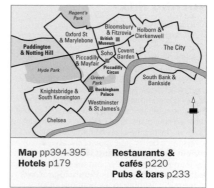

Map pp394-395	Restaurants &
Hotels p179	cafés p220
	Pubs & bars p233

EDGWARE ROAD & PADDINGTON

Edgware Road, Lancaster Gate or Marble Arch tube, or Paddington tube/rail.

Part of the Romans' Watling Street from Dover to Wales, **Edgware Road** rules a definite north–south line marking where the West End stops and central west London begins. It's now the heart of the city's Middle East end: if you want to pick up your copy of *Al Hayat*, cash a cheque at the Bank of Kuwait or catch Egyptian football, head here. North of the Marylebone Road, **Church Street** is home to the wondrous **Alfie's Antique Market** (*see p265*).

The fact that the name Paddington has been immortalised by a certain small, ursine Peruvian émigré is appropriate, given that the area has long been home to refugees and immigrants. It was a country village until an arm of the Grand Union Canal arrived in 1801, linking London to the Midlands, and followed in the 1830s by the railway. **Paddington Station**, with its fine triple roof of iron and glass, was built in 1851 to the specifications of the great engineer Isambard Kingdom Brunel.

Paddington's proximity to central London eventually drew in the developers. The gleaming **Paddington Central** development east of the station is the most recent arrival, a million square feet of office space, canalside apartments and restaurants. East of here in St Mary's Hospital, the old-fashioned **Alexander Fleming Laboratory Museum** gives a sense of what the district used to be like.

Alexander Fleming Laboratory Museum
St Mary's Hospital, Praed Street, W2 1NY (7886 6528, www.imperial.nhs.uk/aboutus/ museumsandarchives/index.htm). Paddington tube/rail. **Open** 10am-1pm Mon-Thur. *By appointment* 2-5pm Mon-Thur; 10am-5pm Fri.

INSIDE TRACK NEW CHINA

The new canalside development called Paddington Central harbours a beautifully designed, top-quality Chinese restaurant: **Pearl Liang** (8 Sheldon Square, 7289 7000, www.pearlliang.co.uk) does delicious dumplings and dim sum.

Admission £2; £1 reductions; free under-5s.
No credit cards. Map p395 D5.
Buzz in at the tatty entrance on your left to find this tiny, dusty, instrument-cluttered lab. Enthusiastic guides conjure up the professor who, in 1928, noticed that mould contamination had destroyed some staphylococcus bacteria on a set-aside culture plate, handing humanity a powerful weapon against bacterial enemies: penicillin. The pub across the street advertised its own healthful properties, claiming the miracle fungus had blown into the lab from them.

NOTTING HILL

Notting Hill Gate, Ladbroke Grove or Westbourne Park tube.

Head north up Queensway from Kensington Gardens and turn west along **Westbourne Grove**. The road starts humble but gets posher the further west you go; cross Chepstow Road and you're in upmarket **Notting Hill**. A host of fashionable restaurants and bars still exploit the lingering street cred of the fast-disappearing black and working-class communities; posh shops are a better reflection of the area's current character. **Notting Hill Gate** is not itself an attractive street, but the leafy avenues to the south of it are; so is **Pembridge Road**, to the north, leading to the boutique-filled streets of Westbourne Grove and Ledbury Road, and to **Portobello Road** and its renowned market (*see p245*).

Portobello Road.

Halfway down, **Blenheim Crescent** boasts three notable independent booksellers. The **Travel Bookshop** (nos.13-15, 7229 5260, www.thetravelbookshop.com) is the store on which Hugh Grant's bookshop was based in the movie *Notting Hill*, a film that did more to undermine the area's bohemian credentials than a fleet of Starbucks. Under the Westway, that elevated section of the M40 motorway linking London with Oxford, is the small but busy **Portobello Green Market**. This is where you'll find Portobello's best vintage fashion stalls. Look out for the excellent second-hand boot and shoe stall and brilliant vintage handbag stall (usually outside the Falafel King), along with vintage clothing stall Sage Femme, often outside the Antique Clothing Shop.

North of the Westway, Portobello's vitality fizzles out. It sparks back to life at **Golborne Road**, the heartland of London's North African community and the address of the excellent, no-frills Moroccan **Tagine** café (no.95, 8968 8055). Here, too, are a pair of rival Portuguese café-delis, the **Lisboa Pâtisserie** (no.57, 8968 5242) and **Café Oporto** (no.62A, 8968 8839). At the north-eastern end of the road stands **Trellick Tower**, an architecturally significant, like-it-or-loathe-it piece of modernism by Ernö Goldfinger. At its western end, Golborne Road connects with Ladbroke Grove, which can be followed north to spooky **Kensal Green Cemetery**.

FREE Kensal Green Cemetery
Harrow Road, Kensal Green, W10 4RA (8969 0152, www.kensalgreen.co.uk). Kensal Green tube. **Open** *Apr-Sept* 9am-6pm Mon-Sat; 10am-6pm Sun. *Oct-Mar* 9am-5pm Mon-Sat; 10am-5pm Sun. *Tours* 2pm Sun; (incl catacombs) 2pm 1st & 3rd Sun of mth. **Admission** free. *Tours* £5 (£4 reductions) donation. **No credit cards.**
Behind a neoclassical gate is a green oasis of the dead. It's the resting place of both the Duke of Sussex, sixth son of George III, and his sister, Princess Sophia; also buried here are Wilkie Collins, Anthony Trollope and William Makepeace Thackeray.

Museum of Brands, Packaging & Advertising
Colville Mews, Lonsdale Road, W11 2AR (7908 0880, www.museumofbrands.com). Notting Hill Gate tube. **Open** 10am-6pm Tue-Sat; 11am-5pm Sun. **Admission** £5.80; £2-£3.50 reductions; free under-7s. **Credit** MC, V. **Map** p394 A6.
Robert Opie began collecting the things most of us throw away when he was 16. Over the years, the collection has grown to include everything from milk bottles to vacuum cleaners and cereal packets. The emphasis is on British consumerism through the last century, though there are items as old as an ancient Egyptian doll. One for nostalgists.

Piccadilly Circus & Mayfair

From traffic chaos to moneyed calm in just a couple of streets.

Top dog since the 1930s, when it was the playground of London's aristocracy, **Mayfair** oozes wealth. The area has recently been the haunt of hedge funders, who defy the recession as they flash cash in restaurants and hotel bars. Vestiges of old Mayfair are still around: the tailors of Savile Row, marginally destuffed; the galleries of Cork Street; the bijou shopping rookery of Shepherd Market. To the north, the neon-lit roundabout of **Piccadilly Circus** remains the one part of town that every Londoner does their best to avoid.

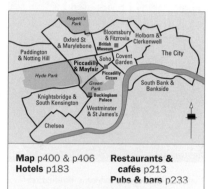

Map p400 & p406	Restaurants &
Hotels p183	cafés p213
	Pubs & bars p233

PICCADILLY CIRCUS & REGENT STREET

Oxford Circus or Piccadilly Circus tube.

Frantic **Piccadilly Circus** is an uneasy mix of the tawdry and the grand, a mix that has little to do with the vision of its architect. John Nash's 1820s design for the intersection of Regent Street and Piccadilly, two of the West End's most elegant streets, was a harmonious circle of curved frontages. But 60 years later, Shaftesbury Avenue muscled in, creating the lopsided and usually pandemonious traffic junction still in place today.

Alfred Gilbert's memorial fountain in honour of child-labour abolitionist Earl Shaftesbury was erected in 1893. It's properly known as the **Shaftesbury Memorial**, with the statue on top intended to show the Angel of Christian Charity, but critics and public alike recognised the likeness of **Eros** and their judgement has stuck. The illuminated advertising panels around the intersection appeared late in the 19th century and have been present ever since; thankfully, they're limited to just one façade. The Coca-Cola sign has been here since 1955, making it the world's longest-running advertisement.

Opposite, the **Trocadero** (www.london trocadero.com) has seen several ventures come

and go, most driven out by high rents and low footfall in this prime but tired location. Tween magnet **Funland** (www.funland.co.uk) seems to be a fixture, and the newest arrival is US crowd-puller **Ripley's Believe It or Not!** (*see p106*). A £100 million revamp of the entire site, to include a hotel complex based on New York's Pod Hotel and smart new retail space, is planned.

Connecting Piccadilly Circus to Oxford Circus to the north and Pall Mall to the south, the broad curve of **Regent Street** was designed by Nash in the early 1800s with the aims of improving access to Regent's Park and

---

INSIDE TRACK JAMMING GOOD WITH WEIRD AND GILLY

Just off Regent Street, **Heddon Street** is where the iconic photograph that graces the cover of David Bowie's *The Rise and Fall of Ziggy Stardust and the Spiders from Mars* was taken. The building against which Bowie leans is now the Moroccan-flavoured **Mô Tea Room**, next door to famed North African eaterie Momo (*see p215*); the bright 'K West' sign visible on the cover has long since been stolen.

Liberty.

bumping up property values in Haymarket and Pall Mall. Much of Nash's architecture was destroyed in the early 20th century, but the grandeur of the street remains impressive. Among the highlights are the mammoth children's emporium **Hamleys** (nos.188-196, 0871 704 1977, www.hamleys.com) and the landmark department store **Liberty** (*see p244*).

Ripley's Believe It or Not!

1 Piccadilly Circus, W1J 0DA (3238 0022, www.ripleyslondon.com). Piccadilly Circus tube. **Open** 10am-10.30pm daily. **Admission** £19.95; free-£17.95 reductions; £65 family. **Credit** MC, V. **Map** p406 W4.

This 'odditorium' follows a formula more or less unchanged since Robert Ripley opened his first display at the Chicago World Fair in 1933: an assortment of 800 curiosities is displayed, ranging from the world's smallest road-safe car to da Vinci's *Last Supper* painted on a grain of rice – via the company's signature shrunken heads.

MAYFAIR

Bond Street or Green Park tube.

The gaiety suggested by the name of Mayfair, derived from a long-gone spring celebration, isn't matched by its latter-day atmosphere today. Even on Mayfair's busy shopping streets, you may feel out of place without the reassuring heft of a platinum card. Nonetheless,

there are many pleasures to enjoy if you fancy a stroll, not least the concentration of blue-chip commercial galleries (*see pp294-297*).

The Grosvenor and Berkeley families bought the rolling green fields that would become Mayfair in the middle of the 17th century. In the 1700s, they developed the pastures into a posh new neighbourhood, focused on a series of landmark squares. The most famous of these, **Grosvenor Square** (1725-31), is now dominated by the supremely inelegant US Embassy, its only decorative touches a fierce eagle and a mass of post-9/11 protective barricades. Out front, pride of place is taken by a statue of President Dwight Eisenhower, who stayed in nearby **Claridge's** when in London (*see p183*); Roosevelt is in the park nearby. Plans are afoot to move everything to Vauxhall.

Brook Street has impressive music credentials: GF Handel lived and died (1759) at no.25, and Jimi Hendrix roomed briefly next door at no.23, adjacent buildings that have been combined into the **Handel House Museum**

INSIDE TRACK WATER, WATER

The water feature in the basement of **Grays Antique Market** (*see above*) is formed from the Tyburn Brook. One of London's buried rivers, it runs underground from Hampstead to Westminster.

(*see below*). For most visitors, however, this
part of town is all about shopping. Connecting
Brook Street with Oxford Street to the north,
South Molton Street is home to the fabulous
boutique-emporium **Browns** (*see p251*) and
the excellent **Grays Antique Market**. And
New Bond Street is an A-Z of every top-end,
mainstream fashion house you can name.

Beyond New Bond Street, **Hanover
Square** is another of the area's big squares,
now a busy traffic chicane. Just south is **St
George's Church**, built in the 1720s and once
everybody's favourite place to be seen and get
married. Handel, who married nobody, attended
services here. South of St George's, salubrious
Conduit Street is where fashion shocker
Vivienne Westwood (no.44) faces staid Rigby
& Peller (no.22A), corsetière to the Queen.

Running south off Conduit Street is the most
famous Mayfair shopping street of all, **Savile
Row**. Gieves & Hawkes (no.1) is a must-visit
for anyone interested in the history of British
menswear; at no.15, the estimable Henry
Poole & Co has cut suits for clients including
Napoleon III, Charles Dickens and 'Buffalo' Bill
Cody. No.3 was the home of the Beatles' Apple
Records and their rooftop farewell concert.

Two streets west, **Cork Street** is known as
the heart of the West End art scene; more than
half a dozen galleries are strung along its few
hundred feet of shopfront. A couple of streets
over is Albemarle Street, where you'll find the
handsomely rejuvenated **Royal Institution**,
home to the **Faraday Museum** (*see right*).

★ Handel House Museum

*25 Brook Street (entrance in Lancashire Court),
W1K 4HB (7399 1953, www.handelhouse.org).
Bond Street tube.* **Open** 10am-6pm Tue, Wed,
Fri, Sat; 10am-8pm Thur; noon-6pm Sun.
Admission £5; £2-£4.50 reductions; free
under-5s. **Credit** MC, V. **Map** p398 H6.
The composer George Frideric Handel moved to
Britain from his native Germany aged 25 and settled in this house 12 years later, remaining here until
his death in 1759. The house has been beautifully
restored with original and recreated furnishings,
paintings and a welter of the composer's scores (in
the same room as photos of Jimi Hendrix, who lived
next door). The programme of events includes
Thursday recitals.

★ FREE Royal Institution
& Faraday Museum

*21 Albemarle Street, W1S 4BS (7409 2992,
www.rigb.org). Green Park tube.* **Open** 9am-5pm
Mon-Fri. **Admission** free. **No credit cards.**
Map p406 U4.
The Royal Institution was founded in 1799 for 'dif-
fusing the knowledge… and application of science
to the common purposes of life'; from behind its neoclassical façade, it's been at the forefront of London's
scientific achievements ever since. In 2008, Sir Terry
Farrell completed a £22 million rebuild, inside and
out, with the brief of improving accessibility and
finding ways to lure people inside. The result is a
more open frontage, a restaurant, a bar and a café.

The Michael Faraday Laboratory, a complete
replica of Faraday's former workspace, is in the
basement, alongside a working laboratory in which
RI scientists can be observed researching their current projects. Some 1,000 of the RI's 7,000-odd scientific objects are on display, including the world's
first electric transformer, a prototype Davy lamp
and a print of the first transatlantic telegraph sig-
nal, sent in 1858. The RI also holds a terrific rolling
programme of talks and demonstrations in its lecture theatre, most famously at Christmas; see the
website for details.

Royal Institution.

SIGHTS

Shepherd Market

Just west of Albemarle Street, **44 Berkeley Square** is one of the original houses in this grand but sadly nightingale-free square. Built in the 1740s, it was described by architectural historian Nikolaus Pevsner as 'the finest terrace house of London'. Curzon Street, which runs off the south-west corner of Berkeley Square, was home to MI5, Britain's secret service, from 1945 until the '90s; it's also the northern boundary of **Shepherd Market**, named after a food market set up here by architect Edward Shepherd in the early 18th century and now a curious little enclave in the heart of this elusive area.

From 1686, this was where the raucous May Fair was held, until it was shut down in the late 18th century due to 'drunkenness, fornication, gaming and lewdness'. You'll still manage the drunkenness easily enough at a couple of good pubs (such as **Ye Grapes**, at 16 Shepherd Market). The cobbler on adjoining White Horse Street ('Don't throw away old shoes, they can be restored!') and the ironmongers on Shepherd Street keep things from becoming too genteel.

PICCADILLY & GREEN PARK

Green Park, Hyde Park Corner or Piccadilly Circus tube.

Piccadilly's name is derived from the picadil, a type of suit collar that was in vogue during the 18th century. The first of the area's main buildings was built by tailor Robert Baker and, indicating the source of his wealth, nicknamed 'Piccadilly Hall'. A stroll through the handful of Regency shopping arcades confirms that the rag trade is still flourishing mere minutes away from Savile Row and Jermyn Street. At the renovated **Burlington Arcade** (*see p245*), the oldest and most stylish of these arcades, top-hatted security staff known as 'beadles' ensure there's no singing, whistling or hurrying in the arcade: such uncouth behaviour is prohibited by archaic bylaws. Formerly Burlington House (1665), the **Royal Academy of Arts** (*see right*) is next door to the arcade's entrance. It hosts several lavish, crowd-pleasing exhibitions each year and has a pleasant courtyard café.

On Piccadilly are further representatives of high-end retail. **Fortnum & Mason** (*see p242*), London's most prestigious food store, was founded in 1707 by a former footman to Queen Anne and was refurbished to celebrate its third century. Look for the fine clock: a 1964 articulated effort, it features 18th-century effigies of Mr Fortnum and Mr Mason, who bow at each other every hour. The simple-looking church at no.197 is **St James's Piccadilly** (*see right*), where William Blake was baptised.

> **INSIDE TRACK**
> **ACHILLES LAID BARE**
>
> The towering statue in Hyde Park behind **Apsley House** (*see below*) of a naked Achilles wielding his sword and buckler was given to the Duke of Wellington 'by the women of England' in 1822. Achilles' fig leaf has been removed by curious admirers twice, most recently in 1961.

West down Piccadilly, smartly uniformed doormen mark the **Wolseley** (*see p216*), a former car showroom reopened in 2004 as a fine if tiresomely lauded restaurant, and the expensive, exclusive **Ritz** (*see p185*). The dull, flat, green expanse just beyond the Ritz is **Green Park**. Work your way along Piccadilly, following the northern edge of Green Park past the queue outside the Hard Rock Café to the Duke of Wellington's old home, **Apsley House** (*see below*), opposite **Wellington Arch** (*see right*). This is hectic Hyde Park Corner; Buckingham Palace (*see p117*) is just a short walk south-east, while Hyde Park (*see p126*) and the upper-crust enclave of Belgravia (*see p123*) are to the west.

Apsley House

149 Piccadilly, W1J 7NT (7499 5676, www.english-heritage.org.uk). Hyde Park Corner tube. **Open** *Nov-Mar* 11am-4pm Wed-Sun. *Apr-Oct* 11am-5pm Wed-Sun. *Tours* by arrangement. **Admission** £5.70; £4.80 reductions. *Tours* phone in advance. *Joint ticket with Wellington Arch* £7; £6 reductions; £17.50 family. **Credit** MC, V. **Map** p400 G8.

Called No.1 London because it was the first London building encountered on the road to the city from the village of Kensington, Apsley House was built by Robert Adam in the 1770s. The Duke of Wellington kept it as his London home for 35 years. Although his descendants still live here, several rooms are open to the public, providing a superb feel for the man and his era. Admire the extravagant porcelain dinner-ware and plates or ask for a demonstration of the crafty mirrors in the scarlet and gilt picture gallery, where a fine Velázquez and a Correggio hang near Goya's portrait of the Iron Duke after he defeated the French in 1812. This was a last-minute edit: X-rays have revealed that Wellington's head was painted over that of Joseph Bonaparte, Napoleon's brother.
▶ *There's a model of the Battle of Waterloo at the National Army Museum; see p122.*

![FREE] Royal Academy of Arts

Burlington House, W1J 0BD (7300 8000, www.royalacademy.org.uk). Green Park or Piccadilly Circus tube. **Open** 10am-6pm

Mon-Thur, Sat, Sun; 10am-10pm Fri. **Admission** free. *Special exhibitions* vary. **Credit** AmEx, DC, MC, V. **Map** p406 U4.

Britain's first art school was founded in 1768 and moved to the extravagant Palladian Burlington House a century later, but it's now best known not for exhibitions but exhibitions. Ticketed blockbusters (such as 'The Real Van Gogh', on until April 2010) are generally held in the Sackler Wing or the main galleries; shows in the John Madejski Fine Rooms are drawn from the RA's holdings, which range from Constable to Hockney, and are free. The Academy's biggest event is the Summer Exhibition, which for more than two centuries has drawn from works entered by the public. There's also an annual arts programme, 'Contemporary', each December, with exhibitions, events and screenings.

FREE St James's Piccadilly
197 Piccadilly, W1J 9LL (7734 4511, www.st-james-piccadilly.org). Piccadilly Circus tube. **Open** 8am-6.30pm daily. *Evening events* times vary. **Admission** free. **Credit** (concerts) AmEx, DC, MC, V. **Map** p406 V4.

Consecrated in 1684, St James's is the only church Sir Christopher Wren built on a new site. A calming building with few architectural airs or graces, it was bombed to within an inch of its life in World War II, but was then painstakingly reconstructed. Grinling Gibbons's delicate limewood garlanding around the sanctuary survived and is one of the few real frills. It's a busy church, staging regular classical concerts, providing a home for the William Blake Society and hosting markets in the churchyard: antiques on Tuesday, arts and crafts from Wednesday to Saturday. There's also a handy café tucked into a corner by the quiet garden.

Wellington Arch
Hyde Park Corner, W1J 7JZ (7930 2726, www.english-heritage.org.uk). Hyde Park Corner tube. **Open** *Apr-Oct* 10am-5pm Wed-Sun. *Nov-Mar* 10am-4pm Wed-Sun. **Admission** £3.50; £1.80-£3 reductions; free under-5s. *Joint ticket with Apsley House £7; £6 reductions; £17.50 family.* **Credit** MC, V. **Map** p400 G8.

Built in the late 1820s to mark Britain's triumph over Napoleonic France, Decimus Burton's Wellington Arch was initially topped by an out-of-proportion equestrian statue of Wellington. However, since 1912 Captain Adrian Jones's 38-ton bronze *Peace Descending on the Quadriga of War* has finished it with a flourish. It has three floors of displays, covering the history of the arch and the Blue Plaques scheme, and great views in winter from the balcony.
▶ *Hyde Park Corner contains one of London's finest war memorials: Charles Sargeant Jagger's moving tribute to the Royal Artillery.*

The Art of Memory

London remembers those killed in recent bomb blasts.

The city has been quick to honour the memory of those killed by suicide bombers on tube and bus on 7 July 2005. Unveiled four years after the bombs, in the south-east corner of Hyde Park between the Lovers' Walk and busy Park Lane, the £1 million monument consists of 52 ten-foot square steel columns, one for each of the fatalities. Each one is marked with the date, time and location of that person's death; they're arranged in four groups, according to which of the four explosions killed the person in question. Designed by architects Carmody Groarke in close consultation with the victims' families, with Antony Gormley as an independent adviser, the monument is an austerely beautiful, quietly modern and human-scale tribute to the atrocity.

Elsewhere, London also has a memorial to the 202 victims of the 2002 Bali bombings, located at the Green Park end of the Foreign Office just by the Cabinet War Rooms. There's also a memorial garden for the victims of 9/11 in Grosvenor Square, close to the American Embassy.

SIGHTS

Westminster & St James's

The gently beating heart of the British establishment.

England is ruled from **Westminster**. The monarchy has resided here since the 11th century, when Edward the Confessor moved west from the City; government also calls it home. Major parts of the area have been designated a UNESCO World Heritage Site.

For such an important area, it's surprisingly spacious. **St James's Park** is one of London's finest parks, **Trafalgar Square** is a tourist hotspot (and is overlooked by the National Gallery), and the **Mall** offers a regal route to Buckingham Palace.

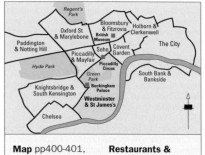

Map pp400-401, pp406-407	Restaurants & cafés p216
Hotels p185	**Pubs & bars** p234

Map pp400-401, pp406-407
Hotels p185
Restaurants & cafés p216
Pubs & bars p234

SIGHTS

TRAFALGAR SQUARE

Leicester Square tube or Charing Cross tube/rail.

Laid out in the 1820s by John Nash, Trafalgar Square is the heart of modern London. Tourists come in their thousands to pose for photographs in front of **Nelson's Column**. It was erected in 1840 to honour Vice Admiral Horatio Nelson, who died at the point of victory at the Battle of Trafalgar in 1805. The statue atop the 150-foot Corinthian column is foreshortened to appear in perfect proportion from the ground. The granite fountains were added in 1845; Sir Edwin Landseer's bronze lions joined them in 1867.

Once surrounded on all sides by busy roads, the square was improved markedly by pedestrianisation in 2003 of the North Terrace,

right in front of the **National Gallery** (*see below*). The mayor's ban on feeding pigeons was another positive step. Around the perimeter of the square are three plinths bearing statues of George IV and two Victorian military heroes, Henry Havelock and Sir Charles James Napier. The fourth plinth was never filled; since 1999, it's displayed temporary, contemporary art, a programme that in 2010 should include sculptor Yinka Shonibare's large-scale model of HMS *Victory* in a glass bottle.

Other points of interest around the square include an equestrian statue of Charles I, dating from the 1630s, with a plaque behind it that marks the original site of Edward I's Eleanor Cross, the official centre of London. At the square's north-east corner is the refurbished **St Martin-in-the-Fields** (*see p112*).

★ FREE National Gallery

Trafalgar Square, WC2N 5DN (7747 2885/ www.nationalgallery.org.uk). Leicester Square tube/Charing Cross tube/rail. **Open** 10am-6pm Mon, Tue, Thur-Sun; 10am-9pm Wed. *Tours* 11.30am, 2.30pm daily. **Admission** free. *Special exhibitions* vary. **Credit** (shop) MC, V. **Map** p407 X5.

Founded in 1824 to display 36 paintings, the National Gallery is now one of the world's great

---

INSIDE TRACK
LIFE WITH THE LIONS

The lions around Trafalgar Square are made from cannons captured from French ships. In the north-west corner of the square, you can find a panel displaying the standard units of imperial measurements.

---

repositories for art. There are masterpieces from virtually every European school of art, from austere 13th-century religious paintings to the sensual delights of Caravaggio and Van Gogh.

Furthest to the left of the main entrance, the modern Sainsbury Wing extension contains the gallery's earliest works: Italian paintings by early masters such as Giotto and Piero della Francesca, as well as the *Wilton Diptych*, the finest medieval English picture in the collection, showing Richard II with the Virgin and Child. The basement of the Sainsbury Wing is also the setting for temporary exhibitions, which in 2010 will include 'Painting History: Paul Delaroche and Lady Jane Grey' (24 Feb-23 May) and the intriguing 'Close Examination: Fakes, Mistakes and Discoveries' (30 June-12 Sept).

In the West Wing (left of the main entrance) are Italian Renaissance masterpieces by Correggio, Titian and Raphael. Straight ahead on entry, in the North Wing, are 17th-century Dutch, Flemish, Italian and Spanish Old Masters, including works such as Rembrandt's *A Woman Bathing in a Stream* and Caravaggio's *Supper at Emmaus*. Velasquez's *Rokeby Venus* is one of the artist's most famous paintings, a reclining nude asking herself – and us – 'How do we look?' Also in this wing are works by the great landscape artists Claude and Poussin. Turner insisted that his Dido Building Carthage and Sun Rising through Vapour should hang alongside two Claudes here that particularly inspired him.

In the East Wing (to the right of the main entrance, and most easily reached via the new street-level entrance on Trafalgar Square) are some of the gallery's most popular paintings: works by the French Impressionists and Post-Impressionists, including Monet's *Water-Lilies*, one of Van Gogh's

Sunflowers and Seurat's *Bathers at Asnières*. Don't miss Renoir's astonishingly lovely *Les Parapluies*.

You shouldn't plan to see everything in one visit, but the free guided tours and audio guides will help you make the best of your time.

★ FREE National Portrait Gallery

St Martin's Place, WC2H 0HE (7306 0055, www.npg.org.uk). Leicester Square tube or Charing Cross tube/rail. **Open** 10am-6pm Mon-Wed, Sat, Sun; 10am-9pm Thur, Fri. **Admission** free. *Special exhibitions* vary. **Credit** AmEx, MC, V. **Map** p407 X4.

Portraits don't have to be stuffy. The excellent National Portrait Gallery has everything from oil paintings of stiff-backed royals to photographs of soccer stars and gloriously unflattering political caricatures. The portraits of musicians, scientists, artists, philanthropists and celebrities are arranged in chronological order from the top to the bottom of the building.

At the top of the escalator up from the main foyer, on the second floor, are the earliest works, portraits of Tudor and Stuart royals and notables, most notably the 'Chandos' Shakespeare, Holbein's 'cartoon' of Henry VIII and the 'Ditchley Portrait' of his daughter, Elizabeth I, her pearly slippers placed firmly on a colourful map of England. On the same floor, the 18th-century collection features Georgian writers and artists, with one room devoted to the influential Kit-Cat Club of bewigged Whig (leftish) intellectuals, Congreve and Dryden among them. More famous names include Wren and Swift. The Duveen Extension contains Regency greats, military men such as Wellington and Nelson, plus Byron, Wordsworth and other Romantics. The first floor is

National Gallery.

SIGHTS

SIGHTS

A Transport of Delight

How long will London have to wait for the next Routemaster?

Ask many Londoners about Routemaster buses, launched in the 1950s, and a faraway look will come into their eyes. They'll talk wistfully about the charm of London's original, open-backed red double-deckers, and they'll praise the convenience of proper bus conductors who accepted coins. The reason for such wistfulness is that these cherished vehicles were ditched in 2005 by former mayor Ken Livingstone,

who scrapped the fleet and replaced them with a collection of charmless, single-decker, 18-metre-long 'bendy buses'.

When Boris Johnson took over from Ken in 2008, it was with a commitment to return the Routemaster to London's streets. In July that year, Johnson launched a competition to design a new, eco-friendly Routemaster, with the aim of reinstating the original's hop-on, hop-off principle. Two designs were chosen, although there's no guarantee that the final bus, due to be unveiled in 2011, will look anything like the winning entries. And there are still large questions about who will pay for the design and construction of a completely new fleet of buses.

Until the new Routemasters come into service, you can experience the joy of the old on two 'heritage routes'. Lovingly refurbished buses from the 1960-64 fleet run on routes 9 (from Aldwych via the Strand, Trafalgar Square and Piccadilly Circus to the Royal Albert Hall) and 15 (from Trafalgar Square to Tower Hill, with glimpses of the Strand, Fleet Street and St Paul's Cathedral); head to stops B or S in the south-west corner of Trafalgar Square. Buses run every 15 minutes from 9.30am; fares match the rest of the bus network, but you must buy a ticket before boarding (*see pp363-364*).

devoted to the Victorians (Dickens, Brunel, Darwin) and, in the Duveen Extension, the 20th century.
▶ *From June to September each year, the NPG exhibits the entrants for the BP Portrait Award.*

FREE St Martin-in-the-Fields
Trafalgar Square, WC2N 4JJ (7766 1122, www. smitf.org). Leicester Square tube or Charing Cross tube/rail. **Open** 8am-6pm daily. *Services* 8am, 1.15pm, 6pm Mon, Tue, Thur, Fri; 8am, 1.15pm, 5.30pm, 6pm Wed; 8am, 10am, 1.15pm (Mandarin), 2.15pm (Cantonese), 5pm, 6.30pm Sun. *Brass Rubbing Centre* 10am-7pm Mon-Wed; 10am-9pm Thur-Sat; 11am-6pm Sun. **Admission** free. *Brass rubbing* £4.50. **Credit** MC, V. **Map** p407 X4.
There's been a church 'in the fields' between Westminster and the City since the 13th century, but the current one was built in 1726 by James Gibbs, using a fusion of neoclassical and baroque styles. The parish church for Buckingham Palace (note the royal box to the left of the gallery), St Martin's benefited from a £36m Lottery-funded refurbishment, completed in 2008. The bright interior has been fully

restored, with Victorian furbelows removed and the addition of a controversial altar window that shows the Cross, stylised as if rippling on water. The crypt, its fine café and the London Brass Rubbing Centre have all been modernised.
▶ *For lunchtime and evening concerts, see p311.*

WHITEHALL TO PARLIAMENT SQUARE
Westminster tube or Charing Cross tube/rail.

The offices of the British government are lined along **Whitehall**, itself named after Henry VIII's magnificent palace, which burned to the ground in 1698. Walking south from Trafalgar Square, you pass the old **Admiralty Offices** and **War Office**, the **Ministry of Defence**, the **Foreign Office** and the **Treasury**, as well as the **Banqueting House** (*see right*), one of the few buildings to survive the blaze. Also here is **Horse Guards**, headquarters of the Household Cavalry, the elite army unit that protects the Queen. The millions who died in the service of the nation in World War I and World War II are commemorated by Sir Edwin Lutyens's dignified **Cenotaph**, focal point of Remembrance Day (*see p277*). Nearby, a separate memorial to the women of World War II, by sculptor John Mills, recalls the seven million women who contributed to the war effort. Churchill planned his war campaigns in the claustrophobic **Cabinet War Rooms** (*see right*), hidden beneath government offices at the west end of King Charles Street. **Downing Street**, home to the prime minister (no.10) and chancellor (no.11), is closed to the public.

The broad sweep of Whitehall is an apt introduction to the monuments of **Parliament Square**. Laid out in 1868, this tiny green space is flanked by the extravagant **Houses of Parliament** (*see right*), the neo-Gothic Middlesex Guildhall (1906-13) and the twin spires of **Westminster Abbey** (*see p115*). Like a pre-pedestrianised Trafalgar Square, it can appear to be little more than a glorified traffic island; an attempt to make it more accessible was scrapped in 2008. Dotted around the square are statues of British politicians, including Disraeli and Churchill, and foreign dignitaries, such as Lincoln and Mandela. In the middle of the green, facing Parliament, you'll see the banners and placards of Brian Haw's one-man, nine-year protest against the wars in Iraq and Afghanistan, which continues despite a government ban designed specifically to shift him from the square.

Parliament itself simply dazzles. An outrageous neo-Gothic fantasy, the seat of the British government is still formally known as the Palace of Westminster, though the only remaining parts of the medieval palace are **Westminster Hall** and the **Jewel Tower** (*see p114*). At the north end of the palace is the clocktower housing the huge 'Big Ben' bell; more than seven feet tall, it weighs over 13 tons.

Banqueting House

Whitehall, SW1A 2EB (0844 482 7777, www.hrp.org.uk). Westminster tube or Charing Cross tube/rail. **Open** 10am-5pm Mon-Sat. **Admission** £4.50; £2.25-£3.50 reductions; free under-5s. **Credit** MC, V. **Map** p401 L8.
This handsome Italianate mansion, designed by Inigo Jones and constructed in 1620, was the first true Renaissance building in London. The sole surviving part of the Tudor and Stuart kings' Whitehall Palace, the Banqueting House features a lavish painted ceiling by Rubens, glorifying James I, 'the wisest fool in Christendom'. Regrettably, James' successor, Charles I, did not rule wisely. After losing the English Civil War to Cromwell's Roundheads, he was executed in front of Banqueting House in 1649 (the event is marked every 31 Jan). Lunchtime

concerts are held on the first Monday of every month except August. Call before you visit: the mansion is sometimes closed for corporate functions.

Cabinet War Rooms & Churchill Museum

Clive Steps, King Charles Street, SW1A 2AQ (7930 6961, www.iwm.org.uk). St James's Park or Westminster tube. **Open** 9.30am-6pm daily. **Admission** £12.95; £10.40 reductions; free under-16s. **Credit** MC, V. **Map** p401 K9.
Out of harm's way beneath Whitehall, this cramped and spartan bunker was where Winston Churchill planned the Allied victory in World War II. Open to the public since 1984, the rooms powerfully bring to life the reality of a nation at war. The cabinet rooms were sealed on 16 August 1945, keeping the complex in a state of suspended animation: every pin stuck into the vast charts was placed there in the final days of the conflict. The 'Undercover' exhibition (until Sept 2010) offered the startling evidence that the Cabinet War Rooms were not bombproof. Churchill complained he'd 'been sold a pup' and authorised the insertion of a protective concrete slab.

The humble quarters occupied by Churchill and his deputies give a tangible sense of wartime hardship, an effect reinforced by the wailing sirens and wartime speeches on the audio guide (free with admission). Adjoining the War Rooms is the engaging Churchill Museum, devoted to the great man and his famous speeches.

▶ *The Cabinet War Rooms is administered by the Imperial War Museum; see p143.*

FREE Houses of Parliament

Parliament Square, SW1A 0AA (7219 4272 Commons information, 7219 3107 Lords information, 0870 906 3773 tours, www.parliament.uk). Westminster tube. **Open** (when in session) *House of Commons Visitors' Gallery* 2.30-10.30pm Mon, Tue; 11.30am-7.30pm Wed; 10.30am-6.30pm Thur; 9.30am-3pm Fri. *House*

INSIDE TRACK
RULES SUPREME

In October 2009, London became home to the UK's first **Supreme Court**, established to achieve a complete separation between the United Kingdom's senior judges and the Upper House of Parliament. This separation was signified by the Justices moving from the House of Lords to a new home in the Middlesex Guildhall, an early 20th-century neo-Gothic building opposite Parliament. The Supreme Court holds permanent and temporary exhibitions in a former cell area that also features a café selling branded trinkets.

SIGHTS

of Lords Visitors' Gallery 2.30-10.30pm Mon, Tue; 3-10pm Wed; 11am-7.30pm Thur; from 10am Fri. *Tours* summer recess only; phone for details. **Admission** *Visitors' Gallery* free. *Tours* £12; £5-£8 reductions; free under-5s. **Credit** MC, V. **Map** p401 L9.

After strict security checks at St Stephen's Gate (the only public access to Parliament), visitors are welcome to observe the debates at the House of Lords and House of Commons, though the experience can be soporific. An exception is Prime Minister's Question Time at noon on Wednesday, when the incumbent PM fields a barrage of predictably hostile questions from the opposition and

SIGHTS

Snapshot
Stuart London

Where to see how London lived.

Peter Paul Rubens' painted ceiling in the **Banqueting House** (*see p113*) is as fine a piece of Stuart propaganda as you could wish to see, its chubby cherubs commissioned by Charles I to celebrate the magnificence of his father James I's rule under bombastic titles: 'The Union of the Crowns', 'The Apotheosis of James I', 'The Peaceful Reign of James I'. The building's architect, Inigo Jones, also built the **Queen's House** (*see p148*) and **St Paul's Covent Garden** (*see p87*).

equally predictable softball questions, fromn loyal backbenchers who want to present the government in a good light. Tickets must be arranged in advance through your embassy or MP, who can also arrange tours. The best time to visit Parliament is during the summer recess, when the main ceremonial rooms, including Westminster Hall and the two houses, are thrown open to the general public as part of an organised tour (book in advance by phone).

The first parliamentary session was held in St Stephen's Chapel in 1275, but Westminster only became the permanent seat of parliament in 1532, when Henry VIII decided to move to a new des-res in Whitehall. Designed by Charles Barry, the Palace of Westminster is now a wonderful mish-mash of styles, dominated by Gothic buttresses, towers and arches. It looks much older than it is: the Parliament buildings were created in 1860 to replace the original Houses of Parliament, destroyed by fire in 1834. The compound contains a staggering 1,000 rooms, 11 courtyards, eight bars and six restaurants, plus a small cafeteria for visitors. Of the original palace, only the Jewel Tower (*see below*) and the ancient Westminster Hall remain.

Jewel Tower

Abingdon Street, SW1P 3JY (7222 2219, www.english-heritage.org.uk). Westminster tube. **Open** *Mar-Oct* 10am-5pm daily. *Nov-Mar* 10am-4pm daily. **Admission** £3; £1.50-£2.60 reductions; free under-5s. **Credit** MC, V. **Map** p401 L9.

This easy-to-overlook little stone tower opposite Parliament was built in 1365 to house Edward III's treasure. It is, with Westminster Hall, all that remains of the medieval Palace of Westminster. It contains a small exhibition on Parliament's history.
▶ *Nowadays, the Crown Jewels are on display in the Tower of London; see p74.*

FREE St Margaret's Church

Parliament Square, SW1P 3PA (7654 4840, www.westminster-abbey.org). St James's Park or Westminster tube. **Open** 9.30am-3.30pm Mon, Tue, Thur, Fri; 9.30am-6pm Wed; 9.30am-1.30pm Sat (times vary due to services). *Services* 10am, 11.15am, 3pm, 6.30pm Sun; phone to check for other times. **Admission** free. **Credit** MC, V. **Map** p401 L9.

Facing the far grander Westminster Abbey, this small church was founded in the 12th century; since 1614, it's served as the official church of the House of Commons. The interior features some of the most impressive pre-Reformation stained glass in London. The east window (1509) commemorates the marriage of Henry VIII and Catherine of Aragon; others celebrate Britain's first printer, William Caxton (buried here in 1491), explorer Sir Walter Raleigh (executed in Old Palace Yard in 1618), and writer John Milton (1608-74), who married his second wife, Katherine Woodcock, here in 1656.

Houses of Parliament. *See p113.*

Westminster Abbey

20 Dean's Yard, SW1P 3PA (7222 5152
information, 7654 4900 tours, www.westminster-
abbey.org). St James's Park or Westminster tube.
Open 9.30am-4.30pm Mon, Tue, Thur, Fri;
9.30am-7pm Wed; 9.30am-4.30pm Sat. *Abbey*
Museum, Chapter House & College Gardens
10am-4pm daily. *Tours* phone for details.
Admission £15; £12 reductions; free under-11s
with adult; £36 family. *Abbey Museum* free.
Tours £3. **Credit** AmEx, MC, V. **Map** p401 K9.
The cultural significance of Westminster Abbey is
hard to overstate, but also hard to remember as
you're shepherded around, forced to elbow fellow
tourists out of the way to read a plaque or see a
tomb. Edward the Confessor commissioned it as a
church to St Peter on the site of a seventh-century
version, but it was only consecrated on 28 Dec 1065,
eight days before he died. William the Conqueror
had himself crowned here on Christmas Day, 1066.
With just two exceptions, every coronation since
then has taken place in the abbey.

Many royal, military and cultural notables are
interred here. The most haunting memorial is the
Grave of the Unknown Warrior, in the nave.
Elaborate resting places in side chapels are taken up
by the tombs of Elizabeth I and Mary Queen of Scots.
In Innocents Corner lie the remains of two lads
believed to be Edward V and his brother Richard
(their bodies were found at the Tower of London), as
well as two of James I's children. Poets' Corner is the
final resting place of Chaucer, the first to be buried
here. Few of the other writers who have stones here
are buried in the abbey, but the remains of Dryden,
Johnson, Browning and Tennyson are all present.
Henry James, TS Eliot and Dylan Thomas have ded-
ications – on the floor, fittingly for Thomas.

In the vaulted area under the former monks' dormitory, one of the abbey's oldest parts, the Abbey
Museum celebrated its centenary in 2008. You'll find
effigies and waxworks of British monarchs, among
them Edward II and Henry VII, wearing the robes
they donned in life. The Choir School is the only
school in Britain exclusively for the education of boy
choristers from eight to 13. Its Christmas services
are truly magnificent. The 900-year-old College
Garden is one of the oldest cultivated gardens in
Britain and a useful place to escape the crowds.

An ongoing refurbishment is scheduled to end in
2010, but the abbey has ambitious plans to create
new visitor facilities, a new gallery and install a new
corona on the roof, something previously suggested
by both Wren and Hawksmoor.

MILLBANK

Pimlico or Westminster tube.

Running south from Parliament along the river,
Millbank leads eventually to **Tate Britain**
(*see p116*), built on the site of an extraordinary
pentagonal prison built to hold criminals
destined for transportation to Botany Bay.
If you're walking south from the Palace of

INSIDE TRACK BIG BEN

Contrary to popular belief, **Big Ben** is
not the iconic clocktower of the New
Year bongs, but the giant bell they're
bonged upon. The template of the bell,
which dates to 1858, is around its
manufacturer's front door: visit the
Whitechapel Bell Foundry (*see p137*)
on a weekday between 9am and 4.15pm
to enter the foyer and see it there.

SIGHTS

Westminster, look out on the left for **Victoria Tower Gardens**, which contain a statue of suffragette leader Emmeline Pankhurst and the Buxton Drinking Fountain commemorating the emancipation of slaves. There's also a version of Rodin's *The Burghers of Calais*.

On the other side of the road, Dean Stanley Street leads to Smith Square, home to the architecturally striking **St John's, Smith Square** (*see p310*), built as a church in grand baroque style and now a popular venue for classical music. **Lord North Street**, the elegant row of Georgian terraces running north from the square, has long been a favourite address of politicians; note, too, the directions on the wall for wartime bomb shelters.

Across the river from Millbank is **Vauxhall Cross**, the oddly conspicuous HQ of the Secret Intelligence Service (SIS), commonly referred to by their old name MI6. In case any enemies of the state were unaware of its location, the cream and green block appeared as itself in the 1999 James Bond film *The World is Not Enough*.

★ FREE Tate Britain

Millbank, SW1P 4RG (7887 8888, www.tate.org. uk). Pimlico tube. **Open** 10am-5.50pm daily; 10am-10pm 1st Fri of mth. *Tours* 11am, noon, 2pm, 3pm Mon-Fri; noon, 3pm Sat, Sun. **Admission** free. *Special exhibitions* vary. **Credit** MC, V. **Map** p401 K11.

Tate Modern (*see p54*) gets all the attention, but the original Tate Gallery, founded by sugar magnate Sir Henry Tate, has a broader and more inclusive brief. Housed in a stately Portland stone building on the riverside, Tate Britain is second only to the National Gallery (*see p110*) when it comes to British art. The historical collection includes work by Hogarth, Gainsborough, Reynolds, Constable (who gets three rooms) and Turner (in the grand Clore Gallery). Many contemporary works were shifted to the other Tate when it opened in 2000, but Stanley Spencer, Lucian Freud, David Hockney and Francis Bacon are well represented here, and the Art Now installations showcase up-and-coming British artists.

Temporary exhibitions include the controversy-courting Turner Prize exhibition (Oct-Jan), a competition in which an outrageous sum of money is awarded to the artist who, it often seems, has invested the least amount of effort in their work. Chris Ofili, one of the prize's more distinguished winners, is honoured with a mid-career retrospective in 2010 (until 16 May), and there's also an exhibition devoted to British comic art (9 June-5 Sept 2010). However, the real blockbuster show this year is devoted to Henry Moore (24 Feb-16 Aug 2010). The gallery has a good restaurant and a well-stocked gift shop. The handy Tate-to-Tate boat service (*see p55*) zips along the river to Tate Modern every 40mins.

VICTORIA

Pimlico tube or Victoria tube/rail.

As you might expect from London's main backpacker hangout, Victoria is colourful and chaotic. Victoria rail station is a major hub for trains to southern seaside resorts and ferry terminals, while the nearby coach station is served by buses from all over Europe. Catering to new arrivals, Belgrave Road provides an almost unbroken line of cheap and often shabby

Tate Britain.

B&Bs, hotels and hostels, most set in fading townhouses. The theatres dotted around Victoria form a western outpost of the West End's Theatreland, with a similar programme of star-vehicle dramas and musicals.

Not to be confused with Westminster Abbey (see p115), **Westminster Cathedral** (see below) is the headquarters of the Roman Catholic church in England. South and east of Victoria station are the impressive Georgian terraces of **Pimlico** and **Belgravia**, made up of some of the most expensive real estate in London. Antiques stores and restaurants line Pimlico Road; the intriguing independent shops of Tachbrook Street are also worth a look.

North of Victoria Street towards Parliament Square is **Christchurch Gardens**, burial site of Thomas ('Colonel') Blood, who stole the Crown Jewels in 1671. He was apprehended making his getaway but, amazingly, managed to talk his way into a full pardon. Also in the area are **New Scotland Yard**, with its famous revolving sign, and the art deco headquarters of **London Underground** at 55 Broadway. Public outrage about Jacob Epstein's graphic nudes on the façade almost led to the resignation of the managing director in 1929.

FREE Westminster Cathedral

42 Francis Street, SW1P 1QW (7798 9055, www.westminstercathedral.org.uk). Victoria tube/rail. **Open** 7am-6pm Mon-Fri; 8am-6.30pm Sat, 8am-7pm Sun. *Bell tower* 9.30am-4.30pm daily. *Services* 7am, 8am, 10.30am, 12.30pm, 1.05pm, 5.30pm Mon-Fri; 8am, 9am, 10.30am, 12.30pm, 6pm Sat; 8am, 9am, 10.30am, noon, 5.30pm, 7pm Sun. **Admission** free; donations appreciated. *Bell tower* £5; £2.50 reductions. **Credit** MC, V. **Map** p400 J10.

With its domes, arches and soaring tower, the most important Catholic church in England looks more Islamic than Christian. There's a reason: architect John Francis Bentley, who built it between 1895 and 1903, was heavily influenced by Istanbul's Hagia Sophia mosque. Compared to the candy-cane exterior, the interior is surprisingly restrained (in fact, it's unfinished), but there are still some impressive marble columns and mosaics. Eric Gill's sculptures of the Stations of the Cross (1914-18) were dismissed as 'Babylonian' when they were first installed, but worshippers have come to love them. A lift runs to the top of the 273ft bell tower for dizzying views over Victoria, Westminster and St James's.

AROUND ST JAMES'S PARK

St James's Park tube.

St James's Park was founded as a deer park for the royal occupants of St James's Palace, and remodelled by John Nash on the orders of George IV. The central lake is home to various species of wildfowl; pelicans have been kept here since the 17th century, when the Russian ambassador donated several of the bag-jawed birds to Charles II. The pelicans are fed at 3pm daily, though they supplement their diet at other times of the day with the occasional pigeon. The bridge over the lake offers views of **Buckingham Palace** (see below).

Along the north side of the park, the Mall connects Buckingham Palace with **Trafalgar Square** (see p110). It looks like a classic processional route, but the Mall was actually laid out as a pitch for Charles II to play 'pallemaille' (an early version of croquet imported from France) after the pitch at Pall Mall became too crowded. On the south side of the park, Wellington Barracks contains the **Guards Museum** (see p118) to the east, Horse Guards contains the **Household Cavalry Museum** (see p118). For the **Changing of the Guard**, see p276 **Standing on Ceremony**.)

Along the north side of the Mall, **Carlton House Terrace** was the last project completed by John Nash before his death in 1835. Part of the terrace now houses the **ICA** (see p118). Just behind is the **Duke of York column**, commemorating Prince Frederick, Duke of York, who led the British Army against the French. He's the nursery rhyme's 'Grand old Duke of York', who marched his 10,000 men neither up nor down Cassel hill in Flanders.

Buckingham Palace & Royal Mews

The Mall, SW1A 1AA (7766 7300 Palace, 7766 7302 Royal Mews, 7766 7301 Queen's Gallery, www.royalcollection.org.uk). Green Park tube or Victoria tube/rail. **Open** *State Rooms* mid July-Sept 9.45am-6pm (last entry 3.45pm) daily. *Queen's Gallery* 10am-5.30pm daily. *Royal Mews* Mar-July, Oct 11am-4pm Mon-Thur, Sat, Sun; Aug; Sept 10am-5pm daily. **Admission** *Palace* £16.50; £9.50-£15 reductions; £44 family; free under-5s. *Queen's Gallery* £8.50; £4.25-£7.50 reductions; £21.50 family; free under-5s. *Royal Mews* £7.50; £4.80-£6.75 reductions; £20 family; free under-5s. **Credit** AmEx, MC, V. **Map** p400 H9.

Although nearby St James's Palace (see p119) remains the official seat of the British court, every monarch since Victoria has used Buckingham Palace as their primary home. Originally known as Buckingham House, the present home of the British royals was constructed as a private house for the Duke of Buckingham in 1703, but George III liked it so much he purchased it for his German bride Charlotte in 1761. George IV decided to occupy the mansion himself after taking the throne in 1820 and John Nash was hired to convert it into a palace befitting a king. Construction was beset with problems, and Nash – whose expensive plans had

SIGHTS

SIGHTS

always been disliked by Parliament – was dismissed in 1830. When Victoria came to the throne in 1837, the building was barely habitable. The job of finishing the palace fell to the reliable but unimaginative Edward Blore ('Blore the Bore'). The neoclassical frontage now in place was the work of Aston Webb in 1913.

As the home of the Queen, the palace is usually closed to visitors, but you can view the interior for a brief period each year while the Windsors are away on their holidays; you'll be able to see the State Apartments, still used to entertain dignitaries and guests of state. At other times of year, you can visit the Queen's Gallery to see the Queen's personal collection of treasures, including paintings by Rubens and Rembrandt, Sèvres porcelain and the Diamond Diadem crown (familiar from Commonwealth postage stamps). Further along Buckingham Palace Road, the Royal Mews is the grand garage for the royal fleet of Rolls-Royces and the home of the splendid royal carriages and the horses, individually named by the Queen herself, that pull them.

Guards Museum
Wellington Barracks, Birdcage Walk, SW1E 6HQ (7414 3428, www.theguardsmuseum.com). St James's Park tube. **Open** 10am-4pm daily. **Admission** £3; £2 reductions; free under-16s. **Credit** (shop) AmEx, MC, V. **Map** p400 J9.
Just down the road from Horse Guards, this small museum tells the 350-year story of the Foot Guards, using flamboyant uniforms, period paintings,

St James's Park. *See p117.*

medals and intriguing memorabilia, such as the stuffed body of Jacob the Goose, the Guard's Victorian mascot, who was regrettably run over by a van in barracks. Appropriately, the shop is well stocked with toy soldiers of the British regiments.
▶ *The Guards form up on the parade ground here before the Changing of the Guard; see p276.*

Household Cavalry Museum
Horse Guards, Whitehall, SW1A 2AX (7930 3070, www.householdcavalry.co.uk). Westminster tube or Charing Cross tube/rail. **Open** *Mar-Sept* 10am-6pm daily. *Oct-Feb* 10am-5pm daily. **Admission** £6; £4 reductions; £15 family ticket; free under-5s. **Credit** MC, V. **Map** p401 K8.
Household Cavalry is a fairly workaday name for the military peacocks who make up the Queen's official guard. They get to tell their stories through video diaries at this small but entertaining museum, which also offers the chance to see medals, uniforms and shiny cuirasses (breastplates) up close. You'll also get a peek – and sniff – of the magnificent horses that parade just outside every day: the stables are separated from the main museum by no more than a screen of glass.

FREE ICA (Institute of Contemporary Arts)
The Mall, SW1Y 5AH (7930 0493 information, 7930 3647 tickets, www.ica.org.uk). Piccadilly Circus tube or Charing Cross tube/rail. **Open** *Galleries* (during exhibitions) noon-7pm Mon-Wed, Fri-Sun; noon-9pm Thur. **Admission** free. **Credit** AmEx, DC, MC, V. **Map** p401 K8.
Founded in 1947 by a collective of poets, artists and critics, the ICA continues to drive the London arts scene forward into brave new territory. The institute moved to the Mall in 1968 and set itself up as a venue for arthouse cinema, performance art, philosophical debates, art-themed club nights and anything else that might challenge accepted notions. Not that this stopped former ICA chairman Ivan Massow dismissing conceptual art as 'pretentious, self-indulgent, craftless tat' in 2002; current artistic director Ekow Eshun made a more valuable contribution to artistic debate by announcing in summer 2008 that admission would henceforth be free.

ST JAMES'S

Green Park or Piccadilly Circus tube.

One of London's most refined residential areas, St James's was laid out in the 1660s for royal and aristocratic families, some of whom still live here. It's a rewarding district, a sedate bustle of intriguing mews and grand squares. Bordered by Piccadilly, Haymarket, the Mall and Green Park, the district is centred on **St James's Square**. It's now home to the members-only **London Library**, founded by Thomas Carlyle in 1841 in disgust at the inefficiency of the British Library.

Just south of the square, **Pall Mall** is lined with exclusive, members-only gentlemen's clubs (in the old-fashioned sense of the word). Polished nameplates reveal such prestigious establishments as the **Institute of Directors** (no.116) and the **Reform Club** (nos.104-105), site of Phileas Fogg's famous bet in *Around the World in Eighty Days*. Around the corner on St James's Street, the **Carlton Club** (no.69) is the official club of the Conservative Party; Lady Thatcher remains the only woman to be granted full membership. Nearby on King Street is **Christie's** (7839 9060, www.christies.com), the world's oldest fine art auctioneers.

At the south end of St James's Street, **St James's Palace** was built for Henry VIII in the 1530s. Extensively remodelled over the centuries, the red-brick palace is still the official address of the Royal Court, even though every monarch since 1837 has lived at Buckingham Palace. From here, Mary Tudor surrendered Calais and Elizabeth I led the campaign against the Spanish Armada; this is also where Charles I was confined before his 1649 execution. The palace is now home to the Princess Royal (the title given to the monarch's eldest daughter, currently Princess Anne); it's closed to the public, but you can attend Sunday services at its historic **Chapel Royal** (1st Sun of mth, Oct-Easter Sunday; 8.30am, 11.15am).

Adjacent to St James's Palace is **Clarence House** (*see below*), the former residence of the Queen Mother; a few streets north is the delightful **Spencer House** (*see right*), the ancestral home of the family of the late Princess Diana. Across Marlborough Road lies the pocket-sized **Queen's Chapel**, designed by Inigo Jones in the 1620s for Charles I's Catholic Queen Henrietta Maria, at a time when Catholic places of worship were officially banned. The Queen's Chapel can only be visited for Sunday services (Easter-July; 8.30am, 11.15am).

Clarence House

The Mall, SW1A 1AA (7766 7303, www.royal collection.org.uk). Green Park tube. **Open** *Aug,*

Buckingham Palace. *See p117.*

Sept 10am-4pm daily. **Admission** £8; £4 under-17s; free under-5s. *Tours* pre-booked tickets only. **Credit** AmEx, MC, V. **Map** p400 J8.
Currently the official residence of Prince Charles and the Duchess of Cornwall, this austere royal mansion was built between 1825 and 1827 for Prince William Henry, Duke of Clarence, who stayed on in the house after his coronation as King William IV. Designed by John Nash, the house has been much altered by its many inhabitants, among them the late Queen Mother. Five receiving rooms and the small British art collection accumulated by the Queen Mother are open to the public in summer. Book in advance.

Spencer House

27 St James's Place, SW1A 1NR (7499 8620, www.spencerhouse.co.uk). Green Park tube. **Open** *Feb-July, Sept-Dec* 10.30am-5.45pm Sun. Last tour 4.45pm. *Gardens* phone or check the website for details. **Admission** £9; £7 reductions. Under-10s not allowed. **Credit** MC, V. **Map** p400 J8.
One of the last surviving private residences in St James's, this handsome mansion was designed for John Spencer by John Vardy, but was completed in 1766 by Hellenophile architect James Stuart, which explains all the mock-Greek flourishes. Lady Georgiana, subject of the recent bodice-ripping film *The Duchess*, lived here all her life. The Spencers left the property generations before Diana married into the Windsor family, but the palatial building is worth visiting for its lavish and painstakingly restored interior decor. It's now mainly used for corporate entertaining, hence the limited access.

Chelsea

Army veterans mix with wealthy fashionistas in south-west London.

Chelsea is where London's wealthy classes play in cultural and geographical isolation. Originally a fishing hamlet, the area was a 'village of palaces' by the 16th century, home to the likes of Henry VIII's ill-fated advisor Sir Thomas More. Artists and poets (Whistler, Carlyle, Wilde) followed from the 1880s, before the fashionistas arrived with the opening of Mary Quant's Bazaar in 1955. These days, you'll find smart shops and street after street of immaculate terraced housing. Cultural pleasures are few, but the Saatchi Gallery is a welcome arrival.

Map pp396-397	Restaurants &
Hotels p187	cafés p219
	Pubs & bars p235

SIGHTS

SLOANE SQUARE & KING'S ROAD

Sloane Square tube then various buses.

Synonymous with the Swinging '60s and immortalised by punk, the dissipated phase of the King's Road is now a matter for historians as the street teems with pricey fashion houses and air-conditioned poodle parlours. Yet on a sunny day, it does make a vivid stroll. For one thing, you don't have to take yourself as seriously as the locals. And for another, the area is figuratively rich with historical associations and literally so, with the expensive red-brick houses that slumber down leafy mews and charming, cobbled side streets.

At the top (east end) of the King's Road is **Sloane Square**. It's named after Sir Hans Sloane, who provided the land for the **Chelsea Physic Garden** (*see p122*), invented milk chocolate in the early 18th century and led to the founding of the British Museum (which was set up to hold his collections when he died); his inventiveness is celebrated at the **Botanist** (*see p219*), the best of the square's eateries. In the middle of the square sits a fountain erected in 1953, a gift to the borough from the Royal Academy of Arts. Sculpted by local man Gilbert Ledward, it depicts Venus; it's an allusion to King Charles II's mistress Nell Gwynne, who lived nearby (hence the road's name). The shaded benches in the middle of the square provide a lovely counterpoint to the looming façades of Tiffany & Co and the enormous Peter Jones department store, in a refurbished 1930s building with excellent views from its top-floor café. A certain edginess is lent to proceedings by the **Royal Court Theatre** (*see p340*), which shocked the nation with its 1956 première of John Osborne's *Look Back in Anger*.

To escape the bustle and fumes, head to the **Duke of York Square**, a pedestrianised enclave of boutiques and restaurants that's presided over by a statue of Hans Sloane. In the summer, the cooling fountains attract hordes of children, their parents sitting to watch from the outdoor areas of the cafés or taking advantage of the Saturday food market. The square is also home to the mercilessly modern art of the **Saatchi Gallery** (*see right*), housed in former military barracks. Around the corner on Chelsea Bridge Road sit more disused army lodgings; the proposed redevelopment of **Chelsea Barracks** has become a controversial topic thanks to the intervention of Prince Charles.

INSIDE TRACK
WHO'S THAT GIRL?

The mother of actress Greta Scacchi was a member of the Bluebell Girls dance troupe, who travelled the world performing for wide-eyed audiences. She was also, though, the model for the statue in the middle of the fountain in **Sloane Square**.

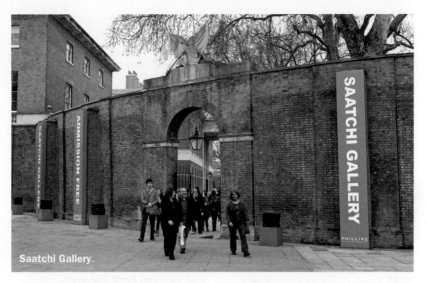

Saatchi Gallery.

The once-adventurous shops on the King's Road are now a mix of trendier-than-thou fashion houses and high street chains, plus a few gems: **John Sandoe Books** (*see p247*) and **Antiquarius** (*see p266*) represent a glorious past, **Shop at Bluebird** (*see p253*) suggests future directions. Wander Cale Street for the likes of jewellery boutique **Felt** (7349 8829, www.felt-london.com) and **Traditional Toys** (7352 1718, www.traditionaltoy.com), or head for the **Chelsea Farmers' Market** on adjoining Sydney Street to find a clutter of artfully distressed rustic sheds housing restaurants and shops selling everything from cigars to garden products. Sydney Street leads to **St Luke's Church**, where Charles Dickens married Catherine Hogarth in 1836.

Towards the western end of the King's Road is **Bluebird**, a dramatic art deco former motor garage housing a café, a restaurant and a popular shop (*see p253*). It's worth a peek even if you can't afford the Chelsea rates to eat here. A little further up the road, the **World's End** store (no.430) occupies what was once Vivienne Westwood's notorious leather and fetish wear boutique Sex; a green-haired Johnny Rotten auditioned for the Sex Pistols here in 1975 by singing along to an Alice Cooper record on the shop's jukebox.

FREE Saatchi Gallery
Duke of York's HQ, off King's Road, SW3 4SQ (7823 2363, www.saatchi-gallery.co.uk). Sloane Square tube. **Open** 10am-6pm daily. **Admission** free. **Credit** (shop) AmEx, MC, V. **Map** p397 F11.

Charles Saatchi's new gallery, here since 2008, offers 50,000sq ft of space for temporary exhibitions. Given his fame as a promoter in the 1990s of what became known as the Young British Artists – Damien Hirst, Tracey Emin, Gavin Turk, Sarah Lucas et al – it will surprise many that the opening exhibition was of new Chinese art. Exhibitions in 2010 cover European sculpture and 'The Power of Paper'.

CHEYNE WALK & CHELSEA EMBANKMENT

Sloane Square tube then various buses.

Chelsea's riverside has long been noted for its nurseries and gardens. The borough's horticultural curiosity is still alive, lending a village air that befits a place of retirement for the former British soldiers living in the **Royal Hospital Chelsea** (*see p122*). In summer, the Chelsea Pensioners, as they're known, regularly don red coats and tricorn hats when venturing beyond the gates. The Royal Hospital's lovely gardens host the **Chelsea Flower Show** (*see p274*) in May each year. Next door is the **National Army Museum** (*see p122*).

West from the river end of Royal Hospital Road is **Cheyne Walk**, less peaceful than it once was due to Embankment traffic. Its river-view benches remain good spots for a sit-down, but the tranquillity of **Chelsea Physic Garden** (*see p122*) is the real treat.

Further west on Cheyne Walk, the park benches of **Chelsea Embankment Gardens** face Albert Bridge, where signs still order troops to 'Break step when marching over

SIGHTS

this bridge'. In the small gardens, you'll find a statue of the great historian Thomas Carlyle – the 'sage of Chelsea', whose home is preserved (*see below*). Nearby, a gold-faced statue of Sir Thomas More looks out over the river from the garden of **Chelsea Old Church** (*see below*), where he once sang in the choir and may well be (partially) buried. Follow Old Church Street north and you'll find the **Chelsea Arts Club** (no.143), founded in 1871 by Whistler.

North of the western extremity of Cheyne Walk are **Brompton Cemetery** (*see p161*) and Chelsea FC's home ground, **Stamford Bridge** (*see p331*). Football fans might be interested in the recently revamped **Chelsea Centenary Museum** (www.chelseafc.com, 10.30am-4.30pm daily except match days; £6, £4 reductions), which contains perhaps the only photograph of Raquel Welch wearing a football kit to be found in any museum in England.

Carlyle's House
24 Cheyne Row, SW3 5HL (7352 7087, www. nationaltrust.org.uk). Sloane Square tube or bus 11, 19, 22, 49, 211, 239, 319. **Open** *Apr-Oct* 2-5pm Wed-Fri; 11am-5pm Sat, Sun. **Admission** £4.90; £12.30 family. **Credit** MC, V. **Map** p397 E12.
Thomas Carlyle and his wife Jane moved to this four-storey, Queen Anne house in 1834. The house was inaugurated as a museum in 1896, 15 years after Carlyle's death, offering an intriguing snapshot of Victorian life. The writer's quest for quiet (details of his valiant attempts to soundproof the attic) strikes a chord today: he was plagued by the sound of revelry from Cremorne Pleasure Gardens.

FREE Chelsea Old Church
Cheyne Walk, Old Church Street, SW3 5DQ (7795 1019, www.chelseaoldchurch.org.uk). Sloane Square tube or bus 11, 19, 22, 49, 319. **Open** 2-4pm Tue-Thur; 1.30-5pm Sun. *Services* 8am, 10am, 11am, 12.15pm Sun. *Evensong* 6pm Sun. **Admission** free; donations appreciated. **No credit cards. Map** p397 E12.
Legend has it that the Thomas More Chapel, which remains on the south side, contains More's headless body buried somewhere under the walls (his head, after being spiked on London Bridge, was 'rescued'

INSIDE TRACK SPIES LIKE US

Chelsea has long been a popular haunt for spies, real and fictional. KGB agent Kim Philby held meetings at the Markham Arms at 138 King's Road, now a branch of the Abbey bank, and both James Bond and George Smiley were given homes in the area by their respective creators.

---

and buried in a family vault in St Dunstan's Church, Canterbury). There's a striking statue of More outside the church. Guides are on hand on Sundays.

★ Chelsea Physic Garden
66 Royal Hospital Road, SW3 4HS (7352 5646, www.chelseaoldchurch.org.uk). Sloane Square tube or bus 11, 19, 239. **Open** *Apr-Oct* noon-5pm Wed-Fri; noon-6pm Sun. *Tours* times vary; phone to check. **Admission** £8-£5 reductions; free under-5s. *Tours* free. **Credit** (shop) AmEx, MC, V. **Map** p397 F12.
The capacious grounds of this gorgeous botanic garden are filled with healing herbs and vegetables, rare trees and dye plants. The garden was founded in 1673 by Sir Hans Sloane with the purpose of cultivating and studying plants for medical purposes. The first plant specimens were brought to England and planted here in 1676, with the famous Cedars of Lebanon (the first to be grown in England) arriving a little later. The garden opened to the public in 1893.
▶ *Sloane's specimens are the oldest items in the botany collection of the Natural History Museum.*

FREE National Army Museum
Royal Hospital Road, SW3 4HT (7730 0717, www.national-army-museum.ac.uk). Sloane Square tube or bus 11, 137, 239. **Open** 10am-5.30pm daily. **Admission** free. **Credit** (shop) AmEx, MC, V. **Map** p397 F12.
More entertaining than its modern exterior suggests, this museum dedicated to the history of the British Army kicks off with 'Redcoats', a gallery that starts at Agincourt in 1415 and ends with the American War of Independence. Upstairs, 'The Road to Waterloo' marches through 20 years of struggle against the French, featuring 70,000 model soldiers. Also on display is the kit of Olympic medal winner Dame Kelly Holmes (an ex-army athlete), while Major Michael 'Bronco' Lane, conqueror of Everest, has donated his frostbitten fingertips.

FREE Royal Hospital Chelsea
Royal Hospital Road, SW3 4SR (7881 5200, www.chelsea-pensioners.org.uk). Sloane Square tube or bus 11, 19, 22, 137, 211, 239. **Open** *June-Apr* 10am-noon, 2-4pm Mon-Sat; 2-4pm Sun. **Admission** free. **Credit** AmEx. **Map** p397 F12.
Roughly 350 Chelsea Pensioners (retired soldiers) live in quarters at the Royal Hospital, founded in 1682 by Charles II and designed by Sir Christopher Wren (with later adjustments by Robert Adam and Sir John Soane). Retired soldiers are still eligible to apply for a final posting here if they're over 65 and in receipt of an Army or War Disability Pension for Army Service. The pensioners have their own club room, bowling green and gardens, and get free tickets to watch Chelsea FC. The museum, open at the same times as the Hospital, has more about their life.
▶ *The Royal Hospital's naval cousin was the Old Royal Naval College; see p147.*

Knightsbridge & South Kensington

Where music and fashion are always the passion.

A certain class of Londoners go to **Knightsbridge** to spend, spend, spend. Or, at least, to hang around people who are spend, spend, spending. Many of the key designer labels have major shops in the area, which gets plenty of foot traffic thanks to its world-famous department stores and high-end restaurants. Nearby, **South Kensington**'s footprint is cultural rather than commercial: you'll find three of the world's greatest museums, some extraordinary colleges, a concert hall and a cutting-edge contemporary art gallery.

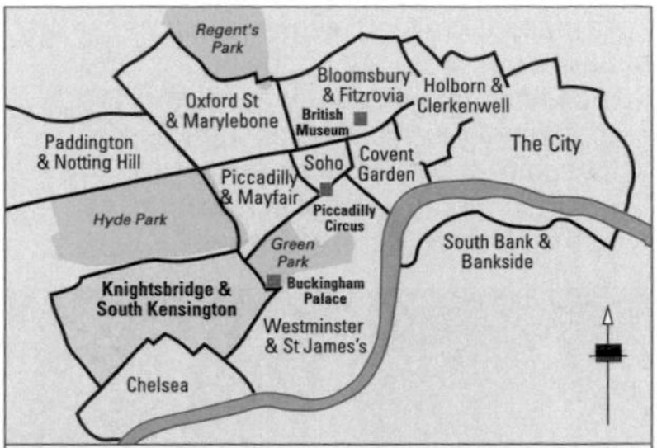

| Map pp394-395 & p397 | Restaurants & cafés p219 |
| Hotels p189 | Pubs & bars p235 |

KNIGHTSBRIDGE

Knightsbridge tube.

Knightsbridge in the 11th century was a village celebrated for its taverns, highwaymen and the legend that two knights once fought to the death on the bridge spanning the Westbourne River (later dammed to form Hyde Park's Serpentine lake). In modern Knightsbridge, urban princesses would be too busy unsheathing the credit card to notice such a farrago. Voguish **Harvey Nichols** (*see p244*) holds court at the top of **Sloane Street**, which leads down to Sloane Square. Expensive brands – Gucci, Prada, Chanel – dominate. East of Sloane Street is **Belgravia**, characterised by a cluster of embassies around **Belgrave Square**. Hidden behind the stucco-clad parades fronting the square are numerous mews, worth exploring for the pubs they conceal, notably the **Nag's Head** (53 Kinnerton Street).

For many tourists, Knightsbridge means one thing: **Harrods** (*see p242*). From its tan bricks and olive green awning to its green-coated doormen, it's an instantly recognisable retail legend. Owner Mohammed Al Fayed continues to add to the richness of eccentricity here, notably with his mawkish memorial to

son Dodi and Princess Diana. Further along is the imposing **Brompton Oratory** (*see below*).

FREE Brompton Oratory

Thurloe Place, Brompton Road, SW7 2RP (7808 0900, www.bromptonoratory.com). South Kensington tube. **Open** 6.30am-8pm daily. **Admission** free; donations appreciated. **No credit cards. Map** p397 E10.
The second-biggest Catholic church in the country (after Westminster Cathedral) is formally the Church of the Immaculate Heart of Mary, but is almost universally known as the Brompton Oratory. Completed in 1884, it feels older, partly because of the baroque Italianate style but also because much of the decoration pre-dates the structure: Mazzuoli's 17th-century

---

INSIDE TRACK
DOWN THE TUBES

Near the Brompton Oratory is the giveaway red-tile covering of **Brompton Road**, one of London's 26 abandoned tube stations. A London businessman is trying to get all of the stations opened for regular public tours; follow his progress at www.theold londonundergroundcompany.com.

SIGHTS

Snapshot
Victorian London

Where to see how London lived.

The legacy of Queen Victoria's reign is everywhere in London, even in buildings that preceded the Victorians: the likes of St Paul's Cathedral (*see p63*) and the Palace of Westminster (*see p113*) received 19th-century alterations to make them look more 'historic'. But South Kensington's palatial museums and monuments are the finest testaments to the self-confidence and ingenuity of the Victorian era, none more so than the extravagant detailing of the **Natural History Museum**.

apostle statues, for example, are from Siena cathedral. The 11am Solemn Mass sung in Latin on Sundays is enchanting, as are Vespers, sung at 3.30pm; the website has details. During the Cold War, KGB agents used the church as a dead-letter box.

SOUTH KENSINGTON

Gloucester Road or South Kensington tube.

As far as cultural and academic institutions are concerned, this is the land of plenty. It was Prince Albert who oversaw the inception of its world-class museums, colleges and concert hall,

using the profits of the 1851 Great Exhibition; the area was nicknamed 'Albertopolis' in his honour. You'll find the **Natural History Museum** (*see below*), the **Science Museum** (*see right*) and the **Victoria & Albert** (*see p126*), **Imperial College**, the **Royal College of Art** and the **Royal College of Music** (Prince Consort Road, 7589 3643; call for details of the musical instrument museum), which forms a unity with the **Royal Albert Hall** (*see p310*), open since 1871 and variously used for boxing, motor shows, marathons, table tennis tournaments, fascist rallies and rock concerts. Opposite is the **Albert Memorial** (*see below*).

FREE Albert Memorial
Kensington Gardens (7495 0916). South Kensington tube. **Tours** 2pm, 3pm, 1st Sun of mth. **Admission** *Tours* £5; £4.50 reductions. **No credit cards. Map** p395 D8.
'I would rather not be made the prominent feature of such a monument,' was Prince Albert's reported response when the subject of his commemoration arose. Hard, then, to imagine what he would have made of this extraordinary thing, unveiled 15 years after his death. Created by Sir George Gilbert Scott, it centres around a gilded Albert holding a catalogue of the 1851 Great Exhibition, guarded on four corners by the continents of Africa, America, Asia and Europe. The pillars are crowned with bronze statues of the sciences, and the frieze at the base depicts major artists, architects and musicians. It's one of London's most dramatic monuments.

★ FREE Natural History Museum
Cromwell Road, SW7 5BD (7942 5000, www.nhm.ac.uk). South Kensington tube. **Open** 10am-5.50pm daily. **Admission** free; charges apply for special exhibitions. *Tours* free. **Credit** (shop) MC, V. **Map** p397 D10.
Both a research institution and a fabulous museum, the NHM opened in Alfred Waterhouse's purpose-built, Romanesque palazzo on the Cromwell Road in 1881. Now joined by the splendid Darwin Centre extension, the original building still looks quite magnificent. The pale blue and terracotta façade just about prepares you for the natural wonders within.
Taking up the full length of the vast entrance hall is the cast of a Diplodocus skeleton. A left turn leads into the west wing or Blue Zone, where long queues form to see animatronic dinosaurs. (Not for nothing do cabbies slyly refer to the museum as the 'Dead Zoo'.) A display on biology features an illuminated, man-sized model of a foetus in the womb along with graphic diagrams of how it might have got there.
A right turn from the central hall leads past the Creepy Crawlies exhibition to the Green Zone. Stars include a cross-section through a Giant Sequoia tree and an amazing array of stuffed birds, including the chance to compare the egg of a hummingbird, smaller than a little finger nail, with that of an

elephant bird (now extinct), almost football-sized. Beyond is the Red Zone. Earth's Treasury is a veritable mine of information on a variety of precious metals, gems and crystals; From the Beginning is a brave attempt to give the expanse of geological time a human perspective. Outside, the delightful Wildlife Garden (Apr-Oct only) showcases a range of British lowland habitats, including a Bee Tree, a hollow tree trunk that opens to reveal a busy hive.

Many of the museum's 22 million insect and plant specimens are housed in the new Darwin Centre, where they take up nearly 17 miles of shelving. With its brand-new eight-storey Cocoon, this is also home to the museum's research scientists, who can be watched at work. But a great deal of this amazing institution is hidden from public view, given over to labs and specialised storage.

Exhibitions promised for 2010 included one on the deep sea, the return of the popular butterfly garden and the Wildlife Photographer of the Year show. There'll also be a new permanent gallery, spotlighting art from the museum's collection.

★ FREE Science Museum

Exhibition Road, SW7 2DD (7942 4000 switchboard, 0870 870 4868 information, www.sciencemuseum.org.uk). South Kensington tube. **Open** 10am-5.45pm daily. **Admission** free; charges apply for special exhibitions. **Credit** MC, V. **Map** p397 D9.

Only marginally less popular with the kids than its natural historical neighbour, the Science Museum is a celebration of the wonders of technology in the service of our daily lives. On the ground floor, the shop – selling wacky toys – is part of the revamped Energy Hall, which introduces the museum's collections with impressive 18th-century steam engines. In Exploring Space, rocket science and the lunar landings are illustrated by dramatically lit mock-ups and models, before the museum gears up for its core

INSIDE TRACK
PULL UP TO THE BUMPER

Exhibition Road is home to an experiment in urban planning called Share Space, which removes street furnishings and encourages pedestrians and drivers to come to a mutual understanding with regard to use of road and pavement.

collection in Making the Modern World. Introduced by *Puffing Billy*, the world's oldest steam locomotive (built in 1815), the gallery also contains Stephenson's *Rocket*. Also here are the Apollo 10 command module, classic cars and an absorbing collection of everyday technological marvels from 1750 to the present. Beyond, bathed in an eerie blue light, is the Wellcome Wing, which celebrates the latest discoveries in the biomedical sciences over three floors. The first-floor Who Am I? gallery, due to reopen in June 2010, explores discoveries in genetics, brain science and psychology.

Back in the main body of the museum, the second floor holds displays on computing, marine engineering and mathematics; the third floor is dedicated to flight, among other things, including the hands-on Launchpad gallery which features levers, pulleys, explosions and all manner of experiments for children (and their associated grown-ups). On the fifth floor, you'll find an intriguing display on the science and art of medicine.

In June 2010, the museum begins its Climate Change Project with a new gallery and a three-year cultural programme. The same month sees the unveiling of the revamped Antenna gallery, looking at contemporary science news.
▶ *The Wellcome Collection makes further connections between art and medicine; see p82.*

SIGHTS

Serpentine Bar & Kitchen in **Hyde Park**.

INSIDE TRACK
MORNING MANOEUVRES

You can watch the Household Cavalry emerge from their South Carriage Drive barracks in **Hyde Park** at 10.30am daily (9.30am on Sundays). They then ride to Horse Guards Parade for the **Changing of the Guard** (*see p276*).

★ FREE Victoria & Albert Museum
Cromwell Road, SW7 2RL (7942 2000, www.vam.ac.uk). South Kensington tube. **Open** 10am-5.45pm Mon-Thur, Sat, Sun; 10am-10pm Fri. *Tours* hourly, 10.30am-3.30pm daily. **Admission** free; charges for special exhibitions. **Credit** (shop) MC, V. **Map** p397 E10.
See right **Profile**.

HYDE PARK &
KENSINGTON GARDENS

Hyde Park Corner, Knightsbridge, Lancaster Gate or Queensway tube.

At one and a half miles long and about a mile wide, **Hyde Park** (7298 2000, www.royalparks.gov.uk) is one of the largest of London's Royal Parks. The land was appropriated in 1536 from the monks of Westminster Abbey by Henry VIII for hunting deer. Although opened to the public in the early 1600s, the parks were favoured only by the upper echelons of society.

At the end of the 17th century, William III, averse to the dank air of Whitehall Palace, relocated to **Kensington Palace** (*see right*). A corner of Hyde Park was sectioned off to make grounds for the palace and closed to the public, until King George II opened it on Sundays to those wearing formal dress. Nowadays, **Kensington Gardens** is delineated from Hyde Park only by the line of the Serpentine and the Long Water. Beside the Long Water is a bronze statue of **Peter Pan**, erected in 1912: it was in Kensington Gardens beside the Round Pond eight years earlier that playwright JM Barrie met Jack Lewellyn Davies, the boy who was the inspiration for Peter. The **Diana, Princess of Wales Memorial Playground** (*see p283*) is a kids' favourite, as is Kathryn Gustafson's ring-shaped **Princess Diana Memorial Fountain**. The year 2009 saw the arrival nearby of Simon Gudgeon's *Isis*, a giant bird that was the first sculpture added to the park for half a century. Nearby is the **Serpentine Gallery** (*see right*).

The **Serpentine** itself, London's oldest boating lake and home to ducks, coots, swans and tufty-headed grebes, is at the bottom of **Hyde Park**, which isn't especially beautiful, but is of historic interest. It was a hotspot for mass demonstrations in the 19th century and remains so today; a march protesting against war in Iraq in 2003 was the largest in British history. The legalisation of public assembly in the park led to the establishment of **Speakers' Corner** in 1872 (close to Marble Arch tube), where political and religious ranters – sane and otherwise – still have the floor. Marx, Lenin, Orwell and the Pankhursts all spoke here.

The park perimeter is popular with skaters, as well as with bike- and horse-riders (for the riding school, *see p336*). If you're exploring on foot and the vast expanses defeat you, look out for the **Liberty Drives** (May-Oct). Driven by volunteers (there's no fare, but offer a donation if you can), these electric buggies pick up groups of sightseers and ferry them around.

Kensington Palace
Kensington Gardens, W8 4PX (0844 482 7777 information, 0844 482 7799 reservations, www.hrp.org.uk). High Street Kensington tube or Queensway tube. **Open** *Mar-Oct* 10am-6pm daily. *Nov-Feb* 10am-5pm daily. **Admission** £12.50; £6.25-£11 reductions; £34 family; free under-5s. **Credit** MC, V. **Map** p394 B8.
Sir Christopher Wren extended this Jacobean mansion to palatial proportions on the instructions of William III. The sections of the palace the public are allowed to see give the impression of intimacy, though the King's Apartments (which you enter via Wren's lofty staircase) are pretty grand. It appears from the Queen's Apartments, however, that William and his wife Mary II lived quite simply in these smaller rooms. The Royal Ceremonial Dress Collection is a display of lavish ensembles worn for state occasions, including a permanent collection of dresses worn by Diana, Princess of Wales, the most famous resident. Make time for tea in Queen Anne's Orangery and admire the Sunken Garden. The palace is currently undergoing renovation but remains open.

★ FREE Serpentine Gallery
Kensington Gardens, near Albert Memorial, W2 3XA (7402 6075, www.serpentinegallery.org). Lancaster Gate or South Kensington tube. **Open** 10am-6pm daily. **Admission** free; donations appreciated. **Credit** (shop) AmEx, MC, V. **Map** p395 D8.
The secluded location to the west of the Long Water makes this small and airy former tea house an attractive destination for lovers of contemporary art. A rolling two-monthly programme of exhibitions featuring up-to-the-minute artists keeps the gallery in the news, as does the annual Serpentine Pavilion: every spring, a renowned architect, who's never before built in the UK, is commissioned to build a new pavilion that opens to the public between June and September. Good little bookshop, too.

Profile Victoria & Albert Museum

A London landmark gets a rolling upgrade.

Its foundation stone laid on this site by Queen Victoria in her last official public engagement in 1899, the V&A (*listings left*) is one of the world's most magnificent museums. As HV Morton said, 'A more wonderful collection of beautiful things does not exist elsewhere in the world.' It's a superb showcase for applied arts from around the world, appreciably calmer than its tearaway cousins on the other side of Exhibition Road.

Some 150 grand galleries on seven floors contain countless pieces of furniture, ceramics, sculpture, paintings, posters, jewellery, metalwork, glass, textiles and dress, spanning several centuries. Items are grouped by theme, origin or age, but any attempt to comprehend the whole collection in a single visit is doomed. For advice, tap the patient staff, who field a formidable combination of leaflets, floorplans, general knowledge and polite concern.

Highlights include the seven Raphael Cartoons painted in 1515 as tapestry designs for the Sistine Chapel; the finest collection of Italian Renaissance sculpture outside Italy; Canova's *Three Graces*; the Ardabil carpet,

the world's oldest and arguably most splendid floor covering, in the Jameel Gallery of Islamic Art; Medici porcelain; and the Luck of Edenhall, a 13th-century glass beaker from Syria. The Fashion galleries run from 18th-century court dress right up to contemporary chiffon numbers; the Architecture gallery has videos, models, plans and descriptions of various styles; and the famous Photography collection holds more than 500,000 images.

The latest instalment in the V&A's FuturePlan is the completely refurbished Medieval & Renaissance Galleries and the Gilbert Collection of silver, gold and gemmed ornaments, here from Somerset House. The Ceramics Galleries have been renovated and supplemented with an eye-catching bridge, there's some lovely Buddhist sculpture in the Robert HN Ho Family Foundation Galleries, and the new Theatre & Performance Galleries take over where Covent Garden's defunct Theatre Museum left off. Further renovation of the Ceramic Galleries is to come in 2010.

SIGHTS

THREE TO SEE
There's more fashion and design at the **Design Museum** (*see p57*), the **Fashion & Textile Museum** (*see p57*) and the **Geffrye Museum** (*see p138*).

North London

Markets, music and London's best park.

North London's list of famous residents gives a good idea of the scope of the area – from Amy Winehouse and Noel Gallagher to Karl Marx, John Keats and Charles Dickens, a huge variety of people have been drawn its mix of pretty, sleepy retreats and buzzing, creative party zones.

First stop is normally **Camden Town**, with its markets, indie pubs and general alternative vibe, but there's further joy to be found in the leafy squares of **Islington** – and, further afield, bohemian **Stoke Newington**

| Hotels p191 | Restaurants & |
| Pubs & bars p236 | cafés p222 |

and newly fashionable **Dalston**. Further to the north, **Hampstead** and **Highgate** offer genteel village life and a glorious public space: Hampstead Heath.

CAMDEN

Camden Town or Chalk Farm tube.

Despite the pressures of modernisation and gentrification, Camden has steadfastly refused to leave behind its grungy history as the cradle of British rock music. Against a backdrop of social deprivation in Thatcher's Britain, venues such as the Electric Ballroom and Dingwalls provided a platform for a generation of musical rebels. More musicians were launched in the 1990s by the Creation label, based in nearby Primrose Hill (*see p131*), among them My Bloody Valentine and the Jesus & Mary Chain. Creation were also responsible for the meteoric rise of Oasis, often seen trading insults with Blur at the **Good Mixer** (30 Inverness Street, 7916 7929). The music still plays at revitalised Camden icon the **Roundhouse** (*see p314*) and at **Koko** (*see p313*), which blazed through the 1970s and '80s first as the Music Machine and then as the Camden Palace.

Being outside the mainstream is nothing new for Camden. Before the Victorian expansion of London, Camden was a watering stop on the highway to Hampstead (*see p131*), with two notorious taverns – the Mother Black Cap and Mother Red Cap (now the **World's End** pub, opposite the tube) – frequented by highwaymen and brigands. After the gaps were filled in with

terraced houses, the borough became a magnet for Irish and Greek railway workers, many of them working in the engine turning-house that is now the Roundhouse. The squalor of the area had a powerful influence on the young Charles Dickens, who lived briefly on Bayham Street; a blue plaque commemorates his stay. He described it as 'shabby, dingy, damp, and as mean a neighbourhood as one would desire not to see'. From the 1960s, things started to pick up for Camden, helped by an influx of students, lured by low rents and the growing arts scene that gave birth first to punk rock, then indie and then Britpop, and nowadays any number of short-lived indie-electro and alt-folk hybrids.

Camden still has a rough quality – dealers and junkies loiter like ghosts around Camden Town tube station – but the hardcore rebellion of the rock 'n' roll years has been replaced by a more laid-back carnival vibe, as goths, indie kids, emos and the last punk rockers vie for attention around the canal. Tourists travel here in their thousands for the sprawling mayhem of **Camden Market** (*see right*), which stretches north from the tube along boutique-lined Camden High Street and Chalk Farm Road. A dozen different countercultures depend on the market for thigh-length Frankenstein boots, studded collars and new leather jackets emblazoned with the mispunctuated mantra 'Punks not Dead'. The market narrowly escaped disaster in February 2008, when fire swept through the Camden Lock Village market, destroying the Hawley Arms, a onetime hangout of Amy Winehouse and Pete Doherty. The rest of the market is still one of London's biggest tourist attractions.

Cutting through the market is **Regent's Canal**, which opened in 1820 to provide a link between east and west London for horse-drawn narrowboats loaded with coal. Today, the canal is used by the jolly tour-boats of the London Waterbus Company (7482 2550, www.london waterbus.com) and Walker's Quay (7485 4433, www.walkersquay.com), which run between Camden Lock and **Little Venice** in summer and on winter weekends. Locals use the canal towpath as a convenient walking route to west Regent's Park and **ZSL London Zoo** (*see p102*), or east to Islington (*see p134*) and through Hackney (*see p141*) all the way to the Thames. West of Camden Town tube on Albert Street, the consolidated **Jewish Museum** (*see p130*) is due to reopen in spring 2010.

Camden is still one of the best places in London to catch a gig. As well as big venues like Koko and the Roundhouse, there are plenty of small pub stages where next year's headliners can be spotted before they make it big. Top spots to catch them include the **Barfly** (*see p315*), the **Underworld** (*see p319*), the **Jazz Café** (*see p318*) and the **Dublin Castle** (94 Parkway, NW1 7AN, 7485 1773), where Madness and, later, Blur were first launched into the limelight.

INSIDE TRACK
CROWD CONTROL

Camden Market's crowds can be awful at the weekends – unfortunately, though, this is the best time to visit. After you're done shopping, slip out sideways on to the canal and stroll five minutes to sedate **Primrose Hill** *(see p131)*, the perfect place to recuperate and assess your purchases.

Camden Market

Camden Lock *Camden Lock Place, off Chalk Farm Road, NW1 8AF (www.camdenlockmarket. com).* **Open** 10.30am-6pm Mon-Fri (reduced stalls); 10am-6pm Sat, Sun.
Camden Lock Village *east of Chalk Farm Road, NW1 (www.camdenlock.net).* **Open** 10.30am-6pm Fri-Sun.
Camden Market *Camden High Street, at Buck Street, NW1 (www.camdenmarkets.org).* **Open** 9.30am-6pm daily.
Inverness Street Market *Inverness Street, NW1 (www.camdenlock.net).* **Open** 8.30am-5pm daily.
Stables Market *off Chalk Farm Road, opposite Hartland Road, NW1 8AH (7485 5511, www. stablesmarket.com).* **Open** 10.30am-6pm Mon-Fri (reduced stalls); 10am-6pm Sat, Sun.
All *Camden Town or Chalk Farm tube.*
Camden Market actually refers to the microcosm of markets that make up the northern Camden Town area. The Camden Market, née Buck Street Market,

Camden.

SIGHTS

Keats House. *See p132.*

is the place for neon sunglasses and pseudo-witty slogan garments. Almost next door, and perennially threatened by proposed Tube station expansions, is the listed building the Electric Ballroom, which sells vinyl and CDs on weekends and is also a music venue. The Inverness Street Market opposite sells similar garb to the Camden Market as well as a diminishing supply of fruit and vegetables. North, next to the railway Bridge, you'll find crafts, clothes, trinkets and small curiosities with a Japanese pop culture influence at Camden Lock and Camden Lock Village, the latter having opened after major fire damage to the market in spring 2009. Just north of here is the Stables Market where you'll find some good vintage clothes shops. Finally, the Horse Hospital area (which once cared for horses injured while pulling barges) is where you'll find more second-hand clothing, more food stands and classic designer furniture. Here, too, is Cyberdog, which probably has London's wackiest-looking sales assistants, sells 'rave toys' and day-glo clubware – if you've pink dreadlocks, Buffalos and a plethora of piercings, you've found retail nirvana.

Jewish Museum

Raymond Burton House, 129-131 Albert Street, Camden, NW1 7NB (7284 7384, www.jewish museum.org.uk). Camden Town tube. **Open** check website for details. **Admission** check website for details. **Credit** MC, V.

Due to reopen in spring 2010 after £10m of investment, London's only museum devoted to Jewish culture and history should provide a fascinating insight into one of Britain's oldest immigrant communities. Planned exhibits include a recreated East End tailor's 'sweatshop', precious ceremonial objects (one recently discovered ritual bath dates back to the 13th century), karaoke Yiddish theatre and a Holocaust Gallery built around the personal story of London-born Auschwitz survivor Leon Greenman.

Around Camden

Primrose Hill, to the west of Camden, is just as attractive as the actors and pop stars who frequent the gastropubs and quaint cafés along **Regent's Park Road** and **Gloucester Avenue**. On sunny Sunday mornings, there's no better spot to read the papers than the pavement tables in front of Ukrainian café, **Trojka** (101 Regent's Park Road, 7483 3765). Other favourite hangouts include the long-established **Primrose Pâtisserie** (no.136, 7722 7848) and upmarket Greek bistro **Lemonia** (no.89, 7586 7454). For a gastropub feed, head to Gloucester Avenue: both the **Engineer** (no.65, 7722 0950) and **Lansdowne** (no.90, 7483 0409) are here. On any clear day, taking a walk up the hill itself is a delight.

ST JOHN'S WOOD

St John's Wood or Swiss Cottage tube.

The woodland that gives St John's Wood its name was part of the great Middlesex Forest, before the land was claimed by the Knights of St John of Jerusalem. Areas of forest were cleared for private villas in the mid-19th century, but the district has retained its green and pleasant glow. Some uncharacteristically sensitive redevelopment during the 1950s has left the area smart and eminently desirable: even a modest semi can cost £2 million. The expensive tastes of locals are reflected in the posh boutiques along the High Street. The main tourist attraction is **Lord's** cricket ground (*see p331*), but a steady stream of music fans pay tribute to the Beatles by crossing the zebra crossing in front of **Abbey Road Studios** (3 Abbey Road). The studio, founded in 1931 by Sir Edward Elgar, is still used to record albums and film scores, including soundtracks to the *Lord of the Rings* trilogy, *Star Wars* prequels and *Harry Potter* films. Up the Finchley Road from St John's Wood is **Swiss Cottage**, worth a visit for the modernist library designed by Sir Basil Spence in the early '60s.

Lord's Tour & MCC Museum

St John's Wood Road, NW8 8QN (7616 8595, www.lords.org). St John's Wood tube. **Tours** *Nov-Mar* noon, 2pm daily. *Apr-Oct* 10am, noon, 2pm daily. **Admission** £14; £6-£8 reductions; £37 family; free under-5s. **Credit** AmEx, MC, V.
Lord's is more than just a famous cricket ground – as the headquarters of the Marylebone Cricket Club (MCC), it is official guardian of the rules of cricket. As well as staging test matches and internationals, the ground is also home to the Middlesex County Cricket Club (MCCC). Visitors can take an organised tour round the futuristic, pod-like NatWest Media Centre and august, portrait-bedecked Long Room. Highlights include the tiny urn containing the Ashes and memorabilia celebrating the achievements of WG Grace, winner of the 1883 Best British Beard Award (not really, but it is an impressive beard).

HAMPSTEAD

Hampstead tube, or Gospel Oak or Hampstead Heath rail.

It may have been absorbed into London during the city's great Victorian expansion, but hilltop Hampstead still feels like a Home Counties' village. It has long been a favoured roost for literary and artistic types: Keats and Constable lived here in the 19th century, and sculptors Barbara Hepworth and Henry Moore took up residence in the 1930s. However, the area is now popular with City workers, who are among the only people able to afford what is some of London's priciest real estate.

The undisputed highlight of the district is **Hampstead Heath**, the relatively vast and in places wonderfully overgrown tract of countryside between Hampstead village and Highgate that is said to have inspired CS Lewis's Narnia. The heath covers 791 acres of woodland, playing fields, swimming ponds and meadows of tall grass that attract picnickers and couples in search of privacy.

At the south end of the heath is dinky Hampstead village, with some genteel shops and cafés, restaurants and lovely pubs such as the **Holly Bush** (*see p236*). While you're here, you can tour the gorgeous sunken gardens and antique collection at **Fenton House** (*see p132*), or gaze at the stars from the **Hampstead Scientific Society Observatory** (Lower Terrace, 8346 1056, www.hampsteadscience.ac.uk/astro), open on clear Friday and Saturday evenings and Sunday lunchtimes from mid September to mid April. A stroll along nearby Judges Walk reveals a line of horse chestnuts and limes virtually unchanged since they appeared in a Constable painting in 1820. Constable was buried nearby at **St John-at-Hampstead Church** (7794 5808), as was Peter Cook. At the top of Hampstead, North End Way divides the

---

INSIDE TRACK
KENWOOD CONCERTS

If you're here in summer, try to catch one of Kenwood's lakeside concerts, which have featured everyone from from Röyksopp to performances of *Carmen*; see www.picnicconcerts.com for details.

SIGHTS

SIGHTS

main heath from the wooded West Heath, one of London's oldest gay cruising areas (but perfectly family-friendly by day). Just off North End Way is Hampstead's best kept secret, the secluded and charmingly overgrown **Hill Garden & Pergola** (open 8.30am-dusk daily), built by Lord Leverhulme using soil from the excavation of the tunnels for the Northern Line.

East of Hampstead tube, a maze of postcard-pretty residential streets shelters **Burgh House** on New End Square (7431 0144, www.burgh house.org.uk), a Queen Anne house with a small local history museum and gallery. Also in the area are **2 Willow Road** (*see right*), architect Ernö Goldfinger's residence in the 1930s, and 40 Well Walk, Constable's home for the last ten years of his life. Downhill towards Hampstead Heath train station is **Keats House** (*see right*).

Further west, and marginally closer to Finchley Road tube, is the **Freud Museum** (*see below*). And almost opposite Finchley Road & Frognal station is the innovative **Camden Arts Centre** (Arkwright Road, corner of Finchley Road, 7472 5500, www.camdenarts centre.org), which hosts edgy art shows, as well as film screenings and performances in the terrace café.

Fenton House

3 Hampstead Grove, NW3 6RT (7435 3471, www.nationaltrust.org.uk). Hampstead tube. **Open** *Mar* 2-5pm Sat, Sun. *Apr-Oct* 2-5pm Wed-Fri; 11am-5pm Sat, Sun. **Admission** *House & gardens* £5.40; £2.70 under-18s; free under-5s. *Gardens* £1. *Joint ticket with 2 Willow Road* £7.30. **Credit** MC, V.

Set in a gorgeous garden, with a 300-year-old apple orchard, this manor house is notable for its 17th- and 18th-century harpsichords, virginals and spinets, which are still played at lunchtime and evening concerts (phone for details). Also on display are European and China porcelain, Chippendale furniture and some artful 17th-century needlework.

▶ *It's possible to combine a visit to Fenton House with 2 Willow Road by buying a joint ticket.*

Freud Museum

20 Maresfield Gardens, NW3 5SX (7435 2002, www.freud.org.uk). Finchley Road tube. **Open** noon-5pm Wed-Sun. **Admission** £6; £4.50 reductions; free under-12s. **Credit** AmEx, MC, V. Driven from Vienna by the Nazi occupation, the great psychoanalyst Sigmund Freud was resident in this quiet suburban house in north London with his wife Martha and daughter Anna until his death in 1939. Now a museum with temporary exhibitions, the house displays Freud's antiques, art and therapy tools, including his famous couch. The building is one of the few in London to have two blue plaques, one for Sigmund and another for Anna, a pioneer in child psychiatry.

Keats House

Keats Grove, NW3 2RR (7332 3868, www.cityoflondon.gov.uk/keatshousehampstead). Hampstead tube, Hampstead Heath rail, or bus 24, 46, 168. **Open** 1-5pm Tue-Sun. **Admission** £5; £3 reductions; free under-12s. **Credit** MC, V. Reopened after refurbishment in 2009, Keats House was the Romantic poet's last British home before tuberculosis forced him to Italy and death at the age of only 25. A leaflet guides you through each room, starting from the rear, as well as providing context for Keats' life and that of his less famous friend and patron, Charles Brown. The 2009 renovation has ensured the decorative scheme is entirely accurate, down to the pale pink walls of Keats' humble bedroom. The garden, in which he wrote 'Ode to a Nightingale', is particularly pleasant. *Photos p130.* ▶ *For the regular poetry readings and other events here, check the website.*

★ FREE Kenwood House/ Iveagh Bequest

Hampstead Lane, NW3 7JR (8348 1286, www.english-heritage.org.uk). Hampstead tube, or Golders Green tube then bus 210. **Open** 11.30am-4pm daily. **Admission** free. *Tours* (for groups by appointment only) £5. **Credit** MC, V. Set in lovely grounds at the top of Hampstead Heath, Kenwood House is every inch the country manor house. Built in 1616, the mansion was remodelled in the 18th century for William Murray, who made the pivotal court ruling in 1772 that made it illegal to own slaves in England. The house was purchased by brewing magnate Edward Guinness, who was

kind enough to donate his art collection to the nation in 1927. Highlights include Vermeer's *The Guitar Player*, a panoramic view of old London Bridge by Claude de Jongh (1630), Gainsborough's *Countess Howe*, and one of Rembrandt's finest self-portraits (dating to c1663).

2 Willow Road

2 Willow Road, NW3 1TH (7435 6166, www.nationaltrust.org.uk). Hampstead tube or Hampstead Heath rail. **Open** *Mar-Nov* noon-5pm Thur-Sun. *Nov* noon-5pm Sat. *Tours* noon, 1pm, 2pm Thur, Fri; 11am, noon, 1pm, 2pm Sat. **Admission** £5.50; £2.70 children; £13.75 family; free under-5s. *Joint ticket with Fenton House* £7.30. **No credit cards**.

A surprising addition to the National Trust's collection of historic houses, this modernist building was designed by Hungarian-born architect, Ernö Goldfinger. The house was designed to be flexible, with movable partitions and folding doors. Home to the architect and his wife until their deaths, it contains a charmingly idiosyncratic collection of art by the likes of Max Ernst and Henry Moore.

▶ *Goldfinger also designed Notting Hill's brutalist Trellick Tower; see p104.*

HIGHGATE

Archway or Highgate tube.

Taking its name from the tollgate that once stood on the High Street, Highgate is inexorably linked with London's medieval mayor, Richard 'Dick' Whittington. As the story goes, the disheartened Whittington fled the City as far as Highgate Hill, but turned back when he heard the Bow Bells peal out 'Turn again, Whittington, thrice Mayor of London'. Today, the area is best known for the atmospheric grounds of **Highgate Cemetery** (*see below*), last resting place of Karl Marx. Adjoining the cemetery is pretty **Waterlow Park**, created by low-cost housing pioneer Sir Sydney Waterlow in 1889, with ponds, a mini-aviary, tennis courts and a cute garden café in 16th-century **Lauderdale House** (8348 8716, www.lauderdalehouse.co.uk), former home of Charles II's mistress, Nell Gwynn. North of Highgate tube, shady **Highgate Woods** are preserved as a conservation area, with a nature trail, adventure playground and café that hosts live jazz during the summer.

★ Highgate Cemetery

Swains Lane, N6 6PJ (8340 1834, www. highgate-cemetery.org). Archway tube. **Open** *East Cemetery* Apr-Oct 10am-4pm Mon-Fri; 11am-4pm Sat, Sun; Nov-Mar 10am-3.30pm Mon-Fri; 11am-3.30pm Sat, Sun. *West Cemetery* by tour only. **Admission** £3. *Tours* £5. **No credit cards**.

The final resting place of some very famous Londoners, Highgate Cemetery is a wonderfully overgrown maze of ivy-cloaked Victorian tombs and time-shattered urns. Visitors are free to wander through the East Cemetery, with its memorials to Karl Marx, George Eliot and Douglas Adams, but the most atmospheric part of the cemetery is the

SIGHTS

Islington. *See p134.*

SIGHTS

foliage-shrouded West Cemetery, laid out in 1839. Only accessible on an organised tour (book ahead, dress respectfully and arrive 30mins early), the shady paths wind past gloomy catacombs, grand Victorian pharaonic tombs, and the graves of notables such as poet Christina Rossetti, scientist Michael Faraday and poisoned Russian dissident Alexander Litvinenko. The cemetery closes during burials, so call ahead. And note that children under eight are not allowed in the West Cemetery.

▶ *Michael Faraday's laboratory can be seen at the refurbished Royal Institution; see p107.*

ISLINGTON

Angel tube or Highbury & Islington tube/rail.

The suburban bower of the *Guardian*-reading middle classes, Islington started life as a small country village beside one of Henry VIII's expansive hunting reserves. It soon became an important livestock market supplying the Smithfield meat yards, before being enveloped into Greater London. During the 19th century, the Regent's Canal brought industry and later industrial decay, but locals kept their spirits up at the local music halls, which launched such working-class heroes as Marie Lloyd, George Formby and Norman Wisdom. From the 1960s, the borough attracted a massive influx of arts and media types, who gentrified the Georgian squares and Victorian terraces and opened cafés, restaurants and boutiques around Upper Street and Essex Road.

Close to the station on Upper Street, the popular **Camden Passage** antiques market (*see p266*) bustles with browsing activity on Wednesdays and Saturdays. The music halls have long gone, but local residents take full advantage of the cultural offerings at the charming **Screen on the Green** cinema (*see p291*), the **Almeida Theatre** (*see p345*) and the often-raucous **King's Head** theatre pub (*see p345*).

East of Angel, Regency-era **Canonbury Square** was once home to George Orwell (no.27) and Evelyn Waugh (no.17A). One of the handsome town houses now contains the **Estorick Collection of Modern Italian Art** (*see below*). Just beyond the end of Upper Street is **Highbury Fields**, where 200,000 Londoners fled in 1666 to escape the Great Fire. The surrounding district is best known as the home of Arsenal Football Club, who abandoned the charming Highbury Stadium in 2006 for the gleaming 60,000-seater behemoth that is the **Emirates Stadium** (*see p331*). Fans can tour the ground or just visit the **Arsenal Museum** (7619 5000, www.arsenal.com). If you fancy a stroll, the Regent's Canal towpath runs east from just

south of Angel tube past Hackney's trendy boho Broadway Market and as far as the Thames, which it joins at **Limehouse Basin** in east London.

★ Estorick Collection of Modern Italian Art

39A Canonbury Square, N1 2AN (7704 9522, www.estorickcollection.com). Highbury & Islington tube/rail or bus 271. **Open** 11am-6pm Wed, Fri, Sat; 11am-8pm Thur; noon-5pm Sun. **Admission** £5; £3.50 reductions; free under-16s, students. **Credit** AmEx, MC, V.

Originally owned by American political scientist and writer Eric Estorick, this is a wonderful depository of early 20th-century Italian art. It is one of the world's foremost collections of futurism, Italy's brash and confrontational contribution to international modernism. The four galleries are full of movement, machines and colour, while the temporary exhibits meet the futurist commitment to fascism full on. There is also a shop and café.

DALSTON & STOKE NEWINGTON

Dalston Kingsland, Rectory Road, Stamford Hill or Stoke Newington rail.

Although scruffy, Dalston scores points for the vibrant African-flavoured market on Ridley Road, and the Turkish *ocakbaşı* (grill restaurants) along Stoke Newington Road, including excellent **Mangal II** (no.4, 7254 7888). Low property prices have attracted a growing contingent of student types, who congregate at the appealingly urban **Dalston Jazz Bar** (4 Bradbury Street, 7254 9728) and the brilliant **Vortex Jazz Club** (*see p320*).

Neighbouring **Stoke Newington**, or Stokey, as it's known to locals, is the richer cousin of Dalston and poorer cousin of Islington, home to a disproportionate number of journalists, TV news presenters and gay women. At weekends, pretty **Clissold Park** (7923 3660) is overrun with picnickers, mums pushing prams and twentysomethings practising capoeira and slacklining.

Most visitors head to Stoke Newington for bijou **Church Street**. This curvy road is lined with second-hand bookshops, cute boutiques and kids' stores, and superior cafés and restaurants – Keralan vegetarian restaurant **Rasa** (no.55, 7249 0344) is probably the best of them. Another local highlight is the simply wonderful **Abney Park Cemetery** (7275 7557, www.abney-park.org.uk), a wild and overgrown Victorian boneyard that looks like a set from a Sam Raimi zombie movie; it's also a nature reserve, with rare butterflies, woodpeckers and bats.

East London

What was once a grim corner of town is now the city's liveliest quarter.

Read the style mags, and it's hard to believe how recently the East End was notorious for its slums and cursed with the smelliest and most unpleasant of London's industries. Jack the Ripper stalked through **Whitechapel**; the presence of the docks later attracted some of the most brutal bombing during the Blitz.

How things change. East London now has three of London's most vital areas. Alongside the City, **Spitalfields** and **Brick Lane** are tourist must-visits, with markets, boutiques, restaurants

Map p403, p405	Restaurants &
Hotels p193	cafés p223
	Pubs & bars p239

and – as they shade into **Shoreditch** – art-student trendy nightlife. **Docklands** now rivals the City as a centre for blue-chip media companies and banks and **Stratford** is the site of 2012's Olympic Park.

SPITALFIELDS

Aldgate East tube/Liverpool Street tube/rail.

Approach this area from Liverpool Street Station, up Brushfield Street, and you'll know you're on the right track when the magnificent spike spire of **Christ Church Spitalfields** (*see below*) comes into sight. The area's other signature sight, **Spitalfields Market** (*see p247*), has emerged from protracted redevelopment and the market stalls have moved back underneath the vaulted Victorian roof of the original building.

Outside, along Brushfield Street, the shops might look as if they're from Dickens's day, but most are recent inventions: the charming grocery shop **A Gold** (no.42; *see p261*) was lovingly restored in the noughties; the owners of the **Market Coffee House** (nos.50-52, 7247 4110) put reclaimed wood panelling and creaky furniture into an empty shell; and the deli **Verde & Co** (no.40, 7247 1924) was opened by its owner, author Jeanette Winterson, inspired by the local food shops she found in – whisper it – France. It's a nice enough stroll, but for another perspective on Spitalfields head a few streets south on a Sunday to find the salt-of-the-earth **Petticoat Lane Market**, hawking knickers

and cheap electronics around Middlesex Street. At the foot of Goulston Street, **Tubby Isaacs** seafood stall has sold whelks and cockles since 1919.

A block north of Spitalfields Market is **Dennis Severs' House** (*see p136*), while across from the market, on the east side of Commercial Street and in the shadow of Christ Church, the **Ten Bells** (84 Commercial Street, 7366 1721) is where one of Jack the Ripper's prostitute victims drank her last gin. The streets between here and Brick Lane to the east are dourly impressive, lined with tall, shuttered Huguenot houses; **19 Princelet Street** (www.19princeletstreet.org.uk) is opened to the public a few times a year. This unrestored 18th-century house was home first to French silk merchants and later Polish Jews who built a synagogue in the garden.

FREE Christ Church Spitalfields

Commercial Street, E1 6QE (7859 3035, www.christchurchspitalfields.org). Liverpool Street tube/rail. **Open** 11am-4pm Tue; 1-4pm Sun. **Admission** free. **No credit cards.** **Map** p403 S5.

Built in 1729 by architect Nicholas Hawksmoor, this splendid church has in recent years been restored to its original state (tasteless alterations had followed a 19th-century lightning strike). Most tourists get no

Spitalfields Market.

further than cowering before the wonderfully over-bearing spire, but the revived interior is impressive, its pristine whiteness in marked contrast to its architect's dark reputation. The formidable 1735 Richard Bridge organ is almost as old as the church. Regular concerts are held here, often from the resident Gabrieli Consort & Players.

▶ *The East End's other Hawksmoor churches are St Anne's Limehouse (Commercial Road, between Limehouse and Westferry DLRs) and St George-in-the-East (on the Highway, near Shadwell DLR).*

★ Dennis Severs' House

18 Folgate Street, E1 6BX (7247 4013, www. dennissevershouse.co.uk). Liverpool Street tube/ rail. **Open** noon-4pm 1st & 3rd Sun of mth; noon-2pm Mon following 1st & 3rd Sun of mth; times vary Mon evenings. **Admission** £8 Sun; £5 noon-2pm Mon; £12 Mon evenings. **Credit** V. **Map** p403 R5.

The ten rooms of this original Huguenot house have been decked out to recreate snapshots of life in Spitalfields between 1724 and 1914. A tour through the compelling 'still-life drama', as American creator Dennis Severs dubbed it, takes you through the cellar, kitchen, dining room, smoking room and upstairs to the bedrooms. With hearth and candles burning, smells lingering and objects scattered apparently haphazardly, it feels as though the inhabitants had deserted the rooms only moments before.

BRICK LANE

Aldgate East tube.

Join the crowds flowing east from Spitalfields Market along Hanbury Street during the weekend, and the direction you turn at the end determines which Brick Lane you see. Turn right and you'll know you're in 'Banglatown', the name adopted by the ward back in 2002: until you hit the bland modern offices beside the kitsch Banglatown arch, it's almost all Bangladeshi cafés, curry houses, grocery stores, money transfer services and sari shops – plus the **Pride of Spitalfields** (3 Heneage Street, 7247 8933), an old-style East End boozer serving ale to all-comers.

Despite the street's global reputation for Indian food (there's even a Brick Lane restaurant in Manhattan), most of the food on offer is disappointing. That said, there are a few exceptions to this rule in the area (*see p224* **Inside Track**), among them the outstanding **Tayyabs** (*see p224*). Alternatively, just opt for some Bengali sweets from the **Madhubon Sweet Centre** at no.42.

Between Fournier Street and Princelet Street, **Jamme Masjid Mosque** is a key symbol of Brick Lane's hybridity. It began as a Huguenot chapel, became a synagogue and was converted, in 1976, into a mosque – in other words, immigrant communities have been layering their experiences on this street at least since 1572, when the St Bartholomew's Day Massacre forced many French Huguenots into exile.

The newest layer is gentrification. On Sunday, there's the lively street market, complemented by the trendier UpMarket – superior, clothes-wise to Spitalfields market – and Backyard Market (for arts and crafts), both held in the **Old Truman Brewery** (nos.91-95). Pedestrianised Dray Walk is crowded every day. It's full of hip independent businesses like **Rootmaster** (www.root-master.co.uk), a vegetarian café in an old red double-decker bus. Heading north on Brick Lane, you'll find the **Vibe Bar** (7377 2899, www.vibe-bar.co.uk) and shops such as second-hand clothes store **Rokit** (nos.101 & 107, 7375 3864, 7247 3777). Further north, Cheshire Street is good for vintage fashion, too – the cavernous **Beyond Retro** (*see p254*) is the stand-out.

WHITECHAPEL

Aldgate East or Whitechapel tube.

Not one of the prettier London thoroughfares, busy but anonymous Whitechapel Road sets the tone for this area. One bright spot is **Whitechapel Art Gallery**, at the foot of Brick Lane (*see p138*), while a little to the east, the **Whitechapel Bell Foundry** (nos.32 & 34, 7247 2599, www.whitechapelbellfoundry. co.uk) continues to manufacture bells, as it has since 1570. It famously produced Philadelphia's Liberty Bell and Big Ben. To join one of the fascinating Saturday tours you'll have to reserve a place (usually well in advance).

At Whitechapel's foremost place of worship, it isn't bells but a muezzin that summons the faithful each Friday: the **East London Mosque**, focal point for the largest Muslim community in Britain, can accommodate 10,000 worshippers. Behind is Fieldgate Street and the dark mass of **Tower House**, a former doss house whose 700 rooms have, inevitably, been redeveloped into flats. This 'sought after converted warehouse building' was a rather dismal –

but decidedly cheaper – proposition when Joseph Stalin and George Orwell (researching his book *Down and Out in Paris and London*) kipped here for pennies. The red-brick alleys give a flavour of Victorian Whitechapel, but this street has also been home to the cheap seekh kebabs of **Tayyabs** (*see p224*) for more than three decades.

East again is the Royal London Hospital and, in a small crypt on Newark Street, the **Royal London Hospital Archives & Museum** (7377 7608, closed Sat, Sun, and Mon). Inside are reproduction letters from Jack the Ripper (including the notorious missive 'From Hell', delivered with an enclosed portion of human kidney) and information on Joseph Merrick, the 'Elephant Man', so named for his congenital deformities. Rescued by surgeon Sir

Shakespeare in Shoreditch

Even then, the young Bard was drawn by the area's cultured credentials.

That Shakespeare's Globe (*see p54*) is located on the South Bank might lead you to believe Britain's greatest playwright spent most of his days fraternising with pimps, prostitutes and even the odd actor around Southwark. But that isn't the case. As biographer-cum-detective Charles Nicholl's book *The Lodger: Shakespeare on Silver Street* makes clear, Shakespeare no more wanted to linger near his playhouse than Quentin Tarantino might hang around the local Odeon. Instead, Nicholl's dogged enquiries reconstruct Shakespeare's life in the rather unliterary milieu of the City.

Thanks to the Great Fire of London and the Blitz, about the closest you can get to Shakespeare's City address is the unromantic underground car park beneath London Wall off the A1211. Instead, you're better off paying homage in Shoreditch. While conducting a survey for a new venue they plan to build on New Inn Broadway, the amateur Tower Theatre troupe (www. towertheatre.org.uk), had a massive scoop when they found the Elizabethan foundations of the Theatre, East End, the stage for Shakespeare's early plays. The site has now become a draw for Shakespeare groupies. 'You wouldn't think a bit of wall and compacted gravel would be so moving, but it is. We've had people in tears, begging to come and stand where people stood to see the first performance of *Romeo & Juliet*.'

Arriving in London in his mid-twenties, Shakespeare made Shoreditch one of his

earliest addresses, perhaps his very first home. This isn't as strange as it sounds. Even in Elizabethan times, Shoreditch was populated by carousing, arty, trend-setting types. The only difference is that their means of artistic expression was writing plays rather than playing indie-electro. And if you walk up Shoreditch High Street, to where it meets Hackney Road – ground zero as far as East End trendiness goes – you'll find St Leonard's, a church built on top of 10,000 graves. Among the bodies buried here is Richard Burbage, Shakespeare's finest tragic actor.

SIGHTS

Brick Lane. See p136.

Frederick Treves, Merrick was given his own room in the Royal London Hospital.

Behind the hospital is the brand new, high-tech **Centre of the Cell** (64 Turner Street, 7882 2562, www.centreofthecell.org), which gives visitors a lively, interactive and occasionally grisly insight into cell biology in a purpose-built pod, suspended over labs investigating cancer and tuberculosis.

★ FREE Whitechapel Gallery
80-82 Whitechapel High Street, E1 7QX (7522 7888, www.whitechapelgallery.org). Aldgate East tube. **Open** 11am-6pm Tue, Wed, Fri-Sun; 11am-9pm Thur. **Admission** free. **Credit** (shop) MC, V. **Map** p405 S6.
This East End stalwart reopened in 2009 following a major redesign and expansion that saw the Grade II listed building nearly triple its amount of exhibition space and transform itself into a vibrant, holistic centre of art complete with a research centre, archives room and café. Since 1901, the Whitechapel Art Gallery has built on its reputation as a pioneering contemporary institution and is well remembered for premiering the talents of exhibitions by Picasso – *Guernica* was shown here in 1939 – Jackson Pollock, Mark Rothko and Frida Kahlo among others. Unlike at Tate or the National Gallery, the Whitechapel is now completely free, so expect the rolling shows to be challenging, risqué exhibitions of British and international work, some of which is usually offered for sale.

SHOREDITCH & HOXTON
Old Street tube/rail.

The story has become familiar: impecunious artists moved into the area's derelict warehouses in the '80s, taking advantage of cheap rent, and quickly turned the triangle formed by Old Street, Shoreditch High Street and Great Eastern Street into the place to be. These days, most of the artists have moved further east, as City workers happy to pay serious money for street cred have driven rents through the roof. Yet this small patch of real estate is clinging on to its reputation as the city's most exciting arts and clubbing centre.

Nightlife permeates the whole area, with centres on Curtain Road, the lower end of Kingsland Road and around Hoxton Square. Nostalgists have to pencil in a visit to **333** (*see p328*) – no longer cutting-edge, but certainly some kind of visually unremarkable landmark – but for the best idea of the nonconformist early days, duck into the **Foundry** (84-86 Great Eastern Street, 7739 6900), a resilient madhouse of impromptu art work, relatively cheap beer and dogs off the leash.

Apart from Hoxton Square galleries **White Cube** (*see p297*) and newcomer **Yvon Lambert** (*see p300*), the area's sole bona fide tourist attraction is the exquisite **Geffrye Museum** (*see below*), a short walk north up Kingsland Road. The surrounding area is dense with good, cheap Vietnamese restaurants with **Sông Quê** (*see p224*) the best known and, perhaps, the best.

★ FREE Geffrye Museum
136 Kingsland Road, E2 8EA (7739 8543, www.geffrye-museum.org.uk). Liverpool Street tube/rail then bus 149, 242, or Old Street tube/rail then bus 243. **Open** 10am-5pm Tue-Sat; noon-5pm Sun. *Almshouse tours* 1st Sat, 1st & 3rd Wed of mth. **Admission** free; donations appreciated. *Almshouse tours* £2; free under-16s. **Credit** (shop) MC, V. **Map** p403 R3.
Housed in a set of 18th-century almshouses, the Geffrye Museum offers a vivid physical history of the English interior. Displaying original furniture, paintings, textiles and decorative arts, the museum recreates a sequence of typical middle-class living rooms from 1600 to the present. It's an oddly interesting way to take in domestic history, with any number of intriguing details to catch your eye – from a bell jar of stuffed birds to a particular decorative flourish on a chair. There's an airy a restaurant overlooking the lovely gardens, which include a walled plot for herbs and a chronological series in different historical styles.
▶ *Charmed by the greenery? Seek out the Chelsea Physic Garden; see p122.*

ᴿᴿᴱᴱ Rivington Place

Rivington Place, EC2A 3BA (7729 9616,
www.rivingtonplace.org). Old Street tube/rail.
Open 11am-6pm Tue, Wed, Fri; 11am-9pm Thur;
noon-6pm Sat. **Admission** free. **Credit** (shop)
MC, V. **Map** p403 R4.

One of Shoreditch's more exciting recent additions,
this public space was designed by David Adjaye and
is the first new-built public gallery in London since
the opening of the Hayward in 1968. The programme champions culturally diverse visual arts.
Two project spaces provide a platform for plenty of
British and international work, including exhibitions, screenings, installations and site-specific commissions. The site has a ground-floor café.

BETHNAL GREEN

Bethnal Green tube/rail/Cambridge Heath rail/
Mile End tube.

Once a suburb of spacious townhouses, by
the mid 19th century Bethnal Green was one
of the city's poorest neighbourhoods. As in
neighbouring Hoxton, a recent upturn in
fortunes has in part been occasioned by
Bethnal Green's adoption as home by a new
generation of artists. The long-standing
Maureen Paley gallery (*see p299*) remains
the key venue, but the new Bethnal Green is
typified by places such as **Herald Street** (*see*

p299) just down the road. The old Bethnal
Green is best experienced by taking a seat
at **E Pellicci** (*see p224*), the exemplary
traditional London caff.

The **V&A Museum of Childhood** (*see
p140*) is positioned close to Bethnal Green tube
station, whereas the area's other main attraction
is a bit of a walk away to the west. Nonetheless,
a visit to the weekly **Columbia Road flower
market** (*see p245*) is a lovely way to fritter
away a Sunday morning. A microcosmic retail
community has grown up around the market:
Treacle (nos.110-112, 7729 0538) for groovy
crockery and cup cakes; **Angela Flanders**
(no.96, 7739 7555) for perfume; **Marcos &
Trump** (no.146, 7739 9008) for vintage fashion.

ᴿᴿᴱᴱ Ragged School Museum

46-50 Copperfield Road, E3 4RR (8980 6405,
www.raggedschoolmuseum.org.uk). Mile End
tube. **Open** 10am-5pm Wed, Thur; 2-5pm 1st Sun
of mth. *Tours* by arrangement; phone for details.
Admission free; donations appreciated. **No
credit cards**.

Ragged schools were an early experiment in public
education: they provided tuition, food and clothes
for destitute children. This one was the largest in
London, and Dr Barnardo himself taught here. It's
now a sweet local museum that contains a complete
mock-up of a ragged classroom, as well as an
Edwardian kitchen.

Whitechapel Gallery.

SIGHTS

SIGHTS

★ FREE **V&A Museum of Childhood**
*Cambridge Heath Road, E2 9PA (8983 5235,
www.museumofchildhood.org.uk). Bethnal Green
tube/rail or Cambridge Heath rail.* **Open** 10am-
5.45pm daily. **Admission** free; donations
appreciated. **Credit** MC, V.

Home to one of the world's finest collections of
children's toys, dolls' houses, games and costumes,
the Museum of Childhood shines brighter than ever
after extensive refurbishment, which has given it an
impressive entrance. Part of the Victoria & Albert
Museum (*see p126*), the museum has been amass-
ing childhood-related objects since 1872 and continues to do so, with *Incredibles* figures complementing
bonkers 1970s puppets, Barbie Dolls and Victorian
praxinoscopes. The museum has lots of hands-on
stuff for kids with regular exhibitions upstairs. The
café on the ground floor, meanwhile, helps revive
flagging grown-ups.

DOCKLANDS

London's docks were fundamental to the
prosperity of the British Empire. Between
1802 and 1921, ten separate docks were
built between Tower Bridge in the west and
Woolwich in the east. These employed tens
of thousands of people. Yet by the 1960s the
shipping industry was changing irrevocably.
The new 'container' system of cargo demanded
larger, deep-draught ships, as a result of which
the work moved out to Tilbury, from where
lorries would ship the containers into the city.
By 1980, the London docks had closed.

The London Docklands Development
Corporation (LDDC), founded in 1981, spent
£790 million of public money on redevelopment
during the following decade, only for a countrywide property slump in the early 1990s to leave
the shiny new high-rise offices and luxury flats
unoccupied. Nowadays, though, as a financial
hub, Docklands is a booming rival to the City
of London, with an estimated 90,000 workers
commuting to the area each day. For visitors,

**INSIDE TRACK
TRINITY BUOY WHARF**

At the mouth of the River Lea, you'll find
Trinity Buoy Wharf (www.trinitybuoywharf.
com) and London's only lighthouse. It's
now a gallery-cum-sound installation, home
to Jem Finer's *Longplayer* (www.longplayer.
com). If the music, which is set to play
for 1000 years, doesn't inspire, the
views across to the former Millennium
Dome should provide food for thought.
Genuine sustenance, meanwhile, comes
from a 1940s diner car.

regular **Thames Clippers** (0870 781 5049,
www.thamesclippers.com) boat connections
with central London and the **Docklands Light
Railway** (DLR) make the area easily accessible.
Just a few stops from where the DLR starts
at Bank station is Shadwell, south of which
is Wapping. In 1598, John Stowe described
Wapping High Street as 'a filthy strait passage,
with alleys of small tenements or cottages,
inhabited by sailors' victuallers', or supplier.
This can still just about be imagined as you
walk along it now, flanked by tall Victorian
warehouses. The historic **Town of Ramsgate**
pub (no.62, 7481 8000), dating from 1545, helps.
Here 'hanging judge' George Jeffreys was
captured in 1688, trying to escape to Europe
in disguise as a woman. Privateer Captain
William Kidd was executed in 1701 at
Execution Dock, near Wapping New Stairs;
the bodies of pirates were hanged from a gibbet
until seven tides had washed over them.
Further east, the **Prospect of Whitby** (57
Wapping Wall, 7481 1095) dates from 1520
and has counted Samuel Pepys and Charles
Dickens among its regulars. It has good
riverside terraces and a fine pewter bar counter.
Opposite sits a rather more modern 'victualler':
Wapping Food (*see p225*) occupies an ivy-clad
Victorian hydraulic power station.

East of here are the Isle of Dogs and Canary
Wharf. The origin of the name 'Isle of Dogs'
remains uncertain, but the first recorded use
is on a map of 1588; one theory claims Henry
VIII kept his hunting dogs here. One thing is
clear: it certainly isn't an island, but rather a
peninsula, extending into the Thames to create
the prominent loop that features in the title
sequence of the BBC soap opera *EastEnders*.
In the 19th century, a huge system of docks
and locks completely transformed what had
been no more than drained marshland; in fact,
the West India Docks cut right across the
peninsula, so the Isle did become some sort
of island.

Almost all the interest for visitors is to be
found in the vicinity of Cesar Pelli's dramatic
One Canada Square, the country's tallest
habitable building since 1991. The only slightly
shorter HSBC and Citygroup towers joined it in
the noughties, and clones are springing up thick
and fast. Shopping options are limited to the
mall beneath the towers (www.mycanarywharf.
com), but you'll find a soothing if rather crisp
Japanese garden beside Canary Wharf tube
station. Across a floating bridge over the dock
to the north, there's the **Museum of London
Docklands** (*see right*).

It's also well worth hopping on the DLR
and heading to Island Gardens station at the
southerly tip of the Isle of Dogs. Nearby, at
Mudchute Park & Farm (Pier Street, Isle

Museum of London Docklands.

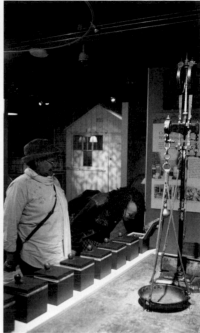

of Dogs, E14 3HP, 7515 5901, www.mudchute. org; *see also p281*) farmyard animals graze in front of the ultramodern skyscrapers. From **Island Gardens** themselves, there are famous views of Greenwich – and the entrance to the Victorian pedestrian tunnel.

Further east, Pontoon Dock is the stop for the beautiful **Thames Barrier Park** (www. thamesbarrierpark.org.uk). Opened in 2001, this was London's first new park in half a century. It has a lush sunken garden of waggly hedges and offers perhaps the best views from land of the fabulously sculptural **Thames Barrier** (*see p150*). Head to King George V for the free ferry (every 15mins daily, 8853 9400) that chugs pedestrians and cars across the river or, if not, the DLR passes under the river to its final stop at **Woolwich Arsenal** (*see p149*).

★ Museum of London Docklands

No.1 Warehouse, West India Quay, Hertsmere Road, E14 4AL (7001 9844, www.museum indocklands.org.uk). Canary Wharf tube or West India Quay DLR. **Open** 10am-6pm daily. **Admission** £5; £3 reductions; free under-16s. **Credit** MC, V.
Housed in a 19th-century warehouse (itself a Grade I-listed building), this huge museum explores the complex history of London's docklands and the river

over two millennia. Displays spreading over three storeys take you from the arrival of the Romans all the way to the docks' 1980s closure and the area's subsequent redevelopment. The Docklands at War section is very moving, while a haunting new permanent exhibition sheds light on the dark side of London's rise as a centre for finance and commerce, exploring the city's heavy involvement in the transatlantic slave trade. You can also walk through full-scale mock-ups of a quayside and a dingy riverfront alley. Temporary exhibitions are frequently set up on the ground floor, where you'll also find a café and a docks-themed play area for kids. Bring plenty of time to this fascinating storehouse, or return later – your ticket is valid for a year.

HACKNEY

London Fields or Hackney Central rail.

Few tourists ever make it out to these tube-less, north-eastern districts, devoid of blockbuster sights, but the area is a good example of lived-in London. Its centre is the refurbished but struggling **Hackney Empire** (291 Mare Street, 8985 2424, www.hackneyempire.co.uk), , a century-old theatre that's set to close 'for a period of reflection' of between six and nine months from January 2009. It's located beside the art deco town hall and the fine little **Hackney Museum** (1 Reading Lane, 8356 3500, www.hackney.gov.uk/museum). Just to the east, **Sutton House** (*see below*) is the oldest house in east London. The area of London Fields demonstrates the borough's ongoing gentrification. Once a lacklustre fruit and veg market, **Broadway Market** is now brimming with young urbanites and trendy young families. As well as the food and vintage garb market on Saturdays, there's a wonderful deli, an inspiring independent bookshop and a fine pub – the **Dove** (nos.24-28, 7275 7617, www.belgianbars.com), with its immense selection of Belgian beers. The old days are respectably represented by **F Cooke** (no.9, 7254 6458), a pie and mash place that's been here since the early 1900s.

Sutton House

2-4 Homerton High Street, E9 6JQ (8986 2264, www.nationaltrust.org.uk). Bethnal Green tube then 254, 106, D6 bus, or Hackney Central rail. **Open** 12.30-4.30pm Thur-Sun. *Café, gallery & shop* noon-4.30pm Thur-Sun. *Tours* phone for details; free tours on 1st Sun of mth. **Admission** £2.80; 70p 5-16s; £6.30 family; free under-5s, National Trust members. **Credit** MC, V.
Built in 1535 for Henry VIII's first secretary of state, Sir Ralph Sadleir, this red-brick Tudor mansion is east London's oldest home. Now beautifully restored in authentic original decor, with a real Tudor kitchen to boot, it makes no secret of its history of neglect: even some 1980s squatter graffiti has been preserved. The house closes for January each year.

THREE MILLS & STRATFORD

Bromley-by-Bow tube/Stratford tube/DLR/rail.

Ignore the thundering roads and gasworks surrounding it and **Three Mills Island** (*see right*) is a delight. A short walk north-east up the canal-like tributary brings you to **Stratford**, nucleus of the transformation for the **2012 Olympics**. Feverish construction work is already under way. After wriggling

---

INSIDE TRACK
TRENDY SPOTTING

If you want to do some serious people-watching, head to **Broadway Market** after midday on a Saturday. Grab a coffee and watch the crème de la crème of east London's hipsterati conga its way around the gourmet food stalls and surrounding boutiques. Shocking hair and frightfully ambitious outfits abound.

---

through the grassland of Hackney Marshes, the river passes the **WaterWorks Nature Reserve** (Lammas Road, 8988 7566, open 8am-9pm or dusk daily). A touchingly odd combination of golf course and nature reserve, these water-filter beds were built in 1849 to purify water during a cholera epidemic.

Three Mills Island

Three Mill Lane, E3 3DU (8980 4626, www.housemill.org.uk). Bromley-by-Bow tube. **Tours** *May-Dec* 1-4pm Sun. **Admission** £3; £1.50 reductions; free under-16s. **No credit cards**.
This pretty island in the River Lea takes its name from the three mills that, until the 18th century, ground flour and gunpowder here. The House Mill, built in 1776, is the oldest and largest tidal mill in Britain and, though out of service, it is occasionally opened to the public. The island offers pleasant walks that can feel surprisingly rural once you're among the undergrowth. There's also a small café and, to puncture the idyll, one of the other mills is a TV studio.

WALTHAMSTOW

Walthamstow Central tube/rail.

2008's sad news that **Walthamstow Stadium** greyhound track had been sold to developers (the 'Save Our Stow' campaign group is still busy trying to buy it back to continue the racing) puts the spotlight firmly on this area's other asset: quaint Walthamstow Village, just a few minutes' walk east of the tube station. Further north, near the junction of Hoe Street and Forest Road, is peaceful Lloyd Park; the grand Georgian house at its entrance is home to the **William Morris Gallery** (*see below*) – the Arts and Crafts pioneer was a Walthamstow boy.

FREE William Morris Gallery

Lloyd Park, Forest Road, E17 4PP (8527 3782, www.walthamforest.gov.uk/william-morris). Walthamstow Central tube/rail or bus 34, 97, 215, 275. **Open** 10am-5pm Wed-Sun. *Tours* phone for details. **Admission** free; donations appreciated. **Credit** (shop) MC, V.
free; donations appreciated. **Credit** (shop) MC, V.
Artist, socialist and source of all that flowery wallpaper, William Morris lived here between 1848 and 1856. There are plenty of wonderful designs in fabric, stained glass and ceramic on show, produced by Morris and his acolytes. The gallery features the medieval-style helmet and sword the designer used as props for some of his murals, but there are also plenty of humbler domestic objects: Morris's coffee cup, for instance, and the satchel he used to distribute his radical pamphlets.
▶ *You can also visit the Red House; see p150.*

South-east London

Delights and curios lie where the tube network fears to tread.

The main obstacle to visiting south-east London is the absence of the London Underground. However, it's worth the effort, not least because it's really not that much of an effort at all. Although there are no tubes down here, overground trains from London Bridge and Charing Cross serve the area, as do extensive bus routes and a constantly expanding DLR network.

The most visited neighbourhood in this part of town is **Greenwich**, an area that rivals South Kensington for historic cultural destinations. Notable diversions elsewhere in the region include the superb Imperial War Museum in **Lambeth**; the Dulwich Picture Gallery in (yes) **Dulwich**; the family-friendly Horniman Museum, a London curio, in the suburb of **Forest Hill**; and, further out, the art deco Eltham Palace.

Hotels p193
Pubs & bars p240

**Restaurants &
cafés** p226

SIGHTS

KENNINGTON & THE ELEPHANT

Kennington tube or Elephant & Castle tube/rail

Even back in the 17th century, the **Elephant & Castle** (named, perhaps, after the ivory-dealing Cutlers Company, or maybe after Charles I's once-intended, the Infanta of Castille) was a busy place. In the early 20th century, it was a tram terminus and south London's West End, before losing its looks to World War II bombs and a grisly '60s makeover. Regeneration of this ugly corner of town has been promised for nearly a decade without ever looking like it might happen. A new skyscraping residential building, the Strata, is due to be completed on the southern roundabout in 2010, but the rest of the £1.5-billion, 170-acre project is still awaiting the green light.

Behind the **Imperial War Museum** (*see right*), Kennington Road leads through an area once blighted by factory stink, young resident Charlie Chaplin's abiding memory. Today, the area's smarter houses are favoured by second-home politicians and lawyers requiring easy access to the city. For many, Kennington means cricket, especially in the beery atmosphere of a Test match at the **Brit Oval** (*see p331*).

★ FREE Imperial War Museum

Lambeth Road, Elephant & Castle, SE1 6HZ (7416 5320, www.iwm.org.uk). Lambeth North tube or Elephant & Castle tube/rail. **Open** 10am-6pm daily. **Admission** free. *Special exhibitions* prices vary. **Credit** MC, V. **Map** p404 N10.

Antique guns, tanks, aircraft and artillery are parked in the main hall of this imposing edifice, built in 1814 as a lunatic asylum (the Bethlehem Royal Hospital, aka Bedlam). After the inmates were moved out in 1930, the central block became the war museum, only to be damaged by World War II air raids. Today, the museum gives the history of armed conflict, especially involving Britain and the Commonwealth, from World War I to today.

Moving on from the more gung-ho exhibits on the ground floor, there are extensive galleries devoted to the two World Wars. The tone of the museum darkens as you ascend. On the third floor, the Holocaust Exhibition (not recommended for under-14s) traces the history of European anti-Semitism and its nadir in the concentration camps. Upstairs, Crimes Against Humanity (unsuitable for under-16s) is a minimalist space in which a film exploring contemporary genocide and ethnic violence rolls relentlessly.

The temporary exhibitions are usually excellent. Outbreak 1939 (until Sept 2010) promises a look at the nation on the eve of war; Horrible Histories: Terrible Trenches (until Oct 2010) is a child-friendly

Overground to the Underground

Take the bus south to explore the art of Camberwell.

Camberwell's blend of run-down Georgian buildings, ugly tower blocks and traffic-choked roads appears, on first glance, less than artful. However, its built-up environs have long proved fertile ground for a flourishing cultural scene, which dates back to Victorian times and has found new life in the early 21st century.

In 1891, William Rossiter opened the pioneering South London Fine Art Gallery. A century later, renamed the **South London Gallery** (*see p300*), it found new renown as the venue that first exhibited *Everyone I Have Ever Slept With 1963-1995*, Tracey Emin's infamous tent. A beacon for Britart during the 1990s, the gallery remains one of London's leading contemporary art venues, and this year unveils its most ambitious scheme since Rossiter's day. In June, a new £1.8-million extension is due to open, swallowing up a neighbouring three-storey Victorian townhouse in order to add a new café, two extra exhibition spaces and a resident artist's flat.

Next door sits the **Camberwell College of Art** (45-65 Peckham Road, 7514 6308, www.camberwell.arts.ac.uk), where the likes ofSyd Barrett and Mike Leigh once studied. Like the SLG, it's also expanding: in early 2010, the college will open **Peckham Space** (7514 2299, www.peckhamspace.com), a new contemporary art venue on nearby Peckham Square that will add to the free public exhibitions and events staged at the college's Camberwell Space. Outside the college, its students continue to colonise Camberwell bars such as the **Sun & Doves** (61-63 Coldharbour Lane, 7733 1525, www.sunanddoves.co.uk), the **Bear** (296A Camberwell New Road, 7274 7037, www.thebear-freehouse.co.uk) and **Art's Bar** (above the Funky Monkey, 25A Camberwell Church Street, 07980 331158).

The modern-day scene isn't limited to the visual arts: the railway arches are vital spaces for clubbing and other diversions. Under Loughborough Junction station, **Arch 468** (Unit 4, 209A Coldharbour Lane, 07973 302908, www.arch468.com) stages work by catch emerging playwrights and theatre companies, with regular free rehearsed readings of new pieces. The more established **Blue Elephant Theatre** (*see p289*) continues to present a vibrant programme of new writing, classic plays, physical theatre and dance.

Talent of all kinds goes into the melting pot in June for the **Camberwell Arts Festival** (www.camberwellarts.org.uk). Last year, visitors were invited to decorate Camberwell Green with their own paintings, join Queer Tango sessions at the Sun & Doves, take part in a tea dance at Myatt's Fields Park (Knatchbull Road), and scour the streets for junk to make instruments for a 'stumble-on-and-hit-upon' orchestra. Getting creative is unavoidable.

SOUTH LONDON GALLERY

recreation of World War I trenches; and from Feb 2010, Ministry of Food will look at rationing, diet and food production in the World War II. In October 2010, the Lord Ashcroft Gallery will open to display the world's largest collection of Victoria Crosses.

CAMBERWELL & PECKHAM

Denmark Hill or Peckham Rye rail.

The Camberwell Beauty butterfly is unlikely to again be found in the area where it was first identified. Head past the traffic and down Church Street to the **Camberwell College of Arts** (Peckham Road, 7514 6300), London's oldest art college, and the **South London Gallery** (*see p300*).

East of here, **Peckham** is still unfairly associated with teenage gangs and dodgy traders, but regeneration schemes continue to spruce up the streets. Rye Lane still resembles old Peckham; Will Alsop's award-winning and frankly odd-looking **Peckham Library**, in an area now known as **Peckham Square**, represents the new. Due south on Rye Lane is **Peckham Rye**, where Blake saw his angels; it's now a prettily laid-out park with well-kept gardens. Keep walking south from Peckham Rye (or take a P4 or P12 bus) to enjoy views over London and Kent from **Honor Oak** and **One Tree Hill**, where Elizabeth I picnicked with Richard Bukeley of Beaumaris in 1602.

DULWICH & CRYSTAL PALACE

Crystal Palace, East Dulwich, Herne Hill, North Dulwich or West Dulwich rail.

Dulwich is a little piece of rural England that fiercely guards its bucolic prosperity. Tasteful fingerposts offer directions: perhaps towards the attractive park (once a duelling spot), the historic boys' public school or the **Dulwich Picture Gallery** (*see right*). It's a pleasant, brisk half-hour's walk from the gallery across the Dulwich Park and up Lordship Lane to the **Horniman Museum** (*see right*) in Forest Hill.

East and west of Dulwich sit **East Dulwich** and **Herne Hill**, the latter home to an exquisite art deco lido in Brockwell Park. The two areas represent the middle(-class) way: not as expensive or charismatic as Dulwich, but less challenging than relentless Brixton.

Crystal Palace is named in honour of Joseph Paxton's famous structure, built for the Great Exhibition in Hyde Park in 1851, moved here three years later and destroyed by fire in 1936. **Crystal Palace Park** contains arches and the sphinx from the Exhibition's Egyptian-themed display; the Dinosaur Park, a lake ringed by Benjamin Waterhouse-Hawkins's

Imperial War Museum. *See p143.*

life-sized dinosaur statues; and the **National Sports Centre** (*see p330*). The **Crystal Palace Museum** (Anerley Hill, SE19 2BA, 8676 0700, www.crystalpalacemuseum. org.uk), opened by volunteers each weekend, has an 'exhibition of the Exhibition'.

★ Dulwich Picture Gallery

Gallery Road, Dulwich, SE21 7AD (8693 5254, www.dulwichpicturegallery.org.uk). North Dulwich or West Dulwich rail. **Open** 10am-5pm Tue-Fri; 11am-5pm Sat, Sun. **Admission** £5; free-£4 reductions. **Credit** MC, V.

Lending weight to the idea that the best things come in small packages, this bijou gallery was designed by Sir John Soane in 1811 as the first purpose-built gallery in the UK. It's a beautiful space that shows off Soane's ingenuity with lighting effects. The gallery displays a small but outstanding collection of work by Old Masters, offering a fine introduction to the baroque era through works by Rembrandt, Rubens, Poussin and Gainsborough. It also has a fine programme of temporary exhibitions (Paul Nash until May 2010) and other events.

▶ *For Sir John Soane's Museum, see p76.*

★ FREE Horniman Museum

100 London Road, Dulwich, SE23 3PQ (8699 1872, www.horniman.ac.uk). Forest Hill rail or bus 363, 122, 176, 185, 312, P4, P13. **Open** 10am-5pm Mon, Tue, Thur-Sat. **Admission** free; donations appreciated. **Credit** MC, V.

SIGHTS

Horniman Museum.
See p145.

SIGHTS

South-east London's premier free family attraction, the Horniman is a museum of many parts. Once the home of tea trader Frederick J Horniman, it's an eccentric-looking art nouveau building (check out the clock tower, which starts as a circle and ends as a square), with a main entrance that gives out on to extensive gardens.

The oldest section is the Natural History gallery, dominated by an ancient walrus (mistakenly over-stuffed by Victorian taxidermists) and now ringed by glass cabinets containing pickled animals, stuffed birds and insect models. Other galleries include the Environment Room, African Worlds, and the Centenary Gallery, which focuses on world cultures. Downstairs, the Music Room contains hundreds of instruments: their sounds can be unleashed via touch-screen tables, while hardier instruments (flip-flop drums, thumb pianos) can be bashed with impunity.

The most popular part of the museum is its show-piece Aquarium, where a series of tanks and rock-pools cover seven distinct aquatic ecosystems. There are mesmerising moon jellyfish, strangely large British seahorses, starfish, tropical fish and creatures from the mangroves. The Evolution 2010 project will bring together the natural history collection, aquarium and gardens to tell the story of how life has evolved on earth.

ROTHERHITHE

Rotherhithe tube.

Once a shipbuilding village and, in the 17th and 18th centuries, a centre for London's whaling trade, the ghostly locale of Rotherhithe has long since seen its docks filled in. Go back in time at the **Brunel Museum** (*see below*) or the mariners' church of **St Mary's Rotherhithe** (St Mary Church Street, SE16 4JE, 7967 0518, www.stmaryrotherhithe.org), which contains maritime oddities; among them is a communion table and bishop's chair made from timber salvaged from the HMS *Temeraire*, immortalised by Turner (the painting is in the National Gallery). Captain Christopher Jones was buried here in 1622; his ship was the *Mayflower*, which set sail from Rotherhithe in 1620, and a waterside pub of the same name marks the spot from which the pilgrims embarked on their journey.

Rotherhithe's road tunnel takes cars across to Limehouse. At the mouth of the tunnel stands the **Norwegian Church & Seaman's Mission**, one of a number of Scandinavian churches in the area. There's also a Finnish church – with a sauna – at 33 Albion Street (7237 1261). Across Jamaica Road, **Southwark Park** has a gallery (7237 1230, www.cafe galleryprojects.com), an old bandstand, a lake and playgrounds.

Brunel Museum

Brunel Engine House, Railway Avenue, Bermondsey, SE16 4LF (7231 3840, www. brunel-museum.org.uk). Rotherhithe tube. **Open** 10am-5pm daily. *Tours* by appointment only. **Admission** £2; £1 reductions; £5 family; free under-5s. **No credit cards**.
This little museum occupies the engine house where the father-and-son team of Sir Marc and Isambard Kingdom Brunel worked to create the world's first tunnel beneath a navigable river. The story of their

achievement is told most entertainingly during guided tours; see the website for details. There's a pleasant riverside café and attractive gardens.
► *Brunel students will love his modest, ingenious Three Bridges at Hanwell, west London. It neatly added a rail line to an existing canal road bridge.*

GREENWICH

Cutty Sark DLR for Maritime Greenwich.

Riverside Greenwich is an irresistible mixture of maritime, royal and horological history, a combination that's earned it recognition as a UNESCO World Heritage Site. The permanent attractions are gathered around **Greenwich Park**, a handsome space with great views.

Royalty has stalked the area since 1300, when Edward I stayed here. Henry VIII was born in Greenwich Palace; the palace was built on land that later contained Wren's Royal Naval Hospital, now the **Royal Naval College** (*see p148*). Based in the college, the **Greenwich Gateway Visitor Centre** (0870 608 2000, www.greenwich.gov.uk) is a useful first port of call. A short walk away, shoppers swarm to **Greenwich Market**, which nervously awaits a controversial redevelopment.

Keeping the river to your left, you'll reach the Thames-lapped **Trafalgar Tavern** (6 Park Row, 8858 2909), haunt of Thackeray and Dickens, and the **Cutty Sark Tavern** (4-6 Ballast Quay, 8858 3146), which dates to 1695. Near the DLR stop is Greenwich Pier; every 15 minutes (peak times), the popular and speedy **Thames Clipper** boats (0870 781 5049, www.thamesclippers.com) shuttles passengers to and from central London.

The pier from which the Thames Clipper service departs is beside the tarp-covered **Cutty Sark** (www.cuttysark.org.uk), built in 1869 and the fastest ever sailing tea clipper in its heyday. In 2007, a conservation project was halted when the boat was devastated by fire, apparently caused by a vacuum cleaner overheating. The restored vessel will be ship-shape, 90 per cent original and, for the first time, raised above curious visitors by spring 2011.

From the riverside, it's a ten-minute walk (or shorter shuttle-bus trip) up the steep slopes of Greenwich Park to the **Royal Observatory** (*see p148*). The building looks even more stunning at night, when the bright green Meridian Line Laser illuminates the path of the Prime Meridian across the London sky.

The riverside Thames Path leads past rusting piers and boarded-up factories to the **Greenwich Peninsula**, dominated by the **O2 Arena**. Designed by the Richard Rogers Partnership as the Millennium Dome, this once-maligned structure's fortunes have improved

considerably since its change of use. Alongside the concerts in the huge arena (*see p314*), club nights in Matter (*see p328*) and movies in the cineplex, attractions include restaurants, big exhibitions and the glossy, permanent **British Music Experience** (*see below*). It's all something of a contrast with the **Greenwich Peninsula Ecology Park** (*see p283*), and with the nearby riverside walks that afford broad, flat, bracing views and various works of art; look out for *Slice of Reality*, a rusting ship cut in half by Richard Wilson and found to the west of the O2.

To the south lies grassy, upmarket **Blackheath**. Smart Georgian homes and stately pubs surround a heath on which some of the world's earliest sports clubs started; among them is the Royal Blackheath Golf Club, said to be the oldest golf club in the world. In August 2009, the heath hosted the week-long Climate Camp of 3,000 anti-capitalist and environmental protesters, a deliberate echo of Blackheath's long history of radical protest that runs back to the Peasants' Revolt in 1381.

British Music Experience

O2 Bubble, Millennium Way, Greenwich, SE10 0BB (8463 2000, www.britishmusicexperience. com). North Greenwich tube. **Open** 10am-8pm daily. **Admission** £15; free-£12 reductions; £40 family. **Credit** AmEx, MC, V.
The memorabilia on show at this new attraction on the O2's top floor includes David Bowie's Ziggy Stardust costume and Noel Gallagher's Union Jack guitar. The main focus, though, is on interactive exhibits: downloading archive music, trying your hand at guitar tutorials, and so on. Workshops, lectures and concerts are also part of the experience.

Fan Museum

12 Crooms Hill, Greenwich, SE10 8ER (8293 1889, www.fan-museum.org). Cutty Sark DLR or Greenwich DLR/rail. **Open** 11am-5pm Tue-Sat; noon-5pm Sun. **Admission** £4; free-£3 reductions; £10 family; free under-7s: free to all 2-5pm Tue. **Credit** MC, V.
The world's most important collection of hand-held fans is displayed in a pair of restored Georgian townhouses. There are about 3,500 fans, including some

---

INSIDE TRACK FANS OF TEA

As well as its fan collection, the **Fan Museum** (*see above*) has a lovely small tearoom, and serves classic English cream teas on Tuesdays and Sundays after 3pm. The orangery overlooks a stunning garden, replete with Japanese themed plantings and fan-shaped flowerbeds.

beauties in the Hélène Alexander collection, but not all are on display at any one time. For details of the regular fan-making workshops and temporary exhibitions, check the website.

★ FREE National Maritime Museum

Romney Road, Greenwich, SE10 9NF (8858 4422, Information 8312 6565, www.nmm.ac.uk). Cutty Sark DLR or Greenwich DLR/rail. **Open** 10am-5pm daily. *Tours* phone for details. **Admission** free; donations appreciated. **Credit** (shop) MC, V.

The world's largest maritime museum contains a huge store of creatively organised maritime art, cartography, models and regalia. Ground-level galleries include Explorers, which covers great sea expeditions back to medieval times, and Maritime London, which concentrates on the city as a port. Upstairs are Your Ocean, which reveals our dependence on the health of the world's oceans, and Nelson's Navy, which holds more than 250 objects drawn from a collection of naval memorabilia from the period. Level two holds the interactive exhibits: the Bridge has a ship simulator, and All Hands lets children load cargo. The Ship of War is the museum's collection of models; Oceans of Discovery commemorates the history of world exploration; and the Atlantic World gallery looks at the relationship between Britian, Africa and the Americas.

▶ *From the museum a colonnaded walkway leads to the Queen's House; see right. Up the hill in the park, the Observatory and Planetarium are also part of the museum; see right.*

FREE Old Royal Naval College

2 Cutty Sark Gardens, Greenwich, SE10 9LW (8269 4747, www.oldroyalnavalcollege.org.uk). Cutty Sark DLR or Greenwich DLR/rail. **Open** 10am-5pm daily. *Tours* by arrangement. **Admission** free. **Credit** (shop) MC, V.

Designed by Wren in 1694, with Hawksmoor and Vanbrugh helping to complete the project, this superb collection of buildings was originally a hospital for the relief and support of seamen and their dependants. Pensioners lived here from 1705 to 1869, before the complex became the Royal Naval College.

The Navy left in 1998, and the neoclassical buildings now house part of the University of Greenwich and Trinity College of Music. The public are allowed into the rococo chapel, where there are free organ recitals, and the Painted Hall, a tribute to William and Mary that took Sir James Thornhill 19 years to complete. Nelson lay in state in the Painted Hall for three days in 1806, before being taken to St Paul's Cathedral for his funeral.

The Pepys building is being transformed into the £5.8-million Discover Greenwich centre. Due to open in spring 2010, it will have an audiovisual exhibition on maritime Greenwich, an information centre and a microbrewery-cum-café on the site of a 1717 brewhouse that once fortified the resident seamen.

FREE Queen's House

Romney Road, Greenwich, SE10 9NF (8312 6565, www.nmm.ac.uk). Cutty Sark DLR or Greenwich DLR/rail. **Open** 10am-5pm daily. *Tours* noon, 2.30pm daily. **Admission** free; occasional charge for temporary exhibitions. *Tours* free. **Credit** (over £5) MC, V.

The art collection of the National Maritime Museum (*see left*) is displayed in what was formerly the summer villa of Charles I's queen, Henrietta Maria. Completed in 1638 by Inigo Jones, the house has an interior as impressive as the paintings on the walls. As well as the stunning 1635 marble floor, look for Britain's first centrally unsupported spiral stair, and the fine painted woodwork and ceilings. The collection includes portraits of famous maritime figures and works by Hogarth and Gainsborough, as well as some from the 20th century.

▶ *Inigo Jones also designed Banqueting House (see p113) and St Paul's Covent Garden (see p87).*

Ranger's House

Chesterfield Walk, Greenwich, SE10 8QX (8853 0035, www.english-heritage.org.uk). Blackheath rail, Cutty Sark DLR or bus 53. **Open** *Apr-Sept* 11am-5pm Sun. *Tours* 11.30am, 2.30pm Mon-Wed. *Oct-Dec* group bookings only. **Admission** £5.70; £2.90-£4.80 reductions; free under-5s. **Credit** MC, V.

The house of the 'Ranger of Greenwich Park' (a post held by George III's niece, Princess Sophia Matilda, from 1815) now contains the collection of treasure – medieval and Renaissance art, jewellery, bronzes, tapestries, furniture, porcelain, paintings – amassed by Julius Wernher, a German who made his fortune in the South African diamond trade. It's all displayed in 12 lovely rooms in this Georgian villa, the back garden of which is the fragrant Greenwich Park rose collection. Check online for details of guided walks.

★ FREE Royal Observatory & Planetarium

Greenwich Park, Greenwich, SE10 9NF (8312 6565, www.rog.nmm.ac.uk). Cutty Sark DLR or Greenwich DLR/rail. **Open** 10am-5pm daily. *Tours* phone for details. **Admission** *Observatory* free. *Planetarium* £6; £4 reductions; £16 family. **Credit** MC, V.

INSIDE TRACK
VIDDY WELL, LITTLE BROTHER

Many unloved 1960s housing estates across south-east London are currently slated for destruction. Perhaps the most infamous of them is the brutalist **Thamesmead Estate** in SE28, which doubled for a dystopian future in Stanley Kubrick's *A Clockwork Orange*.

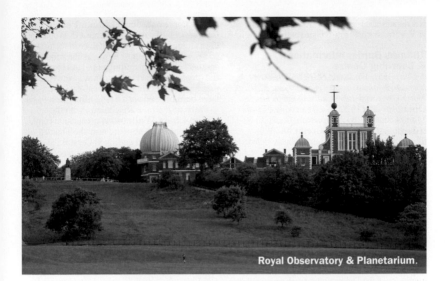

Royal Observatory & Planetarium.

The north site of this two-halved attraction chronicles Greenwich's horological connection. Flamsteed House, the observatory built in 1675 on the orders of Charles II, contains the apartments of Sir John Flamsteed and other Astronomers Royal, as well as instruments used in timekeeping since the 14th century and an onion dome that houses the country's largest refracting telescope. In the courtyard is the Prime Meridian Line, star of a billion snaps of happy tourists with a foot in each hemisphere.

The south site houses the Astronomy Centre, home to the Peter Harrison Planetarium and Weller Astronomy Galleries. The 120-seater planetarium's architecture cleverly reflects its astrological position: the semi-submerged cone tilts at 51.5 degrees, the latitude of Greenwich, pointing to the north star, and its reflective disc is aligned with the celestial equator. Daily and weekend shows include 'Black Holes: The Other Side of Infinity' and 'Starlife', a show describing the birth and death of stars.

WOOLWICH ARSENAL & THE THAMES BARRIER

Woolwich Arsenal DLR/rail or Woolwich Dockyard rail.

Established by the Tudors as the country's main source of munitions, **Woolwich Arsenal** stretched 32 miles along the river by World War I, with its own internal railway system. Much of the land was sold off during the '60s, but the main section has been preserved and is now home to Firepower (*see right*). To the south, the **Royal Artillery Barracks** has the longest Georgian façade in the country.

The river is spanned by another architectural triumph: the **Thames Barrier** (*see p150*).

This is a grim part of London, but regeneration has partly arrived in the form of an extension of the DLR from King George V station under the river to Woolwich Arsenal. More charismatic is the ramshackle **Woolwich Ferry** (8921 5786), diesel-driven boats that take pedestrians (for free) and cars across the river every ten minutes daily. A final river-crossing method in this bridge-free part of town is the **Woolwich Foot Tunnel**, whose sinister and shabby appearance should be corrected by refurbishment in March 2011.

Firepower

Royal Arsenal, Woolwich, SE18 6ST (8855 7755, www.firepower.org.uk). Woolwich Arsenal rail. **Open** 10.30am-5pm Wed-Sun. **Admission** £5; £2.50-£4.50 reductions; free under-5s; £12 family. **Credit** MC, V.

Occupying a series of converted arsenal buildings beside the river, Firepower bristles with preserved artillery pieces, some of them centuries old. An introductory presentation in the Breech Cinema tells the story of the Royal Artillery and leads on to 'Field of Fire', where four screens relay archive film and documentary footage of desert and jungle warfare. Smoke fills the air, searchlights pick out the ordnance that surrounds you and exploding bombs shake the floor. Across the courtyard, another building contains a huge collection of trophy guns and the Cold War gallery, focused on the 'monster bits' (tanks and guns used from 1945 to the present). Army-obsessed kids can get shouted at by real soldiers when they take part in drill call; the website has details of this and other attractions. The on-site café is transformed into a bistro in the evening.

Thames Barrier Information & Learning Centre

1 Unity Way, Woolwich, SE18 5NJ (8305 4188, www.environment-agency.gov.uk/thamesbarrier). North Greenwich tube, Charlton rail or bus 180. **Open** *Apr-Sept* 10.30am-4.30pm daily. *Oct-Mar* 11am-3.30pm daily. **Admission** £2; £1-£1.50 reductions; free under-5s. **Credit** MC, V.

This adjustable dam has been variously called a triumph of modern engineering and the eighth wonder of the world. The shiny silver fins, lined up across Woolwich Reach, are indeed an impressive sight; built in 1982 at a cost of £535m, they've already saved London from flooding some 80 times. The barrier is regularly in action for maintenance purposes; check the website for a current timetable.

To learn more, pay £2 for a look around the learning centre, where you'll find an account of the 1953 flood that led to the barrier's construction, as well displays on wildlife in the Thames and how a flood would affect London. The learning centre is on the south side of the Thames, along with a pleasant café with picnic benches, but some of the best views are from the north side of the river in lovely Thames Barrier Park (*see p141*).

FURTHER SOUTH-EAST

Watling Street, the old pilgrims' way out of London to Canterbury, is now the A207, and the villages it once passed through are suburbs. South of the pilgrims' way, **Eltham** was well known to Londoners – particularly to Geoffrey Chaucer, who served as the clerk of works

Thames Barrier Park.

during improvements to **Eltham Palace** (*see below*) in the reign of Richard II. When the Courtaulds bought Eltham Palace in the early 1930s, it was in deepest Kent. As the suburbs encroached, they acquired more land to keep the great unwashed at bay, an acquisitiveness that has meant Eltham's present-day unwashed have been blessed with a delightful green oasis.

Paths around the area link up with the **Green Chain Walk** (www.greenchain.com), a 40-mile network starting near the Thames Barrier (*see left*) and ending at Crystal Palace (*see p145*), having taken in ancient woodland along the way. South into Kent, the village of **Chislehurst** has some impressive Druids' caves (8467 3264, www.chislehurstcaves.co.uk).

★ Eltham Palace

Court Yard, Eltham, SE9 5QE (8294 2548, www.english-heritage.org.uk). Eltham rail. **Open** *Feb, Mar, Nov, Dec* 11am-4pm Mon-Wed, Sun. *Apr-Oct* 10am-5pm Mon-Wed, Sun. **Admission** *House & grounds* (incl audio tour) £8.20; £4.10-£6.60 reductions; free under-5s; £20.50 family. *Grounds only* £5.10; £2.60-£4.10 reductions; free under-5s. **Credit** MC, V.

When the society couple Stephen and Virginia Courtauld bought this ancient palace in 1931, it had been out of favour as a sovereign residence for centuries. Acquired by Edward II in 1305 and enjoyed by Henry VIII as a child, Eltham was abandoned in favour of Greenwich and fell into disrepair. What remains of the royal residence is the Great Hall, used as a barn for decades but repaired by the Courtaulds in the style they thought fitting. Other medieval remains include the stone bridge over the moat over which you enter the grounds. The Courtaulds lived, briefly, a charmed life here and Stephen, with a sure designer's eye, transformed the house into a paean to art deco glamour. It's a bit of a walk from the station, so hop on a bus (126 or 161).

Red House

13 Red House Lane, Bexleyheath, Kent, DA6 8JF (559799, www.nationaltrust.org.uk). Bexleyheath rail then 15min walk or taxi from station. **Open** *Mar-Nov* 11am-2pm Wed-Sun. *Dec* 11am-4.45pm Fri, Sat. **Admission** £6.90; £3.45 reductions; £17.25 family. *Gardens only* 50p. **Credit** MC, V.

This handsome red-brick house was built in 1859 for William Morris, whose Society for the Protection of Ancient Buildings gave rise to the National Trust. In furnishing Red House, Morris sought to combine his taste for Gothic romanticism with the need for practical domesticity. Beautifully detailed stained glass, tiling, paintings and items of furniture remain in the house, and plenty is being uncovered in the continuing restoration work. The new 50p ticket gives access to the garden, tearoom and shop.

▶ *For Morris fans, the William Morris Gallery in Walthamstow may be more accessible; see p142.*

SIGHTS

South-west London

From parks to palaces, rugby to rowing – whatever floats your boat.

Towards the Surrey border, south-west London starts to feel more like a collection of villages than part of a sprawling metropolis. In **Richmond**, **Barnes** and **Wimbledon**, pretty Georgian houses overlook quaint greens and expansive commons where the blessed clichés of Englishness – tea-drinking, cricket – keep hold. **Stockwell** and **Brixton**, however, are more like their south-east London neighbours: diverse, busy and vibrant, despite creeping gentrification. In the middle, **Wandsworth** and **Clapham**

| Hotels p193 | Restaurants & |
| Pubs & bars p240 | cafés p226 |

are well ahead in terms of gentrification: herds of young professionals picnic on the commons at weekends, fill the bars and restaurants, and fall asleep on Egyptian cotton sheets dreaming of a riverside apartment in **Battersea**. London's rich and royal took advantage of the area's leafy proximity long ago, providing a legacy of world-class attractions that includes Kew Gardens, Hampton Court Palace and Richmond Park.

VAUXHALL, STOCKWELL & BRIXTON

Stockwell tube, or Brixton or Vauxhall tube/rail.

The area now known as Vauxhall was, in the 13th century, home to a big house owned by one Falkes de Bréauté, a soldier rewarded for carrying out King John's dirtier military deeds. Over time, Falkes' Hall became Fox Hall and finally Vauxhall. Vauxhall's heyday was in the 18th century when the infamous Pleasure Gardens, built back in 1661, reached the height of their popularity. As described in William Thackeray's *Vanity Fair*, the wealthy mingled here with the not-so-wealthy, getting into all kinds of trouble on 'lovers' walks'.

The Gardens closed in 1859 and the area became reasonably respectable – all that remains is Spring Garden, behind popular gay haunt the Royal Vauxhall Tavern (aka **RVT**; *see p305*). For a glimpse of old Vauxhall head to lovely, leafy **Bonnington Square**. Down on the river is the cream and emerald **ziggurat** designed by Terry Farrell for the Secret Intelligence Service. On the other side of the south end of Vauxhall Bridge stands

St George's Wharf, a glitzy apartment complex that's been justifiably nicknamed the 'five ugly sisters'.

At the top end of the South Lambeth Road, **Little Portugal** – a cluster of Portuguese cafés, shops and tapas bars – is an enticing oasis. At the other end, **Stockwell** is prime commuter territory, with little to lure visitors except some charming Victorian streets: Albert Square, Durand Gardens, Stockwell Park Crescent and Hackford Road – briefly home to Van Gogh (at no.87).

INSIDE TRACK PARK LIFE

Minutes from Brixton's hectic town centre, **Brockwell Park** (Brixton Water Lane, www.brockwellpark.com) is one of London's most underrated green spaces. Landscaped in the early 19th century for a wealthy glass maker, the park contains his Georgian country house – now a café – an open-air swimming pool, bowling green, walled rose garden, miniature railway and, in July, a traditional country fair.

SIGHTS

SIGHTS

South of Stockwell is **Brixton**, a lively hub of clubs and music, with a long-established Afro-Caribbean community. An interesting, often unpredictable area, Brixton has a big, chaotic street market. Its main roads are modern and filled with chain stores, but there's also some attractive architecture – check out the 1911 **Ritzy Cinema** (Brixton Oval, Coldharbour Lane, 0871 704 2065, www.picturehouses.co.uk) – and a regeneration scheme currently under way includes the creation of a new town square. Brixton's best-known street, **Electric Avenue**, was immortalised during the 1980s by Eddy Grant's eponymous song – it got its name when, in 1880, it became one of the first shopping streets to get electric lights. The Clash's 'Guns of Brixton' famously deals with the tensions felt here in the 1980s, but the rage of the persecuted black community, still finding themselves isolated and under suspicion decades after arriving from the West Indies, is expressed by dub poet Linton Kwesi Johnson – try 'Sonny's Lettah (Anti-Sus Poem)' and 'Five Nights of Bleeding' for starters. The riots of 1981 and 1985 around Railton Road and Coldharbour Lane left the district scarred for years.

BATTERSEA

Battersea Park or Clapham Junction rail.

Battersea started life as an island in the Thames, but it was reclaimed when the surrounding marshes were drained. Huguenots settled here from the 16th century and, prior to the Industrial Revolution, the area was mostly farmland. The river is dominated by Sir Giles Gilbert Scott's magnificent four-chimneyed **Battersea Power Station** (www.battersea powerstation.org.uk), which can be seen close up from all trains leaving Victoria station. Images of this iconic building have graced album covers (notably Pink Floyd's *Animals*) and films (among them Ian McKellen's *Richard III* and Michael Radford's *1984*), and its instantly recognisable silhouette pops up repeatedly as you move around the capital. Work started on what was to become the largest brick-built structure in Europe in 1929, and the power station was in operation through to the early 1980s. Too impressive to be destroyed, its future continues to be the subject of intense public debate – the latest plan by Treasury Holdings UK was submitted in October 2009.

Overlooking the river a little further west, **Battersea Park** (www.batterseapark.org) has beautiful lakes (one with a fine Barbara Hepworth sculpture) and gardens. Much of the park was relandscaped in 2004 according to the

Battersea Power Station.

original 19th-century plans, albeit with some modern additions left in place: the Russell Page Garden, designed for the 1951 Festival of Britain; a Peace Pagoda, built by a Buddhist sect in 1985 to commemorate Hiroshima Day; a petting zoo (7924 5826; *see p281*); and an art gallery (the Pumphouse, 7350 0523, www.wandsworth.gov.uk/gallery). The park extends to the Thames; from the wide and lovely riverside walk you can see both the elaborate **Albert Bridge** and the simpler **Battersea Bridge**, rebuilt between 1886 and 1890 by the sewer engineer, Joseph Bazalgette.

Keep on west of the bridges to find the beautiful church of **St Mary's Battersea** (Battersea Church Road); this was where poet William Blake was married and Benedict Arnold, who contrived to fight on both sides during the American War of Independence, is buried. From here, JMW Turner used to paint the river.

CLAPHAM & WANDSWORTH

Clapham Common tube, or Wandsworth Common or Wandsworth Town rail.

In the 18th and 19th centuries, **Clapham** was colonised by the wealthy upper classes and social reformers, notably abolitionist William Wilberforce's Clapham Sect. But the coming of the railways meant that the posh folk upped sticks, and from 1900 the area fell into decline. Nowadays, it is once again one of the capital's more desirable addresses. **Clapham Common** provides an oasis of peace amid busy traffic, with Holy Trinity Church, which dates from 1776, at its perimeter. From Clapham Common station, turn north into **The Pavement** – it leads to the pubs and shops of Clapham Old Town. Alternatively, head south to the smart shops and cafés of **Abbeville Road**. The area to the west of the common is known as 'Nappy Valley', because of the many young middle-class families who reside there. If you can fight your way between baby carriages, head for **Northcote Road** – especially on weekends, when a lovely little market sets up.

PUTNEY & BARNES

East Putney or Putney Bridge tube, or Barnes or Putney rail.

If you want proof of an area's well-to-do credentials, count the rowing clubs: **Putney** has a couple of dozen. **Putney Bridge** is partly responsible, as its buttresses made it difficult for large boats to continue upstream, creating a stretch of water conducive to rowing. The **Oxford & Cambridge Boat Race** (*see p272*) has started in Putney since 1845. The river has good paths in either direction; heading west along the Putney side of the river will take you past the **WWT Wetland Centre** (*see below*), which lies alongside Barnes Common. The main road across the expanse, Queen's Ride, humpbacks over the railway line below. It was here, on 16 September 1977, that singer Gloria Jones's Mini drove off the road, killing her passenger (and boyfriend) T-Rex singer Marc Bolan. The slim trunk of the sycamore tree hit by the car is covered with notes, poems and declarations of love; steps lead to a bronze bust.

★ WWT Wetland Centre
Queen Elizabeth's Walk, Barnes, SW13 9WT (8409 4400, www.wwt.org.uk). Hammersmith tube then 283 bus, Barnes rail or bus 33, 72, 209. **Open** *Mar-June, Sept-Oct* 9.30am-6pm daily. *July-Aug* 9.30am-6pm Mon-Wed; Fri-Sun; 9.30am-9pm Thur. *Nov-Feb* 9.30am-5pm daily. **Admission** £9.50; £5.25-£7.10 reductions; £26.55 family; free under-4s. **Credit** MC, V.
The 43-acre Wildfowl & Wetlands Trust Wetland Centre may be a mere four miles from central London, but it feels like a world away. Quiet ponds, rushes, rustling reeds and wildflower gardens all teem with bird life – some 150 species – as well as

the now very rare water vole (think Ratty from *The Wind in the Willows*). Naturalists ponder its 27,000 trees and 300,000 aquatic plants and swoon over 300 varieties of butterfly, 20 types of dragonfly, and four species of bat, who now have a stylish new house designed by Turner Prize-winning artist Jeremy Deller. You can hire binoculars on site.

KEW & RICHMOND

Kew Gardens or Richmond tube/rail, or Kew Bridge rail.

Kew's big appeal is its vast and glorious **Royal Botanic Gardens** (*see p155*). The **National Archives** – formerly the Public Records Office – are housed here too, a repository for everything from the Domesday Book to recently released government documents. The place is always full of people researching their family trees. Overlooking the gardens is the **Watermans Arts Centre** (40 High Street, TW8 0DS, 8232 1010, www.watermans.org.uk), which contains a gallery, cinema and theatre focusing on Brit-Asian and South Asian arts. Much of Kew has a rarified air, with leafy streets that lead you into a quaint world of teashops, tiny bookstores and gift shops, a sweet village green, ancient pubs and pleasant riverpaths.

Originally known as the Shene, the wealthy area of **Richmond**, about 15 minutes' walk west down Kew Road, has been linked with royalty for centuries: Edward III had a palace here in the 1300s and Henry VII loved the area so much that in 1501 he built another (naming it Richmond after his favourite earldom); this was where Elizabeth I spent her last summers. Ultimately, the whole neighbourhood took the palace's name, although the building itself is long gone – pretty much all that's left is a small gateway on **Richmond Green**. On the east side of the Green, medieval alleys (such as Brewer's Lane) replete with ancient pubs lead to the traffic-choked high street. The **Church**

INSIDE TRACK
KING OF THE HILL

From the top of **Richmond Hill**, breathe in a vista of lush meadowland, munching cows and meandering river that has remained relatively untouched since the 1700s. England's only view to be protected by its own Act of Parliament, it has been immortalised by artists including Turner and Reynolds. On a clear day, Hampton Court Palace (*see p157*) can be spotted in the distance.

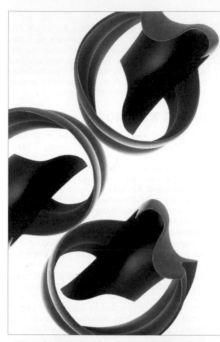

of **St Mary Magdalene**, on Paradise Road, blends architectural styles from 1507 to 1904.

A short walk away in Richmond's Old Town Hall, you'll find the small **Museum of Richmond** (Whittaker Avenue, 8332 1141, www.museumofrichmond.com, closed Mon & Sun). Nearby, the riverside promenade is eminently strollable and dotted with pubs; the **White Cross** (Water Lane, 8940 6844), which has been here since 1835, has a special 'entrance at high tide' – the river floods regularly. The 13 arches of **Richmond Bridge** date from 1774 – this is the oldest surviving crossing over the Thames and offers fine sweeping views.

Richmond Park is the largest of the Royal Parks, occupying some 2,500 acres. There are hundreds of red and fallow deer roaming free across it – presumably much happier without having to listen out for the 'View halloo!' of one of Henry VIII's hunting parties. Within the park's bounds is the Palladian splendour of White Lodge and Pembroke Lodge, childhood home to philosopher Bertrand Russell but now a café. From the park's highest point, there are unobstructed views of St Paul's Cathedral (*see p63*), more than twelve miles in the distance.

★ Royal Botanic Gardens (Kew Gardens)

Kew, Richmond, Surrey, TW9 3AB (8940 1171, www.kew.org). Kew Gardens tube/rail, Kew Bridge rail or riverboat to Kew Pier. **Open** *Apr-Aug* 9.30am-6.30pm Mon-Fri; 9.30am-7.30pm Sat, Sun. *Sept, Oct* 9.30am-6pm daily. *Late Oct early Feb* 9.30am-4.15pm daily, *Early Feb-Mar* 9.30am-5.30pm daily. **Admission** £13; £11 reductions; free under-17s. **Credit** AmEx, MC, V.

Kew's lush, landscaped beauty represents the pinnacle of our national gardening obsession. From the early 1700s until 1840, when the gardens were given to the nation, these were the grounds for two fine royal residences – the White House and Richmond Lodge. Early resident Queen Caroline, wife of George II, was very fond of exotic plants brought back by voyaging botanists. In 1759, the renowned 'Capability' Brown was employed by George III to improve on the work of his predecessors here, William Kent and Charles Bridgeman. Thus began the shape of the extraordinary garden that today attracts hundreds of thousands of visitors each year.

Covering half a square mile, Kew feels surprisingly big – pick up a map at the ticket office and follow the handy signs. Head straight for the 19th-century greenhouses, filled to the roof with plants – some of which have been here as long as the huge glass structures themselves. The sultry Palm House holds tropical plants: palms, bamboo, tamarind, mango and fig trees, not to mention fragrant hibiscus and frangipani. The Temperate House features *Pendiculata sanderina*, the Holy Grail for orchid hunters, with petals some three feet long.

Also worth seeking out are the Princess of Wales Conservatory, divided into ten climate zones; the Marine Display, downstairs from the Palm House (it isn't always open, but when it is you can see the seahorses); the lovely, quiet indoor pond of the Waterlily House (closed in winter); and the Victorian botanical drawings of the Marianne North Gallery, reopened to the public in 2009. For an interesting perspective on 18th-century life, head to Kew Palace (www.hrp.org.uk/KewPalace; £5, free-£4.50 reductions) – Britain's smallest royal palace. On the opposite side of the gardens is the Xstrata Treetop Walkway, a popular addition to the gardens that allows you to walk in the leaf canopy 60ft up.

WIMBLEDON

Wimbledon tube/rail.

Beyond the world-famous tennis tournament, **Wimbledon** is little but a wealthy and genteel suburb. Turn left out of the station on to the uninspiring Broadway, and you'll wonder why you bothered. So turn right instead, climbing a steep hill lined with huge houses. At the top is **Wimbledon Village**, a trendy little enclave of posh shops, eateries and some decent pubs.

From here you can hardly miss **Wimbledon Common**, a huge, wild, partly wooded park, criss-crossed by paths and horse tracks. The

Royal Botanic Gardens.

SIGHTS

windmill (Windmill Road, 8947 2825, www.
wimbledonwindmillmuseum.org.uk) provides
an eccentric touch: Baden-Powell wrote
Scouting for Boys (1910) here; it's now home
to a tearoom and hands-on milling museum.

East of the common lies **Wimbledon Park**,
with its boating lake, and the **All England
Lawn Tennis Club** and **Wimbledon Lawn
Tennis Museum** (*see below*). Two other
attractions are worth seeking out – lovely,
Grade II-listed **Cannizaro Park** (www.
cannizaropark.org.uk) and the gorgeous
Buddhapadipa Temple (14 Calonne Road,
Wimbledon Parkside, 8946 1357, www.
buddhapadipa.org). When it was built in the
early 1980s, this was the only Thai temple in
Europe. The Shrine Room contains a golden
statue of Buddha, a copy of the Buddhasihing
in Bangkok's National Museum.

Wimbledon Lawn Tennis Museum

*Museum Building, All England Lawn Tennis
Club, Church Road, SW19 5AE (8946 6131,
www.wimbledon.org/museum). Southfields tube
or bus 39, 493.* **Open** 10.30am-5pm daily; ticket
holders only during championships. **Admission**
(incl tour) £18; £13-£15.75 reductions; free under-
5s. **Credit** MC, V.
Highlights at this popular museum on the history of
tennis include a 200° cinema screen that allows you
to find out what it's like to play on Centre Court and
a re-creation of a 1980s men's dressing room, complete with a 'ghost' of John McEnroe. Visitors can
also enjoy a behind-the-scenes tour.

FURTHER SOUTH-WEST

*Richmond tube/rail, or Hampton Court or
St Margaret's rail.*

If the water level allows, follow the river from
Richmond west. You could stop at **Petersham**,
home to the **Petersham Nurseries** with its
garden café (Church Lane, off Petersham Road,
8605 3627, www.petershamnurseries.com),
or take in a grand country mansion, perhaps
Ham House (*see below*) or **Marble Hill
House** (*see right*). Next door is the **Orleans
House Gallery** (*see right*).

The river runs on past **Twickenham**, home
to rugby's **Twickenham Stadium** (*see right*),
to **Strawberry Hill** (www.friendsofstrawberry
hill.org), where novelist Horace Walpole's 'little
Gothic castle' is undergoing restoration until
early summer 2010. Several miles further
along the Thames, the river passes beside the
magnificent **Hampton Court Palace** (*see
right*). Few visitors will want to walk this far,
of course – instead take a train from Waterloo
or, for that extra fillip of adventure, a boat.

Ham House

*Ham, Richmond, Surrey, TW10 7RS (8940
1950, www.nationaltrust.org.uk/hamhouse).
Richmond tube/rail then bus 371.* **Open** *Gardens*
mid Feb-mid Dec 11am-5pm Mon-Wed, Sat, Sun;
mid Dec-mid Feb 11am-4pm Mon-Wed, Sat, Sun.
House mid Mar-Nov noon-4pm Mon-Wed, Sat,
Sun.* **Admission** *House & gardens* £9.90; £5.50

Hampton Court Palace.

reductions; £25.30 family; free under-5s. *Gardens only* £3.30; £2.20 reductions; £8.80 family; free under-5s. **Credit** MC, V.

Built in 1610 for one of James I's courtiers, Thomas Vavasour, this lavish red-brick mansion is full of period furnishings, rococo mirrors and ornate tapestries. Detailing is exquisite, down to a table in the dairy with sculpted cows' legs. The restored formal grounds also attract attention: there's a lovely trellised Cherry Garden and some lavender parterres. The tearoom in the old orangery turns out historic dishes (lavender syllabub, for instance) using ingredients from the Kitchen Gardens. Check the website for 400th anniversary events.

▶ *A ferry crosses the river (Feb-Oct, weekends only in winter) to Marble Hill House; see right.*

★ Hampton Court Palace

East Molesey, Surrey, KT8 9AU (0844 482 7777, www.hrp.org.uk). Hampton Court rail, or riverboat from Westminster or Richmond to Hampton Court Pier (Apr-Oct). **Open** *Palace* Apr-Oct 10am-6pm daily; Nov-Mar 10am-4.30pm daily. *Park* dawn-dusk daily. **Admission** *Palace, courtyard, cloister & maze* £14; £7-£11.50 reductions; £38 family; free under-5s. *Maze only* £3.50; £2.50 reductions. *Gardens only* Apr-Oct £4.60; £4 reductions; Nov-Mar free. **Credit** AmEx, MC, V.

It may be a half-hour train ride from central London, but this spectacular palace, once owned by Henry VIII, is well worth the trek. It was built in 1514 by Cardinal Wolsey, the high-flying Lord Chancellor, but Henry liked it so much he seized it for himself in 1528. For the next 200 years it was a focal point of English history: Elizabeth I was imprisoned in a tower by her jealous and fearful elder sister Mary I; Shakespeare gave his first performance to James I in 1604; and, after the Civil War, Oliver Cromwell was so besotted by the building he ditched his puritanical principles and moved in to enjoy its luxuries.

Centuries later, the rosy walls of the palace still dazzle. Its vast size can be daunting, so it's a good idea to take advantage of the guided tours. If you do decide to go it alone, start with Henry VIII's State Apartments, which include the Great Hall, noted for its beautiful stained-glass windows and elaborate religious tapestries; in the Haunted Gallery, the ghost of Catherine Howard – Henry's fifth wife, executed for adultery in 1542 – can reputedly be heard shrieking. The King's Apartments, added in 1689 by Wren, are notable for a splendid mural of Alexander the Great, painted by Antonio Verrio. The Queen's Apartments and Georgian Rooms feature similarly elaborate paintings, chandeliers and tapestries. The Tudor Kitchens are great fun, with their giant cauldrons, fake pies and blood-spattered walls.

More spectacular sights await outside, where the exquisitely landscaped gardens contain superb topiary, peaceful Thames views, a reconstruction of a 16th-century heraldic garden and the famous Hampton Court maze. In summer, there's a music festival and a flower show that rivals that at Chelsea; in winter an ice-skating rink.

Marble Hill House

Richmond Road, Twickenham, Middx, TW1 2NL (8892 5115, www.english-heritage.org.uk). Richmond tube/rail, St Margaret's rail or bus 33, 90, 490, H22, R70. **Open** *Apr-Oct* 10am-2pm Sat; 10am-5pm Sun; group visits Mon-Fri by request. *Nov-Mar* by request. **Admission** £4.40; £2.20-£3.70 reductions; free under-5s. **Credit** MC, V.

King George II spared no expense to win the favour of his mistress, Henrietta Howard. Not only did he build this perfect Palladian house (1724) for his lover, he almost dragged Britain into a war while doing so: by using Honduran mahogany to construct the grand staircase, he managed to spark off a major diplomatic row with Spain. Frankly, it was worth it. Picnic parties are welcome to the grounds here, as are sporty types (there are tennis, putting and cricket facilities). A programme of concerts keeps things busy in the summer, and ferries regularly cross the Thames to Ham House (*see left*).

FREE Orleans House Gallery

Riverside, Twickenham, Middx, TW1 3DJ (8831 6000, www.richmond.gov.uk/orleans_house_gallery). Richmond tube then bus 33, 490, H22, R68, R70, or St Margaret's or Twickenham rail. **Open** *Apr-Sept* 1-5.30pm Tue-Sat; 2-5.30pm Sun. *Oct-Mar* 1-4.30pm Tue-Sat; 2-4.30pm Sun. **Admission** free. **Credit** MC, V.

Secluded in pretty gardens, this Grade I-listed riverside house was constructed in 1710 for James Johnson, Secretary of State for Scotland. It was later named after the Duke of Orleans, Louis-Philippe, who lived in exile here from 1800 until 1817. Though partially demolished in 1926, the building retains James Gibbs's neoclassical Octagon Room, which houses a soothing collection of paintings of the local countryside dating back to the early 1700s. There are also regularly changing temporary exhibitions here and in the nearby Stables Gallery.

World Rugby Museum/ Twickenham Stadium

Twickenham Rugby Stadium, Rugby Road, Twickenham, Middx, TW1 1DZ (8892 8877, www.rfu.com). Hounslow East tube then bus 281, or Twickenham rail. **Open** *Museum* 10am-5pm Tue-Sat; 11am-5pm Sun. *Tours* 10.30am, noon, 1.30pm, 3pm Tue-Sat; 1pm, 3pm Sun. **Admission** £14; £8 reductions; £40 family. **Credit** AmEx, MC, V.

The impressive Twickenham Stadium is the home of English rugby union. Tickets for international matches are extremely hard to come by, but the Museum of Rugby offers some compensation. Tours take in the England dressing room, the players' tunnel and the Royal Box. Memorabilia, selected from some 10,000 pieces, charts the game's development.

SIGHTS

West London

Some of London's oldest money and its newest arrivals.

It's fitting that West London still has
a distinct air of aristocash. This was,
after all, the first of the city's frontiers
to be developed, just outside the City of
Westminster and out of the way of the
westerly smog-carrying winds. Even
today, the elegant Georgian townhouses
of **Holland Park** and **Kensington**
have retained their high status.

Unlike London's north, east and south,
where the posher neighbourhoods are
tucked away in more remote, leafier
suburbs, the smartest parts of the west –
chiefly Fulham, Kensington and Notting
Hill – are conveniently central, while the working-class districts of **Southall**
and **Wembley**, now the first stop for those who've arrived in the country via
Heathrow, are further out.

Hotels p194	**Restaurants &**
Pubs & bars p241	**cafés** p226

Hotels p194   **Restaurants &**
Pubs & bars p241   **cafés** p226

KENSINGTON & HOLLAND PARK

High Street Kensington or Holland Park tube.

There are more millionaires per square mile
in this corner of London than in any other
part of Europe, a hangover from the days
when Kensington was a semi-rural retreat
for aristocrats. Just off **Kensington High
Street**, one of London's smarter mainstream
shopping stretches, an array of handsome
squares are lined with grand 19th-century
houses, many of which still serve as single-
family homes. The houses here are not as
ostentatiously grand as they are in, say,
Belgravia, but nor is the wealth worn as lightly
and subtly it is in many corners of Mayfair.
You're always aware that you're around money.

Linking with Notting Hill (*see p104*) to the
north, **Kensington Church Street** has many
antiques shops selling furniture so fine you
would probably never dare use it. **St Mary
Abbots** (7937 6032, www.stmaryabbotschurch.
org), at the junction of Church Street and High
Street, is a wonderful Victorian neo-Gothic
church, built on the site of the 12th-century
original by Sir George Gilbert Scott between
1869 and 1872. Past worshippers have included
Isaac Newton and William Wilberforce. As well

as beautiful stained-glass windows, it has
London's tallest spire (278 feet).

Across the road is a striking art deco
building, once the department store Barkers
but now taken over by Texan organic food
giant **Whole Foods Market** (nos.63-97,
7368 4500, www.wholefoodsmarket.co.uk).
South down Derry Street, past the entrance
to the **Roof Gardens** – a private members
club and restaurant, which boasts flamingos
and a stream, 100 feet above central London –
is Kensington Square, which boasts one of
London's highest concentrations of blue
plaques. The writer William Thackeray lived
at no.16 and the painter Edward Burne-Jones
at no.41; at no.18, John Stuart Mill's maid made
her bid for 'man from Porlock' status by using
Carlyle's sole manuscript of *The French
Revolution* to start the fire. The houses, though
much altered, date from the development of the
square in 1685, and – hard to believe now –
were surrounded by fields until 1840.

Further to the west is one of London's
finest green spaces: **Holland Park**. Along
its eastern edge, Holland Walk is one of the
most pleasant paths in central London, but
the heart of the park is the Jacobean **Holland
House**. Left derelict after World War II, it
was bought by the London County Council
in 1952; the east wing now houses the city's

best-sited youth hostel (*see p196*). In summer, open-air theatre and opera are staged on the front terrace. Three lovely formal gardens are laid out near the house. A little further west, the Japanese-style **Kyoto Garden** has huge koi carp and a bridge at the foot of a waterfall. Elsewhere, rabbits hop about and peacocks stroll with the confidence of all beautiful creatures. To the south of the park are two more fine historic houses: **Linley Sambourne House**, and, closed for refurbishment until April 2010, **Leighton House** (12 Holland Park Road, W14 8LZ, 7602 3316, www.rbkc.gov.uk/ leightonhousemuseum) with its sternly Victorian red-brick façade.

Linley Sambourne House

18 Stafford Terrace, W8 7BH (7938 1295, www.rbkc.gov.uk/linleysambournehouse). High Street Kensington tube. **Open** *Mar-Dec* by appointment only. **Admission** £6; £1-£4 reductions. **Credit** MC, V. **Map** p396 A9.
The home of cartoonist Edward Linley Sambourne was built in the 1870s and has almost all of its original fittings and furniture. Tours must be booked in advance; they last 90mins, with weekend tours led by an actor in period costume.
▶ *If you enjoy the re-enactment tours here, note that they do something similar at Benjamin Franklin House, see p89.*

EARL'S COURT & FULHAM

Earl's Court, Fulham Broadway or West Brompton tube.

Earl's Court sells itself short, grammatically speaking, since it was once the site of the courthouse of two earls: both the Earl of Warwick and the Earl of Holland. The 1860s saw Earl's Court move from rural hamlet to investment opportunity as the Metropolitan Railway arrived. Some 20 years later it was already much as we see it today, bar the fast food joints. The terraces of grand old houses are mostly subdivided into bedsits and cheap hotels; today, the transient population tends to be Eastern European or South American.

In 1937, the **Earl's Court Exhibition Centre** was built, and in its day was the largest reinforced concrete building in Europe – a phrase that truly makes the heart sing. The centre hosts a year-round calendar of events, from trade shows and pop concerts (Pink Floyd built and tore down *The Wall* here) to the Ideal Home Show. The Exhibition Centre is also close to the new **Metropolitan Police Museum** (*see p181*). Two minutes south down Warwick Road is a tiny venue, with an equally impressive pedigree: the **Troubadour** (263-267 Old Brompton Road, 7370 1434,

SIGHTS

Kensington High Street.

Brompton Cemetery.

www.troubadour.co.uk), a 1950s coffeehouse with a downstairs club that hosted Jimi Hendrix, Joni Mitchell, Bob Dylan and Paul Simon in the 1960s. While it's no longer at the cutting edge, it still delivers a full programme of music, poetry and comedy.

West along Warwick Road are the gates of **Brompton Cemetery**. It's full of magnificent monuments commemorating the famous and infamous, including suffragette Emmeline Pankhurst and, his grave marked by a lion, boxer 'Gentleman' John Jackson – 'Gentleman' John taught Lord Byron to box. The peace and quiet of the cemetery is regularly disturbed at its southern end by neighbouring **Stamford Bridge** (see p331), home of Chelsea FC. **Craven Cottage** (see p331), the home of west London's other Premiership team, Fulham FC, is west of here, at the northern end of the park that surrounds **Fulham Palace**.

★ FREE Fulham Palace & Museum

Bishop's Avenue, off Fulham Palace Road, SW6 6EA (7736 3233, www.fulhampalace.org). Putney Bridge tube or bus 14, 74, 220, 414, 430. **Open** *Museum & gallery* noon-4pm Mon, Tue; 11am-2pm Sat; 11.30am-3.30pm Sun. *Gardens* dawn-dusk daily. *Tours* 2pm 2nd & 4th Sun of mth. **Admission** free; under-16s must be accompanied by an adult. *Tours* £5; free under-16s. **No credit cards.**

Fulham Palace was the episcopal retreat of the Bishops of London. The present building was built in Tudor times, with later significant Georgian and Victorian additions. It would be more accurate to call it a manor house than a palace, but it gives a fine glimpse into the changing lifestyles and architecture of nearly 500 years, from the Tudor hall to the splendid Victorian chapel; try out the echo in the courtyard. There's also access to a glorious stretch of riverside walk. Best of all, these delights still seem largely undiscovered by the majority of Londoners.
▶ *The Drawing Room Café has outdoor tables looking out over an expansive lawn.*

FREE Metropolitan Police Museum

Ground floor of the Empress State Building, Empress Approach, Lillie Road, Earl's Court, SW6 1TR (7161 1234, www.met.police.uk). West Brompton tube/rail. **Open** 10am-4pm Mon-Fri. **Admission** free. **No credit cards.** *See p162* **Police Tactics.**

SHEPHERD'S BUSH

Goldhawk Road or Shepherd's Bush Market tube, or Shepherd's Bush tube/rail.

Shepherd's Bush was once west London's impoverished backwater, the setting for junkyard sitcom *Steptoe & Son*. Now, a couple of decades after house prices started going through the roof, there's visible evidence of gentrification. **Queens Park Rangers** (see p331), the underperforming local football team, has benefited from a huge cash injection from three of the world's richest businessmen, while Shepherd's Bush got a similar boost from the gargantuan **Westfield London** shopping mall (see p245). The **Bush Theatre** (see p345) stages excellent leftfield drama, while **Bush Hall** (see p316), a beautifully restored former snooker hall, and the **O2 Shepherd's Bush Empire** (see p314), an old BBC theatre, have become essential destinations on the music scene. The bar at the **K West** hotel (Richmond Way, W14 OAX, 8008 6600, www.k-west.co.uk) is the place to spot trendy young American bands after they've played at the Shepherd's Bush Empire.

BBC Television Centre

TV Centre, Wood Lane, W12 7RJ (0370 603 0304, www.bbc.co.uk/tours). Wood Lane or White City tube. **Open** by appointment only Mon-Sat. **Admission** £9.50; £8.50 reductions; £7 10-16s, students; £27 family. No under-9s. **Credit** MC, V.

Half a mile north of Shepherd's Bush Green is the BBC TV Centre where, if you book in advance, you can catch a fascinating tour around the temple of British televisual history. Tours include visits to the news desk, the TV studios and the Weather Centre, though children and *Doctor Who* fans might be most excited about the TARDIS on display. Also, if you fancy being part of a BBC television show audience, you can apply for free tickets online at www.bbc.co.uk/whatson.tickets.

HAMMERSMITH

Hammersmith tube.

Dominated by the grey concrete of its flyover, the centre point of Hammersmith is **Hammersmith Broadway**, once a grotty bus garage, now a shiny new shopping mall.

INSIDE TRACK
TRAINSPOTTING IN ACTON

Transport boffins and design classic fans take note: the **London Transport Museum** is now opening its Acton depot to visitors on a few weekends a year. The warehouse contains over 370,000 objects that wouldn't fit into the Covent Garden museum (see p87), including vehicles – a 1950s Routemaster bus prototype among them – and vintage posters and uniforms. See www.ltmuseum.co.uk for details.

Police Tactics

Will the Metropolitan Police Museum transform our view of the city's finest?

In summer 2009, the **Metropolitan Police Museum** (*see p161*) opened in the lobby of their recruiting centre in West Brompton. Since this was the year in which the Met were accused of unnecessary brutality in policing the G20 protests, you can't help thinking a bit of good PR was much needed. Although only a fraction of the force's store of 15,000 historical exhibits is displayed, with half-a-dozen cases available to tell the story of 180 years of London policing, what is on show is certainly interesting: the 100 items range from 19th-century cutlasses to the uniform that Jack Warner wore in the BBC series *Dixon of Dock Green*.

Ghouls will be disappointed: this is not the notorious Black Museum – officially now the Crime Museum (www.met.police.uk/history/crime_museum.htm) to avoid sensitivities about racism – in which

evidence, including countless murder devices, has been stored for instructional purposes since 1874. The Black Museum isn't open to the public, so the nearest you'll get to a visit is to read *Time Out London*'s feature on it: search for 'Black Museum' at www.timeout.com/london. Though, as *Time Out* writer Peter Watts noted: 'the Crime Museum… is one of the most depressing places I have ever been. There is nothing to be gained from seeing this sort of stuff.'

Instead, you're better off either coming here or waiting to see whether a plan, supported by Mayor Boris Johnson, to create an ambitious Blue Light Museum comes to fruition. Bringing together artefacts from the fire brigade, police and ambulance services, it could come to rival the **London Transport Museum** (*see p87*) in significance.

Make it over the road and you'll find the **HMV Hammersmith Apollo** (*see p314*). Opened in 1932 as the Gaumont Palace, it entered rock legend as the Hammersmith Odeon, hosting pivotal gigs by the Beatles, Motörhead and Public Enemy.

Hammersmith Bridge, the city's oldest suspension bridge, is a green and gold hymn to the strength of Victorian ironwork. There's a lovely walk west along the Thames Path from here that takes in a clutch of historic pubs including the **Blue Anchor** (13 Lower Mall, W6 9DJ, 8748 5774); head in the opposite direction for the **Riverside Studios** arts centre (Crisp Road, W6 9RL, 8237 1111, www.riversidestudios.co.uk).

CHISWICK

Turnham Green tube or Chiswick rail.

Once a sleepy, semi-rural suburb, Chiswick is now one of London's swankiest postcodes, its residents including broadcasters, directors, actors, advertising bods and a smattering of rock 'n' roll royalty. In recent years, **Chiswick High Road**, its main thoroughfare, has developed a gastronomic reputation, with dozens of high-end eateries.

Chiswick also has a surprising number of sightseeing attractions. **Chiswick Mall** is a beautiful residential path that runs alongside the river from Hammersmith, and includes **Kelmscott House** (26 Upper Mall, 8741 3735, www.morrissociety.org), once home to pioneering socialist William Morris but now a private house that opens to the public 2-5pm on Thursdays and Saturdays. From here, it's a short walk to **Fuller's Brewery** and **Hogarth's House**, while the **Kew Bridge Steam Museum** and the **Musical Museum** are only a bus ride away; for all, *see below*. It's possible to return to the river path after visiting **Chiswick House** (*see below*), and the wonderful **Royal Botanic Gardens** at Kew (*see p155*) are just over the bridge. Further upstream is **Syon House** (*see p164*), with enough attractions to fill most of a day – among them the **Tropical Forest** animal sanctuary (8847 4730, www.tropicalforest.co.uk, £4.50-£5.50).

Chiswick House

Burlington Lane, W4 2RP (8995 0508, www.chgt.org.uk). Hammersmith tube then bus 190, or Chiswick rail. **Open** *Apr-Oct* 10am-5pm Mon-Wed, Sun. **Admission** £4.40; £3.70 reductions; £2.20 5-16s; free under-5s. **Credit** MC, V.
Richard Boyle, third Earl of Burlington, designed this lovely Palladian villa in 1725 as a place to entertain the artistic and philosophical luminaries of

his day. The Chiswick House & Gardens Trust aims to restore the gardens to Burlington's original design. The restoration will be helped by details from the newly acquired painting *A View of Chiswick House from the South-west* by Dutch landscape artist Pieter Andreas Rysbrack (c1685-1748).

Fuller's Brewery

Griffin Brewery, Chiswick Lane South, W4 2QB (8996 2000, www.fullers.co.uk). Turnham Green tube. **Open** *Tours* hourly 11am-3pm Mon-Fri, by appointment only. *Shop* 10am-8pm Mon-Fri. **Admission** (incl tasting session) £10; £8 reductions. **Credit** MC, V.
Fuller Smith & Turner PLC are London's last family-run brewery. Most of this current building dates back to 1845 but there's been a brewery on this site since Elizabethan times. The two-hour tours need to be booked in advance, but – surprise – there is a pub next door if you can't get on a tour.
▶ *London Pride and ESB are the most popular Fuller's brews, available in pubs across London. For more on good beer, see pp227-241.*

FREE Hogarth's House

Hogarth Lane, Great West Road, W4 2QN (8994 6757). Turnham Green tube or Chiswick rail. **Open** *Apr-Oct* 1-5pm Tue-Fri; 1-6pm Sat, Sun. *Nov, Dec, Feb, Mar1* 1pm Tue Fri; 1 5pm Sat, Sun. **Admission** free; donations appreciated. **No credit cards**.
Recently reopened after a refurbishment, this is the country retreat of the 18th-century painter, engraver and social commentator William Hogarth. On display are most of his engravings, including *Gin Lane*, *Marriage à la Mode* and a copy of *Rake's Progress*.

★ Kew Bridge Steam Museum

Green Dragon Lane, Kew, Surrey, TW8 0EN (8568 4757, www.kbsm.org). Gunnersbury tube/rail or Kew Bridge rail. **Open** 11am-4pm Tue-Sun. **Admission** £9.50; £8.50 reductions; free under-15s. **Credit** MC, V.
One of London's most engaging small museums, this impressive old Victorian pumping station is a reminder that steam wasn't just used for powering trains but also for supplying enough water to the citizens of an expanding London. It's now home to an extraordinary collection of different engines. There are lots of hands-on exhibits for kids, a great dressing-up box and even a miniature steam train.

★ Musical Museum

399 High Street, Kew, Surrey, TW8 0DU (8560 8108, www.musicalmuseum.co.uk). Kew Bridge rail or bus 65, 237, 267. **Open** 11am-5.30pm (last admission 4.30pm) Tue-Sun. **Admission** £8; £6.50 reductions, accompanied under-16s free. **Credit** MC, V.
This recently refurbished museum, housed in a converted church, contains one of the world's foremost

collections of automatic instruments. From tiny Swiss musical boxes to the self-playing Mighty Wurlitzer, the collection embraces an impressive array of sophisticated pianolas, cranky barrel organs, spooky orchestrions, residence organs and violin players, as well as over 30,000 piano rolls.

Syon House

Syon Park, Brentford, Middx, TW8 8JF (8560 0883, www.syonpark.co.uk). Gunnersbury tube/rail then 237, 267 bus. **Open** *House* (mid Mar-Oct only) 11am-5pm Wed, Thur, Sun. *Gardens* (all year) 10.30am-dusk daily. *Tours* by arrangement. **Admission** *House & gardens* £9; £4-£8 reductions; £20 family. *Gardens only* £4.50; £3.50 reductions; £10 family. *Tours* free. **Credit** MC, V.

The Percys, Dukes of Northumberland, were once known as 'the Kings of the North'. Their old house is on the site of a Bridgettine convent, suppressed by Henry VIII in 1534. The building was converted into a house in 1547 for the Duke of Northumberland, its neoclassical interior created by Robert Adam in 1761; there's an outstanding range of Regency portraits by the likes of Gainsborough. The gardens, by Capability Brown, are enhanced by the splendid Great Conservatory and in winter you can take an evening walk through illuminated woodland.

SOUTHALL

Southall rail.

Immigrants used to enter London via the docks and settle in the East End. Now, though, they come via Heathrow and settle here: thus a huge arc of suburban west London – **Hounslow**, **Hayes**, **Southall**, **Harrow**, **Wembley**, **Neasden** – has become home to Europe's biggest South Asian population.

Southall is Britain's best-established immigrant community. From the 1950s onwards, Punjabi Sikhs flocked to the area

INSIDE TRACK
THOMAS HARRIOT

In 1609, Thomas Harriot became the first man to study the moon through a telescope at **Syon House** (*see above*). Because he never published his work, Galileo grabbed the glory, but perhaps Harriot didn't mind: he had already sailed to the New World, learnt Algonquin, written the first English-language publication on the Americas, developed a symbolic notation for algebra (still taught in schools) and conducted a binary number system similar to that used in digital devices today.

to work at the Wolf Rubber Factory and in London Transport; the area soon developed a thriving Asian infrastructure of restaurants, shops and wholesalers that attracted Hindus, Muslims, Tamils, Indian Christians and, more recently, Somalis and Afghans. Take a 607 bus from Shepherd's Bush or a Great Western train from Paddington and, on arrival in Southall, you'll think you're in downtown Delhi – all pounding Bollywood hits, sari fabrics, pungent spices and freshly fried samosas.

Southall Broadway is well worth a visit if only to gawp at **Southall Market**, a unique mix of rural India and cockney London, which until 2007 sold squawking poultry and horses. It still does a brisk trade in general bric-a-brac on Friday and, on Saturday, pretty much everything else. Very difference but, in its own way, equally worthy of diversion is the programme of movies at the three-screen **Himalaya Palace** (14 South Road, 8813 8844), a beautifully restored old movie house dedicated to Bollywood epics.

But it's the food that makes Southall really special; for more, *see p224* **Inside Track**. There's even a Punjabi pub, the **Glassy Junction** (97 South Road, 8574 1626): all the trappings of a white working men's club – patterned carpet, keg beer – plus the considerable boon of hot parathas. It's said to be the only pub in the UK that accepts payment in rupees.

A short walk south of Southall railway station, the **Gurdwara Sri Guru Singh Sabha Southall** (Havelock Road, 8574 4311, www.sgsss.org) is the largest Sikh place of worship outside India. Its golden dome is visible from the London Eye in the east and Windsor Castle to the west; it also provides vegetarian food free to all visitors from the *langar*, or communal kitchen. Non-Sikh visitors are welcome but must take off their shoes before entering, and women must wear a headscarf (they're provided, should you not have one to hand). Enthroned within is the Guru Granth Sahib, the Sikh scripture and supreme spiritual authority of Sikhism.

The suburb of Neasden, six miles north-east of Southall, has its own claim to British Asian fame: the **Shri Swaminarayan Mandir** (105-119 Brentfield Road, 8965 2651, www. mandir.org), the largest Hindu temple outside India to have been built using traditional methods. To this end, nearly 5,000 tons of stone and marble were shipped out to India, where craftsmen carved it into the intricate designs that make up the temple. Then the temple was shipped, piece by piece, to England, where it was assembled on site. The shining marble temple stands incongruously close to one of IKEA's giant blue boxes.

Consume

Modern Pantry. *See p201.*

Hotels	**166**
Pushing the Boundary	186
Playing House	195
Restaurants & Cafés	**197**
Eating In…	198
…and Eating Out	199
Do You Want to Know	
a Secret?	212
The Art of Cooking	217
Pubs & Bars	**227**
In the Mix	237
Profile Sambrook's Brewery	238
Shops & Services	**242**
Where to Shop	243
Top of the Shops	252
Streets Ahead	262

Hotels

A tough year for London's hotels has been a busy one for new openings.

London's hotels have weathered the recession pretty well. Along with a crop of new openings (**Bermondsey Square**, a new **Apex**, Terence Conran's **Boundary**), a number of hotels have presented major upgrades: **Hazlitt's** has added flamboyant new suites, while the **Connaught** moved into a new wing with a pool.

Even so, price is more of a concern than ever. Significantly, both **Dean Street** and **Sanctum** chose to launch with talk of 'crash pads' – their tiniest rooms, offered at lower-than-expected rates. The arrival of hip new B&B options (**Rough Luxe**, **40 Winks**) speaks to the same need.

Big 2010 openings include the refurbished **Savoy** (www.the-savoy.com) and, right on Leicester Square, a **W Hotel** (www.starwoodhotels.com) and the first foray of the **St John** restaurant (*see p203*) into overnight accommodation. Looking a little further ahead, Kit Kemp's **Firmdale** group have acquired property in Soho's Ham Yard for eventual redevelopment. The biggest opening this year, though, will be the giant **Park Plaza Westminster Bridge**: it's set to be the largest new-build hotel in London for 40 years.

STAYING IN LONDON

Hotels in this chapter are classified by the average price of a double room. You can expect to pay more than £300 a night for hotels in the **Deluxe** category, £200-£300 for **Expensive** hotels, £100-£200 for **Moderate** properties and under £100 a night for hotels listed as **Budget**.

The rates we've listed are only for guidance. The variation within these room rates, top to bottom and over the course of the year, can be huge. As a rule, book as far ahead as possible, and always try hotels' own websites first: many offer special online deals throughout the year.

If you can't book ahead, websites such as **www.alpharooms.com**, **www.hotels.com**, **www.expedia.co.uk**, **www.london-discount-hotel.com** and the like may offer keen rates for short-notice bookings, assuming the property in question isn't already fully booked. In addition, the obliging staff at **Visit London** (1 Lower Regent Street, 0870 156 6366, www.visitlondon.com) can look for a room within your selected price range and neighbourhood for free. In general, the geography of London gives some guidance as to the price and type of lodging you're likely to find in a particular part of town. Many of the city's swankier hotels are found in Mayfair (W1), for example, whereas Bloomsbury (WC1) is good for mid-priced hotels and B&Bs. If you're looking for a cheap hotel, try Ebury Street in Victoria (SW1) or Gower Street in Bloomsbury (WC1), as well as Earl's Court (SW5), Bayswater (W2), Paddington (W2) and South Kensington (SW7).

Room rates in this chapter include VAT (sales tax). However, be aware that not all hotels include VAT in the rates they quote – always check before committing to the price. And watch out for added extras that you might otherwise assume to be free. Breakfast can cost around £20, as can internet access, while parking can cost more than £40. We've listed the prices of some extras in this chapter, but again, always check before signing up.

> ❶ Red numbers given in this chapter correspond to the location of each hotel on the street maps. See pp394-407.

At the end of each review, we've listed a selection of services offered by each hotel: restaurants and bars, internet access, spas and the like. The hotel may offer additional services, too: call the hotel or check its website if you're after something specific and unusual. If you're bringing a car to the city (not recommended), always check with the hotel before you arrive: few central hotels offer parking, and those that do tend to charge the earth for it.

In addition to the standard services, note that hotel concierges can often help with additional services: theatre tickets, dinner reservations, babysitters and so on. We've also tried to indicate which hotels offer rooms adapted for disabled customers, but it's always best to confirm the precise facilities with each place before you travel. **Tourism for All** (0845 124 9971, www.tourismforall.org.uk) has details of wheelchair-accessible places.

THE SOUTH BANK & BANKSIDE

Moderate

All Seasons London Southwark Rose
47 Southwark Bridge Road, SE1 9HH (7015 1480, www.southwarkrosehotel.co.uk). London Bridge tube/rail. **Rates** £95-£180 double. **Rooms** 84. **Credit** AmEx, MC, V. **Map** p404 P8 ❶
Just a minute's walk away from Tate Modern and Shakespeare's Globe, this link in the All Seasons chain takes its name from London's most historic theatre, scene of the Bard's earliest productions. The outfit is run on businesslike, rather than classical lines, however. Its rooms are plainly uniform and the look is unadventurously modern, but crisp and clean. The lobby is spacious and impressive, with its gleaming aluminium fittings and walls hung with the work of Japanese photographer Mayumi. Fully

CONSUME

Bermondsey Square Hotel. *See p169.*

Before you book your **London hotel** check the **London Hotelmap™** at LondonTown.com

Visually compare best hotel rates and availability

London's hotels all on one map

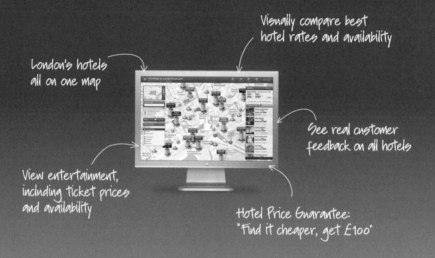

See real customer feedback on all hotels

View entertainment, including ticket prices and availability

Hotel Price Guarantee: "Find it cheaper, get £100"

www.londontown.com/hotels

wired up (for a price in the rooms, although internet access in the restaurant is free), there are even electric blackout blinds. Guests can use the next-door Novotel's gym.

Bar/café. Disabled-adapted rooms. Gym. Internet: wireless (£10/day). Parking: £16/day. Restaurant. Smoking rooms. TV: pay movies.

Bermondsey Square Hotel

Bermondsey Square, Tower Bridge Road, SE1 3UN (0870 111 2525, www.bespokehotels.com). Borough tube or London Bridge tube/rail. **Rates** £109-£169 double. **Rooms** 79. **Credit** AmEx, MC, V. **Map** p405 Q10 **②**

This is a deliberately kitsch new-build on a newly developed square. Suites are named after the heroines of psychedelic rock classics (Lucy, Lily and so on), there are classic discs on the walls, and you can kick your heels from the suspended Bubble Chair at reception. But, although occupants of the Lucy suite get a multi-person jacuzzi (with a great terrace view), and anyone can get sex toys from reception, the real draw isn't the gimmicks – it's well-designed rooms for competitive prices. The Brit food restaurant-bar is a bit hit-or-miss, but the hotel's pretty staff are happy and helpful. *Photos p167.*

Bar/café. Conference facilities. Internet: wireless (free). Restaurant. TV: DVD.

Park Plaza County Hall

1 Addington Street, SE1 7RY (7021 1800, www.parkplaza.com). Waterloo tube/rail. **Rates** £120-£200 double. **Rooms** 398. **Credit** MC, V. **Map** p401 M9 **③**

Approach along the grubby streets from Lambeth North and you'll wonder why we've brought you here, but this is an enthusiastically – if somewhat haphazardly – run new-build. Each room has its own kitchenette with microwave and sink, and room sizes aren't bad across the price range (the floor-to-ceiling windows help them feel bigger). There's a handsomely vertiginous atrium, enabling you to peer down into the central restaurant from the frustratingly infrequent glass lifts, and the ground-floor bar is buzzy with business types after work. The gargantuan Park Plaza Westminster Bridge (200 Westminster Bridge Road, SE1 7UT) is due to open in spring 2010 right in front of the County Hall one.

Bars/cafés (2). Concierge. Conference facilities. Disabled-adapted rooms. Gym. Internet: wireless (£7.95/day). Parking: paid. Restaurant. Room service. Spa facilities. TV: pay movies.

Premier Inn London County Hall

County Hall, Belvedere Road, SE1 7PB (0870 238 3300, www.premierinn.com). Waterloo tube/rail. **Rates** £109-£119 double. **Rooms** 316. **Credit** AmEx, DC, MC, V. **Map** p401 M8 **④**

Its position right by the London Eye, the Thames, Westminster Bridge and Waterloo Station is a gift for out-of-towners on a bargain weekend break.

Extra points are garnered for its friendly and efficient staff, making this newly refurbished branch of the Premier Travel chain the acceptable face of budget convenience. Check-in is quick and pleasant; rooms are spacious, clean and warm with comfortable beds and decent bathrooms with very good showers. Breakfast, a buffet-style affair in a comfortable dining room, is extra but provides ballast for a day of sightseeing/shopping, or indeed meetings. But given the daily cost of the Wi-Fi, you're better off leaving the work at home.

Bars/café. Disabled-adapted rooms. Internet: wireless (£10/day). Restaurant. TV.

THE CITY
Deluxe

Andaz Liverpool Street

40 Liverpool Street, EC2M 7QN (7961 1234, www.london.liverpoolstreet.andaz.com). Liverpool Street tube/rail. **Rates** £245-£605 double. **Rooms** 267. **Credit** AmEx, DC, MC, V. **Map** p405 R6 **⑤**

A faded railway hotel until its £70m Conran overhaul in 2000, the red-brick Great Eastern became in 2007 the first of Hyatt's new Andaz portfolio. The new approach means out with gimmicky menus, closet-sized minibars and even the lobby reception desk, and in with down-to-earth, well-informed service and eco-friendliness. The bedrooms still wear style-mag uniform – Eames chairs, Frette linens – but free services (local calls, wireless internet, healthy minibar) and savvy efforts to connect with the vibey local area are appreciated: witness the

---

INSIDE TRACK
CHAIN YOUR MIND

Chain hotels aren't covered in this section, unless they're new, especially well located (**Premier Inn County Hall**; *see left*) or otherwise unusually praiseworthy. This is simply because the internal logic of chain hotels is that one should be as similar as possible to another, with reliability the main virtue. Of the chains, you can find double rooms for around £100 at **EasyHotel** (www.easyhotel.com), **Express by Holiday Inn** (www.ichotels group.com), **Ibis** (www.ibishotel.com), **Travelodge** (www.travelodge.co.uk); Ibis is perhaps the most appealing of them.

If you've got an awkward departure time from Gatwick or Heathrow, consider the neat and funky 'pod' rooms at the airports' **Yotels** (www.yotel.com). Rates start at £58 a night (they're charged hourly after an initial four hours).

CONSUME

Summer Garden, temporarily installed at the base of the breathtaking atrium as a place to lounge over cocktails or enjoy the Designer Jumble Sale, and entertainment in the hotel's wonderfully gothic Freemasons' Temple.

Bars/cafés (5). Business centre. Concierge. Disabled-adapted rooms. Gym. Internet: wireless & high-speed (free). Restaurants (5). Room service. Smoking rooms. TV.

Expensive

Threadneedles
5 Threadneedle Street, EC2R 8AY (7657 8080, www.theetoncollection.com). Bank tube/DLR. **Rates** £206-£394 double. **Rooms** 69. **Credit** AmEx, MC, V. **Map** p405 Q6 ⑥

Threadneedles boldly slots some contemporary style into a fusty old dame of a building, formerly the grand Victorian HQ of the Midland Bank, bang next to the Bank of England and the Royal Exchange. The etched glass-domed rotunda of the lobby soars on columns over an artful array of designer furniture and shelving that looks like the dreamchild of some powerful graphics software. The bedrooms too are individual, coherent and soothing examples of City-boy chic, in muted beige and textured tones, with limestone bathrooms and odd views of local landmarks: St Paul's, Tower 42 and the Lloyds building.

Bar/café. Concierge. Disabled-adapted rooms. Internet: wireless (£20/day). Restaurant. Room service. TV: pay movies.

Moderate

Apex City of London Hotel
1 Seething Lane, EC3N 4AX (7702 2020, www.apexhotels.co.uk). Tower Hill tube. **Rates** £130-£311 double. **Rooms** 130. **Credit** AmEx, MC, V. **Map** p405 R7 ⑦

Part of a small chain, this dark-toned, modern business hotel on the delightfully named Seething Lane has built a deservedly good reputation – so much so, they opened a new wing overlooking St Olave's church. This also improved the public areas, opening up a handy lounging area to the right of reception where wireless-enabled laptops can be cracked. Staff members are accommodating, room details are obliging (pillow menu, rubber duck in the bathroom, big flatscreen DVDs) and rates can be impressive (especially at weekends or in the surprisingly spacious basement rooms, which have little external light). Above all, the location is terrific – a block from the Tower of London (*see p74*), you're only a stroll from all the City's sights. A new, smaller Apex (7/9 Copthall Avenue, EC2R 7NJ) opened near the Bank of England as we went to press.

Bar/café. Disabled-adapted rooms. Gym. Internet: wireless (free). Restaurant. Room service. Smoking rooms. TV: DVD.

HOLBORN & CLERKENWELL
Expensive

★ Malmaison
Charterhouse Square, EC1M 6AH (7012 3700, www.malmaison.com). Barbican tube/rail. **Rates** £235 double. **Rooms** 97. **Credit** AmEx, DC, MC, V. **Map** p402 O5 ⑧

Malmaison is impressively located, looking out on a lovely cobbled square on the edge of the square mile, near the bars, clubs and better restaurants of the East End. This being design-conscious Clerkenwell, it's no surprise that the decor throughout makes a cool statement (note the Veuve Cliquot ice buckets built into the love seats at reception). The rooms overlooking the square are the pick of the bunch, with the best of the views and morning sunshine that pours through large sash windows on to big, white firm beds. Gripes? Charging for internet access after 30 minutes and the slightly frosty front desk staff – though, to be fair, any stiffness may be offset by the smiley service downstairs in the lovely basement brasserie.

Bars/cafés (2). Disabled-adapted rooms. Gym. Internet: wireless (£10/day). Parking: £20/day. Restaurant. Room service. TV.

★ Rookery
12 Peter's Lane, Cowcross Street, Clerkenwell, EC1M 6DS (7336 0931, www.rookeryhotel.com). Farringdon tube/rail. **Rates** £253 double. **Rooms** 33. **Credit** AmEx, DC, MC, V. **Map** p402 O5 ⑨

Sister hotel to Hazlitt's (*see p177*), the Rookery has long been something of a celebrity hideaway deep in Clerkenwell. Its front door is satisfyingly hard to find, especially when the streets around are teeming with Fabric (*see p323*) devotees; the front rooms can be noisy on these nights. Once inside, guests enjoy an atmospheric warren of creaky rooms, each individually decorated in the style of a Georgian town house: huge clawfoot baths, elegant four-posters and an honesty bar in the drawing room. The ground-floor suite has its own hallway, a cosy boudoir and a subterranean bathroom. Topping it all is the huge split-level Rook's Nest suite, which has views of St Paul's Cathedral (*see p63*).

Bar/café. Concierge. Internet: wireless (free). Room service. TV: DVD.

INSIDE TRACK ONE OF A KIND

If you want to stay at Hampton Court (*see p157*) or in poet John Betjeman's Georgian City house, head to the **Landmark Trust** website (www.landmarktrust.org.uk). The Trust has been restoring such notable old buildings as holiday lets since 1965.

Zetter

86-88 Clerkenwell Road, EC1M 5RJ (7324 4444, www.thezetter.com). Farringdon tube/rail. **Rates** £170-£399 double. **Rooms** 59. **Credit** AmEx, MC, V. **Map** p402 O4 ⑩

Zetter is a fun, laid-back, modern hotel with some interesting design notes. There's a refreshing lack of attitude and a forward-looking approach, with friendly staff and firm eco-credentials (such as occupancy detection systems in the bedrooms). The rooms, stacked up on five galleried storeys overlooking the intimate bar area, are smoothly functional, but cosied up with choice home comforts like hot-water bottles and old Penguin paperbacks, as well as having walk-in showers with Elemis smellies. The hotel keeps popular with not-quite-young creatives through regular art and music events, such as an exhibition of Rob Ryan's paper-cuts.
Bar/café. Concierge. Conference facilities. Disabled-adapted rooms. Internet: wireless (free). Restaurant. Room service. TV: DVD & pay movies.

Moderate

★ Fox & Anchor

115 Charterhouse Street, EC1M 6AA (0845 347 0100, www.foxandanchor.com). Barbican tube or Farringdon tube/rail. **Rates** £112-£280 double. **Rooms** 6. **Credit** AmEx, DC, MC, V. **Map** p402 O5 ⑪

Check in at the handsome attached boozer (*see p228*) and you'll be pointed to the separate front entrance, with lovely floor mosaic, and a handful of well-appointed, atmospheric and surprisingly luxurious rooms. Each of them is different, but the high-spec facilities (big flatscreen TV, clawfoot bath and drench shower) and quirky attention to detail (bottles of ale in the minibar, the 'Nursing hangover' signs to hang out for privacy) are common throughout. Expect some clanking noise in the early mornings, but proximity to the historic Smithfield meat market also means you get a feisty fry-up in the morning in the pub.
Bar/café. Internet: high-speed (free). Restaurant. TV: DVD.

BLOOMSBURY & FITZROVIA

Deluxe

Charlotte Street Hotel

15-17 Charlotte Street, W1T 1RJ (7806 2000, www.firmdale.com). Goodge Street or Tottenham Court Road tube. **Rates** £253-£357 double. **Rooms** 52. **Credit** AmEx, DC, MC, V. **Map** p399 K5 ⑫

Now a fine exponent of Kit Kemp's much imitated fusion of flowery English and avant-garde, this gorgeous hotel was once a dental hospital. Public rooms have genuine Bloomsbury Set paintings, by the likes

Fox & Anchor.

CONSUME

of Duncan Grant and Vanessa Bell, while bedrooms mix English understatement with bold flourishes: soft beiges and greys spiced up with plaid-floral combinations. The huge, comfortable beds and trademark polished granite and oak bathrooms are suitably indulgent, and some rooms have unbelievably high ceilings. The Oscar restaurant and bar are classy and always busy with a smart crowd from the area's media and ad offices. On Sundays, combine a three-course set meal with a classic film screened in the mini-cinema.
Bar/café. Concierge. Disabled-adapted rooms. Gym. Internet: wireless & high-speed (£20/day). Restaurant. Room service. Smoking rooms. TV: DVD.

Sanderson

50 Berners Street, W1T 3NG (7300 1400, www.morganshotelgroup.com). Oxford Circus tube. **Rates** £235-£470 double. **Rooms** 150. **Credit** AmEx, DC, MC, V. **Map** p406 V1 ⑬
No designer flash in the pan, the Sanderson remains a statement hotel, a Schrager/Starck creation that takes clinical chic in the bedrooms to new heights. Colour is generally conspicuous by its absence from many of the rooms. The design throughout is all flowing white net drapes, gleaming glass cabinets and retractable screens. The residents-only Purple Bar sports a button-backed purple leather ceiling and fabulous cocktails; in particular, try the Vesper. The 'billiard room' has a purple-topped pool table, surrounded by strange tribal adaptations of classic dining room furniture.
Bars/cafés (2). Business centre. Concierge. Disabled-adapted rooms. Gym. Internet: wireless & high-speed (£15/day). Parking: £15/day. Restaurant. Room service. Spa facilities. TV: DVD.

Expensive

Myhotel Bloomsbury (11-13 Bayley Street, WC1B 3HD, 7667 6000, www.myhotels.co.uk) is a grown-up, urban brother to Myhotel Chelsea (*see p187*), giving the trademark Asian touches a masculine, minimalist twist.

Academy Hotel

21 Gower Street, WC1E 6HG (7631 4115, www.theetoncollection.com). Goodge Street tube. **Rates** £230-£345 double. **Rooms** 49. **Credit** AmEx, DC, MC, V. **Map** p399 K5 ⑭
One of a family of seven glamorous chics in the Eton Collection, the Academy goes for the country intellectual look to suit Bloomsbury's studious yet decadent history. It's made up of five Georgian town houses, and provides in all its rooms a tranquil generosity of space that's echoed in the Georgian squares sitting serenely between the trafficky rush of Gower Street and Tottenham Court Road. There's a restrained country-house style in the summery florals and

---

checks and a breath of sophistication in the handsome, more plainly furnished suites. The library and conservatory open on to fragrant walled gardens where drinks and breakfast are served in summer.
Bars/cafés (2). Internet: wireless & high-speed (£6.50/hr, £12/day). Room service. TV.

Moderate

Harlingford Hotel

61-63 Cartwright Gardens, WC1H 9EL (7387 1551, www.harlingfordhotel.com). Russell Square tube or Euston tube/rail. **Rates** £110 double. **Rooms** 15. **Credit** AmEx, MC, V. **Map** p399 L4 ⑮
An affordable hotel with bundles of charm in the heart of Bloomsbury, the perkily styled Harlingford has light airy rooms with evident boutique aspirations. The decor is lifted from understated sleek to quirky with the help of vibrant colour splashes from coloured glass bathroom fittings and mosaic tiles. The crescent it's set in has a lovely, leafy private garden where you can lob a tennis ball or just dream under the trees on a summer's night.
Internet: wireless (free). TV.

Morgan

24 Bloomsbury Street, WC1B 3QJ (7636 3735, www.morganhotel.co.uk). Tottenham Court Road tube. **Rates** £110 double. **Rooms** 21. **Credit** MC, V. **Map** p399 K5 ⑯
This brilliantly located, comfortable budget hotel in Bloomsbury looks better than it has for a while after some recent renovations. The rooms have ditched their florals in favour of neutrals. The rooms are well equipped and all geared for the electronic age with wireless, voicemail, flatscreen tellies with freeview and air-conditioning. A good, slap-up English breakfast is served in a good-looking room with wood panelling, London prints and blue and white china plates. The spacious flats are excellent value.
Internet: wireless (free). TV.

Rough Luxe

1 Birkenhead Street, WC1H 8BA (7837 5338, www.roughluxe.co.uk). King's Cross tube/rail. **Rates** £155-£250 double. **Rooms** 9. **Credit** AmEx, MC, V. **Map** p399 L3 ⑰

CONSUME

Rough Luxe. *See p173.*

The latest in hotel design chic is – in the owners' words – Rough Luxe. In a bit of King's Cross that's choked with ratty B&Bs and cheap chains, this Grade II-listed property has walls artfully distressed, torn wallpaper, signature works of art, old-fashioned TVs that barely work and even retains the sign for the hotel that preceded Rough Luxe: 'Number One Hotel'. Each room has free wireless internet, but otherwise have totally different characters: there's the one with the free-standing copper tub, the one with the rose motif and so on. The setup is flexible too: rooms with shared bathrooms can be combined for group bookings, and the owners are more than happy to chat over a bottle of wine in the back courtyard where a great breakfast is served.
Internet: wireless (free). Parking: free. Room service.

Budget

Arosfa

83 Gower Street, WC1E 6HJ (7636 2115, www.arosfalondon.com). Goodge Street tube.
Rates £90 double. **Rooms** 16. **Credit** MC, V.
Map p399 K4 ⑱

Given the eminently reasonable room rates, the trendy swishness of the public areas in this amiable budget hotel comes as a pleasant surprise. You're treated to Philippe Starck chairs, mirrored chests

and a huge New York skyline in the lounge; more stylish embellishments in the halls and tasteful, neutral tones in the well-equipped bedrooms. Recent improvements have given guests flatscreen televisions, as well as the wherewithal for hot drinks in their rooms, plus new showers and toilets in the snug bathrooms.
Internet: wireless & shared terminal (free). TV.

★ Clink Hostel

78 King's Cross Road, WC1X 9QG (7183 9400, www.clinkhostel.com). King's Cross tube/rail.
Rates £40-£50 double; £9-£10 bed. **Beds** 717.
Credit MC, V. **Map** p399 M3 ⑲

Located in a former courthouse, the awesome Clink sets the bar high for hosteldom. There's the setting: the superb original wood-panelled lobby and courtroom where the Clash once stood before the beak (now filled with backpackers surfing the web). Then there's the urban chic ethos that permeates the whole enterprise, from the streamlined red reception counter to the Japanese-style 'pod' beds and the dining area's chunky wooden tables. Guests now have the further delight of a licensed bar and the more pedestrian addition of a coin-op launderette.
Bar/café. Internet: shared terminal (£1/hr). TV.
Other locations Ashlee House, 261-265 Gray's Inn Road, Bloomsbury, WC1X 8QT (7833 9400, www.ashleehouse.co.uk).

Jenkins Hotel

*45 Cartwright Gardens, WC1H 9EH (7387 2067,
www.jenkinshotel.demon.co.uk). Russell Square
tube or Euston tube/rail.* **Rooms** 14. **Credit** MC, V. **Map** p399 K3 ❷⓿

This well-to-do Georgian beauty has been a hotel since the 1920s, when it was converted by Miss Maggie Jenkins. It still has an atmospheric, antique air, although the rooms have mod cons enough – tellies, mini fridges, tea and coffee. Its looks have earned it a role in *Agatha Christie's Poirot*, but it's not chintzy, just quite floral in the bedspread and curtain department. The breakfast room is handsome, with snowy cotton tablecloths and Windsor chairs.
Bar/café. Internet: wireless (free). TV.

COVENT GARDEN & THE STRAND

Deluxe

The **Savoy** (www.the-savoy.com) is due to reopen in spring 2010 after London's most expensive refurbishment.

★ Covent Garden Hotel

*10 Monmouth Street, WC2H 9LF (7806 1000,
www.firmdale.com). Covent Garden or Leicester
Square tube.* **Rooms** 58. **Credit** AmEx, MC, V. **Map** p407 X2 ❷❶

The location and tucked-away screening room of this Firmdale hotel ensure it continues to attract starry customers, with anyone needing a bit of privacy able to retreat upstairs to the lovely panelled private library and drawing room. In the guestrooms, Kit Kemp's distinctive style mixes pinstriped wallpaper, pristine white quilts, floral upholstery with bold, contemporary elements; each room is unique, but each has the Kemp trademark upholstered mannequin and granite and oak bathroom. On the ground floor, the 1920s Paris-style Brasserie Max and its retro zinc bar retain their buzz – outdoor tables give a perfect viewpoint on Covent Garden boutique life in summer.
*Bar/café. Business centre. Concierge. Gym.
Internet: wireless & high-speed (£20/day).
Parking: £37/day. Restaurant. Room service.
Smoking rooms. TV: DVD.*

★ One Aldwych

*1 Aldwych, WC2B 4RH (7300 1000, www.one
aldwych.com). Covent Garden or Temple tube,
or Charing Cross tube/rail.* **Rates** £224-£506 double. **Rooms** 105. **Credit** AmEx, DC, MC, V. **Map** p407 Z3 ❷❷

You only have to push through the front door and enter the breathtaking Lobby Bar to know you're in for a treat. Despite weighty history – the 1907 building was once the offices of the *Morning Post* – One Aldwych is a thoroughly modern place, with Frette linen, bathroom mini-TVs and an environmentally

friendly loo-flushing system. Flowers and fruit are replenished daily and a card with the next day's weather forecast appears at turndown. The location is perfect for the West End theatres and has become a popular with attendees of London Fashion Week (*see p275*), much of which are now held nearby in Somerset House. The three round corner suites are very romantic, and a cosy screening room, excellent spa and a downstairs swimming pool where soothing opera is played may dissuade you from ever stepping outside.
*Bar/café. Concierge. Disabled-adapted rooms.
Gym. Internet: wireless (free), high-speed
(£15.50/day). Parking: £35/day. Pool: indoor.
Restaurants (2). Room service. Smoking rooms.
Spa facilities. TV: DVD & pay movies.*

St Martins Lane Hotel

*45 St Martin's Lane, WC2N 4HX (7300 5500,
www.morganshotelgroup.com). Leicester Square
tube or Charing Cross tube/rail.* **Rates** £230-£450 double. **Rooms** 204. **Credit** AmEx, DC, MC, V. **Map** p407 X4 ❷❸

When it opened a decade ago, the St Martins was the toast of the town. The flamboyant, theatrical lobby was constantly buzzing, and guests giggled like schoolgirls at Philippe Starck's playful decor. The Starck objects – such as the giant chess pieces and gold tooth stools in the lobby – remain, but the space, part of the Morgans Hotel Group, lacks the impact of its heyday. There's still much to be impressed by: the all-white bedrooms have comfortable minimalism down to a T, with floor-to-ceiling windows, gadgetry secreted in sculptural cabinets and sleek limestone bathrooms with toiletries from the spa at sister property Sanderson (*see p173*);
*Bar/café. Business centre. Concierge. Disabled-
adapted rooms. Gym. Internet: high-speed
(£15/day). Parking: £40/day. Restaurant.
Room service. TV: DVD & pay movies.*

SOHO & LEICESTER SQUARE

Deluxe

Soho Hotel

*4 Richmond Mews, W1D 3DH (7559 3000,
www.firmdale.com). Tottenham Court Road tube.* **Rates** £322-£517 double. **Rooms** 50. **Credit** AmEx, DC, MC, V. **Map** p406 W2 ❷❹

You'd hardly know you were in the heart of Soho once you're inside Firmdale's edgiest hotel: the place is wonderfully quiet, with what was once a car park now feeling like a converted loft building. The big bedrooms exhibit a contemporary edge, with modern furniture, industrial-style windows and nicely planned mod cons (digital radios as well as flatscreen TVs), although they're also classically Kit Kemp with bold stripes, traditional florals, plump sofas, oversized bedheads and upholstered tailor's dummies. The quiet drawing room and other public spaces

feature groovy colours – shocking pinks, acid greens – while Refuel, the loungey bar and restaurant, has an open kitchen and, yes, a car-themed mural. *Bar/café. Concierge. Gym. Internet: wireless & high-speed (£20/day). Parking: paid. Restaurant. Room service. Smoking rooms. Spa facilities. TV: DVD.*

Expensive

Dean Street Townhouse & Dining Room

69-71 Dean Street, W1D 3SE (7434 1775, www. sohohouse.com). Leicester Square or Piccadilly Circus tube. **Rates** £165-£295 double. **Rooms** 39. **Credit** AmEx, MC, V. **Map** p406 W3 ㉕

Due to open just as we go to press, Dean Street is the latest enterprise from the people behind Soho House members' club. Above a ground-floor dining room that is to serve classic English food, the four floors of bedrooms run from full-size rooms with early Georgian panelling and reclaimed oak floors up to tiny half-panelled attic rooms for bargain rates. You can expect to enjoy 24hr service and all modern comforts (rainforest showers, up-to-the-minute music systems and flatscreens). Note that sister venue Shoreditch House is due to add 27 bedrooms in 2010. *Bar/café. Disabled-adapted rooms. Internet: wireless (free). Restaurant. Room service. TV: DVD.*

★ Hazlitt's

6 Frith Street, W1D 3JA (7434 1771, www. hazlittshotel.com). Tottenham Court Road tube. **Rates** £253 double. **Rooms** 50. **Credit** AmEx, DC, MC, V. **Map** p406 W2 ㉖

Four Georgian townhouses comprise this absolutely charming place, named after William Hazlitt, the spirited 18th-century essayist who died here in abject poverty. With flamboyance and staggering attention to detail the rooms evoke the Georgian era, all heavy fabrics, fireplaces, free-standing tubs and exquisitely carved half-testers, yet modern luxuries – air-conditioning, TVs in antique cupboards and triple-glazed windows – have been subtly attended to as well. It gets creakier and more crooked the higher you go, culminating in enchanting garret single rooms with rooftop views. Of seven new bedrooms added in 2009, the main suite is a real knock-out: split-level, with a huge eagle spouting water into the raised bedroom bath and a rooftop terrace with sliding roof, it's a joyous extravaganza. *Bar/café. Business centre. Concierge. Conference facilities. Internet: wireless & high-speed (free). Room service. Smoking rooms. TV: DVD.*

Sanctum Soho

20 Warwick Street, W1B 5NF (7292 6100, www.sanctumsoho.com). Oxford Circus or Piccadilly Circus tube. **Rates** £179-£210 double. **Rooms** 30. **Credit** AmEx, MC, V. **Map** p406 V3 ㉗

In a former MI5 research building, Sanctum is Soho club cool with its dark colours, bling room handles and deco lamps, sexed up with a handful of rotating beds and a no-questions-asked policy. The rooms follow one of four colour schemes, broadly deco or powder-puff boudoir in style, with plenty of mirrors and an unspeakable number of TV channels. The residents-only, 24hr-means-24hr bar is small but funky, opening on to a two-level terrace outside, which is topped off with a multi-person jacuzzi. The fun continues with a guitar-tuning service at reception, a smoothly run and darkly handsome bar-restaurant, louche art in each room and a screening room for hire downstairs. *Photos p178.* *Bars/cafés (2). Conference facilities. Disabled-adapted rooms. Internet: wireless (free). Parking: free. Restaurant. Room service. Spa facilities. TV: DVD & pay movies.*

Budget

Piccadilly Backpackers

12 Sherwood Street, W1F 7BR (7434 9009, www. piccadillybackpackers.com). Piccadilly Circus tube. **Rates** £55-£62 double; £12-£22 bed. **Rooms** 50. **Credit** AmEx, MC, V. **Map** p406 V4 ㉘

A hulking presence behind Piccadilly Circus, Backpackers is a brilliant, basic, cosmopolitan hostel with several floors of accommodation and all the facilities a young adventurer could need – a travel shop, laundry, internet café and TV lounge. The bright, airy feel of the place is helped along by teams of graphic art students from all over the world, who are recruited to lend their artistic expertise to the decoration of public areas and the dorms of pod beds (with individual reading lights). *Internet: wireless & shared terminal (£2/hr). TV.*

OXFORD STREET & MARYLEBONE
Expensive

Cumberland

Great Cumberland Place, off Oxford Street, W1H 7DL (0870 333 9280, www.guoman.com). Marble Arch tube. **Rates** £160-£363 double. **Rooms** 900. **Credit** AmEx, DC, MC, V. **Map** p395 F6 ㉙

Perfectly located by Marble Arch tube (turn the right way and you're there in seconds), the Cumberland is a bit of a monster: in addition to the 900 rooms in the main block, there are another 119 in an annexe down the road. The echoing, rather chaotic lobby has some dramatic modern art and sculptures, as well as an impressive but somewhat severe waterfall. The rooms are minimalist, with acid-etched headboards, neatly modern bathrooms and plasma TVs – nicely designed, but rather small. The hotel's excellent dining room is the exclusive Rhodes W1 (*see p213*), but there are also a bar-brasserie and

CONSUME

Sanctum Soho. *See p177.*

boisterous, trash-industrial style, late-night DJ bar. Weekend breakfasts can feel like feeding the 5,000. *Bars/cafés (3). Concierge. Gym. Internet: high-speed (£10/day). Restaurants (3). Room service. TV: pay movies.*

Montagu Place
2 Montagu Place, W1H 2ER (7467 2777, www.montagu-place.co.uk). Baker Street tube. **Rates** £200-£260 double. **Rooms** 50. **Credit** AmEx, DC, MC, V. **Map** p398 G5 ③⓪
A relative newcomer to the city's ranks of small, fashionable townhouse hotels, Montagu Place fills a couple of Grade II-listed Georgian residences with sharply appointed rooms graded according to size. The big ones are entitled Swanky, and have king-size beds and big bathrooms. More modest in size, the Comfy category has queen-size beds and, being at the back of the building, have no street views. All rooms have a cool and trendy look, with cafetières and ground coffee instead of your Nescafé sachets, as well as flatscreen TVs (DVD players are available from reception). The bar in reception means you can get a drink at any time and retire to the graciously modern lounge.
Bar/café. Internet: wireless & high-speed (free). Room service. TV: DVD.

Sherlock Holmes Hotel
108 Baker Street, W1U 6LJ (7486 6161, www.sherlockholmeshotel.com). Baker Street tube. **Rates** £139-£317 double. **Rooms** 119. **Credit** AmEx, DC, MC, V. **Map** p398 G5 ③①
There may be a spot of Victorian detective memorabilia dotted about, but that's the only vaguely kitsch thing about this dashing gentleman's club of a hotel run by Park Plaza. Selling points – and thee are many – include organic and free-range ingredients used in the restaurant, a comfortably chic bar and some stately but fairly handsome rooms (all with nice new fixtures and carpets). The look favours brown leather and beige, with pinstripe scatter cushions and gleaming, spacious bathrooms. Split-level 'loft' suites take advantage of the first floor's double-height ceilings. Hotel guests can use the gym, sauna and steam room free of charge – there's a fee for treatments.
Bar/café. Business centre. Concierge. Disabled-adapted rooms. Gym. Internet: wireless & high-speed (free). Restaurant. Room service. TV: pay movies.

Moderate

Sumner
54 Upper Berkeley Street, W1H 7QR (7723 2244, www.thesumner.com). Marble Arch tube. **Rates** (incl breakfast) £150-£200 double. **Rooms** 20. **Credit** AmEx, DC, MC, V. **Map** p395 F6 ③②
The Sumner's cool, deluxe looks have earned it many fans, not least in the hospitality industry – the

THE BEST HIGH-CLASS HOTELS

Claridge's
The definition of luxury. *See p183.*

Haymarket Hotel
Charming, beautiful, relaxed. *See p185.*

Hazlitt's
For eccentric period drama. *See p177.*

hotel won gold in Visit London's Best Small Hotel Awards in 2008, and had already scooped best London B&B of the Year from the AA. You won't be at all surprised when you get here: from the soft dove and slatey greys of the lounge and halls you move up to glossily spacious accommodation with brilliant walk-in showers. The breakfast room feels soft and sunny, with a lovely, delicate buttercup motif and vibrant Arne Jacobsen chairs to cheer you on your way to the museums.
Concierge. Internet: wireless (free). TV.

22 York Street

22 York Street, W1U 6PX (7224 2990, www. 22yorkstreet.co.uk). Baker Street tube. **Rates** £100-£120 double. **Rooms** 10. **Credit** AmEx, MC, V. **Map** p398 G5 **63**
Bohemian French chic – white furniture, palest pink lime-washed walls, mellow wooden floors, subtly faded textiles and arresting *objets d'époque* – makes this delightfully unpretentious bed and breakfast in the heart of Marylebone a sight to behold. It doesn't announce itself from the outside, so you feel as if you've been invited to stay in someone's arty home, especially when you're drinking good coffee at the gorgeous curved table that dominates the breakfast room-cum-kitchen. Guests are also given free rein with the hot beverages in the elegant lounge upstairs. All the rooms are a decent size and have en suite baths, a rarity in this price range (and in this part of town).
Bar/café. Internet: wireless (free). TV.

PADDINGTON & NOTTING HILL
Deluxe

Hempel
31-35 Craven Hill Gardens, W2 3EA (7298 9000, www.the-hempel.co.uk). Lancaster Gate or Queensway tube or Paddington tube/rail. **Rates** £217-£689 double. **Rooms** 50. **Credit** AmEx, DC, MC, V. **Map** p394 C6 **64**
Since the mid 1990s, the serried white stucco façades of Craven Hill Gardens, a quiet backwater square in Bayswater, have concealed a dramatic alternative universe dreamed up by Anouska Hempel. Though no longer under her ownership, this boutique hotel

started a minimalist design revolution. H is the logo and clinical the look: the coffee tables sunk into the polished stone floor of the lobby; the empty expanses of magnolia paint on the walls; the green plastic turf in the 'Zen-like' garden. Surprisingly the vision still works, though the new owners seem confused about what music to pipe into the public spaces. The rooms, all different but defiantly black and white, have been made more comfortable with the addition of Italian furniture, and the breakfasts are fabulous.
Bar/café. Concierge. Disabled-adapted rooms. Internet: wireless (free). Restaurant. Room service. TV: DVD & pay movies.

Expensive

Miller's Residence

111A Westbourne Grove, W2 4UW (7243 1024, www.millershotel.com). Bayswater or Notting Hill Gate tube. **Rates** (incl continental breakfast) £176-£270 double. **Rooms** 8. **Credit** AmEx, MC, V. **Map** p394 B6 **65**
Owner Martin Miller is an antiques expert, so he knows a thing or two about creating a gloriously atmospheric residence. Indeed, the drawing room, where a buffet breakfast is served, is a gloriously bedecked treasure trove; wherever you look there are aged treasures – chandeliers, vases, paintings and candelabra – lovely to examine while partaking of your free drink from the bar. The rooms are all named after poets: the Browning has a four-poster and a poised elegance; Coleridge is warm and ruddy but not at all trippy; Tennyson has sunny yellow walls and a solid air to it. All come with air-conditioning and CD and DVD players, despite their Romantic reputations.
Bar/café. Concierge. Internet: wireless (free). TV: DVD.

Portobello Hotel

22 Stanley Gardens, W11 2NG (7727 2777, www.portobellohotel.com). Holland Park or Notting Hill Gate tube. **Rates** (incl breakfast) £200-£355 double. **Rooms** 22. **Credit** AmEx, MC, V. **Map** p394 A6 **66**
The Portobello is a hotel with approaching half a century of celebrity status, having hosted the likes of Johnny Depp, Kate Moss, Van Morrison and Alice Cooper, who used his tub to house a boa constrictor, but it remains a pleasingly unpretentious place. There is now a lift to help rockers who are feeling their age up the five floors, but there's still a 24hr bar-restaurant for those who don't yet feel past it. The rooms are themed – the basement Japanese Water Garden, for example, has an elaborate spa bath, its own private grotto and a small private garden – but all are stylishly equipped with a large fan, tall house plants and round-the-clock room service.
Bar/café. Internet: wireless (free). Restaurant. Room service. TV.

CONSUME

AN ENGLISH GARDEN IN CENTRAL LONDON

Run by the Davies family for 40 years, the Cardiff Hotel overlooks a quiet tree-lined square. Enjoy our friendly service and become one of our regular visitors.

WIRELESS INTERNET ACCESS

Singles: £49 - £65 Doubles: £75-£95

DELICIOUS ENGLISH BREAKFAST INCLUDED

CARDIFF HOTEL LONDON

5, 7, 9, Norfolk Square
London W2 1RU
Tel: (020) 7723 9068 / 7723 3513
Fax: (020) 7402 2342
email: stay@cardiff-hotel.com
www.cardiff-hotel.com
Int'l Tel: + 44 20 7723 9068
Int'l Fax: + 44 20 7402 2342

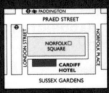

150 metres to
Heathrow Express &
Paddington Station

Moderate

Guesthouse West

163-165 Westbourne Grove, W11 2RS (7792 9800, www.guesthousewest.com). Notting Hill Gate tube. **Rates** (incl continental breakfast) £140-£195 double. **Rooms** 20. **Credit** AmEx, MC, V. **Map** p394 B6 ⑰

By doing away with any stuffy formality – and the vagaries of room service (a list of local restaurants and takeaways is provided in lieu) – this modish little number is an affordable treat. It's blessed with affable staff and an owner with an artistic bent. His connections with art galleries in Spain and London furnish the delightfully retro lobby bar's changing exhibitions, and there's added interest in the summer of a flowery terrace out front where you can sit and preen for the Notting Hill set. Food is served in the downstairs bar (it's only licensed to serve alcohol until 10pm). The minimalist bedrooms – which all have brand new queen-sized beds – have enough extras to keep hip young things happy: wireless internet, flatscreen TVs, Molton Brown toiletries.
Bar/café. Concierge. Disabled-adapted rooms. Internet: wireless (free). Restaurant. TV: DVD & pay movies.

Hotel Indigo

16 London Street, W2 1HL (7706 4444, www. ichotelsgroup.com). Paddington tube/rail. **Rates** £169-£199 double. **Rooms** 64. **Credit** AmEx, DC, MC, V. **Map** p395 D6 ⑱

The first of four boutique properties planned for London from the people behind Crowne Plaza and Holiday Inn has a relaxed all-day bar-restaurant, sharp-witted and friendly staff, and rooms with all mod cons (excellent walk-in showers rather than baths). The decor is a bit try-hard, though: a clinical white foyer gives on to acid-bright striped carpets, and wardrobe interiors are an assault by psychedelic swirl. Photos of Paddington past and ingenious ceiling strips of sky show how less could have been more. The smaller, cheaper attic rooms have most character.
Bar/café. Conference facilities. Disabled-adapted rooms. Internet: wireless (free). Restaurant. Room service. TV: pay movies.

New Linden

59 Leinster Square, W2 4PS (7221 4321, www.newlinden.co.uk). Bayswater tube. **Rates** £95-£149 double. **Rooms** 50. **Credit** AmEx, MC, V. **Map** p394 B6 ⑲

Modern, modish and moderately priced – that's the Mayflower Group for you. This is their Bayswater baby; they prefer to say 'trendy Notting Hill' on their website, but that's stretching the bounds of London geography a little too far. It looks very cool and is fantastically comfortable. The lobby and lounge are slick and glamorous – there's a beautiful teak arch in the lounge and the rooms are creamily low key with some vibrant, twirly eastern influences. Some of the larger family rooms retain their elaborate period pillars and cornicing. The bathrooms are a symphony in marble; the walk-in showers have deluge heads. There's a pleasant little patio for morning coffee and evening drinks.
Concierge. Internet: wireless (free). TV: DVD.

CONSUME

Hotel Indigo.

Connaught.

excellent value for money and impeccable service. The rooms in this grand Victorian terrace have a bright, modern look and plenty of space, and the lounge, with its wood floor, leather covered furniture, sprightly floral wallpaper and elegant mantelpiece is a lovely place to linger. As the name suggests, there's a small walled garden, lushly planted and laden guests might be cheered by the presence of a lift.

Internet: wireless (free, ground floor & 2nd floor), shared terminal (£1/hr). TV.

Pavilion

34-36 Sussex Gardens, W2 1UL (7262 0905, www.pavilionhoteluk.com). Edgware Road tube, or Marylebone or Paddington tube/rail. **Rates** £85-£100 double. **Rooms** 29. **Credit** AmEx, MC, V. **Map** p395 E5 ㊷

A hotel that describes itself as 'fashion rock 'n' roll' is never going to be staid, but Danny and Noshi Karne's Pavilion is quite mind-bogglingly excessive. The rooms have attention-grabbing names, such as 'Enter the Dragon' (Chinese themed), 'Flower Power' (blooming flowery) and 'Cosmic Girl' (way out there, man) and are frequently used for fashion shoots: the website has an impressive list of celebrities who have rocked up here over the years. Bizarre and voluptuous choice of decor notwithstanding, this crazy hotel represents excellent value and has the usual amenities. You might be disappointed if you want cool contemporary elegance and poncey toiletries – the Pavilion's much more fun than that.

Internet: wireless (free). Parking: £10/day. Room service. TV: DVD.

Stylotel

160-162 Sussex Gardens, W2 1UD (7723 1026, www.stylotel.com). Edgware Road tube, or Marylebone or Paddington tube/rail. **Rates** £90 double. **Rooms** 39. **Credit** AmEx, MC, V. **Map** p395 E6 ㊸

Partly due to the enthusiasm of the young manager, it's hard not to like this place. It's a retro-futurist dream: metal floors and panelling, lots of royal blue surfaces (the hall walls, the padded headboards) and pod bathrooms. But the real deal at Stylotel is its bargain-priced studio and apartment (respectively, £120-£150 and £150-£200, breakfast £6 extra). Designed – like the rest of the hotel – by the owner's son, they suggest he's calmed down with age. Here's real minimalist chic: sleek brushed steel or white glass walls panels, simply styled contemporary furniture upholstered in black or white.

Concierge. Internet: wireless (£2/hr). Parking: £10/day. Smoking rooms. TV.

26 Hillgate Place

26 Hillgate Place, W8 7ST (7727 7717, www.26hillgateplace.co.uk). Notting Hill Gate tube. **Rates** £80-£105 double. **Rooms** 2. **No credit cards. Map** p394 A7 ㊹

Vancouver Studios

30 Prince's Square, W2 4NJ (7243 1270, www. vancouverstudios.co.uk). Bayswater or Queensway tube. **Rates** £120-£155 double. **Rooms** 48. **Credit** AmEx, DC, MC, V. **Map** p394 B6 ㊵

Step into the hall or comfortably furnished sitting room of this imposing townhouse and it feels like a large and gracious home, but you have the option of total privacy in the studio or apartment accommodation offered. Each one has its own style – from cool contemporary lines to a softer, more homely style – but all are well equipped with little kitchens so that guests can self-cater, even order in groceries in advance if they wish. With all their mod cons, they're superb value. Zeus the cat lords it over the building and can show you into the pretty garden with its fountain and heady scent of jasmine.

Internet: wireless (free). TV: DVD.

Budget

Garden Court Hotel

30-31 Kensington Gardens Square, W2 4BG (7229 2553, www.gardencourthotel.co.uk). Bayswater or Queensway tube. **Rates** (incl breakfast) £75-£115 double. **Rooms** 32. **Credit** MC, V. **Map** p394 B6 ㊶

Once people have discovered the Garden Court, they tend to keep coming back, says Edward Connolly, owner-manager of this long-established hotel with quiet pride. There aren't many places this close to Hyde Park and Portobello Market that give such

Artist Hilary Dunne has furnished her B&B with paintings of glossy-skinned, doe-eyed women inspired by her travels in the West Indies, as well as the spoils from her former life as textiles importer. The ground-floor room with its large en suite bathroom contains some of the Caribbean collection; the smaller, more colourful downstairs room, with shared bathroom, is bright with wall hangings, throws and cushions from India. The overall effect is of a much-loved, warm and lived-in family home. Breakfast is taken in a busy little space next to the galley kitchen, with French windows opening on to a tiny, ivy-clad courtyard. A slightly larger patio upstairs, home to Hilary's extensive plant collection, looks out over the gardens of Hillgate Place. *Internet: wireless (free). TV.*

PICCADILLY CIRCUS & MAYFAIR

Deluxe

Brown's

Albemarle Street, W1S 4BP (7493 6020, www.roccofortecollection.com). Green Park tube. **Rates** £525-£734 double. **Rooms** 117. **Credit** AmEx, DC, MC, V. **Map** p406 U5 ⑮

Brown's was opened in 1837 by Lord Byron's butler, James Brown. The first British telephone call was made from here in 1876, five years after Napoleon III and Empress Eugenie took refuge in one of the suites after fleeing the Third Republic. Haile Selassie and Rudyard Kipling were also guests. The bedrooms are all large and extremely comfortable, with original art, book collections and, in the suites, fireplaces; the elegant, classic British hotel restaurant, the Albemarle, makes a decorous nod to modernity with a collection of contemporary British art, with pieces by Tracey Emin and Bridget Riley, but the public spaces thrum with history – non-residents can try the £35 afternoon tea in the English Tea Room or a cocktail in the classily masculine Donovan Bar.

Bar/café. Business centre. Concierge. Disabled-adapted rooms. Gym. Internet: wireless (free), high-speed (£15/day). Restaurant. Room service. Spa facilities. TV: pay movies.

★ Claridge's

55 Brook Street, W1K 4HR (7629 8860, www.claridges.co.uk). Bond Street tube. **Rates** £289-£570 double. **Rooms** 203. **Credit** AmEx, DC, MC, V. **Map** p398 H6 ⑯

Claridge's is sheer class and pure atmosphere, with its signature art deco redesign still simply dazzling. Photographs of Churchill and sundry royals grace the grand foyer, as does an absurdly over-the-top Dale Chihuly chandelier. Without departing too far from the traditional, Claridge's bars and restaurant are actively fashionable – Gordon Ramsay is the in-house restaurateur, and the A-listers can gather for

champers and sashimi in the bar. The rooms divide evenly between deco and Victorian style, with period touches such as deco toilet flushes in the swanky marble bathrooms. Bedside panels control the mod-con facilities at the touch of a button. If money's no object, opt for a David Linley suite, done out in gorgeous duck-egg blue and white, or lilac and silver. *Bars/cafés (2). Business centre. Concierge. Disabled-adapted rooms. Gym. Internet: wireless (free). Restaurants (3). Room service. Smoking rooms. Spa facilities. TV: DVD & pay movies.*

★ Connaught

Carlos Place, W1K 2AL (7499 7070, www.the-connaught.co.uk). Bond Street tube. **Rates** £410-£717 double. **Rooms** 125. **Credit** AmEx, DC, MC, V. **Map** p400 H7 ⑰

This isn't the only hotel in London to provide butlers, but there can't be many that offer 'a secured gun cabinet room' for hunting season. This is traditional British hospitality for those who love 23-carat gold leaf trimmings and stern portraits in the halls, but all mod cons in their room, down to flatscreens in the en suite. Too lazy to polish your own shoes? The butlers are trained in shoe care by the expert cobblers at John Lobb. Both of the bars – gentleman's club cosy Coburg and cruiseship deco Connaught (*see p234*) – and the Hélène Darroze restaurant are very impressive; the more modern wing (increasing the number of rooms and adding a gym and spa) was just opening as we went to press. *Bars/cafés (2). Concierge. Disabled-adapted rooms. Gym. Internet: wireless (free). Pool: indoor. Restaurants (2). Room service. Smoking rooms. Spa facilities. TV: DVD.*

★ Dorchester

53 Park Lane, W1K 1QA (7629 8888, www.thedorchester.com). Hyde Park Corner tube. **Rates** £280-£595 double. **Rooms** 250. **Credit** AmEx, DC, MC, V. **Map** p400 G7 ⑱

A Park Lane fixture since 1931, the Dorchester's interior may be thoroughly, opulently classical, but the hotel is cutting-edge in attitude, providing an unrivalled level of personal service. With the grandest lobby in town, amazing views of Hyde Park, state-of-the-art mod cons and a magnificently refurbished (to the tune of £3.2 million) spa, it's small wonder the hotel continues to welcome movie stars (the lineage stretches from Elizabeth Taylor to Tom

CONSUME

Cruise) and political leaders (Eisenhower planned the D-Day landing here). You're not likely to be eating out, either: the Dorchester employs 90 full-time chefs at the Grill Room, Alain Ducasse and China Tang. If you can afford to stay here, you'll want to. *Bar/café. Concierge. Disabled-adapted rooms. Gym. Internet: wireless & high-speed (£19.50/ day). Parking: £30-£40/day. Restaurants (3). Room service. Smoking rooms. Spa facilities. TV: DVD & pay movies.*

★ Haymarket Hotel

1 Suffolk Place, SW1Y 4BP (7470 4000, www.firmdale.com). Piccadilly Circus tube. **Rates** £250-£700 double. **Rooms** 50. **Credit** AmEx, DC, MC, V. **Map** p406 W5 ❹❾
A terrific addition to Kit Kemp's Firmdale portfolio, this block-size building (a private townhouse within the hotel can be rented) was designed by John Nash, the architect of Regency London. The public spaces are a delight, with Kemp's trademark combination of contemporary arty surprises (a giant light-bulb affair over the library's chessboard, a gothic little paper-cut of layered skulls above the tray of free afternoon canapés) and impossible-to-leave, bright, plump, floral sofas. Wow-factors include the surprisingly bling basement swimming pool and bar (shiny sofas, twinkly roof) and the couldn't-be-more central location. Rooms are generously sized (as are bathrooms), individually decorated and discreetly stuffed with facilities, and there's plenty of attention from the switched-on staff. The street-side bar and restaurant are top-notch, the breakfast exquisite. *Bar/café. Concierge. Disabled-adapted rooms. Gym. Internet: wireless (£20/day). Pool: indoor. Restaurant. Room service. Smoking rooms. Spa facilities. TV: DVD.*

Metropolitan

19 Old Park Lane, W1K 1LB (7447 1000, www.metropolitan.como.bz). Hyde Park Corner tube. **Rates** £229-£425 double. **Rooms** 150. **Credit** AmEx, DC, MC, V. **Map** p400 H8 ❺❶
The flashier little sister of the Halkin (*see p189*) may have had its heyday in the 1990s, but it retains that buzzy, relaxed sense of cool. As such, the Met bar and Nobu restaurant continue to attract celebs and models, along with many mere mortals here to rubberneck. The hotel itself is bright and uncluttered. The rooms that are a little clinical and ever-so-slightly dated, but pear-wood furnishings, super-soft mattresses and suede throws keep things very comfortable, and the Shambhala spa toiletries in the bathrooms are a cut above the usual chuck-away fodder. The hotel's greatest asset is the prime location, overlooking a corner of Hyde Park. *Bar/café. Business centre. Concierge. Gym. Internet: wireless, high-speed & shared terminal (free). Parking: £40/day. Restaurant. Room service. Smoking rooms. Spa facilities. TV: DVD & pay movies.*

Ritz

150 Piccadilly, W1J 9BR (7493 8181, www. theritzlondon.com). Green Park tube. **Rates** £586-£646 double. **Room** 136. **Credit** AmEx, DC, MC, V. **Map** p400 J8 ❺❶
If you like the idea of a world where jeans and trainers are banned and jackets must be worn by gentlemen when dining (the requirement is waived for breakfast), the Ritz is for you. Founded by hotelier extraordinaire César Ritz, the hotel is deluxe *in excelsis*. The show-stopper is the ridiculously ornate, vaulted Long Gallery, an orgy of chandeliers, rococo mirrors and marble columns, but all the high-ceilinged, Louis XVI-style bedrooms have been painstakingly renovated to their former glory in restrained pastel colours. Amid the old-world luxury, mod cons include free wireless in most rooms, large TVs and a gym. An elegant afternoon tea in the Palm Court (book ahead) is the way in for interlopers. *Bar/café. Concierge. Gym. Internet: high-speed (£25/day). Restaurant. Room service. Smoking rooms. Spa facilities. TV: DVD.*

Expensive

★ No.5 Maddox Street

5 Maddox Street, W1S 2QD (7647 0200, www.living-rooms.co.uk). Oxford Circus tube. **Rates** £270-£380 double. **Rooms** 12. **Credit** AmEx, DC, MC, V. **Map** p406 U2 ❺❷
This bolthole just off Regent Street is perfect for visiting film directors looking to be accommodated in a chic apartment at a reasonable long-term rate. Here they can shut the discreet brown front door, climb the stairs and flop into a home from home with all contemporary cons, including new flatscreen TVs. The East-meets-West decor is classic 1990s minimalist, but very bright and clean after a gentle refurbishment. Each apartment has a fully equipped kitchen, but room service will shop for you as well as providing usual hotel amenities. There's no bar, but breakfasts and snacks are served, and there's a Thai restaurant (Patara) on the ground floor. *Concierge. Internet: wireless & high-speed (£15/day, £60/wk). Room service. TV: DVD.*

WESTMINSTER & ST JAMES'S

Deluxe

Royal Horseguards

2 Whitehall Court, SW1A 2EJ (0871 376 9033, www.guoman.com). Embankment tube or Charing Cross tube/rail. **Rates** £360-£400. **Rooms** 281. **Credit** AmEx, MC, V. **Map** p401 L8 ❺❸
The Royal Horseguards occupies a French chateau discreetly located off Whitehall. The building was designed by Alfred 'Natural History Museum' Waterhouse for the National Liberal Club in 1887, and club founder, William Gladstone, great reformer that he was, probably would have approved of the

CONSUME

recent refurb of the interior by the Guoman group. It's immaculately clean, 'classic but modern' in style, with welcoming staff. The bedrooms have useful dressing tables, iPod docks and wonderfully comfortable Hypnos beds, and bathrooms come with flatscreen TV and Elemis products. The buffet-style breakfasts are ordinary, but from the upper floors the river views of the City, the London Eye and County Hall – whisper it – rival those of the Savoy. *Bars/cafés (2). Business centre. Concierge. Disabled-adapted rooms. Gym. Internet: wireless (free). Restaurant. Room service. TV.*

Expensive

City Inn Westminster

30 John Islip Street, SW1P 4DD (7630 1000, www.cityinn.com). Pimlico tube. **Rates** £148-£344. **Rooms** 420. **Credit** AmEx, DC, MC, V. **Map** p401 K10 **54**

There's nothing flashy about this new-build hotel, but it is well run, neatly designed and obliging: the rooms have all the added extras you'd want (iMacs, CD/DVD library, broadband, flatscreen TVs) and the floor-to-ceiling windows mean that river-facing

Pushing the Boundary

Conran's freshest enterprise is already one of London's finest places to stay.

Design mogul Sir Terence Conran's **Boundary Project** warehouse conversion (for listings, *see p193*) is evidently a labour of love. The restaurants – which include the Albion (*see p224*), one of the best openings of 2009 – and rooftop bar had already grabbed headlines for their quality and relaxed feel by the time Conran felt ready to open the first of 17 bedrooms. When Time Out was shown around, it was no surprise to find the lepidopterist Sir Terence relaxing in the suite he had himself designed, puffing on a cigar as he looked at the butterflies hung from a central light.

Each bedroom has a wet room and handmade bed, but are otherwise individually

designed, with classic furniture and original art. The five split-level suites range in style from the bright and sea-salt fresh Beach to a new take on Victoriana by Polly Dickens, while the remaining rooms (the slightly larger corner rooms have windows along both external walls) are themed by design style: Mies van der Rohe, Eames, Shaker. There's also a charming Heath Robinson room, decorated with the cartoonist's sketches of hilariously complex machines.

Despite being on the fringes of the madness of Shoreditch, the hotel feels wonderfully calm. And you can enjoy all this cool elegance for just £140, if you opt for a Boundary Room on a Sunday night.

CONSUME

suites on the 12th and 13th floors have superb night views – when the businessmen go home for the weekend you might grab one for £125. With half an eye on near neighbour Tate Britain, the owners have collaborated with the Chelsea College of Art to provide changing art through the lobbies and meeting rooms; outside the rather unconvincing City Café, you can sit on a Ron Arad chair.

Bars/cafés (2). Business centre. Concierge. Disabled-adapted rooms. Gym. Internet: wireless (free). Parking: £30/day. Restaurant. Room service. Smoking rooms. TV: DVD & pay movies.

Trafalgar
2 Spring Gardens, Trafalgar Square, SW1A 2TS (7870 2900, www.thetrafalgar.com). Charing Cross tube/rail. **Rates** £235-£294 double. **Rooms** 129. **Credit** AmEx, DC, MC, V. **Map** p407 X5 ⑮
The Trafalgar is a Hilton, but you'd hardly notice. The mood is young and dynamic at the chain's first 'concept' hotel, for all that it's housed in the imposing edifice that was once headquarters of Cunard (this was where the Titanic was conceived). To the right of the open reception is the Rockwell Bar; breakfast downstairs is accompanied by gentle live music. Yet it's the none-more-central location that's the biggest draw – the few corner suites look directly into Trafalgar Square (prices reflect location), but those without a room with a view can avail themselves of the rooftop bar, open for summer and the run-up to Christmas.
Bars/cafés (2). Business centre. Concierge. Disabled-adapted rooms. Gym. Internet: wireless & high-speed (£15/day). Restaurant. Room service. Smoking rooms. TV: DVD & pay movies.

Moderate

B+B Belgravia
64-66 Ebury Street, SW1W 9QD (7823 4928, www.bb-belgravia.com). Victoria tube/rail. **Rates** (incl breakfast) £120 double. **Rooms** 17. **Credit** AmEx, MC, V. **Map** p400 H10 ⑯
How do you make a lounge full of white and black contemporary furnishings seem cosy and welcoming? Hard to achieve, but they've succeeded at B+B Belgravia who've taken the B&B experience to a new level. It's fresh and sophisticated without being hard-edged: there's nothing here that will make the fastidiously design-conscious wince (leather sofa, arty felt cushions, modern fireplace), but nor is it overly precious. A gleaming espresso machine provides 24/7 caffeine.
Disabled-adapted rooms. Internet: wireless (free). TV.

Windermere Hotel
142-144 Warwick Way, SW1V 4JE (7834 5163, www.windermere-hotel.co.uk). Victoria tube/rail. **Rates** (incl breakfast) £119-£144 double. **Rooms** 20. **Credit** AmEx, MC, V. **Map** p400 H11 ⑰

Heading the procession of small hotels strung along Warwick Way, the Windermere is a comfortable, traditionally decked-out London hotel with no aspirations to boutique status. The decor may be showing its age a bit in the hall, but you'll receive a warm welcome and excellent service – there are over a dozen staff for just 20 rooms. There's a cosy basement restaurant-bar (breakfasts are top-notch) and guests get a discount at the neighbouring car park.
Bar/café. Concierge. Internet: wireless (free). Restaurant. Room service. TV.

Budget

Morgan House
120 Ebury Street, SW1W 9QQ (7730 2384, www.morganhouse.co.uk). Pimlico tube or Victoria tube/rail. **Rates** (incl breakfast) £78-£98 double. **Rooms** 11. **Credit** AmEx, MC, V. **Map** p400 G10 ⑱
The Morgan has the understated charm of the old family home of a posh but unpretentious English friend: a pleasing mix of nice old wooden or traditional iron beds, pretty floral curtains and coverlets in subtle hues, the odd chandelier or big gilt mirror over original mantelpieces, padded wicker chairs and sinks in every bedroom, now with refurbished bathrooms and new carpets. Though there's no guest lounge, guests can sit in the little patio garden, and for Belgravia, the prices are a steal.
Internet: wireless (free). TV.

CHELSEA
Expensive

Myhotel Chelsea
35 Ixworth Place, SW3 3QX (7225 7500, www.myhotels.com). South Kensington tube. **Rates** £148-£290 double. **Rooms** 45. **Credit** AmEx, DC, MC, V. **Map** p397 E11 ⑲
The Chelsea Myhotel feels a world away from its sleekly modern Bloomsbury sister, its aesthetic softer and more English – with a floral sofa and plate of scones in the lobby, and white wicker headboards, velvet cushions and Bee Kind toiletries in the guestrooms. These feminine touches contrast with the mini-chain's feng shui touches, its Eastern-inspired treatment room, and its sleek aquarium. The modernised country farmhouse feel of the bar-restaurant works better for breakfast than it does for a boozy cocktail, but the central conservatory-style library is wonderful. Just sink into one of the ample comfy chairs and listen to the tinkling water feature or your own choice of CD.
Bar/café. Business centre. Concierge. Disabled-adapted rooms. Gym. Internet: wireless & high-speed (free). Restaurant. Room service. Spa facilities. TV: DVD.
Other locations 11-13 Bayley Street, Bloomsbury, WC1B 3HD (7667 6000).

CONSUME

San Domenico House

*29-31 Draycott Place, SW3 2SH (7581 5757,
www.sandomenicohouse.com). Sloane Square
tube.* **Rates** £235-£310 double. **Rooms** 15.
Credit AmEx, MC, V. **Map** p397 F11 ⑥⓪
Along a quiet terrace of late 19th-century red-stone
buildings just off Sloane Square, San Domenico
owes much of its tasteful, historic look to previous
owner Sue Rogers, the interior designer who transformed this former private residence into a boutique
hotel masterpiece. Each of the four categories of gue-
stroom, including the split-level gallery suites, feature original furnishings or antiques. Royal
portraits, Victorian mirrors and Empire-era travelling cases are complemented by fabrics of similar
style and taste, offset by contemporary touches to
bathrooms. The spacious bedrooms enjoy wide-
angle views of London, some from little balconies.
Breakfasts are taken up to guests or laid out in the
room downstairs, while main meals may be taken in
the sumptuous coffee room by the lobby.
*Bar/café. Internet: wireless (free). Restaurant.
Room service. TV.*

KNIGHTSBRIDGE & SOUTH KENSINGTON

Deluxe

Blakes

*33 Roland Gardens, SW7 3PF (7370 6701,
www.blakeshotels.com). South Kensington tube.*
Rates £265-£440 double. **Credit**
AmEx, DC, MC, V. **Map** p397 D11 ⑥①
As original as when Anouska Hempel opened it in
1983 – the scent of oranges and the twittering of a
pair of lovebirds fill the dark, oriental lobby – Blakes
and its maximalist decor have stood the test of time,
a living casebook for interior design students. Each
room is in a different style, with influences from
Italy, India, Turkey and China. Exotic antiques
picked up on the designer's travels – intricately
carved beds, Chinese birdcages, ancient trunks – are
set off by sweeping drapery and piles of plump cushions. Downstairs is the eclectic, Eastern-influenced
restaurant, complemented by a gym and wireless
internet for a celebrity clientele enticed by the discreet, residential location.
*Bar/café. Business centre. Concierge. Gym.
Internet: wireless & high-speed (£12/day).
Parking: paid. Restaurant. Room service.
TV: DVD & pay movies.*

Gore

*190 Queen's Gate, SW7 5EX (7584 6601,
www.gorehotel.com). South Kensington tube.*
Rates £180-£440 double. **Rooms** 50. **Credit**
AmEx, MC, V. **Map** p397 D9 ⑥②
This fin-de-siècle period piece was founded by
descendants of Captain Cook in two grand Victorian
townhouses. The lobby and staircase are close hung
with old paintings, and the bedrooms all have fantastic 19th-century carved oak beds, sumptuous
drapes and shelves of old books. The suites are spectacular: the Tudor Room has a huge stone-faced fireplace and a minstrels' gallery, while tragedy queens
should plump for the Venus room and Judy
Garland's old bed (and replica ruby slippers). Bistrot
190 provides a casually elegant setting for great
breakfasts, while the warm, wood-panelled 190 bar
(see p236) is a charming setting for cocktails.
*Bar/café. Concierge. Internet: wireless & high-
speed (free). Restaurant. Room service. TV.*

Halkin

*Halkin Street, SW1X 7DJ (7333 1000, www.
halkin.como.bz). Hyde Park Corner tube.* **Rates**
£390 double. **Rooms** 41. **Credit** AmEx, DC, MC,
V. **Map** p400 G9 ⑥③
Set up by Singaporean fashion mogul Christina Ong
(who also owns the Metropolitan; *see p185*), the
Halkin marries Eastern charm, style and food with
a central and quiet location in Knightsbridge. The
rooms, all located off black curved, almost trompe
l'oeil wooden corridors are comfortable and full of
Asian artefacts and clever gadgetry (a touch-screen
bedside panel controls everything from the air-con
to the 'do not disturb' sign on the door). Bathrooms
are well equipped and heavy on the marble, and
come stocked with a range of products from Ong's
Shambhala spa. The Michelin-starred Thai restaurant Nahm *(see p220)* is on the ground floor.
*Bar/café. Concierge. Disabled-adapted rooms.
Gym. Internet: wireless & high-speed (free).
Parking. Restaurant. Room service. TV:
DVD & pay movies.*

★ Lanesborough

*1 Lanesborough Place, SW1X 7TA (7259 5599,
www.lanesborough.com). Hyde Park Corner tube.*
Rates £475-£675 double. **Rooms** 95. **Credit**
AmEx, DC, MC, V. **Map** p400 G8 ⑥④
Considered one of London's more historic luxury
hotels, the Lanesborough was in fact redeveloped –
impressively – only in 1991. Occupying an 1820s
Greek Revival building designed as a hospital by
William Wilkins (the man behind the National
Gallery; *see p110*), its luxurious guestrooms are
traditionally decorated with thick fabrics, antique
furniture and lavish Carrera-marble bathrooms.
Electronic keypads control everything from the
air-conditioning to the superb 24hr room service at
the touch of a button. As luxury hotels go, the
Lanesborough's rates are unusually inclusive:
high-speed internet access, movies and calls within
the EU and to the USA are complimentary, as are
personalised business cards stating your residence.
The Library Bar is excellent.
*Bar/café. Business centre. Concierge. Disabled-
adapted rooms. Gym. Internet: wireless & high-
speed (free). Parking: £40/day. Restaurant. Room
service. Spa facilities. TV: DVD & pay movies.*

CONSUME

Milestone Hotel & Apartments

*1-2 Kensington Court, W8 5DL (7917 1000,
www.milestonehotel.com). High Street
Kensington tube.* **Rates** £280-£322 double.
Rooms 57. **Credit** AmEx, DC, MC, V.
Map p394 C8 ⑮

Wealthy American visitors make annual pilgrim-
ages here, their arrival greeted by the comforting,
gravel tones of their regular concierge, as English
as roast beef, and the glass of sherry in the room.
Yet amid old-school luxury (butlers on 24hr call)
thrives inventive modernity (the resistance pool in
the spa). Rooms overlooking Kensington Gardens
feature the inspired decor of South African owner
Beatrice Tillman: the Safari suite contains tent-like
draperies and leopard-print upholstery; the Tudor
Suite has an elaborate inglenook fireplace, minstrels'
gallery and a pouffe concealing a pop-up TV.
*Bar/café. Business centre. Concierge. Disabled-
adapted rooms. Gym. Internet: wireless & high-
speed (free). Pool: indoor. Restaurant. Room
service. Smoking rooms. Spa facilities. TV:
DVD & pay movies.*

Expensive

★ Number Sixteen

*16 Sumner Place, SW7 3EG (7589 5232,
www.firmdale.com). South Kensington tube.*
Rates £190-£310 double. **Rooms** 42. **Credit**
AmEx, DC, MC, V. **Map** p397 D10 ⑯

This may be Kit Kemp's most affordable hotel but
there's no slacking in style or comforts – witness the
fresh flowers and origami-ed birdbook decorations
in the ultra-comfy drawing room. Bedrooms are generously sized, bright and very light, and carry the
Kemp trademark mix of bold and traditional. The
whole place has an appealing freshness about it,
enhanced by a delicious, large back garden with its
central water feature. By the time you finish breakfast in the sweet conservatory, you'll have forgotten
you're in the city.
*Bar/café. Business centre. Concierge. Internet:
wireless & high-speed (£20/day). Parking:
£45/day. Room service. TV: DVD.*

Moderate

Aster House

*3 Sumner Place, SW7 3EE (7581 5888, www.
asterhouse.com). South Kensington tube.* **Rates**
(incl breakfast) £146-£225 double. **Rooms** 13.
Credit MC, V. **Map** p397 D11 ⑰

You'll not find many hotels along this swish archetypal white-terraced South Kensington street. One
of the favoured few, the Aster has become an award-
winner through attention to detail (like impeccable
housekeeping and the mobile phone guests can borrow) and the warmth of its managers, Leona and
Simon Tan. It's all low-key, comfortably soothing
creams with touches of dusty rose and muted green.

Star of the show is the plant-filled conservatory that
serves as a breakfast room and guest lounge – star,
that is, after Ollie and Cordelia, the resident ducks.
*Internet: wireless & high-speed (free). Room
service. TV.*

★ Lux Pod

*38 Gloucester Road, SW7 4QT (7460 3171,
www.theluxpod.com). Gloucester Road tube.*
Rates (min 3 night stay) £107 double. **Rooms** 1.
No credit cards. Map p396 C9 ⑱

This marvellously eccentric little hideaway is the
pride and joy of its owner, Judith Abraham, with
many of the features purpose-designed. Little is the
operative word: it's a tiny space that ingeniously
packs in a bathroom, slide-top kitchenette and
lounge, with the comfy bed high up above the bathroom and accessible only by ladder. All is shiny and
modern, and the room is packed with gadgets (iPod
dock with fine speakers, flatscreen TV, funky cooker
hobs and lighting arrangements, electronic curtains)
and high-style details (leather flooring, hip chairs).
The tight space is ideal for one, a little fiddly to get
round for two, but terrific fun for any design fan,
tech geek or traveller bored of identikit properties.
Internet: wireless (free). TV: DVD & pay movies.

York & Albany.

Vicarage Hotel

*10 Vicarage Gate, W8 4AG (7229 4030,
www.londonvicaragehotel.com). High Street
Kensington or Notting Hill Gate tube.* **Rates**
(incl breakfast) £93-£112 double. **Rooms** 17.
Credit AmEx, MC, V. **Map** p394 B8 ⑥⑨
There are scores of devotees who return regularly
to this tall Victorian townhouse tucked in a quiet
leafy square just off High Street Ken, hard by
Kensington Gardens. It's a comfortable, resolutely
old-fashioned establishment – and that's what the
punters come for. There's a wonderfully grand
entrance hall with red and gold striped wallpaper,
huge gilt mirror and chandelier, with a sweeping
staircase that ascends to an assortment of good-
sized rooms furnished in pale florals and nice old
pieces of furniture.
Internet: wireless (free). TV.

NORTH LONDON

Expensive

York & Albany

*127-129 Parkway, Camden, NW1 7PS (7387
5700, www.gordonramsay.com). Camden Town*

tube. **Rates** £175-£575 double. **Rooms** 10.
Credit AmEx, DC, MC, V.
Overcommitment to TV and transatlantic enterprises might have knocked a little gloss off Gordon
Ramsay's restaurants, but his only hotel is still
going strong. Housed in a grand John Nash building
that was designed as a coaching house but spent the
recent past as a pub, it consists of a restaurant (split
over two levels), bar and delicatessen downstairs;
above them a selection of ten rooms, handsomely
designed by Russell Sage in mellow shades. The
decor is an effective mix of ancient and modern,
sturdy and quietly charismatic furniture married to
modern technology; if you're lucky, you'll have views
of Regent's Park from your bedroom window.
*Bar/café. Disabled-adapted rooms. Internet:
wireless (free). Restaurant. Room service.
TV: DVD.*

Moderate

Colonnade

*2 Warrington Crescent, Little Venice, W9
1ER (7286 1052, www.theetoncollection.com/
colonnade). Warwick Avenue tube.* **Rates** £147-
£213 double. **Rooms** 43. **Credit** AmEx, MC, V.
Map p394 C4 ⑦⓪
Housed in an imposingly sited white Maida Vale
mansion, the Colonnade has been lushly done up in
interior-designer traditional – lots of swagged curtains, deep opulent colours, luxurious fabrics and
careful arrangements of smoothly upholstered furniture. Some of the larger high-ceilinged rooms have
had mezzanine floors added. Guests breakfast in a
subterranean tapas bar. The bar is beneath a front-
of-hotel terrace that makes a good spot for lingering
with a glass of wine on warm evenings.
*Bar/café. Internet: wireless (£15/day). Parking:
£20/day. Restaurant. Room service. TV.*

Rose & Crown

*199 Stoke Newington Church Street, N16 9ES
(7923 3337, www.roseandcrownn16.co.uk).
Bus 73.* **Rates** (incl breakfast) £120-£175 double.
Rooms 6. **Credit** AmEx, MC, V.
The Rose has always been popular as a pub, but now
a separate entrance leads to a contemporary B&B.
Landscape gardener Will, who with Diane runs the
place, in spring 2009 transformed three floors to create individually and tastefully styled guestrooms
(drench showers, quality smellies and furnishings),
a breakfast room and a sun-catching roof terrace
with a large table, a couple of loungers, a patio heater
and a view across to central London from the illuminated glow of 13th-century St Mary's Church
alongside. Pricier rooms feature a stand-alone bathtub, and the suite by the breakfast room is vast.
Truman Brewery touches from yesteryear remain:
the pub sign lettering, a finely carved pre-war stair
rail and the Mystery Arrow games machine.
Internet: wireless (free). TV.

CONSUME

Budget

Hampstead Village Guesthouse

2 Kemplay Road, Hampstead, NW3 1SY
(7435 8679, www.hampsteadguesthouse.com).
Hampstead tube or Hampstead Heath rail.
Rates £80-£95 double. **Rooms** 9. **Credit**
AmEx, MC, V.
Owner Annemarie van der Meer loves to point out
all the quirky space-saving surprises as she shows
you round her wonderful and idiosyncratic bed and
breakfast: here's the folding sink, there's the bed that
pops out of an antique wardrobe… The special
atmosphere at this double-fronted Victorian house,
set on a quiet Hampstead street, means that guests
return year after year. Each room is uniquely decorated with eclectic furnishings – like the French steel
bathtub in one room – and there's a self-contained
studio with its own kitchen. All guests may make
use of a range of home comforts, from hot water bottles to mobile phones, as well as a laptop to borrow.
Breakfast (£7) may be taken in the garden that surrounds this lovely property on three sides.
Internet: wireless (free). Parking: £10/day. TV.

40 Winks.

66 Camden Square

66 Camden Square, Camden, NW1 9XD (7485 4622, rodgerdavis@btinternet.com). Camden Town tube or Camden Road rail. **Rates** (incl continental breakfast) £100 double. **Rooms** 2. **No credit cards.**

A world away from the dreary Eurobustle of Camden Market, lovely 66 Camden Square isn't actually on Camden Square – it's on Murray Street, behind 1 Camden Square, an easy no.29 bus hop to town. A radical design by co-owner/architect Rodger Davis allows natural light to flood through the open-plan interior. Breakfast, taken in the expansive living room or on the terrace, is overseen by Rodger's hospitable other half Sue and a colourful parrot by name of Peckham. The two guestrooms (one double, one single) are upstairs, convivial and comfortable. Neither is en suite, and the owners are keen to point out that they wouldn't have strangers sharing the bathroom. Rates are simple: £50 per person per night, £5 supplement for one-nighters, maximum stay one week. For pedestrians and cyclists, a newly opened path will get you to St Pancras International in 15 minutes. *Internet: wireless (free). TV.*

EAST LONDON
Expensive

★ Boundary

2-4 Boundary Street, Shoreditch, E3 7DD (7729 1051, www.theboundary.co.uk). Liverpool Street tube/rail or bus 8, 26, 48. **Rates** £184-£380 double. **Rooms** 17. **Credit** AmEx, DC, MC, V. **Map** p403 R4 ⓐ

Terence Conran's latest project, in a converted warehouse, includes a restaurant, rooftop bar, ground-floor café (*see p224*) and excellent hotel rooms that opened in 2009. *See p186* **Pushing the Boundary.** *Bar/café. Concierge. Disabled-adapted rooms. Internet: wireless (free). Restaurant. Room service. TV: DVD.*

Moderate

40 Winks

109 Mile End Road, Stepney, E1 4UJ (7790 0259, 07973 653944 mobile, www.40winks.org). Stepney Green tube. **Rates** £135 double. **Rooms** 2. **No credit cards.**

Flamboyant, fashionable and very cool, it's no wonder 40 Winks has been welcoming major film stars over the last year. *See p195* **Playing House.** *Internet: wireless (free). Parking: free.*

Hoxton Hotel

81 Great Eastern Street, Shoreditch, EC2A 3HU (7550 1000, www.hoxtonhotels.com). Old Street tube/rail. **Rates** (incl breakfast) £59-£199 double. **Rooms** 205. **Credit** AmEx, MC, V. **Map** p403 Q4 ⓐ

Famous for its low rates (including some publicity-garnering £1-a-night rooms), the Hoxton deserves credit for many other things. First, there's the hip Shoreditch location – hip enough for Soho House to have taken over the downstairs bar-brasserie in May 2009. Then there are the great design values (the foyer is a sort of postmodern country lodge, complete with stag's head). Finally, the rooms are well thought out, if rather small, with lots of nice touches. The downside? The popularity. If you don't book well in advance and visit during the business week, you could pay as much as at any other big chain. *Bar/café. Business centre. Disabled-adapted rooms. Internet: wireless (free). Restaurant. Room service. TV: pay movies.*

SOUTH-EAST LONDON
Moderate

Church Street Hotel

29-33 Camberwell Church Street, Camberwell, SE5 8TR (7703 5984, www.churchstreethotel. com). Denmark Hill rail or bus 36, 436. **Rates** (incl breakfast) £120-£170 double. **Rooms** 31. **Credit** AmEx, MC, V.

Craftsman José Raido is behind this attractive and original family-run hotel, opened in 2007 near Camberwell Green. Funky bathroom tiles in the bright, high-ceilinged bedrooms, for example, come from Guadalajara, a perfect match for Mexicana such as imported film posters, while the bed frames were forged by José himself. Bathroom products are organic, as are the pastries and cereals served for breakfast in an icon-filled dining room that also operates as a 24-hour honesty bar. You pay only £90 for a double with shared-bathroom, a real bargain. *Bar/café. Internet: wireless (free). Restaurant. TV.*

SOUTH-WEST LONDON
Expensive

★ Bingham

61-63 Petersham Road, Richmond, Surrey, TW10 6UT (8940 0902, www.thebingham. co.uk). Richmond tube/rail. **Rates** £190-£285 double. **Rooms** 15. **Credit** AmEx, DC, MC, V.

CONSUME

Quality boutique hotel, destination restaurant (under Shay Cooper's award-winning supervision) and sun-filled cocktail bar in one, the Bingham makes excellent use of its riverside location by Richmond Bridge. Six of its individually styled, high-ceilinged rooms overlook the river; all of them are named after a poet in honour of the Bingham's artistic past (lesbian aunt-and-niece couple Katherine Harris Bradley and Edith Emma Cooper lived here in the 1890s, hosting members of the aesthetic movement). Each room accommodates an ample bathtub and shower, art deco touches to the furnishings and irresistibly fluffy duck-and-goose feather duvets. Run by the Trinder family for the last 25 years, the Bingham manages to feel both grand and boutique. A treat.
Bar/café. Internet: wireless (free). Parking: £10/day. Restaurant. Room service. TV: DVD.

WEST LONDON
Moderate

Base2Stay
25 Courtfield Gardens, Earl's Court, SW5 0PG (262 8000, www.base2stay.com). Earl's Court tube. **Rates** £115-£152 double. **Rooms** 67. **Credit** AmEx, MC, V. **Map** p396 B10 ⑦
Base2Stay looks good, with its modernist limestone and taupe tones, and keeps prices low by removing inessentials: no bar, no restaurant. Instead, there's the increasingly popular solution of a 'kitchenette' (microwave, sink, silent mini-fridge, kettle), but here with all details carefully attended to (not just token cutlery, but sufficient kitchenware with corkscrew and can opener, and guidance about where to shop). The rooms, en suite (with power showers) and air-conditioned, are as carefully thought out, with desks, modem points and flatscreens, but the single/bunkbed rooms are small. Discount vouchers for nearby chain eateries are supplied by the friendly duo on 24hr reception duty.
Disabled-adapted rooms. Internet: wireless (free). Parking: £30/day. TV: pay movies.

★ Garret
Troubadour, 263-267 Old Brompton Road, Earl's Court, SW5 9JA (7370 1434, www. troubadour.co.uk). West Brompton tube/rail. **Rates** £165 double. **Rooms** 1. **Credit** AmEx, DC, MC, V. **Map** p396 B11 ⑦
For this wonderfully idiosyncratic attic apartment, *see p195* **Playing House.**
Bar/café. Internet: wireless (free). Room service. TV: DVD.

High Road House
162 Chiswick High Road, Chiswick, W4 1PR (8742 1717, www.highroadhouse.co.uk). Turnham Green tube. **Rates** £145-£165 double. **Rooms** 14. **Credit** AmEx, MC, V.

This west London outpost of Nick Jones's ever-fashionable Soho House stable features guestrooms designed by Ilse Crawford, and a members' bar and restaurant above the buzzing ground-floor brasserie. Serving a modern British menu, this has a retro sophisticated-Parisian-bistro-meets-Bloomsbury feel and, as you might expect, the food and service are excellent. Guestrooms are soothing, unadorned, white Shaker Modern with little fizzes of colour (and little hidden treats), the bathrooms well stocked with Cowshed products. There's also a basement games room.
Bars/cafés (2). Disabled-adapted rooms. Internet: wireless (free). Restaurants (2). Room service. TV: DVD & pay movies.

★ Mayflower Hotel
26-28 Trebovir Road, Earl's Court, SW5 9NJ (7370 0991, www.mayflower-group.co.uk). Earl's Court tube. **Rates** (incl continental breakfast) £92-£115 double. **Rooms** 46. **Credit** AmEx, MC, V. **Map** p396 B11 ⑦
After fighting on the frontlines of the Earl's Court budget-hotel style revolution, the Mayflower's taken the struggle to other parts of London (New Linden; *see p181*). But this is where the lushly contemporary house style evolved, proving affordability can be opulently chic. Cream walls and sleek dark woods are an understated background for richly coloured fabrics and intricate wooden architectural fragments sourced from Asia, like the lobby's imposing Jaipuri arch. The facilities too are well up to scratch, featuring marble bathrooms, Egyptian cotton sheets and CD players in the rooms.
Business centre. Internet: wireless (free). Parking: £25/day. TV.

Rockwell
181-183 Cromwell Road, Earl's Court, SW5 0SF (7244 2000, www.therockwell.com). Earl's Court tube. **Rates** £160-£200 double. **Rooms** 40. **Credit** AmEx, MC, V. **Map** p396 B10 ⑦
The Rockwell aims for relaxed contemporary elegance – and succeeds magnificently. The listed premises mean there are no identikit rooms here: they're all different sizes and individually designed, but share gleaming woods and muted glowing colours alongside more sober creams and neutrals. Among the rooms, pleasing eccentricities include a pair of central single rooms with skylights, and basement garden rooms that have tiny patios, complete with garden furniture, looking up at the smartly designed ground-level bridge that leads on to the garden terrace proper from the handsome bar-restaurant. Each room has a power shower, Starck fittings and bespoke cabinets in the bathrooms, and triple glazing ensures you never notice you're on a noisy road.
Bar/café. Concierge. Internet: high-speed (free). Restaurant. TV: pay movies.

CONSUME

Playing House

Two ways to make yourself at home.

Opposite a housing estate and cheap Somali diners, the family home of an interior designer has become the B&B of choice for movie stars and fashion movers. The 'micro-boutique hotel' **40 Winks** (for listings, *see p193*) looks extraordinary (kitchen frescoes, a music room with Beatles drumkit, a lion's head tap in the bath), but each stay is made thoroughly individual by owner David Carter's commitment to his guests, making them feel they're staying with a fabulous friend rather than just renting a room. Too late to book? Intriguing soirées such as Bedtime Stories (for which everyone must wear pyjamas) open the house to a wider audience.

For those who want culture without too much interaction, the **Garret** (for listings, *see left*) is another treat. High above the Troubadour, a 1960s counter-culture café that still hosts poetry and music events, it's unjustly named: yes, the rooms are in the attic and have charming pitched roofs, but there are acres of space. The huge, high main bed lies under a skylight and there's a writing desk, but lingering thoughts of poetic torment are banished by Arts and Crafts decor and the fully equipped lounge-kitchen.

Garret.

Twenty Nevern Square

20 Nevern Square, Earl's Court, SW5 9PD (7565 9555, www.twentynevernsquare.co.uk). Earl's Court tube. **Rates** (incl breakfast) £90-£150 double. **Rooms** 20. **Credit** AmEx, MC, V. **Map** p396 A11 ⑰

Only the less-than-posh location of this immaculate boutique hotel keeps the rates reasonable. Tucked away in a private garden square, it feels far from its locale. The modern-colonial style was created by its well-travelled owner, who personally sourced many of the exotic and antique furnishings (as well as those in sister hotel the Mayflower; see above). In the sleek marble bathrooms, toiletries are tidied away in decorative caskets, but the beds are the real stars: from elaborately carved four-posters to Egyptian sleigh styles, all with luxurious mattresses. The vaguely Far Eastern feel extends into the lounge and the airy conservatory, with its dark wicker furniture.

Bar/café. Internet: wireless & high-speed (free). Parking: £25/day. Room service. TV: DVD.

APARTMENT RENTAL

The companies listed below specialise in holiday lets. Typical daily rates on a reasonably central property run to around £70-£90 for a studio or one-bed apartment to £100 or thereabouts for a two-bed place. However, as with any style of accommodation in London, if you've money to burn, then the sky's the limit. Note that many of these firms operate minimum-stay requirements, which means that apartment rental is only an option if you're planning a relatively protracted visit to the city.

Respected all-rounders with properties around the city include **Holiday Serviced Apartments** (0845 060 4477, www.holiday apartments.co.uk) and **Palace Court Holiday Apartments** (7727 3467, www.palacecourt.c o.uk). **London Holiday Accommodation** (7265 0882, www.londonholiday.co.uk) offers half a dozen decent-priced self-catering options in the West End and on the South Bank. For serviced apartments, try the South Bank or Earl's Court 'campuses' run by **Think Apartments** (0845 602 9437, www.think-apartments.com). **Accommodation Outlet** (7287 4244, www.outlet4holidays.com) is a recommended lesbian and gay agency that has some excellent properties across London in general and in Soho in particular.

CAMPING & CARAVANNING

If putting yourself at the mercy of English weather in a far-flung suburban field doesn't put you off, transport links into central London might do the job instead. Still, you can't really beat the prices.

Crystal Palace Caravan Club *Crystal Palace Parade, Crystal Palace, SE19 1UF (8778 7155). Crystal Palace rail or bus 3.* **Open** *Mar-Sept* 9am-6pm Mon-Sun. *Oct-Feb* 9.30am-5.30pm Mon-Sun. **Rates** *Caravan £5-£8. Tent £5-£15.* **Credit** MC, V.

Lee Valley Campsite *Sewardstone Road, Chingford, E4 7RA (8529 5689, www.leevalley park.org.uk). Walthamstow Central tube/rail then bus 215.* **Open** *Mar-Nov* 8am-9pm daily. **Rates** £7.10; £3.10 under-16s; free under-2s. **Credit** MC, V.

Lee Valley Leisure Centre Camping & Caravan Park *Meridian Way, Pickett's Lock, Enfield, Middx N9 0AR (8803 6900, www. leevalleypark.org.uk). Edmonton Green rail or bus W8.* **Open** 8am-10pm daily. **Rates** £4.20; £2.10 reductions; free under-5s. **Credit** MC, V.

STAYING WITH THE LOCALS

Several agencies can arrange for individuals and families to stay in Londoners' homes. Prices for a stay are around £20-£85 for a single and £45-£105 for a double, including breakfast, and depending on the location and degree of comfort. Agencies include **At Home in London** (8748 1943, www.athomeinlondon. co.uk), **Bulldog Club** (0870 803 4414, www. bulldogclub.com), **Coach House Rentals** (8133 8332, www.rentals.chslondon.com), **Host & Guest Service** (7385 9922, www. host-guest.co.uk), **London Bed & Breakfast Agency** (7586 2768, www.londonbb.com) and **London Homestead Services** (7286 5115, www.lhslondon.com); for an extra classy option, *see below* **Inside Track**. You can usually expect for there to be a minimum length of stay stipulated.

UNIVERSITY RESIDENCES

During university vacations, much of London's dedicated student accommodation is opened up to visitors, providing them with a source of basic but cheap digs. Central locations can make these an absolute bargain.

INSIDE TRACK MOVE UPTOWN

'You may be staying with an artist, an actor or diplomat, a business-man or even a lord!', says www.uptownres.co.uk. Certainly Uptown's 80 hosts offer B&B in some of the most salubrious parts of town – Chelsea, Belgravia, Knightsbridge – for little over £100 a night. Call 7937 2001 or use the form on the website to make a booking.

International Students House *229 Great Portland Street, Marylebone, W1W 5PN (7631 8300, www.ish.org.uk). Great Portland Street tube.* **Open** *Reception* 7.45am-10.30pm Mon-Fri, 8am-10.30pm Sat, Sun. **Rates** £12-£21 (per person) dormitory; £34 single; £53 twin. **No credit cards. Map** p398 H4 ⑦

King's College Conference & Vacation Bureau *Strand Bridge House, 138-142 Strand, Covent Garden, WC2R 1HH (7848 1700, www.kcl.ac.uk/kcvb). Temple tube.* **Rates** £30-£40 single; £52-£60 twin. **No credit cards. Map** p407 Z3 ⑦

LSE *Bankside House, 24 Sumner Street, Holborn, SE1 9JA (7107 5773, www.lse vacations.co.uk). London Bridge tube.* **Rates** £33-£48 single; £45-£70 twin/double. **No credit cards. Map** p404 O8 ⑧
The London School of Economics has vacation rentals across town, but Bankside House (tucked just behind Tate Modern) is the best located.

YOUTH HOSTELS

For Youth Hostel Assocation venues, you can get extra reductions on the rates detailed below. If you're a member of the IYHF (International Youth Hostel Federation), you'll pay £3 less a night. Joining costs only £13 (£6.50 for under-18s), and can be done on arrival or through www.yha.org.uk prior to departure. All under-18s receive a 25 per cent discount, in any case. YHA hostel beds are arranged either in dormitories or in twin rooms.

Earl's Court *38 Bolton Gardens, Earl's Court, SW5 0AQ (7373 7083, www.yha.org.uk). Earl's Court tube.* **Open** 24hrs daily. **Rates** £21.95-£60. **No credit cards. Map** p396 B11 ⑧

Holland Park *Holland Walk, South Kensington, W8 7QU (7937 0748, www.yha.org.uk). High Street Kensington tube.* **Open** 24hrs daily. **Rates** £14.95-£100. **No credit cards. Map** p394 A8 ⑧

Meininger *Baden-Powell House, 65-67 Queen's Gate, South Kensington, SW7 5JS (7590 6910, www.meininger-hostels.com). Gloucester Road or South Kensington tube.* **Rates** £15-£98. **Credit** MC, V. **Map** p397 D10 ⑧

Oxford Street *14 Noel Street, Soho, W1F 8GJ (7734 1618, www.yha.org.uk). Oxford Circus tube.* **Open** 24hrs daily. *Reception* 7am-11pm daily. **Rates** £24.50-£60. **No credit cards. Map** p406 V2 ⑧

St Pancras *79-81 Euston Road, King's Cross, NW1 2QE (0870 770 6044, www.yha.org.uk). King's Cross tube/rail.* **Open** 24hrs daily. **Rates** £21.95-£60. **No credit cards. Map** p399 L3 ⑧

St Paul's *36 Carter Lane, the City, EC4V 5AB (7236 4965, www.yha.org.uk). St Paul's tube or Blackfriars rail.* **Open** 24hrs daily. **Rates** £21.95-£60. **No credit cards. Map** p404 O6 ⑧

Restaurants & Cafés

Finding great food is no longer a challenge in London.

In the last decade, the amount of contemporary British cooking available to London diners has moved from famine to feast. Put it down to the **St John** effect. Fergus Henderson's pioneering restaurant, which is still superb, has been followed by many worthy successors, from **Corrigan's Mayfair** to **Market**. It also inspired an increasing number of Brit-by-numbers places, much in the same way that the **Eagle** unwittingly spawned an array of two-a-penny gastropubs – use this chapter to find the best of both types of venue.

Be sure also to take advantage of the culinary riches London's many immigrants have brought here. Fine Bangladeshi, Moroccan, Lebanese, Turkish and Vietnamese restaurants are listed here, as are top-notch exponents of the cuisines of France, Italy, Japan, Spain, China and Thailand. There are old-school options too: fish and chips, a classic café (**E Pellicci**) and even **M Manze**, the city's finest old pie and mash shop.

ESSENTIAL INFORMATION

Try to book a table in advance. At many places, booking is vital; at a select few restaurants, you may need to book a month ahead. Smoking is banned in all restaurants and cafés. Tipping is standard practice: ten to 15 per cent is usual. Many restaurants add this charge as standard to bills; some do so but still present the credit card slip as 'open', cheekily encouraging the customer to tip twice. Always check the bill.

We've listed a range of meal prices for each place. However, restaurants often change their menus, so treat these prices only as guidelines. Budget venues are marked **£**.

For a selection of the best places to eat with children, *see pp280-281.*

THE SOUTH BANK & BANKSIDE

Borough Market (*see p261*), full of stalls selling all kinds of wonderful food, is a superb forage for gourmet snackers. **Tate Modern**

About the reviews
This chapter is compiled from Time Out's annual London Eating & Drinking Guide (£11.99) and Cheap Eats in London (£7.99), both of which are available from www.timeout.com.

Café: **Level 2** (*see p281*) is superb for those with children, as are the neighbouring outposts of **Wagamama** and **Giraffe** (*see p280*) under the Royal Festival Hall.

Anchor & Hope
36 The Cut, SE1 8LP (7928 9898). Southwark tube or Waterloo tube/rail. **Open** 5-11pm Mon; noon-11pm Tue-Sat; noon-5pm Sun. *Meals served* 6-10.30pm Mon; noon-2.30pm, 6-10.30pm Tue-Sat; 2pm sitting Sun. **Main courses** £11-£22. **Credit** DC, MC, V. **Map** p404 N8 ❶ **Gastropub**
The most common complaint about this relaxed Waterloo gastropub is the no-booking policy. Those who end up having to wait at the bar can salivate over the seasonal British menu on the blackboard, but choose carefully: despite good sourcing, not all dishes are equally successful. Arbroath smokie is a good bet if it's available; other dishes might include cold roast beef and dripping on toast. There's a single sitting on Sundays.
► *If the Anchor's too busy, head down Waterloo Road for no-frills fish and chips at Masters Super Fish (no.191, 7928 6924, closed Sun).*

❶ Blue numbers given here correspond to the location of each restaurant and café on the street maps. See pp394-407.

CONSUME

Eating In...

Our pick of the best winter dining.

Bocca di Lupo
See p208.
A runner-up for *Time Out*'s Best New Italian award in 2009, Jacob Kenedy's welcoming Italian restaurant is a brightly lit, cosy eaterie in the cold streets of Soho. Try meaty specials, such as own-made pork and foie gras sausages with *farro*, or a warming stew.

Giaconda Dining Room
See p203.
Time Out's Best New Restaurant of 2009, Giaconda does bold, meaty flavours that delight but don't overwhelm. For cold winter nights, tuck into braised tripe with chorizo, butter beans and paprika, pumpkin risotto or a trad duck confit with Lyonnaise potatoes.

Rosa's
See p224.
A tiny but efficient Thai café (*pictured*) around the corner from Brick Lane. The curries are piping hot and soul-soothing, and the *som tum* appropriately fiery.

Madsen
See p219.
If it's chilly but you still want to be outside, think Scandinavian. Madsen's pavement tables have no patio heaters, but the restaurant provides thick, soft blankets to keep you cosy while tucking into Nordic specialities and wonderfully nutty Danish beers.

Baltic
74 Blackfriars Road, SE1 8HA (7928 1111, www.balticrestaurant.co.uk). Southwark tube.
Open noon-3pm, 5.30-11.15pm Mon-Sat; noon-10.30pm Sun. **Main courses** £10-£17. **Credit** AmEx, MC, V. **Map** p404 N8 ❷
Eastern European
This stylish spot remains the brightest star on London's east European restaurant scene. The menu combines the best of east European cuisine – from Georgian-style lamb with aubergines to Romanian sour cream *mamaliga* (polenta) – with a light, modern European twist. Great cocktails, a wide choice of vodkas, an eclectic wine list and friendly service add to the appeal. In the high-ceilinged restaurant, gaze up at hundreds of shards of golden amber in the stunning chandelier.

Canteen
Royal Festival Hall, Belvedere Road, SE1 8XX (0845 686 1122, www.canteen.co.uk). Embankment tube or Waterloo tube/rail.
Open 8am-11pm Mon-Fri; 9am-11pm Sat, Sun. **Main courses** £8-£15. **Credit** AmEx, MC, V. **Map** p401 M8 ❸ **British**
Furnished with utilitarian but comfortable tables and booths, this branch of Canteen is handily tucked into the back of the Royal Festival Hall (*see p311*). No surprise, then, that it's often busy. Dishes range from a bacon sandwich and afternoon jam scones to full roasts. Classic breakfasts (eggs benedict, welsh rarebit) are served all day, joined by the likes of macaroni cheese or sausage and mash with onion gravy from lunchtime.
Other locations 2 Crispin Place, off Brushfield Street, Spitalfields, E1 6DW; Park Pavilion, 40 Canada Square, Docklands, E14 5FW; 55 Baker Street, Marylebone, W1U 8EW.

Magdalen
152 Tooley Street, SE1 2TU (7403 1342, www.magdalenrestaurant.co.uk). London Bridge tube/rail. **Open** noon-2.30pm, 6.30-10pm Mon-Fri; 6.30-10pm Sat. **Main courses** £13-£20.
Set lunch £15.50 2 courses, £18.50 3 courses. **Credit** AmEx, MC, V. **Map** p405 Q8 ❹ **British**
Magdalen makes the most of fairly unprepossessing surroundings. A la carte prices are just about reasonable (£17.50 for flavoursome Middle White belly with veg and good gravy, £16.50 for a beautifully presented fish stew), but portions aren't huge; opt instead for the set lunch, a steal at £15.50 for two courses or £18.50 for three. Poached rhubarb with shortbread and crème anglaise is the pick of the puddings, and there's a tempting collection of British cheeses. Staff are young, friendly and efficient.

£ M Manze
87 Tower Bridge Road, SE1 4TW (7407 2985, www.manze.co.uk). Bus 1, 42, 188. **Open** 11am-2pm Mon; 10.30am-2pm Tue-Thur;

10am-2.15pm Fri; 10am-2.45pm Sat.
Main courses £2-£6. **No credit cards.**
Map p405 Q10 **⑤** Pie & mash
Manze's is the finest remaining purveyor of the dirt-cheap traditional foodstuff of London's working classes. It's both the oldest pie shop in town, established in 1902, and the most beautiful, with tiles, marble-topped tables and worn wood benches. Expect mashed potato, minced beef pies and liquor (a parsley sauce); braver souls should try the stewed eels.

More

104 Tooley Street, SE1 2TH (7403 0635, www.moretooleystreet.com). London Bridge tube/rail. **Open** 8am-11pm Mon-Fri; 10am-11pm Sat; 10am-4pm Sun. **Main courses** £10-£16. **Credit** AmEx, MC, V. **Map** p405 Q8 **⑥** Brasserie
A new venture from chef Theodore Kyriakou and business partner Paloma Campbell, More is a true all-day brasserie. Small, sleek and chic, it swings effortlessly from breakfast muesli and fruit plates to full-on lunches and dinners. Mains consist of classics with added touches, along with more unusual, fusion-style dishes. Jolly staff help to create a feel-good atmosphere.

Roast

Floral Hall, Borough Market, Stoney Street, SE1 1TL (7940 1300, www.roast-restaurant.com). London Bridge tube/rail. **Open** 7-9.30am, noon-2.30pm, 5.30-10.30pm Mon-Fri; 8-10.30am, 11.30am-3.30pm, 6-10.30pm Sat; noon-3.30pm Sun. **Main courses** £12-£20. **Credit** AmEx, MC, V. **Map** p404 P8 **❼** British
A big airy restaurant by Borough Market, Roast gets crammed on market days, but staff cope admirably. The restaurant menu (there's a much cheaper bar menu from 3pm) offers the best of British cuisine. Cold poached Devon sea trout with wild garlic salad cream is typical, with Neal's Yard cheeses and trad desserts for afters. Add to this an impressive drinks list, including a fine roster of teas, and you have a great all-rounder.
▶ *Borough Market is also home to the excellent, busy Tapas Brindisa (18-20 Southwark Street, 7357 8880, www.brindisa.com).*

£ Tsuru

4 Canvey Street, SE1 9AN (7928 2228, www.tsuru-sushi.co.uk). Southwark tube or London Bridge tube/rail. **Open** 11am-9pm Mon-Fri. **Main courses** £4-£13. **Credit** MC, V. **Map** p404 O8 **⑧** Japanese
Media honeys from the Blue Fin Building slip away every lunch hour to this tiny yet remarkable canteen, depleting the supply of silky, umami-rich *katsu* curries. On Thursdays and Fridays, the welcoming space becomes a trendy nightspot where *ippin ryori* (Japanese 'tapas') can be enjoyed along with saké and shochu cocktails.

...and Eating Out

Our pick of the best summer dining.

Boundary Project
See p186 and p223.
Terence Conran's three-tiered Shoreditch eaterie not only comprises the laid-back Albion café, which has great pavement tables, but a chic rooftop where barbecues blaze on summer evenings.

Freggo
See p215.
Argentinians may be better known for steak, but ice-cream is a night-time ritual. Imported by Gaucho steakhouses, this chic new ice-cream parlour is the real artisanal deal. Cool off with decadent scoops of dulce de leche or malbec and berries in the alfresco area.

Modern Pantry
See p201.
Anna Hansen's genre-bending cuisine style features gems such as sugar-cured prawn omelette with smoky *sambal*, perfect to be enjoyed in the sun, as well as great brunch options. The outdoor tables (*pictured*) are the perfect for enjoying her Antipodean flair.

Serpentine Bar & Kitchen
See p220.
There are plenty of waterside tables, many shaded by trees, at this Benugo-run café next to the Serpentine lake. Enjoy sun-dappled breakfasts or lunches consisting of seasonal British produce and wood-fired pizzas.

CONSUME

CONSUME

Giaconda Dining Room. *See p203.*

THE CITY

The City remains a working-hours kind of place: in many areas, venues still shut in the evenings and at weekends, and are at their busiest for weekday lunchtimes.

Bodean's
16 Byward Street, EC3R 5BA (7488 3883, www.bodeansbbq.com). Tower Hill tube.
Open noon-3pm, 6-10pm Mon-Fri; 6-10pm Sat.
Main courses £8-£16. **Credit** AmEx, MC, V.
Map p405 R7 ❾ **American**
Bodean's now has five branches: Soho, Westbourne Grove, Fulham, Clapham and, handily, here. The schtick remains unchanged: Kansas City barbecue, with a small informal upstairs and bigger, smarter downstairs with US sport on TV. The food is decent, generous and very, very meaty – bring an appetite.
Other locations throughout the city.

£ Fish Central
149-155 Central Street, EC1V 8AP (7253 4970, www.bodeansbbq.com). Old Street tube/rail or bus 55. **Open** 11am-2.30pm Mon-Sat; 5-10.30pm Mon-Thur; 5-11pm Fri, Sat. **Main courses** £8-£15.
Credit MC, V. **Map** p402 P3 ❿ **Fish & chips**
A large photograph on the wall shows Fish Central as it was pre-makeover: just your everyday chippy. Today, it's quite a lively, trendy set-up. The specials board contains the likes of warm squid salad, but tradition-seekers won't be disappointed. Good chips and mushy peas, decent wines and a welcome choice of tap beers make this a fine local.

Restaurant at St Paul's
St Paul's Cathedral, St Paul's Churchyard, EC4M 8AD (7248 2469, www.restaurantat stpauls.co.uk). St Paul's tube. **Open** noon-4.30pm daily. **Set lunch** £16 2 courses, £20 3 courses.
Credit MC, V. **Map** p404 O6 ⓫ **British**
This is a dull moniker for a handsome, light-filled space in the cathedral crypt, with very sensuous and textural decor – great for a restaurant, surprising in a place of worship. The food is excellent: summery asparagus and poached Gressingham duck egg, treacle-cured salmon with watercress, a prettily pink Trigger Farm barnsley chop, and pastry in a portobello mushroom wellington and pudding of gooseberry cobbler that revealed a very deft pair of hands in the kitchen.
▶ *It's closed in the evening, so try the good-value set dinner at nearby Sauterelle's (Royal Exchange, EC3V 3LR, 7618 2483, www.danddlondon.com).*

Sweetings
39 Queen Victoria Street, EC4N 4SA (7248 3062). Mansion House tube. **Open** 11.30am-3pm Mon-Fri. **Main courses** £12-£28. **Credit** AmEx, MC, V. **Map** p404 P6 ⓬ **Fish & seafood**
No-nonsense British food served in a quintessentially English setting. Diners at the communal tables at the rear can survey walls hung with old cartoons, photos and cricket mementos. Specials might include gull's eggs and smoked salmon pâté while the 'bill of fare' proffers traditional dishes. Sweetings opens only for lunch, takes no bookings, and is full soon after noon, so order a silver pewter mug of Guinness and enjoy the wait.

HOLBORN & CLERKENWELL

Home to the pioneering **St John** (*see p203*) and **Eagle** (*see below*), this scrubby bit of nowhere much is still home to a surprising proportion of London's best eating options.

★ £ Clerkenwell Kitchen

27-31 Clerkenwell Close, EC1R 0AT (7101 9959, www.theclerkenwellkitchen.co.uk). Angel tube or Farringdon tube/rail. **Open** 8am-5pm Mon-Wed, Fri; 8am-11pm Thur. **Main courses** £4-£14. **Credit** MC, V. **Map** p402 N4 ⓭ **Café**

Tucked away in an office development for creatives, the Clerkenwell Kitchen has a ready supply of enthusiastic customers who pop in for coffees, sandwiches, lunch meetings and quiet moments with the Wi-Fi. From noon, high-quality, fairly priced meals made with seasonal produce are served, restaurant-calibre food in a stylishly informal café setting. Enjoy with a glass of wine, a Meantime beer, a Chegworth Valley juice or a well-made Union Hand-Roasted coffee. *See p199* **Eating Out**.

Le Comptoir Gascon

61-63 Charterhouse Street, EC1M 6HJ (7608 0851, www.comptoirgascon.com). Farringdon tube/rail. **Open** noon-2pm, 7-10pm Tue, Wed; noon-2pm, 7-10.30pm Thur, Fri; 10.30am-2.30pm, 7-10pm Sat. **Main courses** £7-£14. **Credit** AmEx, MC, V. **Map** p402 O5 ⓮ **French**

The bistro offshoot of Club Gascon is a deservedly popular spot. A small, convivial brick-lined room that doubles as a deli, it offers the over-30s refuge on a street lined with raucous bars. Even more importantly, the food is great, and nicely priced. Splendid, taste-packed mains of grilled lamb and beef onglet are excellent; sides are worth ordering, especially the mighty french fries cooked in duck fat. Try the own-made ice-creams for dessert.

▶ *The smarter, similarly excellent Club Gascon (57 West Smithfield, EC1A 9DS, 7796 0600, www.clubgascon.com) is just nearby*

Eagle

159 Farringdon Road, EC1R 3AL (7837 1353). Farringdon tube/rail. **Open** noon-11pm Mon-Sat; noon-5pm Sun. *Meals served* 12.30-3pm, 6.30-10.30pm Mon-Fri; 12.30-3.30pm, 6.30-10.30pm Sat; 12.30-3.30pm Sun. **Main courses** £5-£17. **Credit** MC, V. **Map** p402 N4 ⓯ **Gastropub**

Widely credited with being the first gastropub (it opened in 1991), the Eagle is still recognisably a pub with quality food: noisy, often crowded (you'll usually be sharing a table), with no-frills service. The room is dominated by a giant open range at which T-shirted cooks toss earthy grills in theatrical bursts of flame. The kitchen takes up one half of the long bar, with the hearty Med-influenced menu chalked up above it. A short wine list is available by glass or bottle; there are also real ales on tap.

Eastside Inn

40 St John Street, EC1M 4AY (7490 9230, www.esilondon.com). Farringdon tube/rail. **Open** *Bistro* noon-10pm Mon-Sat. *Restaurant* noon-2.30pm, 7-10pm Mon-Fri. **Main courses** *Bistro* £13-£20. **Set meal** *Restaurant* £55 3 courses, £70 tasting menu. **Credit** AmEx, MC, V. **Map** p402 O5 ⓰ **French/haute cuisine**

Bjorn van der Horst's restaurant is a twin enterprise: a restaurant section offering high-priced, limited-choice fine dining, and a bistro, with less expensive and reliably unadventurous French fare. There are plenty of luxury ingredients across both, with lots of big meat flavours and offal, including Van der Horst's signature dish of foie gras with coffee and amaretto foam. Real wow factors are offered by pudding: two orbs, one a gold-plated milk sorbet, the other a meringue that disintegrates when flambéed at the table.

Hix Oyster & Chop House

36-37 Greenhill Rents, off Cowcross Street, EC1M 6BN (7017 1930, www.restaurantsetc ltd.co.uk). Farringdon tube/rail. **Open** noon-3pm, 6-11pm Mon-Fri; 6-11pm Sat; noon-5pm, 6-10pm Sun. **Main courses** £10-£35. **Credit** AmEx, MC, V. **Map** p402 O5 ⓱ **British**

Although the name tells diners what to expect, there's more to Mark Hix's place than chops and oysters: free-range Goosnargh chicken with wild garlic sauce (for two), for example. But oysters (such as Helford natives or Colchester rocks), chops and steaks feature prominently; accordingly, most diners are male. Puddings are nicely retro, albeit with modern twists.

▶ *The same chef opened the eponymous, excellent Hix (66-70 Brewer Street, W1F 9UP, 7292 3518, www.hixsoho.co.uk) in late 2009.*

★ Modern Pantry

47-48 St John's Square, EC1V 4JJ (7250 0833, www.themodernpantry.co.uk). Farringdon tube/rail. **Open** *Café* 8am-11pm Mon-Fri; 9am-11pm Sat; 10am-10pm Sun. *Restaurant* noon-3pm, 6-10.30pm Tue-Fri; 6-10.30pm Sat. **Main courses** £12-£20. **Credit** (both) AmEx, MC, V. **Map** p402 O4 ⓲ **International**

THE BEST BRITISH FOOD

Albion
Conran comes up trumps again. *See p223.*

Fish Central
The finest fish 'n' chips in town. *See left.*

St John
Still the city's best. *See p203.*

CONSUME

A culinary three-parter across two Georgian townhouses, the Modern Pantry feels savvy and of the moment. Both pantry (takeaway) and café (informal) are at street level; upstairs are adjoining dining rooms (still informal). The venue is fashionable without being annoyingly so, and service is spot on. Anna Hansen's menu fuses all kinds of fine ingredients. The weekend brunch is special but popular, so be sure to book. *See also p199* **Eating Out.**

★ Moro

34-36 Exmouth Market, EC1R 4QE (7833 8336, www.moro.co.uk). Farringdon tube/rail or bus 19, 38, 341. **Open** *12.30-10.30pm Mon-Sat.* **Main courses** *£14-£20. Tapas £3-£15.* **Credit** AmEx, DC, MC, V. **Map** p402 N4 **⑲ North African**

A meal that excites the senses is a rarity, but Moro often achieves it. For a restaurant with a big reputation, its decor is unpretentious, the centrepiece being a simple view of the kitchen's big wood-fired oven. You can enjoy tapas at the bar or sit down for a more leisurely wander through the Moorish menu, with inspiration from Egypt to Portugal, Spain to the Lebanon. The drinks list is a point of pride; almost all the wines, sherries and cava come from the Iberian peninsula.

▶ *Opposite, all-day French café Ambassador (no.55, 7837 0009, www.theambassadorcafe. co.uk) serves fine fare, with excellent brunches.*

★ St John

26 St John Street, EC1M 4AY (7251 0848/4998, www.stjohnrestaurant.com). Barbican tube or Farringdon tube/rail. **Open** *noon-3pm, 6-11pm Mon-Fri; 6-11pm Sat; 1-3pm Sun.* **Main courses** *£13-£23.* **Credit** AmEx, DC, MC, V. **Map** p402 O5 **⑳ British**

Chef-patron Fergus Henderson opened the daddy of new-wave British restaurants in the shell of a Smithfield smokehouse in 1995, and hasn't looked back since. The focus is on seasonal and unusual British produce, simply cooked. Although it's a world-famous restaurant, it's completely unstuffy: staff are approachable as well as highly competent and the French wine list won't frighten anyone. And while prices aren't low, they're not excessive for the quality; a cheaper option is to have a snack in the airy bar.

BLOOMSBURY & FITZROVIA

£ Benito's Hat

56 Goodge Street, W1T 4NB (7637 3732, www.benitos-hat.com). Goodge Street tube. **Open** *11.30am-10pm Mon-Wed, Sun; 11.30am-11pm Thur-Sat.* **Main courses** *£5-£6.* **Credit** MC, V. **Map** p398 J5 **㉑ Mexican**

Tex-Mex eateries are currently ten a peso in London; while there's only one Benito's Hat, the branded interior looks ripe for replication. The production line serves some of the best burritos in town. Try the slow-cooked pork, wrapped in a soft, floury tortilla along with fiery salsa brava (made several times daily) and black beans authentically flavoured with avocado leaves. If you're having a drink, the margaritas are suitably merciless.

▶ *El Burrito is a great alternative, a step away on Charlotte Place (see below* **Inside Track***).*

Camino

3 Varnishers Yard, Regents Quarter, N1 9FD (7841 7331, www.camino.uk.com). King's Cross tube/rail. **Open** *Restaurant 8-11.30am, noon-3pm, 6.30-11pm Mon-Fri; 9am-4pm, 7-11pm Sat; 11am-4pm Sun. Bar noon-midnight Mon-Wed; noon-1am Thur-Sat.* **Main courses** *£10-£23. Tapas £3-£8.* **Credit** AmEx, MC, V. **Map** p399 L3 **㉒ Tapas**

Camino's cavernous premises comprise a sleek bar and restaurant; outside, drinkers spill into the courtyard, sipping iced Cruzcampo and nibbling plump, golden-crumbed croquetas. The tapas list is dotted with regional specialities, but the full menu of classical Iberian fare with Modern Euro forays must be sampled in the restaurant, where the stripped-down, self-consciously modern aesthetic is softened by muted candlelight and the hum of conversation.

★ Giaconda Dining Room

9 Denmark Street, WC2H 8LS (7240 3334, www. giacondadining.com). Tottenham Court Road tube. **Open** *noon-2.15pm, 6-9.15pm Mon-Fri.* **Main courses** *£9-£13. Cover £1.* **Credit** AmEx, MC, V. **Map** p407 X2 **㉓ Modern European**

This new arrival is a thoroughly likeable restaurant. The decor is nothing special and the room is a bit cramped, but the food served is what most people want to eat most of the time: the Australian owners describe it as French-ish with a bit of Spain and Italy, but there are also big-flavoured grills, fish of the day and any number of intriguing assemblages (chorizo, chicken liver, trotters and tripe, for instance). *See also p198* **Eating In.** *Photo p200.*

★ Hakkasan

8 Hanway Place, W1T 1HD (7907 1888, www. hakkasan.com). Tottenham Court Road tube. **Open** *Restaurant noon-3pm, 6-11pm Mon-Wed; noon-3pm, 6pm-midnight Thur, Fri; noon-4pm, 6pm-midnight Sat; noon-4pm, 6-11pm Sun.*

INSIDE TRACK
CHARLOTTE PLACE

Just off Goodge Street sits Charlotte Place, surely the best snack alley in town. If you don't fancy **Lantana** (*see p204*), get wraps to go from **El Burrito** (no.5, 7580 5048) or delicious *bánh mì* (baguettes with Vietnamese fillings) from **Viet Baguette** (no.14).

CONSUME

CONSUME

Bar noon-12.30am Mon-Wed; noon-1.30am
Thur-Sat; noon-midnight Sun. **Main courses**
£10-£58. *Dim sum* £3-£20. **Credit** AmEx, MC,
V. **Map** p406 W1 **24** **Chinese**
Creator Alan Yau sold this esteemed restaurant to
an Abu Dhabi-based company in early 2008, but the
changes they've made are minimal. Why mess with
brilliance? It's hard not to be enamoured by the
sultry enclave of chinoiserie that is this underground
restaurant, where sleek staff glide out of the shad-
ows carrying all manner of elegantly presented modern Chinese fare. To dine on dim sum here is a
pleasure, the sweet scallop *siu mai* with glistening
flying-fish roe a highlight.
▶ *On a budget? Visit at lunchtime to enjoy the*
Hakkasan experience for much less.

Konstam at the Prince Albert
2 Acton Street, WC1X 9NA (7833 5040,
www.konstam.co.uk). King's Cross tube/rail.
Open 12.30-3pm, 6.30-10.30pm Mon-Fri;
6.30-10.30pm Sat; 10.30am-4pm Sun. **Main**
courses £11-£17. **Credit** AmEx, MC, V.
Map p399 M3 **25** **British**
Konstam does much with an uninspiring location
and limited (ex-pub) space. Tables are packed close
together, making lunch (when some tables are
empty) preferable to dinner. The USP here is that
more than 85% of the produce is 'grown or reared
within the area covered by the London Underground
network'. Which is not to say that owner/chef Oliver
Rowe's menu is limited or unimaginative. At lunch,
everything is available as a takeaway.
▶ *On parallel Swinton Street, Acorn House*
(no.69, 7812 1842, www.acornhouserestaurant.
com) is another sassy eco-restaurant.

★ Landau
Langham, 1C Portland Place, W1B 1JA (7965
0165, www.thelandau.com). Oxford Circus tube.
Open 7-10.30am, 12.30-11pm Mon-Fri; 7am-noon,
5.30-11pm Sat; 7am-noon Sun. **Main courses**
£19-£30. **Credit** AmEx, DC, MC, V. **Map** p398
H5 **26** **Haute cuisine**
A visit to the Landau brings an immediate sense of
occasion. Chef Andrew Turner presents British
ingredients with molecular gastronomy touches, but
this is still a hotel dining room, so weary (and
wealthy) travellers might also console themselves
with pea soup or grilled dover sole. Desserts allow
the kitchen to unleash its creativity. There are
wonderful views over Nash's All Souls Church and
Broadcasting House if the people-watching opportunities are scant.

★ £ Lantana
13 Charlotte Place, W1T 1SN (7637 3347,
www.lantanacafe.co.uk). Goodge Street tube.
Open 8am-6pm Mon-Wed; 8am-9pm Thur, Fri;
10am-6pm Sat. **Main courses** £4-£10. **Credit**
MC, V. **Map** p398 J5 **27** **Café**

THE BEST CHEAP EATS

Arbutus
Fine haute cuisine in Soho. *See p207.*

Baozi Inn
Nice noodles and more. *See p207.*

Lantana
Café culture comes alive. *See below.*

This cheerful Aussie café won *Time Out*'s Best New
Café award in 2009. It's open for breakfast through
to lunch and sometimes dinner. Sweetcorn fritters
with crispy bacon or smoked salmon with lime aïoli
is a highlight, as is the delicious banana bread, and
the combination of Monmouth beans and a La
Marzocco espresso machine ensures flawless coffee.
▶ *For more spots on Charlotte Place, see p203*
Inside Track.

St Pancras Grand
St Pancras International, Euston Road, NW1
2QP (7870 9900, www.searcys.co.uk/stpancras
grand). King's Cross tube/rail. **Open** 11am-11pm
daily. **Main courses** £14-£22. **Credit** AmEx,
MC, V. **Map** p399 L3 **28** **Brasserie**
The revival of British cuisine had hardly been evi-
dent at its gateways to the world. Now, at last,
London has a station restaurant to be proud of. St
Pancras Grand evokes a grand European café with
contemporary-brasserie style, and the well-sourced
British food is served simply but with ambition.
Even the stripy-aproned staff are first rate.

Salt Yard
54 Goodge Street, W1T 4NA (7637 0657, www.
saltyard.co.uk). Goodge Street tube. **Open** noon-
11pm Mon-Fri; 5-11pm Sat. *Tapas served* noon-
3pm, 6-11pm Mon-Fri; 5-11pm Sat. **Tapas** £2-£9.
Credit AmEx, DC, MC, V. **Map** p398 J5 **29**
Spanish/Italian tapas
The artful menu of Iberian and Italian tapas standards served at this dark, sleek, calm and classy
joint is aimed at diners in search of a slow lunch or
lightish dinner. Fine selections of charcuterie and
cheese front the frequently changing menu, which
features the likes of tuna carpaccio with baby broad
beans, and ham croquettes with manchego. One of
London's top venues for fuss-free tapas.

COVENT GARDEN

£ Abeno Too
17-18 Great Newport Street, WC2H 7JE (7379
1160, www.abeno.co.uk). Leicester Square tube.
Open noon-11pm Mon-Sat; noon-10.30pm Sun.
Main courses £9-£24. **Credit** MC, V. **Map**
p407 X3 **30** **Japanese**

The tables and counter at Abeno Too are all fitted with hot plates for cooking the *okonomiyaki* (pancakes with nuggets of vegetables, seafood, pork and other titbits added to a disc of noodles) that are the speciality of this small chain. The lovely staff cook the pancakes to order, right in front of you: hearty, comforting stuff it is too. If *okonomiyaki* doesn't suit your mood, choose from *katsu* curries, sashimi, salads, rice and noodle dishes and *teppanyaki*.
Other locations 47 Museum Street, Bloomsbury, WC1A 1LY (7405 3211).

L'Atelier de Joël Robuchon
13-15 West Street, WC2H 9NE (7010 8600, www.joel-robuchon.com). Leicester Square tube. **Open** *Restaurant* noon-2.30pm, 5.30-10.30pm daily. *Bar* 2.30pm-2am Mon-Sat; 2.30-10.30pm Sun. **Main courses** £15-£55. **Credit** AmEx, MC, V. **Map** p407 X3 **③** **Modern European**
Joël Robuchon has a clutch of classy restaurants around the globe. The ground-floor dining room here shares the characteristic red and black colour scheme and Japanese-inspired design. Diners sit at high stools around a central area; food is Modern European and beautifully presented. Multi-course tasting menus are the best way to experience the kitchen's skills. Not cheap, but worth it.

£ Food for Thought
31 Neal Street, WC2H 9PR (7836 9072). Covent Garden tube. **Open** noon-8.30pm Mon-Sat; noon-5pm Sun. **Main courses** £4-£8. **No credit cards**. **Map** p407 Y2 **②** **Vegetarian café**

Scoop.

Taking the stairs to this old basement café, where sharing tables is the norm, is like making a steady descent to the 1970s. Of its type, the food is excellent, with big, well-considered flavours and spirited freshness. Prices are very persuasive, too, although service can be sloppy.
▶ *Just after a coffee and a cake? Try Bullet, on the third floor of extreme-sports shop Snow & Rock (4 Mercer Street, WC2H 9QA, 7836 4922, www.bullet-coffee.com).*

★ Great Queen Street
32 Great Queen Street, WC2B 5AA (7242 0622). Covent Garden or Holborn tube. **Open** *Restaurant* noon-2.30pm, 6-10.30pm Mon-Sat; noon-3pm Sun. *Bar* 5-11pm Tue-Sat. **Main courses** £10-£22. **Credit** MC, V. **Map** p407 Z2 **③** **British**
The staff at this casual eaterie are a helpful young bunch. The ex-pub premises have been tarted up, but not too much, and the food is direct and robust food, expect the likes of hare with noodles. Other plus points: desserts are taken seriously, and wines come in glass, carafe and bottle sizes. In the basement, drinks and snacks are served. Pretty much the ideal local, right in the centre of town, which makes booking essential.

£ Rock & Sole Plaice
47 Endell Street, WC2H 9AJ (7836 3785). Covent Garden tube. **Open** 11.30am-10.30pm Mon-Sat; noon-9.30pm Sun. **Main courses** £9-£12. **Credit** MC, V. **Map** p407 Y2 **③** **Fish & chips**
Exactly when the punningly named Rock & Sole Plaice (or its predecessor) first started battering fish is in dispute; some say 1871, while others maintain that it opened just after World War II. Either way, this small corner chippy near Drury Lane is thriving in 2010. West End theatre posters line the walls of the interior; on nice days, you can take your food outside to some pavement tables.

£ Scoop
40 Shorts Gardens, WC2H 9AB (7240 7086, www.scoopgelato.com). Covent Garden tube. **Open** 11am-9pm daily. **Ice-cream** £2.50/scoop. **Credit** AmEx, MC, V. **Map** p407 Y2 **③** **Ice-cream**
The long queues are a testament to the quality of the ice-creams, even the dairy-free health versions, at this Italian artisan's shop. Flavours include ricotta and fig, and a very superior Piedmont hazelnut type.

★ J Sheekey
28-34 St Martin's Court, Leicester Square, WC2N 4AL (7240 2565, www.caprice-holdings. co.uk). Leicester Square tube. **Open** noon-3pm, 5.30pm-midnight Mon-Sat; noon-3.30pm, 6-11pm Sun. **Main courses** £13-£40. **Credit** AmEx, DC, MC, V. **Map** p407 X4 **③** **Fish & seafood**

CONSUME

Unlike many of London's period-piece restaurants (which this certainly is, having first been chartered in the mid 19th century), Sheekey's buzzes with fashionable folk and famous faces. And it seldom turns out a dud from a menu that runs from sparklingly simple seafood platters to dishes that are interesting without being elaborate. You'll pay for the privilege of dining here, and booking ahead is essential, but the rewards are worth both expense and effort.
▶ *Next door, the new J Sheekey Oyster Bar (nos.33-34, WC2N 4AL, 7240 2565, www.j-sheekey.co.uk) serves a similar menu, but with an expanded choice of oysters.*

£ Wahaca

66 Chandos Place, WC2N 4HG (7240 1883, www.wahaca.co.uk). Covent Garden or Leicester Square tube. **Open** noon-11pm Mon-Sat; noon-10.30pm Sun. **Main courses** £3-£10. **Credit** AmEx, MC, V. **Map** p407 Y4 ㊲ **Mexican**
Wahaca has many points in its favour: a central location, colourful and casually fashionable decor, a trendy Mexican menu and achievable prices. To top things off, it's even run by celebrity chef of sorts: Thomasina Miers, a former winner of BBC's *MasterChef*, appears frequently on TV and in the recipe press. The kitchen's aim is to marry locally sourced ingredients with Mexican-inspired recipes, some more authentic than others.
Other locations Southern Terrace, Westfield Shopping Centre, Shepherd's Bush, W12 7GF (8749 4517); Park Pavilion, 40 Canada Square, Docklands, E14 5FW (no phone).

SOHO & CHINATOWN

Chinatown stalwarts such as **Mr Kong** (21 Lisle Street, 7437 7341) and **Wong Kei** (41-43 Wardour Street, 0871 332 8296) still ply their trade, but there's more excitement offered by the newer likes of **Baozi Inn** (*see right*) and **Bar Shu** (*see p208*). On Ganton Street, to the west, there's more Chinese food at **Cha Cha Moon** (*see p209*). Cheaper, non-Chinese cheap eats are served at the **Diner** (nos.16-18, 7287 8962, www.thedinersoho.com) and **Mother Mash** (no.26, 7494 9644, www.mothermash.co.uk).

INSIDE TRACK CHINATOWN

For atmosphere, drop in for a 'bubble tea' (sweet, icy, full of balls of jelly and slurped up with a straw) at the bustling **Jen Café** (4-8 Newport Place, no phone) or late-night fave **HK Diner** (22 Wardour Street, 7434 9544). If you need to eat especially late, Cantonese old-stager the **New Mayflower** (68-70 Shaftesbury Avenue, 7734 9207) is open nightly until 4am.

Baozi Inn.

★ Arbutus

63-64 Frith Street, W1D 3JW (7734 4545, www.arbutusrestaurant.co.uk). Tottenham Court Road tube. **Open** noon-2.30pm, 5-11pm Mon Sat; noon-3pm, 5.30-10.30pm Sun. **Main courses** £14-£20. **Credit** AmEx, MC, V. **Map** p406 W2 ㊳ **Modern European**
Providing very fine cooking at very fair prices isn't an easy trick, but Anthony Demetre makes it look easy. Although it's not cheap to eat à la carte, the set lunch (three courses £15.50) and 'pre-theatre' dinner (three courses £17.50) are famously good value. The restaurant pioneered 250ml carafes for sampling the wines from a well-edited list; try a carafe of macabeo with a juicy, herby mullet with gnocchi, spinach and clams, or a carafe of Rioja for tender rabbit with stewed red peppers, chickpeas and merguez.

★ £ Baozi Inn

25 Newport Court, WC2H 7JS (7287 6877). Leicester Square tube. **Open** 11.30am-10pm daily. **Main courses** £6-£7. **No credit cards**. **Map** p407 X3 ㊴ **Chinese**
Generally speaking, the only useful purpose of a picture menu is for laughing at as you try to reconcile what's on your plate with what's in the picture. But at this cheap, cheerful little brother of Bar Shu and Ba Shan (for both, *see p208*), what you see really is what you get: an interesting choice of dumplings, noodles and hearty soups from China's north and west. It's not the sort of place for lingering, but the folksy commie decor is nicely tongue-in-cheek.

CONSUME

CONSUME

Bar Shu

28 Frith Street, W1D 5LF (7287 6688, www.bar-shu.co.uk). Leicester Square or Tottenham Court Road tube. **Open** noon-11pm Mon-Thur, Sun; noon-11.30pm Fri, Sat. **Main courses** £8-£28. **Credit** AmEx, MC, V. **Map** p406 W3 ⑳
Chinese
A shining example of a regional Chinese restaurant (in this case the chilli- and pepper-laced cuisine of Sichuan) that hasn't compromised on authenticity, Bar Shu serves up fiery food for the brave, with great rewards. The place was refurbished in summer 2009 after a fire destroyed the kitchen.

£ Ba Shan

24 Romilly Street, W1D 5AH (7287 3266). Leicester Square tube. **Open** noon-11pm Mon-Thur, Sun; noon-11.30pm Fri, Sat. **Main courses** £5-£8. **Credit** AmEx, MC, V. **Map** p407 X3 ㉑
Chinese
The latest restaurant from the team behind Bar Shu (*see above*) and Baozi Inn (*see p207*) looks a treat, with wooden screens and splashes of colour breaking up the sleek, dark decor. The menu, based on *xiao chi* (small eats), is similar in concept to Cantonese dim sum, but with many unfamiliar plates. The Sichuanese home-style part of the menu has some of the best dishes.

Bob Bob Ricard

1 Upper James Street, W1F 9DF (3145 1000, www.bobbobricard.com). Piccadilly Circus tube. **Open** 7am-1am Mon-Fri; 8am-1am Sat, Sun. **Main courses** £12-£40. **Credit** AmEx, DC, MC, V. **Map** p406 V3 ㉒ **Brasserie**
The David Collins-designed interior of this louche bar-brasserie is easy on the eye, with lots of marble and leather, gold chainmail and retro lamp fittings, and doesn't take itself too seriously: witness the ridiculous pink waiter uniforms and the champagne buzzer at each table (press to light up your table's number above the bar, like an old-fashioned elevator). The menu is a bit dowdy – lots of retro British comfort food, from a hearty fry-up to shepherd's pie, enlivened by the likes of roast partridge with savoy cabbage – but it is served until 1am.

Bocca di Lupo

12 Archer Street, W1D 7BB (7734 2223, www.boccadilupo.com). Piccadilly Circus tube. **Open** 12.30-3pm, 5.30-11pm Mon-Sat. **Main courses** £8-£22. **Credit** AmEx, MC, V. **Map** p406 W3 ㉓ **Italian**
This busy, informal Italian has a lively open kitchen and tapas-style menu of regional specialities. Select one small dish from several different categories of the menu (raw and cured, fried, pastas and risottos, soups and stews, roasts, and so on) and you should enjoy a fairly balanced meal; for those who prefer not to share, large portions of each dish are also offered. *See also p198* **Eating In**.

Princi.

£ Cha Cha Moon

15-21 Ganton Street, W1F 9BN (7297 9800, www.chachamoon.com). Oxford Circus tube. **Open** 8am-11pm Mon-Fri; 9am-11.30pm Sat, Sun. **Main courses** £4-£8. **Credit** AmEx, MC, V. **Map** p406 U3 ⓪ **Chinese**

Like Wagamama before it, Alan Yau's Cha Cha Moon offers fast food of mixed Asian inspiration at low prices, served on long cafeteria-style tables in a sleek room. The main focus is on excellent noodle dishes, hailing from Hong Kong, Shanghai and elsewhere in China, clocking in at around £5 each.
Other locations 151 Queensway, Bayswater, W2 4YN (7792 0088).

★ Dehesa

25 Ganton Street, W1F 9BP (7494 4170). Oxford Circus tube. **Open** noon-11pm Mon-Sat; noon-5pm Sun. **Tapas** £3.50-£7.25. **Credit** AmEx, MC, V. **Map** p406 U3 ⓪ **Spanish/Italian tapas**

After running a no-reservations policy for a while, this informal yet sophisticated spot now takes bookings, which makes it easier to enjoy its Spanish-Italian tapas. The black-footed Ibérico pig (the place is named after its woodland home) appears in nutty-flavoured ham and other charcuterie, but local sourcing comes to the fore in tapas such as confit Old Spot pork belly with cannellini beans. Staff are bright, well-informed and efficient.

★ £ Fernandez & Wells

73 Beak Street, W1F 9RS (7287 8124, www.fernandezandwells.com). Oxford Circus or Piccadilly Circus tube. **Open** 7.30am-6pm Mon-Fri; 9am-6pm Sat; 10am-6pm Sun. **Main courses** £3-£6. **Credit** (over £5) MC, V. **Map** p406 V3 ⓪ **Café**

If only there were more coffee bars like this in central London. The sandwiches here are far from the cheapest in town, but they are special. Drop by in the morning for, say, a cheese toastie made with sourdough bread, or a breakfast pastry. At lunchtime, seats are at a premium but worth the wait. Fernandez & Wells also runs a takeaway/deli around the corner in Lexington Street, specialising in Spanish products; their new St Anne's Court café is only a short walk from here.
Other locations 43 Lexington Street, Soho, W1F 9AL (7734 1546); 16A St Anne's Court, Soho, W1F 0BG (7494 4242).

★ £ Hummus Bros

88 Wardour Street, W1F 0TH (7734 1311, www.hbros.co.uk). Oxford Circus or Tottenham Court Road tube. **Open** noon-10pm Mon-Wed, Sun; noon-11pm Thur-Sat. **Main courses** £2-£6. **Credit** AmEx, MC, V. **Map** p406 W3 ⓪ **Café**

The simple and hugely successful formula at this café/takeaway is to serve houmous as a base for a selection of toppings, which you scoop up with

excellent, pillowy pitta bread that's toasted while you wait. Sounds too simple? No matter: the food is tasty, nutritious, filling and great value, whether you eat in or take away.
Other locations 37-63 Southampton Row, Bloomsbury, WC1B 4DA (7404 7079).

£ Maison Bertaux

28 Greek Street, W1D 5DQ (7437 6007). Leicester Square tube. **Open** 8.30am-11pm Mon-Sat; 8.30am-7.30pm Sun. **Main courses** £1-£5. **No credit cards. Map** p407 X3 ⓪ **Café**

Oozing arty, bohemian charm, this café dates back to 1871 when Soho was London's little piece of the Continent. Battered old bentwood tables and chairs add to the feeling of being in a pâtisserie in rural France, albeit one with a bit of additional camp Soho flamboyance. The provisions (cream cakes, greasy pastries, pots of tea) are really beside the point.

£ Nosh Bar

39 Great Windmill Street, W1D 7LX (7734 5638). Piccadilly Circus tube. **Open** noon-midnight Mon-Thur; noon-2am Fri, Sat. **Main courses** £3-£5. **Credit** MC, V. **Map** p406 W3 ⓪ **Café**

A Soho institution in the postwar years, the Nosh Bar hosted a stream of ne'er-do-wells drawn by its location and late opening hours. The food was secondary, mainly home-style Jewish snacks such as salt beef on rye, chicken soup and filled bagels. The original Nosh closed in the 1980s, but the new owners have recreated it in the same location. It's much smarter than the original, but prices are still low, the food's decent and the staff are friendly. Brilliantly, it doesn't shut until 2am on Fridays and Saturdays.

★ £ Princi

135 Wardour Street, W1F 0UF (7478 8888, www.princi.co.uk). Leicester Square or Tottenham Court Road tube. **Open** 7am-midnight Mon-Sat; 9am-11pm Sun. **Main courses** £5-£9. **Credit** AmEx, MC, V. **Map** p406 W3 ⓪ **Bakery-café**

Alan Yau has teamed up with an Italian bakery chain for his latest venture, consisting of a vast L-shaped granite counter and communal seating. As well as numerous cakes, tiramisus and pastries, there's a vast range of savoury dishes. The big slices of pizza have a springy base, the margherita variety pungent with fresh thyme; caprese salad comes with creamy balls of buffalo mozzarella and big slices of beef tomato. Princi can get hectic, but it's a solid option for a quick inexpensive snack.

Red Fort

77 Dean Street, W1D 3SH (7437 2115, www.redfort.co.uk). Leicester Square or Tottenham Court Road tube. **Open** *Restaurant* noon-2.15pm, 5.45-11.15pm Mon-Fri; 5.45-11.15pm Sat, Sun. *Bar* 5pm-1am Tue-Sat. **Main courses** £15-£29. **Credit** AmEx, MC, V. **Map** p406 W2 ⓪ **Indian**

CONSUME

Since opening in 1981, Red Fort has seen its ups and downs. But following a stylish and expensive refit in 2001, and the recruitment of a star chef from India (no longer here), the restaurant once again took the crown of the best Indian in Soho. Several years on, it's as sophisticated as ever. Cooking of this standard doesn't come cheap, but it's worth it.

Yauatcha

15 Broadwick Street, W1F 0DL (7494 8888). Piccadilly Circus or Tottenham Court Road tube. **Open** 11am-11.30pm Mon-Thur; 11am-11.45pm Fri, Sat; noon-10.45pm Sun. **Dim sum** £3-£7. **Credit** AmEx, MC, V. **Map** p406 V2 🟢 **Dim sum/tearoom**

Serving dim sum day and night over two floors, Yauatcha happily cocks a snook at traditionalists who believe the treats to 'touch the heart' should never be served past 5pm. Yauatcha's popularity with Soho creatives shows no sign of easing. Much is made of the unusually good (and lengthy) tea list, while the choice of dim sum dishes is extended with congee, noodles and some intriguing stir-fries.

OXFORD STREET & MARYLEBONE

★ L'Autre Pied

5-7 Blandford Street, W1U 3DB (7486 9696, www.lautrepied.co.uk). Baker Street tube. **Open** noon-2.45, 6-10.30pm Mon-Sat; noon-3pm, 6.30-9.30pm Sun. **Main courses** £19-£23. **Credit** AmEx, MC, V. **Map** p398 G5 🟢 **Modern European**

For a far less eye-watering outlay than a meal at Pied à Terre, its older sibling, L'Autre Pied offers nuanced cooking in handsome rooms. With a light touch and subtle use of herbs, chef Marcus Eaves doesn't stint on the dairy, as demonstrated by an intensely creamy mushroom and leek risotto. Despite the trappings of somewhere that takes food very seriously, L'Autre Pied is accessible and relaxing, and the kitchen don't put a foot wrong.

★ £ Busaba Eathai

8-13 Bird Street, W1U 1BU (7518 8080). Bond Street tube. **Open** noon-11pm Mon-Thur; noon-11.30pm Fri, Sat; noon-10pm Sun. **Main**

THE BEST LATE-NIGHT EATS

Bob Bob Ricard
Comfort cooking after hours. *See p208.*

Brick Lane Beigel Bake
Snack around the clock. *See p223.*

Nosh Bar
A Soho legend reborn. *See p209.*

---

courses £5-£11. **Credit** AmEx, MC, V. **Map** p398 G6 🟢 **Thai**

All three branches of this handsome Thai fast food canteen are excellent and busy, but this one is superbly located for Oxford Street shoppers. The interior combines shared tables and bench seats with a touch of dark-toned oriental mystique, and the dishes are always intriguing, as you'd expect of a menu developed by David Thompson of the exemplary Thai fine-dining resto Nahm (*see p220*). **Other locations** 22 Store Street, Bloomsbury, WC1E 7DS (7299 7900); 106-110 Wardour Street, Soho, W1F 0TR (7255 8686).

Fairuz

3 Blandford Street, W1U 3DA (7486 8108, 7486 8182, www.fairuz.uk.com). Baker Street or Bond Street tube. **Open** noon-11.30pm Mon-Sat; noon-11pm Sun. **Main courses** £12-£20. *Set meze* £19.95. *Cover* £1.50. **Credit** AmEx, MC, V. **Map** p398 G5 🟢 **Middle Eastern**

The combination of Lebanese food, neighbourhood-taverna surroundings and West End location has proved enduringly popular for this longstanding Marylebone favourite. Its collection of meze – smooth houmous, zingy *fuul moukala* (green broad beans with olive oil, lemon and coriander), tabouleh, spinach *fatayer* – are brilliantly executed.

£ La Fromagerie

2-6 Moxon Street, W1U 4EW (7935 0341, www.lafromagerie.co.uk). Baker Street or Bond Street tube. **Open** 8am-7.30pm Mon-Fri; 9am-7pm Sat; 10am-6pm Sun. **Main courses** £6-£13. **Credit** AmEx, MC, V. **Map** p398 G5 🟢 **Café**

There aren't many cafés in London where Herefordshire snails cooked in garlic butter make the menu, but Patricia Michelson's high-end deli/café has always ploughed its own, very stylish, culinary furrow, and its communal tables are often packed with devotees. The basic menu, which includes a high-end ploughman's lunch, is supplemented by a separate breakfast offer (own-made baked beans, granola with posh French yoghurt) and a 'kitchen menu' from 12.30pm.

Galvin Bistrot de Luxe

66 Baker Street, W1U 7DJ (7935 4007, www.galvinrestaurants.com). Baker Street tube. **Open** noon-2.30pm, 6-10.30pm Mon-Wed; noon-2.30pm, 6-10.45pm Thur-Sat; noon-3.30pm, 6-9.30pm Sun. **Main courses** £11-£21. **Credit** AmEx, MC, V. **Map** p398 G5 🟢 **French**

Galvin is a destination spot for power-lunching businessmen, but the absence of any stiffness makes it equally suitable for a fun get-together with friends. The cooking is superb: the menu might include crisp-skinned and tender sea bass, served with octopus tossed into a salad, or *pithivier* of quail and wood pigeon. The occasionally offhand service is the only real disappointment.

Do You Want to Know a Secret?

Some of London's most fashionable restaurants aren't even restaurants at all.

CONSUME

Whether you call them 'secret', 'guerrilla' or 'undercover' operations, there's little doubt that thrilling little private kitchens have mushroomed all over the capital during the last year or so. Serving everything from vegetarian Japanese banquets to afternoon teas, dozens of entrepreneurial Londoners have switched the notion of dining out to a new kind of dining in, serving fine food to complete strangers in their own homes.

Some longtime Londoners have argued that the trend isn't new at all, and have pointed to Vauxhall's **Bonnington Centre Café** (www.bonningtoncafe.co.uk) as the original guerrilla dining concept. Set up by a small community, it began life in the 1980s as a café aimed at local squatters; initially, members asked for contributions for meals, with ingredients scavenged from the nearby Covent Garden produce market (it relocated to this part of town in the early 1970s). All the dishes were vegetarian or vegan, and diners were charged less than a fiver for a meal.

Nowadays, the Bonnington Centre Café is licensed, legal and above board. However, the city's taste for illicit food thrills has lingered, no doubt helped by the depth of the recent recession. As a result, a number of enterprising and frequently anonymous individuals have taken to setting up restaurants in their front rooms.

One of the better-known pseudonyms in this new alternative industry is the affable Ms Marmite Lover, whose **Underground Restaurant** (http://marmitelover.blogspot.com) in Kilburn is a showcase for creative contemporary cooking that's booked up weeks in advance. Her reputation is such that she attracted the attentions of the Warner Bros legal team when she planned 'Harry Potter nights' for Halloween; she duly renamed them as 'Generic Wizard nights'. Similar operations to Marmite Lover's include the **Savoy Truffle Supperclub** (www.savoytrufflesupperclub.com), down in Blackheath, and Brixton's **Saltoun Supper Club** (www.eatwithyoureyes.net).

The variety of food on offer is amazing. Housed in a central London flat, Lady Gray's charming **Hidden Tea Room** (www.hiddentearoom.com) serves afternoon teas that are the equal of far pricier institutions in the capital; Hackney's **Bruncheon Club** (http://thebruncheonclub.blogspot.com) provides bloody marys and perfect poached eggs; and the **Secret Ingredient** (contact them on Facebook) features intricate vegetarian Japanese dishes.

The locations vary, although much of the action seems to be out east. Shoreditch-based artists' collective **BEET Happenings** (http://beeteating.wordpress.com) host suppers in the studios of musicians, architects and designers, for instance. But surely the most flamboyant of the current scene is **Pale Blue Door**. Set designer Tony Hornecker (http://tonyhornecker.wordpress.com) has turned his Hackney house into an art and performance installation, which he now regularly converts into a speakeasy-styled restaurant. Find the door down a back alley off Kingsland Road and you're greeted by performers who lead you to a table in one of the rooms, on a balcony or in a secret space in the rafters. There you'll be served a three-course dinner, with transvestite entertainers on hand to provide mid-meal diversions.

Pale Blue Door.

£ Golden Hind

73 Marylebone Lane, W1U 2PN (7486 3644).
Bond Street tube. **Open** noon-3pm, 6-10pm Mon-
Fri; 6-10pm Sat. **Main courses** £5-£11. **Credit**
AmEx, MC, V. **Map** p398 G5 🔢 **Fish & chips**
The Golden Hind's walls are lined with old
black-and-white photos and a blackboard listing the
names of owners back as far as 1914. The current
Hellenic ownership is reflected in a menu that places
mixed Greek pickles and deep-fried feta alongside
standard starters such as fish cakes. Try for a seat
on the ground floor so you can gawp at the stunning
art-deco fryer (sadly, no longer used). Staff are jovial
and service is quick.

★ Providores & Tapa Room

109 Marylebone High Street, W1U 4RX (7935
6175, www.theprovidores.co.uk). Baker Street
or Bond Street tube. **Open** *Providores* noon-
2.45pm, 6-10.30pm Mon-Fri; noon-2.45pm,
6-10.30pm Sat; noon-2.45pm, 6-10pm Sun. *Tapa*
Room 9-10.30pm Mon-Fri; 10am-3pm, 4-10.30pm
Sat; 10am-3pm Sun. **Main courses** £18-£26.
Tapas £2-£15. **Credit** AmEx, MC, V. **Map**
p398 G5 🔢 **International**
Chef-proprietor Kiwi Peter Gordon has long har-
monised ingredients that would form a mishmash
in lesser hands. His latest menu reins in the complexity a little, presenting diners with starter-sized
dishes, flexibly priced as courses per person (rather
than per table). Expect each dish to be an extraordinary fusion of flavours. The serene Providores
restaurant is the calming upstairs counterpoint to
the buzzy street-level Tapa Room.

Rhodes W1

Cumberland, Great Cumberland Place, W1H 7AL
(7616 5930, www.rhodesw1.com). Marble Arch
tube. **Open** noon-2.15pm, 7-10.15pm Tue-Fri;
7-10.15pm Sat. **Set meals** £19.95-£55 2 courses,
£23.95-£65 3 courses. **Credit** AmEx, MC, V.
Map p395 F6 🔢 **Haute cuisine**
Perhaps the most beautiful chandeliers in any
London restaurant are to be found here, but there's
also plenty to look at on the plates. Gary Rhodes'
modern European fine-dining restaurant excels at
unusual presentations of classic ideas, as in a fine
rabbit terrine served with pineapple pickle, and a
beautiful fillet of halibut poised atop wonderful
spiced lentils. Prices are higher for dinner than lunch.
Other locations Rhodes Twenty Four, Tower
42, Old Broad Street, the City, EC2N 1HQ (7877
7703, www.rhodes24.co.uk).

Royal China Club

40-42 Baker Street, NW8 6ER (7486 3898,
www.royalchinagroup.co.uk). Baker Street or
Marble Arch tube. **Open** noon-4.30pm Mon-Thur;
noon-11.30pm Fri, Sat; noon-10.30pm Sun. **Dim**
sum £3-£8. **Main courses** £9-£35. **Credit**
AmEx, MC, V. **Map** p398 G5 🔢 **Dim sum**

The Royal China Club is in the top set of London's
luxury Chinese restaurants, the place to feast on
creative and luxurious dim sum that's completely
Chinese in sensibility and not in the least diluted by
the instinct towards lowest-common-denominator
fusion that is found elsewhere in the capital. As
befits the elegant dining room, even humble *cheung*
fun gets top-notch treatment. Be sure to take some
time over the separate tea menu.
▶ *The Docklands branch (30 Westferry Circus,*
7719 0888) has a fine riverside terrace.

PICCADILLY CIRCUS & MAYFAIR

★ Bentley's Oyster Bar & Grill

11-15 Swallow Street, W1B 4DG (7734 4756,
www.bentleysoysterbarandgrill.co.uk). Piccadilly
Circus tube. **Open** *Oyster Bar* noon-midnight
Mon-Sat; noon-10pm Sun. *Restaurant* noon-3pm,
6-11pm Mon-Fri; 6-11pm Sat; 6-10pm Sun.
Main courses *Oyster Bar* £8-£24. *Restaurant*
£16-£38. **Credit** AmEx, MC, V. **Map** p406 V4
🔢 **Fish & seafood**
There's something timeless about Richard Corrigan's
restoration of this classic oyster house. World War I
was raging when Bentley's first opened, but the
suited gents who flock here today enjoy their seafood
with the same gusto as their great-grandfathers
before them. While the first-floor dining rooms
are more sedate and well-mannered, the downstairs
oyster bar is where the action is.

Chisou

4 Princes Street, W1B 2LE (7629 3931, www.
chisou.co.uk). Oxford Circus tube. **Open** noon-
2.30pm, 6-10.15pm Mon-Sat. **Main courses**
£12-£24. **Credit** AmEx, MC, V. **Map** p406 U2 🔢
Japanese
Chisou looks quiet from the outside; inside, though,
this modestly fashionable restaurant hums with
activity. Friendly waitresses keep things moving at
the blonde-wood tables, while to the rear is a fun
sushi bar. Salted belly pork, and the pure *ume cha*
(rice in a light hot broth with pickled plum) are highlights, and there's a serious saké and shochu list.
Next door is Chisou's noodle and *donburi* bar.

Corrigan's Mayfair

28 Upper Grosvenor Street, W1K 7EH (7499
9943, www.corrigansmayfair.com). Marble
Arch tube. **Open** noon-3pm, 6-10.30pm Mon-Fri;
6-10.30pm Sat; noon-4pm, 6-9.30pm Sun. **Main**
courses £9-£26. **Credit** AmEx, MC, V. **Map**
p400 G6 🔢 **British**
For a fine-dining operation in such a slick setting,
Corrigan's is a remarkably relaxed place. The
welcome starts the moment you walk through the
front door, from formal yet smiling staff. Dishes
from the long menu exceed most expectations: from
octopus carpaccio with baby squid to the enigmatic

CONSUME

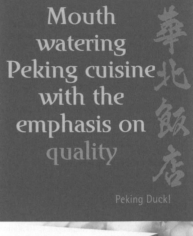

'chocolate, hazelnut' (a medley of wonderful tastes), via ox cheek with mushroom ravioli and garlic leaf, all beautifully arranged.

Gaucho Piccadilly
25 Swallow Street, W1B 4QR (7734 4040, www.gauchorestaurants.co.uk). Piccadilly Circus tube. **Open** noon-10.30pm Mon, Sun; noon-11pm Tue-Sat. **Main courses** £12-£37. **Credit** AmEx, MC, V. **Map** p406 V5 ⑥ **Argentinian**
It's not especially satisfying to admit that a chain restaurant serves some of the best steak in the capital, but ever-expanding Gaucho keeps its focus simple. The cowhide-wallpaper setting is almost too stylish for a grill restaurant, but the beef is top-notch, as are all the extras (morcilla, empanadas, ceviches et al). In 2009, Gaucho brought a bit more Buenos Aires food culture to London with Freggo (7287 9506, www.freggo.co.uk), a late-opening ice-cream parlour that's next door at nos.27-29. **Other locations** throughout the city.

★ Hibiscus
29 Maddox Street, W1S 2PA (7629 2999, www.hibiscusrestaurant.co.uk). Oxford Circus tube. **Open** noon-2.30pm, 6.30-10pm Tue-Fri; 6-10pm Sat. **Set meals** £25-£65 3 courses; £80 tasting menu. **Credit** AmEx, MC, V. **Map** p406 U3 ⑥ **Haute cuisine**
Tables in this simple Mayfair dining room are arranged around a large central workstation topped with an extravagant floral display. The crowd is well-heeled and rather businesslike, even when their intentions are social. Many stick with the set lunch (as usual, far cheaper than the equivalent dinner menu), on which you might find the moussaka of Elwy Valley mutton with feta and anchovy jus that has become something of a signature dish for Hibiscus. For dessert, try clafoutis with almonds and an unusually rich pistachio ice-cream.

Maze
13-15 Grosvenor Square, W1K 6JP (7107 0000, www.gordonramsay.com). Bond Street tube. **Open** noon-2.30pm, 6-10.30pm daily. **Main courses** £15-£30. **Credit** AmEx, DC, MC, V. **Map** p400 G6 ⑥ **Haute cuisine**
Jason Atherton's Maze continues to shine a little brighter than the other starry establishments in the Gordon Ramsay stable. The sleek, handsome room with curved wood veneer and cream leather seating is cheerfully light-filled and offers pleasing leafy views over Grosvenor Square. The set lunch menu is brilliant: from a list of around 13 dishes, you can select any four, five or six courses as desired (they cost £28.50, £35.50 and £42.50 respectively).

Momo
25 Heddon Street, W1B 4BH (7434 4040, www.momoresto.com). Piccadilly Circus tube. **Open** noon-2.30pm, 6.30-11.30pm Mon-Sat;

6.30-11pm Sun. **Main courses** £13-£15. **Credit** AmEx, DC, MC, V. **Map** p406 U3 ⑥ **North African**
Momo is still London's most glamorous Moroccan restaurant. You'll find a funky atmosphere here and some great cooking, but service can be patchy. No matter: it's a fun venue, with the signature Maghrebi soundtrack enough to get everyone rocking.

Parlour
1st floor, Fortnum & Mason, 181 Piccadilly, W1A 1ER (7734 8040, www.fortnumand mason.co.uk). Green Park or Piccadilly Circus tube. **Open** 10am-7.30pm Mon-Sat; noon-5pm Sun. **Ice-cream** £3/scoop. **Credit** AmEx, MC, V. **Map** p406 V5 ⑥ **Ice-cream**
David Collins' quirky design for this café is all ice-cream and chocolate tones, with retro kitchenette seating. It's a great place to meet friends, though prices are high, with sundaes costing £12. The best option is an ice-cream 'flight': three scoops of your choice, served with wonderfully silky Amedei dark- or milk-chocolate sauce for £10.

La Petite Maison
54 Brooks Mews, W1K 4EG (7495 4774, www.lpm.co.uk). Bond Street tube. **Open** noon-2.15pm, 6-10pm daily. **Main courses** £9-£35. **Credit** AmEx, MC, V. **Map** p400 H6 ⑩ **French**
Defiantly bucking the recession with ever-full lunch sittings, La Petite Maison hums loudly with the conversation of heavily tanned men and glossy haired women, all dressed expensively. Tables are styled with bottles of olive oil, lemons and tomatoes on the vine. If this sounds too much, rest assured that the French-Mediterranean food of chef Raphael Duntoye is fabulously uncomplicated in its luxuriousness.

★ Scott's
20 Mount Street, W1K 2HE (7495 7309, www.caprice-holdings.co.uk). Bond Street or Green Park tube. **Open** noon-10.30pm Mon-Sat; noon-10pm Sun. **Main courses** £16-£40. **Cover** £2. **Credit** AmEx, DC, MC, V. **Map** p400 G7 ⑦ **Fish & seafood**
Owner Caprice Holdings is keen to remind diners that Scott's was Ian Fleming's favourite restaurant; certainly, 007 wouldn't look out of place among the monied crowd here. The food is rooted in Anglo-French classics; starters feature dressed crab, while the sea bass is served with lemon and herb butter. The wine list sensibly majors in zingy, mineral whites. Scott's isn't cheap, but it exudes glamour.

Sketch: The Parlour
9 Conduit Street, W1S 2XJ (0870 777 4488, www.sketch.uk.com). Oxford Circus tube. **Open** 8am-9pm Mon-Fri; 10am-9pm Sat. *Tea served* 3-6.30pm Mon-Sat. **Main courses** £4-£9. *Set tea* £9-£24. **Credit** AmEx, MC, V. **Map** p406 U3 ⑦ **Café**

CONSUME

CONSUME

Of the three corners of Pierre Gagnaire's legendarily expensive Sketch, which also including destination dining at the Gallery and the Lecture Room's haute-beyond-haute cuisine, Parlour appeals the most for its tongue-in-cheek sexiness. Saucy nudes illustrate the chairs, and the chandelier appears to be covered with pairs of red fishnet tights. At the launch, the focus was on the pastry counter. Now, the bar takes centre stage. Gagnaire's food menu, includes simple hearty dishes and quirky high-concept creations, such as the club sandwich with red and green bread and a layer of stencilled jelly on top; it's mostly air-dried ham with tiny flecks of grapefruit. Delicious.

£ Tibits

12-14 Heddon Street, W1B 4DA (7758 4110, www.tibits.ch). Oxford Circus tube. **Open** 9am-10.30pm Mon-Wed; 9am-midnight Thur-Sat; 10am-10.30pm Sun. **Buffet** £2/100g. **Credit** MC, V. **Map** p406 U3 🐵 **Vegetarian café**
Designers Guild fabrics in raspberry and lime contrast with a black ceiling and smart wicker chairs at this modern take on the buffet restaurant. Part of a small but impressive Swiss chain, Tibits may be vegetarian but it's not puritanical. Fill your plate from the salads and hot dishes in the central 'boat' and take it to the counter for weighing. There are organic Freedom lagers on tap, plus a handful of wines, and coffees.

Wild Honey

12 St George Street, W1S 2FB (7758 9160, www.wildhoneyrestaurant.co.uk). Bond Street or Oxford Circus tube. **Open** noon-2.30pm, 6-11pm Mon-Sat; noon-3pm, 6-10.30pm Sun. **Main courses** £17-£20. **Credit** AmEx, MC, V. **Map** p398 H6 🐵 **Modern European**
Wild Honey, sister of Arbutus (*see p207*), is calm, composed and in possession of an exceptionally good-value set menu at lunchtime (three courses for £18.95), the best time to relax amid the handsome oak panelling. In contrast, the evenings are encumbered with the time limitations of two sittings and the space limitations of tables penned too close together. Compositions are thoughtful, with each main using two to four key ingredients, often with an English bent.
▶ *Don't get lost! Wild Honey is on St George Street, not plain old George Street close by.*

★ Wolseley

160 Piccadilly, W1J 9EB (7499 6996, www.the wolseley.com). Green Park tube. **Open** 7am-midnight Mon-Fri; 8am-midnight Sat, Sun. *Tea served* 3.30-6.30pm Mon-Fri, Sun; 3.30-5.30pm Sat. **Main courses** £6-£29. *Set tea* £9-£20. *Cover* £2. **Credit** AmEx, DC, MC, V. **Map** p406 U5 🐵 **Brasserie**
An interpretation of the grand cafés of continental Europe, the Wolseley serves breakfast, lunch, tea

and dinner to a smart set of Londoners and visitors in its opulent dining room. Huge bronze doors open up to an art deco dining room, while an entrance table displays a selection of the day's choices. No one comes here just for the food, but breakfast at the Wolseley is a failsafe treat. Attention to detail from beginning to end suggests the place is in no threat of losing its iconic status.

WESTMINSTER & ST JAMES'S

Cinnamon Club

Old Westminster Library, 30-32 Great Smith Street, SW1P 3BU (7222 2555, www.cinnamon club.com). St James's Park or Westminster tube. **Open** 7.30-9.30am, noon-2.30pm, 6-10.45pm Mon-Fri; noon-2.30pm, 6-10.45pm Sat. **Main courses** £11-£29. **Credit** AmEx, DC, MC, V. **Map** p401 K9 🐵 **Indian**
Aiming to create a complete Indian fine-dining experience, Cinnamon Club provides cocktails, fine wines, tasting menus, breakfasts (Indian, Anglo-Indian, British), private dining rooms and all attendant flummery in an impressive, wood-lined space. Executive chef Vivek Singh devises innovative dishes; even the well-priced set meal (£20 for two courses) is invitingly out of the ordinary.
▶ *Cinnamon Kitchen (9 Devonshire Square, EC2M 4WY, 7626 5000, www.cinnamonkitchen. co.uk), a less formal City branch, opened in 2009.*

Inn the Park

St James's Park, SW1A 2BJ (7451 9999, www.innthepark.com). St James's Park tube. **Open** 8-11am, noon-3pm, 5-9pm Mon-Fri; 9-11am, noon-4pm, 5-9pm Sat, Sun. *Tea served* 3-5pm Mon-Fri; 4-5pm Sat, Sun. **Main courses** £10-£19. **Credit** AmEx, MC, V. **Map** p401 K8 🐵 **British**
It's all about the location at this beautifully appointed and designed café-restaurant. The seasonal British cooking isn't always up to expectations, especially given the prices, but there is plenty on the plus side: staff are lovely, and the setting (overlooking the duck lake, with trees all around and the London Eye in the distance) is really wonderful.
▶ *Opened in 2004, Inn the Park was the first Oliver Peyton restaurant associated with a major London sight. For more details of his catering revolution, see right* **Institutional Dining**.

★ National Dining Rooms

Sainsbury Wing, National Gallery, Trafalgar Square, WC2N 5DN (7747 2525, www.the nationaldiningrooms.co.uk). Charing Cross tube/rail. **Open** *Bakery* 10am-5.30pm Mon-Thur, Sun; 10am-8.30pm Fri; 10am-7.30pm Sat. *Restaurant* noon-3.30pm Mon-Thur, Sat, Sun; noon-3.30pm, 5-7.15pm Fri. **Main courses** *Bakery* £5-£10. *Restaurant* £14-£20. **Credit** AmEx, MC, V. **Map** p407 X5 🐵 **British**

The Art of Cooking

The kitchens at London's cultural institutions get a long-overdue upgrade.

Not long ago, London's big galleries and museums fed only the soul, with their cafés and restaurants little more than an afterthought. However, over the past few years, there's been such a dramatic change in the fortunes of museum cafés and restaurants that many have become destinations in their own right. We have one man to thank for bringing the notion of quality cookery to the Big Smoke's revered institutions: Oliver Peyton, who introduced fine-dining concepts to two of London's most elegant art institutions and has since taken his take on modern British food to a variety of other institutions.

Following his interesting but not entirely successful **Inn the Park** (*see left*) in 2004, Peyton launched the **National Dining Rooms** (*see left*) at the National Gallery in 2006, quickly followed by the convivial, later-opening **National Café**. A cut above most establishments of their type, they remain stalwarts of laudable British cookery. Peyton then turned his attention to the **Wallace Collection** (*see p101*), where he opened a classical French eaterie in a gorgeous central atrium, and the **Institute of Contemporary Arts** (**ICA**; *see p118*), where he created the popular ICA Café & Bar. All the while, distinctive Peyton & Byrne bakery-cafés began to pop up across

town, offering sausage rolls and fairy cakes at the **Wellcome Collection** (*see p82*), **St Pancras International** (*see p83*) and the **British Library** (*see p82*).

Other big changes to the capital's eating habits have been provided by Benugo, a catering company named in honour of founders Ben and Hugo Warner. The most recent addition to the duo's portfolio is the mesmerising **Serpentine Bar & Kitchen** (*see p220*), a worthy companion to the Benugo Bar & Kitchen and the Riverfront Bar & Kitchen at **BFI Southbank** (*see p292*), and the fine cafés at the **V&A** (*see p126*) and the **V&A Museum of Childhood** (*see p140*).

Other big cultural names have been followed suit. In 2009, the relaunched Saatchi Gallery introduced **Gallery Mess** (*see p219*), a vivacious contemporary brasserie with a laid-back atmosphere and an ambitious kitchen, and St Paul's Cathedral launched their own restaurant and café, **Restaurant at St Paul's** (*see p200*), to great acclaim. Even acclaimed chefs are getting in on the act. Is the appointment of hotly tipped Maria Elia, former head chef of Delfina, to run the petite **Whitechapel Gallery Dining Room** (*see p225*) a sign that even better things are still to come?

Gallery Mess.

Oliver Peyton's restaurant in the Sainsbury Wing of the National Gallery offers far better food than museum diners are accustomed to, albeit at a price. The weekly-changing set lunch is great value (£18.50 for two courses and a glass of wine), however, especially when it's as satisfying as savoury leek and goat's cheese pancakes followed by a cockle-warming lamb stew. The few window seats have prized views over Trafalgar Square, and the bakery side of the operation ably fulfils the museum café role. *See also p217* **The Art of Cooking**.

Saké No Hana
23 St James's Street, SW1A 1HA (7925 8988). Green Park tube. **Open** noon-2.30pm, 6-11pm Mon-Thur; noon-2.30pm, 6-11.30pm Fri, Sat. **Main courses** £4-£40. **Credit** AmEx, MC, V. **Map** p400 J8 ⓐ **Japanese**
The food presentation at Alan Yau's upmarket venture is unmistakably high-end, as are the smart staff's black uniforms and architect Kengo Kuma's cool tatami and cedar design. Sashimi and sushi account for much of the menu, but pricier cooked dishes such as miso Chilean sea bass in houba leaf make menu-perusing more interesting. The saké and shochu lists remain substantial, and a £25 bento box set meal is available.

CHELSEA

Botanist
7 Sloane Square, SW1W 8EE (7730 0077, www.thebotanistonsloanesquare.com). Sloane Square tube. **Open** 8am-10.30pm Mon-Fri; 9am-10.30pm Sat, Sun. **Main courses** £14-£19. **Credit** AmEx, MC, V. **Map** p400 G10 ⓐ **Modern European**
This all-day bar with adjacent restaurant is decorated with Sir Hans Sloane's botanical illustrations. Less pub-like than the Martin brothers' other ventures (try the Cadogan Arms just down the King's Road; *see p235*), the Botanist attracts upmarket shoppers for well-conceived lunches. Expect fine breakfasts and absolutely superb puddings. At night, cocktails kick in and the bar gets livelier.

Chutney Mary
535 King's Road, SW10 0SZ (7351 3113, www.chutneymary.com). Fulham Broadway tube or bus 11, 22. **Open** 6.30-11.15pm Mon-Fri; 12.30-2.45pm, 6.30-11.15pm Sat; 12.30-2.45pm, 6.30-10.15pm Sun. **Main courses** £14-£26. **Credit** AmEx, DC, MC, V. **Map** p396 C13 ⓐ **Indian**
A pioneer of Anglo-Indian and regional Indian food in London when it opened in 1990, Chutney Mary remains on top form. The expertly prepared food is grounded in tradition but given a modern edge with light sauces and innovative accompaniments. A refurbishment a few years back has left it a more romantic environment.

Gallery Mess
Saatchi Gallery, Duke of York's HQ, King's Road, SW3 4LY (7730 8135). Sloane Square tube. **Open** 9am-9pm daily. **Main courses** £9-£12. **Credit** AmEx, MC, V. **Map** p397 F11 ⓐ **Brasserie**
The Saatchi Gallery welcomed this fabulous new brasserie to its Chelsea premises in May 2009. You can sit inside surrounded by modern art, but the grounds outside – littered with portable tables until 6pm, if the weather's fair – can be a more attractive option in the summer. There's a simple breakfast menu of pastries, eggs and toast or fry-up served until 11.30am, then lunch and dinner take over, with the expected salads, pastas and burgers joined by more ambitious daily specials: perhaps steamed salmon served in a yellow 'curry' broth or saddle of lamb drizzled with a zig-zag of yoghurt. Of the desserts, knickerbocker glory is a triumph.

★ Tom's Kitchen
27 Cale Street, SW3 3QP (7349 0202, www. tomskitchen.co.uk). Sloane Square or South Kensington tube. **Open** 7-10am, noon-3pm, 6-11pm Mon-Fri; 10am-3pm, 6-11pm Sat, Sun. **Main courses** £12-£29. **Credit** AmEx, MC, V. **Map** p397 E11 ⓐ **Brasserie**
White-tiled walls, vast expanses of marble and a busy open kitchen ensure Tom Aikens' place sounds full even when it isn't (though for weekend lunches it usually is). The big draw here is the pancake: well over an inch thick and almost as big as the serving plate, it's categorically London's best, filled with blueberries and drizzled with maple syrup. Lunch and dinner menus make the most of the wood-smoked oven, spit-roast and grill.

KNIGHTSBRIDGE & SOUTH KENSINGTON

Amaya
19 Motcomb Street, 15 Halkin Arcade, SW1X 8JT (7823 1166, www.amaya.biz). Knightsbridge tube. **Open** 12.30-2.15pm, 6.30-11.30pm Mon-Sat; 12.45-2.45pm, 6.30-10.30pm Sun. **Main courses** £8-£25. **Credit** AmEx, DC, MC, V. **Map** p400 G9 ⓐ **Indian**
Slinky by night, when its black leather seating, modish chandeliers and soundtrack of cool beats attract smooching couples, Amaya is light and breezy by day. From the open kitchen, black-aproned chefs display consummate skill at the tawa griddle, the tandoor oven and at the house-speciality charcoal grill.

Madsen
20 Old Brompton Road, SW7 3DL (7225 2772, www.madsenrestaurant.com). South Kensington tube. **Open** noon-10pm Mon; noon-11pm Tue-Thur; noon-midnight Fri, Sat. **Main courses** £11-£18. **Credit** MC, V. **Map** p397 D10 ⓐ **Scandinavian**

CONSUME

Danes might feel frustrated that this chic, serene and very friendly café-cum-restaurant doesn't reflect the current excitement surrounding Copenhagen's food scene, but the straightforward home cooking on offer – chicken breast fillet with horseradish cream sauce and roast root vegetables, *stegt rødspætte* (pan-fried plaice with melted butter and carrots – is pleasing. Skip the brief, international wine list in favour of the wonderful speciality Danish beers from Ærø. *See also p198* **Eating In**.

Nahm
Halkin, Halkin Street, SW1X 7DJ (7333 1234, www.nahm.como.bz). Hyde Park Corner tube.
Open noon-2.30pm, 7-10.45pm Mon-Fri; 7-10.45pm Sat; 7-9.45pm Sun. **Main courses** £11-£17. **Credit** AmEx, DC, MC, V. **Map** p400 G9 **86** **Thai**
Done out in gold and bronze tones, the elegant dining room at the Halkin (*see p189*) feels opulent yet unfussy. Tables for two look out over a manicured garden, and the opportunity to share rare dishes of startling flavour combinations from David Thompson's kitchen makes for a memorable meal.

Olivomare
10 Lower Belgrave Street, SW1W 0LJ (7730 9022). Victoria tube/rail. **Open** noon-2.30pm, 7-11pm Mon-Sat; noon-3pm, 7-10.30pm Sun. **Main courses** £14-£27. **Credit** AmEx, DC, MC, V. **Map** p400 H10 **87** **Fish & seafood**
It's rare to see a contemporary dining room with decor this quirky, but that's not Olivomare's only distinction: this is London's only Sardinian restaurant dedicated to seafood, attracting a cosmopolitan, affluent crowd with a menu that sings of simple luxuries. Typical dishes include the likes of octopus carpaccio with celery salad, or burrata cheese with bottarga (salted fish roe), cherry tomatoes and basil.

Racine
239 Brompton Road, SW3 2EP (7584 4477). Knightsbridge or South Kensington tube, or bus 14, 74. **Open** noon-3pm, 6-10.30pm Mon-Fri; noon-3.30pm, 6-10.30pm Sat; noon-3.30pm, 6-10pm Sun. **Main courses** £12-£21. **Credit** AmEx, MC, V. **Map** p397 E10 **88** **French**
Heavy curtains inside the door allow diners to make a grand entrance into Racine's warm, vibrant 1930s retro atmosphere. The clientele seems to have become less varied in recent times, feeling more male and monied than before, but there's still plenty to enjoy from the menu: try a starter such as garlic and saffron mousse with mussels, or, for dessert, a clafoutis with morello cherries in kirsch.

£ Serpentine Bar & Kitchen
Serpentine Road, Hyde Park, W2 2UH (7706 8114, www.serpentinebarandkitchen.com). Hyde Park Corner tube. **Open** 8am-8pm daily. **Main courses** £4-£10. **Credit** AmEx, MC, V. **Map** p395 F8 **89** **Café**

Perched at the eastern end of the lake in Hyde Park, the Serpentine Bar & Kitchen has a prime location. The interior is an urban take on rural life, using rustic wooden crates and baskets, floral lampshades and colourful bunting; tin buckets on every table hold fresh herbs and flowers. The menu offers plenty of appetising seasonal items that go well beyond the park café norm. There are plenty of seats, with a total of 300 covers inside and out, but things get very busy unless you're here off-peak.
▶ *For more Benugo restaurants, see p217*
The Art of Cooking.

★ Zuma
5 Raphael Street, SW7 1DL (7584 1010, www.zumarestaurant.com). Knightsbridge tube. **Open** *Restaurant* noon-2.15pm, 6-10.45pm Mon-Thur; noon-2.45pm, 6-10.45pm Fri; 12.30-3.15pm, 6-10.45pm Sat; 12.30-3.15pm, 6-10.15pm Sun. *Bar* noon-11pm Mon-Fri; 12.30-11pm Sat; noon-11pm Sun. **Main courses** £14-£70. **Credit** AmEx, DC, MC, V. **Map** p397 F9 **90** **Japanese**
Zuma has established itself as a must-go destination for every rich visitor to London. The stylishly displayed bottles, skilful lighting, and slickly presented sushi and robata bars still impress, and kitchen standards is as high as ever. Two things stand out: the quality of raw ingredients, and the imaginative flavour combinations, such as ginger, lime and coriander on the *tataki* (seared raw beef).
▶ *For Zuma's younger sibling Roka and Shochu Lounge, see p230.*

PADDINGTON & NOTTING HILL

Assaggi
1st floor, 39 Chepstow Place, W2 4TS (7792 5501). Bayswater, Notting Hill Gate or Queensway tube. **Open** 12.30-2.30pm, 7.30-11pm Mon-Fri; 1-2.20pm, 7.30-11pm Sat. **Main courses** £18-£24. **Credit** MC, V. **Map** p394 B6 **91** **Italian**
This Notting Hill icon fills the first floor of a Georgian house above the Chepstow pub. The dining room has a mere dozen tables, so it's clamorous when full – as it always is. The effusive greeting and uncompromising menu, both entirely in Italian, that once gave an exciting sense of place, now come across as a bit affected; and the once-brilliant Sardinian-inspired food can be a little tired at times. Still, its pedigree is so strong that it remains worth a look even now.

★ Le Café Anglais
8 Porchester Gardens, W2 4DB (7221 1415, www.lecafeanglais.co.uk). Bayswater tube. **Open** noon-3.30pm, 6.30-11pm Mon-Thur; noon-3.30pm, 6.30-11.30pm Fri; 11am-3.30pm, 6.30-11.30pm Sat; noon-3.30pm, 6.30-10.15pm Sun. **Main courses** £8-£28. **Cover** £1.50. **Credit** AmEx, MC, V. **Map** p394 B6 **92** **Modern European**

Chef-proprietor Rowley Leigh's fine restaurant opened to great acclaim in 2007 and is still very popular. Despite its location at the Whiteleys shopping centre, the big, white, art deco-style room is glamorous, with floor-to-ceiling leaded windows on one side, and thye open kitchen, rotisserie grill and bar opposite. It's a see-and-be-seen place with a long menu that's a mix-and-match delight perfect for grazers. Among the starters, fish, mains, cheeses and desserts on the traditional large-format carte are hors d'oeuvres and daily roasts, such as roast kid.

Geales

2 Farmer Street, W8 7SN (7727 7528, www.geales.com). Notting Hill Gate tube. **Open** 6-10.30pm Mon; noon-2.30pm, 6-10.30pm Tue-Fri; noon-10.30pm Sat; noon-9.30pm Sun. **Main courses** £8-£17. **Credit** AmEx, MC, V. **Map** p394 A7 ❸ **Fish & seafood**

Don't come here looking for exotic species or fancy cooking: Geales is all about good, classic dishes, served in simple smart premises. The chef's only glance beyond these shores is towards the Continent, with steamed mussels and a tomatoey fish soup. Otherwise it's oysters, smoked salmon, prawn cocktail and firm, white fish in faultlessly crisp batter. Puddings confirm the place's fine British pedigree.

★ Hereford Road

3 Hereford Road, W2 4AB (7727 1144, www. herefordroad.org). Bayswater tube. **Open** noon-3pm, 6-10.30pm Mon-Fri; noon-3.30pm, 6-10.30pm Sat; noon-3.30pm, 6-10pm Sun. **Main courses** £9-£14. **Credit** AmEx, MC, V. **Map** p394 B6 ❸ **British**

Despite having opened as recently as late 2007, Hereford Road has the assurance of somewhere that's been around much longer. It's an easy place in which to relax, with a mixed crowd and a happy buzz. Starters include the likes of (undyed) smoked haddock with white beans and leeks, while mains might feature mallard with braised chicory and lentils. Wines are keenly priced.

£ Kiasu

48 Queensway, W2 3RY (7727 8810). Bayswater or Queensway tube. **Open** noon-11pm daily. **Main courses** £5-£8. **Credit** (minimum £10) MC, V. **Map** p394 C6 ❸ **Malaysian**

This former winner of *Time Out*'s Best Cheap Eats award has had its ups and downs in terms of quality, but lately seems to be on the ascendant again. The casual, modern decor can put a smile on your face with its quirky touches. The stellar *char kway teow* (wok-fried flat noodles) keep a fine balance between sweet and salty, moist and al dente.

Ledbury

127 Ledbury Road, W11 2AQ (7792 9090, www.theledbury.com). Westbourne Park tube. **Open** noon-2.30pm, 6.30-10.30pm Mon-Sat; noon-3pm, 7-10pm Sun. **Set meals** £19-£60. **Credit** AmEx, MC, V. **Map** p394 A6 ❸ **French**

Bull & Last. *See p222.*

The happy buzz that defines a midweek lunch in this residential backwater stands testament to the reputation of Brett Graham's cooking. The imaginative, meticulous dishes are never overwrought, the sourcing is impeccable and the drinks list is exceptional, with as much heft from Austria as the New World. The comfort and noise-level, service and food seamlessly knit together to produce unruffled pleasure.

£ Taqueria
139-143 Westbourne Grove, W11 2RS (7229 4734, www.taqueria.co.uk). Notting Hill Gate tube. **Open** noon-11pm Mon-Thur; noon-11.30pm Fri; noon-10.30pm Sat, Sun. **Main courses** £5-£9. **Credit** MC, V. **Map** p394 A6 ⏱ **Mexican**
Pop-art prints of iconic Mexican revolutionary Emiliano Zapata adorn the walls of this classy cantina. The food isn't exactly revolutionary – classic Mexican street food of tacos, tortas and tostadas, for the most part – but the standard is sound, and Taqueria's traditional Mexican hot chocolate is every bit as spicy and frothy as it should be.
▶ *Nearby García (246 Portobello Rd, 7221 6119, www.cafegarcia.co.uk) is a trad Spanish café.*

NORTH LONDON

For Oriental food, try **Gilgamesh** (*see p236*), which serves assured and sometimes inspired pan Asian food with its extraordinary cocktails.

★ Bull & Last
168 Highgate Road, Kentish Town, NW5 1QS (7267 3641). Kentish Town tube/rail then bus 214, C2, or Gospel Oak rail then bus C11. **Open** noon-11pm Mon-Thur; noon-midnight Fri, Sat; noon-10.30pm Sun. **Meals served** noon-3pm, 6.30-10pm Mon-Fri; 12.30-4pm, 6.30-10pm Sat; 12.30-4pm, 7-9.30pm Sun. **Main courses** £12-£19. **Credit** MC, V. **Gastropub**
With its blackboard menu and real ales, the Bull & Last might look like an archetypal gastropub. However, as at a more formal restaurant, the tables are reserved for diners. Ingredients are of the highest quality – even the charcuterie is made in-house – with mains such as roast Cornish cod with brown shrimps and watercress showing the kitchen's great prowess. Doorstep sandwiches, sensational chips and huge scotch eggs draw daytime fans. *Photo p221.*

Duke of Cambridge
30 St Peter's Street, Islington, N1 8JT (7359 3066, www.dukeorganic.co.uk). Angel tube. **Open** noon-11pm Mon-Sat; noon-10.30pm Sun. *Meals served* 12.30-3pm, 6.30-10.30pm Mon-Fri; 12.30-3.30pm, 6.30-10.30pm Sat; 12.30-3.30pm, 6.30-10pm Sun. **Main courses** £11-£20. **Credit** MC, V. **Map** p402 O2 ⏱ **Gastropub**
Ten years after opening, this light-filled corner pub may no longer be singular in its commitment to an organic menu and drinks list, but it remains near the top in terms of cooking quality. Drinks too are discerning, with Freedom and Pitfield beers, an organic cocktail list and notably palatable wines. There's always an appreciative crowd at the large wooden tables, especially for Sunday lunch.
▶ *Another fine Islington gastro is the Marquess Tavern (32 Canonbury Street, 7354 2975, www.themarquesstavern.co.uk).*

£ Haché
24 Inverness Street, Camden, NW1 7HJ (7485 9100, www.hacheburgers.com). Camden Town tube. **Open** noon-10.30pm Mon-Sat; noon-10pm Sun. **Main courses** £6-£13. **Credit** AmEx, MC, V. **Burgers**
There's a wide choice of gourmet burgers on the menu at Haché, ranging from duck and venison to a welcome vegetarian selection. But the place also excels at top-notch basic burgers, such as steak au naturel and lamb au naturel – portions are large and the meat first-rate, and sides of frites, potato wedges or salad shouldn't disappoint.
Other locations 329 Fulham Road, Chelsea, SW10 9QL (7823 3515).

Manna
4 Erskine Road, Chalk Farm, NW3 3AJ (7722 8028, www.manna-veg.com). Chalk Farm tube, or bus 31, 168. **Open** 6.30-10.30pm Tue-Fri; noon-3pm, 6.30-10.30pm Sat, Sun. **Main courses** £10-£13. **Credit** MC, V. **Vegetarian**
Going strong after upwards of 40 years, Manna appears to have settled into 2008's more mature makeover. The dining space consists of a tiny conservatory and a cosy, curtained snug for more intimate encounters. The menu picks and chooses from around the world, with the ever-popular chef's salad (beetroot, avocado, balsamic-marinated onions, pumpkin seeds and protein from a selection of halloumi, feta or crispy tofu) always a feature.

Market
43 Parkway, Camden, NW1 7PN (7267 9700, www.marketrestaurant.co.uk). Camden Town tube. **Open** noon-2.30pm, 6-10.30pm Mon-Sat; 1-3.30pm Sun. **Main courses** £9-£14. **Credit** AmEx, DC, MC, V. **British**

INSIDE TRACK EAT TURKISH

Dalston Kingsland station north to Stoke Newington Church Street is the Turkish and Kurdish heart of Hackney, which means superb grills: **19 Numara Bos Cirrik** (34 Stoke Newington Road, N16 7XJ, 7249 0400) and **Mangal Ocakbaşı** (10 Arcola Street, E8 2DJ, 7275 8981, www.mangal1.com) are favourites.

Tayyabs. *See p225.*

Parkway doesn't have a reputation as a foodie destination, so hats off to Market for succeeding on this very tricky Camden thoroughfare. Behind an unassuming black frontage, a wide demographic of groups, couples, families and lone diners lap up the good-value, high-quality British fare. Brisk service comes with a smile.

★ £ Ottolenghi
287 Upper Street, Islington, N1 2TZ (7288 1454, www.ottolenghi.co.uk). Angel tube or Highbury & Islington tube/rail. **Open** 8am-11pm Mon-Sat; 9am-7pm Sun. **Main courses** £8-£10. **Credit** AmEx, MC, V. **Map** p402 O1 ⑲
Bakery-café
This is more than an inviting bakery. Behind the pastries piled in the window is a comparatively prim deli counter with lush salads, available day and evening, eat-in or take away. As a stylish daytime café, Ottolenghi is brilliant, but the long canteen-style central table, slow-footed service and bright white decor are not for special occasions.
Other locations 1 Holland Street, Kensington, W8 4NA (7937 0003); 63 Ledbury Road, Notting Hill, W11 2AD (7727 1121); 13 Motcomb Street, Belgravia, SW1X 8LB (7823 2707).

£ S&M Café
4-6 Essex Road, Islington, N1 8LN (7359 5361, www.sandmcafe.co.uk). Angel tube. **Open** 7.30am-11pm daily. **Main courses** £5-£10. **Credit** AmEx, MC, V. **Map** p402 O2 ⑩⑩ **Café**

Preserved by S&M founder Kevin Finch, the decor of the former Alfredo's café is a mix of periods, with panelling covering a probable multitude of building sins, blue Formica tables and tiny red leather chairs. It's cramped, but jovial. The all-day breakfasts are as popular as the eponymous sausage and mash.
Other locations 48 Brushfield Street, Spitalfields, E1 6AG (7247 2252); North Greenwich Centre, Peninsula Square, SE10 0DX (8305 1940); 268 Portobello Road, Ladbroke Grove, W10 5TY (8968 8898).

£ Wagamama
11 Jamestown Road, Camden, NW1 7BW (7428 0800, www.wagamama.com). Camden Town tube. **Open** noon-11pm Mon-Sat; noon-10pm Sun. **Main courses** £6-£10. **Credit** AmEx, DC, MC, V. **Noodles**
Since starting life in 1992, this chain of noodle bars has become an international phenomenon, with branches as far afield as Egypt and New Zealand. The British Wagamamas all serve the same menu: rice plate meals and Japanese ramen, *soba* and *udon* noodles, cooked *teppanyaki*-style on a flat griddle or simmered in huge bowls of spicy soup and all served in double-quick time. The use of high-quality ingredients raises the chain above many of its imitators.
Other locations throughout the city.

EAST LONDON

The famous Indian-food options on Brick Lane don't live up to their reputation; *see p224* **Inside Track**.

★ £ Albion
2-4 Boundary Street, Shoreditch, E2 7DD (7729 1051, www.albioncaff.co.uk). Old Street tube/rail or bus 26, 48, 67, 149, 242. **Open** 8am-midnight daily. **Main courses** £8-£10. **Credit** AmEx, MC, V. **Map** p403 R4 ⑩⑴ **Café**
Almost every new London restaurant seems to be mining the vein of nostalgia for traditional British cuisine, but few have pulled it off as well as Terence Conran's stand-out 'caff', winner of *Time Out*'s Best New Cheap Eats award in 2009. Once you're past the kitsch British products for sale in the shop (HP sauce, Marmite), you're faced with platters of cupcakes and doorstop-thick slices of battenberg, baked on-site. On the main menu, toad in the hole or devilled kidneys sit next to an English breakfast with buttery scrambled eggs and juicy mushrooms. *See also p199* **Eating Out.**
▶ *For more on Conran's Boundary Project, see p186* **Pushing the Boundary.**

★ £ Brick Lane Beigel Bake
159 Brick Lane, E1 6SB (7729 0616). Liverpool Street tube/rail or bus 8. **Open** 24hrs daily. **Main courses** £1-£6. **No credit cards.** **Map** p403 S4 ⑩⑵ **Jewish**

CONSUME

This charismatic little East End institution rolls out perfect bagels (egg, cream cheese, salt beef), superb bread and moreish cakes. Even at 3am, fresh-baked goods are pulled from the ovens at the back; no wonder the queue for bagels trails out the door when the innumerable local bars and clubs begin to close.

£ Chaat

36 Redchurch Street, Shoreditch, E2 7DP (7739 9595, www.chaatlondon.co.uk). Liverpool Street tube/rail then bus 8, 388. **Open** 6-11pm Mon-Sat. **Main courses** £5-£7. **Credit** AmEx, MC, V. **Map** p403 S4 ⑩③ **Indian**

Chaat has a lot going for it. It's located in the hippest street in ultra-fashionable Shoreditch; it has a charming, engaging young female owner, Shanaz Khan; and unusually, it serves simple, home-style Bangladeshi dishes, not the Anglo-Moghul cooking found in most Brick Lane curry houses.

★ Eyre Brothers

70 Leonard Street, Shoreditch, EC2A 4QX (7613 5346, www.eyrebrothers.co.uk). Old Street tube/rail. **Open** noon-2.45pm, 6.30-10.45pm Mon-Fri; 7-11pm Sat. **Main courses** £15-£25. **Credit** AmEx, DC, MC, V. **Map** p403 Q4 ⑩④ **International**

INSIDE TRACK
CURRY IN FAVOUR?

Brick Lane (*see p136*) is an interesting part of town, but the widely fêted Indian food served at its countless popular restaurants is nothing special. For greater authenticity and better cooking, try the few caffs – **Ruchi** (303 Whitechapel Road, E1 1BY, 7247 6666), for example – that offer proper Bangladeshi dishes, especially around the south end of Brick Lane; to the north, **Chaat** (*see above*) is a welcome new addition. A little further off in Whitechapel, try the ever-popular **Tayyabs** (*see right*).

In truth, curry pilgrims are better off in Southall: the East African Punjabi food at **Brilliant** (72-76 Western Road, 8574 1928, UB2 5DZ, www.brilliantrestaurant. com) is superb, while the best kebabs and yoghurt-based snacks can be had at the **New Asian Tandoori Centre** (114-118 The Green, UB2 4BQ, 8574 2597). The less intrepid can enjoy decent Indian food at good prices in central London at **Imli** (167-169 Wardour Street, Soho, W1F 8WR, 7287 4243, www.imli.co.uk) or the often-crowded Covent Garden branch of **Masala Zone** (48 Floral Street, WC2E 9DA, 7379 0101, www.masalazone.com).

This long, attractive room is extremely popular with City gents. Robert and David Eyre have taken the food of the Iberian peninsula into their heart and soul, and reproduce it in a form that's true to its rustic roots yet sophisticated enough to compete with top-level French or Italian cooking. The tapas are sensational, while meat is king on the main menu.

★ £ E Pellicci

332 Bethnal Green Road, E2 0AG (7739 4873). Bethnal Green tube/rail or bus 8. **Open** 7am-4pm Mon-Sat. **Main courses** £5-£6. **No credit cards.** **Café**

This hive of humanity, a family business to the core, has been trading since 1900. It's an aesthetic delight: the art deco wood-panelled interior holds Grade II-listed status. The menu features sandwiches, rolls and ciabattas; big breakfasts; steak pies and lasagnes; and boarding-school classic desserts. Prices remain firmly rooted in the old East End.

★ £ Rosa's

12 Hanbury Street, Spitalfields, E1 6QR (7247 1093, www.rosaslondon.com). Whitechapel tube or Liverpool Street tube/rail. **Open** 11am-10.30pm Mon-Thur, Sun; 11am-1pm Fri, Sat. **Main courses** £6-£14. **Credit** AmEx, MC, V. **Map** p403 S5 ⑩⑤ **Thai**

Rosa's is good-looking for a low-budget, shared-tables place, with wooden architraves cunningly turned into wall sculptures, attractive lighting and a moodier, more spacious dining area in the basement. Although the dishes are (mostly) the familiar Thai roll call, there's a freshness and honesty about the cooking: in the UK, grated green papaya for the *som tam* is often substituted with cheaper carrot or cabbage, but not here. *See also p198 Eating In.*
▶ *A second Rosa's should open in Soho in early 2010, replacing the Noodles pop-up restaurant at 48 Dean Street.*

£ Sông Quê

134 Kingsland Road, Shoreditch, E2 8DY (7613 3222). Liverpool Street tube/rail then bus 67, 149, 242, or Old Street tube/rail then bus 243. **Open** noon-3pm, 5.30-11pm Mon-Sat; 12.30-11pm Sun. **Main courses** £4-£7. **Credit** MC, V. **Map** p403 R3 ⑩⑥ **Vietnamese**

North-east London retains its monopoly on the capital's most authentic Vietnamese restaurants. And Sông Quê, which was the key pioneer, remains the benchmark. It's an efficient, canteen-like operation to which diners of all types are attracted – be prepared to share tables at busy times.

£ Tayyabs

83 Fieldgate Street, Whitechapel, E1 1JU (7247 9543, www.tayyabs.co.uk). Aldgate East or Whitechapel tube. **Open** noon-11.30pm daily. **Main courses** £6-£10. **Credit** AmEx, MC, V. **Indian**

Franco Manca. *See p226.*

Behind the green frontage of a former pub, Tayyabs is a bright, modern Pakistani café that bucks up this down-at-heel backstreet. Droves of City suits are attracted for lunch, along with a few multinational students and locals. The upbeat mood is accentuated by Bollywood beats, a crimson, ochre and mustard colour scheme and the bustle from an open-view kitchen. Food quality can vary. *Photo p223.*

Tea Smith
8 Lamb Street, Spitalfields, E1 6EA (7247 1333, www.teasmith.co.uk). Liverpool Street tube/rail. **Open** 11am-6pm daily. *Set tea* (Sat, Sun) £18-£25. **Credit** MC, V. **Map** p403 R5 **107** Tearoom
As Teasmith's guide states, there are several categories of tea (white, green, oolong, red and black, aged and puer), all of them offered here on a regularly changing menu to drink on the stylish premises or take away. The afternoon tasting menu offers a selection of teas with matched pâtisserie and chocolates by William Curley. As well as top-grade tea, you can also buy beautiful cups, pots and other bits and bobs.
▶ *For more gourmet tea, try Postcard; see p261.*

Les Trois Garçons
1 Club Row, Shoreditch, E1 6JX (7613 1924, www.lestroisgarcons.com). Liverpool Street tube/rail or bus 8, 388. **Open** 7-10pm Mon-Thur; 7-10.30pm Fri, Sat. **Set dinner** £27-£42.50 2 courses, £31-£49.50 3 courses. **Credit** AmEx, DC, MC, V. **Map** p403 S4 **108** French
Behind the sober façade of a converted East End pub, Les Trois Garçons is a paean to decorative excess. Crystal chandeliers hang from the ceiling, while stuffed animals perch on the bar or crane from the walls, swathed in costume jewellery. On the food menu, rich, classical French cuisine is tempered with modern British influences, along with simple but

impeccably sourced ingredients. Excellent service have helped make this a fiercely popular venue.

Wapping Food
Wapping Hydraulic Power Station, Wapping Wall, E1W 3ST (7680 2080, www.thewapping project.com). Wapping tube or Shadwell DLR. **Open** noon-3.30pm, 6.30-11pm Mon-Fri; 10am-4pm, 7-11pm Sat; 10am-4pm Sun. **Main courses** £11-£22. **Credit** AmEx, MC, V. Modern European
Cooking wins out in this enterprise, which is part-Victorian pumping-station museum and part modern art gallery. The fabulous all-Australian wine list eschews that country's mass-produced plonk for top-quality bottles, with by-the-glass options to match almost every dish. Satisfying cooking includes the likes of Brecon lamb on a bed of sprouting broccoli, and roast pork with baked polenta, spring greens and pear chutney.
▶ *In good weather, pop upstairs to see the pretty rooftop lily pond.*

Whitechapel Gallery Dining Room
Whitechapel Gallery, 77-82 Whitechapel High Street, E1 7QX (7522 7888, www.whitechapel gallery.org/dine). Aldgate East tube. **Open** noon-2.30pm, 5.30-11pm Tue-Sat; 11.30am-2.30pm Sun. **Main courses** £13-£18. **Credit** MC, V. **Map** p405 S6 **109** Modern European
The Whitechapel's new restaurant is good-looking but a bit cramped: don't come here for private conversation. It's refreshing to see that while she still uses local and seasonal British ingredients, chef Maria Elia eschews the 'Modern British' slant currently so popular in favour of rich spicing and Mediterranean influences. Expect the likes of eel pâté with tangy marinated beets and braised lamb

CONSUME

shoulder in filo with preserved lemons and dates. Dishes are priced high, but the service is welcoming, helpful and cheerful.

SOUTH-EAST LONDON

Greenwich lacks stand-out eateries. Aside from some over-styled bistros and the high-street chains, **Inside** (*see below*) and some good boozers (*see p240*) are pretty much it.

Inside
19 Greenwich South Street, SE10 8NW (8265 5060, www.insiderestaurant.co.uk). Greenwich rail/DLR. **Open** noon-2.30pm, 6.30-11pm Tue-Fri; 6.30-11pm Sat; noon-3pm Sun. **Main courses** £10-£16. **Credit** AmEx, MC, V. **Modern European**
There are too few neighbourhood restaurants in south-east London that tantalise you anew with fresh flavours, however often or seldom you dine there. With proficient, unobtrusive service, a smart interior, and reasonable prices, Inside serves the whole community. The food, lovingly and often locally sourced, aims pretty high and only occasionally misses. Desserts have been known to convert the resolutely pudding-averse.

£ Pavilion Tea House
Greenwich Park, Blackheath Gate, SE10 8QY (8858 9695, www.companyofcooks.com). Blackheath rail or Greenwich rail/DLR.
Open 9am-5.30pm Mon-Fri; 9am-6pm Sat, Sun. **Main courses** £4-£7. **Credit** MC, V. **Café**
Diagonally opposite the Royal Observatory, set in its own pretty, fenced-in grounds, the Pavilion Tea House provides a convivial cake-and-a-break for weary parents. Its breakfasts, hot meals, salads, snacks and sandwiches are a notch above average.

SOUTH-WEST LONDON

Chez Bruce
2 Bellevue Road, Wandsworth, SW17 7EG (8672 0114, www.chezbruce.co.uk). Wandsworth Common rail. **Open** noon-2pm, 6.30-10pm Mon-Thur; noon-2pm, 6.30-10.30pm Fri; noon-3pm, 6.30-10.30pm Sat; noon-3pm, 7-10pm Sun.
Set meals £25.50-£40 3 courses. **Credit** AmEx, DC, MC, V. **French**
Chez Bruce is still the destination of choice for fine dining in south London, although it has a softer, less minimalist feel to it these days; indeed, it's almost cosy. Some things don't change, though, and the wine list remains a gorgeous (and gorgeously priced) parade through the world's best. The brief menu changes slightly through the week and seasonally, with a backbone of stalwarts.
▶ *If you're in Kew, try proprietor Nigel Platts-Martin's Glasshouse (14 Station Parade, 8940 6777, www.glasshouserestaurant.co.uk).*

★ £ Franco Manca
4 Market Row, Electric Lane, Brixton, SW9 8LD (7738 3021, www.francomanca.com). Brixton tube/rail. **Open** noon-5pm Mon-Sat. **Main courses** £4-£6. **Credit** MC, V. **Pizza**
Since opening inside one of the arches on Brixton Market, Franco Manca has been showered with acclaim. The dining area has a mix of indoor and outdoor seating. The menu is precise (just six pizzas) and cheap. The key to the pizzas' success is the sourdough bases, thin and flavoursome; the organic lemonade is almost as unmissable as the pizzas themselves. A delight. *Photos p225.*

WEST LONDON

Clarke's
124 Kensington Church Street, Kensington, W8 4BH (7221 9225, www.sallyclarke.com). Notting Hill Gate tube. **Open** 12.30-2pm, 6.30-10pm Mon-Fri; noon-2pm, 6.30-10pm Sat; 12.30-2.30pm Sun.
Main courses (lunch) £15-£17. **Set dinner** £39.50 3 courses. **Credit** AmEx, DC, MC, V. **Map** p394 B7 ❿ **Modern European**
Chef-proprietor Sally Clarke has been espousing the 'seasonal and local' ethic since the mid 1980s. The food at this stylishly low-key restaurant shows influences from western Europe, executed with a deft hand, and the wine list has some very good bottles, with California wines particularly well-chosen. Don't miss the breads, for which the deli next door (& Clarke's) is justly famed.

★ Gate
51 Queen Caroline Street, Hammersmith, W6 9QL (8748 6932, www.thegate.tv). Hammersmith tube. **Open** noon-2.45pm, 6-10.45pm Mon-Fri; 6-10.45pm Sat. **Main courses** £10-£14. **Credit** AmEx, MC, V. **Vegetarian**
Having celebrated its 20th birthday, west London's most prominent vegetarian restaurant continues to impress with its innovative dishes and atmospheric, high-ceilinged dining room. The mood is casual and pleasantly noisy with the clatter of cutlery and the chatter of bourgeois meat-avoiders. Dishes can often feature a bewildering number of flavours from around the world. Desserts are equally tempting.

River Café
Thames Wharf, Rainville Road, Hammersmith, W6 9HA (7386 4200, www.rivercafe.co.uk). Hammersmith tube. **Open** 12.30-3pm, 7-9.30pm Mon-Sat; 12.30-3pm Sun. **Main courses** £23-£32. **Credit** AmEx, DC, MC, V. **Italian**
The River Café's popularity shows no sign of waning. Last year's refit hasn't transformed the winning formula, but there's now a bar near the entrance and the wood-fired oven has been made into a focal point. A cheese room has also been added. The wine list, and staff, are friendlier and more relaxed than those in many upmarket restaurants.

Pubs & Bars

Drinking remains a popular pastime in the capital.

Best British invention? You might have thought it was the television, penicillin or the locomotive, but many Londoners will tell you that it's the boozer. From traditional-as-you-like local pubs (the **Lamb**) to slick design bars (the **Connaught**), the city certainly offers a mighty spread.

It's far from a static scene. On the drinks front, the last decade has seen a vast increase in the availability and popularity both of real ale (*see p238* **Profile**) and top-class cocktails. Gourmets will be delighted to see the gastropub revolution continues to yield benefits across the board, with good quality pub grub far easier to find than it was even five years ago. Wine bars have also been making a quiet comeback: the organic and biodynamic list at the wonderful **Terroirs** is one interesting development; the increasing use of wine dispensers (**Kensington Wine Rooms**) another.

CONSUME

THE SOUTH BANK & BANKSIDE

★ Gladstone Arms
64 Lant Street, SE1 1QN (7407 3962). Borough tube. **Open** noon-11pm Mon-Fri; noon-midnight Sat; noon-10.30pm Sun. **Credit** MC, V. **Map** p405 P9 **❶**
While the Victorian prime minister still glares from the massive mural on the outer wall, inside is now funky, freaky and candlelit. Gigs (blues, folk, acoustic, five nights a week) take place at one end of a cosy space; opposite, a bar dispenses ales and lagers. Pies provide sustenance. Retro touches include an old-fashioned 'On Air' studio sign and a Communist-style railway clock.

Skylon
Royal Festival Hall, Belvedere Road, SE1 8XX (7654 7800, www.danddlondon.com). Waterloo tube/rail. **Open** noon-1am daily. *Food* noon-10.45pm daily. **Credit** AmEx, MC, V. **Map** p401 M8 **❷**
There can't be many better views than this in town. Sit at the cocktail bar (between the two restaurant

areas), and gaze at trains trundling out of Charing Cross, cars and red buses whizzing across Waterloo Bridge, and boats and cruisers pootling along the Thames. In spite of its aircraft-hangar proportions, the space feels intimate. Drinks include ten bellinis, a large range of liqueurs and a list of tempting classics (manhattans, sidecars, negronis), all at a price.

Wine Wharf
Stoney Street, SE1 9AD (7940 8335, www.wine wharf.co.uk). London Bridge tube/rail. **Open** noon-11pm Mon-Sat. *Food* noon-10pm Mon-Sat. **Credit** AmEx, DC, MC, V. **Map** p404 P8 **❸**
Part of the Vinopolis complex, Wine Wharf inhabits two storeys of a reclaimed Victorian warehouse, all exposed brickwork and high-ceilinged industrial chic. You could drink very well indeed here: the 250-bin list stretches to 1953 d'Yquem and some very serious prestige cuvée champagnes. But with nearly half the wines available by the glass, there's a great opportunity to experiment.
Other locations Brew Wharf, Stoney Street, SE1 9AD (7378 6601, www.brewwharf.com).

THE CITY

Castle
26 Furnival Street, EC4A 1JS (7405 5470). Chancery Lane tube. **Open** 11am-11pm Mon-Fri. *Food* noon-3pm, 6-9pm Mon-Thur; noon-3pm Fri. **Credit** MC, V. **Map** p404 N5 **❹**

❶ Green numbers given in this chapter correspond to the location of each pub or bar on the street maps. *See pp394-407.*

This cosy, black-fronted pie-slice of a pub in a quiet corner of the City is an unlikely place in which to find such a range of sought-after real ales. The ever-changing range of British brews is supplemented by taps offering Peroni and Erdinger Weissbier; there are also a dozen wines of both colours, by glass and bottle. Doorstep sandwiches, home-made burgers and bangers and mash provide sustenance.

Vertigo 42 Champagne Bar

Tower 42, 25 Old Broad Street, City, EC2N 1HQ (7877 7842, www.vertigo42.co.uk). Bank tube/DLR or Liverpool Street tube/rail. **Open** noon-3pm, 5.30-11pm Mon-Fri. **Credit** AmEx, DC, MC, V. **Map** p405 Q6 ⑤
Stretching above the City, the views from this 42nd-floor bar are breathtaking. So, too, are the prices (white wine from £7.50 a glass), suggesting the economic downturn hasn't hit every banker's bonus. Food is more down to earth: options include wild mushroom tart with artichoke salad, and seared peppered tuna steak, each coming with a recommended tipple. Seating is arranged so that everyone can enjoy the panorama. You'll need to book in advance.

HOLBORN & CLERKENWELL

Clerkenwell has a compelling claim to being the birthplace of the ubiquitous gastropub: the still wonderful **Eagle** (*see p201*) kicked things off. Other food pioneers that provide great drinking are **St John** (*see p203*) and **Cellar Gascon** (59 West Smithfield, EC1A 9DS, 7600 7561, 7796 0600, www.cellargascon.com; *see also p201*).

Café Kick

43 Exmouth Market, EC1R 4QL (7837 8077, www.cafekick.co.uk). Angel tube or Farringdon tube/rail. **Open** *Summer* noon-11pm Mon-Thur; noon-midnight Fri, Sat; 1-10.30pm Sun. *Winter* noon-11pm Mon-Thur; noon-midnight Fri, Sat. **Credit** AmEx, MC, V. **Map** p402 N4 ⑥
Clerkenwell's most likeable bar is this table-football themed gem. The soccer paraphernalia is authentic, retro-cool and mainly Latin (you'll find a Zenit St Petersburg scarf amid the St Etienne and Lusitanian gear); bar staff, beers and bites give the impression you could be in Lisbon. A modest open kitchen ('we don't microwave or deep-fry') dishes out tapas, sandwiches and charcuterie platters.
Other locations Bar Kick, 127 Shoreditch High Street, Shoreditch, E1 6JE (7739 8700).

★ Fox & Anchor

115 Charterhouse Street, EC1M 6AA (7250 1300, www.foxandanchor.com). Barbican tube or Farringdon tube/rail. **Open** 7am-11pm Mon-Fri; 8.30am-11pm Sat; 8.30am-7pm Sun. **Credit** AmEx, MC, V. **Map** p402 O5 ⑦
Pristine mosaic tiling and etched glass scream 'sensitive refurbishment' at this Smithfield treasure. The

dark wood bar is lined with pewter tankards; to the back is the Fox's Den, a series of intimate rooms used for both drinking and dining. Local sourcing is a priority and a pleasure: in addition to the own-label ale, cask beers might include Red Poll and Old Growler from Suffolk's fine Nethergate brewery. There are plenty more delights among the bottles.

★ Seven Stars

53 Carey Street, WC2A 2JB (7242 8521). Chancery Lane or Holborn tube. **Open** 11am-11pm Mon-Fri; noon-11pm Sat; noon-10.30pm Sun. *Food* noon-10pm Mon-Fri; 1-10pm Sat; 1-9pm Sun. **Credit** AmEx, MC, V. **Map** p399 M6 ⑧
Barristers bring their clients to this lovely little pub for champagne after winning a case at the nearby Royal Courts of Justice. In a glass display case sits a copy of *Home from the Inn Contented*, a cookbook by landlady Roxy Beaujolais; it's a sign that the simple pub food advertised on the blackboard (herring with potato salad, say) will be a cut above the norm. Real ales and fairly priced wines by the glass are tipples of choice.

Three Kings of Clerkenwell

7 Clerkenwell Close, EC1R 0DY (7253 0483). Farringdon tube/rail. **Open** noon-11pm Mon-Sat. **No credit cards. Map** p402 N4 ⑨
Rhinoceros heads, Egyptian felines and photos of Dennis Bergkamp provide the decorative backdrop against which a regular bunch of discerning bohos glug Scrumpy Jack, Beck's Vier, Old Speckled Hen or London Pride, and tap the well-worn tables to the Cramps and other gems from an outstanding jukebox. Bottles of Tyskie and Lech point to a recent invasion by jaw-droppingly gorgeous Poles.

INSIDE TRACK
DRINK IN HISTORY

In the vicinity of the City are some London's most impressive historic pubs. Some, like the **Jerusalem Tavern** (55 Britton Street, EC1M 5UQ, 7490 4281, www.stpetersbrewery.co.uk), on the site of a former coffee house, and **Ye Old Mitre** (1 Ely Court, Ely Place side of 8 Hatton Garden, EC1N 6SJ, 7405 4751), charmingly hidden between two streets, are great boozers in their own right. The **Black Friar** (174 Queen Victoria Street, EC4V 4EG, 7236 5474) may not be London's best pub, but has an absolutely superb Arts and Crafts interior. The **Cittie of York** (22 High Holborn, WC1V 6BN, 7242 7670) is another pub to gladden the eye – so long as you push past the dull front room into the massive banqueting hall of a back room.

Lamb. *See p231.*

CONSUME

Vinoteca
*7 St John Street, EC1M 4AA (7253 8786, www.
vinoteca.co.uk). Farringdon tube/rail.* **Open** noon-
11pm Mon-Sat; noon-5pm Sun. *Food* noon-2.45pm,
6.30-10pm Mon-Fri; noon 3pm, 6-10pm Sat; noon-
4pm Sun. **Credit** MC, V. **Map** p402 O5 ⑩
Inspired in name and approach by the Italian *enoteca*
(a blend of off-licence and wine bar, with snacks
thrown in), Vinoteca is more of a serious gastropub
in spirit. But even if you're not in the mood for much
more than a plate of bread and olive oil, it's worth
heading here for the impressive 200-bottle wine list,
of which 25 are available by the glass. Bonus: all
wines are available to take away at retail price.

BLOOMSBURY & FITZROVIA

For sheer style, try the bar at **Hakkasan** (*see
p203*). In King's Cross, **Camino** (*see p203*) has
a courtyard off the spacious bar, while the **Big
Chill House** (*see p224*) is for music fans.

★ All Star Lanes
*Victoria House, Bloomsbury Place, WC1B 4DA
(7025 2676, www.allstarlanes.co.uk). Holborn
tube.* **Open** 5-11.30pm Mon-Wed; 5pm-midnight
Thur; noon-2am Fri, Sat; noon-11pm Sun. **Main
courses** £9.50-£14.50. *Bowling* £7.50-£8.50/
game. **Credit** AmEx, MC, V. **Map** p399 L5 ⑪
Of Bloomsbury's two subterranean bowling dens,
this is the one with aspirations. Walk past the lanes
and smart, diner-style seating, and you'll find yourself in a comfortable, subdued side bar with chilled
glasses, classy red furnishings, an unusual mix of
bottled lagers (try Anchor Steam) and impressive
cocktails. There's an American menu and, at week-

ends, DJs. A much bigger location opened in late
2008 in Brick Lane (no.87, 7422 8370).
▶ *Nearby, Bloomsbury Bowling Lanes (Bedford
Way, 7183 1979, www.bloomsburybowling.com)
offers a pints-and-worn-carpets take on the game,
complete with private karaoke booths.*

Bradley's Spanish Bar
*42-44 Hanway Street, W1T 1UT (7636 0359).
Tottenham Court Road tube.* **Open** noon-11pm
Mon-Sat; 3-10.30pm Sun. **Credit** MC, V. **Map**
p406 W1 ⑫
There's something of the Barcelona dive bar about
this pub, but other than that it's not really that
Spanish. A hotchpotch of local workers, shoppers
and foreign exchange students fills the cramped
two-floor space, enraging taxi drivers as they spill
on to the narrow street. All that's changed since the
'90s is the staff, now mainly Hungarian. If you're on
the verge of an Oxford Street meltdown, escape here.

Champagne Bar at St Pancras
*St Pancras International Station, Pancras Road,
King's Cross, NW1 2QP (7870 9900, www.
searcystpancras.co.uk). King's Cross tube/rail.*
Open 7am-11.30pm daily. *Food* 7am-10pm daily.
Credit AmEx, DC, MC, V. **Map** p399 L3 ⑬
The Eurostar station's Champagne Bar lies beneath
William Henry Barlow's magnificent Victorian roof.
The champagne list is comprehensive, with every
significant Grand Marque featured in depth. It's pos-
sible to spend £880 on a bottle of 1996 Krug Clos de
Mesnit, but tempting choices start at around £50 a
bottle and there are 15 by the glass (the house De
Nauroy Brut NV is £7.50 a glass). The short food
menu focuses on British ingredients.

CONSUME

Shochu Lounge.

★ Lamb

94 Lamb's Conduit Street, WC1N 3LZ (7405 0713). Holborn or Russell Square tube. **Open** 11am-midnight Mon-Sat; noon-10.30pm Sun. *Food* noon-9pm daily. **Credit** AmEx, MC, V. **Map** p399 M4 ⓮

The standard range of Young's beers are dispensed from a central horseshoe bar in this 280-year-old pub, around which are ringed original etched-glass snob screens, used to prevent Victorian gentlemen from being seen when liaising with 'women of dubious distinction'. A sunken back area gives access to a convenient square of summer patio. *Photo p229.*

Shochu Lounge

Basement, Roka, 37 Charlotte Street, W1T 1RR (7580 9666, www.shochulounge.com). Goodge Street or Tottenham Court Road tube. **Open** 5pm-midnight daily. *Food* 5.30-11.30pm Mon-Sat; 5.30-10.30pm Sun. **Credit** AmEx, DC, MC, V. **Map** p398 J5 ⓯

Beneath landmark Japanese restaurant Roka, the chic Shochu Lounge offers drinks based on the vodka-like distilled spirit of the same name. Shochu is often overlooked for its more widespread counterpart, saké, but it's here used in healthy tonics (75ml measures, £6.90) in cocktails (£8.30), and sold by the 50ml measure. With a 13.5% service charge, drinks run to around £10. The full Roka menu is available.

COVENT GARDEN & THE STRAND

★ Gordon's

47 Villiers Street, Strand, WC2N 6NE (7930 1408, www.gordonswinebar.com). Embankment tube or Charing Cross tube/rail. **Open** 11am-11pm Mon-Sat; noon-10pm Sun. *Food* noon-10pm Mon-Sat; noon-9pm Sun. **Credit** AmEx, MC, V. **Map** p407 Y5 ⓰

Gordon's was established in its present form in 1890, but the atmospheric exposed brickwork and flickering candlelight make this basement feel older still. Although this is the definitive old-school wine bar, it gets packed with a young and lively crowd, half of whom seem to be on first dates. The wine list is surprisingly modern; still, in such surroundings, it seems a shame not to drink the fortified wines, drawn directly from casks behind the bar.

Lamb & Flag

33 Rose Street, WC2E 9EB (7497 9504). Covent Garden tube. **Open** 11am-11pm Mon-Thur; 11am-11.30pm Fri, Sat; noon-10.30pm Sun. *Food* noon-3pm Mon-Fri; noon-4.30pm Sat, Sun. **Credit** MC, V. **Map** p407 Y3 ⓱

This dog-leg alleyway used to be a pit of prostitution and bare-knuckle bashes, the latter hosted at this historic, low-ceilinged tavern back when it was called the Bucket of Blood; poet John Dryden was beaten up here in 1679. Space is always at a premium, hence the pavement cluster on summer evenings. Two centuries of mounted cuttings and caricatures amplify the sense of character.

▶ *If it's too busy, try the Benelux-themed Lowlander (36 Drury Lane, 7379 7446, www.lowlander.com).*

Princess Louise

208-209 High Holborn, WC1V 7BW (7405 8816). Holborn tube. **Open** 11am-11pm Mon-Fri; noon-11pm Sat; noon-10.30pm Sun. *Food* noon-2.30pm, 6-8.30pm Mon-Thur; noon-2.30pm Fri, Sat. **Credit** AmEx, MC, V. **Map** p407 Z1 ⓲

With half-a-dozen ornately carved, sumptuously tiled bar areas under one high, stucco ceiling, the Princess Louise is a classic example of the Victorian public house in which drinking was segregated according to class. Today, it's an across-the-board Sam Smith's pub, prices starting at an egalitarian £1.88 for a pint of bitter. Sandwiches, baguettes and pub food satisfy hungrier diners, who are also accommodated in the upstairs bar (mealtimes only). *Photo p232.*

★ Terroirs
5 William IV Street, WC2N 4DW (7036 0660, www.terroirswinebar.com). Charing Cross tube/rail. **Open** noon-11pm Mon-Sat. **Credit** AmEx, MC, V. **Map** p407 Y4 ⑲
It may be a gimmick or it may be the future of winemaking. Either way, many of the new generation of organic and biodynamic, sulphur-, sugar- or acid-free wines on offer here are well made, and the line-up of Calvados and Armagnac bottles is impressive. Food is terrific: a tapas-style selection of French bar snacks, charcuterie and seafood, along with plats du jour.
▶ *Terroirs has been so successful it expanded in late 2009 into a large basement two floors down.*

SOHO & LEICESTER SQUARE

Soho is also one of the focal points of the city's gay nightlife scene. For more, *see pp305 307.*

Amuse Bouche
21-22 Poland Street, W1F 8QG (7287 1661, www.abcb.co.uk). Oxford Circus tube. **Open** 4-11.30pm Mon-Thur; 4pm-midnight Fri; 5pm-midnight Sat. **Credit** AmEx, DC, V. **Map** p406 V2 ⑳
Dedicated to the democratisation of champagne, Amuse Bouche has hit on a winning formula: relaxed, modern surroundings, and a list of 40 or so champagnes, with more than ten also offered by the glass. Food comes in the form of tapas-style global nibbles, and prices are admirably restrained.
Other locations 51 Parsons Green Lane, Parsons Green, SW6 4JA (7371 8517).

Dog & Duck
18 Bateman Street, W1D 3AJ (7494 0697). Tottenham Court Road tube. **Open** 10am-11.30pm Mon-Sat; noon-10.30pm Sun. *Food* 10am-10pm Mon-Sat; noon-9pm Sun. **Credit** AmEx, MC, V. **Map** p406 W2 ㉑
This Soho landmark is known for its literary heritage, vintage interior (etched mirrors, carved mahogany) and ever-changing ale selection, ranging from the familiar likes of London Pride to altogether rarer beers from the Newman Brewery. Sausages are another feature. The George Orwell room upstairs, where the writer once celebrated a book launch, offers more room; downstairs, punters spill out on to the pavement.

★ French House
49 Dean Street, W1D 5BG (7437 2799, www.frenchhousesoho.com). Leicester Square or Piccadilly Circus tube. **Open** 4-11.30pm Mon-Thur; 4pm-midnight Fri; 5pm-midnight Sat. **Credit** AmEx, DC, MC, V. **Map** p406 W3 ㉒
Through the door of this venerable Gallic establishment have passed many titanic drinkers of the pre- and post-war era, the Bacons and the Behans. The venue's French heritage also enticed De Gaulle to run a Resistance operation from upstairs. His image is still in place behind the bar, where beer is served in half-pints and litre bottles of Breton cider (£7) are still plonked on the famed back alcove table.

★ LAB
12 Old Compton Street, W1D 4TQ (7437 7820, www.lab-townhouse.com). Leicester Square or Tottenham Court Road tube. **Open** 4pm-midnight Mon-Sat; 4-10.30pm Sun. *Food* 6-11pm Mon-Sat; 6-10.30pm Sun. **Credit** MC, V. **Map** p407 X2 ㉓
Newer spots have overtaken the '70s-meets-'90s decor, but few can match the sheer enthusiasm and knowledge of the staff at the London Academy of Bartending. Cocktails are king here, and many original combinations are mixed using LAB's own

Lamb & Flag.

CONSUME

Princess Louise. *See p230.*

infusions and syrups (chorizo tequila, anyone?). Pull up a chair and let one of the ultra-helpful mixologists guide you through the menu. The unashamed party vibe means this place fills up early.

Lucky Voice
52 Poland Street, W1F 7LR (7439 3660, www. luckyvoice.co.uk). Oxford Circus tube. **Open** 5.30pm-1am Mon-Thur; 3pm-1am Fri, Sat; 3-10.30pm Sun. **Credit** AmEx, MC, V. **Map** p406 V2 ㉔
There are nine rooms at this karaoke venue, each with space for four to 12 singers; some come with props such as hats, wigs and inflatable electric guitars. A drinks menu includes cocktails (£7), saké and spirits, brought to your room when you press the 'thirsty' button; food is limited to pizzas and snacks. The perfect place to discover your inner Susan Boyle. **Other locations** 173-174 Upper Street, Islington, N1 1RG (7354 6280).

★ Milk & Honey
61 Poland Street, W1F 7NU (7292 9949, www.mlkhny.com). Oxford Circus tube. **Open** *Non-members* 6-11pm Mon-Fri; 7-11pm Sat. **Credit** AmEx, DC, MC, V. **Map** p406 V2 ㉕
You could walk past the inconspicuous door of this semi-mythical, dimly lit Soho speakeasy every day and never know it was here, and that's probably just how they like it. It's members-only most of the time, but mere mortals can book a table until 11pm. While the place may not be at its best, what it lacks in atmosphere it more than makes up for with its outstanding cocktails.

OXFORD STREET & MARYLEBONE

Artesian
Langham Hotel, 1C Portland Place, W1B 1JA (7636 1000, www.artesian-bar.co.uk). Oxford Circus tube. **Open** 2pm-1am daily. **Credit** AmEx, DC, MC, V. **Map** p398 H5 ㉖
David Collins' redesign of the historic Langham hotel artfully blends Victorian decadence with modern detail. Rum is a passion: the impressive drinks menu offers more than 60, from a £9 Gosling's Black Seal to a £300 Havana Club Maximo. There's also a clever 'cocktail grazing menu', which allows you to work your way through the extensive selection with less impact on both wallet and sobriety.

Duke of Wellington
94A Crawford Street, W1H 2HQ (7723 2790, www.thedukew1.co.uk). Baker Street tube or Marylebone tube/rail. **Open** noon-11pm Mon-Sat; noon-10.30pm Sun. *Food* noon-3pm, 6.30-10pm Mon-Fri; noon-4pm, 6.30-10pm Sat; 12.30-4pm, 7-9pm Sun. **Credit** AmEx, MC, V. **Map** p395 F5 ㉗
Since its makeover by the owners of the Brown Dog in Barnes (28 Cross Street, SW13 0AP, 8392 2200, www.thebrowndog.co.uk), the Duke has attracted a moneyed clientele happy to splash out £30 on a decent Pouilly-Fumé or £55 on a better red from Pauillac. They're mostly here, though, for the food: for the pork chops with apple sauce, leeks and prunes or splendidly comforting cottage pie, served with greens, say.

PADDINGTON & NOTTING HILL

★ Kensington Wine Rooms
*127-129 Kensington Church Street, W8 7LP
(7727 8142, www.greatwinesbytheglass.com).
Notting Hill Gate tube.* **Open** noon-11pm
Mon-Sat; noon-10.30pm Sun. **Credit** MC, V.
Map p394 B7 ㉓
With about 100 varieties, the wine list here isn't the
longest in the capital, but the mix of lesser-known
Old World styles and contemporary New World
wines is exceptionally well chosen. Bottles can be
taken away, but it's really all about the 40 wines by
the glass, dispensed from five Enomatic machines
in the cosy front room. The dining room is usually
filled with well-to-do locals.

★ Lonsdale
*44-48 Lonsdale Road, W11 2DE (7727 4080,
www.thelonsdale.co.uk). Ladbroke Grove or
Notting Hill Gate tube.* **Open** 6pm-midnight Mon-
Thur; 6pm-1am Fri, Sat; 6-11.30pm Sun. **Credit**
AmEx, MC, V. **Map** p394 A6 ㉙
It's been five years or more since he mixed drinks
here, but bartender Dick Bradsell's influence can be
felt in the outstanding contemporary cocktails: try
the elderflower fizz (elderflower cordial, lemon juice
and champagne). Comprising a sun-catching front
terrace, a long bar counter and a wide, candlelit seating area at the back, the Lonsdale treats cocktail history with reverence; drinks invented in London
between 1914 and 1934 are a specialist subject.

Portobello Star
*171 Portobello Road, W11 2DY (7229 8016).
Ladbroke Grove tube.* **Open** 11am-11pm Mon-
Thur; 11am-12.30am Fri, Sat; 11am-11.30pm Sun.
Credit MC, V. **Map** p394 A6 ㉚
This 'cocktail tavern' deftly blends discerning bar
and traditional boozer. The bountifully stocked bar
is manned by friendly staff educated in the art of
adult refreshment; 'Drink less but better' is the
mantra of leading mixologist Jake Burger. His
impeccable, approachable directory of discerning
drinks is the last word on sophisticated intoxication.
There are DJs on Friday and Saturday nights.

PICCADILLY CIRCUS & MAYFAIR

★ Connaught Bar
*Connaught, Carlos Place, W1K 2AL (7499 7070,
www.the-connaught.co.uk). Bond Street tube.*
Open 4pm-1am Mon-Sat. **Credit** AmEx, DC,
MC, V. **Map** p400 H7 ㉛
The main bar of the swish Connaught hotel (*see
p183*) is grown-up, darkly elegant and reminiscent
of a cruise liner, with unobtrusive lighting and a
deco feel. The expensive drinks and the service have
a lot to live up to in the surroundings, but the
Connaught martini is worth ordering for the table-
side theatre alone and the staff are faultless –
slightly formal, but never standoffish. *Photos p234.*
▶ *Across the lobby, the hotel's cosy and discreet
Coburg Bar is another winner.*

Kensington Wine Rooms.

CONSUME

Connaught Bar. See p233.

CONSUME

Galvin at Windows

London Hilton, Park Lane, W1K 1BE (7208 4021, www.galvinatwindows.com). Green Park or Hyde Park Corner tube. **Open** noon-3pm, 6-11pm Mon-Fri; 5-11pm Sat; 11.45am-3pm Sun. **Credit** AmEx, DC, MC, V. **Map** p400 G8 ⓐ
There's no more remarkable site for a bar in London than Windows, offering remarkable panoramic views from the 28th floor of the Park Lane Hilton. Add a sleek interior that mixes art deco glamour with a hint of '70s petrodollar kitsch, and you can't go wrong. Admittedly, it's not cheap – £11.95 for a cocktail – but the drinks are assembled with care, and service is attentive without being obsequious.

Only Running Footman

5 Charles Street, W1J 5DF (7499 2988, www.the runningfootman.biz). Green Park tube. **Open** 7.30am-midnight daily. *Food* 7.30am-10.30pm daily. **Credit** AmEx, MC, V. **Map** p400 H7 ⓑ
Despite a dramatic recent refurbishment, this place still looks as if it's been here forever. On the ground floor, jolly chaps prop up the mahogany bar, enjoying three decent ales and an extensive menu. A full English breakfast is served for only £7.50, a fraction of the price you'd pay in nearby Claridge's. On the first floor, there's a quieter, formal dining room.

WESTMINSTER & ST JAMES'S

Albannach

66 Trafalgar Square, WC2N 5DS (7930 0066, www.albannach.co.uk). Charing Cross tube/rail. **Open** 5pm-1am Wed; 5pm-3am Thur-Sat. **Credit** AmEx, DC, MC, V. **Map** p407 X5 ⓒ
Right on Trafalgar Square, Albannach (as opposed to 'sassanach') specialises in Scotch whiskies and cocktails thereof. A map in the menu details the origins of these Highland and Island malts, the pages brimming with 17-year-old Glengoynes, 12-year-old Cragganmore and 29-year-old Auchentoshan. That said, kilted staff, illuminated reindeer and too many loud office groups detract from the quality on offer.

Boisdale of Belgravia

13-15 Eccleston Street, SW1W 9LX (7730 6922, www.boisdale.co.uk). Victoria tube/rail. **Open** noon-1am Mon-Fri; 7pm-1am Sat. *Food* noon-2.30pm, 7-11.15pm Mon-Fri; 7-11.15pm Sat. **Credit** AmEx, DC, MC, V. **Map** p400 H10 ⓓ
There's nowhere quite like this posh, Scottish-themed enterprise, and that includes its sister branch in the City. If you're here to drink, you'll be drinking single malts from a terrific range. That said, the outstanding wine list is surprisingly affordable, with house selections starting at under £20. Additional appeal comes from live jazz (six nights a week) and a heated cigar terrace.
Other locations Boisdale of Bishopsgate, Swedeland Court, 202 Bishopsgate, the City, EC2M 4NR (7283 1763).

★ Dukes Hotel
35 St James's Place, SW1A 1NY (7491 4840, www.dukeshotel.co.uk). Green Park tube. **Open** noon-11pm Mon-Sat; noon-10.30pm Sun. *Food* noon-4pm daily. **Credit** AmEx, DC, MC, V. **Map** p400 J8 ⑥
This titchy bar looks like an upper-class Georgian sitting room. The martinis are among the best in London and priced accordingly. Sipping one amid the polite murmur of the very adult clientele, while munching on complimentary nuts and Puglian olives, is a soothing experience. Alternatives include nearly a dozen good wines by the glass.

St Stephen's Tavern
10 Bridge Street, SW1A 2JR (7925 2286). Westminster tube. **Open** noon-3pm, 5.30-11pm Mon-Fri. **Credit** MC, V. **Map** p401 L9 ⑰
Done out with dark woods, etched mirrors and lovely Arts and Crafts-style wallpaper, this is a lovely old pub. The food is reasonably priced and the ales are excellent, but drinks can be expensive. Opposite Big Ben, its location is terrific, yet it's neither too touristy nor too busy. If the downstairs bars are full, head upstairs and look for a seat on the mezzanine.
▶ *Its nearest rival is the Red Lion (48 Parliament Street, SW1A 2NH, 7930 5826), popular with politicians and those that love them.*

1707
Fortnum & Mason, 181 Piccadilly, W1A 1ER (7734 8040, www.fortnumandmason.com). Piccadilly Circus tube. **Open** noon-9pm Mon-Sat. **Credit** AmEx, MC, V. **Map** p406 V5 ⑱
Although it's named after the year in which Fortnum & Mason was founded, 1707 looks firmly towards the future. Unpolished wooden slats line the walls, and the lines are clean and modern, but the star is the wine and champagne list; note that you can drink any of the wines sold within the wine department if you're willing to pay £10 corkage on the retail price. By comparison, food is a bit of an afterthought.
▶ *For Fortnum & Mason itself, see p242.*

CHELSEA
On the corner of Sloane Square, the **Botanist** (*see p219*) is a handsome venue for a drink.

★ Cadogan Arms
298 King's Road, SW3 5UG (7352 6500, www.thecadoganarmschelsea.com). Sloane Square tube. **Open** 11am-11pm daily. **Credit** AmEx, DC, MC, V. **Map** p397 E12 ⑲
In 2009, this 19th-century Chelsea pub was given a rebuild by the Martin brothers, the men behind the Botanist up the road. It now has a countrified air, complete with antlers, a stuffed rabbit and fly-fishing paraphernalia, and a smoothly run dining area, but it's a proper boozer with a bar built for drinking. Dishes are expertly cooked and attractively presented; there's also a good cheeseboard, if you've still room after dinner.

Tini
87-89 Walton Street, SW3 2HP (7589 8558, www.tinibar.com). Knightsbridge or South Kensington tube. **Open** 6pm-midnight Mon-Thur; 6pm-1am Fri, Sat; 6pm-12.30am Sun. **No credit cards.** **Map** p397 E10 ⑳
Located around the point where the noblesse of Knightsbridge gives way to swanky Chelsea, Tini is a cocktail lounge hangout for haves and have-yachhts, proper posh and a bit ridiculous. Serviced by genteel Gianfrancos in suits and spread under low ceilings, it's laced with traces of pink neon and fancy fleshiness courtesy of an Italian-leaning drinks list and Pirelli calendars from yesteryear.

KNIGHTSBRIDGE & SOUTH KENSINGTON

Anglesea Arms
15 Selwood Terrace, SW7 3QG (7373 7960, www.capitalpubcompany.com). South Kensington tube. **Open** 11am-11pm Mon-Sat; noon-10.30pm Sun. **Credit** AmEx, MC, V. **Map** p397 D11 ㉑
Formerly the local of both Charles Dickens and DH Lawrence, this old boozer is packed tight on summer evenings, with the front terrace and main bar filled with professional blokes chugging ale, and their female equivalents putting bottles of Sancerre on expenses. But the Anglesea has always had more aura than the average South Kensington hostelry; perhaps it's the link with the Great Train Robbery, reputedly planned here.

Blue Bar
Berkeley, Wilton Place, SW1X 7RL (7235 6000, www.the-berkeley.co.uk). Hyde Park Corner tube. **Open** 4pm-1am Mon-Sat; 4-11pm Sun. **Credit** AmEx, DC, MC, V. **Map** p400 G9 ㉒

CONSUME

THE BEST PUB INTERIORS

Fox & Anchor
A Smithfield Market mainstay, beautifully reconstructed. *See p228.*

Lamb
Peer through old-fashioned 'snob screens' to order your pint. *See p230.*

Princess Louise
A stunning gin-palace-turned-boozer, all dark wood and mirrors. *See p230.*

It isn't just a caprice: this David Collins-designed bar really lives up to its name. The sky-blue bespoke armchairs, the deep-blue ornate plasterwork and the navy-blue leather-bound menus combine with discreet lighting to striking effect. It's more a see-and-be-seen place than somewhere to kick back, but don't let the celeb-heavy reputation put you off: staff treat everyone like royalty, and the cocktails are a masterclass in sophistication.

190 Queensgate

Gore Hotel, 190 Queensgate, SW7 5EX (7584 6601, www.gorehotel.co.uk). Gloucester Road or South Kensington tube. **Open** noon-1am Mon-Sat. **Credit** AmEx, MC, V. **Map** p397 D9 ⑱

In a library atmosphere of dark wood and low lighting, this hotel bar provides varied, classy cocktails – including 20 flavoured mojitos – to a varied, classy clientele. Beaumont des Crayères is the bubbly of choice; wines and beers display a Spanish touch. The Iberian management could do far better than the desultory tapas on offer. Still, on a happier note, the service is excellent.

▶ *For the hotel, see p189.*

NORTH LONDON

The **Lockside Lounge** (75-89 West Yard, Camden Lock Place, Camden, NW1 8AF, 7284 0007, www.locksidelounge.com) is an excellent Camden DJ bar, while the big terrace-cum-car park at Torquil's Bar at the **Roundhouse** (*see p314*) is typically north London urban, with a fine terrace. In Islington, the boisterous **King's Head** (*see p346*) is as good a pub as it is a theatre, and the **Duke of Cambridge** (*see p222*) might be a better pub than restaurant.

Crown & Goose

100 Arlington Road, Camden, NW1 7HP (7485 8008, www.crownandgoose.co.uk). Camden Town tube. **Open** noon-midnight Mon-Thur, Sun; noon-2am Fri, Sat. **Credit** MC, V. **Map** p398 J2 ⑭

Its popularity breeds contempt among some people, but the C&G remains a near-perfect local: far enough

---

off the beaten track to elude the hordes and packed with Victorian charm, from the scrubbed furniture to the antique portraits and gilt-framed mirrors on its pea-green walls. Small and cosy, never more so than when evening comes and staff draw blinds, the Crown also turns out simple but superb pub food.

Driver

2-4 Wharfdale Road, King's Cross, N1 9RY (7278 8827, www.driverlondon.co.uk). King's Cross tube/rail. **Open** 10am-midnight Mon-Fri; 10am-4am Sat; noon-midnight Sun. **No credit cards.** **Map** p399 M2 ⑮

Spread over five floors, with decor alternating from urban to intricate, this soaring yet svelte Swiss army knife of a venue encompasses a pub-style restaurant, a small roof terrace, a members' bar, a lounge and a dining room that, later, transforms *Bugsy Malone*-style into a dancefloor with decks. The Driver has given a green-fingered salute to convention by planting its garden vertically on the outside wall.

Gilgamesh

Stables Market, Chalk Farm Road, Chalk Farm, NW1 8AH (7482 5757, www.gilgameshbar.com). Chalk Farm tube. **Open** 6pm-2.30am Mon-Thur; noon-2.30am Fri-Sun. *Food* noon-3pm, 6pm-midnight daily. **Credit** AmEx, MC, V.

Reached by escalator, Gilgamesh feels part Mesopotamian epic, part Cecil B DeMille. Once you've been shown to your seat in the expansive main room (reserve at weekends), you'll still be gawping long after the thick drinks menu has been delicately offered. Drinks are themed along Babylonian lines: even the mocktails are named after the Tigris and Euphrates.

★ Holly Bush

22 Holly Mount, Hampstead, NW3 6SG (7435 2892, www.hollybushpub.com). Hampstead tube or Hampstead Heath rail. **Open** noon-11pm Mon-Sat; noon-10.30pm Sun. *Food* noon-10pm daily. **Credit** (over £10) MC, V.

As the trend for gutting old pubs claims yet more Hampstead boozers, this place's cachet increases. Located on a quiet hilltop backstreet, it was built as a house in the 1790s and used as the Assembly Rooms in the 1800s, before becoming a pub in 1928. A higgledy-piggledy air remains, with three low-ceilinged bar areas and one bar counter at which are poured decent pints. Sound food (rock oysters, roast beef sandwiches) and a good choice of wines by the glass are further draws.

★ 69 Colebrooke Row

69 Colebrooke Row, Islington, N1 8AA (07540 528593, www.69colebrookerow.com). Angel tube. **Open** 5pm-midnight Mon-Wed; 5pm-1am Thur; 5pm-2am Fri, Sat. **Credit** AmEx, MC, V. **Map** p402 O2 ⑯

See right In the Mix.

THE BEST COCKTAIL BARS

LAB
The London Academy of Bartending is perfect for a big night out. *See p231.*

Milk & Honey
Find this Soho speakeasy and you'll be in for a treat. *See p232.*

69 Colebrooke Row
Invention in Islington courtesy of star bartender Tony Conigliaro. *See right.*

In the Mix

Cocktail maestro Tony Conigliaro gets a place to call his own.

Tony Conigliaro started out in the bar trade 14 years ago, working with, among others, the brother of his current business partner, Camille Hobby-Limon. After time spent at the likes of Isola and Shochu Lounge, Conigliaro joined Hobby-Limon in 2009 to open **69 Colebrooke Row** (for listings, *see left*), a tiny, quietly handsome room (book ahead if you can) where discerning drinkers are fed a selection of unusual, flavourful cocktails. Last autumn, *Time Out* magazine chose it as the Best New Bar of 2009.

Time Out (TO): Our reviewer dubbed 69 Colebrooke Row 'the El Bulli of booze' in our first review. Would you agree?
Tony Conigliaro (TC): I think that might be an exaggeration, but it's a big compliment! What they've been doing there [chef Ferran Adrià's 'molecular gastronomy'] is a 28-year project. We're using modern methods and modern ideas, but they're not necessarily that obvious. Our dry martinis, for example, have an essence of dry, which is basically a distillation of polyphenols, tannins and grape seeds. It doesn't have a flavour, but it does have an effect: it slightly dries out your tongue as you're drinking your martini. It's not whizz-bang fireworks.

TO: Have drinkers lagged behind foodies, then, or bartenders behind chefs?
TC: I think the history is different. Food goes back centuries. The history of cocktails only goes back 200 years.

TO: What is it about cocktails that first appealed to you?
TC: I really like all the different aspects of them. It's not just about the drinks: it's about being a host, making a venue, about the history of drinks.

TO: What drew you to this quiet Islington sidestreet?
TC: It was more the venue that sold it for us. Camille knew I wanted to open a very small, Tokyo-style bar just off the beaten track. Our references are more 1950s film noir than anything else. It also had a garret-style room upstairs, which has become a kind of workshop where we work on new ideas.

TO: Are you proudest of any one particular creation?
TC: I like whatever I'm working on, pushing things forward. Right now, we're working on a Somerset sour for the autumn. It's basically Somerset cider brandy made sour, but we've created a diorama around it, adding cider; for garnish, there's a little apple that floats up and down inside the drink, a reference to the apple-bobbing at Halloween. The garnish is infused with the scent of hay using a vacuum cooker.

TO: What do you find most rewarding about the work?
TC: Customers coming back!

CONSUME

CONSUME

Profile Sambrook's Brewery

A boutique brewer brings beer back to Battersea.

Over the last few years, real ale has seen a surprising but welcome spike in popularity in London. Also known as cask-conditioned ale, real ale differs from most tap beers in that it's not filtered or pasteurised, it's pulled from a barrel using a handpump without recourse to nitrogen or carbon dioxide pressure, and it doesn't contain added preservatives.

The biggest brewery remaining in London is Fuller Smith & Turner of Chiswick. Commonly known simply as Fuller's, the company manufactures a range of ales, among them the widely available London Pride. And, despite the increased popularity of ale in the city, few locals can name a London-brewed beer that isn't part of the Fuller's stable. One such Londoner, alarmed at the paucity of brewing in the capital, was Duncan Sambrook.

One evening at a beer festival in the city, Sambrook found himself wondering why there weren't many native beers on offer. Having studied chemistry

at university and then become an accountant in the City, he realised he had two of the skills under his belt. So Sambrook took the plunge and set up shop in an industrial unit not far from Clapham Junction, in south-west London. All his brewing equipment was imported from Canada and assembled like an Ikea kit, except for the fact that this kit cost £200,000.

Currently, Sambrook's Brewery produces Wandle Ale, named in honour of a nearby river and available on tap in about 30 pubs; among them is the Betjeman Arms at St Pancras International. You can also try it at the tiny, standing-room-only bar and shop at the brewery, which sells the beer in bottles or polypins (small, barrel-like containers) for customers to take away.

'We do tours followed by tastings, and so far we've had a lot of interest from the corporate sector,' says Sambrook. 'It seems bankers and the financial sector are keen to show that they can, in fact, organise a piss-up in a brewery.'

TASTE IT
For more on Sambrook's, including stockists, tours and the shop's hours, call 7228 0598 or see www. sambrooks brewery.co.uk.

★ Wenlock Arms

26 Wenlock Road, Hoxton, N1 7TA (7608 3406, www.wenlock-arms.co.uk). Old Street tube/rail. **Open** noon-midnight Mon-Thur, Sun; noon-1am Fri, Sat. *Food* noon-9pm daily. **No credit cards. Map** p402 P3 ㊼

Peek through the door of this traditional boozer and you'll immediately see its raison d'être: real ales, around eight of them at one time. The scruffy decor is a perfect match for the down-at-heel location, but there's a real community feel to the place: how many Islington pubs have cricket and football teams, or offer up free triangle sandwiches on a Sunday night as an impromptu jazz session unfolds in the corner? More formal jazz gigs take place on Friday and Saturday nights, and there's a quiz each Thursday.

EAST LONDON

Late-night **Charlie Wright's International Bar** *(see p320)* is as much about drinking as it is about live music. For the thriving gay scene in Shoreditch, *see pp305-307*. And for nightclubs in this part of town, *see pp325-328*.

★ Callooh Callay

65 Rivington Street, Shoreditch, EC2A 3AY (7739 4781). Old Street tube. **Open** 5-11pm Mon-Thur, Sun; 4pm-1am Fri; 5pm-1am Sat. **Credit** MC, V. **Map** p403 R4 ㊽

Only a pair of intertwined Cs divulges Callooh Callay's location. Inside, it's warm and whimsical; the neo-Victorian decor is as eclectic as *Jabberwocky*, the poem by Lewis Carroll from which the bar gets its name. A laid-back lounge, a mirrored bar and loos tiled in old cassettes lie behind an oak Narnia wardrobe. Stake out seats here to people-watch: lots of vintage fabrics and fixed-gear cyclists.

Carpenter's Arms

73 Cheshire Street, Brick Lane, E2 6EG (7739 6342, www.carpentersarmsfreehouse.com). Liverpool Street tube/rail. **Open** 4-11.30pm Mon; noon-11.30pm Tue-Thur, Sun; noon-12.30am Fri, Sat. *Food* 4-10pm Mon; 1-10pm Tue-Sun. **Credit** MC, V. **Map** p403 S4 ㊾

At one time, this cosy boozer took centre stage in East End gangsterland. It was bought by the Kray twins in 1967 for their dear old mum, and it was here that Ronnie tanked up on dutch courage before murdering Jack 'the Hat' McVitie. Today, Hoxtonites, fashionistas, the odd ironic moustache and a few ambitious hats fill the snug space. The drinks selection is great, and the cut-above food (boards of cheese, Sunday roasts) isn't sold at stupid prices.

Commercial Tavern

142 Commercial Street, Spitalfields, E1 6NU (7247 1888). Aldgate East tube or Liverpool Street tube/rail. **Credit** AmEx, MC, V. **Map** p403 R5 ㊿

The inspired chaos of retro-eccentric decor and warm, inclusive atmosphere make this landmark flatiron corner pub very likeable. It seems to have escaped the attentions of the necking-it-after-work masses, perhaps because of the absence of wall-to-wall lager pumps. The bar itself is made up of colourful art deco tiles, and there's a distinct decorative playfulness throughout; it's a great example of how a historic pub can be lit up with new life.

► *Down the street is the fabulous Golden Heart (110 Commercial Street, E1 6LZ, 7247 2158), a famous, crowded nursery for East End arty types.*

Grapes

76 Narrow Street, Limehouse, E14 8BP (7987 4396). Westferry DLR. **Open** noon-3pm, 5.30-11pm Mon-Wed; noon-11pm Thur-Sat; noon-10.30pm Sun. *Food* noon-2.30pm, 7-9.30pm Mon-Sat; noon-3.30pm Sun. **Credit** AmEx, MC, V.

If you're trying to evoke the feel of the Thames docks before their Disneyfication into Docklands, these narrow, ivy and etched-glass 1720 riverside premises are a good place to start: the downstairs is all wood panels and nautical jetsam. It's a fairly blokey pub: expect good ales and a half-dozen wines of each colour by glass and bottle, plus jugs of kir royale or strawberry fizz for summer and port for winter.

► *Nearby, Gordon Ramsay's Narrow (44 Narrow Street, 7592 7950, www.gordonramsay.com) does great bar snacks.*

CONSUME

★ Green & Red

51 Bethnal Green Road, Shoreditch, E1 6LA (7749 9670, www.greenred.co.uk). Liverpool Street tube/rail or bus 8, 26, 48. **Open** 5.30pm-midnight Mon-Thur; 5.30pm-2am Fri, Sat; 5.30-10.30pm Sun. *Food* 6-11pm Mon-Sat; 6-10pm Sun. **Credit** AmEx, MC, V. **Map** p403 S4 (51)

Named after the green and red of the Mexican flag, G&R attracts people going to the nearby Rich Mix cineplex and couples happy to pick at plates of meatballs or octopus ceviche upstairs. There's also some serious drinking to be done, for which the slouchy sofas and late-night basement bar may be more suitable. Young professionals neck Negra Modelo lager and smoke on the titchy front terrace, but specialist tequilas and tequila cocktails are the real joy.

Loungelover

1 Whitby Street, Shoreditch, E1 6JU (7012 1234, www.loungelover.co.uk). Liverpool Street tube/rail. **Open** 6pm-midnight Mon-Thur, Sun; 5.30pm-1am Fri; 6pm-1am Sat. *Food* 6-11.30pm Mon-Fri, Sun; 7-11.30pm Sat. **Credit** AmEx, DC, MC, V. **Map** p403 S4 (52)

This louche cocktail lounge parades low-lit decadence in its decor, a mish-mash of baroque, kitsch and exotic with distressed wooden armoires, vintage palm-frond chandeliers, a stuffed hippo's head and tea lights set on elegant, glass-topped tables. It may all be a little pretentious, but the staff are helpful; if

you're looking for somewhere that will impress, the place can hardly be bettered. Cocktails involved deft mixes; food includes sushi and hot Japanese snacks.
▶ *The same folks are behind the nearby Les Trois Garçons restaurant (see p225).*

SOUTH-EAST LONDON

Dartmouth Arms
7 Dartmouth Road, Forest Hill, SE23 3HN (8488 3117, www.thedartmoutharms.com). Forest Hill rail or bus 122, 176, 185. **Open** noon-11pm Mon-Sat; noon-10.30pm Sun. *Food* noon-3pm, 6-9.30pm Mon-Sat; noon-9pm Sun. **Credit** MC, V.
This gastropub is ideally located for the Horniman Museum *(see p145)*. The front bar is now a well-aired, sepia-tinted space perfect for relaxing with the papers or the free Wi-Fi; there's also an adjoining 'snug bar' (the red walls of which boast exhibitions by local artists) and a rear dining room. Cocktails are just £5.50-£6.25, and there's a long wine list, but beers are limited: Brakspear and Bombardier, Staropramen and Kronenbourg.

Gipsy Moth
60 Greenwich Church Street, Greenwich, SE10 9BL (8858 0786, www.thegipsymothgreenwich. co.uk). Cutty Sark DLR. **Open** noon-11pm Mon-Thur; noon-midnight Fri; 10am-midnight Sat; 10am-10.30pm Sun. *Food* noon-10pm Mon-Fri; 11am-10pm Sat; 11am-9.30pm Sun. **Credit** AmEx, MC, V.
This moderately funky pub offers an impressive range of beers (Schneider Weisse, Früli, Budvar, Paulaner and at least six others), well-priced wines and pretty decent food, from full breakfasts through bar snacks (pint of prawns, aïoli) to solid mains such as glazed bacon loin with free-range eggs and chips. The split level garden and roomy interior are ideal for a sit-down after roaming around Greenwich.
▶ *In good weather, grab a riverside seat at the nearby Cutty Sark Tavern (4-6 Ballast Quay, SE10 9PD, 8858 3146).*

Greenwich Union
56 Royal Hill, Greenwich, SE10 8RT (8692 6258, www.greenwichunion.com). Greenwich rail/DLR. **Open** noon-11pm Mon-Fri; 11am-11pm Sat; 11.30am-10.30pm Sun. *Food* noon-10pm Mon-Fri, Sun; 11am-10pm Sat. **Credit** MC, V.
The Union is the headquarters of Alistair Hook's Meantime Brewery, the result of his mission to bring beers brewed according to true German tradition to the British public. Six draught beers, including a pale ale and a stout, are joined by two dozen or more international labels by the bottle, including the little-seen Schneider Aventinus. Food runs from a humble bacon butty to chargrilled ribeye Angus steak; you'll also find decent wines.

SOUTH-WEST LONDON

Also worth a look here are the **Dogstar** *(see p328)* on Brixton's Coldharbour Lane, and the scruffy but likeable **Windmill** *(see p319).*

Effra
38A Kellet Road, Brixton, SW2 1EB (7274 4180). Brixton tube/rail. **Open** noon-11pm Mon-Thur; noon-midnight Fri; 10am-midnight Sat; 10am-10.30pm Sun. *Food* noon-10pm Mon-Fri; 11am-10pm Sat; 11am-9.30pm Sun. **No credit cards.**
This old-school pub has more of an Afro-Caribbean community feel than many Brixton watering holes. The daily-changing menu offers the likes of sea-weed callaloo and jerk pork, and palm fronds tower over drinkers in the cosy patio garden. One look at the fading Victorian splendour of the gold-corniced ceiling and pretty domed glass lamps, and it's no wonder locals pack the place out each night.

Loft
67 Clapham High Street, Clapham, SW4 7TG (7627 0792, www.theloft-clapham.co.uk). Clapham North or Clapham South tube. **Open** 6pm-midnight Tue-Thur; 5pm-1.30am Fri, Sat; noon-midnight Sun. *Food* 6-10pm Tue-Thur; 5-10pm Fri; 5-9pm Sat; noon-7pm Sun. **Credit** AmEx, MC, V.
This first-floor bar is often missed by the party-hunting 20-year-olds who trawl Clapham High Street. There's little reason to pass through the inconspicuous doorway unless you already know what lies within: the best selection of cocktails in SW4 amid spacious, slightly industrial surroundings, with nine black swivel chairs lining a long slab of bar counter. Tables around the corner from the main bar accommodate diners tucking into burgers of Scottish beef.

Lost Angel
339 Battersea Park Road, Battersea, SW11 4LF (7622 2112, www.lostangel.co.uk). Battersea Park rail. **Open** noon-11pm Tue, Wed; noon-midnight Thur; noon-2am Fri, Sat; noon-11pm Sun. *Food* noon-10pm Mon-Thur; noon-10.30pm Fri, Sat; noon-9pm Sun. **Credit** AmEx, MC, V.

INSIDE TRACK POP-UP BARS

From cocktail supremo Douglas Ankrah's Opera Quarter Bar in Covent Garden to arty Frank's Campari Bar in a Peckham multi-storey car park, summer 2009 was all about the pop-up bar. Making use of credit-crunched vacant properties and a full optic-row of imagination, pop-up bars are exactly what they sound like – open for a few months, then gone forever. To catch the hottest new ones before they close, check www.timeout.com.

CONSUME

Lost Angel.

You might not expect to find a bar as likeable as this along such a sorry-looking stretch of the Battersea Park Road. The range of drinks covers most bases: the three ales may include Wandle from nearby Sambrook's Brewery, while the cocktail list is split between classics, reinventions and shouldn't-work but-do corruptions. They're all served within an eye-catching interior that falls pleasingly between corner pub and modish bar (trombones on the ceiling, white phone box). The kitchen offers poshed-up bar food and entertainment runs from DJs to quiz nights.

▶ Not far away, the same owners run the award-winning Lost Society (697 Wandsworth Road, 7652 6526, www.lostsociety.co.uk).

★ White Horse
1-3 Parsons Green, Parsons Green, SW6 4UL (7736 2115, www.whitehorsesw6.com). Parsons Green tube. **Open** 9.30am-11.30pm Mon-Wed, Sun; 9.30am-midnight Thur-Sat. *Food* 10am-10.30pm daily. **Credit** AmEx, MC, V.
Only a lack of ceiling fans stops the main bar of this renowned hostelry from feeling like something from the days of the Raj. The Victorian ceilings are airily high, and wide windows with wooden venetian blinds let in plenty of light. Chesterfield-style sofas surround huge tables, though the umbrella-covered pavement tables are most coveted. Expect plenty of turned-up collars, rugby shirts and pashminas, although the mix of customers is wider than you might imagine. There are usually six to eight hand-pumped ales alongside the 135 bottled beers.

WEST LONDON
Botanist on the Green
3-5 Kew Green, Kew, Surrey, TW9 3AA (8948 1838, www.thebotanistkew.com). Kew Gardens tube/rail or bus 65, 391. **Open** noon-11pm Mon-Thur; noon-midnight Fri, Sat; noon-10.30pm Sun. **Credit** AmEx, MC, V.
The name is a nod to its floral neighbour, the Royal Botanic Gardens (*see p155*); certainly, this pub's position on the corner of Kew Green makes it a perfect place for a relaxing pint after a mooch around the gardens. The space has cosy nooks – one with a fabulous double-sided fireplace – and raised areas that give it a more intimate feel. The outdoor space is as twinkly as a fairy grotto.

Ladbroke Arms
54 Ladbroke Road, Holland Park, W11 3NW (7727 6648, www.capitalpubcompany.com). Holland Park tube. **Open** 11.30am-11pm Mon-Sat; noon-10.30pm Sun. *Food* noon-2.30pm, 7-9.30pm Mon-Fri; 12.30-2.45pm, 7-9.30pm Sat, Sun. **Credit** AmEx, MC, V. **Map** p394 A7 ⑤
The Ladbroke caters to both monied fortysome-things sinking Sancerre on the front terrace, and ale aficionados after a pint of Sharp's Cornish Coaster. The decor in the light main bar is noteworthy, with a original 1920s poster for Fap'Anis on one side and a pre-war French ad for olive oil on the other. A back room fills with middle-aged chatter, while a narrow corridor behind provides peace for book-readers.

Shops & Services

A city bursting with street-culture craziness and time-honoured style.

In its celebration of both tradition and cutting-edge style, the recent revamp of department store **Liberty** captured what's great about the capital's shopping scene. For every fashion-forward new opening and pop-up store in London (Soho's **Newburgh Quarter** has beeen particularly lively this year), you'll find a classic, centuries-old independent that's still going strong (take a bow, **James Smith & Sons**, umbrella specialists).

Between those extremes lies a changing kaleidoscope of places in which to part with your cash: multicultural street markets, deluxe department stores, flashy food shops and, of course, chain-store flagships. You'll also find some of the best places in Europeto buy books, records and second-hand clothes. Despite credit crunches and chopped-up credit cards, London is one of the world's most exciting, exhaustive and exhausting retail centres.

SHOPPING IN LONDON

The listings in this chapter concentrate on British brands and shops that are not only unique to the city, but also relatively central. For the key shopping areas around London, *see right* **Where to Shop**.

Most goods – with the notable exceptions of books, food and children's clothes – are subject to value added tax (VAT), which is almost always included in the prices advertised by shops. VAT was levied at 15 per cent during 2009, but looked likely to rise back up to its former level of 17.5 per cent early in 2010. Some shops operate a scheme allowing visitors from outside the EC to claim back VAT; for details, *see p373*. Central London shops stay open late (7pm or 8pm) one night a week (Thursday in the West End; Wednesday in Chelsea and Knightsbridge).

General

DEPARTMENT STORES

High-street favourite for undies and ready meals, **Marks & Spencer** (www.marksandspencer.co.uk) also offers several fashion ranges, including its designer Autograph collection for men and women, and the younger, trend-led Per Una line and Limited Collection.

★ Fortnum & Mason
181 Piccadilly, St James's, W1A 1ER (7734 8040, www.fortnumandmason.co.uk). Green Park or Piccadilly Circus tube. **Open** 10am-8pm Mon-Sat; noon-6pm Sun. **Credit** AmEx, DC, MC, V. **Map** p406 V4.

The revamped F&M is stunning. A sweeping spiral staircase soars through the four-storey building, while light floods down from a central glass dome. The iconic *eau de nil* blue and gold colour scheme with flashes of rose pink abound on both the store design and the packaging of the fabulous ground-floor treats, such as the chocolates, biscuits, teas and preserves. The five restaurants, all redesigned by David Collins (of Wolseley fame), are equally impressive. A food hall in the basement has a huge range of fresh produce and more wines than ever before; beehives installed on top of the building in 2008 mean that F&M's honey, which went on sale in September 2009, is as local as it gets. The shop is redolent of a time when luxury meant the highest degree of comfort rather than ostentation, but that's not to say it's beyond the means of a modest budget. The famous hampers start from £35 for the Teatime Hamper, going up to £500.

Harrods
87-135 Brompton Road, Knightsbridge, SW1X 7XL (7730 1234, www.harrods.com). Knightsbridge tube. **Open** 10am-8pm Mon-Sat; noon-6pm Sun. **Credit** AmEx, DC, MC, V. **Map** p397 F9.

Where to Shop

London's best shopping neighbourhoods in brief.

COVENT GARDEN & SOHO

The famous former flower market is choked with chains and crowds, but **Neal Street** and the streets radiating off **Seven Dials** rule for trainers and streetwear. Another urbanwear hotspot is Soho's **Carnaby Street**, which has traded tacky tourist shops for hip chains and independents. **Berwick Street** is still hanging on to some record shops, while **Charing Cross Road** and **Cecil Court** are prime browsing territory for bookish types.

OXFORD STREET & MARYLEBONE

London's commercial backbone, **Oxford Street** heaves with department stores and big chains, which spill over on to elegant **Regent Street**. In contrast, **Marylebone** has a villagey atmosphere and small shops that sell everything from designer jewellery to artisan cheeses. Venture further north to **Church Street** for antiques.

NOTTING HILL

Best known for its antiques market on **Portobello Road**, Notting Hill also has an impressive cache of push boutiques around the intersection of **Westbourne Grove** and **Ledbury Road** – a laid-back alternative to the West End and Chelsea. The area is also good for rare vinyl and vintage clothes.

MAYFAIR & ST JAMES'S

The traditional home of tailors (**Savile Row**) and shirtmakers (**Jermyn Street**), this patch also retains venerable specialist hatters, cobblers and perfumers. **Bond Street** glitters with jewellers and designer stores.

CHELSEA & KNIGHTSBRIDGE

King's Road is pretty bland these days, but punctuated with some interesting shops. Designer salons line **Sloane Street** and mix with chains on **Knightsbridge**, which is anchored by deluxe department stores.

KENSINGTON

Once a hub of hip fashion, **Kensington High Street** has surrendered to the chains, but it's still worth exploring the backstreets leading up to Notting Hill Gate. Rarefied antiques shops gather on **Kensington Church Street**. In South Ken, **Brompton Cross** has glossy contemporary furniture showrooms and designer boutiques.

EAST LONDON

East London is great for independent shops and some of the city's best markets (all on Sundays). Head for **Brick Lane** and its offshoots, especially up-and-coming Redchurch Street, for clothing, accessories and home goods that have been made or adapted by idiosyncratic young designers, and heaps of vintage fashion. **Shoreditch** and **Hoxton** have hip boutiques, furniture stores and bookshops, while Hackney's **Broadway Market** hosts a farmers' market as well as a clutch of cool indie stores.

NORTH LONDON

The grungy markets of **Camden** are best left to the under-25s, but nearby **Primrose Hill** has an exquisite selection of small shops selling, among other things, quirky lingerie and vintage clothes. Antiques dealers are thinning out on Islington's **Camden Passage**, but there's a growing number of other indies, including a gourmet chocolatier and an ethical boutique.

Foyles. *See p247.*

CONSUME

All the glitz and marble can be a bit much, but in the store that boasts of selling everything, it's hard not to leave with at least one thing you'll like. New additions to the legendary food halls and restaurants include a branch of the historical Venetian coffee bar Caffè Florian, and the 5J ham and tapas bar from Sanchez Romero Carvajal, Spain's oldest Jabugo ham-producing company. It's on the fashion floors that Harrods really comes into its own, though, with well-edited collections from the heavyweights. Recent launches have included the eagerly awaited revival of Halston, the iconic 1970s design house, in 2008, and the 2009 opening of a Louis Vuitton menswear boutique in the newly refurbished ground floor menswear department.

▶ *Nearby Harvey Nichols (109-125 Knightsbridge, SW1X 7RJ, 7235 5000, www.harveynichols.com) is coasting a little these days, but you'll still find a worthy clutch of unique fashion brands, plus a new, belle epoque-style champagne bar.*

Liberty

Regent Street, Soho, W1B 5AH (7734 1234, www.liberty.co.uk). Oxford Circus tube. **Open** 10am-9pm Mon-Sat; noon-6pm Sun. **Credit** AmEx, DC, MC, V. **Map** p406 U2.

Charmingly idiosyncratic, Liberty is housed in a 1920s mock Tudor structure. The store was given a major revamp in February 2009 (dubbed the 'Liberty Renaissance'), with new lines and the creation of a dedicated scarf room, as well as a frequently changing Bazaar area – referencing the days when the store was famous for offering never-seen-before items from far-flung places. Walk in the main entrance on Great Marlborough Street, flanked by

Paula Pryke's exuberant floral concession, and you'll find yourself in a room devoted to the store's own label, in the middle of a galleried atrium. Shopping here is about more than just spending money; artful and arresting window displays, exciting new collections and luxe labels make it an experience to savour for its own sake.

Despite being up with the latest fashions, Liberty still respects its dressmaking heritage with an extensive range of cottons in the third-floor haberdashery department. Stationery also pays homage to the traditional, with beautiful Liberty of London notebooks, address books, photo albums and diaries embossed with the art nouveau 'Ianthe' print. From August to December 2009, the fourth floor was host to the 'Prints Charming' exhibition, celebrating the company's iconic textiles with the launch of several new print designs by British artists, including Turner Prize-winner Grayson Perry.

▶ *Liberty's stand-alone store (197 Sloane Street, 7573 9695) sells select own-brand products.*

★ Selfridges

400 Oxford Street, Marylebone, W1A 1AB (0800 123 400, www.selfridges.com). Bond Street or Marble Arch tube. **Open** 9.30am-9pm Mon-Sat; noon-6pm Sun. **Credit** AmEx, DC, MC, V. **Map** p398 G6.

Selfridges celebrated its 100th anniversary in 2009 with a big party and Centenary Exhibition. And it remains the best London department store: its concession boutiques, store-wide themed events and collections from the hottest new brands make a great option for stylish, one-stop shopping, while useful floor plans make navigating the store easy-peasy.

It stocks a winning combination of new talent, hip and edgy labels, smarter high-street labels, and mid- and high-end brands. In 2009, hip yet affordable brands LnA and AY Not Dead (from California and Buenos Aires respectively) joined the hallowed womenswear halls on the second floor, while a new Diesel shop opened to much fanfare in the first floor menswear department.

SHOPPING CENTRES & ARCADES

The **Royal Arcades** in the vicinity of Piccadilly are a throwback to shopping past – the Burlington Arcade (*see below*) is the largest.

★ Burlington Arcade
Piccadilly, St James's, W1 (7630 1411, www. burlington-arcade.co.uk). Green Park tube. **Open** 8am-6.30pm Mon-Wed; Fri 8am-7pm Thur; 9am-6.30pm Sat; 11am-5pm Sun. **No credit cards. Map** p408 U4.
In 1819, Lord Cavendish commissioned Britain's very first shopping arcade. Nearly two centuries later, the Burlington is still one of London's most prestigious shopping streets, patrolled by 'beadles' decked out in top hats and tailcoats. Highlights include collections of classic watches, iconic British brands Mackintosh and Globe-Trotter (*see p258*), and Sermoneta, selling Italian leather gloves in a range of bright colours. High-end food shops comes in the form of Luponde Tea and Laduree; head to the latter for exquisite Parisian macaroons.

Kingly Court
Carnaby Street, opposite Broadwick Street, Soho, W1B 5PW (7333 8118, www.carnaby.co.uk). Oxford Circus tube. **Open** 10am-7pm Mon-Sat; noon-6pm Sun. **No credit cards. Map** p408 U3.
Kingly Court has helped Carnaby Street reclaim some of its 1960s reputation as the heart of swinging London. The three-tiered complex boasts a funky mix of chains and independents, as well as a branch of Triyoga.

Westfield London
Ariel Way, Shepherd's Bush, W12 7GF (7333 8118, www.uk.westfield.com/london). White City or Wood Lane tube, or Shepherd's Bush tube/rail. **Open** 10am-10pm Mon-Wed, Fri; 10am-10pm Thur; 9am-9pm Sat; noon-6pm Sun. **No credit cards. Map** p408 U3.
Occupying 46 acres and covering nine different postcodes, Westfield London took the crown of Europe's largest shopping centre when it opened in autumn 2008. The impressive site, which held the 1908 Olympics, cost around £1.6 billion to build, and houses some 265 shops. Popular labels that have never had stand-alone stores in the UK, such as Hollister and Ugg, have shops here; you'll also find luxury fashion houses, including Louis Vuitton and

Burberry. Highlights from the boutique-like labels include Sienna Miller's Twenty8Twelve, Tabio, Myla lingerie and Cos. Michelin-starred chefs Pascal Aussignac and Vincent Labeyrie can soothe away any shopping-induced stress with their gastronomic creations at Croque Gascon. If they don't manage to tempt your taste buds, then one of the other 50 eateries (including branches of Balans, Square Pie and Wahaca) surely will.

MARKETS

London's exuberant street markets are a great place to sample street life while picking up some bargains. Below is a selection of the best; for **Camden Market** (*see p129*); for food markets, *see p261*.

★ Columbia Road Market
Columbia Road, Bethnal Green, E2. Liverpool Street tube/rail then bus 26, 48, or Old Street tube/rail then bus 55, 243. **Open** 8am-2pm Sun. **Map** p403 S3.
On Sunday mornings, this unassuming East End street is transformed into a swathe of fabulous plant life and the air is fragrant with blooms and the shouts of old-school Cockney stallholders (most offering deals for 'a fiver'). But it's not just about flora: alongside the market is a growing number of shops selling everything from pottery, Mexican glassware and prints (don't miss Ryantown at no.126, 7613 1510) to cupcakes and perfume. Get there early for the pick of the crop, or around 2pm for the bargains; refuel at Jones Dairy (23 Ezra Street, 7739 5372, www.jonesdairy.co.uk).

Portobello Road Market
Portobello Road, Notting Hill, W10 (www.portobelloroad.co.uk). Ladbroke Grove or Notting Hill Gate tube. **Open** *General* 8am-6.30pm Mon-Wed, Fri, Sat; 8am-1pm Thur. *Antiques* 4am-4pm Fri, Sat. **No credit cards. Map** p394 A6.

CONSUME

CREATIVITY AT THE LOWEST PRICE
WE'RE CONFIDENT OUR PRICES CAN'T BE BEATEN
ASK IN STORE FOR DETAILS
OF CASS PRICE GUARANTEE

CASS PRICE PROMISE

LET'S FILL THIS TOWN
WITH ARTISTS

PAINTS | BRUSHES | PADS | CANVAS | PORTFOLIOS | SETS

Best known for antiques and collectibles, this is actually several markets rolled into one: antiques start at the Notting Hill end; further up are food stalls; under the Westway and along the walkway to Ladbroke Grove are emerging designer and vintage clothes on Fridays (usually marginally less busy) and Saturdays (invariably manic).

Spitalfields Market
Commercial Street, between Lamb Street & Brushfield Street, City, E1 6AA (7247 8556, www.oldspitalfieldsmarket.com). Liverpool Street tube/rail. **Open** *General* 9.30am-5pm Thur, Fri, Sun. *Antiques* 8.30am-4.30pm Thur. *Food* 10am-5pm Fri-Sun. *Fashion* 9.30am-5pm Fri. *Records & books* 10am-4pm 1st & 3rd Fri of the mth. **No credit cards. Map** p405 R5.
Recent redevelopments have given a new lease of life to this East End stalwart. Spitalfields now consists of the refurbished 1887 covered market and an adjacent modern shopping precinct. Around the edge of Old Spitalfields Market, stands sell food from around the world. The busiest day is Sunday, when nearby Brick Lane Market and Sunday (Up)Market in the Old Truman Brewery (strong on edgy designer and vintage fashion; www.sundayupmarket.co.uk) create a fashion shoot-meets-Bangladeshi-bazaar vibe in the neighbourhood.

Specialist
BOOKS & MAGAZINES
Central branches of the big chains include **Borders** (22 Charing Cross Road, WC2H 0JR, 7379 8877, www.borderstores.co.uk) and the **Waterstone's** flagship (203-206 Piccadilly, SW1Y 6WW, 7851 2400, www.waterstones. co.uk), with a fine bar-café and an on-site branch of the Trailfinders travel agency.

General

Foyles
113-119 Charing Cross Road, Soho, WC2H 0EB (7437 5660, www.foyles.co.uk). Tottenham Court Road tube. **Open** 9.30am-9pm Mon-Sat; noon-6pm Sun. **Credit** AmEx, MC, V. **Map** p407 X2.
Probably the single most impressive independent bookshop in London, Foyles built its reputation on the sheer volume and breadth of its stock: there are 56 specialist subjects in this flagship store. Its five storeys accommodate other shops, too: Ray's Jazz (*see p267*) is now on the third floor, having moved to give more space to a first-floor café that hosts low-key recitals and readings from the likes of Douglas Coupland and Sebastian Faulks, as well as gigs. In addition to branches in the Southbank Centre and at St Pancras International, a fourth branch has now opened in Westfield (*see p245*). *Photo p244.*

INSIDE TRACK BOOK ALLEY

Bookended by Charing Cross Road and St Martin's Lane, picturesque **Cecil Court** (www.cecilcourt.co.uk) is known for its antiquarian book, map and print dealers. Notable residents include children's specialist **Marchpane** (no.16, 7836 8661) and 40-year veteran **David Drummond at Pleasures of Past Times** (no.11, 7836 1142), who specialises in theatre and magic.

John Sandoe
10 Blacklands Terrace, Chelsea, SW3 2SR (7589 9473, www.johnsandoe.com). Sloane Square tube. **Open** 9.30am-5.30pm Mon, Tue, Thur-Sat; 9.30am-7.30pm Wed; noon-6pm Sun. **Credit** AmEx, DC, MC, V. **Map** p397 F11.
Tucked away on a Chelsea sidestreet, this independent looks just as a bookshop should and, after being in business for over half a century, remains a firm local favourite. The stock is packed to the rafters; of the 25,000 books here, 24,000 are a single copy, so there's serious breadth.

★ London Review Bookshop
14 Bury Place, Bloomsbury, WC1A 2JL (7269 9030, www.lrbshop.co.uk). Holborn tube. **Open** 10am-6.30pm Mon-Sat; noon-6pm Sun. **Credit** AmEx, MC, V. **Map** p399 L5.
From the inviting and stimulating presentation to the quality of the books selected, this is an inspiring bookshop. Politics, current affairs and history are well represented on the ground floor; downstairs, audio books lead on to exciting poetry and philosophy sections, everything you'd expect from a shop owned by the *London Review of Books*. Browse through your purchases in the adjoining London Review Cakeshop.

Specialist

Books for Cooks
4 Blenheim Crescent, Notting Hill, W11 1NN (7221 1992, www.booksforcooks.com). Ladbroke Grove tube. **Open** 10am-6pm Tue, Wed, Fri, Sat; 10am-5.30pm Thur. **Credit** MC, V.
Books in this celebrated shop cover hundreds of cuisines, chefs and cookery techniques. Even better, the shop's kitchen-café tests different recipes every day, sold to eager customers from noon.

Magma
117-119 Clerkenwell Road, Holborn, EC1R 5BY (7242 9503, www.magmabooks.com). Chancery Lane tube or Farringdon tube/rail. **Open** 10am-7pm Mon-Sat. **Credit** AmEx, MC, V. **Map** p402 N4.

CONSUME

If it's a visual medium or phenomena, this art and design specialist has got a book on it. Magazines, DVDs, trendy toys, T-shirts, toy and pin-hole cameras and a series of commissioned limited-edition posters and cards are also sold.
Other locations 8 Earlham Street, WC2H 9RY (7240 8498); 16 Earlham Street, WC2H 9LN (7240 7571).

★ Stanfords
12-14 Long Acre, Covent Garden, WC2E 9LP (7836 1321, www.stanfords.co.uk). Covent Garden or Leicester Square tube. **Open** 9am-7.30pm Mon, Wed, Fri; 9.30am-7.30pm Tue; 9am-8pm Thur; 10am-8pm Sat; noon-6pm Sun. **Credit** MC, V. **Map** p407 Y3.
Three floors of travel guides, travel literature, maps, language guides, atlases and magazines. The basement houses the full range of British Ordnance Survey maps; you can plan your next trip over Fairtrade coffee in the Natural Café.

Used & antiquarian

Biblion
1-7 Davies Mews, Mayfair, W1K 5AB (7629 1374, www.biblionmayfair.co.uk). Bond Street tube. **Open** 10am-6pm Mon-Sat. **Credit** MC, V. **Map** p398 H6.
Around 70 dealers display their various wares at these spacious premises in Grays Antique Market. The prices are as broad as the stock.

Simon Finch Rare Books
26 Brook Street, Mayfair, W1K 5DQ (7499 0974, www.simonfinch.com). Bond Street or Oxford Circus tube. **Open** 10am-6pm Mon-Fri. **Credit** MC, V. **Map** p398 J6.
This era-spanning, idiosyncratic collection has wonderful surprises, from one of the original copies of *Last Exit to Brooklyn* to esoterica like *Mushrooms, Russia & History*. Prices start at around £20.

Skoob
Unit 66, The Brunswick, Bloomsbury, WC1N 1AE (7278 8760, www.skoob.com). Russell Square tube. **Open** 10.30am-8pm Mon-Sat; 10.30am-6pm Sun. **Credit** MC, V. **Map** p399 L4.
A back-to-basics basement beloved of students from the nearby University of London, Skoob showcases some 50,000 titles covering virtually every subject, from philosophy and biography to politics and the occult. Prices are very reasonable.

CHILDREN
Fashion

In addition, try baby superstore **Mamas & Papas** (256-258 Regent Street, W1B 3AF, 0870 850 2845, www.mamasandpapas.co.uk).

Caramel Baby & Child
291 Brompton Road, South Kensington, SW3 2DY (7589 7001, www.caramel-shop.co.uk). South Kensington tube. **Open** 10am-6pm Mon-Sat; noon-5pm Sun. **Credit** AmEx, MC, V. **Map** p397 E10.
Now more than a decade old, Caramel is a great place to head to for tasteful togs for children, from babies to 12-year-olds. The look is relaxed, but the clothes are well finished in modern, muted colour schemes. While the styles have clearly been inspired by the sturdy clothes of the past, they never submit to full-blown nostalgia.
Other locations 77 Ledbury Road, Notting Hill, W11 2AG (7727 0906); 259 Pavilion Road, Chelsea, SW1X 0BP (7730 2564); 82 Hill Rise, Richmond, Middx TW10 6UB (8940 6325).

Their Nibs
214 Kensington Park Road, Notting Hill, W11 1NR (7221 4263, www.theirnibs.com). Ladbroke Grove or Notting Hill Gate tube. **Open** 10am-6pm Mon-Sat; noon-5pm Sun. **Credit** AmEx, MC, V. **Map** p394 A6.
A visit to this shop is a treat. The vintage-inspired gear encompasses quirky dungarees for crawling babes and demure summer frocks for preening girls; there's also a play corner with a blackboard, books and toys to occupy tinies while older ones browse.

Toys

Early Learning Centre (www.elc.co.uk) has many branches dedicated to imaginative play. Their **Nibs** (*see left*) has a great toy selection, and **Selfridges** (*see p244*) and **Harrods** (*see p242*) have dedicated toy departments.

Benjamin Pollock's Toyshop

44 The Market, Covent Garden, WC2E 8RF (7379 7866, www.pollocks-coventgarden.co.uk). Covent Garden tube. **Open** 10.30am-6pm Mon-Sat; 11am-4pm Sun. **Credit** AmEx, MC, V. **Map** p407 Z3.
Best known for its toy theatres (from £2.95 for a tiny one in a matchbox to about £70 for elaborate models), Pollock's is also superb for traditional toys, such as knitted animals, china tea sets, masks, glove puppets, cards, spinning tops and fortune-telling fish.
▶ *For the associated toy museum, see p83.*

Honeyjam

267 Portobello Road, Notting Hill, W11 1LR (7243 0449, www.honeyjam.co.uk). Ladbroke Grove tube. **Open** 9.30am-5.30pm Mon-Sat; 11am-4pm Sun. **Credit** MC, V. **Map** p394 A6.
Despite the hype (the shop is co-owned by former model Jasmine Guinness), Honeyjam is full of fun, with a good selection of pocket money-priced trinkets.

Store Rooms. *See p253.*

★ Playlounge

19 Beak Street, Soho, W1F 9RP (7287 7073, www.playlounge.co.uk). Oxford Circus or Piccadilly Circus tube. **Open** 11am-7pm Mon-Sat; noon-5pm Sun. **Credit** AmEx, MC, V. **Map** p406 V3.
Compact but full of fun, this groovy little shop has action figures, gadgets, books and comics, e-boy posters, T-shirts and clothes that appeal to kids and adults alike. Those nostalgic for illustrated children's literature shouldn't miss the Dr Seuss PopUps and *Where the Wild Things Are* books.

ELECTRONICS & PHOTOGRAPHY

General

Ask

248 Tottenham Court Road, Fitzrovia, W1T 7QZ (7637 0353, www.askdirect.co.uk). Tottenham Court Road tube. **Open** 10am-7pm Mon-Wed, Fri, Sat; 10am-8pm Thur; noon-6pm Sun. **Credit** AmEx, DC, MC, V. **Map** p399 K5.
Some shops on Tottenham Court Road feel gloomy and claustrophobic, but Ask has four capacious, well-organised floors that give you space to browse. Stock, spanning digital cameras, MP3 players, radios and laptops, as well as hi-fis and TVs and all the requisite accessories, concentrates on the major consumer brands. Prices are competitive.

Specialist

Behind its grand façade, the **Apple Store** (235 Regent Street, 7153 9000, www.apple.com) offers all the services you'd expect, including the trademark 'Genius Bar' for technical support. Several shops on Tottenham Court Road offer laptop repairs; instead, consider **Einstein Computer Services** (07957 557065, www.einsteinpcs.co.uk), which operates on a call-out basis for £20 per hour. **Adam Phones** (2-3 Dolphin Square, Edensor Road, W4 2ST, 0800 123 000, www.adamphones.com) rents mobile phone handsets for £1 a day with reasonable call charges. For film processing, try **Snappy Snaps** (www.snappysnaps.co.uk) and **Jessops** (www.jessops.com).

Calumet

93-103 Drummond Street, Somers Town, NW1 2HJ (7380 1144, www.calumetphoto.co.uk). Euston tube/rail. **Open** 8.30am-5.30pm Mon-Fri; 9.30am-5.30pm Sat; 10am-4pm Sun. **Credit** AmEx, MC, V. **Map** p398 J3.
Calumet caters mainly for professionals, students and darkroom workers, with lights, power packs, gels, tripods and storage stock complementing top-end digital gear. It does repairs and rentals, too.
Other locations 175 Wardour Street, Soho, W1F 8WU (7434 1848).

CONSUME

FASHION
Boutiques

Some of London's best fashion boutiques are to be found in Stoke Newington (**Hub**; www.hub shop.co.uk), Islington (**Diverse**; www.diverse clothing.com) and Notting Hill (**Aimé**; www. aimelondon.com).

Albam
23 Beak Street, Soho, W1F 9RS (3157 7000, www.albamclothing.com). Oxford Circus tube. **Open** noon-7pm Mon-Sat; noon-5pm Sun. **Credit** AmEx, MC, V. **Map** p406 V3.
With its refined yet rather manly aesthetic, this menswear label dresses well-heeled gents, fashion editors and regular guys who like no-nonsense style. The focus is on classic, high-quality design with a subtle retro edge; Steve McQueen is an inspiration.

Junky Styling
12 Dray Walk, Old Truman Brewery, 91-95 Brick Lane, Brick Lane, E1 6RF (7247 1883, www.junkystyling.co.uk). Liverpool Street tube/ rail. **Open** 11am-7pm daily. **Credit** AmEx, MC, V. **Map** p403 S5.
Junky offers an innovative take on second-hand clothes that fits in with increased eco-awareness. Owners Kerry Seager and Anni Saunders take two or more formal garments (a pinstripe suit and a tweed jacket, say) and recycle them into an entirely new piece (skirts £50-£200, jackets £100-£350).

★ No-one
1 Kingsland Road, Shoreditch, E2 8AA (7613 5314, www.no-one.co.uk). Old Street tube/rail. **Open** 11am-7pm Mon-Sat; noon-6pm Sun. **Credit** AmEx, MC, V. **Map** p403 O1.
A favourite of Shoreditch locals and noncomformist style icons such as Björk, this shop/café stocks a melange of cool merchandise: jeans from Lee and Cheap Monday; T-shirts by Jaguar Shoes,; tassle dresses from new label White Trumpet, ruffled skirts from Elton & Jacobsen; shoes by Opening Ceremony and Bernhard Wilhelm; and accessories by Jessican Dance.

★ Three Threads
47-49 Charlotte Road, Shoreditch, EC2A 3QT (7749 0503, www.thethreethreads.com). Old Street tube/rail. **Open** 11am-7pm Mon-Sat; noon-5pm Sun. **Credit** AmEx, MC, V. **Map** p403 R4.
The laid-back vibe at the Three Threads tempts even the most shop-phobic male, but its increased women's stock is equally covetable. Threads themselves come in the form of exclusive, cult labels such as Japan's Tenderloin, as well as stalwart streetwear labels like Carhartt. Bags from Mimi, casual Pointers shoes, jewellery from Sabrina Dehoff and a good range of Ray-Bans round off the show.

Designer stores

Key British designers include **Vivienne Westwood** (44 Conduit Street, W1S 2YL, 7439 1109, www.viviennewestwood.com), **Paul Smith** (Westbourne House, 120 Kensington Park Road, W11 2EP, 7727 3553, www.paulsmith. co.uk), **Alexander McQueen** (4-5 Old Bond Street, W1S 4PD, 7355 0088, www.alexander mcqueen.com) and **Stella McCartney** (30 Bruton Street, W1J 6QR, 7518 3100, www.stella mccartney.com). Luxury Italian brand **Missoni** recently opened its first UK store on Sloane Street (no.193; SW1X 9QX, www.missoni.com).

★ B Store
24A Savile Row, Mayfair, W1S 3PR (7734 6846, www.bstorelondon.com). Oxford Circus tube. **Open** 10.30am-6.30pm Mon-Fri; 10am-6pm Sat. **Credit** AmEx, MC, V. **Map** p406 U3.
A platform for cutting-edge designers, B Store is the place to preview next big things, such as Austrian Ute Ploier, alongside established iconoclasts such as Peter Jensen and Opening Ceremony. The eponymous own label, offering stylish basics and shoes, is going from strength to strength.

★ Browns
23-27 South Molton Street, Mayfair, W1K 5RD (7514 0000, www.brownsfashion.com). Bond Street tube. **Open** 10am-6.30pm Mon-Wed, Fri, Sat; 10am-7pm Thur. **Credit** AmEx, MC, V. **Map** p398 H6.
Among the 100-odd designers jostling for attention in Joan Burstein's five interconnecting shops (menswear is at no.23) are Chloé, Derek Lam and Marc Jacobs. New labels include Felipe Oliveira Baptista, with on-trend oversized blazers and print leggings, as well as exclusives from Balenciaga, James Perse and Osman Yousefzada. Browns Focus is younger and more casual; Labels for Less is loaded with last season's leftovers.
Other locations 11-12 Hinde Street, W1U 3BE (7514 0056); 6C Sloane Street, Chelsea, SW1X 9LE (7514 0040); Browns Focus, 38-39 South Molton Street, Mayfair, W1K 5RN (7514 0063); Browns Labels for Less, 50 South Molton Street, W1K 5SB (7514 0052).

THE BEST FASHION

Dover Street Market
Edgy capsule collections. See p253.

No-one
For the right sort of Shoreditch. See left.

Three Threads
To get the boyf shopping too. See left.

CONSUME

Top of the Shops

The capital's most-talked-about emporium is still great for a cheap fashion fix.

The Oxford Street branch of **Topshop** (no.214, W1W 8LG, 7636 7700, www. topshop.com) lays claim to being the world's largest fashion shop. Size is important, sure, but it's not the only reason for the brand's unstoppable success.

SIZE AND SIZES

Topshop is big. Some 200,000 people visit each week, squeezing into 40,000 pairs of jeans. But the shop's strength lies in the variety that being so enormous allows. Everything from socks to tights to jeans come in a gargantuan range of cuts and styles, with tall and petite ranges alongside larger sizes in sensible quantities. Be warned, though: London's skinny fashion boys snap up Topman's smaller sizes at astonishing speeds.

TOPMAN

Topman is catching up with its big sister. It recently opened a new floor above the existing one, stocking labels such as Garbstore, WESC and Baracuta, and has also found space for an outpost of indie

record store Rough Trade (*see p268*), a suit shop, a denim shop, another EAT café and a 'trainer boutique' from Office.

CAPSULE COLLECTIONS

Following on from the massive success of the the Kate Moss collection (fashion's first lady even has her own office in the building), September 2009 saw the launch of the feverishly anticipated Christopher Kane for Topshop range, followed in November by Stella McCartney for Topman. Look out, as well, for Topshop's more exclusive EDIT range and Topman's various ongoing collaborations and concessions such as LENS, TM Designs and LTD, featuring hotly tipped and recently established names such as Dexter Wong, Self and James Long.

FREE PERSONAL SHOPPERS

Take a seat in a private room while a stylist does the rail-trawling for you – with no obligation to buy. If the idea fills you with TV makeover dread, glean style tips from the free weekly Stylemail emails.

CONSUME

Diverse

294 Upper Street, Islington, N1 2TU (7359 8877, www.diverseclothing.com). Angel tube. **Open** 10.30am-6.30pm Mon-Wed, Fri, Sat; 10.30am-7.30pm Thur; 11.30am-5.30pm Sun. **Credit** AmEx, DC, MC, V. **Map** p402 O1.

Islington stalwart Diverse does a fine job of keeping N1's style queens in fashion-forward mode. Despite the cool clobber, chic layout and striking window displays, this is the sort of place where you can rock up in jeans and scuzzy Converse and not feel uncomfortable trying on next season's See by Chloé.

★ Dover Street Market

17-18 Dover Street, Mayfair, W1S 4LT (7518 0680, www.doverstreetmarket.com). Green Park tube. **Open** 11am-6pm Mon-Sat. **Credit** AmEx, MC, V. **Map** p400 J7.

Comme des Garçons designer Rei Kawakubo's ground-breaking six-storey space combines the edgy energy of London's indoor markets – concrete floors, tills inside corrugated iron shacks, Portaloo dressing rooms – with rarefied labels. Recent additions include the store's own relaxed menswear label, DSM; a new satellite collection for women from Comme des Garçons; trendy multi-fabric hats from Bernstock Spiers; and Gitman & Co's 1980s-style oxford and gingham check shirts.

Margaret Howell

34 Wigmore Street, Marylebone, W1U 2RS (7009 9009, www.margarethowell.co.uk). Bond Street tube. **Open** 10am-6pm Mon-Wed, Fri, Sat; 10am-7pm Thur. **Credit** AmEx, DC, MC, V. **Map** p398 H5.

Howell's wearable clothes are made in Britain with an old-fashioned attitude to quality. These principles combine with her elegant designs to make for the best 'simple' clothes for sale in London. Her pared-down approach means prices seem steep, but these are clothes that get better with time.

Shop at Bluebird

350 King's Road, Chelsea, SW3 5UU (7351 3873, www.theshopatbluebird.com). Sloane Square tube. **Open** 10am-7pm Mon-Sat; noon-6pm Sun. **Credit** AmEx, MC, V. **Map** p397 D12.

Part lifestyle boutique and part design gallery, the Shop at Bluebird offers a shifting showcase of clothing for men, women and children (Ossie Clark, Peter Jensen, Marc Jacobs), accessories, furniture, books and gadgets. A recent refurbishment left the shop with a retro feel, with vintage furniture, reupholstered seating and hand-printed fabrics. The menswear range has also had an overhaul, with the addition of various exclusive and sophisticated brands.

Discount

Tussle with teens for bargains at cheap-as-chips retailer **Primark** (499-517 Oxford Street,

7495 0420, www.primark.co.uk), one of the few stores to prosper during the recession, despite growing distrust of disposable fashion for ethical reasons. Grown-ups might prefer **Browns Labels for Less** (*see p251*).

Burberry Factory Shop

29-31 Chatham Place, Hackney, E9 6LP (8328 4287). Hackney Central rail. **Open** 10am-6pm Mon-Sat; 11am-5pm Sun. **Credit** AmEx, MC, V.

This warehouse space showcases seconds and excess stock reduced by 50% or more. Classic men's macs can be had for around £199 or less.

Paul Smith Sale Shop

23 Avery Row, Mayfair, W1X 9HB (7493 1287, www.paulsmith.co.uk). Bond Street tube. **Open** 10.30am-6.30pm Mon-Wed, Fri, Sat; 10.30am-7pm Thur; 1-5.30pm Sun. **Credit** AmEx, DC, MC, V. **Map** p400 H7.

Samples and previous season's stock at a 30-50% discount. Stock includes clothes for men, women and children, as well as a range of accessories.

Store Rooms

43 Pitfield Street, Hoxton, N1 6DA (7608 1105, www.thestorerooms.com). Old Street tube/rail. **Open** 10am-7pm Mon-Fri; 11am-6pm Sat; 11am-5pm Sun. **Credit** MC, V. **Map** p403 Q3.

A timely idea, this: a crisply styled sale shop where all items are discounted 35-70%, all the time. The stock changes constantly, but you might find Penfield gilets or Sibin Linnebjerg's 1960s-inspired cardigans among the bargains. *Photos pp248-249.*

High street

The best of the high-street chains are young, designer-look **Reiss** (Kent House, 14-17 Market Place, Fitzrovia, W1H 7AJ, 7637 9112, www.reiss.co.uk), which has recently launched its much-anticipated 71 Reiss collection; H&M's upmarket sibling **COS** (222 Regent Street, W1B 5BD, 7478 0400, www.cosstores.com); and **Uniqlo** (311 Oxford Street, W1C 2HP, 7290 7701, www.uniqlo.co.uk), a favourite among fashionistas. **Topshop**'s massive, throbbing flagship (*see left* **Top of the Shops**) has recently really upped the ante with a new floor for men, while **American Apparel** (www.americanapparel.net) is expanding at breakneck speed, selling its range of retro loungewear, spandex leggings and cool hoodies.

Tailors

Chris Kerr

52 Berwick Street, Soho, W1F 8SL (7437 3727, www.eddiekerr.co.uk). Oxford Circus tube. **Open** 8am-5.30pm Mon-Fri; 8.30am-1pm Sat. **Credit** AmEx, MC, V. **Map** p406 V2.

CONSUME

Hurwundeki.

Chris Kerr, son of legendary 1960s tailor Eddie Kerr, is the man to visit if Savile Row's prices or attitude aren't to your liking. The versatile Kerr has no house style; instead, he makes every suit to each client's exact specifications, and those clients include Johnny Depp and David Walliams. A good place to get started with British tailoring.
▶ *For the Savile Row tailors, see p107.*

Timothy Everest

35 Bruton Place, Mayfair, W1J 6NS (7629 6236, www.timothyeverest.co.uk). Bond Street tube. **Open** 10am-6pm Mon-Fri; 11am-5pm Sat. **Credit** AmEx, MC, V. **Map** p400 H7.
One-time apprentice to the legendary Tommy Nutter, Everest is a star of the latest generation of London tailors. He's well known for his relaxed 21st-century definition of style.

Used & vintage

Luna & Curious (*see p264*) has a reasonably priced selection of reconditioned pieces, while **Dover Street Market** (*see p253*) houses an outpost of LA store Decades.

★ Beyond Retro

112 Cheshire Street, Shoreditch, E2 6EJ (7613 3636, www.beyondretro.com). Liverpool Street tube/rail. **Open** 10am-7pm Mon-Wed, Fri, Sat; 10am-8pm Thur; 10am-6pm Sun. **Credit** MC, V. **Map** p405 S4.

This enormous palace of second-hand clothing and accessories is the starting point for many an expert stylist, thrifter or fashion designer on the hunt for bargains and inspiration. The 10,000 items on the warehouse floor include 1950s dresses, cowboy boots and denim hot pants, many under £20. In-store events, such as live bands, add to the lively and supremely east London vibe.
Other locations 58-59 Great Marlborough Street, Soho, W1F 7JY (7434 1406).

Brick Lane Thrift Store

68 Sclater Street, Spitalfields, E1 6HR (7739 0242, www.theeastendthriftstore.com). Liverpool Street tube/rail. **Open** noon-7pm daily. **Credit** AmEx, MC, V. **Map** p403 S4.
Almost everything is a magical £10 or less at this second-hand shop, sister to the older East End Thrift Store. Two levels hold a refined collection of best-sellers and popular lines from the East End warehouse, such as checked Western shirts. Men looking for the perfect trans-seasonal jacket should have a look at the rails of Harringtons.
▶ *There's more at the Camden Thrift Store (51 Chalk Farm Road, NW1 8AN, 07748 406537).*

Girl Can't Help It

Alfie's Antique Market, 13-25 Church Street, Marylebone, NW8 8DT (7724 8984, www. thegirlcanthelpit.com). Edgware Road tube or Marylebone tube/rail. **Open** 10am-6pm Tue-Sat. **Credit** AmEx, MC, V. **Map** p395 E4.

New Yorker Sparkle Moore and her Dutch partner Jasja Boelhouwer preside over the cache of vintage Hollywood kitsch. For ladies, there are red-carpet gowns and 1950s circle skirts (£100-£350), plus glam accessories. The suave menswear encompasses Hawaiian shirts (from £50).
▶ For more on Alfie's Antique Market, see p266.

Hurwundeki
34 Marshall Street, Soho, W1F 7EU (7734 1050, www.hurwundeki.com). Oxford Circus tube. **Open** noon-7.30pm Mon-Sat; noon-6pm Sun. **Credit** AmEx, MC, V. **Map** p406 V2.
This stripped-pine and exposed-brick offshoot of a Spitalfields vintage store-cum-hair salon is furnished with lovingly sourced curios and antiques. Shopping here is an instant passport to east London chic-boho fashion.
Other locations 98 Commercial Street, Spitalfields, E1 6LZ (7392 9194).

Rellik
8 Golborne Road, Ladbroke Grove, W10 5NW (8962 0089, www.relliklondon.co.uk). Westbourne Park tube. **Open** 10am-6pm Tue-Sat. **Credit** AmEx, MC, V.
This celeb fave was set up in 2000 by three Portobello market stallholders: Fiona Stuart, Claire Stansfield and Steven Philip. The trio have different tastes, which means there's a mix of pieces by the likes of Halston, Vivienne Westwood, Bill Gibb, Christian Dior and the ever-popular Ossie Clark.

FASHION ACCESSORIES & SERVICES
Clothing hire

Lipman & Sons
22 Charing Cross Road, Soho, WC2H 0HR (7240 2310, www.lipmanandsons.co.uk). Leicester Square tube. **Open** 9am-6pm Mon-Wed, Fri, Sat; 9am-8pm Thur. **Credit** AmEx, DC, MC, V. **Map** p407 X4.
A reliable, long-serving formalwear specialist.

Cleaning & repairs

British Invisible Mending Service
32 Thayer Street, Marylebone, W1U 2QT (7935 2487, www.invisible-mending.co.uk). Bond Street tube. **Open** 8.30am-5.30pm Mon-Fri; 10am-1pm Sat. **No credit cards.** **Map** p398 G5.
A 24hr service is offered.

Celebrity Cleaners
9 Greens Court, Soho, W1F 0HJ (7437 5324, www.invisible-mending.co.uk). Piccadilly Circus tube. **Open** 8.30am-6.30pm Mon-Fri. **No credit cards.** **Map** p406 W3.

Dry-cleaner to West End theatres and the ENO.
Other locations Neville House, 27 Page Street, Pimlico, SW1P 4JJ (7821 1777).

Fifth Avenue Shoe Repairers
41 Goodge Street, Fitzrovia, W1T 2PY (7636 6705, www.invisible-mending.co.uk). Goodge Street tube. **Open** 8am-6.30pm Mon-Fri; 10am-6pm Sat. **Credit** AmEx, MC, V. **Map** p398 J5.
High-calibre, speedy shoe repairs.

Hats

For bold hats by the king of couture headgear, head to **Philip Treacy** (69 Elizabeth Street, SW1 9PJ, 7730 3992, www.philiptreacy.co.uk).

Bates the Hatter
21A Jermyn Street, SW1Y 6HP (7734 2722, www.bates-hats.co.uk). Piccadilly Circus tube. **Open** 9am-5pm Mon-Fri; 9.30am-4pm Sat. **Credit** AmEx, DC, MC, V. **Map** p400 J7.
With its topper-shaped sign and old-fashioned interior, Bates is a specialist gem. The traditional headwear spans panamas to tweed deerstalkers by way of dapper flat caps and, of course, classy top hats.

Bernstock Spiers
234 Brick Lane, Brick Lane, E2 7EB (7739 7385, www.bernstockspeirs.com). Aldgate East tube. **Open** 10am-6pm Tue-Fri; 11am-5pm Sat, Sun. **Credit** AmEx, MC, V.
Paul Bernstock and Thelma Spiers' unconventional hats for men and women have a loyal following, being both wearable and fashion-forward. Past ranges have included collaborations with Peter Jensen and Emma Cook, while the latest collection has been inspired by old-school skiwear. This boutique store opened in 2004; the brand also opened a concession in Dover Street Market (*see p253*) in 2009. A woollen beanie costs £36.

INSIDE TRACK
NEWBURGH QUARTER

The area comprising the fork tines of Carnaby Street, Newburgh Street and Marshall Street, rebranded the 'Newburgh Quarter', is an increasingly cutting-edge shopping spot. Highlights include **Beyond the Valley** (2 Newburgh Street), **Hurwundeki** (*see above*) and ethical, outdoorsy **Howies** (42 Carnaby Street). Lots of pop-up shops (recently, Sienna Miller's Twenty8Twelve shop) home in on this area, which is always great for denim and trainers: Puma, Lee, Wrangler, Pepe, Onitsuka Tiger, Size? and Levi's vintage denim shop Cinch are all here.

CONSUME

Jewellery

There are also some lovely pieces for sale in **Contemporary Applied Arts** (*see p264*).

Ec one

41 Exmouth Market, Clerkenwell, EC1R 4QL (7713 6185, www.econe.co.uk). Farringdon tube/rail. **Open** 10am-6pm Mon-Wed, Fri; 11am-7pm Thur; 10.30am-6pm Sat. **Credit** MC, V. **Map** p402 N4.

Jos and Alison Skeates showcase jewellery from more than 50 designers. Playful pieces by Stephen Webster (now creative director for Garrard) are stocked; there's also plenty of choice for those on tighter budgets, including simple but stylish earrings and bangles by Alexis Bittar, and Alex Monroe's gorgeous fripperies for under £200. **Other locations** 56 Ledbury Road, Notting Hill, W11 2AJ (7243 8811).

Garrard

24 Albemarle Street, Mayfair, W1S 4HT (0870 871 8888, www.garrard.com). Bond Street or Green Park tube. **Open** 10am-6pm Mon-Fri; 10am-5pm Sat, Sun. **Credit** AmEx, DC, MC, V. **Map** p406 U5.

The Crown Jeweller's diamond-studded designs have appealed to a new generation of bling-seekers since the brand was modernised by Jade Jagger. It's now in the hands of London-based jeweller Stephen Webster, who took over as creative director in 2009.

Kabiri

37 Marylebone High Street, Marylebone, W1U 4QE (7224 1808, www.kabiri.co.uk). Baker Street tube. **Open** 10am-6.30pm Mon-Sat; noon-5pm Sun. **Credit** AmEx, MC, V. **Map** p398 G5.

The work of more than 100 jewellery designers, from emerging talent to established names, is showcased at Kabiri's flagship in Covent Garden. Innovation and sophistication are both highly prized, and the pieces cover a good range of price categories. Several designers are exclusive to Kabiri, including K Brunini and Roberto Marroni. There's a smaller shop on Marylebone High Street, as well as a concession in Selfridges (*see p244*). **Other locations** 37 Marylebone High Street, W1U 4QE (7224 1808).

Lingerie & underwear

Agent Provocateur is now a glossy international chain, but the original outpost of the shop that popularised high-class kink is still in Soho (6 Broadwick Street, W1F 8HL, 7439 0229, www.agentprovocateur.com). **Alice & Astrid** (30 Artesian Road, W2 5DD, 7985 0888, www.aliceandastrid.com) sells pretty lingerie and loungewear in light cottons and silks from its cutesy Notting Hill shop. For a serious bespoke service, try royal corsetière **Rigby & Peller** (22A Conduit Street, Mayfair, W1S 2XT, 0845 076 5545, www.rigbyandpeller.com).

Bordello

55 Great Eastern Street, Shoreditch, EC2A 3HP (7503 3334, www.bordello-london.com). Liverpool Street tube/rail. **Open** 11am-7pm Tue-Sat; 1-5pm Sun. **Credit** MC, V. **Map** p403 R4.

Seductive yet welcoming, Bordello stocks luxurious lingerie by Damaris, Mimi Holliday, Myla, Buttress & Snatch and Pussy Glamore. Pistol Panties bikinis are also stocked. The edgy vibe appeals to East End glamazons, first-daters and off-duty burlesque stars.

Myla

74 Duke of York Square, King's Road, Chelsea, SW3 4LY (7730 0700, www.myla.com). Sloane Square tube. **Open** 10am-6.30pm Mon-Sat; noon-5pm Sun. **Credit** AmEx, MC, V.

Luxury lingerie brand Myla has acquired a devoted following. There are now seven London stores, including one in Westfield shopping centre, which makes getting one's hands on the label's stylish, high-quality bras, knickers, toys and accessories a breeze.

Luggage & bags

Harrods (*see p242*) and **Selfridges** (*see p244*) have excellent selections of luggage and bags, while **Mimi**'s (40 Cheshire Street, 7729 6699, www.mimiberry.co.uk) leather satchels, shoulder bags in muted tones and cool clutches have become staples of the East End fashion-pack

★ Ally Capellino

9 Calvert Avenue, Shoreditch, E2 7JP (7613 3073, www.allycapellino.co.uk). Liverpool Street tube/rail. **Open** noon-6pm Wed-Fri; 10am-6pm Sat; 11am-4pm Sun. **Credit** AmEx, MC, V. **Map** p403 R4.

INSIDE TRACK SAMPLE SALES

Nothing beats sample sales for designer bargains. The Shopping & Style section of *Time Out* magazine rounds up the best every week, but it's also worth getting on a few mailing lists for advance notice. **Designer Warehouse Sales** (www.designerwarehousesales.com), **Secret Sample Sale** (www.secretsamplesale.co.uk), **Designer Sales UK** (www.designersales.co.uk), **London Designer Sale** (www.londondesignersale.co.uk) and the slightly more imaginatively named **Billion Dollar Babes** sales (www.billiondollarbabes.com) run several sales a year, covering everything from luxe brands to up-and-coming labels.

CONSUME

The full range of Ally Capellino's stylishly under-stated unisex bags, wallets and purses. Prices start at £39 for a cute leather coin purse, rising to around £300 for larger, more structured models. If prices are too high, hold on until sale time when there are very generous discounts.

Globe-Trotter
54-55 Burlington Arcade, Mayfair, W1J 0LB (7529 5950, www.globe-trotterltd.com). Green Park tube. **Open** 10am-6pm Mon-Sat. **Credit** AmEx, MC, V. **Map** p400 J7.
Globe-Trotter's indestructible steamer-trunk luggage, available here in various sizes and colours, accompanied the Queen on honeymoon. Iconic Mackintosh coats share shop space.
▶ *Looking for luggage that's a solution rather than an investment? Marks & Spencer (www.marksandspencer.co.uk) does reliable basics.*

Shoes

Among the best footwear chains are **Office** (57 Neal Street, Covent Garden, WC2H 4NP, 7379 1896, www.office.co.uk), which offers funky styles for guys and girls at palatable prices; **Kurt Geiger** (198 Regent Street, W1B 5TP, 3238 0044, www.kurtgeiger.com) and **Russell & Bromley** (24-25 New Bond Street, W1S 2PS, 7629 6903, www.russellandbromley.co.uk), which both turn out classy takes on key trends for both sexes; and **Clarks** (476 Oxford Street, W1C 1LD, 0844 499 9302, www.clarks.co.uk), inventor of Wallabes.

Carnaby Street is a great place for trainers (*see p255* **Inside Track**), with branches of **Size?** (nos.33-34, www.size.co.uk), **Puma** (nos.52-55, www.puma.com) and **Vans** (no.47, www.vans.eu) among the options.

Black Truffle
4 Broadway Market, Hackney, E8 4QJ (7923 9450, www.blacktruffle.co.uk). London Fields rail or bus 394. **Open** 11am-6pm Tue-Sat; noon-6pm Sun. **Credit** AmEx, MC, V.
This Hackney favourite sells quirky, stylish yet wearable footwear for women, men and kids. Now in a new, much larger space near the canal, the shop remains a Broadway Market stalwart. Look out for shoes by Chie Mihara, Melissa, F Troupe and Falke, knee-high boots by Alberto Fermani and bags from Ally Capellino and Matt & Nat.
Other locations 52 Warren Street, Fitzrovia, W1T 5NJ (7388 4547).

Georgina Goodman
44 Old Bond Street, Mayfair, W1F 4GD (7493 7673, www.georginagoodman.com). Green Park tube. **Open** 10am-6pm Mon-Wed, Fri, Sat; 10am-7pm Thur. **Credit** AmEx, DC, MC, V. **Map** p400 H8.

Goodman started her business crafting sculptural, made-to-measure footwear from a single piece of untreated vegetan leather; a couture service is still available at her airy, gallery-like shop (shoes start at £750 for women, or £1,200 for men). The excellent ready-to-wear range (from £165 for her popular slippers) has brought Goodman's individualistic approach to a wider customer base. Her latest range features a plethora of snakeskin, satin and an ultra-shiny patent leather, and each shoe bears Goodman's signature stripe on the bottom, with the stamp 'Made in Love'.

★ Sniff
1 Great Titchfield Street, Fitzrovia, W1W 8AU (7299 3560, www.sniff.co.uk). Oxford Circus tube. **Open** 10am-6pm Mon-Wed, Fri, Sat; 10am-7pm Thur. **Credit** AmEx, MC, V. **Map** p406 U1.
Sniff's two boutique-like stores, one in town and one out east, provide an alternative to average high-street shoe stores, selling ranges of shoes for men and women that cover every eventuality from sports to parties. There's a well-balanced mix of brands, both established (Opening Ceremony, Ed Hardy, Fornarina, Converse) and lesser known (eccentric British designer Miss L Fire, stylish but very wearable brand Velvet Bee, cult Argentinian label Mishka). The company closed its St Christopher's Place store in 2009, but its Spitalfields stores remains a first port of call with the area's fashionistas.
Other locations 115 Commercial Street, Spitalfields, E1 6BG (7375 1580).

FOOD & DRINK

Bakeries

Konditor & Cook
22 Cornwall Road, Waterloo, SE1 8TW (7261 0456, www.konditorandcook.com). Waterloo tube/rail. **Open** 7.30am-6.30pm Mon-Fri; 8.30am-2.30pm Sat. **Credit** AmEx, MC, V. **Map** p404 N10.
Gerhard Jenne caused a stir when he opened this bakery on a South Bank sidestreet in 1993, selling gingerbread people for grown-ups and lavender-flavoured cakes. Success lay in lively ideas such as magic cakes that spell the recipient's name in a series of individually decorated squares. Quality prepacked salads and sandwiches are also sold. The brand is now a mini-chain, with several branches.
Other locations throughout the city.

Primrose Bakery
69 Gloucester Avenue, Primrose Hill, NW1 8LD (7483 4222, www.primrosebakery.org.uk). Chalk Farm tube. **Open** 8.30am-6pm Mon-Sat; 10am-5.30pm Sun. **Credit** MC, V.
Catch a serious sugar high from Martha Swift's pretty, generously sized cupcakes in vanilla, coffee

and lemon flavours. The tiny, retro-styled shop also sells peanut butter cookies and layer cakes. **Other locations** 42 Tavistock Street, Covent Garden, WC2E 7PB (7836 3638).

Drinks

Algerian Coffee Stores
52 Old Compton Street, Soho, W1V 6PB (7437 2480, www.algcoffee.co.uk). **Open** 9am-7pm Mon-Wed; 9am-9pm Thur, Fri; 9am-8pm Sat. **Credit** AmEx, DC, MC, V. **Map** p406 W3.
For 120 years, this unassuming little shop has been trading over the same wooden counter. The range of coffees is broad, with house blends sold alongside single-origin beans, and some serious teas and brewing hardware are also available.
▶ *Passing? Take away a single or double espresso for 90p, or a cappuccino or a latte for £1.10.*

Berry Bros & Rudd
3 St James's Street, Mayfair, SW1A 1EG (7396 9600, www.bbr.com). Green Park tube. **Open** 10am-6pm Mon-Fri; 10am-5pm Sat. **Credit** AmEx, DC, MC, V. **Map** p400 J8.
Britain's oldest wine merchant has been trading on the same premises since 1698, and its heritage is reflected in its panelled sales and tasting rooms. Burgundy- and claret-lovers will drool at the hundreds of wines, but there are also decent selections from elsewhere in Europe and the New World. Prices are generally fair.

Cadenhead's Covent Garden Whisky Shop
26 Chiltern Street, Marylebone, W1U 7QF (7935 6999, www.whiskytastingroom.com). Baker Street tube. **Open** 10.30am-6.30pm Mon-Sat. **Credit** DC, MC, V. **Map** p407 Z3.

Borough Market. *See p261.*

CONSUME

Cadenhead's is a survivor of a rare breed: the independent whisky bottler. And its shop is one of a kind, at least in London. Cadenhead's selects barrels from distilleries all over Scotland and bottles them without filtration or any other intervention.

▶ For a wider range of spirits – the widest selection in London, they say – try Gerry's (74 Old Compton Street, Soho, W1D 4UW, 7734 4215, www.gerrys.uk.com). It's not far from Milroy's (3 Greek Street, Soho, 7437 2385, www.milroys.co.uk), another whisky specialist.

★ Postcard Teas
9 Dering Street, Mayfair, W1S 1AG (7629 3654, www.postcardteas.com). Bond Street or Oxford Circus tube. **Open** 10.30am-6.30pm Tue-Sat. **Credit** AmEx, MC, V. **Map** p398 H6.
The range in Timothy d'Offay's exquisite little shop is not huge, but it is selected with care: for instance, all its Darjeeling teas (£3.50-£5.95/50g) are currently sourced from the Goomtee estate, regarded as the best in the region. There's a central table for those who want to try a pot; or book in for one of the tasting sessions held on Saturdays between 10am and 11am. Tea-ware and accessories are also sold.

General

You'll find outposts of supermarket chains **Sainsbury's** (www.sainsburys.co.uk) and **Tesco** (www.tesco.com) across the city. Superior-quality **Waitrose** (www.waitrose.com) has central branches on Marylebone High Street and in Bloomsbury's Brunswick Centre (www.brunswick.co.uk).

Whole Foods Market
63-97 Kensington High Street, South Kensington, W8 5SE (7368 4500, www.whole foodmarket.com). High Street Kensington tube. **Open** 8am-10pm Mon-Sat; 10am-6pm Sun. **Credit** AmEx, DC, MC, V.
The London flagship of the American health-food supermarket chain occupies the handsome deco department store that was once Barkers. There are several eateries on the premises.

Markets

A resurgence of farmers' markets in the capital reflects Londoners' growing concern over provenance and environmental issues. Two of the most central are in Marylebone (Cramer Street car park, corner of Moxton Street, off Marylebone High Street, 10am-2pm Sun) and Notting Hill (behind Waterstone's, access via Kensington Place, W8, 9am-1pm Sat). For a fashion show and farmers' market in one, head to **Broadway Market** on a Saturday. For more, contact **London Farmers' Markets** (7833 0338, www.lfm.org.uk).

★ Borough Market
Southwark Street, Borough, SE1 (7407 1002, www.boroughmarket.org.uk). London Bridge tube/rail. **Open** 11am-5pm Thur; noon-6pm Fri; 8am-5pm Sat. **No credit cards. Map** p404 P8.
The food hound's favourite market occupies a sprawling site near London Bridge. Gourmet goodies run the gamut, from Flour Power City Bakery's organic loaves to chorizo and rocket rolls from Spanish specialist Brindisa, plus rare-breed meats, fruit and veg, cakes and all manner of preserves, oils and teas; head out hungry to take advantage of the numerous free samples. The market is now open on Thursdays, when it tends to be quieter than at always-mobbed weekends. A rail viaduct planned for above the space is still going ahead, despite a campaign against it, but a recent plan for the market to expand into the adjacent Jubilee Market area means that space shouldn't be lost. The new area will be reserved for 'raw food' specialists. *Photos p259.*

Specialist

A Gold
42 Brushfield Street, Spitalfields, E1 6AG (7247 2487). Liverpool Street tube/rail. **Open** 9.30am-5.30pm Mon-Fri; 11am-6pm Sat; 10am-6pm Sun. **Credit** AmEx, MC, V. **Map** p405 R5.
A Gold was flying the flag for British foods long before it became fashionable to do so. Opposite Spitalfields Market, it resembles a village shop from a bygone era. The baked goods alone take customers on a whistlestop tour of Britain: Cornish saffron cakes, Dundee cakes, Welsh cakes, and (of course) Eccles cakes made in Lancashire. English mead, proper marmalade and teas, unusual chutneys and traditional sweets make great gifts.

Daylesford Organic
44B Pimlico Road, Belgravia, SW1W 8LJ (7881 8060, www.daylesfordorganic.com). Sloane Square tube. **Open** 8am-8pm Mon-Sat; 10am-4pm Sun. **Credit** AmEx, MC, V. **Map** p400 G11.
Part of a new wave of chic purveyors of health food, this impressive offshoot of Lady Carole Bamford's Cotswold-based farm shop is set over three floors, and includes a café. Goods include ready-made dishes, store-cupboard staples such as pulses, pasta and sauces, cakes and breads, charcuterie and cheeses.

Hope & Greenwood
1 Russell Street, Covent Garden, WC2B 5JD (7240 3314, www.hopeandgreenwood.co.uk). Covent Garden tube. **Open** 11am-7.30pm Mon-Wed; 11am-8pm Thur, Fri; 10.30am-7.30pm Sat 11.30am-5.30pm Sun. **Credit** MC, V. **Map** p407 Z3.
The central branch of this Victorian-style sweetshop is always packed with customers searching for a sweet brand of nostalgia. It's the perfect place to find

CONSUME

Streets Ahead

Two very different roads that are right on London's fashion satnav.

REDCHURCH STREET, E1

There's been a distinct buzz surrounding Redchurch Street of late, spurred on in no small part by the media hype surrounding Conran's new Boundary Rooms and nearby members club Shoreditch House. Tucked inside the square formed by Bethnal Green Road, Shoreditch High Street, Calvert Avenue and Club Row, the street has long been ripe for fashion-focused gentrification thanks to its excellent location in the very thick of the east London action. However, the road is changing by the minute – get here before it loses its energy.

Vintage homewares specialist **Caravan** (no.3, 7033 3532, www.caravanstyle.com), which relocated from Spitalfields Market in 2009, was quick to catch on to the street's increasing stature. Selling an assortment of homely oddities, such as vintage cushions, retro desk lamps and plastic birds that tweet, it's a regular first-port-of-call for stylists. Further up the street, **Jeanette's** (no.64-66, entrance on Club Row; www. jeanettesshop.blogspot.com) was one of the fashion pack's most eagerly awaited openings of 2009, stocking ultra-rare one-off pieces by James Main's (aka Jeanette, of Boombox fame) mates, including Christopher Kane, Jessica Ogden and Richard Nicoll.

For something equally English, but of the edible rather than sartorial variety, head to **Albion** (*see p223*), on the corner of Redchurch and Boundary Street. You'll find a wealth of home-grown brands in the shop, from HP Sauce to Daylesford Organic via Neal's Yard. Have yourself some brunch in the well-priced café or head to Italian coffeeshop/deli **Franzè & Evans** (no.101, 7033 1910, www.franzeevans.com) for a lemon and polenta cake and a cappuccino. If you're about in the afternoon/evening, head to the **Jago** (no.77, 07501 469474, www.thejago.com), a contemporary art gallery-cum-bar.

MOUNT STREET, W1

If your idea of an afternoon's browsing has more to do with impressive window displays than graffiti-strewn converted squats, then Mayfair may be more your thing. With its dignified Victorian terracotta façades and by-appointment-only galleries, this section of W1 still harbours a superior vibe; consider, for example, traditional vendors such as master butcher **Allens Butchers of Mount Street** (no.117) and cigar shop **Sautter** (no.106, 7499 4866, www.sautter cigars.com). But Mount Street has recently become home to a raft of top-notch new openings, giving the area's traditional luxury aesthetic a youthful twist.

Towards the east end of the street sits the **Balenciaga** flagship (no.12, 7317

CONSUME

4400), its super-chic clothing set off by a glowing interior. A few doors along, you'll encounter two more of the high-end fashion brands that have recently moved into the street: **Wunderkind** (no.16, 7493 4312, www.wunderkind.de), Joop's fantastical diffusion line, which occupies the former site of Boss, and the shop of revered shoe designer **Christian Louboutin** (no.17, 7491 0033, www.christianlouboutin.com). Next door, treat yourself the best highlights in London at **Jo Hansford** (no.19, 7495 7774, www.johansford.com), a Mount Street stalwart.

Slightly further along sits the first UK boutique for **Marc Jacobs** (nos.24-25, 7399 1690, www.marcjacobs.com), one of the superbrands cherry-picked for the street by real-estate consultants Wilson McHardy, who were put in charge of reinvigorating the area in 2006. An stand-alone **Marc by Marc Jacobs** store followed at the corner of Mount Street and South Audley Street (entrance on the latter, no.56; 7408 7050) in spring 2009. On the other side of the street sits niche Australian skin, hair and body brand **Aesop** (no.91, 7409 2358, www.aesop.net.au), making Mount Street something of a one-stop destination for bleeding-edge international design and luxury British quirks.

the sweets, sherbets, chews and chocolates that were once the focus of a proper British childhood. Tall glass jars filled with a wish list of suckable pleasures line the back wall, delicate plates of chocolates are displayed on the counter, and various gift sets fill the rest of the shop. A 400g glass jar of lemon bonbons will set you back £7.99; alternatively, you can just pop in for a sugar pig, a Curly Wurly or a packet of sherbet Dip Dabs.

Other locations 20 Northcross Road, East Dulwich, SE22 9EU (8613 1777).

Neal's Yard Dairy

17 Shorts Gardens, Covent Garden, WC2H 9UP (7240 5700, www.nealsyarddairy.co.uk). Covent Garden tube. **Open** 11am-7pm Mon-Thur; 10am-7pm Fri, Sat. **Credit** MC, V. **Map** p407 Y2.

Neal's Yard buys from small farms and creameries and matures the cheeses in its own cellars until they're ready to sell in peak condition. Names such as Stinking Bishop and Lincolnshire Poacher are as evocative as the aromas in the shop. It's best to walk in and ask what's good today: you'll be given tasters by the well-trained staff. There's another shop at Borough Market (6 Park Street, 7367 0799).

▶ *In Marylebone, there are more great cheeses at La Fromagerie (2-6 Moxon Street, W1U 4EW, 7935 0341, www.lafromagerie.co.uk).*

Paul A Young Fine Chocolates

33 Camden Passage, Islington, N1 8EA (7424 5750, www.payoung.net). Angel tube. **Open** 11am-6pm Wed, Thur, Sat; 11am-7pm Fri; noon-5pm Sun. **Credit** AmEx, MC, V. **Map** p402 O2.

A gorgeous boutique with almost everything – chocolates, cakes, ice-cream – made in the downstairs kitchen and finished in front of customers. Young is a respected pâtissier as well as a chocolatier and has an astute chef's palate for flavour combinations: the white chocolate with rose masala is divine, as are the salted caramels.

▶ *England's oldest chocolatier, Prestat (14 Princes Arcade, St James's, SW1Y 6DS, 0800 0213 023, www.prestat.co.uk) offers unusual and traditional flavours in brightly coloured gift boxes.*

GIFTS & SOUVENIRS

★ Coco de Mer

23 Monmouth Street, Covent Garden, WC2H 9DD (7836 8882, www.coco-de-mer.com). Covent Garden tube. **Open** 11am-7pm Mon-Wed, Fri, Sat; 11am-8pm Thur; noon-6pm Sun. **Credit** AmEx, MC, V. **Map** p407 Y2.

London's most glamorous erotic emporium sells a variety of tasteful books, toys and lingerie, from glass dildos that double as objets d'art to a Marie Antoinette costume of crotchless culottes and corset. Trying on items is fun as well: peepshow-style velvet changing rooms allow your lover to watch you undress from a 'confession box' next door.

CONSUME

Contemporary Applied Arts

2 Percy Street, Fitzrovia, W1T 1DD (7436 2344, www.caa.org.uk). Goodge Street or Tottenham Court Road tube. **Open** 10am-6pm Mon-Sat. **Credit** AmEx, MC, V. **Map** p399 K5.

This airy gallery, run by a charitable arts organisation, represents more than 300 makers. The work embraces the functional – jewellery, tableware, textiles – but also includes unique, purely decorative pieces. The ground floor hosts exhibitions by individual artists, or themed by craft; in the basement shop, you'll find pieces for all pockets. Glass is always exceptional here.

★ James Smith & Sons

53 New Oxford Street, Holborn, WC1A 1BL (7836 4731, www.james-smith.co.uk). Holborn or Tottenham Court Road tube. **Open** 9.30am-5.15pm Mon-Fri; 10am-5.15pm Sat. **Credit** AmEx, MC, V. **Map** p407 Y1.

More than 175 years after it was established, this charming shop, with Victorian fittings still intact, is holding its own in the niche market of umbrellas and walking sticks. The stock here isn't the throwaway type of brolly that breaks at the first sign of bad weather. Lovingly crafted 'brellas, such as a classic City umbrella with a hickory crook at £110, are built to last. A repair service is also offered.

Luna & Curious

198 Brick Lane, Mayfair, E1 6SA (7033 4411, www.lunaandcurious.com). Aldgate East tube or Liverpool Street tube/rail. **Open** noon-6pm Wed-Sun. **Credit** MC, V. **Map** p405 S4.

The stock here, from vintage cocktail dresses to ultra-English teacups, is collated by a collective of young artisans. There's jewellery made from ceramics, feathers and old embroidery from military jackets. Prices are surprisingly reasonable for products so lovingly put together.

★ Shelf

40 Cheshire Street, Spitalfields, E2 6EH (7739 9444, www.helpyourshelf.co.uk). Liverpool Street tube/rail. **Open** 1-6pm Fri, Sat; 11am-6pm Sun. **Credit** MC, V. **Map** p403 S4.

Artist Katy Hackney and costume designer Jane Petrie's gift shop-cum-gallery is a great place to pick up unique presents, such as Prague-based sculptor Pravoslav Rada's enigmatic ceramics, or one of the limited-edition collaborations with east London artist Rob Ryan. The handcrafted Magno wooden radio (around £160) was a new feature for 2009.

HEALTH & BEAUTY

Complementary medicine

Hale Clinic

7 Park Crescent, Marylebone, W1B 1PF (7631 0156, www.haleclinic.com). Great Portland Street or Regent's Park tube. **Open** 9am-9pm Mon-Fri; 9am-5pm Sat. **Credit** MC, V. **Map** p398 H4.

Around 100 practitioners are affiliated to the Hale Clinic, which was founded with the aim of integrating complementary and conventional medicine and opened by the Prince of Wales in 1988. The treatment list is a veritable A-Z of alternative therapies, while the shop stocks supplements, skincare products and books.

Hairdressers & barbers

If the options listed below are out of your range, try a branch of **Mr Topper's** (7631 3233; £6 men, £10-£12 women).

Daniel Hersheson

45 Conduit Street, Mayfair, W1F 2YN (7434 1747, www.danielhersheson.com). Oxford Circus tube. **Open** 9am-6pm Mon-Wed, Sat; 9am-8pm Thur, Fri. **Credit** AmEx, MC, V. **Map** p406 U3.

Despite its location in the heart of upmarket Mayfair, this modern two-storey salon isn't at all snooty, with a staff of very talented cutters and colourists. Prices start at £55 (£40 for men), though you'll pay £250 for a cut with Daniel (£125 for men). There's also a menu of therapies; the swish Harvey Nichols (*see p244*) branch has a dedicated spa. Hersheson's Blow Dry Bar at Topshop (*see p252*; call 7927 7888 to book) offers catwalk looks for £22.

F Flittner

86 Moorgate, City, EC2M 6SE (7606 4750, www.fflittner.com). Moorgate tube/rail. **Open** 8am-6pm Mon-Wed, Fri; 8am-6.30pm Thur. **Credit** AmEx, MC, V. **Map** p405 Q6.

In business since 1904, Flittner seems not to have noticed that the 21st century has begun. Hidden behind beautifully frosted doors (marked 'Saloon') is a simple, handsome room, done out with an array of classic barber's furniture that's older than your gran. Within these hushed yet welcoming confines, up to six black coat-clad barbers deliver straightforward haircuts (dry cuts £13.50-£15.50, wet cuts £18-£22) and shaves with skill and dignity.

▶ *For a modern take on the art of the wet shave, try Murdock (340 Old Street, Shoreditch, EC1V 9DS, 7729 2288, www.murdocklondon.com).*

Tommy Guns

65 Beak Street, Soho, W1F 9SN (7439 0777, www.tommyguns.com). Oxford Circus or Picadilly Circus tube. **Open** 10am-8pm Mon-Fri; 10am-8pm Sat. **Credit** AmEx, MC, V.

Now over a decade old, and with new branches on Brewer Street and all the way over in New York City, Tommy Guns remains a very cool prospect indeed. This original Soho space, complete with retro fittings, is filled with youthful colourists and cutters and there's a friendly, relaxed buzz to the place most

days. Men's cuts start from £39, and women's cuts can be had from £49.
Other locations 49 Charlotte Road, Shoreditch, EC2A 3QT (7739 2244); 65 Brewer Street, Soho, W1F 9TQ (7287 0011).

Opticians

Dollond & Aitchison (www.danda.co.uk) and **Specsavers** (www.specsavers.com) are chains with branches on most high streets.

Cutler & Gross
16 Knightsbridge Green, Knightsbridge, SW1X 7QL (7581 2250, www.cutlerandgross.com). Knightsbridge tube. **Open** 9.30am-7pm Mon-Sat; noon-4pm Sun. **Credit** AmEx, MC, V. **Map** p397 F9.
C&G celebrated its 40th anniversary in 2009, and its stock of handmade frames is still at the cutting-edge of optical style. Stock runs from Andy Warhol-inspired glasses to naturally light buffalo-horn frames, and recent collaborations have included frames with trend-leaders Comme des Garçons. Vintage eyewear from the likes of Ray-Ban and Courrèges is at the sister shop down the road.
Other locations 7 Knightsbridge Green, Knightsbridge, SW1X 7QL (7590 9995).
▶ *For cool vintage frames and sunglasses, check out the Klasik stall (http://klasik.org) at Old Spitalfields Market (see p247) every Sunday.*

Pharmacies

National chain **Boots** (www.boots.com) has branches across the city, offering dispensing pharmacies and photo processing. The store on Piccadilly Circus (44-46 Regent Street, W1B 5RA, 7734 6126) is open until midnight (except Sunday, when it closes at 6pm).

DR Harris
29 St James's Street, St James's, SW1A 1HB (7930 3915, www.drharris.co.uk). Green Park or Piccadilly Circus tube. **Open** 8.30am-6pm Mon-Fri; 9.30am-5pm Sat. **Credit** AmEx, MC, V. **Map** p400 J8.

Founded in 1790, this venerable chemist has a royal warrant. Wood-and-glass cabinets are filled with bottles, jars and old-fashioned shaving brushes and manicure kits. The smartly packaged own-brand products such as the bright blue Crystal Eye Gel have a cult following.

Shops

Eco pioneer **Neal's Yard Remedies** (15 Neal's Yard, Covent Garden, WC2H 9DP, 7379 7222, www.nealsyardremedies.com) now has several central London locations, offering excellent organic products, a herbal dispensary and complementary therapies. Beauty chain **Space NK** (8-10 Broadwick Street, Soho, W1F 8HW, 7734 3734, www.spacenk.com) is a great source of niche skincare and make-up brands.

Liz Earle Naturally Active Skincare
38-39 Duke of York Square, Chelsea, SW3 4LY (7730 9191, www.lizearle.com). Sloane Square tube. **Open** 10am-7pm Mon, Wed-Sat; 10.30am-7pm Tue; 11am-5pm Sun. **Credit** AmEx, MC, V. **Map** p397 F11.
Former beauty writer Liz Earle's hugely successful botanical skincare range was previously only available from her HQ on the Isle of Wight. The new London flagship is still on Duke of York Square, but in a larger space across from the previous shop, and stocks the streamlined range of products, based on a simple, no-fuss regime of cleansing, toning and moisturising. Highlights include the Instant Boost Skin Tonic (£11 for 200ml). The 'minis' and essentials packs are a great introduction to the range.
▶ *On a corner of Sloane Square, Ortigia's sleek flagship (no.55, 7730 2826, www.ortigia-srl.com) sells divinely packaged smellies.*

★ Lost in Beauty
117 Regent's Park Road, Primrose Hill, NW1 8UR (7586 4411, www.lostinbeauty.com). Chalk Farm tube. **Open** 10am-7pm Mon-Fri; 10am-6pm Sat; 11am-5pm Sun. **Credit** AmEx, MC, V.
Kitted out with vintage shop fittings, this chic boutique stocks a well-edited array of beauty brands, including Phyto, Australian brand Jurlique, Caudalie, Dr Hauschka, Rodial, REN, ZO1 suncare products and cult cosmetics brand Becca.

Miller Harris
21 Bruton Street, Mayfair, W1J 6QD (7629 7750, www.millerharris.com). Bond Street or Green Park tube. **Open** 10am-6pm Mon-Sat. **Credit** AmEx, MC, V. **Map** p400 H7.
Grasse-trained British perfumer Lyn Harris's distinctive, long-lasting scents, in their lovely decorative packaging, are made with quality natural extracts and oils. Noix de Tubéreuse (£75/100ml), a lighter and more palatable tuberose scent than many

CONSUME

on the market, is a perennial favourite, while new scent Fleurs de Bois (£55/100ml) evokes a traditional English garden.

Other locations 14 Needham Road, Notting Hill, W11 2RP (7221 1545); 14 Monmouth Street, Covent Garden, WC2H 9HB (7836 9378).

Spas & salons

Many of London's luxury hotels – including the **Sanderson** (*see p173*) and the **Dorchester** (*see p183*) – make their excellent spa facilities available to the public.

Cowshed

119 Portland Road, Notting Hill, W11 4LN (7078 1944, www.cowshedclarendoncross.com). Holland Park tube. **Open** 9am-8pm Mon-Fri; 9am-7pm Sat; 10am-5pm Sun. **Credit** AmEx, MC, V.

The London outpost of Babington House's Cowshed does the chic, white country cousin proud. The chic, white ground floor is buzzy, with a tiny café area on one side, and a manicure/pedicure section on the other, complete with groovy retro mini-TVs. For facials, massages, waxing and more, head downstairs.

★ Elemis Day Spa

2-3 Lancashire Court, Mayfair, W1S 1EX (7499 4995, www.elemis.com). Bond Street tube. **Open** 9am-9pm Mon-Sat; 10am-6pm Sun. **Credit** AmEx, MC, V. **Map** p398 H6.

This leading British spa brand's exotic, unisex retreat is tucked away down a cobbled lane off Bond Street. The elegantly ethnic treatment rooms are a lovely setting in which to relax and enjoy a spot of pampering, from wraps to facials.

HOUSE & HOME

Antiques

Although boutiques have encroached on their territory, some quirky dealers remain on Islington's **Camden Passage** (off Upper Street, 7359 0190, www.camdenpassage antiques.com), especially in Pierrepont Arcade. Marylebone's **Church Street** is now a major area for vintage homewares, and host to Alfie's Antique Market (*see below*), but **Portobello Road** (*see p245*) remains the biggest, best-known market for antiques.

Alfie's Antique Market

13-25 Church Street, Marylebone, NW8 8DT (7723 6066, www.alfiesantiques.com). Edgware Road tube or Marylebone tube/rail. **Open** 10am-6pm Tue-Sat. **No credit cards. Map** p395 E4.

Alfie's hosts more than 100 dealers in vintage furniture and fashion, art, accessories, books, maps and more. Dodo Posters do 1920s and '30s ads.

Antiquarius

131-141 King's Road, Chelsea, SW3 5PH (7823 3900, www.antiquarius.co.uk). Sloane Square tube then bus 11, 19, 22, 319, 211. **Open** 10am-6pm Mon-Sat. **No credit cards. Map** p397 E12.

This longstanding King's Road landmark houses around 60 dealers, with specialisms from vintage trunks and jewellery to original film art.

Core One

Gas Works, 2 Michael Road, Fulham, SW6 2AD (7823 3900). Sloane Square tube then bus 11, 19, 22, 319, 211. **Open** 10am-6pm Mon-Fri; 11am-4pm Sat. **No credit cards.**

A group of antiques and 20th-century dealers has colonised this industrial building in Fulham, including Dean Antiques (7610 6997, www.deanantiques. co.uk) for dramatic pieces, and De Parma (7736 3384, www.deparma.com) for elegant mid-century design.

Grays Antique Market & Grays in the Mews

58 Davies Street, W1K 5LP & 1-7 Davies Mews, Mayfair, W1K 5AB (7629 7034, www.grays antiques.com). Bond Street tube. **Open** 10.30am-6.30pm Mon-Wed, Fri, Sat; 10.30am-7.30pm Thur; noon-5pm Sun. **No credit cards. Map** p398 H6.

More than 200 dealers in this smart covered market sell everything from jewellery to rare books.

General

Habitat (121 Regent Street, W1B 4TB, 0844 499 1134, www.habitat.co.uk) is a good source of affordable modern design.

Conran Shop

Michelin House, 81 Fulham Road, Fulham, SW3 6RD (7589 7401, www.conran.co.uk). South Kensington tube. **Open** 10am-6pm Mon, Tue, Fri; 10am-7pm Wed, Thur; 10am-6.30pm Sat; noon-6pm Sun. **Credit** MC, V. **Map** p397 E10.

Sir Terence Conran's flagship store in the Fulham Road's beautiful 1909 Michelin Building showcases furniture and design for every room in the house as well as the garden; there are plenty of portable accessories, gadgets, books, stationery and toiletries that make great gifts or souvenirs.

Other locations 55 Marylebone High Street, W1U 5HS (7723 2223).

Labour & Wait

18 Cheshire Street, off Brick Lane, Spitalfields, E2 6EH (7729 6253, www.labourandwait.co.uk). Aldgate East tube or Liverpool Street tube/rail. **Open** 11am-5pm Wed, Fri; 1-5pm Sat; 10am-5pm Sun. **Credit** MC, V. **Map** p403 S4.

This much-celebrated shop pays homage to timeless, unfaddy domestic goods that combine beauty with utility: think Victorian pantry crossed with 1950s kitchen. The quintessentially British homewares include traditional feather dusters (£8), tins of twine (£6.50), simple enamelware and sturdy canvas bags. Labour & Wait also has a space at concept store Dover Street Market (*see p253*).

MUSIC & ENTERTAINMENT
CDs, records & DVDs

Oxford Street's Zavvi bit the dust in 2009, but the street is still host to megastore **HMV** (www.hmv.co.uk), offering a comprehensive line-up of CDs and DVDs, plus some vinyl. Serious browsers, however, head south into Soho, where indie record stores are still clinging on around Berwick and D'Arblay Streets.

Flashback
50 Essex Road, Islington, N1 8LR (7354 9356, www.flashback.co.uk). Angel tube then bus 38, 56, 73, 341. **Open** 10am-7pm Mon-Sat; 11.30am-6pm Sun. **Credit** AmEx, MC, V. **Map** p402 O1.
Stock is scrupulously organised at this second-hand treasure trove. The ground floor is dedicated to CDs, while the basement is vinyl-only: an ever-expanding jazz collection jostles for space alongside soul, hip hop and a carpal tunnel-compressing selection of library sounds. A range of rarities is pinned in plastic sleeves to the walls.

Honest Jon's
278 Portobello Road, Notting Hill, W10 5TE (8969 9822, www.honestjons.com). Ladbroke Grove tube. **Open** 10am-6pm Mon-Sat; 11am-5pm Sun. **Credit** AmEx, MC, V.
Honest Jon's found its way to Notting Hill in 1979, where it was reportedly the first place in London to employ a Rastafarian. The owner helped James Lavelle set up Mo'Wax records. You'll find jazz, hip hop, soul, broken beat, reggae and Brazilian music on the shelves.

Pure Groove Records
6-7 West Smithfield, Clerkenwell, EC1A 9JX (7778 9278, www.puregroove.co.uk). Farringdon tube/rail. **Open** noon-7pm Mon-Fri. **Credit** MC, V. **Map** p402 O5.
Pure Groove is a stylish, multimedia collection of vinyl, poster art and CD gems covering all things indie, alternative and cutting-edge in guitar and electronic music. The rear, housing T-shirts, cotton bags and posters, doubles as a stage for the regular live-band sets and film screenings.
► *A stiff walk up Farringdon Road, Brill (27 Exmouth Market, 7833 9757) is a small CD shop-cum-café with a fine curated selection.*

Ray's Jazz at Foyles
3rd floor, Foyles Bookshop, 113-119 Charing Cross Road, Soho, WC2H 0EB (7440 3205, www.foyles.co.uk). Tottenham Court Road tube.

Rough Trade East. *See p268.*

Open 9.30am-9pm Mon-Sat; 11.30am-6pm Sun. Credit AmEx, MC, V. Map p407 X2.
London's least beardy jazz shop has left its cramped first-floor quarters in Foyles (see p247) and ascended to the third floor. The predominantly CD-based stock remains as it was: you'll find a good selection of blues, avant-garde, gospel, folk and world, but modern jazz is the main draw.

Rough Trade East

Dray Walk, Old Truman Brewery, 91 Brick Lane, Spitalfields, E1 6QL (7392 7788, www.rough trade.com). Liverpool Street tube/rail. Open 8am-9pm Mon-Thur; 8am-8pm Fri, Sat; 11am-7pm Sun. Credit AmEx, DC, MC, V. Map p403 S5.
Despite the fading fortunes of many record shops, Rough Trade added this warehouse-style, 5,000sq ft store, café and gig space to the cluster of boutiques and bars off Brick Lane. It's a temple to things alternative, where staff will blitz you with releases so new they've barely been recorded. *Photo p267.*
Other locations 130 Talbot Road, Notting Hill, W11 1JA (7229 8541).

Musical instruments

Site of the legendary recording studio Regent Sounds in the 1960s, Denmark Street, off Charing Cross Road, is now a hub for music shops, especially if you're looking for a new, second-hand or rare vintage guitar.

Chappell of Bond Street

152-160 Wardour Street, Soho, W1F 8YA (7432 4400, www.chappellofbondstreet.co.uk). Tottenham Court Road tube. Open 9.30am-6pm Mon-Fri; 10am-5.30pm Sat. Credit AmEx, MC, V. Map p406 V2.
It's retained its old name, but Chappell recently moved from Bond Street (its home for nearly 200 years) to this amazing three-storey musical temple. This is the leading Yamaha stockist in the UK, and the collection of sheet music (classical, pop and jazz) is reputedly the largest in Europe.

SPORTS & FITNESS

Harrods (see p242) has a good fitness department, including specialist concessions. Bike chains Evans Cycles (www.evans cycles.com) and Cycle Surgery (www.cycle surgery.com) each have a number of branches across the city. For the best places to find fashion trainers, see p258.

Decathlon

Canada Water Retail Park, Surrey Quays Road, Rotherhithe, SE16 2XU (7394 2000, www. decathlon.co.uk). Canada Water tube. Open 9am-9pm Mon-Fri; 9am-7pm Sat; 11am-5pm Sun. Credit MC, V.

The warehouse-sized London branch of this French chain offers London's biggest single collection of sports equipment. You'll find a vast array of reasonably priced equipment and clothing for all mainstream racket and ball sports as well as for swimming, running, surfing, fishing, ice-skating, skiing and more.

Run & Become

42 Palmer Street, Victoria, SW1H 0PH (7222 1314, www.runandbecome.com). St James's Park tube. Open 9am-6pm Mon-Wed, Fri, Sat; 9am-8pm Thur. Credit MC, V. Map p400 J9.
The experienced staff here, most of them enthusiastic runners, are determined to find the right pair of shoes for your particular physique and running style. The full gamut of running kit, from clothing to speed monitors, is also available.

TICKETS

For London performances, whether musical, theatrical or in some other cultural orbit, it's worth booking ahead – surprisingly obscure acts sell out, and high-profile gigs and sporting events can do so in seconds. It's almost always cheaper to bypass ticket agents and go direct to the box office: agents charge booking fees that often top 20 per cent. If you have to use an agent, booking agencies include Ticketmaster (0870 277 4321, www.ticketmaster.co.uk), Stargreen (7734 8932, www.stargreen.com), Ticketweb (0844 477 1000, www.ticketweb. co.uk), See Tickets (0870 264 3333, www.see tickets.com) and Keith Prowse (0870 840 1111, www.keithprowse.com). However, there are several ways to save money on tickets. For specific tips on where to get tickets (and how to keep the cost down) for the theatre, see p339; for gigs and concerts, see p308 & p312.

TRAVELLERS' NEEDS

Independent travel specialist Trailfinders (European travel 0845 050 5945, worldwide flights 0845 058 5858, www.trailfinders.com) has several branches in the capital, including in the Piccadilly Waterstone's (nos.203-206, SW1Y 6WW, 7851 2400, www.waterstones.co.uk).

Excess Baggage Company

4 Hannah Close, Great Central Way, Wembley, Middx, NW10 0UX (0800 783 1085, www. excess-baggage.com). Credit AmEx, MC, V.
Ships goods to over 300 countries and territories worldwide, including the USA, Canada, Australia, New Zealand and South Africa, from a single suitcase to complete household removal. Prices are reasonable and include cartons and other packing materials. There are branches in the city's main rail stations, as well as Heathrow and Gatwick airports.

Arts & Entertainment

Royal Ballet. *See p288.*

Calendar	**270**	
Small is Beautiful	273	
Standing on Ceremony	276	
Children	**278**	
Festivals Children	282	
Comedy	**284**	
Stand Up to Be Counted	286	
Dance	**287**	
Let's Get Physical	288	
Festivals Dance	289	
Film	**290**	
Festivals Film	293	
Galleries	**294**	
Festivals Art & Design	298	

Gay & Lesbian	**301**
Dressing Up, Getting Out	303
Festivals Gay & Lesbian	304
Music	**308**
Profile Kings Place	309
Festivals Classical	310
Festivals Rock, Pop & Roots	313
Picture This	317
Festivals Jazz	319
Nightlife	**321**
All Bar None	324
Profile Mr C	327
Sport & Fitness	**329**
Ride Cycle the Sights	334
Theatre	**337**
The Cheap Seats	339
Profile Wilton's Music Hall	342
Festivals Theatre	344

Calendar

The city's most exciting goings-on – all year round.

All over London, festivals and events play ever more elaborate variations on the themes of parading, dancing and the arts. Weather plays a part in the timing, with a concentration of things to do in the hotter months, but the city's calendar is pretty busy for most of the year.

Alongside this chapter, a series of boxes detail events dedicated to dance (*see p289*), film (*see p293*), art (*see p298*), music (*see p310, p313 and p319*), theatre (*see p344*), families (*see p282*) and gay culture (*see p304*); for a calendar of sporting events, *see p329*. The weekly *Time Out London* magazine, in print and online (www.timeout.com/london), is a great source of information. If you're planning your trip around a particular event, always confirm the details in advance – events can be cancelled and dates may change.

ARTS & ENTERTAINMENT

ALL YEAR ROUND

For the Changing of the Guard, *see p276* **Standing on Ceremony**.

Ceremony of the Keys

Tower of London, Tower Hill, the City, EC3N 4AB (0844 482 7777, www.hrp.org.uk). Tower Hill tube/Tower Gateway DLR. **Date** 9.30pm daily (advance bookings only). **Map** p405 R7.
Join the Yeoman Warders after-hours at the Tower of London as they ritually lock the fortress's entrances in this 700-year-old ceremony. You enter the Tower at 9.30pm and it's all over just after 10pm, but places are hotly sought after – apply at least two months in advance; full details are on the website.

Gun Salutes

Green Park, Mayfair & St James's, W1, & Tower of London, the City, EC3. **Dates** 6 Feb (Accession Day); 21 Apr & 14 June (Queen's birthdays); 2 June (Coronation Day); 10 June (Duke of Edinburgh's birthday); 15 June (Trooping the Colour); State Opening of Parliament (*see p277*); 13 Nov (Lord Mayor's Show); 14 Nov (Remembrance Sunday); also for state visits. **Map** p400 H8.
There are gun salutes on many state occasions. A cavalry charge features in the 41-gun salutes mounted by the Kings Troop Royal Horse Artillery in Hyde Park at noon (opposite the Dorchester; *see p185*), whereas, on the other side of town, the Honourable Artillery Company ditches the ponies and piles on the firepower with their 62-gun salutes (1pm at the Tower of London). If the dates happen to fall on a Sunday, the salute is held on Monday.

JANUARY-MARCH

This is a good time of year for dance events, among them **Resolution!** at the Place and **Spring Dance** and Sadler's Wells; for both, *see p289* **Festivals**. For **National Storytelling Week** and the **Imagine** children's literature festival, *see p282*; for the **London Lesbian & Gay Film Festival**, *see p293*.

★ London International Mime Festival

7637 5661, www.mimefest.co.uk. **Date** 13-31 Jan.
This long-running festival aims to explode any prejudices you may have against mime and its related theatrical forms. Expect innovative and visually stunning theatre from across the globe.

Joseph Grimaldi Memorial Service

*Holy Trinity Church, Beechwood Road, Dalston,
E8 3DY (www.clowns-international.co.uk).
Dalston Kingsland rail.* **Date** 7 Feb.
Join hundreds of motley-clad 'Joeys' for their annual service commemorating the legendary British clown, Joseph Grimaldi (1778-1837).

★ Chinese New Year Festival

*Around Gerrard Street, Chinatown, W1,
Leicester Square, WC2, & Trafalgar Square,
WC2 (7851 6686, www.chinatownchinese.co.uk).
Leicester Square or Piccadilly Circus tube.*
Date 14 Feb. **Map** p406 W3.
Launch the Year of the Tiger in style at celebrations that engulf Chinatown and Leicester Square. Dragon dancers writhe alongside a host of impressive acts in the grand parade to Trafalgar Square, while the restaurants of Chinatown get even more packed than usual.
▶ *For sights around Chinatown, see pp95-96.*

Pancake Day Races

Great Spitalfields *Dray Walk, Brick Lane,
Spitalfields, E1 6QL (7375 0441, www.
alternativearts.co.uk). Liverpool Street tube/rail.*
Poulters Annual *Guildhall Yard, City, EC2P
2EJ (www.poulters.org.uk). Bank tube/DLR or
Moorgate tube/rail.*
Both Date 16 Feb.
Shrove Tuesday brings out charity pancake racers across the capital. Don a silly costume and join in the fun at the Great Spitalfields Pancake Race (you'll need to register in advance) or watch City livery companies race in full regalia at the event organised by the Worshipful Company of Poulters.

Jewish Book Week

*Royal National Hotel, Bedford Way, Bloomsbury,
WC1 0DG (7446 8771). Russell Square tube.*
Date 27 Feb-7 Mar. **Map** p399 K4.
One of London's biggest literature festivals, Jewish Book Week is renowned for its livelydebates and Q&A sessions with authors and intellectuals.

Who Do You Think You Are? Live

*Olympia, Hammersmith Road, Kensington,
W14 8UX (www.whodoyouthinkyouarelive.co.uk).
Kensington Olympia tube/rail.* **Date** 26-28 Feb.
A spin-off from the hugely successful BBC TV series that keeps Brits glued to the box watching weepy celebs uncover their ancestry, this enormous family history event could help you trace yours.

National Science & Engineering Week

0870 770 7101, www.the-ba.net.
Date 12-21 Mar.
From the weirdly wacky to the profound, this annual series of events engages the public in celebrating science, engineering and technology.

St Patrick's Day Parade & Festival

7983 4100, www.london.gov.uk. **Date** 14 Mar.
Join the London Irish out in force for this huge annual parade through central London followed by toe-tapping tunes in Trafalgar Square.

Chinese New Year.

ARTS & ENTERTAINMENT

★ Kew Spring Festival

For listings, *see p155* **Royal Botanic Gardens**.
Date early Mar-Apr.
Kew Gardens is at its most beautiful in spring, with five million flowers carpeting the grounds.

APRIL-JUNE

Early summer is terrific for outdoor events, among them excellent alfresco theatre at the **Greenwich & Docklands International Festival** and, on the South Bank, **Watch this**

London Mela. *See p275.*

Space (for both, *see p344* **Festivals**). Sport fans can go racing (**Royal Ascot**, the **Epsom Derby**), queue for **Wimbledon** tickets or watch a football playoff; for all, *see pp329-330*. For classical music at the **City of London Festival** and the **Hampton Court Palace Festival**, *see p310* **Festivals**; for rockier fare at the **Camden Crawl**, the **Wireless Festival** and the **Summer Series** at Somerset House, *see p313* **Festivals**.

Oxford & Cambridge Boat Race

River Thames, from Putney to Mortlake (www.theboatrace.org). Putney Bridge tube, or Barnes Bridge, Mortlake or Putney rail. **Date** 3 Apr.
Blue-clad Oxbridge students race each other in a pair of rowing eights, watched by tens of millions worldwide. Experience the excitement from the riverbank (along with 250,000 other fans) for the 156th instalment of the historic race.

Alternative Fashion Week

Spitalfields Traders Market, Crispin Place, Brushfield Street, Spitalfields, E1 6AA (7375 0441, www.alternativearts.co.uk). Liverpool Street tube/rail. **Date** 19-23 Apr.
Map p403 R5.
Forget London Fashion Week, this is the place to discover the edgiest new designers – more than 60 took part in 2009.

Shakespeare's Birthday

For listings, *see p54* **Shakespeare's Globe**.
Date wknd closest to 23 Apr.
To celebrate the Bard's birthday, the Globe Theatre throws open its doors for a series of events.

★ Virgin London Marathon

Greenwich Park to the Mall via the Isle of Dogs, Victoria Embankment & St James's Park (7902 0200, www.london-marathon.co.uk). Blackheath & Maze Hill rail (start), or Charing Cross tube/rail (end). **Date** 25 Apr.
One of the world's elite long-distance races, the London Marathon is also one of the world's largest fund-raising events – nearly 80% of participants run for charity, so zany costumes abound among the 35,000 starters. If you haven't already applied to run, you're too late: just go along to watch.

Covent Garden May Fayre & Puppet Festival

Garden of St Paul's Covent Garden, Bedford Street, Covent Garden, WC2E 9ED (7375 0441, www.alternativearts.co.uk). Covent Garden tube. **Date** 9 May. **Map** p407 Y4.
All-day puppet mayhem (10.30am-5.30pm) devoted to celebrating Mr Punch at the scene of his first recorded sighting in England in 1662. Mr P takes to the church's pulpit at 11.30am.

Chelsea Flower Show
Royal Hospital, Royal Hospital Road, Chelsea, SW3 4SR (7649 1885, www.rhs.org.uk). Sloane Square tube. **Date** 25-29 May. **Map** p397 F12. Elbow past the crowds of rich old ladies to admire perfect blooms, or get ideas for your own humble plot. The first two days are reserved for Royal Horticul-tural Society members and tickets for the open days are hard to come by. The show closes at 5.30pm on the final day; display plants are sold off from 4.30pm.

Story of London
www.london.gov.uk/storyoflondon. **Date** throughout June.
The Mayor of London's newest extravaganza, held for the first time in 2009 and hopefully returning again in 2010 (check the website) is an all-encompassing celebration of the past, present and future of the capital. With a month-long programme of over 400 activities from which to choose, you're spoilt for choice – from the thrills and spills of a Tudor joust to enjoying a London-related film at BFI Southbank.

Small is Beautiful

Introduce yourself to London's unstoppable micro-festival scene.

The trend can be traced back to the **Camden Crawl** (www.thecamdencrawl.com), which launched back in the early '90s. But it's only been in the last few years that pub crawl-style multi-venue music festivals have become an established feature of the city's musical life, offering Londoners a little slice of festival culture without requiring them to get out of town.

The idea is simple. Festivalgoers are issued with a wristband, which allows access to a number of venues in the same part of town, and are left to chart their own route. Some venues are big, as are some of the acts. Others are tiny pub backrooms, hosting shows by young up-and-comers. A few surprise shows add a little extra spice.

Organised fans plan their evenings with military precision. However, most people end up missing many of the acts they originally wanted to see, usually due to some combination of drunken confusion and full-to-capacity venues, only to stumble across all manner of great new groups by accident. The line-ups capture London's hyperactive listening habits perfectly,

veering from maniacal electro-pop to maudlin Americana.

The micro-festival trend really took flight in May 2008 with the first **Stag & Dagger** festival (www.staganddagger.com), the first of east London's several versions of the Crawl. The concentration of muso pubs and bars around Shoreditch – the likes of the Old Blue Last (*see p326*) and Cargo (*see p316*), among others – is perfectly suited to the micro-festival template, which helps explain the arrival in October 2008 of the artier but not entirely dissimilar **Concrete & Glass** (www.concreteandglass.co.uk).

Now sponsored by *Vice* magazine, Stag & Dagger returned in 2009 and will be back this year (28 May 2010), while the Camden Crawl will also return (1-2 May 2010). And it's worth looking out for the possible return of other events that debuted in 2009, such as the **Brick Lane Takeover** (www.bricklanetakeover.org.uk), in aid of cancer support charity Macmillan, and the **Land of Kings** (www.landofkings.co.uk), which took over a dozen or so venues in Dalston. Check *Time Out* magazine for details.

ARTS & ENTERTAINMENT

Coin Street Festival
Bernie Spain Gardens (next to Oxo Tower Wharf), South Bank, SE1 9PH (7021 1600, www.coinstreet.org). Southwark tube or Waterloo tube/rail. **Date** June-Aug. **Map** p404 N8.
Celebrating London's cultural diversity, this free, summer-long Thameside festival features a series of music-focused events. One of the best sessions is Pulse in June, a wild mix of Eastern and Central European music from gypsy to new wave.

Open Garden Squares Weekend
www.opensquares.org. **Date** 12-13 June.
Secret – and merely exclusive – gardens are thrown open to the public. You can visit roof gardens, prison gardens and children-only gardens, as well as a changing selection of those tempting oases railed off in the middle of the city's finest squares. Some charge an entrance fee.

Exhibition Road Music Day
Exhibition Road, SW7 (www.exhibitionroad musicday.org). South Kensington tube. **Date** last wknd of June. **Map** p397 D9.
London's counterpart to France's midsummer Fête de la Musique ranges through institutions that border Exhibition Road and spills into Hyde Park. With Imperial College and the Ismaili Centre among the participants, you can expect anything from experimental music to Sufi chants.

JULY-SEPTEMBER
Summer sees some of the most important music festivals of the year – namely, the **BBC Sir Henry Wood Promenade Concerts** (more commonly, the Proms), the **Lovebox Weekender**, the **English Heritage Picnic Concerts** at Kenwood House and the teenager-friendly **Underage** festival (for all, *see p310 and p313*) – as well as the city's major gay event, **Pride London** (*see p304* **Festivals**). There are also two cutting-edge dance events, the **Place Prize** and **Dance Umbrella** (for both, *see p289* **Festivals**).

Music Village
Hyde Park, W1 (7264 0000, www.culturalcooperation.org). **Date** 1st wknd of July. **Map** p395 F7.
Europe's longest-running festival of world cultures is always inspirationally themed, bringing global musicians together and showcasing London's own diaspora performers.

London Literature Festival
Southbank Centre, Belvedere Road, SE1 8XX (0871 663 2501, www.londonlitfest.com). Waterloo tube/rail. **Date** 1st 2 wks of July. **Map** p401 M8.
Now in its fifth year, the London Literature Festival usually combines superstar writers with stars from

Notting Hill Carnival.

other fields: architects, comedians, sculptors and cultural theorists examining anything from queer literature to migration.

★ Chap Olympiad
www.thechap.net. **Date** second wknd of July.
English eccentrics are in full cry at this annual event mounted by *The Chap* magazine, which starts with the lighting of the Olympic Pipe. 'Sports' include cucumber sandwich discus and hop, skip and G&T. Check the venue closer to the time: it was held in Bloomsbury in 2009.

Broadwalk Ballroom
Regent's Park, Marylebone, NW1 (www.dancealfresco.org). Regent's Park tube. **Date** July-Aug. **Map** p398 G3.
Regent's Park's Broadwalk is transformed into a dancefloor over two weekends in July and August, with dancing from 2pm to 6pm. Ballroom is held on Saturdays and tango on Sundays, with lessons for novices at 1pm.

Carnival del Pueblo
Various locations from City Hall to Burgess Park (www.carnavaldelpueblo.co.uk). Elephant & Castle tube/rail. **Date** 1st wknd of Aug.

This vibrant outdoor parade and festival is more than just a loud-and-proud day out for South American Londoners: it attracts people from all walks of life (60,000 in 2009) looking to inject a little Latin spirit into the weekend.

Great British Beer Festival

Earl's Court Exhibition Centre, Warwick Road, SW5 9TA (01727 867201, www.camra.org.uk). Earl's Court tube. **Date** 3-7 Aug. **Map** p396 A11.
Real ale is the star at this huge event devoted to British brews, including cider and perry (a pear cider). Foreign beers and lagers get a look-in at what's been called 'the biggest pub in the world'.

London Mela

Gunnersbury Park, Ealing, W3 (7387 1203, www.londonmela.org). Acton Town or South Ealing tube. **Date** mid Aug.
Thousands flock to west London for this exuberant celebration of Asian culture, dubbed the Asian Glastonbury. You'll find urban, classical and experimental music, circus, dance, visual arts, comedy, children's events, and great food. *Photos p272.*

★ Notting Hill Carnival

Notting Hill, W10, W11 (7727 0072, www.the nottinghillcarnival.com). Ladbroke Grove, Notting Hill Gate or Westbourne Park tube. **Date** 29-30 Aug. **Map** p394 A6.
Two million people stream in to Notting Hill to Europe's largest street party, full of the smells, colours and music of the Caribbean. Massive sound systems dominate, but there's tradition, too: calypso and a spectacular parade.
▶ *For sightseeing in Notting Hill, see p104.*

Great River Race

River Thames, from Ham House, Richmond, Surrey TW10, to Island Gardens, Isle of Dogs, E14 (8398 9057, www.greatriverrace.co.uk). **Date** 5 Sept.
The alternative Boat Race (*see p272*) is much more fun, with an exotic array of around 300 traditional rowing boats from across the globe racing the 22 miles from Richmond to Greenwich. Hungerford Bridge, the Millennium Bridge and Tower Bridge all provide good viewpoints.

Mayor's Thames Festival

Between Westminster Bridge & Tower Bridge (7928 8998, www.thamesfestival.org). Waterloo tube/rail or Blackfriars rail. **Date** mid Sept. **Map** p404 N7.
A giant end-of-the-season party along the River Thames, this is the largest free arts festival in London. It's a spectacular and family-friendly mix of carnival, pyrotechnics, art installations, river events and live music alongside craft and food stalls. The highlight is the last-night lantern procession and firework finale.

London Fashion Week

Somerset House, WC2R 1LA (7759 1999, www.londonfashionweek.co.uk). Embankment tube or Charing Cross tube/rail. **Date** Sept.
The biannual showcase (it returns each February) embellishes London's reputation for cutting-edge street style and sartorial innovation. Until recently, it was considered the least significant of the big four trade shows, behind New York, Milan and Paris. Not any more. But in 2009, its 25th anniversary was celebrated with a new principal venue (Somerset House; *see p90*) and renewed energy: Vivienne Westwood, Luella Bartley and Burberry returned, alongside more recent stars such as Christopher Kane and Peter Jensen.

Skyride

www.londonfreewheel.com. **Date** 3rd Sun of Sept.
Held annually since 2007, this cycling festival is very popular: last year, nearly 50,000 people rode the main traffic-free route from Buckingham Palace to the Tower and a number of subsidiary routes, enjoying music, the car-less roads and the chance to meet Olympic cyclists along the way. *Photos p277.*
▶ *For cycle hire in London, see p333.*

★ Open House London

3006 7008, www.openhouse.org.uk. **Date** 18-19 Sept.
Londoners' favourite opportunity to snoop round other people's property: palaces, private homes, corporate skyscrapers, pumping stations, bomb-proof bunkers et al, many of which are normally closed to the public. Along with the building openings, there's a programme of debates on architecture, plus the 20-mile London Night Hike.
▶ *For more on architecture, see pp34-41.*

Brick Lane Festival

www.bricklanefestival.co.uk. Algate East tube. **Date** late Sept.
Diners, dancers and musicians spill on to the streets during this display of Brick Lane's vivid cultural diversity. Alongside a live music marathon, the street's plethora of Indian restaurants create special menus for the event.

INSIDE TRACK
TRAFALGAR SQUARE

Among ex-mayor Ken Livingstone's most popular initiatives was pedestrianising the north side of Trafalgar Square, and then programming almost weekly events in it. Even under budget-slashing Boris, expect all kinds of entertainment here – music, film, theatre, dance – and usually for free. For details, check www.london. gov.uk/trafalgarsquare.

ARTS & ENTERTAINMENT

Great Gorilla Run
Mincing Lane, the City, EC3 (7916 4974, www.greatgorillas.org/london). Monument or Tower Hill tube, or Fenchurch Street rail. **Date** 25 Sept. **Map** p405 R7.
Go ape with a 1,000-strong pack of gorilla-suited runners, who take on a 7km course through the City in aid of gorilla conservation.

Pearly Kings & Queens Harvest Festival
St Martin-in-the-Fields, Trafalgar Square, Westminster, WC2N 4JJ (7766 1100, www. pearlysociety.co.uk). Leicester Square tube or Charing Cross tube/rail. **Date** late Sept/early Oct. **Map** p407 Y4.
London's Pearlies assemble for their annual thanksgiving service dressed in spangly (and colossally heavy) Smother Suits covered in hundreds of pearl buttons. The sensational outfits evolved from Victorian costermongers' love of decorating their clothes with buttons.

OCTOBER-DECEMBER
Along with the launch of the Turner Prize, the **Frieze Art Fair** and **Zoo** (for both, *see p298* **Festivals**) are huge art events. The **London Film Festival** (*see p293* **Festivals**) takes place in October, and this is also the season for the **London Jazz Festival** (*see p319* **Festivals**) and the winter instalment of the **Spitalfields Festival** (*see p310* **Festivals**).

Big Draw
8351 1719, www.campaignfordrawing.org. **Date** 1-31 Oct.
Engage with your inner artist at the Big Draw, a nationwide frenzy of drawing using anything from pencils to vapour trails. The British Library's Big Picture Party brings out heavy hitters such as Quentin Blake, a festival patron.

London to Brighton Veteran Car Run
Serpentine Road, Hyde Park, W2 2UH (01327 856024, www.lbvcr.com). Hyde Park Corner tube. **Date** 1st Sun of Nov. **Map** p395 E8.
A sedate procession of around 500 pre-1905 cars. The first pair trundles off at sunrise (7am-8.30am), but you can catch them a little later crossing Westminster Bridge or view them in repose on a closed-off Regent's Street the day before (11am-3pm).

Diwali
Trafalgar Square, WC2 (7983 4100, www.london.gov.uk). Charing Cross tube/rail. **Date** 5 Nov. **Map** p407 X5.
A vibrant celebration of the annual Festival of Light by London's Hindu, Jain and Sikh communities. There are fireworks, food, music and dancing.

Standing on Ceremony
Nowhere does pomp and circumstance better than London.

On alternate days from 10.45am (see www.changing-the-guard.com/sched.htm for details), one of the five Foot Guards regiments lines up in scarlet coats and tall bearskin hats in the forecourt of Wellington Barracks; at exactly 11.27am, the soldiers start to march to Buckingham Palace (*see p117*), joined by their regimental band, to relieve the sentries there in a 45-minute ceremony for the **Changing of the Guard**.

Not far away, at Horse Guards Parade in Whitehall, the Household Cavalry mount the guard daily at 11am (10am on Sunday). Although this ceremony isn't as famous as the one at Buckingham Palace, it's a little more visitor-friendly: the crowds aren't as thick here as they are at the palace, and spectators aren't held far back from the action by railings. After the old and new guard have stared each other out in the centre of the parade ground, you can nip through to the Whitehall side to catch the departing old guard perform their hilarious dismount choreography, a synchronised,

firm slap of approbation to the neck of each horse before the gloved troopers all swing off.

As well as these near-daily ceremonies, London sees other, less frequent parades on a far grander scale. The most famous is **Trooping the Colour**, staged to mark the Queen's official birthday on 13 June (her real one's in April). At 10.45am, the Queen rides in a carriage from Buckingham Palace to Horse Guards Parade to watch the soldiers, before heading back to Buckingham Palace for a midday RAF flypast and the impressive gun salute from Green Park.

Also at Horse Guards, on 3-4 June, a pageant of military music and precision marching begins at 7pm when the Queen (or another royal) takes the salute of the 300-strong drummers, pipers and musicians of the Massed Bands of the Household Division. This is known as **Beating the Retreat** (7414 2271, tickets 7839 5323).

Bonfire Night

Date 5 Nov & around.

Diwali pyrotechnics segue seamlessly into Britain's best-loved excuse for setting off fireworks: the celebration of Guy Fawkes' failure to blow up the Houses of Parliament in 1605. Try Battersea Park, Alexandra Palace or Victoria Park for fireworks, or pre-book a late ride on the London Eye (*see p47*).

★ Lord Mayor's Show

Through the City (7332 3456, www.lordmayors show.org). **Date** 13 Nov.

This big show marks the traditional presentation of the new Lord Mayor for approval by the monarch's justices. The Lord Mayor leaves Mansion House in a fabulous gold coach at 11am, along with a colourful procession of floats and marchers, heading to the Royal Courts of Justice (*see p60*). There he makes his vows, and is back home easily in time for afternoon tea. At 5pm, there's a fireworks display from a Thames barge. (Note that the Lord Mayor is a City officer, elected each year by the livery companies and with no real power as such; don't confuse him with the Mayor of London, Boris Johnson.)

Remembrance Sunday Ceremony

Cenotaph, Whitehall, Westminster, SW1. Charing Cross tube/rail. **Date** 14 Nov. **Map** p401 L8.

Held on the Sunday nearest to 11 November – the day World War I ended – this solemn commemoration honours those who died fighting in the World Wars and later conflicts. The Queen, the Prime Minister and other dignitaries lay poppy wreaths at the Cenotaph (*see p113*). A two minute silence at 11am is followed by a service of remembrance.

State Opening of Parliament

Palace of Westminster, Westminster, SW1A 0PW (7219 4272, www.parliament.uk). *Westminster tube.* **Date** Nov. **Map** p401 L9.

Pomp and ceremony attend the Queen's official reopening of Parliament after its summer recess. She arrives and departs in the state coach, accompanied by troopers of the Household Cavalry.

Christmas Celebrations

Covent Garden (0870 780 5001, www.covent gardenmarket.co.uk); Bond Street (www.bond streetassociation.com); St Christopher's Place (7493 3294, www.stchristophersplace.com), Marylebone High Street (7580 3163, www. marylebonevillage.com); Trafalgar Square (7983 4100, www.london.gov.uk). **Date** Nov-Dec.

Of the big stores, Fortnum & Mason (*see p242*) still creates enchantingly old-fashioned Christmas windows, and Harvey Nichols (*see p244*) usually produces show-stopping displays. Otherwise, though, skip the commercialised lights on Oxford and Regent's Streets and head, instead, for smaller shopping areas such as St Christopher's Place, Bond Street, Marylebone High Street and Covent Garden.

Skyride. *See p275.*

It's traditional to sing carols beneath a giant Christmas tree in Trafalgar Square (*see p110*) – an annual gift from Norway in gratitude for Britain's support during World War II – but you can also join in a mammoth singalong at the Royal Albert Hall (*see p310*) or an evocative carol service at one of London's historic churches. Londoners have also taken to outdoor ice-skating in a big way; *see p335.*

New Year's Eve Celebrations

Date 31 Dec.

The focus of London's public celebrations has officially moved from the traditionally overcrowded Trafalgar Square (though it's still sure to be packed) to the full-on fireworks display launched from the London Eye and rafts on the Thames. The best view is from nearby bridges, but you'll have to get there early. Otherwise, overpriced festivities in clubs, hotels and restaurants take place across the capital. Those with stamina can take in the New Year's Day Parade the next day.

ARTS & ENTERTAINMENT

Children

London offers big fun for the little ones.

With so many parks, farms and museums clamouring for their attention, kids will never get bored in London. Many key attractions, such as the **Natural History Museum** and the **Science Museum**, are free; many of those that aren't, such as the **Tower of London**, give you a lot of fun for your buck. Over-stimulation is more likely to be a problem: bustle the kids around too many landmarks and you risk sulks and tantrums.

For event listings, check the Around Town pages in *Time Out* magazine. For useful tips, visit the Mayor's site at www.london.gov.uk/young-london.

WHERE TO GO

The South Bank & Bankside (pp44-56)

There's so much to see and do here for children – just tell them to watch out for joggers and cyclists. The expensive end is around the ever popular **London Eye** (*see p47*) and, across the way, the **Sea Life London Aquarium** and the **Movieum** (for both, *see p49*). Moving east, visit the **Southbank Centre** (*see p51 and p311*) to see what's happening in the Royal Festival Hall foyer: free shows and workshops take place during holidays and weekends. Next, the **Royal National Theatre** (*see p339*) offers free entertainment during summer.

Keep going, past Gabriel's Wharf, a riverside cluster of shops and restaurants, towards the Millennium Bridge, where **Tate Modern** (*see p55*) looms large. Try the gallery trails and browse books in the Family Zone or take part in an event at the Bloomberg Learning Zone on Level Five. (If you're up for more art, there's a boat service to **Tate Britain**, *see p116*.)

Once you've emerged, pick up the Bankside Walk, ducking under the southern end of Southwark Bridge. Walk down cobbly Clink Street towards the **Golden Hinde** (*see p54*) and **Southwark Cathedral** (*see p56*), having passed the **Clink Prison Museum** (*see p53*), a cheaper alternative to the **London Dungeon** (*see p56*). From Tooley Street, march through Hays Galleria to regain the riverside path, which takes you to the warship museum **HMS Belfast** (*see p57*) and on, past the dancing

fountains to **City Hall** (*see p57*) and **Tower Bridge** (*see p72*).

The City (pp57-71)

It seems pricey, but the **Tower of London** (*see p72*) is a top day out for all ages. If it's free stuff you're after, though, look no further than the excellent **Museum of London** (*see p67*), undergoing a £20-million revamp in time for spring 2010). Lots of family events are held in school holidays, and creative workshops and storytelling sessions happen throughout the year. There are also activity sheets to guide children through the permanent exhibitions. The **Bank of England Museum** (*see p68*) is a surprising hit with bullion-obsessed youth.

Bloomsbury & Fitzrovia (pp75-80)

Children are captivated by the mummies at the **British Museum** (*see p79*). However, it's a tad overwhelming, so children may prefer the short

---

THE BEST LONDON LESSONS

For history
Tower of London. *See p72.*

For geography
Greenwich Meridian Line. *See p147.*

For English literature
Shakespeare's Globe. *See p54.*

Eyeopener family tour to a wander around the galleries. Events and workshops are often held; there are free backpacks for kids, filled with puzzles and games, as well as a range of trails. At weekends and during school holidays, Ford Centre for Young Visitors provides a family-friendly picnic-style eating area.

Central London's best playground, **Coram's Fields** (*see p283*), is close, and the **Foundling Museum** (*see p81*) next door is also worth a visit. The **Cartoon Museum** (*see p81*) holds children's workshops and family fun days every second Saturday of the month. Not far from here, **Pollock's Toy Museum** (*see p83*) is a nostalgia trip for parents, though kids will appreciate the shop. It stocks a great range of pop-up theatres as well as traditional wooden and handcrafted toys.

Covent Garden & the Strand (pp81-87)

London Transport Museum (*see p87*) is a joyful place with buses, trains and taxis that children can climb on. It has a programme of school-holiday events. For freestyle fun, the acts pulling in the crowds in front of **St Paul's Covent Garden** (*see p87*) are worth watching. On the south side of the Strand, **Somerset House** (*see p90*) allows kids to play outside among the fountains in summer, skate on the winter ice rink or attend regular art workshops.

Trafalgar Square (pp107-110)

London's central square (www.london.gov.uk/ trafalgarsquare) has been a free playground for children since time immemorial – those lions beg to be clambered on. Various festivals take place most weekends. Even if all is quiet in the Square, the **National Gallery** (*see p110*) has paper trails and audio tours, as well as regular kids' and teens' workshops and storytelling sessions for under-fives. For three- to 12-year-olds, the **National Portrait Gallery** (*see p111*) runs Family Faces art workshops and storytelling sessions once a month, as well as a range of weekend and holiday events.

Just nearby, the newly refurbished church of **St Martin-in-the-Fields** (*see p112*) has London's only brass-rubbing centre, an absorbing activity beloved by tweenies, as well as a fine café that does plenty of the type of food that goes down well with children.

South Kensington (pp121-123)

Top on any Grand Day Out itinerary is this cultural goldmine. The **Science Museum** (*see p125*) offers plenty of excitement, with six play zones for all ages, from the Garden in the basement for under-sixes to the relaunched Launchpad upstairs, where children can try some 50 experiments. Dinosaur fans won't rest until they've visited the **Natural History**

Pollock's Toy Museum.

ARTS & ENTERTAINMENT

Museum (*see p124*), but there's far more to this monster museum than prehistoric lizards. Though natural beasts may capture your attention, the real Beauty is the **Victoria & Albert Museum** (*see p126*). Its free weekend and school holiday drop-in family events (featuring trails, activity-based backpacks, and interactive workshops) provide great ways of focusing on the collection. Educational resources are available in the Sackler Centre studios and the Theatre & Performance Galleries. (Its sister gallery, Bethnal Green's **Museum of Childhood**, *see p140*, has an excellent programme of events for children.)

Greenwich (pp144-147)

Magical Greenwich provides a lovely day out away from the mayhem of the West End. Arrive by boat to appreciate its riverside charms, then take time to get the latest on the restoration work to the **Cutty Sark** (due for completion in 2011) and to explore the very child-friendly **National Maritime Museum** (*see p148*). From here it's a pleasant leg-stretch in the Royal Park for views from the very top of the hill, crowned by the spectacular **Royal Observatory & Planetarium** (*see p148*). When the stars come out, keep an eye out for the luminous green Meridian Line that cuts across the sky towards the city.

Somerset House. *See p279.*

EATING & DRINKING

Of the venues listed in the Restaurants & Cafés chapter, **Inn the Park** (*see p216*) and **Masala Zone** (*see p224* **Inside Track**) are particularly child-friendly.

Frizzante@Hackney City Farm

1A Goldsmith's Row, Hackney, E2 8QA (7739 2266, www.frizzanteltd.co.uk). Liverpool Street tube/rail then bus 26, 48, or Old Street tube/rail then bus 55. **Open** 10am-5.30pm Tue-Sun. **Main courses** £4.50-£7.50. **Credit** AmEx, DC, MC, V. A family-friendly farmhouse kitchen in the heart of Hackney. Once you've trotted around visiting pigs, poultry and sheep, you can settle down to eat their relatives (or stick to vegetarian options). The oil-cloth-covered tables heave with families tucking into healthy nosh, including farm breakfasts.
▶ *Frizzante also runs the café at the Unicorn Theatre; see p283.*

Giraffe

Riverside Level 1, Royal Festival Hall, Belvedere Road, Waterloo, SE1 8XX (7928 2004, www.giraffe.net). Embankment tube or Waterloo tube/rail. **Open** 8am-11pm Mon-Fri; 9am-11pm Sat; 9am-10.30pm Sun. **Main courses** £7.95-£14.95. **Set meal** (5-7pm Mon-Fri) £7.25 2 courses. **Credit** AmEx, MC, V. This popular branch of the global mini-chain pulls families in with balloons and babycinos. Burgers are juicy and the brunch menu lists favourites such as pancakes and eggs and bacon. The kids' lunchtime deal (noon-3pm) includes a drink and dessert for £5.75. There are several branches all over the city.
▶ *If nothing on the menu appeals, branches of noodle-bar Wagamama and pizzeria Strada are right next door.*

Mudchute Kitchen

Mudchute Park & Farm, Pier Street, Isle of Dogs, Docklands, E14 3HP (7515 5901, www.mudchute.org). Mudchute DLR. **Open** 9.30am-4.30pm Tue-Sun. **Main courses** £3-£8. **Credit** MC, V. **Map** p401 M8.

A farm fenced in by skyscrapers is an amusing place for anyone to eat lunch, but it's ideal for families. Eat at farmhouse kitchen-tables, while your babies roll around on a big futon or in the toy corner. Other distractions include the irresistible cakes.

Rainforest Café
20 Shaftesbury Avenue, Piccadilly, W1D 7EU (7434 3111, www.therainforestcafe.co.uk). Piccadilly Circus tube. **Open** noon-10pm Mon-Thur; noon-8pm Fri; 11.30am-8pm Sat; 11.30am-10pm Sun. **Main courses** £10.25-£16. **Credit** AmEx, DC, MC, V. **Map** p401 K7.
The themed restaurant is designed to thrill children with animatronic wildlife, cascading waterfalls and jungle-sound effects. The menu has lots of family-friendly fare, from 'paradise pizza' and 'Bamba's bangers' to a host of amusing dishes for grown-ups. The children's menu costs £11.50 for two courses.

★ Tate Modern Café: Level 2
Tate Modern, Sumner Street, Waterloo, SE1 9TG (7401 5014, www.tate.org.uk). St Paul's tube or Blackfriars rail. **Open** 10am-5.30pm Mon-Thur, Sat, Sun; 10am-9.30pm Fri. **Main courses** £6.95-£10.50. **Credit** AmEx, MC, V. **Map** p404 O7.
In addition to views from the windows framing the busy Thames, there are literacy and art activities on the junior menu, handed out with a pot of crayons. Children can choose haddock fingers with chips, pasta bolognese with parmesan or macaroni cheese bake, with an ice-cream or fruit salad, for £4.95; a free kids' main is offered when an adult orders a main from the regular menu. There is also a range of half-price dishes from the adult menu.

TGI Friday's
6 Bedford Street, Covent Garden, WC2E 9HZ (7379 0585, www.tgifridays.co.uk). Covent Garden tube or Charing Cross tube/rail. **Open** 11am-11.30pm Mon-Sat; noon-11pm Sun. **Main courses** £6.95-£17. **Credit** AmEx, MC, V. **Map** p401 L7.
The cheery staff, handing out balloons and crayons, are on a mission to make children welcome. The food is varied, but veers towards barbecues, Tex-Mex dishes, burgers and chips. The children's menu has all the fried regulars, but also pasta dishes and fruity sundaes for pudding – or dirt and worm pie for chocolate fiends.

That Place on the Corner
1-3 Green Lanes, Stoke Newington, N16 9BS (7704 0079, www.thatplaceonthecorner.co.uk). Canonbury rail then bus 73, 141, 341. **Open** 10.30-6pm Mon-Thur; 10.30-8pm Fri; 10.30am-2.30pm Sat, Sun. **Main courses** £4.85-£8.25. **Credit** MC, V. **Map** p401 L7.
London's only child-friendly café that won't let in unaccompanied grown-ups. There's a library, play

Camley Street Natural Park *See p282.*

shop and dressing-up corner, as well as baking, dance and music classes. The menu sticks to the trusted pasta/panini/big breakfast formula, with brasserie staples like fish cakes.

ENTERTAINMENT
City farms & zoos

There's always something new at ZSL **London Zoo** (*see p102*); the interactive Animal Adventure children's zoo opened recently, as well as the wonderful Blackburn Pavilion for exotic birds. The admission charge seems high, but there's loads to do. Easier on the budget is the adorable **Battersea Park Children's Zoo** (www.batterseaparkzoo. co.uk), where ring-tailed lemurs, giant rabbits, inquisitive meerkats, playful otters and kune kune pigs are among the inhabitants. Activity days are held throughout the summer.

City farms all over London charge nothing to get in. Try **Freightliners City Farm** (www.freightlinersfarm.org.uk) and **Kentish Town City Farm** (www.aapi.co.uk/cityfarm) or, in the east, **Mudchute City Farm** (www.mudchute.org) and **Hackney City Farm** (www.hackneycityfarm.co.uk), both of which have cafés (for both, *see left*).

Festivals Children

What not to miss this year.

Many of London's best family-friendly festivals are held in summer. One of the best is **Watch this Space** (www.national theatre.org.uk/wts), which makes the **Royal National Theatre**'s Theatre Square the jolliest piece of astroturf in town.

Held in Hackney's **Victoria Park** in early August, the **Underage Festival** (www.under agefestivals.com) was launched a few years ago the world's first music festival aimed at under-17s. In the last couple of years, it's attracted around 7,000 teens, donning free T-shirts and grooving to the likes of Patrick Wolf, Ladyhawke and the Horrors. And now, even babies are getting into the groove, thanks to organisations such as **Babygroove** (www.babygroove.co.uk), **Baby Loves Disco** (www.babyloves disco.co.uk) and **Planet Angel** (www.planet angel.net). All of them run regular club nights and days for cutting-edge or cutting-teeth customers and their parents.

Also in mid August, the **Free Time Festival** (www.somerset-house.org.uk) is a fresh-air festival offering arts, dance, music and storytelling among the fountains in Somerset House (*see p90*). Meanwhile, **Kids Week** (www.officiallondontheatre.co.uk) livens up London's Theatreland for a fortnight, during which five- to 16-year-olds can see West End shows for free, if accompanied by a full-paying adult.

The cosy **Children's Book Week** (www.booktrust.org.uk) in early October gets libraries, schools and celebrated children's authors involved in encouraging children to read. In November, the **Children's Film Festival** (www.londonchildrenfilm.org.uk) offers a week of screenings at the **Barbican** (*see p291*); it includes the First Light Young Juries scheme, in which children aged from seven to 16 are invited to be film critics.

In the first week of February, **National Storytelling Week** (www.sfs.org.uk) presents events for tellers and listeners of all ages all across town. In the dog days of winter, there's nothing better than curling up with your thumb in your mouth to listen to a good yarn, well told. Also in February, the **Imagine** children's literature festival at the **Southbank Centre** (www.southbank centre.co.uk) includes storytelling, comedy, workshops and all sorts of other frolics across the site. Children as young as five can have great fun here.

Watch This Space.

Puppets

★ Little Angel Theatre

14 Dagmar Passage, off Cross Street, Islington, N1 2DN (7226 1787, www.littleangeltheatre.com). Angel tube or Highbury & Islington tube/rail. **Open** *Box office* 10am-6pm daily. **Tickets** £6-£12. **Credit** MC, V.

Established by John Wright in 1961, London's only permanent puppet theatre stages diverse productions, devised here or by visiting companies, that cover all aspects of puppetry. There's a Saturday Puppet Club and a Puppet Academy.

Puppet Theatre Barge

Opposite 35 Blomfield Road, Little Venice, W9 2PF (07836 202745 summer, 7249 6876 winter, www.puppetbarge.com). Warwick Avenue tube. **Open** *Box office* 10am-8pm daily. **Tickets** £10; £8.50 reductions. **Credit** AmEx, MC, V.

This intimate waterborne stage is the setting for quality puppet shows that put a modern twist on traditional tales. The barge is here between October and July; shows are held at 3pm on Saturday and Sunday, daily during school holidays. The barge also holds performances in Richmond and central London.

Science & nature

FREE Camley Street Natural Park

12 Camley Street, King's Cross, N1C 4PW (7833 2311, www.wildlondon.org.uk). King's Cross tube/rail. **Open** 10am-5pm daily. **Admission** free. **No credit cards. Map** p399 L2.

A small green space on the site of a former coal yard, Camley Street is a lovely oasis at the heart of renovated King's Cross. London Wildlife Trust's flagship reserve, it hosts pond-dipping and nature-watching for children; its wood-cabin visitor centre is used by the Wildlife Watch Club. *Photo p281.*

FREE Greenwich Peninsula Ecology Park

Thames Path, John Harrison Way, Greenwich, Greenwich, SE10 0QZ (8293 1904, www.urban ecology.org.uk). North Greenwich tube or bus 108, 161, 422, 472, 486. **Open** 10am-5pm (or dusk) Wed-Sun. **Admission** free. **No credit cards.** **Map** p399 L2.

This wetland haven on the Greenwich Peninsula is a pleasant riverside walk away from the O2. Family fun days, and all-summer play activities, such as bat-box making and den building, are part of a busy calendar of events.

Theatre

Half Moon Young People's Theatre

43 White Horse Road, Limehouse, E1 0ND (7709 8900, www.halfmoon.org.uk). Limehouse DLR/rail. **Open** Box office 10am-6pm Mon-Fri; 10am-5pm Sat. **Tickets** £5. **Credit** MC, V.

The Half Moon's inclusive policy places particular emphasis on engaging those often excluded by ethnicity and disabilities. Two studios provide a calendar of performances for children aged from six months, and kids can join one of the seven youth theatre groups (for five- to 17-year-olds).

Unicorn Theatre

147 Tooley Street, Bankside, SE1 2HZ (7645 0560, www.unicorntheatre.com). London Bridge tube/rail. **Open** Box office 9.30am-6pm Mon-Fri; 10am-6pm Sat; noon-5pm Sun. **Tickets** £10-£18; £7-£12 reductions. **Credit** MC, V. **Map** p405 Q8.

This light, bright building near Tower Bridge, with its huge white unicorn in the foyer has two performance spaces. Its small ensemble company of actors perform in all Unicorn shows and focus on an outreach programme for local children.

Theme parks

Three theme parks are within easy reach, west of London. **Legoland** (Winkfield Road, Windsor, Berks SL4 4AY, 0870 504 0404, www.legoland. co.uk) is always a hit with youngsters, with rides including the wet 'n' wild Viking's River Splash, and the extraordinary Miniland London, made of 13 million Lego bricks. **Thorpe Park** (Staines Road, Chertsey, Surrey KT16 8PN, 0870 444 4466, www.thorpepark.com) has the fastest rollercoaster in Europe, called Stealth, and the terrifying horror-movie ride, Saw; it's best for older kids and teens. And **Chessington World of Adventures** (Leatherhead Road, Chessington, Surrey KT9 2NE, 0870 444 7777,

www.chessington.com) is a gentler option. This theme park, open since the 1930s, is partly a zoo, and children can pay to be zoo keeper for a day.

Always call or check the websites for opening times, which vary throughout the year. Only Thorpe Park is open all year; the others close in November until February or March. All cost about £30-£35 per adult, with different pricing schemes for families. Arrive early in the morning to avoid the worst queues, and note that height and health restrictions apply on some rides.

SPACES TO PLAY

London's parks are great escapes for little 'uns. **Hyde Park** (*see p126*) and lovely **St James's Park** (*see p117*) are in the centre of town, but it isn't far to **Regent's Park** (*see p101*) or even **Hampstead Heath** (*see p131*).

FREE Coram's Fields

93 Guilford Street, Bloomsbury, WC1N 1DN (7837 6138, www.coramsfields.org). Russell Square tube. Apr-Sept 8am-8pm Mon-Fri; 9am-8am Sat, Sun. *Oct-Mar* 8am-dusk Mon-Fri; 9am-dusk Sat, Sun. **Admission** free (adults only admitted if accompanied by child under 16). **No credit cards.** **Map** p399 L4.

No adult can enter Coram's Fields without a child. The historic site dates to 1747, when Thomas Coram established the Foundling Hospital, but only opened as a park in 1936. It has sandpits, a paddling pool, a football pitch and a zip wire.

▶ *For the Foundling Hospital museum, see p81.*

★ FREE Diana, Princess of Wales Memorial Playground

Near Black Lion Gate, Broad Walk, Kensington Gardens, South Kensington, W8 2UH (7298 2141, www.royalparks.gov.uk). Bayswater or Queensway tube. **Open** *Summer* 10am-6.45pm daily. *Winter* 10am-dusk daily. **Admission** free; adults only admitted if accompanied by under-12s. **No credit cards.** **Map** p395 E8.

A firm favourite with young children who bring buckets and spades, as the pirate ship at its centre is moored in a sea of sand.

Discover

1 Bridge Terrace, Stratford, E15 4BG (8536 5555, www.discover.org.uk). Stratford tube/rail/ DLR. **Open** *Term-time* 10am-5pm Tue-Sun. *School holidays* 10am-5pm daily. **Admission** *Garden* free. *Story trail* £4; £3.50 reductions; free under-2s. **Credit** MC, V. **Map** p395 E8.

The UK's first creative learning centre for children is committed to promoting cultural diversity and providing learning opportunites for socially and economically disadvantaged children. The new interactive Pirates Ahoy! exhibition allows kids to find hidden treasure, explore secret caves and scrub the decks.

ARTS & ENTERTAINMENT

Comedy

What's so funny – and, more importantly, where.

London is the best city in Britain, and one of the best in the world, for comedy. New talents are constantly arriving in town, hoping for their own BBC show or – failing that – work writing for one the capital's innumerable production companies. The result is around 250 gigs a week, ranging from open-mic nights in pubs all the way up to arena tours, and a weight of competition that ensures the comedians here stay at the top of their game. Where to begin? Probably at the **Comedy Store**, the fail-safe home of alternative laughs and a must for anyone into stand-up. But the variety is great: London's comedy scene is always lively, even during the mass comedy-industry exodus to Edinburgh every August. For weekly line-ups, check *Time Out* magazine and www.timeout.com.

CENTRAL

Amused Moose Soho
Moonlighting, 17 Greek Street, Soho, W1D 4DR (7287 3727, www.amusedmoose.com). Leicester Square or Tottenham Court Road tube. **Shows** 8.30pm Sat. **Admission** £9-£12.50. **Credit** MC, V. **Map** p406 W2.
Hils Jago's rosters are invariably strong, with big names such as Bill Bailey, Noel Fielding and Eddie Izzard continuing to justify the club's multi-award-winning status. Jago has a lot of special guests who can't be named – in other words, really top names trying out new material – and runs the annual Amused Moose Laugh Offs, past finalists of which have included Jimmy Carr and Simon Amstell.
Other locations Walkabout's DownUnder Bar, 11 Henrietta Street, Covent Garden, WC2E 8PS (7287 3727); Comedy Cellar at the Washington, 50 England's Lane, Chalk Farm, NW3 4UE (7287 3727).

Comedy Camp
Barcode, 3-4 Archer Street, Soho, W1D 7AP (7483 2960, www.comedycamp.co.uk). Leicester Square or Piccadilly Circus tube. **Shows** 8.30pm Tue. **Admission** £10. **Credit** MC, V. **Map** p406 W3.
This intimate, straight-friendly gay club in Soho is one of the best nights out anywhere in town. The audiences are always up for a big evening, and resident host and promoter Simon Happily only books fabulous acts.

★ Comedy Store
1A Oxendon Street, Soho, SW1Y 4EE (0844 847 1728, www.thecomedystore.co.uk). Leicester Square or Piccadilly Circus tube. **Shows** phone for details Mon; 8pm Tue-Thur, Sun; 8pm & midnight Fri, Sat. **Admission** £15.25-£17.50; £8 reductions. **Credit** AmEx, MC, V. **Map** p406 W4.
Alternative line-ups at this, the daddy of British comedy clubs, helped launched esteemed jokers such as Alexei Sayle, Dawn French and Paul Merton. The legendary gong show, in which would-be stand-ups are given as much time on stage as the audience will allow, is on the last Monday of the month.

Funny Side of Covent Garden
Corner Store, 33-35 Wellington Street, Covent Garden, WC2E 7BN (0870 446 0616, www.the funnyside.info). Covent Garden tube. **Shows** 8pm Wed-Sat; 7.30pm Sun. **Admission** £12.50. **Credit** AmEx, MC, V. **Map** p407 Z3.
This medium-sized club hosts comedy five nights a week in the basement of a decent bar. It's one of the nicer rooms in which to watch comedians, and you can nearly always be certain of a cracking line-up of well-established acts.
Other locations Downstairs at the Spectator, 6 Little Britain, the City, EC1A 7BX.

Just the Tonic
Leicester Square Theatre, 6 Leicester Place, Leicester Square, WC2H 7BX (0844 847 2475, www.justthetonic.com). Leicester Square tube.

Shows 7.30pm Fri, Sat. **Admission** £12.50. **Credit** AmEx, MC, V. **Map** p407 X4.

Darrell Martin's London outpost of the acclaimed Nottingham comedy fixture never fails to deliver a cracking night of top-flight comics.

Lowdown at the Albany
240 Great Portland Street, Marylebone, W1W 5QU (7387 5706, www.lowdownatthealbany. com). Great Portland Street tube. **Shows** times vary. **Admission** £6-£10. **No credit cards. Map** p398 H4.

This rough-around-the-edges basement venue is a simple set-up that hosts stand-up, sketch shows and the odd play. It's great for Edinburgh previews.

★ Soho Theatre
For listings, *see p346.*

The Soho Theatre has become one of the best places in London to see comics break out of their normal club sets to perform more substantial solo shows. There's always a good mix of home-grown and international talent on display.

NORTH LONDON

Downstairs at the King's Head
2 Crouch End Hill, Crouch End, N8 8AA (8340 1028, www.downstairsatthekingshead.com). Finsbury Park tube/rail then W7 bus. **Shows** 8.30pm Tue, Thur, Sat, Sun. **Admission** £4-£10. **No credit cards.**

Founded in 1981, this venue is still run with huge enthusiasm by immensely knowledgeable promoter Pete Grahame. It's an easy-going, comfortable place where comedians can experiment and play around

with complete freedom. It's popular with comics wanting to do warm-up shows for TV and tours.

★ Hen & Chickens
109 St Paul's Road, Highbury Corner, Islington, N1 2NA (7704 2001, www.henandchickens.com). Highbury & Islington tube/rail. **Shows** times vary. **Admission** £5.50-£12. **No credit cards.**

This dinky theatre, located above a cosy Victorian corner pub, is well known as the best place to see great solo shows, especially from big-name comics warming up for a tour. Past acts include the likes of Jimmy Carr, Frankie Boyle and Rhona Cameron.

EAST LONDON

Comedy Café
66-68 Rivington Street, Shoreditch, EC2A 3AY (7739 5706, www.comedycafe.co.uk). Liverpool Street or Old Street tube/rail. **Shows** 9pm Wed, Thur; 8pm Fri; 8.30pm Sat. **Admission** free Wed; £8 Thur; £10 Fri; £15 Sat. **Credit** MC, V. **Map** p403 R4.

The Comedy Café is another purpose-built club set up by a comedian. Noel Faulkner mainly keeps to the back room now but, with the emphasis on inviting bills and satisfied punters, his influence can still be felt. The atmosphere is fun and, as the name suggests, food is an integral part of the experience.

Theatre Royal Stratford East
For listings, *see p316.*

A gem of a comedy night is held here every Monday at 8pm, and it's free. The gig, which takes place in the long bar upstairs, has great line-ups, especially considering you're not paying a penny.

Comedy Café.

ARTS & ENTERTAINMENT

SOUTH LONDON

Banana Cabaret

Bedford, 77 Bedford Hill, Balham, SW12 9HD (8682 8940, www.bananacabaret.co.uk). Balham tube/rail. **Shows** 9pm Fri, Sat. **Admission** £13, £9 reductions Fri; £16, £13 reductions Sat. **Credit** MC, V.

Satisfaction is pretty much guaranteed every Friday and Saturday at this exciting, long-running club in the big roundhouse setting of the Bedford Arms pub in Balham. A safe bet.

Jongleurs Battersea

The Rise, 49 Lavender Gardens, Clapham, SW11 1DJ (0844 499 4060, www.jongleurs.com). Clapham Junction rail. **Shows** 9pm Fri, Sat. **Admission** £14-£17. **Credit** AmEx, MC, V.

Established back in 1983, this is the flagship branch of the countrywide Jongleurs chain, a chain with an unashamedly business-like approach to comedy. In other words, you get many of the biggest names on the circuit, but you also get boozed-up punters who would laugh at anything.

Other locations 11 East Yard, Chalk Farm, NW1 8AB (0844 499 4064).

Up the Creek

302 Creek Road, Greenwich, SE10 9SW (8858 4581, www.up-the-creek.com). Greenwich DLR/ rail. **Shows** 9pm Fri; 8.30pm Sat. **Admission** £10, £6 reductions Fri; £15, £12 reductions Sat. **Credit** MC, V.

Set up by the late and legendary Malcolm Hardee ('To say that he has no shame is to drastically exaggerate the amount of shame he has,' quipped one critic several years ago), this purpose-built club has been around since the 1990s, and is still one of the best places to see live comedy. It's renowned for its lively, bearpit atmosphere.

WEST LONDON

Headliners

George IV, 185 Chiswick High Road, Chiswick, W4 2DR (8566 4067, www.headlinerscomedy. com). Turnham Green tube. **Shows** 9pm Fri, Sat. **Admission** £12. **No credit cards.**

The only purpose-built club in west London has the experienced Simon Randall at the helm, who also runs Ha Bloody Ha. In late 2009, Randall was looking to open a second space to replace Headliners' previous gigs at Ealing Studios.

Stand Up to Be Counted

Meet Jack Whitehall, one of London's fastest-rising stand-ups.

Jack Whitehall won the Amused Moose New Act of the Year 2007 at Edinburgh. His *Nearly Rebellious* show was nominated for Best Edinburgh Newcomer 2009 and later transferred to London.

TO (Time Out): Age?
JW (Jack Whitehall): 21. Born on 7/7/88, which means I really hate radical Islam!

TO: Describe yourself in no more than 50 words.
JW: A comic who's constantly being prefixed with the word 'young', which means, what with the linear temporal nature of existence, in about six years, I'm fucked. I'll need a new gimmick. Maybe I'll black up.

TO: Nicest thing a reviewer has said about you?
JW: All the lovely things in *Time Out*. An unhinged fan on the internet once said she'd take a bullet for me. *Heat* once called me 'cute', the accolade all comics strive for.

TO: Worst thing a reviewer has said about you?
JW: A woman once wrote she'd rather stick needles in her eyes than watch me, which is little harsh. Unless she's a heroin addict looking for an entry point, in which case I'll take it as a compliment.

TO: What gets you in the mood to be funny?
JW: The trailer to *Con Air* gets me pumped. It's my psych-up music!

TO: What's the most memorable heckle you've ever received?
JW: Student from Warrington University: 'Shut up! Get on with your jokes. I came here because of the comedy.' Me: 'No you didn't. You came here 'cause you fucked up your A-levels.' Student: something aggressive that's too rude to print.

TO: What's your biggest fear?
JW: Silence. And violence from an audience member.

Dance

The scene just keeps on moving

London's dance culture is based on strong traditions, and is sometimes thought of as lagging a little behind the cutting edge. However, there's a lot of invention here. Many choreographers here feed off the unbridled creativity for which London is renowned, while others use the vibrant cross-cultural pollinations that are part and parcel of the city. Even the 79-year-old Royal Ballet is producing groundbreaking new work at present, thanks to resident choreographer Wayne McGregor. And there are plenty of chances to get moving yourself. Look out, especially, for the city's tea dances and old-time balls, inspired in part by the success of TV series *Strictly Come Dancing*.

For information on upcoming events and classes, pick up *Time Out* magazine or see www.timeout.com/london/dance.

ARTS & ENTERTAINMENT

DANCE COMPANIES

Although the **Rambert Dance Company** (www.rambert.org.uk) has been around since before World War II, a regular turnover of great dancers and new works keeps the troupe fresh, and its programmes of contemporary dance are always accessible. Another popular name is **Matthew Bourne** (www.new-adventures.net), who reimagines classic tales (from *Swan Lake* to *Edward Scissorhands*) with great sets and plenty of humour. On a smaller scale, comedy takes a central role for the **New Art Club** (www.newartclub.org), a duo whose work lies between contemporary dance, theatre and stand-up. The career of **Michael Clark** (www.michaelclarkcompany.com) has had its controversial moments, but he's now reconciled his classical roots with his punk spirit.

New ballet companies don't come along that often, but two new arrivals look like they're here to stay. Based in London and New York, Christopher Wheeldon's **Morphoses** (www.morphoses.org) perform regularly in the city. And the small group of dancers who make up **Ballet Black** (www.balletblack.co.uk), the UK's first black and Asian ballet company, are as happy playing a room above a pub as they are at the Royal Opera House.

About the author

Lyndsey Winship is the dance editor of Time Out *magazine.*

Many London choreographers absorb cross-cultural influences into their work. **Shobana Jeyasingh** (www.shobanajeyasingh.co.uk), **Akram Khan** (www.akramkhancompany.net) and Nina Rajarani's **Srishti** (www.srishti.co.uk) all work to varying degrees with South Asian dance, while Zimbabwean **Bawren Tavaziva** (www.tavazivadance.com) is one of several figures in the city adding African dance to the melting pot.

MAJOR VENUES

Barbican Centre

For listings, see p308.

Conceived in the 1960s and completed in 1982, the Barbican attracts and nurtures experimental dance, especially in the perfectly intimate Pit Theatre. The year-round Barbican International Theatre Events

ARTS & ENTERTAINMENT

Let's Get Physical

It is dance, it just doesn't have all that much dancing.

The blurring of the boundaries separating dance from physical theatre and performance art is nothing new. The late Pina Bausch made Tanztheater famous back in the 1980s, for instance. However, Britain has traditionally preferred its dance based on technique, athleticism and musical moves to the more conceptual European approach – until now. Companies such as Belgium's Les Ballets C de la B have made an impact in London both on artists and on audiences, who are opening up to boundary-blurring work that often doesn't contain much of what you'd call 'dance' at all.

Physical theatre has been presented in the UK for years by groups such as the politically pointed **DV8** (www.dv8.co.uk) and the witty **Protein Dance** (www.protein dance.co.uk), and by choreographers such as **Jasmin Vardimon** (www.jasminvardimon. com), who combines quirky characters with explosive physicality. Young names to look out include **Maresa von Stockert** (www. tilted.org.uk), **Lost Dog** (www.lostdog dance.co.uk) and **MIKS** (www.miks.org.uk)

Outside these confines, other established names in British dance have been moving in a more theatrical direction.

Choreographer **Akram Khan** (www.akram khancompany.net) collaborated with actress Juliette Binoche, for example. And the big venues have started to get in on the act: Sadler's Wells recently welcomed a transfer of *I Am Falling*, a collaboration between choreographer Anna Williams and theatre director Carrie Cracknell that opened at the Gate Theatre.

'Because theatre is such an important part of our culture, we have a history that sometimes weighs us down a little,' says Alistair Spalding, the artistic director of Sadler's Wells. 'I think it's important to stop thinking in that way, that dance has got to be separate. We definitely don't want to be stuck in a dance ghetto.'

The Lilian Baylis Studio, the theatre's smaller space, has been repositioned as a home for more experimental work, presenting the likes of Dutch director Lotte van den Berg and French conceptualists Jerome Bel and Xavier Le Roy. 'Some of these artists have hardly ever been represented in London and they're quite well known in the rest of Europe, so we're playing a bit of catch-up,' says Spalding. Hopefully it shouldn't take too long to get up to speed.

series (BITE; www.barbican.org.uk/theatre) offers plenty of noteworthy dance performances.

★ Place
17 Duke's Road, Bloomsbury, WC1H 9PY (7121 1100, www.theplace.org.uk). Euston tube/rail.
Box office noon-6pm Mon-Sat; noon-8pm on performance days. **Tickets** £5-£15. **Credit** MC, V. **Map** p401 K3.
For genuinely emerging dance, look to the Place. The theatre is behind the Place Prize for choreography, which rewards the best in British contemporary dance as well as regular seasons of new work such as Resolution! (short works; Jan/Feb) and Spring Loaded (Apr/May).

★ Royal Opera House
For listings, see p311.
For the full ballet experience, nothing beats the Royal Opera House, home of the Royal Ballet. The current incarnation of the building is an appropriately grand space in which to see the likes of Carlos Acosta. Tours of the building sometimes take in a ballet rehearsal. There's edgier fare in the Linbury Studio Theatre and the Clore Studio Upstairs.

★ Sadler's Wells
Rosebery Avenue, Finsbury, EC1R 4TN (0844 412 4300, www.sadlerswells.com). Angel tube.
Box office *In person* 9am-8.30pm Mon-Sat. *By phone* 24hrs daily. **Tickets** £10-£60. **Credit** AmEx, MC, V. **Map** p404 N3.
Purpose-built in 1998 on the site of a 17th-century theatre of the same name, this dazzling complex is home to impressive local and international performances. The smaller Lilian Baylis Studio offers smaller-scale new works and works-in-progress, and the Peacock Theatre (on Portugal Street in Holborn) operates as a satellite venue. A specially chartered bus departs after each performance to Farringdon, Victoria and Waterloo stations.

Siobhan Davies Dance Studios
85 St George's Road, Southwark, SE1 6ER (7091 9650, www.siobhandavies.com). Elephant & Castle tube/rail. **Box office** 9am-9pm Mon-Fri; 10am-2pm Sat, Sun. **Tickets** £3-£18. **Credit** MC, V. **Map** p404 N10.
Opened in 2006, this award-winning studio was designed in consultation with dancers, ensuring that the building met their needs. As well as being home

to Davies's own company, the studio hosts talks and performances at the more experimental end of the scale. The performance programme is sporadic, however, so check details before setting out.

Southbank Centre
For listings, see p311.
The refurbishment of the Royal Festival Hall (RFH) has led to a revival in the dance programme of the cluster of venues collectively known as the Southbank Centre: the mammoth RFH, the medium-sized Queen Elizabeth Hall, the intimate Purcell Room and the riverside terrace. The appointment in 2009 of Nicky Molloy as the new head of dance here should mean some exciting and progressive programming in the near future.

OTHER VENUES

Blue Elephant
59A Bethwin Road, Camberwell, SE5 0XT (7701 0100, tickets 0844 477 1000, www.blueelephant theatre.co.uk). Oval tube. **Box office** *In person* 1hr before performance. *By phone* 24hrs. **Tickets** £7-£12.50. **No credit cards**.
Hidden away in the wilds of south London, the Blue Elephant Theatre is a little off the beaten path. However, its accessible programme of quality contemporary dance, which runs alongside theatre and other performance, is worth seeking out.

Greenwich Dance Agency
Borough Hall, Royal Hill, Greenwich, SE10 8RE (8293 9741, www.greenwichdance.org.uk). Greenwich DLR/rail. **Box office** 9.30am-9pm Mon-Thur; 9.30am-5.30pm Fri; 10am-3pm Sat, Sun. **Tickets** £7-£15. **Credit** MC, V.
Home to resident artist Temujin Gill, of the Temujin Dance Company, and Noel Wallace, who made history as the English National Ballet's first black dancer, this fun art deco venue in Greenwich hosts classes and workshops, as well as the surely unique GDA cabaret, short bursts of dance performed among punters who are tucking into full table-service meals.

Laban Centre
Creekside, Deptford, SE8 3DZ (information 8691 8600, tickets 8469 9500, www.laban.org). Deptford DLR or Greenwich DLR/rail. **Open** 10am-6pm Mon-Sat. **Tickets** £6-£15. **Credit** MC, V.
The home of Transitions Dance Company, this beautiful independent conservatoire for dance training was founded by Rudolf Laban (1879-1958), creator of a unique and enduring discipline for movement. Designed by Herzog & de Meuron of Tate Modern fame, the premises include a 300-seat auditorium.
▶ *Also in Deptford, the Albany (Douglas Way, SE8 4AG, 8692 4446, www.thealbany.org.uk) specialises in hip hop theatre.*

Festivals Dance

What not to miss this year.

For more than 30 years, **Dance Umbrella** (Oct-Nov, www.danceumbrella.co.uk) has been the daddy of London dance festivals, staging a stimulating mix of local and international artists, established names and brand new talent across a number of London venues.

Although it's a relative newcomer to the festival calendar, **Spring Dance** (Mar-Apr, www.sadlerswells.com) is a big hitter, bringing major companies to the 2,400-seater London Coliseum (*see p311*). The line-up for 2010 features the Ballet Nacional de Cuba, among others. At the other end of the scale, the Place's **Resolution!** festival (Jan-Feb, www.theplace.org.uk) presents young choreographers, many of whom are presenting their first works. Also at the Place, the biennial **Place Prize** (Sept, www.theplaceprize.com) sees established choreographers competing against unknowns for a big-money prize.

Other festivals take a niche: the four-day, Thames-side **London International Tango Festival** (Sept, http://rivertango. co.uk), the **Flamenco Festival** (Mar, www.sadlerswells.com) and hip hop weekend **Breakin' Convention** (May, www.sadlerswells.com). If you'd rather take part, the **Big Dance** (July, www. london.gov.uk/bigdance), offers classes, workshops and performances in everything from disco to folk dance.

Film

A cosmopolitan cinema showcase.

Giant picture palaces that host red-carpet premières attended by A-list actors? Check. Cheap-as-chips repertory cinema? Right around the corner. Refurbished art deco gems? You'll find wonderful independents just out of central London, some with sofas and in-cinema bars. A world-class film festival? Every autumn. Outdoor screenings in remarkable settings, ciné clubs, film seasons devoted to every genre and national cinema under the sun? Yes, yes and yes. And it isn't until you stroll round London that you realise how often the city has played a starring role itself, with both its iconic sights (rampaging mummies at the British Museum) and characterful neighbourhoods (a floppy-haired bookseller in Notting Hill) giving visitors a visual preview of the capital. Sit back and enjoy.

ARTS & ENTERTAINMENT

WHERE TO GO

While Leicester Square has the biggest first-run cinemas, it also has the biggest prices. By contrast, the independents provide a cheaper and often more enjoyable night out.

Among the rep cinemas, **BFI Southbank** (formerly the National Film Theatre; *see p292*) gets top billing, screening seasons exploring and celebrating various genres of cinema and TV. After the BFI, London's best repertory cinema is found at the **Riverside Studios** (*see p292*), where you'll find special seasons and film events. It's also worth checking out the self-explanatory Directorspectives at the **Barbican** (*see right*).

Unexpected venues for film-viewing include the big museums and galleries, which programme film seasons linked to current exhibitions. In particular, try the **British Museum** (*see p79*), the **National Gallery** (*see p110*) and the **Imperial War Museum** (*see p143*), or **Tate Modern** (*see p55*) for avant-garde art films. The small cinemas at several luxury hotels run public screenings; among them are those at the **Soho Hotel** and **One Aldwych** (for both, *see p175*).

Outdoor summertime screens have popped up across the capital. The most glamorous is the **Somerset House Summer Screen** (www.somersethouse.org.uk/film), for which recent blockbusters and old classics are run in a magnificent Georgian courtyard, and Park Nights at the **Serpentine Gallery** (*see p126*), where you can watch films in the gallery's annual summer pavilion. The latest trend is to mix cinema with other forms of entertainment, from DJs to pub quizzes, themed fancy dress to secret locations (*see right* **Inside Track**).

A new venue in Notting Hill, **Cinéphilia West** (171 Westbourne Grove, 7792 4433, www.cinephilia.co.uk) combines every interest under one roof. Here you'll find a gallery with rare film posters, a bookshop and a café, alongside screenings and seminars.

The lowdown

Consult *Time Out* magazine's weekly listings or visit www.timeout.com/film for full details of what's on; programmes change on a Friday.

INSIDE TRACK REEL DEALS

Many first-run cinemas charge less before 5pm on weekdays; some offer cheap tickets on Monday evenings too. The **Prince Charles** (*see p292*; from £4, the earlier in the day you go, the cheaper the ticket) and the **Riverside Studios** (*see p292*; double-bills for £7.50) offer great bargains, but informal screenings can be even cheaper – the **British Museum** (*see p79*) sometimes shows movies for £3.

Films released in the UK are classified under the following categories: **U** – suitable for all ages; **PG** – open to all, parental guidance is advised; **12A** – under-12s only admitted with an over-18; **15** – no one under 15 is admitted; **18** – no one under 18 is admitted.

FIRST-RUN CINEMAS
Central London

Barbican
Silk Street, City, EC2Y 8DS (7638 8891, www. barbican.org.uk). Barbican tube or Moorgate tube/rail. **Tickets** £9.50; £4.50-£7.50 reductions; £5.50 Mon. **Screens** 3. **Credit** AmEx, MC, V. **Map** p402 P5.
The three screens at the concrete behemoth show new releases of world and independent cinema alongside an inventive range of seasons, such as the Bad Film Club and the always-excellent Directorspective strand, featuring surveys of the likes of Werner Herzog and Jacques Tati.

Curzon Cinemas
Chelsea *206 King's Road, SW3 5XP (7351 3742, tickets 0871 703 3990). Sloane Square then bus 11, 19, 22, 319.* **Screens** 1. **Map** p397 E12.
Mayfair *38 Curzon Street, Mayfair, W1J 7TY (7495 0500, tickets 0871 703 3989). Green Park or Hyde Park Corner tube.* **Screens** 2. **Map** p400 H8.
Soho *99 Shaftesbury Avenue, W1D 5DY (7292 7686, tickets 0871 703 3988). Leicester Square tube.* **Screens** 3. **Map** p407 X3.
All *www.curzoncinemas.com.* **Tickets** £7-£12; £5-£9 reductions. **Credit** MC, V.
Expect a superb range of shorts, rarities, double bills and seasons alongside new international releases at the Curzons. There's 1970s splendour in Mayfair (it's sometimes used for premières) and comfort in Chelsea, perfect for a Sunday screening after a King's Road brunch. Coolest of the bunch, the Soho outpost has a buzzing café and a decent basement bar. But the newest addition, **Hmvcurzon** (*see p292* **Inside Track**), is the most interesting development for the future of London cinema.

★ ICA Cinema
Nash House, the Mall, Westminster, SW1Y 5AH (7930 0493, tickets 7930 3647, www.ica.org.uk). Charing Cross tube/rail. **Tickets** £8; £7 reductions; £5 Mon. **Screens** 2. **Credit** MC, V. **Map** p401 K8.
London's leading contemporary arts centre (*see p118*) meets its brief not only by screening a hugely eclectic range of cinema, but by distributing some of the most noteworthy films of recent years.
▶ *Need somewhere to dissect what you've just seen? The Reel Deal gets you a very decent burger and beer in the spiffy ICA Café for just £8.*

Odeon Leicester Square
Leicester Square, WC2H 7LQ (0871 224 4007, www.odeon.co.uk). Leicester Square tube. **Tickets** £20; £7.80-£14.50 reductions. **Screens** 1. **Credit** AmEx, MC, V. **Map** p407 X4.
You'll often find the red carpets and crush barriers up outside this art deco gem – it's London's leading site for star-studded premières. If you're lucky, you might catch one of the sporadic silent film screenings, with accompaniment on a 1937 Compton organ that really does come up through the floor. Otherwise, it's big-volume mainstream hits.

Outer London

Electric Cinema
191 Portobello Road, Notting Hill, W11 2ED (7908 9696, www.electriccinema.co.uk). Ladbroke Grove or Notting Hill Gate tube. **Tickets** £7.50-£15; £7.50-£10 Mon. **Screens** 1. **Credit** AmEx, MC, V.
The Electric has gone from past-it fleapit to luscious luxury destination with leather seats and sofas, footstools and a bar inside the auditorium. It also has a fashionable brasserie next door.

Everyman & Screen Cinemas
Everyman *5 Hollybush Vale, Hampstead, NW3 6TX. Hampstead tube.* **Tickets** £12.50-£15; £7.50 reductions. **Screens** 2.
Screen on the Green *83 Upper Street, Islington, N1 0NP. Angel tube.* **Tickets** £12.50-£15; £7.50 reductions. **Screens** 2. **Map** p402 O2.
Both *0870 066 4777, www.everymancinema. com.* **Credit** MC, V.
London's most elegant cinema, the Everyman has a glamorous bar and two-seaters (£30) in its 'screening lounges', complete with foot stools and wine coolers. The Everyman now also owns three Screen cinemas, of which the Islington's Screen on the Green is the best.

ARTS & ENTERTAINMENT

★ **Phoenix**
52 High Road, East Finchley, N2 9PJ (8444 6789, www.phoenixcinema.co.uk). East Finchley tube. Tickets £6-£9; £6 reductions. Screens 1. Credit MC, V.
Built in 1910, revamped in the 1930s and currently undergoing a project to restore its art deco glory, the Phoenix offers real old-fashioned glamour. Owned by a charitable trust enjoying strong community support, it runs a varied programme including live theatre and opera transmissions.

Rio Cinema
107 Kingsland High Street, Dalston, E8 2PB (7241 9410, www.riocinema.org.uk). Dalston Kingsland rail. Tickets £6-£8; £3.50-£6 reductions. Screens 1. Credit AmEx, MC, V.
Another great deco survivor restored to its original sleek lines, the Rio is east London's finest independent. Alongside mainstream releases, the Rio is well known for its Turkish and Kurdish film festivals.

Vue Westfield London
Westfield London, Shepherd's Bush, W12 7SL (0871 224 0240, www.myvue.com). White City or Wood Lane tube, or Shepherd's Bush tube/rail. Tickets check website for details. Screens 14. Credit MC, V.
Due to open in spring 2010, the newest multiplex in town is 3D-ready and has stadium seating. Its location in a huge new shopping centre (*see p245*) should make it a good Plan B for rainy days. There's a further Vue planned for Westfield Stratford City, due to open in 2011, and Vue West End (in the north-east corner of Leicester Square) remains a key venue for London Film Festival screenings (*see right*).

REPERTORY CINEMAS

Several first-run cinemas also offer rep-style fare – check *Time Out* magazine for locations.

★ **BFI Southbank**
South Bank, SE1 8XT (7928 3535, tickets 7928 3232, www.bfi.org.uk). Embankment tube or

---

INSIDE TRACK FILM IN STORE

The small Curzon chain (*see p291*) has teamed up with HMV record shops (*see p267*) to launch the first **Hmvcurzon** in the Wimbledon HMV store (23 The Broadway, www.hmvcurzon.com) in October 2009. With its mix of mainstream and world cinema (in small screening rooms, the largest holding 103 people), film talks and a bar, it's aiming to compete with the reps and independents as much as provide an alternative to the multiplexes.

Waterloo tube/rail. Tickets £8.60; £5-£6.25 reductions; £5 Tue. Screens 3. Credit AmEx, MC, V. Map p401 M8.
With an expansion in 2007, the former National Film Theatre gained a new name, a cool bar-restaurant (from Benugo) and the Mediatheque. With its newly chic promenade-facing café-bar (also run by Benugo), the BFI is packing in crowds like never before, but the place's success is still built on excellent, thought-provoking seasons and the opportunity to see rare British and foreign films.
▶ *The Mediatheque is a room where computers and headphones give free access to the BFI's huge and illuminating film and documentary archive.*

Ciné Lumière
Institut Français, 17 Queensberry Place, South Kensington, SW7 2DT (7073 1350, www.institut-francais.org.uk). South Kensington tube. Tickets £7-£9; £5-£7 reductions; £7 Mon. Screens 1. Credit MC, V. Map p397 D10.
Ciné Lumière reopened in January 2009 with more comfortable seating and a refreshed art deco interior. No longer screening French films only, it's now a standard-bearer for world cinema in the capital.

Prince Charles
7 Leicester Place, Leicester Square, WC2H 7BY (0870 811 2559, www.princecharlescinema.com). Leicester Square tube. Tickets £4-£9.50. Screens 2. Credit MC, V. Map p407 X3.
Central and cheap, the Prince Charles sits just up an alley from the pricey Leicester Square monsters; even films on the new screen are a relative bargain. It's perfect for catching up on still-fresh films you missed first time round, and is particularly renowned for riotous singalong screenings.

★ **Riverside Studios**
Crisp Road, Hammersmith, W6 9RL (8237 1111, www.riversidestudios.co.uk). Hammersmith tube. Tickets £7.50; £6.50 reductions. Screens 1. Credit MC, V. Map p407 X3.
Regular double-bills slot between special seasons, many spotlighting Eastern European cinema. The café-bar and riverside terrace are usually packed with a voluble mix of film- and theatregoers.

IMAX

BFI IMAX
1 Charlie Chaplin Walk, South Bank, SE1 8XR (0870 787 2525, www.bfi.org.uk/imax). Waterloo tube/rail. Tickets £13.50-£15; £8.75-£11 reductions. Screens 1. Credit AmEx, MC, V. Map p401 M8.
The biggest screen supplements made-for-IMAX fare with mainstream blockbusters (either very big, or very big and in disorienting 3D) such as *Avatar*.
▶ *There's also an exhibition-themed programme at an IMAX at the Science Museum; see p125.*

Festivals Film

What not to miss this year.

There's a film festival in the capital pretty much any given week, but the **London Film Festival** (www.bfi.org.uk/lff, October) is far and away the most prestigious. Nearly 200 new British and international features are screened, mainly at BFI Southbank and Leicester Square's Vue West End. It's preceded by the delightfully left-field **Raindance Festival** (www.raindance.co.uk), which offers independent features and a terrific shorts programme.

The **London Lesbian & Gay Film Festival** (7928 3232, www.bfi.org.uk/llgff), in late March, is the UK's third largest film festival. Earlier in the month comes **Birds Eye View** (www.birds-eye-view.co.uk), a highly rated celebration of women filmmakers. Also in the spring, the **Human Rights Watch International Film Festival** (7713 2773, www.hrw.org/iff, 17-26 Mar) aims to put a human face on threats to individual freedom and dignity, while the **East End Film Festival** (www.eastendfilm festival.com, 22-29 Apr) explores cinema's great potential to cross cultural boundaries, reserving a special place for films starring London's East End.

Several festivals screen the output of a particular foreign territory. Among them are the Polish Cultural Institute's **Kinoteka** (www.kinoteka.org.uk, Mar); June's wonderful **Mosaïques** festival at the Ciné Lumière; and, in November, the **Discovering Latin America Film Festival** (www.discoveringlatinamerica.com), which offers films, documentaries and shorts that rarely get distribution, and the **Latin American Film Festival** (www.latinamerican filmfestival.com), which showcases some of the latest commercial features.

Short films are featured at the **London Short Film Festival** (www.shortfilms.org.uk) in the new year. In July, the **Rushes Soho Shorts** festival (www.sohoshorts.com) features everything from documentaries to music promos, while August's **London International Animation Festival** (www. liaf.org.uk) screens 300-plus animated shorts from around the globe. Last but by no mean least, there's the **Portobello Film Festival** (www.portobellofilmfestival.com, early Sept), which offers an eclectic programme of screenings that are all free of charge to the public.

ARTS & ENTERTAINMENT

Galleries

There's still action out east, but London's art scene continues to travel.

London's galleries may have evaded financial armageddon, but a more cautious atmosphere hangs palpably over the commercial scene. The most interesting developments have been in the non-profit sector, with **Raven Row** leading the way in Spitalfields and the **Showroom** bringing its nurturing presence to Marylebone, having been an East End stalwart for decades. For listings, check *Time Out* magazine or www.timeout.com, or the free *New Exhibitions of Contemporary Art*, available from most galleries and at www.newexhibitions.com.

FINE ART

Mayfair's reputation as prime art hunting territory has been challenged recently by the rejuvenated Fitzrovia, with **Pilar Corrias**, **Stuart Shave Modern Art** and **Gallery One One One** just minutes from one another.

Alison Jacques Gallery

16-18 Berners Street, Fitzrovia, W1T 3LN (7631 4720, www.alisonjacquesgallery.com). Goodge Street or Oxford Circus tube. **Open** 10am-6pm Tue-Sat, or by appointment. **No credit cards**. **Map** p398 J5.

Jacques shows emerging and established names such as Jon Pylypchuk and André Butzer, plus works from the estates of Robert Mapplethorpe and Hannah Wilke. In 2010, expect shows by Americans Tomory Dodge and Liz Craft.

Bloomberg Space

50 Finsbury Square, the City, EC2A 1HD (7330 7959, www.bloombergspace.com). Moorgate tube/rail. **Open** 11am-6pm Mon-Sat. **No credit cards**. **Map** p403 Q5.

Instead of simply leasing or buying art for its European HQ, Bloomberg dedicates a space within its London building to an ongoing exhibition programme of contemporary and commissioned art. 'Comma', the latest incarnation, is a lively schedule of new commissions by artists who are given the opportunity to experiment and expand their practice.

About the author

Martin Coomer writes about art for a number of publications in London and abroad, including Art Review, Big Issue *and* Time Out *magazine.*

★ Gagosian

6-24 Britannia Street, King's Cross, WC1X 9JD (7841 9960, www.gagosian.com). King's Cross tube/rail. **Open** 10am-6pm Tue-Sat. **No credit cards**. **Map** p399 M3.

Visitors flock to this vast space, part of US super-dealer Larry Gagosian's expanding empire, to see big names such as Cy Twombly, Jeff Koons and Howard Hodgkin, plus a second tier of fashionable US and European artists including Mark Grotjahn and 2009 Turner Prize nominee Richard Wright. **Other locations** 17-19 Davies Street, Mayfair, W1K 3DE (7493 3020).

Gallery One One One

111 Great Titchfield Street, Fitzrovia, W1W 6RY (7637 0868, www.davidrobertsartfoundation.com). Warren Street tube. **Open** 10am-6pm Tue-Fri; 11am-4pm Sat. **No credit cards**. **Map** p399 M3.

David Roberts is the latest in a line of collectors to start a charitable foundation and open premises in which to show their acquisitions. The programme is a mix of solo presentations and group shows organised by invited curators. In 2010, expect to see work by Damien Roach and a collaboration with the MFA Curating programme at Goldsmith's College.

Haunch of Venison

6 Haunch of Venison Yard, off Brook Street, Mayfair, W1K 5ES (7495 5050, www.haunch ofvenison.com). Bond Street tube. **Open** 10am-6pm Mon-Wed, Fri; 10am-7pm Thur; 11am-5pm Sat. **Credit** AmEx, MC, V. **Map** p398 H6.

Now owned by auction house Christie's, the Haunch has moved to palatial premises behind the Royal Academy of Arts, where it mounts shows by major names (Turner Prize winners Keith Tyson and

Richard Long), mid-career artists (Diana Thater, Zarina Bhimji) and emerging talent (Jitish Kallat). A survey of Russian art from the 1980s and '90s can be seen in 2010.

★ Hauser & Wirth London
196A Piccadilly, Mayfair, W1J 9DY (7287 2300, www.hauserwirth.com). Piccadilly Circus tube. Open 10am-6pm Tue-Sat. No credit cards. Map p406 U5.
This Swiss-owned gallery opened in 2003 in a former bank, with intact basement vaults. H&W represents big name artists including Louise Bourgeois, international names such as Anri Sala, and home-grown talents such as Martin Creed.
Other locations Hauser & Wirth Colnaghi, 15 Old Bond Street, Mayfair, W1S 4AX (7287 2300).

Jerwood Space
171 Union Street, Borough, SE1 0LN (7654 0171, www.jerwoodspace.co.uk). Borough or Southwark tube. Open noon-6pm Tue-Sun. No credit cards. Map p404 O8.
Part of a larger set-up of theatre and dance spaces (and a great café), the Jerwood had an erratic visual arts presence until recently. Now various awards, including Jerwood Contemporary Painters (21 Apr-30 May), Jerwood Contemporary Makers (17 June-25 July) and the Jerwood Drawing Prize (29 Sept-7 Nov) are grouped under the banner Jerwood Visual Arts.

Lisson
29 & 52-54 Bell Street, Marylebone, NW1 5DA (7724 2739, www.lissongallery.com). Edgware Road tube. Open 10am-6pm Mon-Fri; 11am-5pm Sat. No credit cards. Map p395 E5.
The Lisson is a superb platform for major international names, including the Lisson Sculptors: Anish

INSIDE TRACK
MAJOR COLLECTIONS

For non-commercial spaces, see the following pages:

Barbican Art Gallery p65
Courtauld Gallery p89
Design Museum p57
Dulwich Picture Gallery p145
Embankment Galleries p90
Hayward p53
ICA p118
National Gallery p110
National Portrait Gallery p111
Rivington Place p139
Royal Academy of Arts p108
Saatchi Gallery p121
Serpentine Gallery p126
Tate Britain p116
Tate Modern p55
V&A p126
Whitechapel Gallery p138

Kapoor, Tony Cragg and Richard Wentworth. 'Lisson Presents' is a new introduction to the programme, featuring work by selected artists shown alongside classics from the Lisson archive.
Other locations 29 Bell Street, Marylebone, NW1 5BY (7535 7350).

Pilar Corrias
54 Eastcastle Street, Fitzrovia, W1W 8EF (7323 7000, www.pilarcorrias.com). Oxford Circus tube. Open 10am-6pm Mon-Fri; 11am-6pm Sat. No credit cards. Map p406 V1.

ARTS & ENTERTAINMENT

176. *See p297.*

Formerly a director at the Lisson (see p295) and Haunch of Venison (see p294), Corrias opened this Rem Koolhaas-designed gallery in 2008 with a giant aluminium Christmas tree by Philippe Parreno. Look out for works by Charles Avery, as well as a rare London showing by Rirkrit Tiravanija in 2010.

★ **Sadie Coles HQ**
69 South Audley Street, Piccadilly, W1K 2QZ (7434 2227, www.sadiecoles.com). Oxford Circus or Piccadilly Circus tube. **Open** 10am-6pm Tue-Sat. **No credit cards. Map** p406 U3.
Coles represents some of the hippest artists from both sides of the Atlantic: her 2010 programme includes work by Raymond Pettibon, Matthew Barney and Andrea Zittel. A second space in nearby Balfour Mews has been used for installations by Urs Fischer and Gabriel Kuri and, in 2009, a gem of a show by the German artist Daniel Sinsel.

Showroom
63 Penfold Street, Marylebone, NW8 8PQ (7724 4300, www.theshowroom.org). Edgware Road tube. **Open** noon-6pm Wed-Sat. **No credit cards. Map** p395 E4.
In 2009, 25 years after its inception, the Showroom moved into these new premises. Its mission remains the same: to support artists at pivotal stages of their careers. New films by Emily Wardill, a collaboration with the Wispa Institute, Gdansk, and a project by Cinenova, which distributes films and videos made by women, are scheduled for 2010.

Sprüth Magers London
7A Grafton Street, Mayfair, W1S 4EJ (7408 1613, www.spruethmagers.com). Green Park tube. **Open** 10am-6pm Tue-Sat. **No credit cards. Map** p400 H7.
Fischli & Weiss, Cindy Sherman, John Baldessari and Robert Morris are just a few of the major-league international artists that have shown in this handsome gallery housed in an 18th-century building just off Old Bond Street.

Stuart Shave/Modern Art
23-25 Eastcastle Street, Fitzrovia, W1W 8DF (7299 7950, www.modernart.net). Oxford Circus tube. **Open** 11am-6pm Tue-Sat. **No credit cards. Map** p406 V1.
This always on-trend gallery shows the likes of Jonathan Meese, Matthew Monahan, Eva Rothschild and Barry McGee.

★ **White Cube**
25-26 Mason's Yard, St James's, SW1 6BU (7930 5373, www.whitecube.com). Green Park tube. **Open** 11am-6pm Tue-Sat. **Credit** AmEx, MC, V. **Map** p406 V5.
Jay Jopling's famous gallery reasserted its West End presence in 2006 with the opening of this purpose-built 5,000sq ft space. White Cube Hoxton Square

still runs an excellent programme of shows by the gallery's expanding stable, but this larger space seems designated for A-list Young British Artists, such as Tracey Emin and Jake and Dinos Chapman. **Other locations** 48 Hoxton Square, Shoreditch, N1 6PB (7930 5373).

North London

★ **Camden Arts Centre**
Arkwright Road, Finchley, NW3 6DG (7472 5500, www.camdenartscentre.org). Finchley Road tube or Finchley Road & Frognal rail. **Open** 10am-6pm Tue, Thur-Sun; 10am-9pm Wed. **Credit** MC, V.
Under the directorship of Jenni Lomax, Camden Arts Centre has eclipsed larger venues. The annual artist-curated shows – by, among others, Tacita Dean – have been among the most memorable in recent history. The Centre also hosts a comprehensive programme of talks, events and workshops and boasts a good bookshop and a great café, which opens on to a surprisingly tranquil garden.

★ **176**
176 Prince of Wales Road, Chalk Farm, NW5 3PT (7491 5720, www.projectspace176.com). Chalk Farm tube or Kentish Town West rail. **Open** 10am-6pm Tue-Sat. **Credit** MC, V.
Launched in September 2007, this former Methodist chapel – a remarkable neoclassical building – holds three shows a year, enabling artists to create experimental new work and curators to build exhibitions around the Zabludowicz Collection of global emerging art in all media. *Photo p295.*

Parasol Unit
14 Wharf Road, Islington, N1 7RW (7490 7373, www.parasol-unit.org). Angel tube or Old Street tube/rail. **Open** 10am-6pm Tue-Sat. **No credit cards. Map** p402 P3.
This former warehouse (adjacent to Victoria Miro) has been beautifully converted by architect Claudio Silverstrin into exhibition spaces on two floors and a reading area. The Unit shows work by emerging and major-league figures: in 2010, expect film by the Finnish artist Eija-Liisa Ahtila and the first London solo show for the Japanese artist Tabaimo.

Festivals Art & Design

What not to miss this year.

The main event is the **Frieze Art Fair** (14-17 Oct, www.friezeartfair.com), which sees 150 of the world's best galleries descend on Regent's Park for four days of trading and schmoozing. Held in the same time-frame, **Zoo** (www.zooartenterprises.com) features younger galleries, project and non-profit spaces and collectives, though its thunder was stolen in 2009 when Frieze announced that it too would dedicate part of its fair to emerging galleries.

Spring sees **Collect** (14-17 May, www.craftscouncil.org.uk), a contemporary applied arts fair at the Saatchi Gallery (*see p121*). The biennial **London Festival of Architecture** (19 June-4 July, www.lfa2010.org) mixes stunts and serious-minded discussions. And the **London Design Festival** (18-26 Sept, www.londondesignfestival.com) is a monster celebration of architecture and design.

May and June see London's many art schools present their degree shows. Among

the best are the two shows staged by the **Royal College of Art** (www.rca.ac.uk): the first devoted to painting and photography (28 May-6 June), the second dedicated to design (25 June-4 July). And over at the Old Truman Brewery off Brick Lane, **Free Range** (4 June-26 July, www.free-range.org.uk) is an eight-week degree show bonanza featuring dozens of colleges.

★ Victoria Miro
16 Wharf Road, Islington, N1 7RW (7336 8109, www.victoria-miro.com). Angel tube or Old Street tube/rail. **Open** 10am-6pm Tue-Sat. **Credit** MC, V. **Map** p402 P3.
A visit to this canalside, ex-Victorian furniture factory rarely disappoints. High-calibre artists on show include Chris Ofili, Peter Doig and Doug Aitken. In 2007, the gallery opened Victoria Miro 14, a sleek space next door to the original that's used for exhibitions and special projects including Grayson Perry's mammoth 'The Walthamstow Tapestry'.

East London

Hoxton Square, **Cambridge Heath Road** and **Vyner Street** are all good places to start an exploration of east London's galleries, but it's worth planning your visit carefully (*see p297* **Inside Track**). For grass-roots alternatives, head east to **Hackney Wick**, where you'll find studios and galleries such as **Elevator** (www.elevatorgallery.co.uk). Some stare demolition in the face: the area is in the shadow of the Olympics 2012 site).

★ Approach E2
1st floor, 47 Approach Road, Bethnal Green, E2 9LY (8983 3878, www.theapproach.co.uk). Bethnal Green tube or Cambridge Heath rail. **Open** 10am-6pm Tue-Sat. **No credit cards.**

Occupying an elegant former pub function room, the Approach has a reputation for showing both emerging artists and more established names such as John Stezaker, Rezi van Lankveld and Germaine Kruip, all of whom will show at the gallery in 2010.

Calvert 22
22 Calvert Avenue, Shoreditch, E2 7JP (7613 2141, www.calvert22.org). Old Street tube/rail or bus 8, 55, 67, 149, 242, 243. **Open** 10am-6pm Wed-Sat; 11am-5pm Sun. **No credit cards.** **Map** p403 R4.
London's first not-for-profit foundation specialising in art from Russia and Central and Eastern Europe, founded by Russian art collector and economist Nonna Materkova, presents three curated exhibitions a year that showcase talent from the region. Among the shows for 2010 are a survey of photography and a look at post-1990s art from the region.

Chisenhale Gallery
64 Chisenhale Road, Bow, E3 5QZ (8981 4518, www.chisenhale.org.uk). Bethnal Green or bus 8, 277, D6. **Open** 10am-6pm Tue-Sat. **No credit cards.** **Map** p403 R4.
The Chisenhale commissions up to five shows a year by emerging artists. Famous works such as Rachel Whiteread's *Ghost*, the concrete cast of a house, and Cornelia Parker's exploded shed *Cold Dark Matter* were Chisenhale commissions. A sound installation by Florian Hecker will be on show in 2010.

Flowers East

82 Kingsland Road, Hoxton, E2 8DP (7920 7777, www.flowerseast.com). Old Street tube/rail. **Open** 10am-6pm Tue-Sat. **Credit** AmEx, MC, V. **Map** p403 E3.

Flowers East might not garner the press attention of some of its neighbours, but it's an admired East End institution. It represents more than 40 artists, including Patrick Hughes, Derek Hirst and Nicola Hicks. The main gallery also houses Flowers Graphics; and there's a smaller West End space. **Other locations** Flowers Central, 21 Cork Street, Mayfair, W1S 3LZ (7439 7766).

Herald Street

2 Herald Street, Bethnal Green, E2 6JT (7168 2566, www.heraldst.com). Bethnal Green tube/rail. **Open** 11am-6pm Tue-Fri; noon-6pm Sat, Sun. **No credit cards**. **Map** p403 R4.

Herald Street shows fashionable young things such as Oliver Payne and Nick Relph, as well as work by a slightly older generation. Genre-crossing sculpture by Matthew Darbyshire and Donald Urquhart's sparky drawings are part of the 2010 programme. The gallery houses Donlon Books, selling rare and out-of-print art, photography and fashion tomes.

★ Matt's Gallery

42-44 Copperfield Road, Mile End, E3 4RR (8983 1771, www.mattsgallery.org). Mile End tube. **Open** 10am-6pm Wed-Sun; or by appointment. **No credit cards**. **Map** p403 R4.

Few galleries in town are as well respected as Matt's, named after founder/director Robin Klassnik's dog. Since 1979, Klassnik has supported artists in their often ambitious ideas for projects. Richard Wilson's sump oil installation *20:50* (now in the Saatchi Gallery) and Mike Nelson's *Coral Reef* were both Matt's commissions. Melanie Jackson, Graham Fagen and Alison Turnbull will show during 2010.

★ Maureen Paley

21 Herald Street, Bethnal Green, E2 6JT (7729 4112, www.maureenpaley.com). Bethnal Green tube/rail. **Open** 11am-6pm Wed-Sun; or by appointment. **No credit cards**. **Map** p403 R4.

Maureen Paley opened her East End gallery long before the area became the art hive it is today. The gallery represents high-profile artists such as Turner Prize winners Wolfgang Tillmans and Gillian Wearing, plus Paul Noble and sculptor Rebecca Warren. Highlights of 2010 include paintings by Londoner Kaye Donachie and work by the influential American photographer James Welling.

MOT International

54 Regents Studios, 8 Andrew's Road, Hackney, E8 4QN (7923 9561, www.motinternational.org). Bethnal Green tube or Cambridge Heath rail. **Open** 11am-6pm Wed-Sun; or by appointment. **No credit cards**. **Map** p403 R4.

Successfully making the transition from artist-run space to commercial enterprise, Chris Hammond's gallery shows rapidly emerging names including Amanda Beech, Clunie Reid and Simon Bedwell, in a fifth-floor space overlooking Regent's Canal.

★ Raven Row

56 Artillery Lane, Spitalfields, E1 7LS (7377 4300, www.ravenrow.org). Liverpool Street tube/rail. **Open** 11am-6pm Wed-Sun. **No credit cards**. **Map** p403 R5.

Occupying two stunning, 18th-century buildings in Spitalfields, Raven Row opened in 2009 with a survey of proto-Pop artist Ray Richardson, and quickly set itself up as the non-profit space to watch. The beautifully restored rooms have so far been used for cracking shows by David Hullfish Bailey and Nils Norman and a reappraisal of Eduardo Paolozzi's work for the art and literature magazine *Ambit*. There's also a residency programme.

▶ *Raven Row is the newest of the city's non-profit venues; others include Calvert 22 (see left), the Parasol Unit (see p297), the Louise T Blouin Institute (see p300) and 176 (see p297).*

Vilma Gold

6 Minerva Street, Bethnal Green, E2 9EH (7729 9888, www.vilmagold.com). Bethnal Green tube or Cambridge Heath rail. **Open** 11am-6pm Wed-Sun. **No credit cards**. **Map** p403 R4.

No longer the new kid on the block, Vilma Gold still attracts the cognoscenti who come for such fashionable fare as the neo-expressionist paintings of Sophie von Hellermann and the anti-heroic assemblages of Brian Griffiths, as well as work by international newcomers such as London-based sculptor Alexandre da Cunha.

Wilkinson Gallery

50-58 Vyner Street, Bethnal Green, E2 9DQ (8980 2662, www.wilkinsongallery.com). Bethnal Green tube or Cambridge Heath rail. **Open** 11am-6pm Wed-Sat; noon-6pm Sun; or by appointment. **No credit cards**. **Map** p403 R4.

INSIDE TRACK
DEPTFORD ART MAP

Deptford in south London has been touted as a hot new district for years, but its location has kept it low profile. A more galvanised approach to publicity occurred in 2009 with the launch of the **Deptford Art Map** (www.deptfordartmap.co.uk), a map of local galleries and studios that includes the **Agency**, a recent arrival from Shoreditch, and the evocatively named **Goth on Bus** gallery. Wander at your leisure or book for a monthly walking tour.

ARTS & ENTERTAINMENT

Anthony and Amanda Wilkinson's gallery, the first purpose-built gallery in E2, dominates Vyner Street and has an international reputation for showing high-calibre artists including the German painters Thoralf Knobloch and Matthias Weischer. Quirkier fare can be found in the first-floor project space

★ Yvon Lambert
20 Hoxton Square, Shoreditch, N1 6NT (7729 2687, www.yvon-lambert.com). Old Street tube/rail. **Open** 10am-6pm Mon-Sat. **No credit cards. Map** p403 R3.
This former warehouse (adjacent to Victoria Miro, *see below*) has been beautifully converted by architect Claudio Silverstrin into exhibition spaces on two floors and a reading area. The Unit shows work by emerging and major-league figures: in 2009, expect works by Robert Mangold and a group show themed around parades and processions.

South London

Corvi-Mora/Greengrassi
1A Kempsford Road, Kennington, SE11 4NU (Corvi-Mora 7840 9111, Greengrassi 7840 9101, www.corvi-mora.com, www.greengrassi. com). Kennington tube. **Open** 11am-6pm Tue-Sat. **No credit cards.**
These two galleries share a building that comprises a warehouse space on the ground floor and a smaller gallery upstairs. Greengrassi's artists include painters Lisa Yuskavage and Tomma Abts; among those on show in 2010 are Vincent Fecteau and Stefano Arienti. Jim Isermann, Tomoaki Suzuki and Dee Ferris are part of Corvi-Mora's eclectic stable.

South London Gallery
65 Peckham Road, Peckham, SE5 8UH (7703 9799, www.southlondongallery.org). Oval tube then bus 436 bus, or Elephant & Castle tube/rail then bus 12, 171. **Open** noon-6pm Tue-Sun. **No credit cards.**
See p144 **Overground to the Underground.**

West London

Louise T Blouin Institute
3 Olaf Street, Shepherd's Bush, W11 4BE (7985 9600, www.ltbfoundation.org). Latimer Road tube. **Open** 10am-6pm Tue, Wed, Fri; 10am-9pm Thur. **Admission** £5; £3 reductions. **Credit** MC, V.
Head of the LTB Group of Companies, Louise T Blouin MacBain opened this non-profit space in 2006 over three storeys of a 1920s coachworks. The Institute has galleries, a conference centre, a cinema and a café. Experimentation, debate and learning are key principles, with crossovers between politics, science, art and design the subject of regular events. A highlight of 2009 was a still voy of the great American sculptor Louise Nevelson.

ARCHITECTURE & DESIGN

Architectural Association
36 Bedford Square, Fitzrovia, WC1B 3ES (7887 4000, www.aaschool.net). Tottenham Court Road tube. **Open** 9am-5pm Mon, Wed-Fri; 9am-9pm Tue; 9am-5pm Sat. **Credit** MC, V. **Map** p399 K5.
Talks, events, exhibitions: three good reasons for visiting these elegant premises. The café makes that four. During the summer months, the gallery shows work by students graduating from the AA School in a display that often spills into the square.

Royal Institute of British Architects
66 Portland Place, Marylebone, W1B 1AD (7580 5533, www.architecture.com). Great Portland Street tube. **Open** 9.30am-5.30pm Tue-Fri; 10am-1pm Sat. **Credit** MC, V. **Map** p398 H5.
Temporary exhibitions such as the annual Housing Design Awards are held in RIBA's Grade II-listed headquarters, which houses a bookshop, a first-floor café and one of the finest architectural libraries in the world. It also hosts an excellent lecture series.

PHOTOGRAPHY

Michael Hoppen Gallery
3 Jubilee Place, Chelsea, SW3 3TD (7352 4499, www.michaelhoppengallery.com). Sloane Square tube. **Open** noon-6pm Tue-Fri; 10.30am-5pm Sat; or by appointment. **Credit** MC, V. **Map** p397 E11.
This three-storey space in Chelsea shows a mixture of classic vintage photography by the likes of Garry Winogrand and William Klein, and contemporary work, including Japanese photographer Nobuyoshi Araki.

★ Photographers' Gallery
16-18 Ramillies Street, Soho, W1A 1AU (0845 262 1618, www.photonet.org.uk). Oxford Circus tube. **Open** 11am-6pm Tue-Wed, Sat, Sun; 11am-8pm Thur, Fri. **Credit** AmEx, DC, MC, V. **Map** p406 U2.
Home of the £30,000 Deutsche Börse Photography Prize (5 Feb-10 Apr), this gallery hosts a diverse range of exhibitions and events. In late 2008, the gallery, along with its café and shop, to this transitionary space, which will be redeveloped from mid 2010 until 2011. The gallery will continue to programme shows and events around the Soho area during this time.

INSIDE TRACK BUILT TO LAST

New London Architecture (26 Store Street, WC12E 7BT 7636 4044, www.new londonarchitecture.org), which features excellent exhibitions on urban planning as well as a 12-metre 3D model of London.

Gay & Lesbian

London's queer scene is still very much in the pink.

Sydney's got the sun, New York City and San Francisco have the history and Rio's got the bodies, but – right now, at least – London's got the buzz. Whatever your taste in music, from thunderous indie to thumping disco, you'll find a gay club that specialises in it, on a nightlife scene that runs around the clock and throughout the week. Add in an array of cabaret nights and literary salons, a handful of cafés and restaurants, a major gay and lesbian film festival and the ever-popular annual Pride celebration, and there should be something to keep you busy.

THE GAY SCENE IN LONDON

Roughly speaking, London's gay scene is split into three distinct zones: **Soho**, **Vauxhall** and **east London**. Each of these three districts has its own character: in a nutshell, Soho is the most mainstream, Vauxhall is the the most decadent and east London is the most outré.

Centred on Old Compton Street, the Soho scene continues to attract the crowds. Luvvies take in a singalong at the **Green Carnation**, fit freaks work out at **Sweatbox** and everyone else mills around the plethora of gay-slanted bars and cafés. And just down the road, close to Charing Cross station, sits the legendary **Heaven**, home to **G-A-Y**. If your dream has always been to see Madonna or Kylie in a club, here's your chance – the list of singers who've done live PAs here reads like a *Who's Who* of squeal-tastic gay pop icons.

Down south, Vauxhall is more hedonistic. You could arrive in London on a Friday evening and dance non-stop here for an entire weekend before flying out of town again. But it's not all about going wild: venues such as the **RVT** and the **Eagle** draw loyal local followings.

The most alternative and creative of the capital's queer scenes is in east London. In the likes of the **George & Dragon** and the **Dalston Superstore**, you'll be rubbing shoulders with fashion and music's movers and shakers, to soundtracks built by ferociously underground DJs. With so much coolness going on, it can get a little snooty, but a lot of the bars and clubs round Shoreditch and Dalston are also properly mixed, which makes the area ideal for night out with straight mates.

Keen to cut to the chase? **Chariots** remains the sauna chain of choice, although **Vault 139** and **Pleasuredrome** (Arch 124, Cornwall Road, 7633 9194, www.pleasuredrome.com) also have their followers. Most regular bars don't have backrooms, but some club nights in Vauxhall can get raunchy. The monthly **Hard On** (www.hardonclub.co.uk) is the top pick on the calendar for lovers of fetish and leather.

For lesbians, the clubby **Candy Bar** (4 Carlisle Street, W1D 3BJ, 7287 5041, www.candybarsoho.com) operates in Soho under new management, **First Out** café is jammed with gals and the women-only **Glass Bar**, having survived threats of closure, is back in vogue. New stand-alone nights pop up all the time, with **Mannequin Social** one current fave.

RESTAURANTS & CAFES

More or less every café and restaurant in London welcomes gay custom, though some do so more than others. Nowhere in or around Soho is going to bat an eyelid at you and your other half having a romantic dinner; in particular, **J Sheekey** (*see p205*), the **Wolseley** (*see p216*), **Quo Vadis** (*see p92*), **Arbutus** (*see p207*) and **Wild Honey** (*see p216*) all have particularly enthusiastic gay followings.

Balans

60 Old Compton Street, Soho, W1D 4UG (7439 2183, www.balans.co.uk). Leicester Square or Piccadilly Circus tube. **Open** 8am-5am Mon-Thur; 8am-6am Fri, Sat; 8am-2am Sun. **Admission** £5 after midnight Mon-Thur; £7 Fri, Sat. **Credit** AmEx, MC, V. **Map** p406 W3.
The gay café-restaurant of choice for many years, Balans is all about location, location, location (plus hot waiters, decent food and ridiculous opening hours). Situated across from Compton's bar and next door to Clone Zone, it's the beating heart of the Soho scene. The nearby Balans Café (no.34) serves a shorter version of the menu. Both are open almost all night and are good for a post-club bite.
Other locations 239 Old Brompton Road, Earl's Court, SW5 9HP (7244 8838); 187 Kensington High Street, Kensington, W8 6SH (7376 0115); 214 Chiswick High Road, Chiswick, W4 1BD (8742 1435).

First Out

52 St Giles High Street, Covent Garden, WC2H 8LH (7240 8042, www.firstoutcafebar.com). Tottenham Court Road tube. **Open** noon-11pm Mon-Sat; 4-10pm Sun. **Credit** MC, V. **Map** p407 X1.
This lesbian and gay café was London's first homosexual café when it opened back in 1986, and still packs in a mostly lesbian crowd. A busy notice-board, friendly service and a yummy vegetarian menu give the place a genuine community feel right in the centre of town, while a licence for cocktails and beer makes it a handy spot in which to enjoy pre-club drinks.

Randall & Aubin

16 Brewer Street, Soho, W1F 0SQ (7287 4447, www.randallandaubin.com). Piccadilly Circus tube. **Open** noon-11pm Mon-Sat; 4-10pm Sun. **Credit** AmEx, MC, V. **Map** p406 W3.
Established in 1906, this French seafood charcuterie and boucherie is an experience, if you can bear the the inevitable queues. A massive mirror ball and an exuberant and camp waiting staff have helped make it a well-known gay dining destination, although it attracts clients from everywhere. If the food isn't always quite up to scratch, the joyous ambience usually makes up for it.

NIGHTCLUBS

London's club scene is particularly subject to change: venues close, nights end and new soirées start. Check *Time Out* magazine or www.timeout.com for details on what's on when you're here. And in particular, look out for one-off electro nights from **Hot Boy Dancing Spot** (www.myspace.com/hotboydancingspot), **Bastard Batty Bass** (www.battybass.com) and **Trailer Trash** (www.clubtrailertrash.com).
If you want to stay up all night and all day, head to Vauxhall. At **Fire** (South Lambeth Road, SW8 1UQ, www.fireclub.co.uk), nights such as Gravity, Later, Orange and Open keep dancers furnished with funky house from Friday morning through until Tuesday; perhaps the best night is the monthly Horizon, (11pm-8am, second Sat of the month). Other clubs in the area include **Union** and **Area**, on the Albert Embankment (no.66 and no.67-68).

Club Caribana

Factory, 65 Goding Street, Vauxhall, SE11 5AW (07931 395 395 mobile, www.caribana club.com). Vauxhall tube/rail. **Open** 11pm-6am 1st Sat of mth. **Admission** £5-£8 before midnight, then £10. **Credit** MC, V.
Held monthly, this mixed gay Caribbean night features R&B, soca and funky house. Look out for occasional theme nights and PAs.

Club Kali

Dome, 1 Dartmouth Park Hill, Tufnell Park, N19 5QQ (7272 8153, www.clubkali.com). Tufnell Park tube. **Open** 10pm-3am 3rd Fri of mth. **Admission** £8; £5 reductions. **No credit cards**.
The world's largest LGBT Asian dance club offers Bollywood, bhangra, Arabic tunes, R&B and dance classics spun by DJs Ritu, Riz & Qurra.

Eagle London

349 Kennington Lane, Vauxhall, SE11 5QY (7793 0903, www.horsemeatdisco.co.uk). Vauxhall tube/rail. **Open** Horse Meat Disco 8pm-3am Sun. **Admission** £6. **No credit cards**.
Formerly South Central, this place has become a hub for those wishing to try a bit of leather without a strict dress code. It also hosts Sunday's much-loved Horse Meat Disco, where old bears and young fashionistas come together for an disco-centric party.

Exilio Latino

Guy's Bar, Boland House, St Thomas Street, Bankside, SE1 9RT (07956 983230 mobile, www.exilio.co.uk). London Bridge tube/rail. **Open** 10pm-3am Sat. **Admission** £5 before 11pm; £8 after 11pm. **No credit cards**. **Map** p401 M6.
This is London's principal queer Latino spot, with girls and guys getting together for merengue, salsa, cumbia and reggaeton.

Dressing Up, Getting Out

How to make sure that your clubbing gear cuts the mustard.

At some of the cooler clubs on London's gay scene – Wet Yourself every Sunday at **Fabric** (*see p323*), Hannah Holland's forward-thinking **Bastard Batty Bass** (*see left*), anything at **Dalston Superstore** (*see p305*) – you can expect to see some mind-blowing outfits. Fashion students show up having spent a week perfecting their David Bowie make-up, models wear 'something they found at Beyond Retro' (*see p254*), and impossibly hip-looking kids rock looks that they just invented earlier that evening.

However, the presence on the scene of such style mavens doesn't mean you need to bring a whole suitcase just for clubbing. For a city as wound-up as London, nightlife fashions are surprisingly relaxed, with a focus on individuality and DIY. The ultimate fashion faux pas is turning up in a 'look' ripped off from a shop-window mannequin or – worse – from Kate Moss. Turn up in head-to-toe Topshop and people will cringe. But turn up in your mother's stonewashed jeans, customised and patched by you, and people will (discreetly) take notes.

The first thing to remember is that most venues are hot. If you leave a coat with a cloakroom, put your coat-check ticket in your purse or wallet and not in your pocket, where it will get damp, fall apart and leave you stuck at the club until everyone has left so you can claim the last remaining jacket.

Skinny jeans on boys and girls still reign supreme, from black to acid stonewash via faded grunge, travel-unfriendly white and good ol' blue. Couple them with a vest or cool T-shirt. Boys? Not too baggy (this isn't Brooklyn). Girls? Draped off a shoulder, accessorised with a chain-strap handbag.

The 1980s are still an influence, but the cool kids have been working the early '90s of late: from music to plenty of gold bling, dressed head-to-toe in black. Don't even think about nu-rave gear, best described as what would happen if someone shut their eyes, rifled through all of the trends from '85 to '95, and put them all on at once.

For girls, heels that work with jeans work just as well with a dress (and the dress works just as well with flats). Comfortable ballerina pumps or Converse are equally reliable options. For boy, trainers ('80s Nike Airs, perhaps) or a pair of brogues (for snappy dressers) should go down well. Add colour-rimmed sunglasses and some oversized jewellery picked up at the market.

Make-up won't take up much space. In fact, swing by MAC at the airport and get them to suggest a makeover: bright red Lady Courage lipstick, perhaps; gold over outer eyelid and upper cheekbone; or, simply, plenty of kohl. And finally, pack some gel for that directional haircut, spiky, flat-top or geek-inspired side parting.

Ultimately, confidence is key. No one here really knows what to wear or how to wear it. Even so, that doesn't excuse you not knowing how to own the dancefloor…

stivals
.ay & Lesbian

Principal dates in the queer year.

In June, **Pride London** (www.pridelondon. org) remains popular, perhaps more for the street party in a traffic-free Soho than for the long-standing parade from Oxford Street to Victoria Embankment – these days, it seems to be as much about the corporate quest for the pink pound than making a political point. A two-week cultural festival precedes the big day. **Soho Pride** (www.sohopride.net) sees the same West End streets overrun in late summer. In Regent's Park, **Black Pride** (www.ukblackpride.org.uk), a queer alternative to the Notting Hill Carnival (*see p275*) – which still, sadly, has zero gay presence – continues to grow every year. In spring, there's the annual **London Lesbian & Gay Film Festival** (*see p293*), with an emphasis on edgier fare in the wake of *Brokeback Mountain*. Also worth checking out is July's **London Literature Festival** (*see p274*), which often hosts gay-oriented readings and talks.

★ Ghetto
58 Old Street, City, EC1V 9AJ (7287 3726, www.ghetto-london.co.uk). Old Street tube/rail. **Open** 10pm-1am Mon, Tue; 10pm-3am Wed, Thur; 10pm-5am Fri, Sat; 10pm-2am Sun. **Admission** varies. **No credit cards. Map** p402 P4.
Ghetto's hip enough to attract the local queer scenester crowd, but friendly enough to get Soho-ites to come out east. As such, the range of nights here caters for guys and girls from all over. Special mention goes to Saturday's Wigout, the pop night fag hags beg their gay best friends to take them to. Upstairs is the Trash Palace bar; arrive early enough and you can get tickets for downstairs. *Photo p306.*

★ Heaven
Underneath the Arches, Villiers Street, Covent Garden, WC2N 6NG (7930 2020, www.heaven-london.com). Embankment tube or Charing Cross tube/rail. **Open** hrs vary. **Admission** prices vary. **No credit cards. Map** p407 X4.
London's most famous gay club is a bit like *Les Misérables* – it's camp, it's full of history and tourists love it. Popcorn (Mon) has long been a good bet, but it's really all about G-A-Y (Thur-Sat). For years, divas with an album to flog (Madonna, Kylie, Girls Aloud) have turned up to play here at the weekend. Expect big things.

★ Mannequin Social
Sosho, 2 Tabernacle Street, Shoreditch, EC2A 4LU (07879 846671 mobile, www.mannequin-social.com). Moorgate or Old Street tube/rail. **Open** 8pm-3am 2nd Sat of mth. **Admission** £10. **Credit** MC, V. **Map** p403 Q4.
Two pals set up this night for Shoreditch girls and their male guests; by autumn 2009, it was so popular that it had to move to this bigger venue. It's usually held on the second Saturday of the month. Tunes run from indie to electro; a chatty vibe prevails.
▶ *The Commercial Tavern (see p239) is a great queer-friendly pre-club watering hole.*

Popstarz
Den & Centro, 16A West Central Street, Covent Garden, WC1A 1JJ (7240 1864, www.popstarz. org). Holborn or Tottenham Court Road tube. **Open** 10pm-4am Fri. **Admission** free before 11pm, then £8. **Credit** MC, V. **Map** p407 Y1.
What G-A-Y is to cheese, Popstarz is to indie. It's studenty, drunken, attitude-free and popular – so popular, in fact, that the club has spawned imitators from New York to Paris, as well as a mini alt gay empire in London (*see above* Ghetto and Trash Palace). There are also occasional PAs from in-demand acts such as Maxïmo Park.

★ RVT
Royal Vauxhall Tavern, 372 Kennington Lane, Vauxhall, SE11 5HY (7820 1222, www.rvt. org.uk). Vauxhall tube/rail. **Open** 7pm-midnight

Mon-Fri; 9pm-2am Sat; 2pm-midnight Sun. **Admission** £5-£7. **Credit** MC, V.
This pub-turned-legendary-gay-venue, a much-loved stalwart on the scene for years, operates an anything-goes booking policy. The most famous fixture is Saturday's queer performance night Duckie (www. duckie.co.uk), with Amy Lamé hosting performances at midnight that range from strip cabaret to porn puppets; Sunday's Dame Edna Experience drag show, from 5pm, is also essential, drawing quasi-religious devotees. The aim is always to please the crowd of regulars, reliably vocal with their feedback. Punters verge on the bear, but the main dress code is 'no attitude'. The monthly Kimono Krush night packs in arty bears and bearded trannies.

XXL

51-53 Southwark Street, Borough, SE1 1RU (7403 4001, www.xxl-london.com). London Bridge tube/rail. **Open** 9pm-3am Wed; 9pm-6am Sat. **Admission** £3-£12. **Credit** AmEx, MC, V. **Map** p404 P8.
The world's biggest club for bears and their friends, XXL is nirvana for the chubbier, hairier and blokier of London's gay men and their twinky admirers. True to its name, the venue is bigger than average, with two dancefloors, two bars and even an outdoor beer garden.

PUBS & BARS

Unless otherwise indicated, all the pubs and bars listed here are open to both gay men and lesbians. In the Shoreditch area, Trash Palace, the bar section of **Ghetto** (*see left*), is good for pre-club drinks.

Barcode Vauxhall

Arch 69, Goding Street, Vauxhall, SE11 4AD (7582 4180, www.bar-code.co.uk). Vauxhall tube. **Open** 4pm-1am Mon-Thur; 4pm-4am Fri, Sat; 5pm-1am Sun. **Admission** £4 after 10pm Fri, Sat. **Credit** AmEx, MC, V.
Prior to the arrival of BCV, Vauxhall was mostly for clubbing, with pre-dance drinks to be enjoyed any-where-else-but. Now those pre-dancing punters are joined by folks just after a drink at this massive, lavish venue, which attracts a blokey-ish crowd despite its shiny surfaces.
▶ *BCV's forerunner Barcode, off Shaftesbury Avenue, hosts the mostly gay and thoroughly excellent Comedy Camp night (see p284).*

Box

Seven Dials, 32-34 Monmouth Street, Covent Garden, WC2H 9HA (7240 5828, www.box bar.com). Leicester Square tube. **Open** 11am-11pm Mon-Sat; noon-10.30pm Sun. **Credit** AmEx, MC, V. **Map** p407 X2.
Muscle boys and theatre luvvies adore this place, which sits near the historic Seven Dials monument,

INSIDE TRACK GAY SALONS

Craving queer culture that's a little more cerebral? Try out London's new breed of queer salons, essentially literary or cultural get-togethers. In particular, look out for the **House of Homosexual Culture** (www.myspace.com/homoculture), **Tart Women's Salon** (www.tartsalon.co.uk/home.php) and **Polari** (www.myspace.com/polarigaysalon).

a popular perching point for Sunday-afternoon drinkers. It's also opposite Dress Circle, a music shop specialising in Broadway and West End musicals. Just so you know.

★ Dalston Superstore

117 Kingland High Street, Dalston, E8 2PB (7254 2273). Dalston Kingsland rail. **Open** 11am-2am daily. **Credit** MC, V.
The opening of this gay arts space-cum-bar in summer 2009 cemented Dalston's status as the final frontier of the East End's gay scene. Come during the day for the café grub, Wi-Fi and art exhibitions on the walls; at night, you can expect queues for an impressive roster of guest DJs spinning anything from garage to pop.

Horse Meat Disco. *See p302.*

ARTS & ENTERTAINMENT

Freedom Bar

66 Wardour Street, Soho, W1F 0TA (7734 0071, www.freedombarsoho.com). Piccadilly Circus tube. **Open** 5pm-3am Mon-Fri; 2pm-3am Sat; 2-11.30pm Sun. **Credit** MC, V. **Map** p406 W3.

Shaun Given, who gave the Edge an edge back in 2005, began to work his magic on Freedom in early 2008. Once the favourite haunt of the gay glitterati, it now has softer lighting and friendlier staff. The huge basement, a ballroom with pink vinyl seating and the obligatory poles, hosts varied entertainment.
► *In winter, the cosy alcoves of nearby retro-styled basement bar Friendly Society (no.79, 7434 3805) are great for cocktails and first dates.*

G-A-Y Bar

30 Old Compton Street, Soho, W1D 4UR (7494 2756, www.g-a-y.co.uk). Leicester Square tube. **Open** noon-midnight daily. **Credit** MC, V. **Map** p406 W3.

The G-A-Y night at Heaven (*see p304*) gets the celebrity cameos, but this popular bar is still a shrine to queer pop idols, with nightly drinks promos every time they play a video from the current diva du jour. There's also a popular women's bar in the basement, called (delightfully) Girls Go Down.
► *Just round the corner (5 Goslett Yard, off Charing Cross Road), you'll find G-A-Y bar's plush late-night sibling, G-A-Y Late.*

George & Dragon

2 Hackney Road, Bethnal Green, E2 7NS (7012 1100). Old Street tube/rail or bus 26, 48, 55. **Open** 6pm-midnight daily. **Credit** AmEx, MC, V. **Map** p403 S3.

The trendy location of this mini pub ensures a stylish and up-for-it clientele, while the decor (a wall-mounted horse's head, creepy puppets, random garbage) keeps the vibe fun. The music here – pop, indie and accessible electronica – is often delivered with a healthy sense of humour. Gay pub or not, this is one of London's best boozers.
► *Just up the road is another east London gay institution: rough-round-the-edges watering hole the Joiners Arms (116-118 Hackney Road).*

Green Carnation

4-5 Greek Street, Soho, W1D 4DB (7434 3323, www.greencarnationsoho.co.uk). Tottenham Court Road tube. **Open** 4pm-2am Mon-Sat; 4pm-12.30am Sun. **Admission** £5 Mon-Thur, after 11pm Fri, Sat. **Credit** AmEx, MC, V. **Map** p406 W2.

Formerly Element (itself formerly Sanctuary), the Green Carnation has had a major refit to spectacular effect. Head upstairs for cocktails in posh surroundings, with chandeliers and piano music to heighten the senses and raise the tone. There's a bar and a dancefloor downstairs. It's a haven for West

Ghetto. *See p304.*

End Wendies, always on hand to belt out a minor Sondheim in the wee hours.

Hoist

Arches 47B & 47C South Lambeth Road, Vauxhall, SW8 1RH (7735 9972, www.the hoist.co.uk). Vauxhall tube/rail. **Open** 8pm-midnight 3rd Thur of mth; 10pm-3am Fri; 10pm-4am Sat; 2-8pm, 10pm-2am Sun. **Admission** £7 Fri, Sun; £10 Sat; varies Thur. **No credit cards**.

One of two genuine leather bars in town, this club sits under the arches and makes the most of its underground and industrial setting. Wear leather, uniforms, rubber, skinhead or boots only – trainers will see you shunned at the door. There's a weekly Sunday afternoon event called SBN (Stark Bollock Naked); the clue is in the name.

KW4

77 Hampstead High Street, Hampstead, NW3 1RE (7435 5747, www.kingwilliamhampstead. co.uk). Hampstead tube or Hampstead Heath rail. **Open** 11am-11pm Mon-Thur; 11am-midnight Fri-Sun. **Credit** MC, V.

The perfect evening ending (or beginning) to time spent on the Heath, this fabulous old local – the King William IV, or even the King Willy to those with longer memories – attracts a very Hampstead crowd (read: well-off and ready for fun). On summer weekends, the cute little beer garden tends to fill up with a mix of gay and straight punters keen to put down their shopping bags.

Pendulum

56 Frith Street, Soho, W1D 3JG (0871 971 5840). Tottenham Court Road tube. **Open** 4-11.30pm Mon-Thur; 4pm-midnight Fri, Sat; 4-10.30pm Sun. **Credit** AmEx, MC, V. **Map** p406 W2.

This new bar-restaurant was opened in summer 2009 by the team behind a clutch of London's gay bars and nights, and they know a thing or two about what the Soho scene is after. There's a large, futuristic bar space for cocktails downstairs; above it is the Outsider Tart restaurant, serving southern American comfort food (macaroni cheese, Cajun potato salad, brownies).

Retro Bar

2 George Court, off the Strand, Covent Garden, WC2N 6HH (7839 8760). Charing Cross tube/ rail. **Open** noon-11pm Mon-Fri; 5-11pm Sat; 5-10.30pm Sun. **Credit** AmEx, MC, V. **Map** p407 Y4.

Iggy Pop and Kate Bush are on the walls of this bar of the Popstarz ilk (*see p304*), where nights are dedicated to indie rock and Eurovision hits. The crowd here is mixed in every sense: gay/straight, gay/ lesbian and scene queen/true eccentric. Quiz nights are popular, and the bar on occasion lets punters be the DJ – bring your iPod.

Shadow Lounge

5 Brewer Street, Soho, W1F 0RF (7287 7988, www.theshadowlounge.co.uk). Piccadilly Circus tube. **Open** 10pm-3am Mon-Sat. **Admission** £5-£10. **Credit** AmEx, MC, V. **Map** p406 W3.

For celebrity sightings, suits, cutes and fancy boots, this is your West End venue. Expect a hefty cover charge and a queue on the weekends, but there's often a sublime atmosphere inside.

Yard

57 Rupert Street, Soho, W1V 7BJ (7437 2652, www.yardbar.co.uk). Piccadilly Circus tube. **Open** 2-11.30pm Tue-Sat; 2pm-midnight Fri, Sat. **Credit** AmEx, MC, V. **Map** p406 W3.

Come for the courtyard in summer, stay for the Loft Bar in winter. This unpretentious bar offers a great open-air courtyard in a great location, which attracts pretty boys, blokes and lesbians in equal measure.
▶ *A similar crowd can be found at Rupert Street (no.57), particularly popular with professional chaps after work or pre-partying at the weekends.*

SEX CLUBS & SAUNAS

Chariots

1 Fairchild Street, Shoreditch, EC2A 3NS (7247 5333, www.gaysauna.co.uk). Liverpool Street tube/rail. **Open** noon-9am daily. **Admission** £15. **Credit** MC, V. **Map** p403 R4.

Chariots is a sauna chain with outlets all over town. The original is this one in Shoreditch, the biggest and busiest, although not necessarily the best. That accolade probably goes to the one on the Albert Embankment at Vauxhall (nos.63-64, 7735 6709). The Waterloo branch (101 Lower Marsh, 7401 8484) has the biggest sauna in the UK.
Other locations throughout the city.

★ Sweatbox

Ramillies House, 1-2 Ramillies Street, Soho, W1F 7LN (3214 6014, www.sweatboxsoho.com). Oxford Circus tube. **Open** noon-2am Mon-Thur, Sun; noon-7am Fri, Sat. **Admission** £20/day; £10/day reductions. **Spa only** £15/day. **Credit** MC, V. **Map** p406 U2.

Sweatbox Soho looks more like a nightclub than a typical gym, with the sleek design offset by friendly staff. Though small, the space is well laid out, with a multigym and a free weights room. Qualified masseurs offer treatments. If that doesn't do the trick, there's a sauna downstairs.

Vault 139

139 Whitfield Street, Fitzrovia, W1T 5EN (7388 5500, www.vault139.com). Warren Street tube. **Open** 4pm-1am Mon-Sat; 1pm-1am Sun. **Admission** £5-£6. **No credit cards**. **Map** p398 J4.

This cruise bar is located right in the middle of town, only a short walk from Soho.

Music

Take note – there's plenty here to hear.

Few cities can rival London's music scene for diversity and choice. Thanks in part to an open-minded culture that sees dubstep producers rubbing shoulders with free-jazz musicians, grime artists rapping with rock bands and classical conductors going to nightclubs with drum 'n' bass DJs, London exerts a magnetic pull on the world's top musicians. But there's lots to note outside cross-cultural collaborations, with scenes dedicated to everything from cosy folk music to grubby indie, and the capital can service any musical fancy. Check *Time Out* magazine for the weekly picture.

About the author
Chris Parkin writes on music for Time Out magazine, the NME and BBC.co.uk.

Classical & Opera

London's classical scene has never looked or sounded more current. With the Southbank Centre, the Barbican Centre and Kings Place all working with strong programmes, and youthful music directors such as the English National Opera's Edward Gardner keen to retain a spirit of adventure, the capital is looking forward.

Tickets & information

Tickets for most classical and opera events are available direct from the venues, online or by phone. Always book ahead. Several venues, such as the Barbican and the Southbank Centre, operate standby schemes, offering unsold tickets at cut-rate prices just before the show.

CLASSICAL VENUES

In addition to the major venues below, you can hear what tomorrow's classical music might sound like at the city's music schools, which stage regular concerts by pupils and visiting professionals. Check the websites of the **Royal Academy of Music** (7873 7300, www.ram.ac.uk), the **Royal College of Music** (7589 3643, www.rcm.ac.uk), the **Guildhall School of Music & Drama** (7628 2571, www.gsmd.ac.uk) and **Trinity College of Music** (8305 4444, www.tcm.ac.uk).

★ Barbican Centre

Silk Street, City, EC2Y 8DS (7638 4141 information, 7638 8891 tickets, www.barbican.org.uk). Barbican tube or Moorgate tube/rail. **Box office** 9am-9pm Mon-Sat. **Tickets** £7-£32. **Credit** AmEx, MC, V. **Map** p402 P5.

Europe's largest multi-arts centre is easier to navigate than ever after a renovation. And the programming remains rich: alongside the London Symphony Orchestra, guided by principal conductor Valery Gergiev, and the BBC Symphony Orchestra, under Jiri Belohlávek, the Great Performers series presents recitals from major musicians, and there's a laudable amount of contemporary classical music.

Cadogan Hall

5 Sloane Terrace, Chelsea, SW1X 9DQ (7730 4500, www.cadoganhall.com). Sloane Square tube. **Box office** 10am-8pm Mon-Sat. **Tickets** £10-£35. **Credit** MC, V. **Map** p400 G10.

Jazz groups and rock bands have been attracted by the acoustics in this former Christian Science church, renovated and reopened in 2004. However, the programming at the austere yet comfortable 900-seat hall is dominated by classical music. The Royal Philharmonic Orchestra are resident; other orchestras also perform, and there's regular chamber music (including lunchtime concerts during the Proms).

★ Kings Place

90 York Way, King's Cross, N1 9AG (0844 264 0321, www.kingsplace.co.uk). King's Cross tube/rail. **Box office** noon-8pm Mon-Sat; noon-8pm Sun (performance days only). **Tickets** £6.50-£34.50. **Credit** MC, V. **Map** p399 L2. *See right* **Profile**.

ARTS & ENTERTAINMENT

Profile Kings Place

Might this be the most enterprising music venue in London?

Scruffy and neglected, the streets around King's Cross Station have rarely had much to recommend them. However, things are changing, and fast. The renovation of St Pancras Station and the opening of the new Eurostar terminal have coincided with plenty of other new developments in and around the area, of which the most impressive is tucked away up York Way.

Aware that office blocks are an 'unfriendly building type', property developer Peter Millican wanted Kings Place to be a little different from the norm. It starts with the building itself: designed by the architectural firm of Dixon Jones, it's tidily integrated with the adjacent canal basin. Above the airy lobby, the top seven floors of the building are given over to offices; the *Guardian* newspaper is the most high-profile resident. There's a gallery, a restaurant and a café on the ground floor. But the real appeal lies in the basement, where you'll find one of the city's most exciting music venues.

With just over 400 seats, the main hall is a beauty, dominated by wood carved from a single, 500-year-old Black Forest oak tree and ringed by invisible rubber pads that kill unwanted ambient noise. Whether for amplified jazz or small-scale chamber music, the sound is always immaculate. There's also a versatile second hall and a number of smaller rooms, given over to workshops, lectures and other special events.

And the programming, overseen by Millican himself, is tremendous. Each week, the selection of concerts takes a different theme: anything from baroque opera to Norwegian jazz, 21st-century classical music to English folk. Some series are built around the London Sinfonietta and the Orchestra of the Age of Enlightenment, the two resident ensembles. These weekly themes are supplemented by other strands (chamber music on Sundays, experimental music on Mondays) and other special events. It's all part of an ethos that dares to be different.

MORE DETAILS
For listings information on Kings Place, *see left.*

ARTS & ENTERTAINMENT

LSO St Luke's

161 Old Street, City, EC1V 9NG (7490 3939 information, 7638 8891 tickets, www.lso.co.uk/ lsostlukes). Old Street tube/rail. **Box office** 9am-8pm Mon-Sat; 11am-8pm Sun. **Tickets** free-£32. **Credit** AmEx, MC, V. **Map** p402 P4.

This Grade I-listed church, built by Nicholas Hawksmoor in the 18th century, was beautifully converted into a performance and rehearsal space by the LSO several years ago. The orchestra occasionally welcomes the public for open rehearsals (book ahead); the more formal side of the programme takes in global sounds and some pop alongside classical music, including lunchtime concerts every Thursday that are broadcast on BBC Radio 3.
▶ *Hawksmoor also designed Christ Church Spitalfields; see p135.*

Royal Albert Hall

Kensington Gore, South Kensington, SW7 2AP (7589 3203 information, 7589 8212 tickets, www.royalalberthall.com). South Kensington tube or bus 9, 10, 52, 452. **Open** 9am-9pm daily. **Tickets** £4-£150. **Credit** AmEx, MC, V. **Map** p397 D9.

In constant use since opening in 1871, the Royal Albert Hall continues to host a wide array of events throughout the year. The classical side of the programming is dominated by the Proms, which runs every night for two months each summer (*see below*) and sees a wide array of orchestras and other ensembles battling rising temperatures and a far-from-ideal acoustic. Otherwise, rock and pop dominates.

St James's Piccadilly

197 Piccadilly, Piccadilly, W1J 9LL (7381 0441, www.st-james-piccadilly.org). Piccadilly Circus tube. **Box office** 8am-6.30pm Mon-Sat. **Tickets** free-£15. **No credit cards. Map** p406 V4.

This community-spirited Wren church holds free lunchtime recitals (Mon, Wed, Fri at 1.10pm) and offers regular evening concerts in a variety of fields. The church has a café attached.

St John's, Smith Square

Smith Square, Westminster, SW1P 3HA (7222 1061, www.sjss.org.uk). Westminster tube. **Box office** 10am-5pm Mon-Fri. **Tickets** £10-£50. **Credit** MC, V. **Map** p401 K10.

This 18th-century church hosts concerts more or less nightly. Down in the crypt is the Footstool restaurant, so named after Queen Anne's demand that architect Thomas Archer make the church look like a footstool she'd kicked over.

St Martin-in-the-Fields

Trafalgar Square, Westminster, WC2N 4JJ (7766 1100, www.stmartin-in-the-fields.org). Charing Cross tube/rail. **Box office** *In person* 8am-5pm Mon, Tue; 8am-8pm Wed-Sat. *By phone* 10am-5pm Mon-Sat. **Tickets** £6-£25. **Credit** MC, V. **Map** p407 X4.

Festivals Classical

What not to miss this year.

The **Proms** – or, as they're officially known, the BBC Sir Henry Wood Promenade Concerts (www.bbc.co.uk/proms) – overshadows all other classical music festivals in the city. Held between mid July and mid September at the Royal Albert Hall (*see above*), with a few supplementary events at other venues, the season includes around 70 concerts, covering everything from early music recitals to orchestral world premières. You can buy tickets in advance, but many prefer to queue on the day for £5 'promenade' tickets, which allow entry to the standing-room stalls or the gallery at the very top of the auditorium.

Held in June and July, the **City of London Festival** (7583 3585, www.colf.org) presents a wide array of concerts in a variety of genres, with an emphasis on classical music and jazz. Many concerts are held in unusual venues (historic churches, handsome courtrooms, the halls of the ancient livery companies); there's always a strong programme of free events. Close by, the enterprising **Spitalfields Festival** (www.spitalfields festival.org.uk) stages two short series of concerts every June and December, though 2009 saw the event dramatically downsized. Also in June, the **Chelsea Arts Festival** (www.chelseaartsfestival.org) offers a small spread of concerts around south-west London.

The height of summer sees concerts held in the grounds of several palaces and stately homes. The **Hampton Court Palace Festival** (www.hamptoncourt festival.com) and the **English Heritage Picnic Concerts** at Kenwood House (www.picnicconcerts.com; *see p132*) both fit into this category. Another alfresco event is the excellent **Opera Holland Park** (0845 230 9769, www.operahollandpark. com), which sees a canopied theatre host a season of opera.

This church is one of the capital's most amiable, populist venues, hosting performances of Mozart and Vivaldi by candlelight, jazz in the crypt's café and lunchtime recitals (Mon, Tue, Fri) from young musicians, many students at the city's music colleges.
▶ *For more on the church, see p112.*

★ Southbank Centre
Belvedere Road, South Bank, SE1 8XX (0871 663 2501 information, 0871 663 2500 tickets, www.southbankcentre.co.uk). Embankment tube or Waterloo tube/rail. **Box office** *In person* 10am-8pm. *By phone* 9am-8pm. **Tickets** £7-£75. **Credit** AmEx, MC, V. **Map** p401 M8.
A £90m renovation has improved the Royal Festival Hall, externally and acoustically. There are three main halls here: the Royal Festival Hall, which holds nearly 3,000 seats and counts the Philharmonia and the Orchestra of the Age of Enlightenment as residents; the Queen Elizabeth Hall, which has room for around 900 concertgoers; and the 365-capacity Purcell Room, about one-third the size of the QEH and the scene for regular recitals. Programming is rich in variety; the same is true of the foyer stage, which hosts hundreds of free concerts every year.

★ Wigmore Hall
36 Wigmore Street, Marylebone, W1U 2BP (7935 2141, www.wigmore-hall.org.uk). Bond Street tube. **Box office** *In person* 10am-8.30pm daily. *By phone* 10am-7pm daily. **Tickets** £5-£75. **Credit** AmEx, DC, MC, V. **Map** p398 G6.
Built in 1901 as the display hall for Bechstein Pianos, the world-renowned Wiggy has perfect acoustics for the 400-plus concerts that take place each year. Music from the classical and romantic periods are mainstays, but a recent broadening in the remit has seen more baroque and an increased jazz line-up, with Brad Mehldau curating a series of concerts through until 2011. Monday-lunchtime recitals are broadcast live on BBC Radio 3.

OPERA VENUES

In addition to the two big venues below, look out for occasional concert performances at **Cadogan Hall** (*see p308*), summer's **Opera Holland Park** (*see left* **Festivals**) and sporadic appearances by **English Touring Opera** (www.englishtouringopera.org.uk).

English National Opera, Coliseum
St Martin's Lane, Covent Garden, WC2N 4ES (0871 911 0200 tickets, www.eno.org). Leicester Square tube or Charing Cross tube/rail. **Box office** *In person* 10am-6pm Mon-Sat. *By phone* 24hrs daily. **Tickets** £22-£87. **Credit** MC, V. **Map** p407 X4.
Built as a music hall in 1904, the home of the English National Opera (ENO) is in sparkling condition following a renovation in 2004. And after a shaky

period several years ago, ENO itself is in solid shape under the youthful stewardship of music director Edward Gardner, notwithstanding the occasional dud (such as Rupert Goolde's critically panned 2009 production of *Turandot*). All works are performed in English, and prices are generally a good deal cheaper than at the Royal Opera House.

★ Royal Opera, Royal Opera House
Covent Garden, WC2E 9DD (7304 4000, www.roh.org.uk). Covent Garden tube. **Box office** 10am-8pm Mon-Sat. **Tickets** £8-£110. **Credit** AmEx, MC, V. **Map** p407 Z3.
Thanks to a turn-of-the-century refurbishment, the ROH once again sits among the ranks of the world's great opera houses. Critics suggest that the programming can be a little spotty, especially so given the famously elevated ticket prices, and not all of chief executive Tony Hall's attempts to win a new audience seem suitably dignified. But there are still fine productions here, many under the baton of Antonio Pappano, and the modern outlook taken by Hall and his comrades is generally laudable. Potential high-lights in 2010 include new productions of Prokofiev's *The Gambler* (Feb) and Verdi's *Aida* (Apr/May), and the return of Thomas Adès's *Powder Her Face* (June).
▶ *The Royal Ballet are also based here; see p288.*

Rock, Pop & Roots

The longtime London cliché of indie bands playing in a sticky dive endures, but the capital's rock and pop scene is far from predictable. Close your eyes and stick a pin in *Time Out*'s weekly gig listings, and you might find yourself watching an American country star in a tiny basement, an African group under a railway arch or a torch singer in an ancient church.

Of late, big firms from outside the industry – record retailer HMV, phone company O2 – have been investing in many of the capital's large venues. The results of their involvement have been both welcome (improved sound systems, smarter decor) and undesirable (overpriced bars, edgeless ambience). Regardless of who runs the venues, the range of acts playing in them is as good as it's ever been.

ARTS & ENTERTAINMENT

Koko.

Tickets & information

Your first stop should be *Time Out* magazine, which lists hundreds of gigs every week. Most venues' websites detail future shows. Check ticket availability before setting out: venues large and small can sell out weeks in advance. The main exceptions are pub venues, which sell tickets only on the day. Prices vary wildly: you could pay £150 to see Madonna at the O2 Arena or see a superb singer-songwriter for free. Many venues offer tickets online via their websites, but beware: most online box offices are operated by ticket agencies, which add booking fees that can raise the ticket price by as much as 30 per cent. Try to pay cash in person if possible (*see below*); for details of London's ticket agencies, *see p268*.

There's often a huge disparity between door times and stage times; the Jazz Café opens at 7pm, for instance, but the gigs often don't start until after 9pm. Some venues run club nights after the gigs, which means the show has to be wrapped up by 10.30pm; but at other venues, the main act won't even start until 11pm. If in doubt, call ahead.

MAJOR VENUES

In addition to the venues below, the **Barbican Centre** (*see p308*), the **Southbank Centre** (*see p311*) and the **Royal Albert Hall** (*see p310*) stage regular gigs.

HMV Forum
9-17 Highgate Road, Kentish Town, NW5 1JY (7428 4099 information, 0844 847 2405 tickets, www.kentishtownforum.com). Kentish Town tube/rail. **Box office** *In person* 4-8pm performance days. *By phone* 24hrs daily. **Tickets** £5-£30. **Credit** MC, V. **Map** p402 N2. Built as a cinema in 1934, this cramped, 2,000-capacity art deco hall is now co-owned by HMV, part of the music retailer's attempt to shore up its business by diversifying into the increasingly lucrative live market. The high calibre of alt-rock bands who play here (Sonic Youth, Kasabian, White Lies) is a sign of their strong pulling power.
▶ *The time-honoured choice for a pre-gig pint is the nearby Bull & Gate, which also stages gigs.*

INSIDE TRACK AVOID THE FEES

You can avoid the brutal booking fees levied by many major venues by buying your tickets in cash from two box offices. Tickets for shows at the **Borderline**, the **HMV Apollo**, the **HMV Forum**, the **Jazz Café** and the **Relentless Garage** cost face value if purchased with cash at the Jazz Café's box office (10.30am-5.30pm Mon-Sat). And tickets for the **O2 Academy Brixton**, the **O2 Academy Islington** and the **O2 Shepherd's Bush Empire** can be bought for face value at the O2 Academy Islington's box office (noon-4pm Mon-Sat).

HMV Hammersmith Apollo

45 Queen Caroline Street, Hammersmith,
W6 9QH (8563 3800 information, 0844 844
4748 tickets, www.hammersmithapollo.net).
Hammersmith tube. **Box office** *In person*
4pm-8pm performance days. *By phone* 24hrs
daily. **Tickets** £10-£35. **Credit** MC, V.
This 1930s cinema doubles as a 3,600-capacity all-seater theatre (popular with big comedy acts and children's shows) and a 5,000-capacity standing-room-only gig space, hosting shows by major rock bands and others not quite ready for the O2.

IndigO2

For listings, see p314 **O2 Arena**.
The little brother of the vast O2 Arena (*see p314*)
isn't really all that little: with a capacity of 2,350
(part-standing room, part-amphitheatre seating,
sometimes part-table seating), IndigO2 is impressive
in its own right. Its niche roster of MOR acts is dominated by soul, funk, pop-jazz and wearied old pop
acts, though it also hosts after-show parties for those
headlining the O2.

★ Koko

1A Camden High Street, Camden, NW1 7JE
(0870 432 5527 information, 0844 847 2258
tickets, www.koko.uk.com). Mornington Crescent

tube. **Box office** *In person* 1-5pm Mon-Fri
(performance days only). *By phone* 24hrs daily.
Tickets £3-£25. **Credit** AmEx, MC, V.
Avoid standing beneath the sound-muffling over-
hang downstairs and you may find that this former
music hall, formerly the Camden Palace, is among
London's finest venues. The 1,500-capacity hall
stages weekend club nights and gigs by indie rockers, from the small and cultish to those on the up.

★ 02 Academy Brixton

211 Stockwell Road, Brixton, SW9 9SL (7771
3000 information, 0844 477 2000 tickets,
www.o2academybrixton.co.uk). Brixton tube/rail.
Box office *In person* 2hrs before doors on
performance days. *By phone* 24hrs daily.
Tickets £10-£40. **Credit** AmEx, MC, V.
Brixton is still the preferred venue for metal, indie
and alt-rock bands looking to play their triumphant
'Look, ma, we've made it!' headline show. Built in
the 1920s, this ex-cinema is the city's most atmospheric big venue. And with its sloping floor, everyone's guaranteed a decent view.

02 Academy Islington

N1 Centre, 16 Parkfield Street, Islington, N1 0PS
(7288 4400 information, 0844 477 2000 tickets,
www.o2academyislington.co.uk) Angel tube.

Festivals Rock, Pop & Roots

What not to miss this year.

Both Camden and Shoreditch are home to a handful of rock and pop festivals that take in a multitude of venues. April's two-day **Camden Crawl** (www.thecamdencrawl.com) sees a mix of hip indie acts spread across Camden's clubs and pubs. And down in Shoreditch, look out for the indie-friendly **Stag & Dagger** (www.staganddagger.com, late May) and the multi-arts **Concrete & Glass** (www.concreteandglass.co.uk, autumn), both of which take in a number of venues. For more on these, *see p273* **Small is Beautiful**.

Outdoor events take over in summer. As well as one-off gigs, Hyde Park hosts heritage-rock weekender **Hard Rock Calling** (www.hardrockcalling.co.uk) and the poppier, more contemporary **Wireless Festival** (www.wirelessfestival.co.uk) in late June. In July, Victoria Park is home to the leftfield **Field Day** (www.fielddayfestivals.com), the under-18s-only **Underage Festival** (www.underagefestivals.com) and Groove Armada's **Lovebox Weekender** (www.lovebox.net). And Clapham Common lords it over the August Bank Holiday with

its **SW4** rave-up (www.southwestfour.com) and the band-packed **Get Loaded** (www.getloadedinthepark.com).

There's more mainstream fare at **Somerset House** (*see p90*), where the Summer Series welcomes an array of big and generally pretty mainstream acts for roughly ten days of open-air shows. Autumn sees Camden host the **BBC Electric Proms** (www.bbc.co.uk/electricproms), with most major events staged at the Roundhouse. And in summer, the Southbank Centre (*see p311*) invites a guest artist to curate **Meltdown**, a fortnight of gigs, films and other events. Scott Walker and Ornette Coleman are among the previous curators.

Other events are limited to a single genre. The best of them include the Southbank Centre's **London African Music Festival** (7328 9613, www.londonafricanmusicfestival.com, late Sept); **La Linea** (8693 1042, www.comono.co.uk, from mid Apr), a fortnight of contemporary Latin American music; and the terrific, ever-changing series of thematic folk and world events at the **Barbican** (*see p308*).

O2 Arena.

Box office *In person* noon-4pm Mon-Sat. *By phone* 24hrs daily. **Tickets** £3-£20. **Credit** AmEx, MC, V. **Map** p402 N2.

Located in the heart of a shopping mall, this 800-capacity room was never likely to be London's edgiest venue. Still, as a stepping stone between the pubs of Camden and the city's larger venues, it's a good place to catch fast-rising indie acts and reformed '80s bands, not least because of the great sound system. The adjacent Bar Academy hosts smaller bands.

★ O2 Arena
Millennium Way, North Greenwich, SE10 0BB (8463 2000 information, 0844 856 0202 tickets, www.theo2.co.uk). North Greenwich tube. **Box office** *In person* noon-7pm daily. *By phone* 24hrs daily. **Tickets** £10-£100. **Credit** AmEx, MC, V.

Since its launch in July 2007, this conversion of the former Millennium Dome has been a huge success, taking over from Wembley Arena and Earl's Court as the arena venue of choice. With its outstanding sound, unobstructed sightlines and the potential for artists to perform 'in the round', even the biggest acts (Prince, Britney, Led Zep) don't feel far away.

▶ *There are two other substantial venues on the site: IndigO2 (see p313) and Matter (see p328).*

INSIDE TRACK BOAT TO THE O2

You can get to the O2 Arena (*see above*), IndigO2 (*see p313*) and Matter (*see p328*) by tube, but it's more fun to take the 20-minute river ride on **Thames Clipper** (*see p364*) from London Bridge or Waterloo.

O2 Shepherd's Bush Empire
Shepherd's Bush Green, Shepherd's Bush, W12 8TT (8354 3300 information, 0844 477 2000 tickets, www.o2shepherdsbushempire.co.uk). Shepherd's Bush Market tube or Shepherd's Bush tube/rail. **Box office** *In person* 6-8pm performance days. *By phone* 24hrs daily. **Tickets** £8-£40. **Credit** AmEx, MC, V.

Holding 2,000 standing or 1,300 seated, this former BBC theatre is a fine mid-sized venue. Sightlines are good, the sound is decent (with the exception of the alcove behind the stalls bar and the scarily vertiginous top floor) and the roster of shows is quite varied, with acts at the poppier end of the scale joined by everyone from folkies to grizzled '70s rockers.

★ Roundhouse
Chalk Farm Road, Camden, NW1 8EH (7424 9991 information, 0844 482 8008 tickets, www.roundhouse.org.uk). Chalk Farm tube. **Box office** *In person* 11am-6pm Mon-Sat. *By phone* 9am-7pm Mon-Sat; 9am-4pm Sun. **Tickets** £5-£50. **Credit** MC, V.

The main auditorium's supporting pillars mean there are some poor sightlines, but this one-time railway turntable shed, used for hippie happenings in the 1960s before becoming a famous rock (and punk) venue in the '70s, has been a fine addition since its reopening in 2006. Expect a mix of arty rock gigs, dance performances, theatre and multimedia events.

Scala
275 Pentonville Road, King's Cross, N1 9NL (7833 2022, www.scala-london.co.uk). King's Cross tube/rail. **Box office** 10am-6pm Mon-Fri. **Tickets** £8-£15. **Credit** MC, V. **Map** p399 L3.

Built as a cinema after World War I, the TARDIS-like Scala stages an agreeably broad range of indie, electronica, hip hop and folk. Its chilly air-con isn't rivalled anywhere in London.

Wembley Arena
Arena Square, Engineers Way, Wembley, HA9 0DH (8782 5566 information, 0844 815 0815 tickets, www.livenation.co.uk/wembley). Wembley Park tube. **Box office** *In person* 10.30am-9pm performance days; 10.30am-4.30pm non-performance days. *By phone* 24hrs daily. **Tickets** £5-£100. **Credit** AmEx, MC, V.
Wembley Arena may have seen its commercial heyday draw to a close with the arrival of the O2. Still, although it's hardly anyone's favourite venue, not least because the food and drink could be both cheaper and better, a £30m refurbishment has improved this 12,500-capacity venue.

CLUB & PUB VENUES

In addition to the venues below, a handful of nightclubs stage gigs. Try the **Notting Hill Arts Club** (*see p328*), **Madame JoJo's** (*see p323*), **Proud** (*see p325*) and the **ICA** (*see p118*). And it's also worth checking the schedules at the excellent **Café Oto** (*see p319*).

Amersham Arms
388 New Cross Road, New Cross, SE14 6TY (8469 1499, www.amersham-arms.co.uk). New Cross or New Cross Gate rail, or bus 21, 36, 136, 171, 177, 225, 321, 436, 453. **Open** noon-midnight Mon-Wed, Sun; noon-2am Thur; 10am-3am Fri, Sat. **Tickets** vary. **Credit** MC, V.
South-east London's finest venue brings together the character (and prices) of a traditional pub with a modern sound system, an upstairs arts space, a walled garden for smokers and a 3am booze licence. The roster is dominated by indie and electro bands.

★ Bardens Boudoir
36-44 Stoke Newington Road, Dalston, N16 7XJ (7249 9557, www.bardensboudoir.co.uk). Dalston Kingsland rail or bus 67, 76, 149, 243. **Open** hrs vary. **Tickets** £4-£6. **No credit cards.**
Located below a furniture store in Turkish London, the well-loved, 300-capacity and rough-around-the-edges Bardens is a home from home for the city's artier rock kids. Shows include terrific noise, alt-rock and cabaret-themed gigs, plus club nights.

Barfly
49 Chalk Farm Road, Chalk Farm, NW1 8AN (7688 8994 information, 0844 847 2424 tickets, www.barflyclub.com). Chalk Farm tube. **Open** 6.30pm-1am Mon-Thur; 6.30pm-3am Fri, Sat; noon-midnight Sun. *Shows* from 7pm daily. **Admission** £5-£8. **No credit cards.**
As other similarly sized venues open with smarter decor and less conventional booking policies, this 200-capacity venue's star has begun to fade. Still, it's part of London's indie-rock fabric and the capital's original nexus between guitars and electro.
▶ *The same people run Fly (36-38 New Oxford Street, Bloomsbury, WC1A 1EP, 7636 9176).*

Bloomsbury Bowling Lanes
Basement, Tavistock Hotel, Bedford Way, Bloomsbury, WC1H 9EU (7183 1979, www.bloomsburybowling.com). Russell Square tube. **Open** 1pm-2am Mon-Thur; noon-3am Fri, Sat; 1pm-midnight Sun. **Admission** varies. **Credit** AmEx, MC, V. **Map** p399 K4.

Amersham Arms.

INSIDE TRACK FREE LOVE

London's live music scene sometimes offers something for nothing. Regular events include the indie rock-dominated RoTa, held every Saturday between 4pm and 8pm at the **Notting Hill Arts Club** (see p328), and the fine programme of after-work concerts staged in the foyer of the Royal Festival Hall at the **Southbank Centre** (see p311); for others, see the weekly listings in *Time Out* magazine.

Offering a late night drink away from Soho, BBL has been putting on live bands and DJs for a while now. If you get bored of the bands, or if you find bowling tough with the elbows of dancers knocking you off your game, hole up in one of the karaoke booths.

★ Borderline
Orange Yard, off Manette Street, Soho, W1D 4JB (0844 847 2465, www.meanfiddler.com). Totteham Court Road tube. **Open** hrs vary. **Admission** £3-£20. **Credit** AmEx, MC, V. **Map** p406 W2.
A small, sweaty dive bar-slash-juke joint right in the heart of Soho, the Borderline has long been a favoured stop-off for touring American bands of the country and blues varieties, though you'll also find a variety of indie acts and singer-songwriters down here. Be warned, though, that it can get very, very cramped.

Corsica Studios.

★ Bush Hall
310 Uxbridge Road, Shepherd's Bush, W12 7LJ (8222 6955 information, 0870 060 0100 tickets, www.bushhallmusic.co.uk). Shepherd's Bush Market tube. **Box office** By phone 24hrs daily. **Tickets** £6-£20. **Credit** AmEx, MC, V.
Over the years, this handsome room has been a dance hall, a soup kitchen and a snooker club. But now, with its original fittings intact, it plays host to big bands performing stripped-down shows, top folk outfits and rising indie rockers.

Cargo
83 Rivington Street, Shoreditch, EC2A 3AY (7739 3440, www.cargo-london.com). Old Street tube/rail. **Open** noon-1am Mon-Thur; noon-3am Fri; 6pm-3am Sat; 1pm-midnight Sun. **Admission** free-£12. **Credit** MC, V. **Map** p403 R4.
Located down a side street and under a bridge, the bricks 'n' arches of Cargo keeps Shoreditch music fans in a blissful state of whatever-next-ness. Gigs run the gamut from indie also-rans to global imports. Check out the great street-food café and the Shepard Fairey-styled street art in the garden.

Corsica Studios
Elephant Road, Elephant & Castle, SE17 1LB (7703 4760, www.corsicastudios.com). Elephant & Castle tube/rail. **Open** hrs vary. **Tickets** £5-£12. **No credit cards. Map** p404 O10.
This flexible performance space is increasingly being used as one of London's most adventurous live music venues and clubs, supplementing bands with sundry poets, live painters and lunatic projectionists. It's open until midnight or 1am for gigs, and until 6am for some club nights.

Green Note
106 Parkway, Camden, NW1 7AN (7485 9899, www.greennote.co.uk). Camden Town tube. **Open** 7-11pm Wed, Thur, Sun; 7pm-midnight Fri; 6.30pm-midnight Sat. **Tickets** £7-£15. **Credit** MC, V.
A stone's throw from Regent's Park, this cosy little venue and vegetarian cafe-bar opened in 2005 and has proven to be a welcome addition to the city's roots circuit. Singer-songwriters, folkies and blues musicians make up the majority of the gig roster, with a handful of big names in among the listings.

Hoxton Square Bar & Kitchen
2-4 Hoxton Square, Shoreditch, N1 6NU (7613 0709, www.hoxtonsquarebar.com). Old Street tube/rail. **Open** 11am-midnight Mon; 11am-1am Tue-Thur; 11am-2am Fri, Sat; 11am-12.30am Sun. **Tickets** £5-£10. **Credit** MC, V. **Map** p403 R3.
Set in hipsterland, this 450-capacity venue is more than just a place to be seen: the venue's finger-on-the-pulse line-ups are always cutting edge and fun, with the venue often hosting a band's first London outing. Get there early or prepare to queue.

ARTS & ENTERTAINMENT

Picture This

Ten album covers that show various corners of the capital.

ABBEY ROAD
THE BEATLES (1969)
Abbey Road, NW8
You probably know this one already.

MEATY BEATY BIG AND BOUNCY
THE WHO (1971)
Railway Hotel, Railway Approach, HA3
The cover of this greatest-hits compilation
shows seminal mod hangout the Railway
Hotel in Harrow. It's now the site of
four blocks of flats, each named after
a member of the Who.

THE RISE AND FALL OF ZIGGY
STARDUST AND THE SPIDERS
FROM MARS
DAVID BOWIE (1972)
Heddon Street, W1
The red telephone phone box was put
back in its original location during Heddon
Street's recent makeover.

NEW BOOTS AND PANTIES!!
IAN DURY (1977)
Vauxhall Bridge Road, SW1
The title referred to the only clothes a
thrifty Dury wouldn't buy from charity shops.
The cover was shot outside a now-defunct
clothing store called Axford's; the kid is
Baxter Dury, Ian's son.

THIS IS THE MODERN WORLD
THE JAM (1977)
Under the Westway, W10
Behind Paul Weller, Rick Buckler and Bruce
Foxton rise the towers of the Silchester
West council estate, not far from Latimer
Road tube station.

ANIMALS
PINK FLOYD (1977)
*Battersea Power Station, east of Chelsea
Bridge, SW8*
During the photo shoot, the inflatable
pig came loose from its moorings and
disappeared into the London sky.

PARKLIFE
BLUR (1994)
*Walthamstow Stadium, 300 Chingford
Road, E4*
A visual hymn to the East End. The album
was launched at the stadium, with Blur
sponsoring a race.

**(WHAT'S THE STORY) MORNING
GLORY OASIS (1995)**
Berwick Street, W1
The two men passing each other on this
Soho street are believed to be Oasis art
director Brian Cannon and DJ Sean Rowley.

ORIGINAL PIRATE MATERIAL
THE STREETS (2002)
Kestrel House, City Road, EC1
The photograph was taken in 1995 by
German snapper Rut Blees Luxemburg,
the same photographer who supplied the
similarly evocative cover shot for Bloc
Party's *A Weekend in the City*.

BURIAL
BURIAL (2006)
Wandsworth, SW18
William Bevan's dystopian dubstep is
coloured by his life in south London.
This shot looks down from the sky
towards Wandsworth Prison.

★ 100 Club
100 Oxford Street, Soho, W1D 1LL (7636
0933, www.the100club.co.uk). Oxford Circus
tube. **Open** *Shows* 7.30pm-midnight Mon; 7.30-
11.30pm Tue-Thur; 7.30pm-12.30am Fri; 7.30pm-
1am Sat; 7.30-11pm Sun. **Tickets** £6-£20.
Credit MC, V. **Map** p406 V1.
Perhaps the most adaptable venue in London, this
wide, famous, 350-capacity basement room has long
provided a home for trad jazz, pub blues, northern
soul and, famously, punk: the venue staged a historic show in 1976 that featured the Sex Pistols, the
Clash and the Damned. These days, it offers jazz,
indie acts and ageing rockers.

Jazz Café
5 Parkway, Camden, NW1 7PG (7688 8899
information, 0844 847 2514 tickets, www.jazz
cafe.co.uk). Camden Town tube. **Box office**
In person 10.30am-5.30pm Mon-Sat. *By phone*
24hrs daily. **Tickets** £10-£30. **Credit** MC, V.
There's some jazz on the schedule, but this two-floor
club deals more in soul, R&B and hip hop these
days, and has become the first port of call for soon-
to-be-huge US acts: Mary J Blige, John Legend and
the Roots all played their first European dates here.

★ Lexington
96-98 Pentonville Road, Islington, N1 9JB
(7837 5371, www.thelexington.co.uk). Angel
tube. **Open** noon-2am Mon-Thur; noon-4am
Fri, Sat; noon-midnight Sun. **Tickets** £5-£10.
Credit AmEx, MC, V. **Map** p402 N2.
They've put a lot of thought into things at the
Lexington. Downstairs, there's a lounge bar offering
a vast array of US beers and bourbons, above-par

bar food and a Rough Trade music quiz (every
Monday). And upstairs is a 200-capacity venue, with
a superb sound system in place for the leftfield indie
that dominates.

★ Luminaire
311 Kilburn High Road, Kilburn, NW6 7JR
(7372 7123 information, 0844 477 1000
tickets, www.theluminaire.co.uk). Kilburn tube
or Brondesbury rail. **Open** hrs vary. **Tickets**
£6-£20. **Credit** AmEx, MC, V.
The Luminaire won *Time Out's* Venue of the Year
accolade in 2006, and remains one of the best music
clubs in town. The policy is fantastically broad, taking in everything from alt-country hero Howe Gelb
to noise-mongers Jesu. The sound system is top-
notch, the decor is stylish and the staff are lovely.

93 Feet East
150 Brick Lane, E1 6QL (7770 6006, www.93feet
east.co.uk). Aldgate East tube. **Open** 5-11pm Mon-
Thur; 5pm-1am Fri; noon-1am Sat; noon-10.30pm
Sun. *Shows* vary. **Admission** free-£5. **No credit
cards. Map** p403 S5.
With three rooms, a balcony and a wrap-around
courtyard that's great for barbecues, 93 Feet East
manages to overcome the otherwise crippling lack of
a proper late licence. Expect tech-house DJs, a mix of
indie-dance bands and art-rockers, and short films.

Relentless Garage
20-22 Highbury Corner, Highbury, N5 1RD
(7619 6720 information, 0844 847 1878 tickets,
www.thegarage.co.uk). Highbury & Islington
tube/rail. **Box office** *By phone* 24hrs daily.
Tickets £3-£20. **Credit** AmEx, MC, V.

Vortex Jazz Club. *See p320.*

This 650-capacity Highbury venue has reopened after three years and an impressive refurbishment. It now books an exciting calendar of indie, art-rock and punk gigs. Upstairs is a smaller venue.

12 Bar Club
22-23 Denmark Place, Soho, WC2H 8NL (7240 2622, www.12barclub.com). Tottenham Court Road tube. **Open** *Café* 11am-7pm Mon-Sat; noon-7pm Sun. *Bar* 7pm-3am Mon-Sat; 6-10.30pm Sun. *Shows* from 7.30pm; nights vary. **Admission** £5-£15. **No credit cards. Map** p407 X2.
A London treasure, this easy-to-miss hole-in-the-wall venue books a grab-bag of low-key stuff, though its tiny size (capacity of 100, minuscule stage) dictates a predominance of singer-songwriters.

Underworld
174 Camden High Street, Camden, NW1 0NE (7734 1932, www.theunderworldcamden.co.uk). Camden Town tube. **Box office** *In person* 11am-11pm Mon-Sat; noon-10.30pm Sun. *By phone* 24hrs daily. **Shows** hrs vary. **Admission** £5-£20. **No credit cards.**
A dingy maze of pillars and bars below Camden, this subterranean oddity is an essential for metal and hardcore fans who want their ears bludgeoned by bands with names such as the Atomic Bitchwax, Skeletonwitch and Decrepit Birth.

Union Chapel
Compton Terrace, Islington, N1 2XD (7226 1686, www.unionchapel.org.uk). Highbury & Islington tube/rail. **Open** hrs vary. **Tickets** free-£40. **No credit cards.**
This Victorian Gothic church still holds regular services each Sunday, but it's also one of London's most atmospheric gig venues, booking acts such as Joan as Policewoman. Look out for their many thematic series, as well as freebie Daylight gigs on Sundays. The acoustic is better suited to smaller line-ups.

★ Windmill
22 Blenheim Gardens, Brixton, SW2 5BZ (8671 0700, www.windmillbrixton.co.uk). Brixton tube/rail. **Open** *Shows* 8-11pm Mon-Thur; 8pm-1am Fri, Sat; 5-11pm Sun. **Admission** free-£6. **No credit cards.**
If you can live with the iffy sound and the amusingly taciturn barflies, you might think this pokey little L-shaped pub is one of the city's best venues. Mark it down to the adventurous bookings (punk, country, techno, folk, metal) and cheap admission.

Jazz

The international big hitters keep on visiting, but these are exciting times for London's homespun jazz scene. Inspired by freewheeling attractions at the **Vortex** (*see p320*), the

Festivals Jazz

What not to miss this year.

Showcasing London's thriving jazz scene while simultaneously welcoming an array of big names from abroad, November's excellent **London Jazz Festival** (7324 1880, www.londonjazzfestival.org.uk) covers most bases, from trad to free improv. It's comfortably the biggest jazz festival of the year, though you may also find some interesting events at the all-free, open-air **Ealing Jazz Festival** (8825 6064, www.ealing.gov.uk, July) and Greenwich's **Riverfront Jazz Festival** (www.riverfrontjazz.co.uk, late Sept). In addition, look out for the occasional showcases organised by the **Loop Collective** (www.loopcollective.org) and the **F-IRE Collective** (www.f-ire.com), which feature some of the best young talents in the country.

sporadic **Boat-Ting Club** nights (www.boat-ting.co.uk) and Hugh Metcalfe's roaming **Klinker** (www.iotacism.com/klinkerizer), acts such as Portico Quartet and Led Bib have both bothered the Mercury Prize with recent albums, and the F-IRE and Loop Collectives are sheltering boundary-pushing future stars.

In addition to the venues below, the **100 Club** (*see left*) hosts trad groups, while the **Spice of Life** at Cambridge Circus (6 Moor Street, W1, 7739 3025) has solid mainstream jazz. The **Jazz Café** (*see left*) lives up to its name from time to time; there's a good deal of jazz at the excellent **Kings Place** (*see p308*); and both the **Barbican** (*see p308*) and the **Southbank Centre** (*see p311*) host dozens of big names. For the increasingly excellent **London Jazz Festival**, *see above* **Festivals**.

Bull's Head
373 Lonsdale Road, Barnes, SW13 9PY (8876 5241, www.thebullshead.com). Barnes Bridge rail. **Open** 11am-11pm Mon-Sat; noon-11pm Sun. *Shows* 8.30pm Mon-Sat; 1-3.30pm, 8.30-11pm Sun. **Admission** £5-£12. **Credit** AmEx, MC, V.
This venerable, ancient Thamesside pub won a reputation for hosting modern jazz in the '60s but today specialises in mainstream British jazz and swing. Regular guests include ace veteran pianist Stan Tracey and sax maestro Peter King.

★ Café Oto
18-22 Ashwin Street, Dalston, E8 3DL (7923 1231, www.cafeoto.co.uk). Dalston Kingsland rail/bus 30, 38, N38, 67, 76, 149, N149, 56,

ARTS & ENTERTAINMENT

277, 242. **Open** 9.30am-1am Mon-Fri; 10am-midnight Sat, Sun. *Shows* from 8pm; days vary. **Admission** £3-£8. **No credit cards**.
Opened in April 2008, this 150-capacity café and music venue can't easily be categorised, though its website offers the tidy definition that it specialises in 'creative new music that exists outside of the mainstream'. That means Japanese noise rockers ('Oto' is Japanese for 'sound'), electronica pioneers, improvising noiseniks and artists from the stranger ends of the rock, folk and classical spectrums.

★ Charlie Wright's International Bar
45 Pitfield Street, Hoxton, N1 6DA (7490 8345, www.myspace.com/charliewrights). Old Street tube/rail. **Open** noon-1am Mon-Wed, Sun; noon-4am Thur, Fri; 6pm-4am Sat. *Shows* 8-10pm daily. **Admission** free-£10. **Credit** MC, V. **Map** p403 Q3.
When Zhenya Strigalev and Patsy Craig began programming the line-up here in 2006, London's jazz fans were given a reason to visit. Now this agreeably scruffy venue stages a fine jazz programme on all nights except Saturdays. Gigs don't usually start until 10pm, and run late on Thursdays and Fridays.

Forge
3-7 Delancey Street, Camden, NW1 7NL (7383 7808, www.forgevenue.org). Camden Town tube. **Open** hrs vary. **Admission** free-£15. **Credit** AmEx, MC, V.

Forge.

This environmentally friendly, 125-capacity venue has just about everything – solar panels, a natural ventilation system, fantastic acoustics, a first-class restaurant (Caponata) that opens up into the performance space and a line-up that runs the gamut from Swedish noodling to minimalism.

Pizza Express Jazz Club
10 Dean Street, Soho, W1D 3RW (7439 8722, www.pizzaexpresslive.com). Tottenham Court Road tube. **Shows** 9-11pm daily. **Admission** £15-£25. **Credit** AmEx, DC, MC, V. **Map** p406 W2.
The upstairs restaurant (7437 9595) is jazz-free, but the 120-capacity basement is one of the best mainstream jazz venues in town. Singers such as Kurt Elling and Lea DeLaria join instrumentalists from home and abroad on the nightly bills.

★ Ronnie Scott's
47 Frith Street, Soho, W1D 4HT (7439 0747, www.ronniescotts.co.uk). Leicester Square or Tottenham Court Road tube. **Shows** 7pm daily. **Admission** (non-members) £15-£100. **Credit** AmEx, MC, V. **Map** p406 W2.
Opened (on a different site) by the British saxophonist Ronnie Scott in 1959, this jazz institution was completely refurbished in 2006. The capacity was expanded to 250, the food got better and the bookings become drearier. Happily, though, Ronnie's has got back on track of late, with jazz heavyweights once more dominating in place of the mainstream pop acts who held sway for a while.

606 Club
90 Lots Road, Chelsea, SW10 0QD (7352 5953, www.606club.co.uk). Imperial Wharf rail, or bus 11, 211. **Shows** 7.30pm Mon; 7pm Tue-Thur; 8pm Fri, Sat; 12.30pm, 7pm Sun. **Tickets** £8-£12. **Credit** AmEx, MC, V.
Since 1976, Steve Rubie has run this spot, which relocated to this 150-capacity club in 1987. Alongside its Brit-dominated bills, expect informal jams featuring musos who've come from gigs elsewhere. There's no entrance fee as such; bands are funded from a music charge added to bills at the end of the night. Alcohol can only be served to non-members with food.

★ Vortex Jazz Club
Dalston Culture House, 11 Gillet Street, Dalston, N16 8JN (7254 4097, www.vortexjazz.co.uk). Dalston Kingsland rail. **Shows** 8.45pm daily. **Admission** free-£12. **Credit** MC, V.
Before Café Oto (*see p319*) joined the fray, the Vortex was the capital's centre for leftfield jazz, avant-garde and other marginalised talent, and it retains a fearsome reputation. Since relocating to Dalston in 2005, the venue has gone from strength to strength, hosting its own strand of the London Jazz Festival and various other forward-thinking events. The bar stays open late for further cosmic discussions.

Nightlife

Want to party? Time to explore the city's hidden corners.

A couple of years ago, many of the most popular venues were a short stroll from a central tube station. Today, though, finding the best clubs requires a little more effort. You'll have to head to no-tube-land out east for the likes of **Dalston Superstore**, go down cobbled backstreets in London Bridge to find **Cable** or schlep out to Greenwich for **Matter**. But do so and the payoff is enormous: you're finding the most cutting-edge nightlife in London and, perhaps, the world.

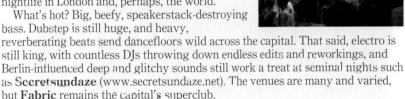

What's hot? Big, beefy, speakerstack-destroying bass. Dubstep is still huge, and heavy, reverberating beats send dancefloors wild across the capital. That said, electro is still king, with countless DJs throwing down endless edits and reworkings, and Berlin-influenced deep and glitchy sounds still work a treat at seminal nights such as **Secretsundaze** (www.secretsundaze.net). The venues are many and varied, but **Fabric** remains the capital's superclub.

NIGHTCLUBS

Shoreditch remains the hub of the capital's nightlife scene, especially around Brick Lane (which offers plenty of late-night bars at the northern end of the strip) and across towards Hoxton Square. The city's cool kids, though, are now taking the bus north up the Kingsland Road from here to **Dalston**. It can be difficult to find the clubs, much less what's happening in them, but a few moments spent perusing the Clubs section of *Time Out* magazine or hunting on Facebook will unearth some fabulous happenings at the likes of the **Dalston Superstore** (*see p305*) and **Visions Video** (588 Kingsland Road).

With the demise of the End and AKA, the **West End** no longer retains the appeal it once had; with the exception of **Madame JoJo's** (*see p323*), there's little here besides bars and pubs. And although **Egg** (*see p325*) remains a great clubbing spot, **King's Cross** lost out when the Cross, Canvas and the Key closed due to rail development.

About the author

Time Out*'s features editor,* **Simone Baird** *has written about nightlife and edgy cabaret for publications such as the* Sunday Times Style *magazine and* NME.

There's more of interest further out. The gay village in **Vauxhall** (*see p301*) is just as welcoming to straight-rolling, open-minded types, with club promoters looking more and more towards south-of-the-river venues such as **Area** (67 Albert Embankment, SE1 7TP, www.areaclublondon.com) and the **Lightbox** (6A South Lambeth Place, SW8 1SP) as occasional homes for their parties. The calendar is usually even fuller at **Cable** (*see p323*) in London Bridge, and, further out still, at **Matter** (*see p328*) in the old Millennium Dome. Meanwhile, the cabaret juggernaut rolls on, smashing through into mainstream clubland. To see the best, head to **Volupté** (*see p324*), which hosts opulent burlesque nights and the always-interesting **Bethnal Green Working Men's Club** (*see p325*). Whatever you do, go with an open mind.

London rewards those who are willing to chance something new, but not all risks are worth taking. Before you head out, find which night bus gets you home and where you need to catch it (the tube doesn't start until around 7am on Sundays). But if the bus network still proves too mind-boggling at stupid o'clock, then check out our guide to catching a cab (*see p326 and p328*). And always make sure that your cab is licensed; to find out how to tell, and for more on the public transport network, *see pp363-365*.

Find London's best bars, clubs and restaurants in one place.

LATE**NIGHTLONDON**.CO.UK
Tel: 0870 7777 080

CENTRAL

Bathhouse
*7-8 Bishopsgate Churchyard, City, EC2M 3TJ
(7920 9207, www.thebathhousevenue.com).
Liverpool Street tube/rail.* **Open** 5pm-midnight
Mon-Wed; 5pm-2am Thur; 5pm-5am Fri; 9pm-
5am Sat. **Admission** £5-£8. **Credit** MC, V.
This Victorian Turkish bathhouse is now a fresh
London party space. All marble and gilt mirrors, it
seems almost too appropriate for decadent Sunday
happening the Boom Boom Club and its showgirl
burlesque and young neo-cabaret stars. Dress to the
nines in your vintage finest, then drink wildly to fit
in. Saturday sees Rock-a-Billy Rebels draw dressed-
up fans of '50s-vintage rock 'n' roll.

★ Cable
*33A Bermondsey Street, Borough, SE1 2EG
(7403 7730, www.cable-london.com). London
Bridge tube/rail.* **Open** 11pm-6am Fri, Sat; 10pm-
5am Sun. **Admission** £5-£15. **Credit** MC, V.
All old-style brickwork and industrial air-con ducts,
this new spot has a similar feel to Fabric. No tiny
basement, the venue boasts two dance arenas, a bar
with a spot-and-be-spotted mezzanine, plenty of
seating and a great covered smoking area out the
back. High-calibre nights include forward-thinking
electro session Bugged Out and ace tech house rave-
up Mute. Don't hesitate when staff ask to take your
thumbprint when you check your coat; if you lose
your ticket, you won't need to wait for the club to
clear before you can claim it back.

Fabric
*77A Charterhouse Street, Clerkenwell, EC1M
3HN (7336 8898, www.fabriclondon.com).
Farringdon tube/rail.* **Open** 10pm-6am Fri; 11pm-
8am Sat; 11pm-6am Sun. **Admission** £8-£18.
Credit AmEx, MC, V. **Map** p402 O5.
Fabric remains the club that most visitors come to
see in London, and with good reason. Fridays
always and forever belong to the bass; highlights
include DJ Hype, who takes over all three rooms once
a month for his drum 'n' bass and dubstep night
Playaz, and Switch & Sinden's electro bass-heavy
Get Familiar party, a sell-out every other month.
Saturdays descend into techy, minimal, deep house
territory, with original resident Craig Richard joined
by performances from artists that you just can't hear
anywhere else. Sunday nights feature East End
down-and-dirty electro jump-up Wet Yourself.

Madame JoJo's
*8-10 Brewer Street, Soho, W1F 0SE (7734 3040,
www.madamejojos.com). Leicester Square or
Piccadilly Circus tube.* **Open** 8pm-3.30am Tue;
9pm-3.30am Thur; 10pm-3.30am Fri, Sun; 7pm-
3.30am Sat. **Admission** £4-£10. **Credit** AmEx,
MC, V. **Map** p408 W3.
The red and slightly shabby basement space at
JoJo's is a beacon for those seeking to escape the
West End's post-work chain pubs. Treasured nights
include variety (the London Burlesque Social Club,
first Thursdays; Kitsch Cabaret, every Saturday;
Finger in the Pie Cabaret's talent-spotting show-
cases) and Keb Darge's long-running Deep Funk.

ARTS & ENTERTAINMENT

Paradise by Way of Kensal Green.
See p325.

All Bar None

Not all of London's best club nights happen in clubs.

A number of major clubs closed for good in 2008 and 2009, among them the Cross, the Key, Canvas, Turnmills and the End. But despite their demise, Londoners didn't suddenly stop clubbing. Quite the opposite – indeed, in some ways, the final parties at these era-defining venues helped to revitalise the capital's clubland.

As these bigger venues closed, pubs have become more popular among promoters, and a host of fabulous boozers have flexed late licences in order to provide cutting-edge entertainment for savvy clubbing folk. Whereas 'proper' clubs often have a short time frame in which to make money (six hours a night, three nights a week), pubs don't suffer such limitations. And the numerous small rooms they offer can provide a cheap canvas for promoters wishing to try something different.

Brixton has long had the **Dogstar** (*see p328*), the three-floored Coldharbour Lane watering hole referenced in the Streets' 'Too Much Brandy'. And now it's also got **Dex** (*see p328*). On top of the Prince hotel, the venue has an enormous roof terrace, full of sun loungers and capacious bedouin tents, and a varied programme of events. Also south of the river, the **Amersham Arms** (*see p315*) attracts a young indie crowd, while north-west London has **Paradise by Way of Kensal Green** (*see right*).

Across on the other side of town, the **Star of Bethnal Green** (*see p326*) has outstanding rave credentials thanks to Mulletover's promoter Rob Star. Decked out in wild and flamboyant murals with a great sound system, and offering free admission every night, the venue draws in east London's young turks. While the Amersham leans more towards guitar-based gigs, the Star is a straight-up, hands-in-the-air rave, and canny swap parties, queer disco-a-thons and Sunday roasts mean that it's never far from rammed.

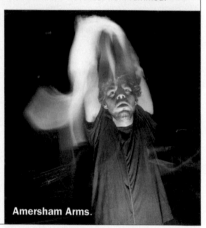

Amersham Arms.

Social

5 Little Portland Street, Marylebone, W1W 7JD (7636 4992, www.thesocial.com). Oxford Circus tube. **Open** noon-midnight Mon-Wed; noon-1am Thur, Fri; 6pm-1am Sat; hrs vary Sun. **Admission** free-£5. **Credit** AmEx, MC, V. **Map** p408 U1.
A discreet, opaque front hides this daytime diner and DJ bar of supreme quality, set up by Heavenly Records nearly a decade back. After drinks upstairs, its clientele of music industry workers, alt-rock nonebrities and other scenesters shamble down to an intimate basement space rocked by DJs six nights a week. The monthly Hip Hop Karaoke (www.hiphopkaraokelondon.blogspot.com) is a giggle.

★ Volupté

7-9 Norwich Street, Holborn, EC4A 1EJ (7831 1622, www.volupte-lounge.com). Chancery Lane tube. **Open** 5pm-1am Tue, Wed; 5pm-3am Thur, Fri; 2pm-2am Sat. **Admission** £5-£15. **Credit** MC, V. **Map** p406 N5.

Expect to suffer wallpaper envy as you enter the ground-floor bar and then descend to the club. Punters enjoy some of the best cabaret talent in town from tables set beneath absinthe-inspired vines. Afternoon Tease combines burlesque with high tea most Saturday afternoons; the Black Cotton Club turns goes back to the 1920s.

NORTH LONDON

Better known as gig venues, **Koko** (*see p313*) and the **Barfly** (*see p315*) also have good reputations for feisty club nights.

★ Big Chill House

257-259 Pentonville Road, King's Cross, N1 9NL (7427 2540, www.bigchill.net). King's Cross tube/rail. **Open** noon-midnight Mon-Wed, Sun; noon-1am Thur; noon-3am Fri, Sat. **Admission** £5 after 10pm Fri, Sat. **Credit** MC, V. **Map** p399 M3.

ARTS & ENTERTAINMENT

A festival, a record label, a bar and now also a club venue, the Big Chill empire rolls on. A good thing too, if it keeps offering such interesting things as this three-floor space. The likes of A Skillz and owner Pete Lawrence regularly handle deck duties, and there's great terrace.

Egg
200 York Way, King's Cross, N7 9AP (7609 8364, www.egglondon.net). King's Cross tube/rail then free shuttle from York Way. **Open** 10pm-6am Fri; 10pm Sat-noon Sun. **Admission** £5-£15. **Credit** MC, V. **Map** p399 L2.
With its Mediterranean-styled three floors, garden and enormous terrace (complete with a small pool), EGG is big enough to get lost in, but manages to retain an intimate atmosphere. The upstairs bar in red ostrich leather is rather elegant, but the main dancefloor downstairs has a warehouse rave feel. Highlights include forward-looking electro session Always Fridays.
▶ *Looking for some kinky fun? Cabaret club Apothecary (3 Vale Royal, N7 9AP, 7609 8364, www.apothecarybar.co.uk) is just next door.*

★ Paradise by Way of Kensal Green
19 Kilburn Lane, Kensal Green, W10 4AE (8969 0098, www.theparadise.co.uk). Kensal Green tube or Kensal Rise rail. **Open** noon-midnight Mon-Wed; noon-1am Thur; noon-2am Fri, Sat; noon-11.30pm Sun. **Credit** MC, V.
This is one of the fastest rising stars in the pub-restaurant-club market, thanks to canny promotion by DJ Tayo. Themed supper clubs, vintage burlesque shows and kicking rave-ups from the likes of Justin Robertson and Tayo himself make it more than just a good local spot – it's become a destination in its own right. *Photos p323.*

Proud
Horse Hospital, Stables Market, Camden, NW1 8AH (7482 3867, www.proudcamden.com). Chalk Farm tube. **Open** 11am-1.30am Mon-Wed; 11am-2.30am Thur-Sat; 11am-12.30am Sun. **Admission** free-£10. **Credit** AmEx, MC, V. **Map** p399 L2.
North London guitar-slingers do rockstar debauchery at this former equine hospital, whether draping themselves – cocktail in hand – over the luxurious textiles in the individual stable-style booths, sinking into deck chairs on the outdoor terrace, or spinning around in the main band room to trendonista electro, indie and alternative sounds.

EAST LONDON

East London is now the heart of London's clubland, with most venues of note based in Hoxton, Shoreditch and, increasingly, Dalston. In addition to the venues below, it's also worth checking **Cargo** (*see p316*), which offers club nights alongside its strong programme of live music, and gay hangout the **Dalston Superstore** (*see p305*).

Bethnal Green Working Men's Club
42-44 Pollard Row, Bethnal Green, E2 6NB (7739 7170, www.workersplaytime.net). Bethnal Green tube. **Open** hrs vary. **Admission** free-£8. **Credit** AmEx, MC, V. **Map** p403 R4.
Sticky red carpet and broken lampshades perfectly suit the programme of quirky lounge, retro rock 'n' roll and fancy-dress burlesque parties from spandex-lovin' dance husband-and-wife Duotard or Grind a Go Go, for which burlesque starlets get a hip 1960s dancefloor. The mood is friendly, the playlist upbeat and the air full of artful, playful mischief.

Dalston Superstore.

INSIDE TRACK GETTING HOME FROM SHOREDITCH

According to Dimi, a local cab driver, 'You'll always catch a cab where Bethnal Green Road meets Shoreditch High Street, by the members' club Shoreditch House. Many cabbies will have stopped at the Brick Lane Beigel Bake (*see p223*), so there are a lot around there. You can also find cabs at the junction of Hackney Road and Kingsland Road, by Browns bar and the church.'

Book Club
100-106 Leonard Street, Shoreditch, EC2A 4RH (7684 8618, www.wearetbc.com). Old Street tube/rail. **Open** 8am-midnight Mon-Wed; 8am-2am Thur, Fri; 10am-2am Sat; 10am-midnight Sun. **Admission** £5. **Credit** MC, V.
Taking over the two-floored site formerly known as Home, the Book Club aims to fuse lively creative events with late-night drinking seven nights of the week. Out of the gates with a programming roster that includes live art battle-cum-hip hop party Secret Wars and tranny superstar Jonny Woo's Dance Class, it might just succeed.

Catch
22 Kingsland Road, Hoxton, E2 8DA (7729 6097, www.thecatchbar.com). Old Street tube/rail. **Open** 6pm-midnight Mon, Tue, Wed; 6pm-2am Thur-Sat; 7pm-1am Sun. **Admission** free-£12. **Credit** AmEx, MC, V. **Map** p403 R3.
Located at the southern end of the Kingsland Road, Catch doesn't look like much and its staff can be somewhat surly, but the small upstairs room attracts a great mix of adventurous young promoters. The arty, film noir-inspired Decasia Club attracts hip things dressed in black; the monthly Meat Raffle offers up space disco, new wave power pop and the odd helping of gothic rock.

★ East Village
89 Great Eastern Street, Shoreditch, EC2A 3HX (7739 5173, www.eastvillageclub.com). Old Street tube/rail. **Open** 5pm-midnight Tue, Wed; 5pm-1am Thur; 5pm-4am Fri; 9pm-4am Sat; 2-11pm Sun. **Admission** free-£10. **Credit** AmEx, MC, V. **Map** p403 Q4.
Stuart Patterson, one of the Faith crew who've been behind all-day house-music parties across London since 1999, has transformed what was once the Medicine Bar into this two-floor, 'real house' bar-club that punches above its weight. The top-notch DJs should suit any sophisticated clubber; expect to see the likes of Chicago house don Derrick Carter, legendary reggae selector Aba Shanti-I and London's own Mr C (*see right* **Profile**).

Herbal
10-14 Kingsland Road, Hoxton, E2 8DA (7613 4462, www.herbaluk.com). Old Street tube/rail. **Open** 9pm-2am Tue-Thur; 9pm-3am Fri, Sat; 8pm-2am Sun. **Admission** free-£10. **Credit** AmEx, MC, V. **Map** p403 R3.
The lines outside this loved but under-the-weather two-floor venue still stretch down the block, leaving queuers and smokers with a wildly insalubrious view of gridlocked Kingsland Road as they wait. Bass-fuelled dancefloor devastation rules on Fridays at rotating nights such as Doctor's Orders, Fiver and Viper Recordings; Saturdays offer house music all night long, with nights such as Bobby & Steve Presents and the soulful We Love Soul.

Old Blue Last
38 Great Eastern Street, Shoreditch, EC2A 3ES (7739 7033, www.theoldbluelast.com). Liverpool Street or Old Street tube/rail. **Open** noon-midnight Mon-Wed; noon-12.30am Thur, Sun; noon-1.30am Fri, Sat. **Admission** free-£5. **Credit** AmEx, MC, V. **Map** p403 R4.
This shabby two-floor Victorian boozer was transformed by hipster handbook *Vice* in 2004. The Klaxons, Amy Winehouse and Lily Allen have all played secret shows in the sauna-like upper room, but its high-fashion rock 'n' rollers also dig regular club nights from girlie indie DJ troupe My Ex Boyfriend's Records and Sean McLusky's scuzzy electro rock nights.

Plastic People
147-149 Curtain Road, Shoreditch, EC2A 3QE (7739 6471, www.plasticpeople.co.uk). Old Street tube/rail. **Open** 9pm-2am 2nd Thur of mth; 10.30pm-4am Fri, Sat; 9pm-1.30am Sun. **Admission** £5-£10. **Credit** MC, V. **Map** p405 R4.
The long-established and long-popular Plastic People subscribes to the old-school line that all you need for a kicking party is a dark basement and a sound system (the rig here embarrasses those in many larger clubs). The programming remains true to form: deep techno to house, all-girl DJ line-ups and many a star DJ squeezing through the doors for a secret gig.

Star of Bethnal Green
359 Bethnal Green Road, Bethnal Green, E2 6LG (07932 869705, www.starofbethnalgreen. com). Bethnal Green tube. **Open** 11.30am-midnight Mon-Thur, Sun; 11.30am-2am Fri, Sat. **Admission** free-£5. **Credit** MC, V. **Map** p405 R4.
A bold red and silver star stamps the wall behind the stage in this intimate boozer, which offers low-key gigs from big bands and an eclectic yet funky-fresh line-up of disco to house to indie nights, burlesque freak shows and madcap quiz nights (cash for the winners, free pasta for everyone).

Profile Mr C

A clubland pioneer comes full circle as he returns to SE1.

Richard West got his stage name in the days when he used a CB radio and needed a handle. He later told journalists that the 'C' came from 'cunt', but the truth is more prosaic: as a supporter of Chelsea FC, he called himself Chelsea Boy, shortening it to Mr C when he started as an MC.

Cutting his rapping teeth on pirate radio in the mid '80s, Mr C joined forces with Colin Faver and Evil Eddie Richards to become the resident rapper at Camden Palace. The following year, he debuted as a DJ at his birthday party on January 2 1988, and was soon offered a night of his own. The result was Fantasy, one of London's very first acid house parties, and it was through this he met Paul Rip, promoter of the RiP nights on Clink Street near London Bridge. Following his successes here, he went on to organise a string of other nights, among them Harmony, the Main Buzz, the Drop Club, Vapour Space and Cyclone, while also topping the charts as a member of the Shamen on the cheeky drug anthem 'Ebeneezer Goode'.

In 1995, Mr C joined forces with fellow DJ Layo Pashkin to open the End. Despite being located in unfashionable central London, it quickly became one of the city's most important and most beloved dance music clubs, thanks to a top-drawer sound system and some forward-looking programming. The sadness when the venue shut up shop at the start of 2009 was genuine and heartfelt.

However, despite the end of the End, its founder is still on the scene. Having started at the End back in 2002, his club night Superfreq has now found a new home at **Cable** (*see p323*), a new venue that's just around the corner from Clink Street. It neatly brings this clubland veteran back to the neighbourhood in which he first built his reputation, while also keeping him at the heart of London's changing clubland. He should be there for a while yet.

ARTS & ENTERTAINMENT

333

*333 Old Street, Hoxton, EC1V 9LE (7739
5949, www.333mother.com). Old Street tube/rail.*
Open *Club* 10.30pm-3am Fri, Sat; 10pm-5am Sat.
Bar 8pm-3am daily. **Admission** *Club* free-£7.
Credit MC, V. **Map** p405 Q4.
While it's no longer the be-all and end-all of East End
clubbing, this three-floored clubbing institution still
draws queues for indie-rave mash-ups at the weekends. The basement's dark and intense, which
works well for the dubstep talent on show. Upstairs
is just like a house party, complete with broken loos
and random strangers falling over your shoes.

SOUTH LONDON

Dex

*467-469 Brixton Road, Brixton, SW9 8HH
(7326 4455, www.princeanddex.com). Brixton
tube/rail.* **Open** 10pm-6am Fri, Sat. **Admission**
£10. **Credit** AmEx, MC, V.
This plush members' club and boutique hotel is a
beacon for a new young professional media crowd
looking for somewhere sexy for post-work and late-
night drinks. Its USP is a two-tiered rooftop bar with
a hot tub and panoramic views over Brixton; the
soundtrack runs to fidget house (Slide), hip hop
(Mind Yuh Business) and even Balkan music (raucous rompers Stranger than Paradise).

Dogstar

*389 Coldharbour Lane, Brixton, SW9 8LQ
(7733 7515, www.antic-ltd.com/dogstar). Brixton
tube/rail.* **Open** 4pm-2am Mon-Thur; 4pm-4am
Fri; noon-4am Sat; noon-2am Sun. **Admission**
£5 after 10pm Fri, Sat. **Credit** MC, V.
A Brixton institution from back when Coldharbour
Lane was an uncrossed frontier, the Dogstar is a
big street-corner pub that exudes the kind of urban
authenticity beloved by clubbers. The atmosphere
can be intense, but it's never less than vibrant and
is usually pretty friendly. The music policy varies,
but quality generally stays high.

Matter

*O2 Arena, Peninsula Square, Greenwich, SE10
ODY (0844 477 1000, www.matterlondon.com).
North Greenwich tube.* **Open** 10pm-6am Fri;

INSIDE TRACK GETTING
HOME FROM BRIXTON

Getting back from Brixton isn't always
easy. 'It can be tough to get a cab here,
so pick a night when there's a big gig
on at the Brixton Academy (*see p313*),'
says one driver. 'Try outside the Fridge
nightclub on Brixton Hill, because there's
a taxi rank there too.'

10pm-7am Sat. **Tickets** £10-£15. **Credit**
AmEx, MC, V.
Meet Fabric's dream venue, a 2,600-capacity spot
under the former Millennium Dome. Sightlines are
great and the sound is amazing: the 'BodyKinetic'
floor is a step forward from Fabric's 'BodySonic'
dancefloor, designed to vibrate to the frequencies
of the bass speakers directly below it. Expect similar programming to the venue's older brother, with
state-of-the-art 3D mapped audiovisuals on inter-
locking screens. It's rather far from central London
at 6am, but Thames Clipper boats operate half-
hourly to Waterloo Bridge and Thames Pier.
► *For IndigO2, see p313; for the O2 Arena,
see p314; for Fabric, see p323.*

Ministry of Sound

*103 Gaunt Street, off Newington Causeway,
Elephant & Castle, SE1 6DP (0870 060 0010
Premium, www.ministryofsound.com). Elephant
& Castle tube/rail.* **Open** 10.30pm-6am Fri;
11pm-7am Sat. **Admission** £12-£20. **Credit**
AmEx, MC, V. **Map** p404 O10.
Cool it ain't (there's little naffer in London clubland
than the VIP rooms here), but home to a killer sound
system the Ministry most certainly is. Long-running
trance and epic house night the Gallery has made its
home here on Fridays, with large sets from Paul
Oakenfold and Sander van Doorn; the Saturday
Sessions chop and change between deep techno,
fidget house, electro and more, through Sasha's 18,
Erick Morillo's Subliminal Sessions and the summery house Soul Heaven.

Plan B

*418 Brixton Road, Brixton, SW9 7AY (0870
116 5421, www.plan-brixton.co.uk). Brixton
tube/rail.* **Open** 10pm-6am Fri; 10pm-8am Sat;
10pm-5am Sun. **Admission** £8-£12. **Credit**
AmEx, MC, V. **Map** p404 O10.
It may be small, but Plan B punches well above its
weight. Having been refurbished after a fire, it
reopened in autumn 2009 and the flow of hip hop
and funk stars resumed with a kicking relaunch
weekend that featured DJ sets from the likes of Hot
Chip and Goldie.

WEST LONDON

Notting Hill Arts Club

*21 Notting Hill Gate, Notting Hill, W11 3JQ
(7460 4459, www.nottinghillartsclub.com).
Notting Hill Gate tube.* **Open** 7pm-2am Tue-
Thur; 6pm-2am Fri; 4pm-2am Sat; 4pm-1am Sun.
Admission £5-£8; free before 8pm. **Credit** MC,
V. **Map** p394 A7.
Cool west London folk are grateful for this small,
basement club. It isn't much to look at, but it almost
single-handedly keeps this side of town on the radar
thanks to nights such as Thursday's YoYo: for fans
of crate-digging, it runs from funk to 1980s boogie.

Sport & Fitness

Olympics or no Olympics, London has always held a torch for sport.

Right now, you can't discuss London sport without discussing the 2012 Olympics. Anticipation is building, but there's plenty here to occupy visitors in the meantime. Alongside a multitude of week-in week-out matches featuring professional teams, the calendar is dotted with major one-off events, from the none-more-British Wimbledon championships to the all-American razzle-dazzle bestowed on the city by the NFL's annual visit. And more active types will also find plenty of easily accessible facilities for all manner of sports. For more on sport in London, see www.timeout.com/london/sport.

Spectator Sports

THE SPORTING YEAR

Below is a list of major sporting events in 2010. For all events held in stadiums or otherwise-enclosed spaces (basically, everything except the Boat Race, the London Marathon and the cycling events), book tickets in advance.

Spring

Rugby Union: Six Nations
Twickenham (see p332). **Date** 6 Feb, 27 Feb.
England take on Wales (6 Feb) and Ireland (27 Feb) at Twickenham in this tournament, which also features Scotland, France and Italy.

Football: Carling Cup Final
Wembley Stadium (see p331). **Date** 28 Feb.
The League Cup is seen as the lesser of the country's domestic tournaments, though victory ensures a place in the UEFA Europa League.

★ Rowing: The Boat Race
River Thames. **Date** 3 Apr.
See p272.

Rugby Union: EDF Energy Cup Final
Twickenham (see p332). **Date** 19-21 Apr.
The showpiece domestic knockout competition reaches its climax.

★ Athletics: Virgin London Marathon
Around London. **Date** 25 Apr.
See p272.

Summer

★ Cricket: Internationals
Brit Oval (see p331). **Dates** *Tests* 18-22 Aug: Eng v Pakistan. *One-day internationals* 30 June: Eng v Australia. 17 Sept: Eng v Pakistan.
Lord's (see p331). **Date** *Tests* 27-31 May: Eng v Bangladesh. 13-17 July: Pakistan v Australia. 26-30 Aug: Eng v Pakistan. *One-day internationals* 3 July: Eng v Australia. 20 Sept: Eng v Pakistan.
England play a series of Test matches (five-day fixtures) and one-day internationals (50 overs per side).

Football: Play-off Finals
Wembley Stadium (see p331). **Dates** 22, 29-30 May.
A promotion place is up for grabs for the winners of these enthralling end-of-season games between teams from the Championship and Leagues 1 and 2.

Football: FA Cup Final
Wembley Stadium (see p331). **Date** 15 May.
The climax of the historic tournament. Portsmouth, who beat Championship side Cardiff City in 2008, showed that smaller clubs can still win big trophies.

★ Horse Racing: Epsom Derby
Epsom Racecourse (see p332). **Date** 5 June.
One of Britain's best-known flat races.

Tennis: Aegon Championships
Palliser Road, West Kensington, W14 9EQ (7386 3400, www.queensclub.co.uk). Barons Court tube. **Date** 7-13 June.
The pros tend to treat this grass-court tournament as a summer warm-up to Wimbledon.

Olympic Park.

Horse Racing: Royal Ascot
Ascot Racecourse (see p332). **Date** 15-19 June.
Major races include the Ascot Gold Cup on the Thursday, which is Ladies' Day. Expect sartorial extravagance and fancy hats.

★ Cycling: Smithfield Nocturne
Around Smithfield Market (www.smithfield nocturne.co.uk). **Date** 19 June.
This exciting cycling event features everything from elite riders to City commuters taking part in a folding-bike race.

★ Tennis: Wimbledon Championships
All England Lawn Tennis Club, Church Road, Wimbledon, SW19 5AE (8971 2700, www. wimbledon.org). Southfields tube. **Date** 21 June-4 July.
Getting into Wimbledon requires forethought. Seats on the show courts are distributed by a ballot, which closes the previous year; enthusiasts who queue on the day may gain entry to the outer courts. You can also turn up later in the day and pay reduced rates for seats vacated by spectators who've left early.

Rowing: Henley Royal Regatta
Henley Reach, Henley-on-Thames, Oxon, RG9 2LY (01491 572153/www.hrr.co.uk). Henley-on-Thames rail. **Date** 30 June-4 July.
First held in 1839, and under royal patronage since 1851, Henley is a posh, five-day affair.

Athletics: Norwich Union London Grand Prix
Crystal Palace National Sports Centre (see right). **Date** last wknd of July.
Big names in athletics turn out each year for this annual track and field event.

Rugby Union: Middlesex Sevens
Twickenham (see p332). **Date** 14 Aug.
A curtain-raiser to the rugby union season, featuring short, fast seven-a-side matches.

Rugby League: Challenge Cup Final
Wembley Stadium (see right). **Date** 28 Aug.
The north's big day out, drawing boisterous, convivial crowds. St Helens have won the title for the last three seasons.

Autumn

Cycling: Tour of Britain
Around London. **Date** mid Sept.
Join thousands on the streets for a stage of British cycling's biggest outdoor event.

American Football: NFL
Wembley Stadium (see right). **Date** Oct.
The NFL took a regular-season fixture out of North America for the first time in 2007, and plans to do so every year until 2012.

Winter

★ Darts: PDC World Championshop
Alexandra Palace (www.pdcworldchampionship. co.uk). **Date** Dec-Jan.
The raucous, good-humoured PDC Championships are widely regarded as being of greater stature than the rival BDO tournament in January at Frimley Green (www.bdodarts.com).

Horse Racing: Stan James Christmas Festival
Kempton Park (see p332). **Date** 26-27 Dec.
The King George VI three-mile chase on Boxing Day is the highlight of this festival, a Christmas staple for racing fans.

MAJOR STADIUMS

There's a mass of building work at the Olympic site near Stratford, east London. In 2012, the **Olympic Park** will include a £600-million, 80,000-capacity stadium (due to be remodelled after the event), an aquatic centre, a velopark, a hockey centre and the Olympic village. See www.london2012.com for more.

The **O2 Arena** *(see p314)* hosts sporadic events, including ice hockey and basketball; **Wembley Arena** *(see p315)* offers boxing, snooker, basketball and show jumping.

Crystal Palace National Sports Centre
Ledrington Road, Crystal Palace, SE19 2BB (8778 0131, www.gll.org). Crystal Palace rail.

Until the Olympic stadium in Stratford is completed, this Grade II-listed building and leisure centre remains the major athletics venue in the country, and hosts popular summer Grand Prix events.

★ Wembley Stadium

Stadium Way, Wembley, Middx, HA9 0WS (0844 980 8001, www.wembleystadium.com). Wembley Park tube or Wembley Stadium rail.
Britain's most famous sports venue reopened in early 2007 after an expensive redevelopment. Designed by Lord Foster, the 90,000-capacity stadium is some sight, its futuristic steel arch now an imposing feature of the skyline. England football internationals and cup finals are played here, as are a number of one-off sporting events. There has been criticism of the high volume of seats set aside for corporate guests at big matches; guided tours offer alternative access.

INDIVIDUAL SPORTS

Basketball

Playing at the Capital City Academy in Willesden, the **London Capital** (838 8726, www.iwonder.co.uk) are the city's sole representatives in the British Basketball League (www.bbl.org.uk); perhaps regular pre-season NBA games at the **O2** (*see p.314*) will generate more enthusiasm. Contact the **English Basketball Association** (0114 223 5693, www.englandbasketball.co.uk) for more details.

Cricket

Typically, the English national team hosts Test and one-day series against two international sides each summer. For this summer's international fixtures, *see p329*.

Seats are easier to come by for county games, both four-day and one-day matches. The season runs from April to September. Surrey play at the Brit Oval and Middlesex play at Lord's.

Brit Oval *Kennington Oval, Kennington, SE11 5SS (0871 246 1100, www.surreycricket.com). Oval tube.* **Tickets** *International* £15-£100. *County* £12-£20.
★ **Lord's** *St John's Wood Road, St John's Wood, NW8 8QN (7432 1000, www.lords.org). St John's Wood tube.* **Tickets** *International* call for details. *County* £14-£20.

Football

Playing in the lucrative Barclays Premier League, **Arsenal** and **Chelsea** are the city's major players. Arsenal are based in the 60,000-capacity Emirates stadium; Chelsea depend on the transfer-market largesse of Russian oil tycoon Roman Abramovich, perhaps stymied by a ban on signing new players until 2011. Other Premier League clubs include **Fulham**, inconsistent **Tottenham**, and financially troubled **West Ham**. Chelsea, Arsenal and West Ham each have museums.

Tickets for Premier League games can be hard to obtain, but a visit to Fulham is a treat: a superb setting by the river, a historic ground and seats in the 'neutral' section often available on the day. For clubs in the lower leagues (the Championship, Football Leagues 1 and 2, all sponsored by Coca-Cola), tickets are cheaper and easier to obtain. Prices given are for adult non-members. The English national team plays its home fixtures at **Wembley Stadium** (*see left*). Tickets can be hard to come by.

Arsenal *Emirates Stadium, Ashburton Grove, Highbury, N7 7AF (0844 277 3625, www.arsenal.com). Arsenal tube.* **Tickets** £30-£70. Premier League.
Chelsea *Stamford Bridge, Fulham Road, Chelsea, SW6 1HS (0871 984 1905, www.chelseafc.com). Fulham Broadway tube.* **Tickets** £40-£65. Premier League.
Crystal Palace *Selhurst Park, Whitehorse Lane, South Norwood, SE25 6PU (0871 200 0071, www.cpfc.co.uk). Selhurst rail/468 bus.* **Tickets** £25-£35. Championship.
Fulham *Craven Cottage, Stevenage Road, Fulham, SW6 6HH (0870 442 1234, www.fulhamfc.com). Putney Bridge tube.* **Tickets** £25-£55. Premier League.
Leyton Orient *Matchroom Stadium, Brisbane Road, Leyton, E10 5NF (8926 1111, www.leytonorient.com). Leyton tube.* **Tickets** £20-£22. League 1.
Queens Park Rangers *Loftus Road Stadium, South Africa Road, Shepherd's Bush, W12 7PA (0870 112 1967, www.qpr.co.uk). White City tube.* **Tickets** £20-£35. Championship.
Tottenham Hotspur *White Hart Lane Stadium, 748 High Road, Tottenham, N17 0AP (0844 844 0102, www.tottenhamhotspur.com). White Hart Lane rail.* **Tickets** £37-£49. Premier League.

INSIDE TRACK
FOOTBALL MUSEUMS

If you failed to get tickets to a game, you can still see the inside of a football stadium by going on a tour. However, you'll need to decide who to support: **Chelsea** (0871 984 1955, www.chelseafctours.com), **West Ham** (0871 222 2700, www.whufc.com), **Tottenham Hotspur** (0844 844 0102, www.tottenhamhotspur.com) or **Arsenal** (7619 5000, www.arsenal.com) all offer tours.

West Ham United *Upton Park, Green Street, West Ham, E13 9AZ (0871 222 2700, www.whu fc.com). Upton Park tube.* **Tickets** *£35-£63. Premier League.*

Greyhound racing

In the absence of Walthamstow Stadium, sold for development in 2008 (although campaigners hope to save it), head to **Wimbledon** (Plough Lane, 0870 880 1000, www.lovethedogs.co.uk). Further afield, head to chirpy **Romford** (London Road, 01708 762345, www.romford greyhoundstadium.co.uk) or relaxed **Crayford** (Stadium Way, 01322 557836, www.crayford. com). For more, visit www.thedogs.co.uk.

Horse racing

The racing year is divided into the flat-racing season, from April to September, and the National Hunt season over jumps, from October to April. For more information about the 'sport of kings', visit www.discover-racing.com.

The Home Counties around London are liberally sprinkled with a fine variety of courses, each of which offers an enjoyable day out from the city. Impressive **Epsom** hosts the Derby in June, while cultured **Royal Ascot** offers the famous Royal Meeting in June and the King George Day in July; book ahead for them all. **Sandown Park** hosts the Whitbread Gold Cup in April and the Coral Eclipse Stakes in July. There's also racing at popular **Kempton Park** and delightful **Windsor**.

Epsom *Epsom Downs, Epsom, Surrey, KT18 5LQ (01372 726311 information, 0844 579 3004 tickets, www.epsomdowns.co.uk). Epsom Downs or Tattenham Corner rail.* **Admission** *£15-£50.*
Kempton Park *Staines Road East, Sunbury-on-Thames, TW16 5AQ (01932 782292 information, 0844 579 3004 tickets, www.kempton.co.uk). Kempton Park rail.* **Admission** *from £12.*
★ **Royal Ascot** *Ascot Racecourse, Ascot, Berks, SL5 7JX (0870 722 7227, www.ascot.co.uk). Ascot rail.* **Admission** *phone for details.*
Sandown Park *Portsmouth Road, Esher, Surrey, KT10 9AJ (01372 464348 information, 0844 579 3004 tickets, www.sandown.co.uk). Esher rail.* **Admission** *£18-£30.*
Windsor *Maidenhead Road, Windsor, Berks, SL4 5JJ (01753 498400, www.windsor-race course.co.uk). Windsor & Eton Riverside rail.* **Admission** *£13-£23.*

Motorsport

Every other Sunday, bangers, hot rods and stock cars come together at **Wimbledon Stadium** (8946 8000, www.spedeworth.co.uk)

for pedal-to-the-metal, family-oriented mayhem. **Rye House Stadium** (01992 440400) in Hoddesdon, on the northern edges of London, also hosts speedway, providing a home for the **Rye House Rockets** (www.ryehouse.com). Matches usually take place on Saturday nights.

Rugby

For more than a century, there have been two rival rugby 'codes', each with their own rules and traditions: rugby union and rugby league.

Rugby union dominates in the south of England. The Guinness Premiership runs from early September to May; most games are played on Saturday and Sunday afternoons. Look out, too, for matches in the Heineken Cup, a pan-European competition. Local Premiership teams – including Harlequins, infamous for 2009's 'Bloodgate' scandal – are listed below; for a full list of clubs, contact the Rugby Football Union (8892 2000, www.rfu.com).

The English national team's home games in the Six Nations Championship (Jan-Mar; *see p329*) are held at **Twickenham** (Rugby Road, Twickenham, Middx, 8892 2000, www.rfu.com), the home of English rugby union. Tickets are almost impossible to get hold of, but other matches are more accessible. There are also internationals in October and November.

Rugby league's heartland is in the north of England: London's sole Super League club is **Harlequins RL**. However, in late summer, the sport moves south as Wembley hosts the Challenge Cup final; *see p330*.

Harlequins *Stoop Memorial Ground, Langhorn Drive, Twickenham, Middx, TW2 7SX (8410 6000 information, 0871 527 1315 tickets, www. quins.co.uk). Twickenham rail.* **Tickets** *£10-£35.*
Harlequins Rugby League *Stoop Memorial Ground, Langhorn Drive, Twickenham, Middx, TW2 7SX (8410 6000 information, 0871 527 1315 tickets, www.league.quins.co.uk). Twickenham rail.* **Tickets** *£10-£35.*
London Irish *Madejski Stadium, Shooters Way, Reading, Berks, RG2 0FL (0844 249 1871, www.london-irish.com). Reading rail then £2 shuttle bus.* **Tickets** *£20-£35.*
London Wasps *Adams Park, Hillbottom Road, High Wycombe, Berks, Bucks HP (0844 225 2990, www.wasps.co.uk). High Wycombe rail.* **Tickets** *£15-£45.*
Saracens *Vicarage Road Stadium, Watford, Herts, WD18 0EP (01727 792800, www.saracens. com). Watford High Street rail.* **Tickets** *£15-£40.*

Tennis

For **Wimbledon**, *see p330*; for the **Aegon Championships**, *see p329*.

Arsenal v Chelsea. *See p331.*

Participation & Fitness

CYCLING

Cycling in London is more popular than ever, and it's set to grow even further with the introduction of a new, City Hall-sponsored bike rental scheme. Scheduled to launch in summer 2010, the scheme will see 6,000 bikes available for quick-and-easy rental from one of 400 self-service docking stations around central London. It should work like the successful Vélib' scheme in Paris: users will rent bikes with a credit card, and will be charged a fee based on the length of time they take before parking the bike at another docking station. For more on the scheme, see www.tfl.gov.uk/cycling.

This new scheme will be good for short journeys, but those in need of a longer rental should try one of the firms below. **Velorution** rent folding bikes, also with local delivery; and the **London Bicycle Tour Company** offers bikes from their South Bank base.

Serious riders should try the **Herne Hill Velodrome** (Burbage Road, Herne Hill, SE24, www.vcl.org.uk), the world's oldest circuit, or the newly opened **Redbridge Cycle Centre** (Forest Road, Hainault, Essex, IG6, 8500 9359), which boasts a road circuit, a mountain bike track and seven different circuit combinations.

London Bicycle Tour Company *1A Gabriel's Wharf, 56 Upper Ground, South Bank, SE1 9PP (7928 6838, www.londonbicycle.com). Southwark tube.* **Open** 10am-6pm daily. **Hire** £3/hr; £19/1st day, then £9/day. *Deposit* with credit card, or £180 cash. **Credit** AmEx, MC, V. **Map** p404 N7.
Velorution *18 Great Titchfield Street, Fitzrovia, W1W 8BD (7637 4004, www.velorution.biz). Oxford Circus tube.* **Open** 9am-7pm Mon-Fri; 10.30am-6.30pm Sat. **Hire** £20/day. **Credit** AmEx, MC, V. **Map** p398 J5.

GOLF

You don't have to be a member to tee off at the many public courses in the London area, but you will need to book in advance. There's a list of clubs at www.englishgolfunion.org; two accessible beauties are the lovely **Dulwich & Sydenham Hill Golf Club** in Dulwich (8693 8491, www.dulwichgolf.co.uk, £40, members only Sat & Sun) and the testing **North Middlesex Golf Club** near Arnos Grove (8445 3060, www.northmiddlesexgc.co.uk, £15-£30, members only before 1pm Sat & Sun).

HEALTH CLUBS & SPORTS CENTRES

A lot of London hotels have gym facilities. But if you're looking for something more serious, many health clubs and sports centres admit non-members and allow them to join classes. Some of the best are listed below; for a list of all venues in Westminster, call 7641 1846, or for Camden, call 7974 1542. Note that last entry is normally 45-60 minutes before the listed closing times. For more independent spirits, Hyde Park, Kensington Gardens and Battersea Park have good jogging trails.

★ Central YMCA

112 Great Russell Street, Bloomsbury, WC1B 3NQ (7343 1844, www.centralymca.org.uk). Tottenham Court Road tube. **Open** 6.30am-10pm Mon-Fri; 10am-8pm Sat; 10am-7pm Sun. **Credit** MC, V. **Map** p407 X1.
Conveniently located and user-friendly, the Y has a good range of cardiovascular and weight-training equipment, a pool and a sports hall, as well as a full timetable of excellently taught classes.

Jubilee Hall Leisure Centre

30 The Piazza, Covent Garden, WC2E 8BE (7836 4835, www.jubileehallclubs.co.uk). Covent

Ride Cycle the Sights

Use London's new bike hire scheme to take in the city's highlights.

With London taking its cue from Paris's pick-up, drop-off bike rental scheme (*see* p333), it's easier than ever to see the city's sights by bike. This route, taking in many of London's highlights, is easily accessible on two wheels: when the scheme launches in the summer, there should be docking stations at the beginning of the tour, in front of the V&A and on the western side of the Natural History Museum, and at the end, by Tate Modern. And if you want to stop and look around at any point, you'll never be too far from a docking station en route.

Start in South Kensington with a visit to one or more of the major museums (the

Natural History Museum, the **Science Museum** and the **V&A**; *see pp124-126*). Once you're done, ride up Exhibition Road to Alexandra Gate and into Hyde Park, passing the **Albert Memorial**, the **Serpentine Gallery** and the **Princess of Wales Memorial Fountain** (*see pp124-126*) before crossing the Serpentine.

Turn right along Serpentine Road to where it ends at **Hyde Park Corner**, on Park Lane at the southern tip of Mayfair. Crossing Hyde Park Corner on the bike line, take the second left into leafy Constitution Hill. Beyond that massive wall on your right is **Buckingham Palace** (*see p117*). There's

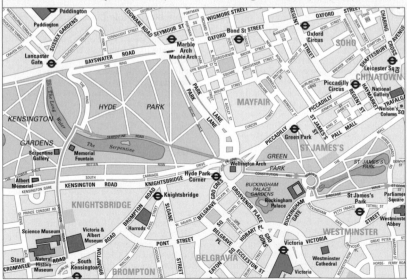

Garden tube. **Open** 6.45am-10pm Mon-Fri; 9am-9pm Sat; 10am-5pm Sun. **Map** p407 Z3.
A reliable and very central venue that provides calm surroundings for workouts, Jubilee Hall also offers a selection of therapies and treatments. There are other Jubilee Hall centres in Southwark, Westminster and Hampstead.

Westway Sports Centre

1 Crowthorne Road, Ladbroke Grove, W10 6RP (8969 0992, www.westwaysportscentre.org). Ladbroke Grove or Latimer Road tube. **Open** 8am-10pm Mon-Fri; 8am-8pm Sat; 10am-10pm Sun. **Map** p407 Z3.

A smart sports centre with a diverse range of activities on offer, including all-weather pitches, tennis courts, a swim centre and gym, plus the largest indoor climbing facility in the country.

ICE SKATING

There's a permanent indoor rink in Bayswater: **Queens Ice & Bowl** (17 Bayswater, W2 4QP, 7229 0172, www.queensiceandbowl.co.uk). But at Christmas, a variety of temporary rinks spring up all over town. **Somerset House** (*see p90*) set the trend; it's since been followed by **Hampton Court Palace** (*see p157*), the

a better view from the Queen Victoria Memorial, which helps explain the tourists clambering all over it.

From the memorial, turn left into Birdcage Walk, which follows St James's Park all the way to **Parliament Square** and **Big Ben** (*see pp112-115*). Take a left up Whitehall, past 10 Downing Street and the Horse Guards, to **Trafalgar Square** (*see pp110-112*), then negotiate the traffic and turn right into the Strand. Once you've crossed Ludgate Circus, **St Paul's Cathedral** (*see p83*) will hover into view.

After St Paul's, keep cycling along Cheapside and you'll come to **Bank** (*see*

pp67-71), quiet at weekends but busy with financiers, lawyers and other suit-wearing types during the week. From here, head to the **Tower of London** (*see p74*), which sits at the northern end of **Tower Bridge** (*see p74*). If you're lucky, you'll catch one of regular bridge openings.

Having crossed Tower Bridge, turn right into Tooley Street, passing the lengthy queues outside the **London Dungeon** and perhaps stopping for a bite to eat at **Borough Market** (Thur-Sat only; *see p261*). Duly revived, cycle along Southwark Street to Great Guilford Street and **Tate Modern** (*see p55*).

ARTS & ENTERTAINMENT

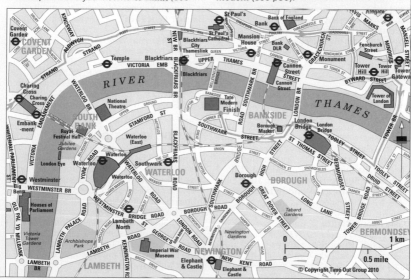

Tower of London (*see p74*) and **Kew Gardens** (*see p155*), among others. Check the weekly *Time Out* magazine for a full list.

RIDING

There are various stables in and around the city; for a list, see www.bhs.org.uk. Those below run classes for all ages and abilities.

Hyde Park & Kensington Stables *63 Bathurst Mews, Paddington, W2 2SB (7723 2813, www.hydeparkstables.com). Lancaster Gate tube.* **Open** *Summer* 7.15am-5pm Mon-Fri; 9am-5pm Sat, Sun. *Winter* 7.15am-3pm Mon-Fri; 9am-3pm Sat, Sun. **Lessons** *Group* £55-£59/hr. *Individual* £79-£95/hr. **Map** p395 D6.

Wimbledon Village Stables *24 High Street, Wimbledon, SW19 5DX (8946 8579, www.wv stables.com). Wimbledon tube/rail.* **Open** 9am-12.15pm Tue; 9am-5pm Wed-Sun. **Lessons** *Group* £50-£55/hr. *Individual* £70-£75/hr.

STREET SPORTS

Under the Westway in Acklam Road, W10, **Baysixty6 Skate Park** (www.baysixty6.com) has a large street course and four halfpipes, all wooden and covered. **Stockwell Skate Park** (Stockwell Park Road, SW9, www.stockwell skatepark.com) is one of the city's most popular outdoor parks; it's rivalled by **Cantelowes Skatepark** (Cantelowes Gardens, Camden Road, NW1, www.cantelowesskatepark.co.uk) and **Mile End Skatepark** (corner of Burdett Road and St Pauls Way, E3), which opened in May 2009. Many skateboarders and BMXers prefer unofficial street spots such as the **South Bank** under the Royal Festival Hall. Inliners should keep an eye on www.londonskaters.com.

SWIMMING

There are indoor pools scattered all over London, with the **Central YMCA** (*see p334*) and the **Oasis Sports Centre** (*see below*) both worth a visit. To find your nearest pool, see www.activeplaces.co.uk. For pools suited to children, check www.britishswimming.co.uk.

If alfresco swimming is more your thing, there are open-air lidos at **Parliament Hill Fields**, the **Serpentine**, **Tooting Bec**, **Brockwell Park** and **London Fields**. For more, see www.londonpoolscampaign.com.

Oasis Sports Centre *32 Endell Street, Covent Garden, WC2H 9AG (7831 1804, www.gll.org). Holborn tube.* **Open** *Indoor* 6.30am-9pm Mon-Fri; 9.30am-5.30pm Sat, Sun. *Outdoor* 6.30am-9pm Mon-Fri; 9.30am-5pm Sat, Sun. **Admission** £3.90; £1 reductions. **Map** p407 Y2.

TENNIS

Many parks around the city have council-run courts that cost little or nothing to use; keener players should try the indoor and outdoor courts at the **Islington Tennis Centre**, though non-members may only book up to five days ahead. For grass courts, phone the Lawn Tennis Association's Information Department (8487 7000, www.lta.org.uk).

Islington Tennis Centre *Market Road, Islington, N7 9PL (7700 1370, www.aquaterra. org). Caledonian Road tube or Caledonian Road & Barnsbury rail.* **Open** 7am-11pm Mon-Thur; 7am-10pm Fri; 8am-10pm Sat, Sun. **Court rental** £9-£20/hour.

TEN-PIN BOWLING

Queens Ice & Bowl *17 Queensway, Bayswater, W2 4QP (7229 0172, www.queensiceandbowl. co.uk). Bayswater tube.* **Open** 10am-11pm daily. Bowling £6.50/game. **Lanes** £12. **Map** p394 C7.
Rowans Bowl *10 Stroud Green Road, Finsbury Park, N4 2DF (8800 1950, www.rowans.co.uk). Finsbury Park tube/rail.* **Open** 10.30am-12.30am Mon-Thur, Sun; 10.30am-2.30am Fri, Sat. Bowling £2.90-£4.10. **Lanes** 24.

YOGA & PILATES

For something more than just a quick stretch in your hotel room, check out the yoga activities and classes (and fully equipped Pilates studio) at Triyoga. You may also want to consult the **British Wheel of Yoga** (www.bwy.org.uk).

Triyoga *6 Erskine Road, Primrose Hill, NW3 3AJ (7483 3344, www.triyoga.co.uk). Chalk Farm tube.* **Open** 6am-10pm Mon-Fri; 8am-8.30pm Sat; 9am-9pm Sun. **Admission** £12-£15/session. **Other locations** Wallacespace, 2 Dryden Street, Covent Garden, WC2E 9NA (7483 3344); Kingly Court, Soho, W1B 5PW (use main number).

INSIDE TRACK SURF BUS

It might not be as convenient as Malibu, Hawaii or Bondi Beach (or, for that matter, as sunny), but a weekend of surfing can still be enjoyed from a London base. Come Friday after work, surfers can hop on to a biodiesel-powered coach and take a six-hour ride to Newquay in Cornwall for a weekend of lessons and associated beachside hilarity. Trips run throughout the summer; for a full schedule, see www.bigfriday.com.

Theatre

Star power continues to illuminate the theatres of London's West End.

With the highest concentration of playhouses in the world, London's West End is a beacon for lovers of stage performance, drawing more theatregoers in an average year than Broadway. The biggest attractions in town remain the indomitable musicals, some of which have been running for two decades, that line Shaftesbury Avenue. However, straight plays have been making something of a comeback; productions tend towards the conservative but frequently attract the biggest names in showbiz from both sides of the Atlantic. And away from the commercial sector,  political debate and formal innovation are mainstays at a handful of subsidised venues and a broad variety of fringe theatres, fed by the capital's multicultural influences and the increasing cross-pollination of its arts scene.

THEATRE IN LONDON

Escapist entertainment thrives when times are tough, so it's no surprise that the West End developed a rosy glow as the recession sank its fangs into Britain. Summer 2009 saw audience numbers rise by eight per cent on the previous year, with feelgood musicals benefiting the most: Broadway import *Wicked* announced its highest-grossing year to date (since 2006, it's taken £80 million at the box office). Yet the downturn also encouraged musical producers to stick safely to the Yellow Brick Road, with a legion of new shows based on hit movies – *Legally Blonde*, *Sister Act*, *Priscilla Queen of the Desert* – joining the already-established likes of *Dirty Dancing*, *Billy Elliot* and *Hairspray*. Producers of straight plays are at it, too, with *The Shawshank Redemption* and *Breakfast at Tiffany's* just the two most recent arrivals.

Impresarios such as Lord Lloyd Webber have developed another canny way to find success: casting leading ladies and gents through 'reality TV' competitions, which run for weeks on end and generate untold millions in free publicity for the show in advance of its opening. The fevered publicity generated by BBC show *I'd Do Anything*, for instance, helped make the 2009 revival of *Oliver!* one of the fastest-selling shows in West End history. Yet all the critical acclaim went to a production that originated at the tiny Menier Chocolate Factory: a sparkling revival of *La Cage aux Folles*.

Drama producers continue to rely on star casting as they fight the musical tide. The diminutive **Donmar Warehouse** shuffled over to the Wyndham's Theatre for a sell-out season that mixed compelling dramas with big-shot actors (Jude Law as Hamlet, for instance), and looks set to present equally high-profile stars back at its Earlham Street home during 2010. And the **Theatre Royal Haymarket**, meanwhile, continues its unique practice of operating as a producing house overseen by annually-changing artistic directors. Keep an eye out for the latest productions in Sean Mathias' season, which has already provided a successful *Waiting for Godot* starring Ian McKellen and Patrick Stewart.

The two main subsidised theatres continue to do well. Shows that start life at the **National Theatre** regularly transfer to the West End; the most notable production of late has been Michael Morpurgo's *War Horse*, whose life-sized equine puppets are now taking centre stage at the **New London Theatre**. The **Barbican Centre**, meanwhile, continues to programme visually exciting and physically expressive work from around the world. And on a smaller scale, the **Lyric Hammersmith** and the **BAC** are breeding grounds for young, experimental companies.

For details of what's on when you're in town, see the Theatre section of the weekly *Time Out* magazine, which offers reviews and full listings information for all notable shows.

Theatre districts

In strictly geographical terms, the **West End** refers to London's traditional theatre district, a busy area bounded by Shaftesbury Avenue, Drury Lane, the Strand and the Haymarket. Most major musicals and big-money dramas run here, alongside transfers of successful smaller-scale shows. However, the 'West End' appellation is now also applied to other major theatres elsewhere in town, including subsidised venues such as the **Barbican Centre** (in the City), the **National Theatre** (on the South Bank) and the **Old Vic** (near Waterloo).

Off-West End denotes theatres with smaller budgets and smaller capacities. These venues, many of them sponsored or subsidised, push the creative envelope with new writing, often brought to life by the best young acting and directing talent. The **Soho Theatre** and the **Bush** are good for up-and-coming young playwrights, while the **Almeida** and **Donmar Warehouse** offer elegantly produced shows with the occasional big star. One rung below these venues is the **Fringe** (*see p346* **Inside Track**), a disparate collection of small theatres within which quality and style varies wildly.

Buying tickets

If there's a specific show you want to see, aim to book ahead. And, if possible, always try to do so at the theatre's box office, at which booking fees are generally smaller than they are with agents such as Ticketmaster (*see p268*).

If you're more flexible about your choice of show, consider buying on the day from one of the **Tkts** booths, or taking your chances with standby seats (*see right* **The Cheap Seats**).

THE WEST END
Major theatres

Barbican Centre
Silk Street, the City, EC2Y 8DS (0845 120 7550, www.barbican.org.uk). Barbican tube or Moorgate tube/rail. **Box office** *In person* 9am-9pm Mon-Sat. **Tickets** £7-£32. **Credit** AmEx, MC, V. **Map** p402 P5.
The annual BITE (Barbican International Theatre Events) season continues to cherry-pick exciting and eclectic theatre companies from around the globe. The big draw in 2010 is revered director Peter Brook, who teams up with Theatre des Bouffes du Nord for *11 and 12*, based on the true story of Sufi sage Tierno Bokar and set in 1930s French-occupied Mali. In 2009, Barbican stalwarts Cheek By Jowl had punters queuing for returns to their *Andromaque*; expect a similar buzz around their *Macbeth* in March 2010.
▶ *For music at the Barbican, see p308.*

The Cheap Seats
Getting the most out of the box office.

At the two **Tkts** booths (Clocktower Building, Leicester Square, WC2H 7NA, www.officiallondontheatre.co.uk/tkts; also at the Brent Cross Shopping Centre in north-west London), anybody can buy tickets for big shows at much-reduced rates, either on the day or up to a week in advance. It's not uncommon to find the best seats for West End blockbusters sold at half price. The Leicester Square branch opens at 10am (noon on Sundays); you can check which shows are available on any given day by checking the website. And before buying, be sure you're at the correct booth, in a stand-alone building on the south side of Leicester Square – the square is ringed with other ticket brokers, where the seats are worse and the prices are higher.

Many West End theatres also offer their own reduced-price tickets for shows that haven't sold out on the night; these are known as 'standby' seats. Some standby deals are limited to those with student ID. The time these tickets goes on sale varies; check before setting out.

If you'd rather book ahead, subsidised theatres offer better value than purely commercial playhouses. For the Travelex-sponsored season at the **National Theatre** (*see below*), two-thirds of the seats go for £10. Some of the best offers are found at the **Royal Court Theatre** (*see p340*), where productions can be seen for as little as 10p if you're willing to stand in the slips. They also present 'Cheap Mondays', with all tickets at £10.

★ National Theatre
South Bank, SE1 9PX (7452 3400 information, 7452 3000 tickets, www.nationaltheatre.org.uk). Embankment or Southwark tube, or Waterloo tube/rail. **Box office** 9.30am-8pm Mon-Sat. **Tickets** *Olivier & Lyttelton* £10-£42.50. *Cottesloe* £10-£31. **Credit** AmEx, MC, V. **Map** p401 M8.
No theatrical tour of London is complete without a visit to the National Theatre (officially the Royal National Theatre), a concrete-clad, 1960s modernist building that's home to three auditoria and a rolling repertory programme that generally offers a choice of three or four productions in any given week. After some controversy in 2009 over the racial politics of its *England People Very Nice* and a distinctly mixed reception for Helen Mirren's *Phèdre*, artistic director Nicholas Hytner is playing it safer in 2010 with the

return of 2009 sell-out show *Every Good Boy Deserves Favour* and the latest in a recent flurry of *Hamlet*s to hit the capital, while NT heavyweights Simon Russell Beale and Fiona Shaw team up for foppish farce *London Assurance*.

Old Vic

The Cut, Waterloo, SE1 8NB (0844 871 7628, www.oldvictheatre.com). Waterloo tube/rail. **Box office** *In person* 10am-7.30pm Mon-Sat. *By phone* 9am-10pm Mon-Sat. **Tickets** £10-£48.50. **Credit** AmEx, MC, V. **Map** p404 N9.
The combination of Oscar-winner Kevin Spacey and producer David Liddiment at this 200-year-old theatre continues to be a commercial success; it's sometimes a critical hit, too, especially when Spacey takes to the stage. Sam Mendes' Bridge Project, an Anglo-American collaboration between Mendes, Spacey's Old Vic and Joseph V Melillo's Brooklyn Academy of Music, has proved a highlight; it returns in 2010 with *The Tempest* and *As You Like It*, performed by a transatlantic cast that includes Christian Camargo, Stephen Dillane and Juliet Rylance.

Open Air Theatre

Regent's Park, Inner Circle, Marylebone, NW1 4NR (0844 826 4242, www.openairtheatre.org). Baker Street tube. **Tickets** £10-£35. **Credit** AmEx, MC, V. **Map** p398 G3.
The verdant setting of this alfresco theatre lends itself perfectly to summery Shakespeare romps in a season that runs from June to September. Standards are well above village-green dramatics, and the 2010 season features *The Crucible*, *The Comedy of Errors*, and a production of *Macbeth* for children. If you don't want to bring a picnic, good-value, tasty food can be bought at the Garden Café; alternatively, plump for traditional tea or Pimm's on the lawn.

★ Royal Court Theatre

Sloane Square, Chelsea, SW1W 8AS (7565 5000, www.royalcourttheatre.com). Sloane Square tube. **Box office** 10am-6pm Mon-Sat. **Tickets** 10p-£25; all tickets £10 Mon. **Credit** AmEx, MC, V. **Map** p400 G11.
From John Osborne's *Look Back in Anger*, staged in the theatre's opening year of 1956, to the numerous discoveries of the past decade, among them Sarah Kane, Joe Penhall and Conor McPherson, the emphasis at the Royal Court has always been on new voices in British theatre. Artistic director Dominic Cooke has injected plenty of politics into the programme, and successfully lowered the age of his audiences in the process. Expect to find rude, lyrical new work set on the London streets by first-time playwrights such as Bola Agbaje and the more established but no less cool Debbie Tucker Green; American and European writers with a message also feature. Look out for quality shorts programmed at 6pm and 9pm, and more of the usual vividly produced British and international work by young writers.

Royal Shakespeare Company

01789 403444 information, 0844 800 1110 tickets, www.rsc.org.uk. **Box office** *By phone* 9am-8pm Mon-Sat. **Tickets** £10-£48. **Credit** AmEx, MC, V.
Britain's flagship company hasn't had a London base since it quit the Barbican in 2002, although it may turn its mind towards finding one as the £100m redevelopment of its Stratford-upon-Avon home reaches completion. In the meantime, it continues its itinerant existence, striking deals with West End theatres for major transfers (usually for three months from December) and popping up in smaller venues to stage the ambitious new plays that artistic director Michael Boyd has championed. In 2010, the latter (at the Hampstead Theatre, www.hampsteadtheatre.com) include Dennis Kelly's *The Gods Weep*, about an unravelling CEO.

★ Shakespeare's Globe

21 New Globe Walk, Bankside, SE1 9DT (7401 9919, www.shakespeares-globe.org). Southwark tube or London Bridge tube/rail. **Box office** *Off season* 10am-5pm Mon-Fri. *Theatre* 10am-5pm daily. **Tickets** £5-£32. **Credit** AmEx, MC, V. **Map** p404 O7.
Sam Wanamaker's dream to recreate the theatre where Shakespeare first staged many of his plays has become a successful reality, underpinned by outreach work (you can drop in for regular free Q&As with cast and director). The open-air, standing-room Pit tickets are excellent value, if a little marred by low-flying aircraft. Expect a range of Shakespeare classics alongside new plays on parallel themes.

Long-runners & musicals

★ Billy Elliot the Musical

Victoria Palace Theatre, Victoria Street, SW1E 5EA (0844 248 5000, www.victoriapalacetheatre. co.uk). Victoria tube/rail. **Box office** 10am-8.30pm Mon-Sat. **Tickets** £19.50-£62.50. **Credit** AmEx, MC, V. **Map** p400 H10.
The combination of Elton John's music and a heart-melting yarn about a northern working-class lad with an unlikely talent for ballet has scooped more awards internationally than any other British musical.

Dirty Dancing

Aldwych Theatre, Aldwych, Covent Garden, WC2B 4DF (0844 847 2330, www.dirtydancing london.com). Covent Garden tube or Charing Cross tube/rail. **Box office** *In person* 10am-8pm daily. *By phone* 24hrs daily. **Tickets** £15-£60. **Credit** AmEx, MC, V. **Map** p399 M6.
With its raunchy choreography, archetypal ugly duckling story and powerful hit of nostalgia, it's no wonder *Dirty Dancing* took record advance bookings. Repeated flashes of visual wit in James Powell's production and the infectious music should have you whooping and cheering by the end.

ARTS & ENTERTAINMENT

Hairspray.

Profile Wilton's Music Hall

A beautiful old East End theatre is hanging on for dear life.

ARTS & ENTERTAINMENT

In the last decade, a couple of London's grandest old music halls have been refurbished to something close to their former glory. Built in 1901, the Hackney Empire received a £15-million restoration in 2004, the same year that the Coliseum – first an variety hall, now an opera house (*see p311*) – benefited from a plush renovation to celebrate its centenary. However, one music hall dates back even further than this esteemed pair – and does it ever look the part.

London's last surviving example of the giant pub halls of the mid 19th century, **Wilton's Music Hall** (*listings p346*) once entertained the masses with acts ranging from Chinese performing monkeys to acrobats, contortionists to opera singers . It was here that Victorian music hall star George Leybourne made

his name in character as Champagne Charlie, and that the can-can first scandalised London. Roughly 150 years after opening, Wilton's still serves as a theatre – but only just.

Wilton's Music Hall started life in the 19th century not as a theatre but as a pub called the Prince of Denmark, nicknamed the 'Mahogany Bar' on account of its handsome wood fittings. (The theatre's current bar is on the site of the old pub.) In 1853, John Wilton, the tavern's owner, turned a purpose-built concert room behind the pub into the site's first music hall, before acquiring adjoining properties to build a larger, grander theatre to the rear in 1858. The space boasts a high proscenium arch stage, a balcony supported by unusual, twisting columns, and a decorative vaulted ceiling.

Charred roof timbers bear witness to the huge 'sun-burner' chandelier, complete with 300 gas jets, that once lit the room.

In 1888, the hall was acquired by the Methodist Church and became a mission, serving the local community for the next seven decades. Thousands of striking dockers were fed here during their landmark fight against dock owners in 1889; in the 1930s, the hall sheltered locals fighting Oswald Mosley's fascist blackshirts. Most notably (indeed, almost miraculously), it was one of the few buildings in the area to survive the Blitz.

In the years after Sir John Betjeman launched a successful campaign for Wilton's to be granted listed-building status in the 1960s, saving it from the threat of demolition, the property fell into disrepair. But after Fiona Shaw and Deborah Warner brought their interpretation of TS Eliot's *The Waste Land* here in 1997, it was rediscovered, and has since hosted opera, theatre (in 2010, an all-male *Pirates of Penzance*), music (from the Kreutzer Quartet to Marc Almond) and even occasional film screenings. Private-hire events such as weddings and film shoots help keep it afloat.

Much of the theatre's charm is down to its unvarnished condition. However, this same state of repair is also causing serious problems, to the point where the World Monuments Fund Repairs, a non-profit group dedicated to architectural preservation, placed the building on its most-endangered list in 2008. Repairs totalling an estimated £4 million are needed to stop the hall collapsing in the next few years, and funding has so far proved difficult to secure. Unless the money is found soon, the long history of this wonderful old room could soon enter its final chapter.

THREE TO SEE
More classic auditoriums.

Coliseum
From music hall to opera.
See p311.

Masonic Temple
Under Andaz.
See p169.

Wigmore Hall
Classical in Marylebone.
See p311.

ARTS & ENTERTAINMENT

Festivals Theatre

What not to miss this year.

In 2009, the **Greenwich & Docklands International Festival** (www.festival.org) presented a five-metre-high 'aquatic queen' riding across the water on a penny-farthing bicycle at Millwall Dock, and aerialists performing on top of giant, perilous sway poles at Cutty Sark Gardens. Expect equally eye-catching stunts at this year's free, four-day street art and outdoor theatre spectacular, held in late June. At around the same time of year, **LIFT** (the **London International Festival of Theatre**; www.liftfest.org.uk) promises to take off in new directions under new director Mark Ball.

In July and August, the National Theatre (*see p339*) rolls out a large square of astroturf by the river for **Watch This Space** (www.nationaltheatre.org.uk), a programme of alfresco theatre, dance and circus. Also in August, an eclectic bunch of new, experimental and short shows sprint through the **Camden Fringe** (www.camdenfringe.org). Finally, more outré work can be seen at January's **London International Mime Festival** (www.mimefest.co.uk), from haunting visual theatre to puppetry for adults.

Hairspray

Shaftesbury Theatre, 210 Shaftesbury Avenue, Covent Garden, WC2H 8DP (7379 5399, www.shaftesbury-theatre.co.uk). Holborn or Tottenham Court Road tube. **Box office** 10am-6pm daily. **Tickets** £22.50-£62.50. **Credit** MC, V. **Map** p407 Y2.

Chubby heroine Tracy Turnblad, victim of high school anti-fat bimbos, teams up with the black kids from Special Ed to overthrow '60s American racial prejudice and fulfil her dreams by busting their non-white dance moves on TV. Preposterous and uplifting; bouffant for the spirits. *Photos p241.*

★ Jersey Boys

Prince Edward Theatre, 28 Old Compton Street, Soho, W1D 4HS (0844 482 5151, www.delfont mackintosh.co.uk). Leicester Square tube. **Box office** 10am-8pm Mon-Sat. *Seetickets* 24hrs daily. **Tickets** £20-£62.50. **Credit** AmEx, MC, V. **Map** p406 W2.

This Broadway import had the critics singing the praises of Ryan Molloy, who hits the high notes in Frankie Valli & the Four Seasons' doo-wop standards. This standard tale of early struggle, success and break-up is elevated by pacy direction.

Lion King

Lyceum Theatre, 21 Wellington Street, Covent Garden, WC2E 7RQ (7492 1581, www.disney.co.uk). Covent Garden tube. **Box office** *In person* 10am-8pm daily. *By phone* 8am-7pm daily. **Tickets** £20-£58.50. **Credit** AmEx, MC, V. **Map** p407 Z3.

After ten years, the vibrant yellow hoardings advertising this Disney show are as much a part of the Lyceum's exterior as its original 19th-century portico. There's nothing subtle about Lebo M, Elton John and Tim Rice's show, but Simba's flight and return to his rightful destiny as king of the pride strikes a chord in theatregoers (including Michelle Obama, who saw the show in June 2009).

Love Never Dies

Adelphi Theatre, Strand, WC2R 0NS (7492 1581, www.reallyuseful.com). Charing Cross tube/rail. **Box office** *By phone* 8am-7pm daily. **Tickets** £32.50-£67.50. **Credit** AmEx, MC, V. **Map** p407 Y4.

The Phantom of the Opera, the world's most commercially successful piece of entertainment, returns to London in a new guise in February: this time he's ensconsed in Coney Island during its heyday. Can Lord Lloyd Webber repeat the success of the original, with its hackle-raising melodies and 1980s goth-meets-Paris design?

▶ *The original Phantom is still playing at Her Majesty's Theatre on the Haymarket (0844 277 4321, www.reallyuseful.com).*

Les Misérables

Queen's Theatre, Shaftesbury Avenue, Soho, W1D 6BA (0844 482 5160, www.lesmis.com, www.delfontmackintosh.co.uk). Leicester Square or Piccadilly Circus tube. **Box office** *In person* 10am-8pm Mon-Sat. *Seetickets* 24hrs daily. **Tickets** £15-£59. **Credit** AmEx, MC, V. **Map** p406 W3.

It's more than two decades since the RSC's version of Boublil and Schönberg's musical came to the London stage. When you've been singing these songs since your first audition, it's easy to take it that half-inch too far. Still, the voices are lush, the revolutionary sets are film-fabulous, and the lyrics and score (based on Victor Hugo's novel) will be considerably less chirpy than whatever's on next door.

Mousetrap

St Martin's Theatre, West Street, Cambridge Circus, Covent Garden, WC2H 9NZ (0844 499 1515, www.the-mousetrap.co.uk). Leicester Square tube. **Box office** 10am-8pm Mon-Sat. **Tickets** £13.50-£37.50. **Credit** AmEx, MC, V. **Map** p407 X3.

Running in the West End since 1952, Agatha Christie's drawing-room whodunnit is a murder mystery Methuselah, and will probably still be booking when the last trump sounds.

Priscilla Queen of the Desert
Palace Theatre, Cambridge Circus, Soho, W1D 5AY (0871 297 0777, www.priscillathemusical. com). Leicester Square tube. **Box office** *By phone* 24hrs daily. **Tickets** £20-£65. **Credit** AmEx, MC, V. **Map** p407 X3.
Its hyperactive mix of high heels, high camp and low humour may have divided the critics, but this flamboyant stage version of the 1994 drag queen road movie can't fail to make an impression.

OFF-WEST END THEATRES

Almeida
Almeida Street, Islington, N1 1TA (7359 4404, www.almeida.co.uk). Angel tube. **Box office** *In person* 10am-6pm Mon-Sat. *By phone* 24hrs daily. **Tickets** £6-£29.50. **Credit** AmEx, MC, V. **Map** p402 O1.
Well groomed and with a rather funky bar, the Almeida turns out thoughtfully crafted theatre for grown-ups. Under artistic director Michael Attenborough it has drawn top directors like Thea Sharrock and Rupert Goold, and premières from the likes of Neil LaBute.

Battersea Arts Centre.

★ Battersea Arts Centre (BAC)
Lavender Hill, Battersea, SW11 5TN (7223 2223, www.bac.org.uk). Clapham Common tube, Clapham Junction rail or bus 77, 77A, 345. **Box office** 10am-6pm Mon-Fri; 2-6pm Sat. **Tickets** £5-£10; pay what you can Tue (phone ahead). **Credit** MC, V. **Map** p402 O1.
Housed in the old Battersea Town Hall, the forward-thinking BAC hosts young theatre troupes; expect quirky, fun and physical theatre from the likes of cult companies Kneehigh and 1927. May's Burst Festival is a launchpad for new contemporary theatre and performance art; you can see stand-up comedians hone their Edinburgh Festival routines during the N20 season in July.

★ Bush
Shepherd's Bush Green, Shepherd's Bush, W12 8QD (8743 5050, www.bushtheatre.co.uk). Goldhawk Road tube or Shepherd's Bush tube/ rail. **Box office** noon-8pm Mon-Sat (performance days); 10am-6pm Mon-Sat (non-performance days). **Tickets** £7-£15. **Credit** AmEx, MC, V. **Map** p402 O1.
This diminutive venue punches above its weight, with well-designed productions and an impressive record of West End transfers. It's famous for its championing of new writers; alumni include Stephen Poliakoff and David Edgar.

★ Donmar Warehouse
41 Earlham Street, Covent Garden, WC2H 9LX (0844 871 1624, www.donmarwarehouse.com). Covent Garden or Leicester Square tube. **Box office** *In person* 10am-7.30pm Mon-Sat. *By phone* 9am-10pm Mon-Sat; 10am-8pm Sun. **Tickets** £12-£30. **Credit** AmEx, MC, V. **Map** p407 Y2.
The Donmar is less a warehouse than a boutique chamber. Artistic director Michael Grandage has kept the venue on a fresh, intelligent path, and the combination of artistic integrity and intimate space is hard to resist. Perhaps that's why so many high-profile film actors clamour to tread the boards here, among them Nicole Kidman, Gwyneth Paltrow, Gillian Anderson and Ewan McGregor.

Gate Theatre
Prince Albert, 11 Pembridge Road, Notting Hill, W11 3HQ (7229 0706, www.gatetheatre.co.uk). Notting Hill Gate tube. **Box office** *By phone* 10am-6pm Mon-Fri. **Tickets** £16; £11 reductions. **Credit** MC, V. **Map** p394 A7.
A doll's house of a theatre, with rickety wooden chairs as seats, the Gate is the only producing theatre in London dedicated to international work, often in specially commissioned new translations.

King's Head Theatre
115 Upper Street, Islington, N1 1QN (7226 8561 information, 0844 209 0326 tickets, www.kings headtheatre.org). Angel tube. **Box office** *In*

ARTS & ENTERTAINMENT

person 10am-7.30pm daily. *By phone* 24hrs daily. **Tickets** £10-£20. **Credit** AmEX, MC, V. **Map** p402 N2.
Started in the 1910s on a tiny budget, this theatre is a tiny space tucked away at the back of a charming if somewhat ramshackle Victorian boozer. In the past, it's launched a raft of stars, among them Hugh Grant. It's also a favourite crossover spot for television actors to exercise their comedy muscles.

★ Lyric Hammersmith
Lyric Square, King Street, Hammersmith, W6 0QL (0871 221 1722, www.lyric.co.uk). Hammersmith tube. **Box office** *By phone* 10am-5.30pm Mon-Sat. *In person* 9.30am-7.30pm on perfomance days. **Tickets** £10-£25. **Credit** MC, V. **Map** p402 N2.
Artistic director Sean Holmes launched his tenure in 2009 with a pledge to bring writers back into the building, making space for neglected modern classics and new plays alongside the cutting-edge physical and devised work for which the Lyric is best known. Highlights in 2010 include a version of Chekhov's *Three Sisters*, directed by Holmes with experimental theatre company Filter.

Soho Theatre
21 Dean Street, Soho, W1D 3NE (7478 0100, www.sohotheatre.com). Tottenham Court Road tube. **Box office** *In person* 10am-6pm Mon-Sat; 10am-7.30pm performance nights. *By phone* 10am-7pm Mon-Sat. **Tickets** £5-£20. **Credit** MC, V. **Map** p397 K6.
Its cool blue neon lights and front-of-house café help it blend it into the Soho landscape, but this theatre has made quite a name for itself since opening in 2000. It attracts a younger, hipper crowd than most theatres, and brings on aspiring writers with a free script-reading service and workshops.
▶ *For comedy at the Soho, see p285.*

Theatre Royal Stratford East
Gerry Raffles Square, Stratford, E15 1BN (8534 0310, www.stratfordeast.com). Stratford tube/ rail/DLR. **Box office** *In person* 10am-7pm Mon-Sat. *By phone* 10am-6pm Mon-Sat. **Tickets** £10-£20. **Credit** MC, V. **Map** p397 K6.
The Theatre Royal is a community theatre, with many shows written, directed and performed by black or Asian artists. Musicals are big here: ex-Kinks frontman Ray Davies penned *Come Dancing*, which may follow home-grown success *The Harder They Come* to the West End following a national tour.
▶ *There's a great comedy night too; see p285.*

★ Tricycle
269 Kilburn High Road, Kilburn, NW6 7JR (7372 6611 information, 7328 1000 tickets, www.tricycle.co.uk). Kilburn tube. **Box office** 10am-9pm Mon-Sat; 2-8pm Sun. **Tickets** £8.50-£25. **Credit** MC, V. **Map** p397 K6.

Passionate and political, the Tricycle consistently finds original ways into difficult subjects. In the last few years, it has pioneered 'tribunal' docu-dramas – transcript-based theatre that investigates subjects such Guantanamo Bay, the murder of black teenager Stephen Lawrence, and the official case made for the Iraq War. 'Pay What You Can' every Tuesday at 8pm and Saturday at 4pm.

Wilton's Music Hall
Graces Alley, off Ensign Street, E1 8JB (7702 9555, www.wiltons.org.uk). Aldgate East or Tower Hill tube. **Box office** hrs vary. **Tickets** prices vary. **Map** p405 S7.
See pp342-343 **Profile.**

★ Young Vic
66 The Cut, Waterloo, SE1 8LZ (7922 2922, www.youngvic.org). Waterloo tube/rail. **Box office** 10am-6pm Mon-Sat. **Tickets** £10-£29.50. **Credit** MC, V. **Map** p404 N8.
As the name would suggest, this Waterloo venue has more youthful bravura than its older sister up the road, and draws a younger crowd, who pack out the open-air balcony at its popular restaurant and bar on the weekends. They come to see European classics with a distinctly modern edge, new writing with an international flavour and collaborations with leading companies such as the English National Opera – in 2010, there'll be a production of Hans Werner Henze's 1961 *Elegy for Young Lovers*.

Escapes & Excursions

Dungeness. *See p356.*

Getting Around   **348**
   Map Escapes & Excursions   349

Brighton   **351**

Canterbury   **352**
   Country Flavours   353

Dungeness, Romney & Rye 356

Cambridge   **359**

Escapes & Excursions

Sometimes the best bit of London is leaving it all behind.

There's so much in London that you could easily spend a lifetime exploring the city. Which isn't at all the same thing as *wanting* to spend a lifetime exploring the city. Everyone who lives here sometimes feels an irresistible urge to leave, so why would visitors be any different?

We've suggested four overnight excursions and a day-trip that should refresh and reinvigorate you. Two of the excursions are by the sea, but could hardly be more different: **Brighton** offers traditional seaside kitsch and a full-on nightlife scene, while **Dungeness, Rye & Romney** come with cranky charm and an other-worldly atmosphere. Inland and nestling happily in the lee of the North Downs, **Canterbury** is a lively medieval city, its cathedral and ruined abbey of such historical significance that they're listed as a UNESCO World Heritage Site. And **Cambridge**, as flat as the fenlands it sits upon, is perfect for those who like peeking into cloistered courts and college chapels. A day-trip to **Middle Farm** in Lewes rounds out the selection.

GETTING AROUND

All of the destinations included in this chapter are within easy reach of London, perfect either for a day trip or an overnight stay. **Brighton** and **Cambridge** are the easiest of the four to reach by train; they're both within an hour of London, with rail services running from early in the morning until relatively late at night; **Canterbury** is also a simple rail ride from London. It's more of an effort to reach **Dungeness**, **Romney** and **Rye**, but it's worth the work (and if you don't fancy negotiating the train network, it's an easier journey by road should you wish to hire a car).

For the main attractions, we've included details of opening times, admission prices and transport details, but be aware that these can change without notice: always phone to check. Major sights are open all through the year, but many of the minor ones close out of season, often from November to March. Before setting out, drop in on the **Britain & London Visitor Centre** (*see p375*) for additional information.

By train

Notwithstanding the occasional strike or weather-related line closure, Britain's rail network is generally reliable. However, ticket prices on some services are insultingly high, and the splintering of the network caused by privatisation has made it harder to source reliable information on train times and prices.

For information on train times and ticket prices, call **National Rail Enquiries** on 0845 748 4950. Ask about the cheapest ticket for the journey you're planning; be aware that for long journeys, tickets may be considerably cheaper the earlier you book. Timetables can be found at **www.nationalrail.co.uk**; buy tickets online at **www.thetrainline.com**.

If you need extra help, there are rail travel centres in London's mainline stations, as well as at Heathrow and Gatwick airports. Staff can give you guidance on timetables and booking. We specify departure stations in the 'Getting there' section for each destination; the journey times cited are the fastest available.

Escapes & Excursions

© Copyright Time Out Group 2010

40 km

20 miles

Thaxted
Stansted
Clacton-on-Sea
Colchester
Burnham-on-Crouch
Maldon
Chelmsford
ESSEX
Southend
Sheerness
Whitstable
Reculver
Margate
Broadstairs
Ramsgate
Sandwich
Deal
Dover
Folkestone
New Romney
Old Romney
Dungeness (pp365-366)
Camber Sands
Winchelsea
Rye (pp355-359)
Hastings
Battle
Eastbourne
Newhaven
EAST SUSSEX
THE SOUTH DOWNS
Middle Farm (p363)
Lewes
Brighton (pp351-352)
Worthing
Littlehampton
Bognor Regis
Chichester
WEST SUSSEX
Arundel
Midhurst
Petersfield
Portsmouth
Gosport
Fareham
SOUTHAMPTON
NEW FOREST
HAMPSHIRE
Winchester
Andover
Basingstoke
Alton
Aldershot
Farnham
Guildford
Woking
SURREY
Leatherhead
Dorking
Horsham
Crawley
Gatwick
Reigate
East Grinstead
Royal Tunbridge Wells
Sevenoaks
KENT
Maidstone
Ashford
Canterbury (pp353-354)
Rochester
Chatham
THE NORTH DOWNS
M20
M2
M25
Redhill
Sutton
Croydon
Chessington World of Adventures (p362)
Kingston-upon-Thames
Richmond
GREATER LONDON
pp390-391
City
Bexleyheath
Erith
Rainham
Dartford
Swanley
Chislehurst
Tilbury
Thorpe Park (p363)
Legoland (p363)
Staines
Heathrow
Windsor
Slough
Maidenhead
Cookham
Marlow
Henley-on-Thames
Reading
Newbury
BERKSHIRE
M4
A4
Thame
High Wycombe
Amersham
Beaconsfield
BUCKINGHAM-SHIRE
CHILTERN HILLS
Aylesbury
Bicester
Buckingham
Woodstock
Oxford
OXFORDSHIRE
River Thames
A44
A40
A361
A429
Stow-on-the-Wold
THE COTSWOLDS
Wantage
Wallingford
WILT-SHIRE
A420
BERKSHIRE
Winchester
M3
M27
A303
A34
A338
A36
A31
A35
Watford
St Albans
Hatfield
Hertford
Stevenage
Luton
BEDS
HERTFORDSHIRE
M1
M25
A1(M)
Harlow
Bishop's Stortford
M11
Chelmsford
A12
A414
A13
A5
A41
Time Out London 349

By coach

Coaches operated by **National Express** (0870 580 8080, www.nationalexpress.com) are scheduled to run throughout the country. Services depart from Victoria Coach Station (*see below*), ten minutes' walk from Victoria rail and tube stations. **Green Line Travel** (0870 608 7261, www.greenline.co.uk) also operates coaches.

Victoria Coach Station

164 Buckingham Palace Road, Victoria, SW1W 9TP (7222 1234, www.tfl.gov.uk). Victoria tube/rail. **Map** p400 H11.
Britain's most wide-ranging coach services are run by National Express (*see above*) from Victoria Coach Station, as are services run many other companies to and from Europe; some depart from Marble Arch.

By car

If you're in a group of three or four, it may be cheaper to hire a car (*see p365*), especially if you plan to take in several sights within an area. The road directions in the listings below should be used in conjunction with a proper map.

By bicycle

Capital Sport (01296 631671, www.capital-sport.co.uk) offers gentle cycling tours along the Thames from London. Leisurely itineraries include plenty of time to explore royal palaces, parks and historic attractions; the website contains full details. Alternatively, try **Country Lanes** (www.countrylanes.co.uk), which leads cycling tours all over the beautiful New Forest in Hampshire (01590 622627).

Brighton.

London-on-Sea

BRIGHTON

Britain's youngest city, England's most popular tourist destination after London and the host to the nation's biggest annual arts festival outside Edinburgh, Brighton is thriving. A welter of exciting new projects are reaching fruition, but novelty is nothing new to Brighton, which has evolved throughout its existence.

Brighton began life as Brighthelmstone, a small fishing village; it remained so until 1783, when the future George IV transformed it into a fashionable retreat. George kept the architect John Nash busy converting a modest abode into a faux-oriental pleasure palace; it's now the **Royal Pavilion** (*see below*), and remains an ostentatious sight. Next door, the **Brighton Museum & Art Gallery** (Royal Pavilion Gardens, 01273 292882) has entertaining displays and a good permanent art collection.

Only two of Brighton waterfront's three Victorian piers are still standing. Lacy, delicate **Brighton Pier** is a clutter of hot-dog stands, karaoke and fairground rides, filled with customers in the summertime. Still, with seven miles of coastline, Brighton retains all the traditional seaside resort trappings. Look out for the free **Brighton Fishing Museum** (201 King's Road Arches, on the lower prom between the piers, 01273 723064) and the **Sea-Life Centre** (*see right*), the world's oldest functioning aquarium.

A gay hub, a major student town and a child-friendly spot, Brighton still welcomes weekend gaggles of hen parties, ravers, nudists, discerning vegetarians, surfers, sunseekers and all-around wastrels. Many are satisfied to tumble from station to seafront, calling in at a couple of bars down the hill – and, perhaps, visiting the huge number of independent shops in and around **North Laine**, and in the charming network of narrow cobbled streets known as the **Lanes** – before plunging on to the pier or the pebbles. But to get the best out of Brighton, seek out its unusual little pockets: the busy gay quarter of **Kemp Town**, the savage drinking culture of **Hanover**, the airy terraces of **Montpelier**. Although hilly, all of the city is readily accessible by an award-winning bus network, with an all-night service on main lines.

★ Royal Pavilion

Brighton, BN1 1EE (01273 292820, www.royal pavilion.org.uk). Open Apr-Sept 9.30am-5.45pm daily. *Oct-Mar* 10am-5.15pm daily. *Tours* by appointment. Last entry 45mins before closing. **Admission** £8.80; £6.90 reductions; £5.10 under-15s; free under-5s. **Credit** AmEx, MC, V.

Sea-Life Centre

Marine Parade, BN2 1TB (01273 604234, www.sealifeeurope.com). Open Mar-Sept 10am-6pm daily (last admission 5pm). *Oct-Feb* 10am-5pm (last admission 4pm). **Admission** £14.50; £10-£12.50 reductions; free under-3s. **Credit** AmEx, MC, V.

Where to eat & drink

Brighton offers a ridiculous amount of dining possibilities for a town of its size, a handful of which would hold their head in any city in the UK. **Gingerman** (21A Norfolk Square, 01273 326688, www.gingermanrestaurants.com) offers top-quality continental (mainly French) cuisine at accessible prices. Located in a former bank, **Seven Dials** (1 Buckingham Place, 01273 885555, www.sevendialsrestaurant.co.uk) does two- and three-course deals. **Terre à Terre** (71 East Street, 01273 729051, www. terreaterre.co.uk) is an inventive vegetarian restaurant. **La Capannina** (15 Madeira Place, 01273 680839) is the best Italian in town. And **Riddle & Finns** (12B Meeting House Lane, 01273 323008, www.riddleandfinns.co.uk) is an accomplished champagne and oyster bar.

Of the city's drinking holes, **Brighton Rocks** (6 Rock Place, 01273 601139) is Kemp Town's most talked-up small bar, with a heated terrace, sparkling cocktails and superb organic cuisine. The **Hand in Hand** (33 Upper St James Street, 01273 699595) is a small, traditional boozer that attracts an older, discerning clientele thanks to its fine range of ales. The **Lion & Lobster** (24 Sillwood Street, 01273 327299) is a wonderful little pub with a nice vibe, cool and communal. The **Sidewinder** (65 Upper St James Street, 01273 679927) is a pre-club bar with DJs. Of the gay bars, the most fun is to be had at the **Amsterdam Hotel** (11-12 Marine Parade, 01273 688825, www.amsterdam.uk.com). **Doctor Brighton's** (16-17 King's Road, 01273 208113), on the seafront, is also worth a punt, with regular DJs playing house and techno.

INSIDE TRACK PARK LIFE

In 1947, a government-commissioned report by Arthur Hobhouse suggested that the **South Downs** should be one of a dozen UK regions to be protected as National Parks. Six decades later, it finally happened. In 2009, the government announced that a 625-square-mile area stretching roughly from Winchester to Eastbourne will become a National Park, hopefully by 2011.

Where to stay

Given Brighton's popularity with tourists, it's unsurprising that hotel prices can be on the high side. **Drakes** (43-44 Marine Parade, 01273 696934, www.drakesofbrighton.com, doubles £125-£250) is one of Brighton's high-end designer hotels. The in-house restaurant is run by the best chef in town, Ben McKellar of Gingerman fame (*see p351*). Another worthwhile option is the typically chic **myhotel Brighton** (17 Jubilee Street, 01273 900300, www.myhotels.com, doubles £140-£600), which has a penthouse suite containing a 400-year-old carousel horse.

On the recently developed Brighton Marina, the **Alias Hotel Seattle** (Brighton Marina, 01273 679799, www.aliashotels.com, doubles £125-£180) feels much like a state-of-the-art liner. **Blanch House** (17 Atlingworth Street, 01273 603504, www.blanchhouse.co.uk, doubles £130-£230) is an unassuming Georgian terrace house with a dozen rooms themed after snowstorms, plus roses, rococo decor and a 1970s disco. The pampering **Nineteen** (19 Broad Street, 01273 675529, www.hotelnineteen.co.uk, doubles £80-£250) has just seven rooms in a stylish townhouse.

Good quality stops on Ship Street are the classy **Hotel du Vin** (nos.2-6, 01273 718588, www.hotelduvin.com, doubles £170-£480) and, next door, its slightly cheaper new sister the **Pub du Vin** (no.7, 01273 718588, www.hoteldu vin.com/pubduvin, doubles £170-£340), where a pie and a pint cost a fiver. The **Amherst** (2 Lower Rock Gardens, 01273 670131, www. amhersthotel.co.uk, doubles £100-£130) is one of the best bargains among Brighton's contemporary hotels, while the **George IV** (34 Regency Square, 01273 321196, www.georgeiv. hotel.co.uk, doubles £80-£180) is surely *the* best bargain, offering sea views from the city.

Getting there

By train Trains for Brighton leave from Victoria (50mins; map p400 H10) or King's Cross/ St Pancras and London Bridge (1hr 10mins; map p399 L3 & p405 Q8).
By coach National Express coaches for Brighton leave from Victoria Coach Station (1hr 50mins).
By car Take A23, the M23, then the A23 again to Brighton (approx 1hr 20mins).

Tourist information

Tourist Information Centre *Royal Pavilion, Brighton, East Sussex, BN1 1JS (0906 711 2255, www.visitbrighton.com).* **Open** *Summer* 10am-5pm Mon-Sat; 10am-4pm Sun. *Winter* 10am-5pm Mon-Sat.

Ancient History

CANTERBURY

The home of the Church of England since St Augustine was based here in 597, the ancient city of Canterbury is rich in atmosphere. Gaze up at its soaring spires, or around you at the enchanting medieval streets, and you'll soon feel blessed, even if you're not an Anglican.

The town's busy tourist trade and large university provide a colourful counterweight to the brooding mass of history present in its old buildings. And, of course, to the glorious **Canterbury Cathedral** (*see p355*); it's at its most inspirational just before dusk, especially if there's music going on within and the coach parties are long gone. Inside, you'll find superb stained glass, stone vaulting and a vast Norman crypt. A plaque near the altar marks what is believed to be the exact spot where Archbishop Thomas à Becket was murdered; the Trinity Chapel contains the site of the original shrine, plus the tombs of Henry IV and the Black Prince. Be prepared to shell out for entry, but it's well worth it.

A pilgrimage to Becket's tomb was the focus of one of the earliest and finest long poems in all English literature: Geoffrey Chaucer's *Canterbury Tales*, written in the 14th century. At the exhibition named after the poem (*see p355*), visitors are given a device that they point at tableaux inspired by Chaucer's tales of a knight, a miller, a Wife of Bath, and others, enabling them to hear the stories.

Just down the road from Christ Church Gate lies the **Royal Museum & Art Gallery** (High Street, 01227 452747), a monument to high Victorian values. It's currently closed for refurbishment, expected to reopen in 2011, when its permanent collections of art by cattle painter Thomas Sidney Cooper, as well as work by Van Dyck and Sickert, will be on display once again.

Founded to provide shelter for pilgrims, **Eastbridge Hospital** (25 High Street, 01227 471688) retains the smell of ages past. Visitors can tour the hospital and admire the undercroft with its Gothic arches, the Chantry Chapel, the Pilgrims' Chapel and the refectory with an enchanting early 13th-century mural showing Christ in Majesty (there's only one other like this, and it's in France).

The **Roman Museum** (*see p355*) has the remains of a townhouse and mosaic floor among its treasures, augmented with computer reconstructions and time tunnels. From here, you get a super view of the cathedral tower. After the Romans comes St **Augustine**, or at least the ruins of the abbey he built (Longport, 01227 767345, www.english-heritage.org.uk).

Country Flavours

Take a day trip to a farm full of epicurean delights.

Between the picturesque Sussex towns of Firle and Lewes – easily reached by train from London (Victoria to Lewes in just over an hour, then a ten-minute train to Glynde, whence it's a 15-minute walk) – lies **Middle Farm** (Firle, Lewes, East Sussex, BN8 6LJ, 01323 811411, www.middlefarm.com). This family-run working farm once sold only marmalade and eggs, but it's gradually expanded. It now encompasses the National Collection of Cider & Perry, an acclaimed farm shop overflowing with artisan produce and a pretty garden centre, gift shop and restaurant, all within 625 acres of glorious countryside. It's an ideal destination for a day trip from London.

If you arrive in need of some grown-up refreshment, head for the stable block. Bolstered by the vogue for all things traditional, cider and perry (pear cider) are making an extraordinary comeback. Proper cider and perry are made by using the fruit's juice and nothing else: only the length of ripening, the blend of fruit cultivars or the depth of filter are adjusted. With more than 6,000 cultivars of British apple, there have always been plenty of local variations. Take a taster cup and work your way around the 100 or so casks here. Another 150 different ciders and perries are available by the bottle, and there's a tempting array of fresh apple juices, sloe gin, country wines and Sussex ales.

High animal-welfare and environmental standards are central to Middle Farm's ethos, and the owners are committed to transparency: kids (and big kids) get to watch activities in the milking shed every day at 3pm. You can sample the results in the shop, where more than 50 cheeses are sold. Three on-site butchers specialise in custom cuts of Middle Farm's own pork, lamb and beef with free-range Sussex poultry and local game, and there are countless different types of sausage. Squeezing your way past the fruit and veg, you'll find baskets overflowing with fresh bread and trays of cakes and scones; row after row of jams and chutneys are crammed on to the shelves.

Any kids in tow will be entertained while you shop by shire horses, rabbits and guinea pigs, patrolling geese and noisy peacocks, but adults have their own programme of events: there's a traditional Christmas Fair and a raucous Apple Festival. Even if there are no seasonal events when you visit, the local area has plenty to keep you occupied: a stroll up Firle Beacon or over the Downs, a trip to the antiques shops of Lewes and, of course, a fantastic selection of local pubs.

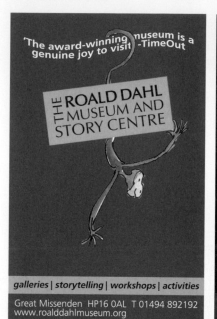

It's now in the capable hands of English Heritage, which has attached a small museum and shop to the site.

Everything you want to see, do or buy in Canterbury is within walking distance. And that includes the seaside – at least, it does if you fancy a long (seven-mile) walk or cycle along the Crab & Winkle Way, a disused railway line to pretty Whitstable.

★ Canterbury Cathedral
The Precincts, CT1 2EH (01227 762862, www. canterbury-cathedral.org). **Open** *Easter-Sept* 9am-5pm Mon-Sat; 12.30-2pm Sun. *Oct-Easter* 9am-4.30pm Mon-Sat; 12.30-2pm Sun. Admission restricted during services and special events. **Admission** £7.50; £6.50 reductions; free under-5s. **Credit** MC, V.

Canterbury Tales
St Margaret's Street, CT1 2TG (01227 479227, www.canterburytales.org.uk). **Open** *Mid Feb-June, Sept, Oct* 10am-5pm daily. *July, Aug* 9.30am-5pm daily. *Nov-mid Feb* 10am-4.30pm daily. **Admission** £7.75; £5.75-£6.75 reductions; free under-4s. **Credit** MC, V.

Roman Museum
Butchery Lane, CT1 2JR (01227 785575, www.canterbury-museums.co.uk). **Open** *Nov-May* 10am-5pm Mon-Sat. *June-Oct* 10am-5pm Mon-Sat; 1.30-5pm Sun. Last entry 1hr before closing. **Admission** £3.10; £2.10 reductions; free under-5s. **Credit** MC, V.

Where to eat & drink

Michael Caines has brought a touch of Michelin glamour to the Canterbury eating scene. As well as his fine dining restaurant and champagne bar at his hotel **ABode** (*see right*), there's also his **Old Brewery Tavern** (High Street, 01227 826682, www.michaelcaines.com, mains £9-£19), where prints of grizzled coopers rolling barrels hang on the walls. But the newest notable opening is **Deeson's** (25-26 Sun Street, 01227 767854, www.deesonsrestaurant.co.uk, mains £10-£18), serving Modern British seasonal dishes made with locally sourced produce (Romney Marsh lamb, Kentish wines and beers, and so on.

Elsewhere, the **Goods Shed** (Station Road West, 01227 459153, mains £10-£18) occupies a lofty Victorian building, which was formerly a railway freight store. On a raised wooden platform, diners sit at scrubbed tables and choose from the specials chalked on the board. Only ingredients on sale in the farmers' market below them are used in the restaurant. For people who care about their food and its provenance, this is heaven.

Pub-wise, Canterbury is in thrall to its students, who take over the **West Gate Inn** Wetherspoons when they're tired of drinking on campus. Most of the better pubs are owned by Shepherd Neame, the local brewery based up the road in the town of Faversham, and the best both happen to be in St Dunstan's Street: the **Unicorn** (no.61, 01227 463187) has a kitsch garden and real ales, while the **Bishop's Finger** (no.13, 01227 768915) and attracts both students and more mature clientele. Built in 1370, the **Parrot** (1-9 Church Lane, St Radigands, 01227 762355) is the oldest pub in Canterbury and also one of the oldest buildings. A good choice of ales and cider is served in a charming setting.

Where to stay

The third in a small chain of smart hotels created by Andrew Brownsword, **ABode** (30-33 High Street, 01227 766266, www.abode hotels.co.uk, doubles £150-£425) has brought a welcome breath of chic into Canterbury's chintzy accommodation options. The 72 rooms are ordered by price and size ranging from 'comfortable', through 'desirable' and 'enviable' to 'fabulous' (a penthouse with superior views and a tennis court-sized bed). **Michael Caines Fine Dining Restaurant** (01227 826684, www.michaelcaines.com, main courses £19-£25) has a young, two Michelin-starred chef at the helm. The most satisfying part of a meal here may be the selection of British cheeses.

Elsewhere, **Canterbury Cathedral Lodge** (The Precincts, 01227 865350, www. canterburycathedrallodge.org, doubles £89-£109) is right inside the cathedral precincts. The hotel is hardly historic (indeed, it's only five years old) but the views certainly are, with bright and comfortable accommodation in a private courtyard. Nearby, the **Cathedral Gate Hotel** (36 Burgate, 01227 464381, www.cathgate.co.uk, doubles £60-£135) is a splendid old hotel built in 1438 and pre-dates the Christ Church Gate it sits alongside. Its 25 rooms, with atmospheric sloping floors and ceilings, are reached via dark narrow corridors and low doorways.

INSIDE TRACK IN TRAINING

If the Romney, Hythe & Dymchurch line has whetted your appetite for adventures on the iron horse, the **Bluebell Railway** (01825 720825, www.bluebell-railway. co.uk) runs beautifully preserved old steam locomotives along the nine miles of line between Sheffield Park and Kingscote.

Greyfriars (6 Stour Street, 01227 456255, www.greyfriars-house.co.uk, doubles £55-£75) is a ancient but comfortable city-centre hotel; however, like all the others it's booked up at graduation time and in high season. **Magnolia House** (36 St Dunstan's Terrace, 01227 765121, www.magnoliahousecanterbury.co.uk, doubles £95-£125) is compact but recommended; the breakfast is delicious and well worth lingering over. The walk to and from town takes you through peaceful Westgate Gardens. Further out, the **Ebury Hotel** (65-67 New Dover Road, 01227 768433, www.ebury-hotel.co.uk, doubles £105-£145) is really quite grand-looking, with a sweeping drive and a Gothic exterior. The best bedrooms have views of the garden, but most of them are large, light and comfortable.

Getting there

By train From Victoria to Canterbury East (1hr 20mins; map p400 H10), or from Charing Cross (map p401 L7) to Canterbury West (1hr 30mins). A new high-speed train service from St Pancras International brings the journey time down to about an hour.
By coach National Express from Victoria Coach Station (1hr 50mins).
By car Take the A2, the M2, then the A2 again (approx 2hrs).

Tourist information

Tourist Information Centre *12-13 Sun Street, Buttermarket, Canterbury, Kent, CT1 2HX (01227 378100, www.canterbury.co.uk).* **Open** 9.30am-5pm Mon-Sat; 9.30am-4.30pm Sun.

Wild Horizons
DUNGENESS, ROMNEY & RYE

Perhaps because it's difficult to reach from London (though there are rail links to Rye and Hastings), Romney Marsh is other-worldly in a way that conjures up science fiction scenarios in Tarkovsky movies; you half expect to see Steed and Mrs Peel in *The Avengers* supping ale in the eerily unchanged villages. It's a strange but appealing mix of olde-worlde cobbled streets and ancient inns, sandy beaches, the world's largest expanse of shingle and event-horizoned marshland, criss-crossed by canals and studded with tiny medieval churches and strange concrete defence constructions dating back to post-World War I. So long as the transport links remain as poor as they are, there probably – hopefully – won't be any real changes here for decades to come. Hastings is the ideal starting point for a circular tour (by car) that takes in

the towns of Winchelsea and Rye, Romney Marsh and Dungeness.

Winchelsea was built on a never-completed medieval grid pattern, first laid out by King Edward I, when the 'old' settlement was swept into the sea in the storms of 1287. The place is proud of its status as England's smallest town, but really it's a sleepy village of 400 residents. It's almost too quaint to be true – like **Rye**, which is a photogenic jumble of Norman, Tudor and Georgian architecture perched on one of the area's few hills. It's worth taking a look at the medieval Landgate gateway and the **Castle Museum** and 13th-century **Ypres Tower** (*see below*). The **Rye Art Gallery** (107 High Street, 01797 222433, www.ryeartgallery.co.uk) offers a changing series of excellent exhibitions, mostly by local artists.

East from Rye lies **Romney Marsh**, flat as a pancake and laced with cycle paths. Bikes can be hired from **Rye Hire** (1 Cyprus Place, Rye, 01797 223033); it's an ideal way to explore the lonely medieval churches that dot the level marsh. Heading out of Rye along the coast road takes you to **Camber Sands**, a vast sandy beach that's a great spot for kite-flying, riding, sand-yachting and invigorating walking.

Beyond is **Dungeness Point**, a huge beach of flint shingle stretching miles out into the sea. Clustered on this strange promontory are a lighthouse that offers wonderful views and a good café. The light on this remote, gloriously bleak patch of land is odd, reflected from the sea on both sides, and the oddness of the landscape is enhanced by the presence of the massive Dungeness nuclear power station that dominates the horizon; such man-made wonders are set against a magnificent natural backdrop.

When the miniature **Romney, Hythe & Dymchurch Railway** train barrels by, you know you're in an episode of *The Prisoner*. Proudly proclaiming to be the 'world's smallest public railway', it's fully functioning but one-third of the standard size. The diminutive train, built by millionaire racing driver Captain Howey in 1927, even includes a buffet car. Sitting in one of the tiny carriages is a surreal experience, as you meander from the wide-open shingle of the Point behind back gardens and caravan parks, through woodland and fields to arrive at **Hythe** (roughly 13 miles away).

Rye Castle Museum & Ypres Tower
3 East Street, TN31 7JY (01797 226728, www.ryemuseum.co.uk). **Open** *Museum* Easter-Oct 2-5pm Mon, Thur, Fri; 10.30am-1pm, 2-5pm Sat, Sun. Closed Oct-Easter. *Tower* Easter-Oct 10.30am-5pm Mon, Thur-Sun. **Admission** *Museum* £2.50; £2 reductions. *Tower* £2.95; £2 reductions. *Both* £5; £4 reductions. **No credit cards.**

Where to eat & drink

You'll find some of the finest food on the south-east coast here. In Rye, the **Landgate Bistro** (5-6 Landgate, Rye, 01797 222829, www.land gatebistro.co.uk, mains £13-£17) once ruled the roost with its attractive, inventive and pleasingly unfussy dishes, but now faces real competition from the **George in Rye** (98 High Street, 01797 222114, www.thegeorge inrye.com, mains £15-£30), where the chef is Rod Grossmann, previously at London's Moro. It's also a hotel – luxurious, stylish, welcoming and altogether very likeable.

The light and informal **Fish Café** (17 Tower Street, 01797 222226, www.thefishcafe.com, mains £10-£19) serves some of the best seafood in town. If fancy isn't your thing, Rye has plenty of simpler eateries: pasta at **Simply Italian** (The Strand, 01797 226024, www. simplyitalian.co.uk, £5-£13) or sound pub food at any number of lovely boozers in town.

The finest option on the seaside is the **Place** (New Lydd Road, Camber, 01797 225057, www. theplacecambersands.co.uk, mains £10-£18) at Camber Sands, which prides itself on its use of locally sourced and eco-friendly produce.

Further east, the **Pilot** (Battery Road, Lydd, 01797 320314, www.thepilot.uk.com, mains £7-£13) serves some of the best fish and chips in Kent. For dinner with a difference, try the Sunday Fly 'n' Dine at **Lydd Airport** (Lydd, Romney Marsh, 01797 322207, www.lyddair. com/flyanddine.html), a low-level 20-minute flight over the Kent coast and a three-course carvery meal – all for £49.95.

Of the many pubs, the **Woolpack Inn** (Beacon Lane, nr Brookland, 01797 344321, mains £5-£24) is one of the best, with low ceilings and original 15th-century beams sourced, enterprisingly, from local shipwrecks. The tiny, multi-award-winning **Red Lion** (Snargate, Romney Marsh, 01797 344648) is something of a Romney Marsh institution, famed for the fact that its interior hasn't been touched since World War II. It doesn't offer food, but you're welcome to bring your own.

Where to stay

Even in the winter months, accommodation in Rye needs to be booked as far in advance as possible. If the tweeness of many of Rye's B&Bs is overly intimate for your tastes but you still

Dungeness.

want a place with character and also some individuality, the **Hope Anchor Hotel** (Watchbell Street, 01797 222216, www.thehope anchor.co.uk, doubles £85-£200) is a reliable bet. It's set in a lovely location at the end of a pretty, cobbled street. The **White Vine House** (24 High Street, 01797 224748, www. whitevinehouse.co.uk, doubles £125-£165) has seven tastefully decorated rooms.

Wonderfully located on Rye's quaintest cobbled street, the atmospheric 17th-century **Jeake's House** (Mermaid Street, 01797 222828, www.jeakeshouse.com, doubles £102-£125) has 11 individually decorated rooms; the gold room features an impressive inglenook fireplace in which a lovely wood stove nestles. The 16th-century **Mermaid Inn** (Mermaid Street, 01797 223065, www.mermaidinn.com, doubles £160-£200) offers olde-worlde tradition at its finest (including an accomplished restaurant), complete with stone fireplaces, four posters, wonky floors and secret passages.

Winchelsea's **Strand House** (Tanyard's Lane, 01797 226276, www.thestrandhouse. co.uk, doubles £70-£120) is a 15th-century house with ten rooms and a delightful garden. The **Romney Bay House Hotel** (Coast Road, Littlestone-on-Sea, New Romney, 01797 364747, doubles £92-£164) is a ten-bedroom mansion designed for Hollywood gossip columnist Hedda Hopper by Sir Clough Williams-Ellis of Portmeirion fame. It's perched on the seafront, right at the end of the bumpy coastal road, with welcoming, individually styled rooms (two with four-posters). And if you're looking for lovingly prepared food with an emphasis on locally sourced ingredients, you'd be hard pushed to find a better place to eat on the peninsula. In Hastings, the **Zanzibar International Hotel** (9 Eversfield Place, 01424 460109, www. zanzibarhotel.co.uk, doubles £99-£215) is a tall, thin seafront house that feels like a private house rather than a boutique hotel.

Getting there

By train From London Bridge or Cannon Street to Rye via Ashford International (approx 1hr 45mins; map p404 P7 & p405 Q8). From Charing Cross, Waterloo East or London Bridge to Hastings (approx 1hr 30mins; map p401 L7). **By car** Take the A20, the M20, then the A259 (approx 2hrs 30mins).

Tourist information

Hastings Tourist Information *Queen Square, Hastings, East Sussex TN34 1TL (0845 274 1001, www.visit1066country.com).* **Open** 8.30am-6.15pm Mon-Fri; 9am-5pm Sat; 10.30am-4.30pm Sun.
Folkestone Tourist Office *01303 258 594, www.discoverfolkstone.co.uk.* **Open** 9am-5pm Mon-Fri for email and telephone enquiries only.
Rye Tourist Information *4 Lion Street, Rye, East Sussex TN31 7LB (01797 229049, www.visitrye.co.uk).* **Open** *Easter-Oct* 10am-5pm daily.

Cambridge.

Colleges & Culture

CAMBRIDGE

Gorgeous, intimidating Cambridge has the feel of an enclosed city. With the narrow streets and tall old buildings of the town centre, it has a way of conveying disapproval to visitors architecturally – and that's before you even reach the 'Keep off the Grass' signs. But pluck up the courage to pass through those imposing gates with their stern porters: within and behind the colleges are pretty green meadows and the idle River Cam, a place where time seems to have stopped back in the 18th century.

Cambridge first became an academic centre when a fracas at Oxford – involving a dead woman, an arrow and a scholar holding a bow – led to some of the learned monks bidding a hasty farewell to Oxford and a hearty hello to Cambridge. Once the dust settled, the monks needed somewhere to peddle their knowledge: the first college, **Peterhouse** (01223 338200, www.pet.cam.ac.uk), was established in 1284. The original hall survives, though most of the present buildings are from the 19th century. Up the road is **Corpus Christi** (01223 338000, www.corpus.cam.ac.uk), founded in 1352. Its Old Court dates from that time and is linked by a gallery to the 11th-century **St Bene't's Church** (Bene't Street, www.stbenetschurch. org), the oldest surviving building in town.

Past Corpus Christi, grand **King's College** (01223 331100, www.kings.cam.ac.uk) was founded by Henry VI in 1441. Its chapel (01223 331155), built between 1446 and 1515 on a scale that would humble many cathedrals, has breathtaking interior fan vaulting and the original stained glass. Attend a service in term-time to hear its wonderful choirboys.

Continue north to find pretty **Trinity** (01223 338400, www.trin.cam.ac.uk), a college founded in 1336 by Edward III and then refounded by Henry VIII in 1546. A fine crowd of Tudor buildings surrounds the Great Court where, legend has it, Lord Byron would bathe naked in the fountain with his pet bear. Wittgenstein studied and taught here, and the library (a cool and airy design by Wren) is open to visitors at certain times (noon-2pm Mon-Fri all year, 10.30am-12.30pm Sat term-time, 01223 338488). Within, covered cases contain such treasures as a lock of Newton's hair, a Shakespeare first folio and Otto Robert Frisch's crisp and moving account of the first atomic bomb test. From behind the library, you can see the neo-Gothic Bridge of Sighs that connects the major courts of **St John's** (01223 338600, www.joh.cam. ac.uk) across the Cam.

Each of the 31 Cambridge colleges is an independent entity, so entry times (and, for the more famous ones, prices) vary considerably: www.cam.ac.uk/cambuniv/colleges.html has the details. But Cambridge isn't only about the colleges. Behind its impressive neoclassical façade, the **Fitzwilliam Museum** (*see p360*) has a superb collection of paintings and sculpture (masterpieces by Titian, Modigliani and Picasso), as well as ancient artefacts from Egypt, Greece and Rome. A short walk south, the 40 relaxing acres of the **Botanic Gardens** (*see below*) have 8,000 plants, among them delightfully modest alpine plants in a glasshouse and, at the entrance, a descendant of Sir Isaac Newton's apple tree.

Fans of eccentric and ghoulish museums should head to Downing Street. On the south side are both the towering totem poles and toucan-shaped 'lime scoop' of the **Museum of Archaeology & Anthropology** (01223 333516, www.maa-cambridge.org) and the fossils and scintillating gemstones of the **Sedgwick Museum of Earth Sciences** (01223 333456, www.sedgwickmuseum.org). On the north side, you'll find the strange scientific devices and grand orreries of the **Whipple Museum of the History of Science** (01223 330906, www.hps.cam.ac.uk/whipple) and, beneath a suspended whale skeleton, the animal skeletons and stuffed birds of the **Museum of Zoology** (01223 336650, www.zoo.cam ac.uk/museum).

One of the real treats during a visit to Cambridge is **Kettle's Yard** (*see p360*), once Tate curator Jim Ede's home and now a magnificently atmospheric collection of early 20th-century artists – Miró, Brancusi, Hepworth – arranged just as he left it. Ring the doorbell and you can settle in one of Ede's chairs and read a book from his shelves.

Behind the main colleges, the beautiful meadows bordering the willow-shaded Cam are known as **the Backs**. Carpeted with crocuses in spring, the Backs are idyllic for summer strolling and 'punting' (pushing flat boats with long poles). Punts can be hired; **Scudamore's Boatyard** (01223 359750, www.scudamores. com) is the largest operator. If you get handy at the surprisingly difficult skill of punting, you can boat down to the **Orchard Tea Rooms** (45-47 Mill Way, CB3 9ND, 01223 551 125, www.orchard-grantchester.com), where Ted Hughes and Sylvia Plath courted and Rupert Brooke lodged as a student.

Cambridge University Botanic Gardens

1 Brookside, CB2 1JE (01223 336265, www.botanic.cam.ac.uk). **Open** *Apr-Sept* 10am-6pm daily. *Oct, Feb, Mar* 10am-5pm daily. *Nov-Jan* 10am-4pm daily. **Admission** £4; £3.50 reductions.

Trumpington Street, CB2 1RB (01223 332900, www.fitzmuseum.cam.ac.uk). **Open** 10am-5pm Tue-Sat; noon-5pm Sun. **Admission** free.

★ FREE Kettle's Yard
Castle Street, CB3 0AQ (01223 748100, www.kettlesyard.co.uk). **Open** *House* 1.30-4.30pm Tue-Sun & bank hol Mon in summer; 2-4pm Tue-Sun & bank hol Mon in winter. *Gallery & bookshop* 11.30am-5pm Tue-Sun & bank holiday Mon. **Admission** free.

Where to eat & drink

Occupying an enviable riverside spot, **Midsummer House** (Midsummer Common, 01223 369299, www.midsummerhouse.co.uk, £47.50 2 courses, £65 3 courses) produces Michelin-starred French food that rises to the occasion. Service is as fussy as you'd expect, but the food is perfectly presented and painstakingly prepared in flavour combinations that are never less than intriguing.

The **Cambridge Chop House** (1 King's Parade, 01223 359506, www.cambscuisine.com/thechophouse, mains £9-£17) is a great come-one-come-all bistro opposite King's College, where you can tuck into British comfort food, complemented by a few wines and a couple of excellent draught ales. Nearby, the busy subterranean **Rainbow Café** (9A King's Parade, 01223 321551, www.rainbowcafe.co.uk, mains £8-£10) serves cheap, hearty vegetarian food. For a teatime treat, follow the example of generations of students and tuck into a Chelsea bun from **Fitzbillies** (52 Trumpington Street, 01223 352500, www.fitzbillies.co.uk).

Cambridge has many creaky old inns in which to settle down and enjoy one of the city's decent local ales. The **Eagle** on Bene't Street (01223 505020) is the most famous – Crick and Watson drank here after fathoming the mysteries of DNA – but there are many others, including the **Pickerel Inn** (30 Magdalene

Street, 01223 355068) and, down a back alley a little off the beaten track, the sweet little **Free Press** (Prospect Row, 01223 368337, www.freepresspub.com).

Where to stay

Because of the university's prominence here, there are plenty of guesthouses in town, with a cluster of B&Bs nicely located just across the Cam from the centre of town to the north of Midsummer Common. **Harry's** (39 Milton Road, 01223 503866, www.welcometoharrys.co.uk, doubles £75), **Worth House** (152 Chesterton Road, 01223 316074, www.worth-house.co.uk, doubles £60) and **Victoria Guest House** (57 Arbury Road, 01223 350086, www.victoria-guesthouse.co.uk, doubles £65) are all good value.

The pick of the luxury hotels is the **Hotel du Vin** (15-19 Trumpington Street, 01223 227330, www.hotelduvin.com, doubles £155-£170), a cheerfully but carefully run operation, painstakingly converted from listed terraced houses. A basement bar (with wine cellar) extends the whole length of the hotel, the busy all-day restaurant occupies one end of the ground floor and there's a heated and covered cigar 'room' outside.

DoubleTree by Hilton (Granta Place, Mill Lane, 01223 259988, www.doubletreebyhilton.co.uk, doubles £150) is located right on the Cam behind Peterhouse, and has an indoor swimming pool. Finally, the **Hotel Felix** (Whitehouse Lane, Huntingdon Road, 01223 277977, www.hotelfelix.co.uk, doubles £180-£230), a modern hotel centred on a characterful 1852 Victorian mansion, is a little remote for walkers, but it has loads of parking space and a good decked area outside its twinkly bar-restaurant.

Getting there

By train Trains to Cambridge leave from King's Cross (50mins; map p399 L3) or Liverpool Street (map p405 R5; 1hr 15mins).
By coach National Express coaches to Cambridge leave from Victoria Coach Station (1hr 50mins).
By car Take Junction 11 or Junction 12 off the M11.

Tourist information

VisitCambridge Visitor Information Centre
The Old Library, Wheeler Street (0871 226 8006, www.visitcambridge.org). **Open** *Oct-Easter* 10am-5.30pm Mon-Fri; 10am-5pm Sat. *Easter-Sept* 10am-5.30pm Mon-Fri; 10am-5pm Sat; 11am-5pm Sun & bank hols.

INSIDE TRACK DING DING!

Apart from punts, the classic Cambridge mode of transport is the bicycle: staff at **Cambridge Station Cycles** (01223 307125, www.stationcycles.co.uk) in the car park to the right out of the train station are very helpful (and will store luggage at a reasonable rate). Wind on a long scarf and toss some books in your basket, and you'll feel exactly like a student.

Directory

Getting Around	**362**
Resources A-Z	**367**
Travel Advice	367
The Local Climate	376
Further Reference	**377**
Index	**379**
Advertisers' Index	**388**

Getting Around

ARRIVING & LEAVING

For information on short breaks outside London, *see pp348-350*.

By air

Gatwick Airport *0844 335 1802, www.gatwickairport.com. About 30 miles south of central London, off the M23.*
Of the three rail services that link Gatwick to London, the quickest is the **Gatwick Express** (0845 850 1530, www.gatwickexpress.com) to Victoria; it takes 30mins and runs 3.30am-12.30am daily. Tickets cost £16.90 single or £28.80 for an open return (valid for 30 days). Under-15s pay £8.45 for a single and half-price for returns; under-5s go free.
Southern (0845 748 4950, www. southernrailway.com) also runs a rail service between Gatwick and Victoria, with trains every 5-10mins (every 25mins between 1am and 4am). It takes about 35 mins, and costs £10.90 for a single, £11 for a day return (after 9.30am) and £23.80 for an open period return (valid for one month). Under-16s get half-price tickets; under-5s go free.
If you're staying in King's Cross or Bloomsbury, consider trains run by **Thameslink** (0845 748 4950, www.firstcapitalconnect.co.uk) to St Pancras. Tickets cost £8.90 single, £9.50 day return (after 9.32am) or £17 for a 30-day open return.
By road, **National Express dot2dot** (08453 682 368, www.dot2. com) offers a coach service at £20 each way (£21 online). A **taxi** costs about £100 and takes ages.

Heathrow Airport *0870 000 0123, www.heathrowairport.com. About 15 miles west of central London, off the M4.*
The **Heathrow Express** train (0845 600 1515, www.heathrow express.co.uk) runs to Paddington every 15mins (5.10am-11.25pm daily), and takes 15-20mins. The train can be boarded at the tube station that serves Terminals 1, 2 and 3 (aka Heathrow Central), or the separate station serving the new Terminal 5; passengers travelling to or from Terminal 4 can connect with a shuttle train at Heathrow Central. Tickets cost £16.50 single or £32 return (£1 less online, £2

more if you buy on board); under-16s go half-price. Many airlines have check-in desks at Paddington.
The journey by tube into central London is longer but cheaper. The 50-60min **Piccadilly Line** ride into central London costs £4 one way (£2 under-16s). Trains run every few minutes from about 5am to 11.57pm daily (6am-11pm Sun).
The **Heathrow Connect** (0845 678 6975, www.heathrowconnect. com) rail service offers direct access to Hayes, Southall, Hanwell, West Ealing, Ealing Broadway and Paddington stations in west and north-west London. The trains run every half-hour, with stops at two stations at Heathrow: one serving Terminals 1, 2 and 3, and the other serving Terminal 4; there's a shuttle from the T4 station to Terminal 5. A single from Paddington is £7.40; an open return is £14.80.
National Express (0871 781 8181, www.nationalexpress.com) runs daily coach services to London Victoria (90mins, 5am-9.35pm daily), leaving Heathrow Central bus terminal every 20-30mins. It's £5 for a single (£2.50 under-16s) or £9 (£4.50 under-16s) for a return.
By road, **National Express dot2dot** (*see above*) offers an airport-to-hotel coach service for £21.50 each way. A **taxi** into town will cost roughly £100 and take an hour or more, depending on traffic.

London City Airport *7646 0000, www.londoncityairport.com. About 9 miles east of central London.*
The **Docklands Light Railway (DLR)** now includes a stop for London City Airport. The journey to Bank station in the City takes around 20mins, and trains run 5.30am-12.30am Mon-Sat or 7am-11.30pm Sun. By road, a **taxi** costs around £30 to central London; less to the City or to Canary Wharf.

Luton Airport *01582 405100, www.london-luton.com. About 30 miles north of central London, J10 off the M1.*
It's a short bus ride from the airport to Luton Airport Parkway station. From here, the **Thameslink** rail service (*see above*) calls at many stations (St Pancras International and City among them); journey time is 35-45mins. Trains leave every

15mins or so and cost £11.50 single one-way and £20.50 return, or £12 for a cheap day return (after 9.30am Mon-Fri, all day weekends). Trains between Luton and St Pancras run at least hourly all night.
By coach, the Luton to Victoria journey takes 60-90mins. **Green Line** (0870 608 7261, www.green line.co.uk) runs a 24-hour service. A single is £11 and returns cost £16; under-16s go half-price. A **taxi** into London will cost upwards of £50.

Stansted Airport *0870 000 0303, www.stanstedairport.com. About 35 miles north-east of central London, J8 off the M11.*
The **Stansted Express** train (0845 748 4950, www.stansted express.com) runs to and from Liverpool Street station; the journey time is 40-45mins. Trains leave every 15-45mins, and tickets cost £19 single, £28.80 return; under-16s travel half-price, under-5s free.
The **Airbus** (0871 781 8181, www.nationalexpress.com) coach service from Stansted to Victoria takes at least 80mins. Coaches run roughly every 30mins (24hrs daily), more frequently at peak times. A single is £10 (£5 for under-16s), return is £17 (£8.50 for under-16s). A taxi to London is about £80.

By coach

Coaches run by **National Express** (0871 781 8181, www. nationalexpress.com), the biggest coach company in the UK, arrive at **Victoria Coach Station** (164 Buckingham Palace Road, SW1W 9TP, 7730 3466, www.tfl. gov.uk) near Victoria tube station. This is also where companies such as Eurolines (01582 404511, www.eurolines.com) dock their European services. Major station redevelopment is planned, which may begin this year.

By rail

Trains from mainland Europe run by Eurostar (0870 518 6186, www. eurostar.com) arrive at **St Pancras International** (Pancras Road, King's Cross, NW1 2QP, 0870 518 6186, www.stpancras.com). In late 2009, services should also begin to Stratford station in east London.

PUBLIC TRANSPORT

Getting around London on public transport is easy but expensive.

Information

Details on timetables and other travel information are provided by **Transport for London** (7222 1234, www.tfl.gov.uk/journey planner). Complaints or comments on most forms of public transport can also be taken up with **London TravelWatch** (7505 9000, www.londontravelwatch.org.uk).

Travel Information Centres

TfL's Travel Information Centres provide help with the tube, buses and Docklands Light Railway (DLR; see p364). You can find them in **Camden Town Hall**, opposite St Pancras (9am-5pm Mon-Fri), and in the stations below. Call 7222 1234 for more information.

Euston station 7 15am-9.15pm Mon-Fri; 7.15am-6.15pm Sat; 8.15am-6.15pm Sun.
Heathrow Terminals 1, 2 & 3 tube station 6.30am-9pm daily.
Liverpool Street tube station, 7.15am-9.15pm Mon-Sat; 8.15am-8pm Sun.
Piccadilly Circus tube station 9.15am-7pm daily.
Victoria station 7.15am-9.15pm Mon-Sat; 8.15am-8.15pm Sun.

Fares & tickets

Tube and DLR fares are based on a system of six zones, stretching 12 miles out from the centre of London. A flat cash fare of £4 per journey applies across zones 1-4 on the tube, and £4.50 for zones 1-6; customers save up to £2.50 per journey with a pre-pay Oyster card (see below). Anyone caught without a ticket or Oyster card is subject to a £50 on-the-spot fine (reduced to £25 if you pay within three weeks).

Oyster cards A pre-paid smart-card, Oyster is the cheapest way of getting around on buses, tubes and the DLR. You can charge up standard Oyster cards at tube stations, Travel Information Centres (see above), some rail stations and newsagents. There is a £3 refundable deposit payable on each card; to collect your deposit, call 0845 330 9876.

In addition to standard Oyster cards, new **Visitor Oyster** cards are available from Gatwick Express

outlets, National Express coaches, Superbreak, visitlondon.com, visitbritaindirect.com, Oxford Tube coach service and on Eurostar services. The only difference between Visitor Oysters and 'normal' Oysters is that they come pre-loaded with money.

A tube journey in zone 1 using Oyster pay-as-you-go costs £1.80 (65p for under-16s), compared to the cash fare of £4. A single tube ride within zones 2, 3, 4, 5 or 6 costs £1.30 (65p for under-16s); single journeys from zones 1-6 using Oyster are £4.20 (7am-7pm Mon-Fri) or £2.40 (all other times), or £1.10 for children. Up to four children pay just £1 each for their fares when accompanied by an adult with a Travelcard.

If you make a number of journeys using Oyster pay-as-you-go on a given day, the total fare deducted will always be capped at the price of an equivalent Day Travelcard. However, if you only make one journey using Oyster pay-as-you-go, you will only be charged a single Oyster fare.

Day Travelcards If you're only using the tube, DLR, buses and trams, using Oyster to pay as you go will always be capped at the same price as an equivalent Day Travelcard. However, if you're also using National Rail services, Oyster may not be accepted: opt, instead, for a Day Travelcard, a standard ticket with a coded stripe that allows travel across all networks.

Anytime Day Travelcards can be used all day. They cost from £7.20 for zones 1-2 (£3.60 child), up to £14.80 for zones 1-6 (£7.40 child). Tickets are valid for journeys started by 4.30am the next day. The cheaper **Off-Peak Day Travelcard** allows travel after 9.30am Mon-Fri and all day at weekends and public holidays. It costs from £5.60 for zones 1-2 up to £7.50 for zones 1-6.

Children Under-5s travel free on buses and trams without the need to provide any proof of identity. 5- and 10-year-olds can also travel free, but need to obtain a 5-10 Oyster photocard. For details, visit www.tfl.gov.uk/fares or call 0845 330 9876.

An 11-15 Oyster photocard is needed by 11- to 15-year-olds to pay as they go on the tube/DLR and to buy 7-Day, monthly or longer period Travelcards, and by 11- to 15-year-olds if using the tram to/from Wimbledon.

Photocards Photocards are not required for 7-Day Travelcards or Bus Passes, adult-rate Travelcards or Bus Passes charged on an Oyster card. For details of how to obtain 5-10, 11-15 or 16+ Oyster photocards, see www.tfl.gov.uk/fares or call 0845 330 9876.

London Underground

Delays are fairly common, with lines closing at weekends for engineering works. Trains are hot and crowded in rush hour (8-9.30am and 4.30-7pm Mon-Fri). Even so, the 12 colour-coded lines that together comprise the underground rail system – also known as 'the tube' – remain the quickest way to get around London. Comments or complaints are dealt with by **LU Customer Services** on 0845 330 9880 (8am-8pm daily); for lost property, see p371.

Using the system You can get Oyster cards from www.tfl.gov.uk/oyster, by calling 0870 849 9999, at tube stations, Travel Information Centres, some rail stations and newsagents. Single or day tickets can be bought from ticket offices or machines. You can buy most tickets and top up Oyster cards at self-service machines. Some ticket offices close early (around 7.30pm); carry a charged-up Oyster card to avoid being stranded.

To enter and exit the tube using an Oyster card, simply touch it to the yellow reader, which will open the gates. Make sure you also touch the card to the reader when you exit the tube, or you'll be charged a higher fare when you next use your card to enter a station. On certain lines, you'll see a pink reader – touch it in addition to the yellow entry/exit readers and on some routes it will reduce your fare.

To enter using a paper ticket, place it in the slot with the black magnetic strip facing down, then pull it out of the top to open the gates. Exiting is done in much the same way; however, if you have a single journey ticket, it will be retained by the gate as you leave.

Timetables Tube trains run daily from around 5am (except Sunday, when they start an hour or so later depending on the line, and Christmas Day, when there's no service). You shouldn't have to wait more than ten minutes for a train; during peak times, services should run every two or three minutes. Times of last trains vary; they're

DIRECTORY

usually around 12.30am daily (11.30pm on Sun). The tubes run all night only on New Year's Eve; otherwise, you're limited to night buses (*see below*).

Fares The single fare for adults across the network is £4. Using Oyster pay-as-you-go, the fare varies by zone: zone 1 costs £1.60; zones 1-2 costs £1.60 or £2.20, depending on the time of day; zones 1-6 is £2.20 or £3.80. The single fare for children aged 11-15 is £2 for any journey that includes zone-1 travel and £1.60 for others. Under-11s travel free (*see also p363*).

National Rail & London Overground services

Independently run commuter services coordinated by **National Rail** (0845 748 4950, www.national rail.co.uk) leave from the city's main rail stations. Visitors heading to south London, or to more remote destinations such as Hampton Court Palace, will need to use these overground services. Travelcards are valid on these services within the right zones, but not all routes accept Oyster pay-as-you-go; check before you travel.

Operated by Transport for London, meaning it does accept Oyster, the **London Overground** rail line runs through north London from Stratford in the east to Richmond in the south-west. New spurs connect Willesden Junction in the north-west to Clapham Junction in the south-west, and Gospel Oak in the north to Barking in the east, as well as heading north-west from Euston. Trains run about every 20mins (every 30mins on Sun).

For lost property, *see p371*.

Docklands Light Railway (DLR)

DLR trains (7363 9700, www.tfl. gov.uk/dlr) run from Bank station (where they connect with the tube system's Central and Waterloo & City lines) or Tower Gateway, close to Tower Hill tube (Circle and District lines). At Westferry station, the line splits east and south via Island Gardens to Greenwich and Lewisham; a change at Poplar can take you north to Stratford. The easterly branch forks after Canning Town to either Beckton or London City Airport; the latter is due to extend across the river to Woolwich Arsenal this year. Trains run 5.30am-12.30am daily. For lost property, *see p371*.

Fares Adult single fares on the DLR are the same as for the tube (*see p363*) except for DLR-only journeys in zones 2-3, which cost £1.60 (£1.10 with Oyster pay-as-you-go) or 80p for 11-15s (55p with Oyster pay-as-you-go).

The DLR also offers one-day Rail & River Rover tickets, which add one day's DLR travel to hop-on, hop-off travel on **City Cruises** riverboats (10am-6pm, *see p366*) between Westminster, Waterloo, Tower and Greenwich Piers.

Starting at Tower Gateway, trains leave hourly from 10am for a special tour, with a guide adding commentary. It costs £12 for adults or £6 for kids; a family pass (two adults and up to three under-16s), which must be bought in person from the piers, costs £28. Under-5s go free.

Buses

You must have a ticket or valid pass before boarding any bus in zone 1, and before boarding any articulated, single-decker bus ('bendy buses', which are in the process of being phased out) anywhere in the city. You can buy a ticket (or a 1-Day Bus Pass) from machines at bus stops, although they're often not working; better to travel with an Oyster card or some other pass (*see p363*). Inspectors patrol buses at random; if you don't have a ticket or pass, you may be fined £50.

All buses are now low-floor vehicles that are accessible to wheelchair-users and passengers with buggies. The only exceptions are Heritage routes 9 and 15, which are served by the world-famous open-platform Routemaster buses.

For lost property, *see p371*.

Fares Using Oyster pay-as-you-go costs £1.20 a trip; your total daily payment, regardless of how many journeys you take, will be capped at £3.90. Paying with cash at the time of travel costs £2 for a single trip. Under-16s travel for free (using an Under-11 or 11-15 Oyster photocard as appropriate; *see p363*). A 1-Day Bus Pass gives unlimited bus and tram travel for £3.80.

Night buses Many bus routes operate 24 hours a day, seven days a week. There are also some special night buses with an 'N' prefix, which run from about 11pm to 6am. Most night services run every 15-30mins, but busier routes run a service around every 10mins. Fares are the same as for daytime buses;

Bus Passes and Travelcards can be used at no extra fare until 4.30am of the morning after they expire.

Green Line buses Green Line buses (0844 801 7261, www.green line.co.uk) serve the suburbs within 40 miles of London. Its office is opposite **Victoria Coach Station** (*see p362*); services run 24 hours.

Tramlink

In south London, trams run between Beckenham, Croydon, Addington and Wimbledon. Travelcards that cover zones 3, 4, 5 or 6 are valid, as are Bus Passes. Cash fares are £2 (£1.20 with Oyster pay-as-you-go).

For lost property, *see p371*.

Water transport

Most river services operate every 20-60mins between 10.30am and 5pm, and may run more often and later in summer. For commuters, **Thames Clippers** (0870 781 5049, www.thamesclippers.com) runs a service between Embankment Pier and Royal Arsenal Woolwich Pier; stops include Blackfriars, Bankside, London Bridge, Canary Wharf and Greenwich. A standard day roamer ticket (valid 10am-5pm) costs £12, while a single from Embankment to Greenwich is £5, but Oyster cardholders get a third off. **Thames Executive Charters** (www.thamesexecutivecharters.com) also offers travelcard discounts on its River Taxi between Putney and Blackfriars, calling at Wandsworth, Chelsea Harbour, Cadogan Pier and Embankment, meaning a £4.50 standard single becomes £3. **Westminster Passenger Service Assocation** (7930 2062, www.wpsa.co.uk) runs a daily service from Westminster Pier to Kew, Richmond and Hampton Court from April to October. At around £12 for a single, it's not cheap, but it is a lovely way to see the city, and there are discounts of 30-50% for Travelcard holders.

Thames River Services (www.westminsterpier.co.uk) operates from the same pier, offering trips to Greenwich, Tower Pier and the Thames Barrier. A trip to Greenwich costs £10.40, though £14 buys you a Rivercard, which allows you to hop on and off at will. Travelcard holders get a third off.

For commuter service timetables, plus a full list of leisure operators and services, see www.tfl.gov.uk.

For lost property, *see p371*.

DIRECTORY

TAXIS

Black cabs

The licensed London taxi, aka 'black cab' (although, since on-car advertising, they've come in many colours), is a much-loved feature of London life. Drivers must pass a test called 'the Knowledge' to prove they know every street in central London, and the shortest route to it.

If a taxi's orange 'For Hire' sign is lit, it can be hailed. If a taxi stops, the cabbie must take you to your destination if it's within seven miles. It can be hard to find an empty cab, especially just after the pubs close. Fares rise after 8pm on weekdays and at weekends.

You can book black cabs from the 24hr **Taxi One-Number** (0871 871 8710, a £2 booking fee applies, plus 12.5% if you pay by credit card), **Radio Taxis** (7272 0272) and **Dial-a-Cab** (7253 5000; credit cards only, with a booking fee of £2). Comments or complaints about black cabs should be made to the **Public Carriage Office** (0845 602 7000, www.tfl.gov.uk/pco). Note the cab's badge number, which should be displayed in the rear of the cab and on its back bumper.

For lost property, *see p371*.

Minicabs

Minicabs (saloon cars) are generally cheaper than black cabs, but can be less reliable. Only use licensed firms (look for a disc in the front and rear windows), and avoid those who illegally tout for business in the street: drivers may be unlicensed, uninsured and dangerous.

Trustworthy and fully licensed firms include **Addison Lee** (7387 8888), which will text you when the car arrives, and **Lady Cabs** (7272 3300), **Ladybirds** (8295 0101) and **Ladycars** (8981 7111), which employ only women drivers. Otherwise, text HOME to 60835 ('60tfl'). Transport for London will then text you the numbers of the two nearest licensed minicab operators and the number for Taxi One-Number, which provides licensed black taxis in London. The service costs 35p plus standard call rate. No matter who you choose, always ask the price when you book and confirm it with the driver.

Motorbike taxis

For speedy journeys or airport dashes, weave through traffic on the back of a motorbike. Both **Passenger Bikes** (0844 561 6147, www.passengerbikes.com) and **Taxybikes** (7255 4269, www.addisonlee.com/services/taxybikes) have a minimum £25 charge, and offer fixed airport rates; the bikes are equipped with panniers, and can carry a small to medium suitcase. You pay a premium for the thrill: central London to Gatwick currently costs £110-£120.

DRIVING

London's roads are often clogged with traffic and roadworks, and parking (*see below*) is a nightmare. Walking or using public transport are better options. But if you do hire a car, you can use any valid licence from outside the EU for up to a year after arrival. Speed limits in the city are generally 20 or 30mph on most roads. Don't use a mobile phone (unless it's hands-free) while driving or you risk a £1,000 fine.

Car hire

All firms below have branches at the airport; several also have offices in the city centre. Shop around for the best rate; always check the level of insurance included in the price.

Alamo *UK: 0870 400 4562, www.alamo.co.uk. US: 1-877 222 9075, www.alamo.com.*
Avis *UK: 0844 544 3407, www.avis.co.uk. US: 1-800 331 1212, www.avis.com.*
Budget *UK: 0844 544 3439, www.budget.co.uk. US: 1-800 472 3325, www.budget.com.*
Enterprise *UK: 0870 350 3000, www.enterprise.co.uk. US: 1-800 261 7331, www.enterprise.com.*
Europcar *UK: 0870 607 5000, www.europcar.co.uk. US: 1-877 940 6900, www.europcar.com.*
Hertz *UK: 0870 844 8844, www.hertz.co.uk. US: 1-800 654 3001, www.hertz.com.*
National *UK: 0870 400 4552, www.nationalcar.co.uk. US: 1-800 222 9058, www.nationalcar.com.*
Thrifty *UK: 01494 751500, www.thrifty.co.uk. US: 1-800 847 4389, www.thrifty.com.*

Congestion charge

Drivers coming into central London between 7am and 6pm Monday to Friday have to pay £8, a fee known as the congestion charge. The congestion charge zone is bordered by Marylebone, Euston and King's Cross (N), the Old Street roundabout (NE), Tower Bridge (E), Elephant & Castle (S), Vauxhall, Chelsea, Kensington (SW), and Holland Park, Bayswater, Paddington (W); see the map on pp392-393. You'll know when you're about to drive into the charging zone from the red 'C' signs on the road. You can also enter the postcode of your destination at http://cclondon.tfl.gov.uk/cclondon/zone/default.aspx to discover if it's within the charging zone.

The thoroughfare formed by Vauxhall Bridge Road, Grosvenor Place and Park Lane is the sole toll-free route through the zone. If you stick to this road while crossing central London, you won't have to pay. After a consultation period, the mayor announced in late 2008 that he would be removing the Western Extension Zone (essentially, the area west of Park Lane), although the change wouldn't take place until 2010, in spring at the earliest; check www.tfl.gov.uk for the latest.

There are no tollbooths – the scheme is enforced by numberplate recognition from CCTV cameras. Passes can be bought from some newsagents, garages and NCP car parks; you can also pay online at www.cclondon.com, by phone on 0845 900 1234 or by SMS (you'll need to pre-register at the website for the latter option). You can pay any time during the day; payments are also accepted until midnight on the next charging day, although the fee is £10 if you pay then. Expect a fine of £50 if you fail to pay, rising to £100 if you delay payment.

Breakdown services

If you're a member of a motoring organisation in another country, check if it has a reciprocal agreement with a British one. The AA and the RAC offer schemes that cover Europe in addition to the UK.

AA (Automobile Association) *0870 550 0600 information , 08457 887766 breakdown, www.theaa.com.*
ETA (Environmental Transport Association) *0845 389 1010, www.eta.co.uk.*
RAC (Royal Automobile Club) *0870 572 2722 information, 0800 828282 breakdown, www.rac.co.uk.*

Parking

Central London is scattered with parking meters, but free spots are rare. Meters cost £1.10 for 15mins, and are limited to two hours. Parking on a single or double yellow line, a red line or

DIRECTORY

in residents' parking areas during the day is illegal, and you may end up being fined, clamped or towed.

However, in the evening (from 6pm or 7pm in much of central London) and at various times at weekends, parking on single yellow lines is legal and free. If you find a clear spot on a single yellow line during the evening, look for a sign giving the local regulations. Meters also become free at certain times during evenings and weekends. Parking on double yellow lines and red routes is illegal at all times.

NCP 24-hour car parks (0845 050 7080, www.ncp.co.uk) are numerous but pricey (£2-£7.20 for two hours). Central ones include Arlington House, Arlington Street, St James's, W1; Snowsfields, Southwark, SE1; and 4-5 Denman Street, Soho, W1.

Clamping & vehicle removal

The immobilising of illegally parked vehicles with a clamp is commonplace in London. There will be a label on the car telling you which payment centre to phone or visit. You'll have to stump up an £80 release fee and show a valid licence. The payment centre will de-clamp your car within four hours. If you don't remove your car at once, it may get clamped again, so wait by your vehicle.

If your car has disappeared, it's either been stolen or, if it was parked illegally, towed to a car pound by the local authorities. A release fee of £200 is levied for removal, plus £40 per day from the first midnight after removal. To add insult to injury, you'll also probably get a parking ticket of £60-£100 when you collect the car (reduced by a 50% discount if paid within 14 days). To find out how to retrieve your car, call the **Trace Service** hotline (7747 4747).

CYCLING

London isn't the friendliest of towns for cyclists, but the **London Cycle Network** (www.londoncyclenetwork.org.uk) and **London Cycling Campaign** (7234 9310, www.lcc.org.uk) help make it better. **Transport for London** (7222 1234) offers a printable route-finder for cyclists. For **cycle hire**, including information on the city's new bike-rental scheme, see p333.

WALKING

The best way to see London is on foot, but the city's street layout is very complicated – even locals often

carry maps. We've included street maps of central London in the back of this book (starting on p394), with essential locations clearly marked; the standard Geographers' *London A-Z* and Collins' *London Street Atlas* are useful supplements. There's also route advice at www.tfl.gov.uk/gettingaround.

GUIDED TOURS

By bicycle

The **London Bicycle Tour Company** (see p333) runs a range of tours in central London.

By boat

City Cruises: Rail River Rover 7740 0400, www.citycruises.com. **Rates** £11; £5.50 reductions. Combines hop-on, hop-off travel on any regular City Cruise route (pick-ups at Westminster, Waterloo, Tower and Greenwich Piers) with free travel on the DLR.
Jason's Trip Canal Boats 7286 3428, www.jasons.co.uk. **Rates** £7.50-£8.50; £6.50-£7.50 reductions. These 90min narrowboat tours between Little Venice and Camden are unremittingly popular.
Thames RIB Experience 7930 5746, www.thamesribexperience. com. **Rates** £29-£45; £16-£27 reductions.
Our favourite of the growing number of Thames RIB tours (a RIB is a powerful speedboat) zooms you from the Embankment, either to Canary Wharf (50mins) or the Thames Barrier (90mins), and back. You'll need to book in advance.
Thames River Adventures 07931 845 345, http://thamesriveradventures.co.uk. **Tours** from £65. Want to investigate Tower Bridge, Hampton Court Palace or Regent's Canal under your own steam? Guided kayak tours are offered between March and October.

By bus

Big Bus Company 7233 9533, www.bigbustours.com. **Rates** £25; £10 reductions; free under-5s. These open-top buses (8.30am-6pm, or until 4.30pm in winter) cover more than 70 stops in town, among them Haymarket, Green Park (near the Ritz) and Marble Arch. There's live commentary in English, and recorded commentary in eight other languages. Passengers can hop on and hop off as many times as they like. Tickets include a river cruise.

Original London Sightseeing Tour 8877 1722, www.theoriginaltour.com. **Rates** £24; £12 reductions; £84 family; free under-5s. OLS's hop-on, hop-off bus tours cover 90 stops in central London, including Marble Arch and Trafalgar Square. Commentary comes in seven languages. Tickets include a free river cruise.
London Duck 7928 3132, www. londonducktours.co.uk. **Rates** £20; £14-£16 reductions; £58 family. Tours of Westminster in an amphibious vehicle. The 75min road/river trip starts on Chicheley Street (behind the London Eye) and enters the Thames at Vauxhall.

By helicopter

Cabair 8953 4411, www.cabair helicopters.com. **Rates** £150/person. Cabair runs half-hour tours (Sun, some Sat) that depart from Elstree Aerodrome in north London and follow the Thames.

By car

Black Taxi Tours of London 7935 9363, www.blacktaxitours. co.uk. **Rates** £100-£110. Tailored two-hour tours for up to five people. **Small Car Big City** 7585 0399, www.smallcarbigcity.com. **Rates** £89-£119. Feeling a little retro? Tour town in a classic Mini Cooper.

On foot

Head to **www.walklondon. org.uk** for a massive variety of free walks and events. Good choices for paid group tours on a variety of subjects, both mainstream and arcane, include **And Did Those Feet** (8806 3742, www.chr.org.uk), **Performing London** (01234 404774, www.performinglondon. co.uk), **Silver Cane Tours** (07720 715295, www.silvercane tours.com) and **Urban Gentry** (8149 6253, www.urbangentry.com). The **Original London Walks** (7624 3978, www.walks.com) provide an astonishing 140 different walks on a variety of themes, the most popular being their daily Jack the Ripper walks around the East End. More idiosyncratic walks – such as a Cuban Cigar Walk around Mayfair & St James's – can be downloaded from **www.citiesinsound.com**. And if walking's too slow for you, pull on your trainers for a guided run from **www.londonsightseeing runs.com**.

Resources A-Z

TRAVEL ADVICE

For up-to-date information on travel to a specific country – including the latest on safety and security, health issues, local laws and customs – contact your home country government's department of foreign affairs. Most have websites with useful advice for would-be travellers.

AUSTRALIA
www.smartraveller.gov.au

CANADA
www.voyage.gc.ca

NEW ZEALAND
www.safetravel.govt.nz

REPUBLIC OF IRELAND
foreignaffairs.gov.ie

UK
www.fco.gov.uk/travel

USA
www.state.gov/travel

ADDRESSES

London postcodes are less helpful than they could be for locating addresses. The first element starts with a compass point – N, E, SE, SW, W and NW, plus the smaller EC (East Central) and WC (West Central). However, the number that follows relates not to geography (unless it's a 1, which indicates central) but to alphabetical order. So N2 is way out in the boondocks (East Finchley), while W2 covers the very central Bayswater.

AGE RESTRICTIONS

Buying/drinking alcohol 18.
Driving 17.
Sex 16.
Smoking 18.

ATTITUDE & ETIQUETTE

Don't mistake reserve for rudeness or indifference: strangers striking up a conversation are likely to be foreign, drunk or mad. The weather is a safe subject on which to broach a conversation. Avoid personal questions or excessive personal contact beyond a handshake.

If you want to rile a Londoner in the underground, stand blocking the escalator during rush hour (stand on the right, walk on the left). While use of a map doesn't mark you out as a tourist in this sometimes bewildering city, trying to flag down a black cab with its orange light off surely does, as this means it's occupied (see p365).

BUSINESS

As the financial centre of Europe, London is well equipped to meet the needs of business travellers. The financial action is increasingly centred on Canary Wharf. Marketing, advertising and entertainment companies have a strong presence in the West End.

Conventions & conferences

Visit London 7234 5800, www.visitlondon.com. Enquiries.
Queen Elizabeth II Conference Centre Broad Sanctuary, Westminster, SW1P 3EE (7222 5000, www.qeiicc.co.uk). Westminster tube **Open** 8am-6pm Mon-Fri. Conference facilities 24hrs daily. **Map** p401 K9. Excellent conference facilities.

Couriers & shippers

DHL 08701 100 300, www.dhl.co.uk.
FedEx 0845 607 0809, www.fedex.com.

Office services

ABM Alternative Business Machines 111 Freston Road, W11 4BD (7486 5634, www.abm ltd.com). Latimer Road tube. **Open** 9am-5pm Mon-Fri. **No credit cards. Map** p398 G5.
British Monomarks 27 Old Gloucester Street, Holborn, WC1N 3XX (7419 5000, www.british monomarks.co.uk). Holborn tube. **Open** Mail forwarding 9.30am-5.30pm Mon-Fri. Phone answering 9am-6pm Mon-Fri. **Credit** AmEx, MC, V. **Map** p399 L5.

CONSUMER

Consumer Direct 0845 4040 506, www.consumerdirect.gov.uk. Funded by the government's Office of Fair Trading, this is a good place to start for consumer advice on all goods and services.

CUSTOMS

Citizens entering the UK from outside the EU must adhere to duty-free import limits:

● 200 cigarettes or 100 cigarillos or 50 cigars or 250g of tobacco
● 2 litres still table wine plus either 1 litre spirits or strong liqueurs (above 22% abv) or 2 litres fortified wine (under 22% abv), sparkling wine or other liqueurs
● 60cc/ml perfume
● 250cc/ml toilet water
● other goods to the value of no more than £145

The import of meat, poultry, fruit, plants, flowers and protected animals is restricted or forbidden; there are no restrictions on the import or export of currency.

People over the age of 17 arriving from an EU country are able to import unlimited goods for their own personal use, if bought tax-paid (so not duty-free). For more details, see www.hmrc.gov.uk.

DISABLED

As a city that evolved long before the needs of disabled people were considered, London is difficult for wheelchair users, though access and facilities are slowly improving. The capital's bus fleet is now low-floor for easier wheelchair access; there are no steps for any of the city's trams; and all DLR stations have either lifts or ramp access. However, steps and escalators to the tube and overland trains mean they are often of only limited use to wheelchair users. A blue symbol on the tube map (see p416) indicates stations with step-free access. The Tube Access Guide booklet is free; call 7222 1234 for more details.

DIRECTORY

Most major attractions and hotels offer good accessibility, though provisions for the hearing- and sight-disabled are patchier. Enquire about facilities in advance. *Access in London* is an invaluable reference book for disabled travellers, available for a £10 donation (sterling cheque, cash US dollars or via PayPal to gordon. couch@virgin.net) from **Access Project** (39 Bradley Gardens, W13 8HE, www.accessproject-phsp.org).

Artsline *21 Pine Court, Wood Lodge Gardens, Bromley, Kent BR1 2WA (7388 2227, www.artsline. org.uk).* Open 9.30am-5.30pm Mon-Fri. Map p399 K3. Information on disabled access to arts and culture.
Can Be Done *11 Woodcock Hill, Harrow, Middx HA3 0XP (8907 2400, www.canbedone.co.uk). Kenton tube/rail.* Open 9.30am-5pm Mon-Fri. Disabled-adapted holidays and tours in London, around the UK and worldwide.
Royal Association for Disability & Rehabilitation *12 City Forum, 250 City Road, Islington, EC1V 8AF (7250 3222, 7250 4119 textphone, www.radar.org.uk). Old Street tube/rail.* Open 9am-5pm Mon-Fri. Map p402 P3.
A national organisation for disabled voluntary groups that also publishes books and the bimonthly magazine *New Bulletin* (£35/yr).
Tourism for All *0845 124 9971, www.tourismforall.org.uk.* Open Helpline 9am-5pm Mon-Fri. Information for older people and people with disabilities in relation to accessible accommodation and other tourism services.
Wheelchair Travel & Access Mini Buses *1 Johnston Green, Guildford, Surrey GU2 9XS (01483 233640, www.wheelchair-travel.co.uk).* Open 9am-6pm Mon-Fri; 9am-noon Sat. Hires out converted vehicles (driver optional), plus cars with hand controls and wheelchair-adapted vehicles.

DRUGS

Illegal drug use remains higher in London than the UK as a whole, though it's becoming less visible on the streets and in clubs. Despite fierce debate, cannabis remains a Class C drug, meaning that possession may only result in a warning and confiscation. More serious Class B and A drugs (ecstasy, LSD, heroin, cocaine and the like) carry stiffer penalties, with a maximum of seven years in prison for possession.

ELECTRICITY

The UK uses the European 220-240V, 50-cycle AC voltage. British plugs use three pins, so travellers with two-pin European appliances should bring an adaptor, as should anyone using US appliances, which run off 110-120V, 60-cycle.

EMBASSIES & CONSULATES

American Embassy *24 Grosvenor Square, Mayfair, W1A 2LQ (7499 9000, http://london.usembassy.gov). Bond Street or Marble Arch tube.* Open 8.30am-5.30pm Mon-Fri. Map p400 G7.
Australian High Commission *Australia House, Strand, Holborn, WC2B 4LA (7379 4334, www. uk.embassy.gov.au). Holborn or Temple tube.* Open 9am-5pm Mon-Fri. Map p401 M6.
Canadian High Commission *38 Grosvenor Street, Mayfair, W1K 4AA (7258 6600, www. canada.org.uk). Bond Street or Oxford Circus tube.* Open 8am-4pm Mon-Fri. Map p400 H7.
Embassy of Ireland *17 Grosvenor Place, Belgravia, SW1X 7HR (7235 2171, 7225 7700 passports & visas, www.embassyofireland.co.uk). Hyde Park Corner tube.* Open 9.30am-5.30pm Mon-Fri. Map p400 G9.
New Zealand High Commission *New Zealand House, 80 Haymarket, St James's, SW1Y 4TQ (7930 8422, www.nzembassy.com). Piccadilly Circus tube.* Open 9am-5pm Mon-Fri. Map p406 W4.

EMERGENCIES

In the event of a serious accident, fire or other incident, call **999** – free from any phone, including payphones – and ask for an ambulance, the fire service or police. For hospital Accident & Emergency departments, *see below*; for helplines, *see right*; for police stations, *see p373*.

GAY & LESBIAN

Time Out Gay & Lesbian London (£12.99) is the ultimate handbook to the capital. The phonelines below offer help and information; for HIV and AIDS, *see right*.

London Friend *7837 3337, www.londonfriend.org.uk.* Open 7.30-9.30pm Tue, Wed, Fri.
London Lesbian & Gay Switchboard *7837 7324, www. llgs.org.uk.* Open 10am-11pm daily.

HEALTH

British citizens or those working in the UK can go to any general practitioner (GP). People ordinarily resident in the UK, including overseas students, are also permitted to register with a National Health Service (NHS) doctor. If you fall outside these categories, you will have to pay to see a GP. Your hotel concierge should be able to recommend one.

A pharmacist may dispense medicines on receipt of a prescription from a GP. NHS prescriptions cost £7.20; under-16s and over-60s are exempt from charges. Contraception is free for all. If you're not eligible to see an NHS doctor, you'll be charged cost price for any medicines prescribed.

Free emergency medical treatment under the NHS is available to:
● EU nationals and those of Iceland, Norway and Liechtenstein; all may also be entitled to state-provided treatment for non-emergency conditions with an EHIC (European Health Insurance Card)
● nationals of New Zealand, Russia, most former USSR states and the former Yugoslavia
● residents (irrespective of nationality) of Anguilla, Australia, Barbados, the British Virgin Islands, the Falkland Islands, Iceland, the Isle of Man, Montserrat, Poland, Romania, St Helena and the Turks & Caicos Islands
● anyone who has been in the UK for the previous 12 months, or who has come to the UK to take up permanent residence
● students and trainees whose courses require more than 12 weeks in employment in the first year
● refugees and others who have sought refuge in the UK
● people with HIV/AIDS at a special STD treatment clinic

There are no NHS charges for services including:
● treatment in A&E wards
● emergency ambulance transport to a hospital
● diagnosis and treatment of certain communicable diseases
● family planning services
● compulsory psychiatric treatment

Accident & emergency

Listed below are most of the central London hospitals that have 24-hour Accident & Emergency (A&E) departments.

Charing Cross Hospital *Fulham Palace Road, Hammersmith, W6 8RF (8846 1234, www.imperial.nhs.uk). Barons Court or Hammersmith tube.*

Chelsea & Westminster Hospital *369 Fulham Road, Chelsea, SW10 9NH (8746 8000, www.chelwest.nhs.uk). South Kensington tube.* **Map** p396 C12.

Royal Free Hospital *Pond Street, Hampstead, NW3 2QG (7794 0500, www.royalfree.nhs.uk). Belsize Park tube or Hampstead Heath rail.*

Royal London Hospital *Whitechapel Road, Whitechapel, E1 1BB (7377 7000, www.bartsandthe london.nhs.uk). Whitechapel tube.*

St Mary's Hospital *Praed Street, Paddington, W2 1NY (7886 6666). Paddington tube/rail.* **Map** p395 D5.

St Thomas' Hospital *Lambeth Palace Road, Lambeth, SE1 7EH (7188 7188, www.guysandst thomas.nhs.uk). Westminster tube or Waterloo tube/rail.* **Map** p401 L9.

University College Hospital *235 Grafton Road, NW1 2BU (0845 155 5000, www.uclh.nhs.uk). Euston Square or Warren Street tube.* **Map** p398 J4.

Complementary medicine

British Homeopathic Association *0870 444 3950, www.trust homeopathy.org.* **Open** *Enquiries* 9am-5pm Mon-Fri. Referrals.

Contraception & abortion

Family planning advice, contraceptive supplies and abortions are free to British citizens on the NHS, and to EU residents and foreign nationals living in Britain. Phone 0845 310 1334 or visit www.fpa.org.uk for your local Family Planning Association. The 'morning after' pill (around £25), effective up to 72 hours after intercourse, is available over the counter at pharmacies.

British Pregnancy Advisory Service *0845 730 4030, www. bpas.org.* **Open** *Helpline* 8am-9pm Mon-Fri; 8.30am-6pm Sat; 9.30am-2.30pm Sun. Callers are referred to their nearest clinic for treatment.

Brook Advisory Centre *7284 6040, 0808 802 1234 helpline, www.brook.org.uk.* **Open** *Helpline* 9am-5pm Mon-Fri. Information on sexual health, contraception and abortion, plus free pregnancy tests for under-25s.

Marie Stopes House *Family Planning Clinic/Well Woman Centre, 108 Whitfield Street,*

Fitzrovia, W1T 5BE (0845 300 8090, www.mariestopes.org.uk). Warren Street tube. **Open** *Clinic* 8.30am-4.30pm Mon-Fri. *Helpline* 24hrs daily. **Map** p398 J4. Contraceptive advice, emergency contraception, pregnancy testing, an abortion service, cervical and health screening or gynaecological services. Fees may apply.

Dentists

Dental care is free for resident students, under-18s and people on benefits. All others must pay. To find an NHS dentist, contact the local Health Authority or a Citizens' Advice Bureau (*see right*).

Dental Emergency Care Service *Guy's Hospital, St Thomas Street, Borough, SE1 9RT (7188 0511). London Bridge tube/rail.* **Open** 9am-5pm Mon-Fri. **Map** p404 Q8. Queues start forming at 8am; arrive by 10am if you're to be seen at all.

Hospitals

For a list of hospitals with Accident & Emergency departments, *see left*; for other hospitals, consult the *Yellow Pages* directory.

Opticians

See p264.

Pharmacies

Also called 'chemists' in the UK. Branches of Boots and larger supermarkets have a pharmacy, and there are independents on the high street (*see p264*). Staff can advise on over-the-counter medicines. Most pharmacies keep shop hours (9am-6pm Mon-Sat).

STDs, HIV & AIDS

NHS Genito-Urinary Clinics (such as the Centre for Sexual Health) are affiliated to major hospitals. They provide free, confidential treatment of STDs and other problems, such as thrush and cystitis, offer counselling about HIV and other STDs, and can conduct blood tests.

The 24-hour **Sexual Healthline** (0800 567 123, www.playingsafely. co.uk) is free and confidential. See online for your nearest clinic. For other helplines, *see right*; for abortion and contraception, *see left*.

Mortimer Market Centre for Sexual Health *Mortimer Market, off Capper Street, Bloomsbury,*

WC1E 6JB (7530 5050). Goodge Street or Warren Street tube. **Open** 9am-6pm Mon, Thur; 9am-7pm Tue; 1-6pm Wed; 8.30am-3pm Fri. **Map** p398 J4.

Terrence Higgins Trust Lighthouse *314-320 Gray's Inn Road, King Cross, WC1X 8DP (0845 122 1200, www.tht.org.uk). King's Cross tube/rail.* **Open** *Helpline* 10am-10pm Mon-Fri; noon-6pm Sat, Sun. **Map** p399 M5. Advice for those with HIV/AIDS, their relatives, lovers and friends. It also offers free leaflets about AIDS and safer sex.

HELPLINES

Helplines dealing with sexual health issues are listed under STDs, HIV & AIDS (*see above*).

Alcoholics Anonymous *7835 0022, www.alcoholics-anonymous. org.uk.* **Open** 10am-10pm daily.

Citizens' Advice Bureaux *www.citizensadvice.org.uk.* The council-run CABs offer free legal, financial and personal advice. Check the phone book or see the website for your nearest office.

Missing People *0500 700 700, www.missingpeople.org.uk.* **Open** 24hrs daily. Information on anyone reported missing.

NHS Direct *0845 4647, www.nhs direct.nhs.uk.* **Open** 24hrs daily. A free, first-stop service for medical advice on all subjects.

Rape & Sexual Abuse Support Centre *8683 3300, www.rape crisis.org.uk.* **Open** noon-2.30pm, 7-9.30pm Mon-Fri; 2.30-5pm Sat, Sun. Information and support.

Samaritans *0845 790 9090, www.samaritans.org.uk.* **Open** 24hrs daily. General helpline.

Victim Support *0845 450 3936, www.victimsupport.org.uk.* **Open** 8am-8pm Mon-Fri. **Map** p398 H5. Emotional and practical support to victims of crime.

ID

You're unlikely to be asked for ID in London when buying alcohol or tobacco, although many shops and some bars check anyone who looks 21 or under. Passports and photographic driver's licences are acceptable forms of ID.

INSURANCE

Insuring personal belongings can be difficult to arrange once you have arrived, so do so before you leave home. Medical insurance is

DIRECTORY

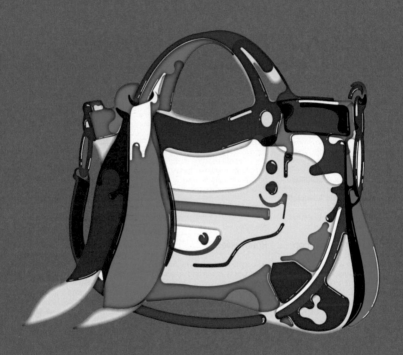

Ask New York City about New York City fabulous
nycgo.com

usually included in travel insurance packages. Unless your country has an arrangement with the UK (*see p368*), it's important to ensure you have adequate health cover.

INTERNET

Many hotels now have high-speed internet access, whether via a cable or as wireless. Many cafés have wireless access; see below for three central establishments. And you'll also find internet terminals in public libraries (*see right*).

Benugo Bar & Kitchen
BFI Southbank, Belvedere Road, South Bank, SE1 8XT (7401 9000, www.benugo.com). Waterloo tube/ rail. **Open** 11am-11pm Mon-Sat; 11am-10.30pm Sun.
Hummus Brothers *88 Wardour Street, Soho, W1F 0TH (7734 1311, www.hbros.co.uk). Oxford Circus tube.* **Open** noon-10pm Mon-Wed, Sun; noon-11pm Thur-Sat.
Peyton & Byrne *Wellcome Collection, 183 Euston Road, Bloomsbury, NW1 2BE (7611 2138, www.peytonandbyrne.com). Euston tube/rail.* **Open** 10am-6pm Mon-Wed, Fri, Sat; 10am-10pm Thur; 11am-6pm Sun.

LEFT LUGGAGE
Airports

Gatwick Airport *01293 502014 South Terminal, 01293 569900 North Terminal.*
Heathrow Airport *8745 5301 T1, 8897 9541 T2, 8759 3344 T3, 8897 6874, T4, 8283 5073 T5.*
London City Airport *7646 0162.*
Stansted Airport *01279 663213.*

Rail & bus stations

Security precautions mean that London stations tend to have left-luggage desks rather than lockers. Call 0845 748 4950 for details.

Charing Cross *7930 5444.* **Open** 7am-11pm daily.
Euston *7387 8699.* **Open** 7am-11pm daily.
King's Cross *7837 4334.* **Open** 7am-11pm daily.
Paddington *7313 1514.* **Open** 9am-5.30pm Mon-Fri.
Victoria *7963 0957.* **Open** 9am-5.30pm Mon-Fri.

LEGAL HELP

Those in difficulties can visit a Citizens' Advice Bureau (*see p369*)

or contact the groups below. Try the **Legal Services Commission** (0845 345 4345, www.legalservices. gov.uk) for information. If you're arrested, your first call should be to your embassy (*see p368*).

Joint Council for the Welfare of Immigrants *7251 8706, www.jcwi.org.uk.* **Open** 2-5pm Tue, Thur. JCWI's legal advice line offers guidance and referrals.
Law Centres Federation *7839 2998, www.lawcentres.org.uk.* **Open** 10am-5.30pm Mon-Fri. Free legal help for people who can't afford a lawyer and livee or work in the immediate area; this office connects you with the nearest centre.

LIBRARIES

Unless you're a resident, you won't be able to join a lending library. At the British Library (*see p83*), only exhibition areas are open to non-members, but the libraries below can be used for reference by all.

Barbican Library *Barbican Centre, Silk Street, City, EC2Y 8DS (7638 0569, www.cityoflondon.gov.uk/ barbicanlibrary). Barbican tube.* **Open** 9.30am-5.30pm Mon, Wed; 9.30am-7.30pm Tue, Thur; 9.30am-2pm Fri; 9.30am-4pm Sat. **Map** p402 P5.
Holborn Library *32-38 Theobald's Road, Bloomsbury, WC1X 8PA (7974 6345). Chancery Lane tube.* **Open** 10am-7pm Mon-Fri; 10am-5pm Sat. **Map** p399 M5.
Kensington Central Library *12 Philimore Walk, Kensington, W8 7RX (7937 2542, www.rbkc.gov.uk/ libraries). High Street Kensington tube.* **Open** 9.30am-8pm Mon, Tue, Thur; 9.30am-5pm Wed, Fri, Sat.
Marylebone Library *109-117 Marylebone Road, Marylebone, NW1 5PS (7641 1300, www. westminster.gov.uk/libraries). Baker Street tube or Marylebone tube/rail.* **Open** 9.30am-8pm Mon, Tue, Thur, Fri; 10am-8pm Wed; 9.30am-5pm Sat; 1.30-5pm Sun. **Map** p395 F4.
Victoria Library *160 Buckingham Palace Road, Belgravia, SW1W 9UD (7641 4258, www.westminster.gov. uk/libraries). Victoria tube/rail.* **Open** 9.30am-8pm Mon; 9.30am-7pm Tue, Thur, Fri; 10am-7pm Wed; 9.30am-5pm Sat. **Map** p400 H10.
Westminster Reference Library *35 St Martin's Street, Westminster, WC2H 7HP (7641 4636, www. westminster.gov.uk/libraries). Leicester Square tube.* **Open** 10am-8pm Mon-Fri; 10am-5pm Sat. **Map** p407 X4.

Women's Library *25 Old Castle Street, Whitechapel, E1 7NT (7320 2222, www.thewomenslibrary. ac.uk). Aldgate or Aldgate East tube.* **Open** *Reading room* 9.30am-5pm Tue, Wed, Fri; 9.30am-8pm Thur; 10am-4pm Sat. **Map** p405 S6.

LOST PROPERTY

Always inform the police if you lose anything, if only to validate insurance claims; *see p373* or the *Yellow Pages* for police station locations. Only dial 999 if violence has occurred; use 0300 1231212 for non-emergencies. Report lost passports both to the police and to your embassy (*see p368*).

Airports

For items left on the plane, contact the relevant airline. Otherwise, phone the following:

Gatwick Airport *01293 503162.*
Heathrow Airport *8745 7727.*
London City Airport *7646 0000.*
Luton Airport *01582 395219.*
Stansted Airport *01279 663293.*

Public transport

If you've lost property in an overground station or on a train, call 0870 000 5151, and give the operator the details.

Transport for London *Lost Property Office, 200 Baker Street, Marylebone, NW1 5RZ (7918 2000, www.tfl.gov.uk). Baker Street tube.* **Open** 8.30am-4pm Mon-Fri. **Map** p398 G4. Allow three working days from the time of loss. If you lose something on a bus, call 7222 1234 and ask for the numbers of the depots at either end of the route. For tube losses, pick up a lost property form from any station.

Taxis

The Transport for London office (*see p363*) deals with property found in registered black cabs. Allow seven days from the time of loss. For items lost in a minicab, contact the relevant company.

MEDIA
Magazines

Time Out remains London's only quality listings magazine. Widely available in central London every Tuesday, it gives listings for the week from Thursday. If you want to know what's going on and whether it's any good, look here.

Nationally, *Loaded*, *FHM* and *Maxim* are big men's titles, while women often buy *Glamour* and *Grazia* alongside *Vogue*, *Marie Claire* and *Elle*. The appetite for gossip rags such as *Heat*, *Closer* and *OK* has abated only slightly.

The *Spectator*, *Prospect*, the *Economist* and the *New Statesman* are at the serious, political end of the market, with the satirical *Private Eye* bringing some levity to the subject. The *London Review of Books* ponders life and letters in considerable depth. The laudable *Big Issue* is sold across the capital by registered homeless vendors.

For webzines, *see p378*.

Newspapers

London's main daily paper is the sensationalist *Evening Standard*, published Monday to Friday. It became a freesheet in autumn 2009, after a major revamp under a new owner failed to bring in enough sales. In the mornings, you'll still find *Metro*, the free *Standard* spin-off that led a deluge of low-quality free dailies, in tube station dispensers and discarded on trains.

Quality national dailies include, from right to left, the *Daily Telegraph*, *The Times* (best for sport), the *Independent* and the *Guardian* (best for arts). All go into overdrive on Saturdays and have bulging Sunday equivalents bar the *Guardian*, which has a sister Sunday paper, the *Observer*. The pink *Financial Times* (daily except Sunday) is the best for business.

In the middle market, the leader is the right-wing *Daily Mail* (and *Mail on Sunday*); the *Daily Express* (and *Sunday Express*) competes. The tabloid leader is the *Sun* (and Sunday's *News of the World*). The *Daily Star* and the *Mirror* are the main lowbrow contenders.

Radio

The stations below are broadcast on standard wavebands as well as digital, where they are joined by some interesting new channels (mostly from the BBC). The format is not yet widespread, but you may be lucky enough to have digital in your hotel room or hire car.

Absolute *105.8 FM.* Laddish rock.
BBC Radio 1 *98.8 FM.* Youth-oriented pop, indie and dance.
BBC Radio 2 *89.1 FM.* Bland during the day; better after dark.

BBC Radio 3 *91.3 FM.* Classical music dominates, but there's also discussion, world music and arts.
BBC Radio 4 *93.5 FM, 198 LW.* The BBC's main speech station is led by news agenda-setter *Today* (6-9am Mon-Fri, 7-9am Sat).
BBC Radio 5 Live *693, 909 AM.* Rolling news and sport. Avoid the morning phone-ins.
BBC London *94.9 FM.* Danny Baker (3-5pm Mon-Fri) is brilliant.
BBC World Service *648 AM.* Some repeats, some new shows, transmitted globally.
Capital FM *95.8 FM.* Pop and chat.
Classic FM *100.9 FM.* Easy-listening classical.
Heart FM *106.2 FM.* Capital for grown-ups.
Kiss *100 FM.* Dance music.
LBC *97.3 FM.* Phone-ins and talk.
Magic *105.4 FM.* Familiar pop.
Smooth *102.2 FM.* Aural wallpaper.
Resonance *104.4 FM.* Arts radio – an inventively oddball mix.
Xfm *104.9 FM.* Alternativish rock.

Television

With a multiplicity of formats, there are plenty of pay-TV options. However, the relative quality of free TV keeps subscriptions from attaining US levels.

The five main free-to-air networks are as follows:
BBC1 The Corporation's mass-market station. Relies too much on soaps, game shows and lifestyle TV, but does have quality offerings. As with all BBC stations, there are no commercials.
BBC2 A reasonably intelligent cultural cross-section, but now upstaged by BBC4 (*see below*).
ITV1 Monotonous weekday mass-appeal shows. ITV2 does much the same on digital.
Channel 4 Extremely successful US imports (the likes of *Ugly Betty* and *ER*), more or less unwatchable homegrown entertainments and the occasional great documentary.
Five From high culture to lowbrow filth. A strange, unholy mix.

Satellite, digital and cable channels include the following:
BBC3 Appalling homegrown comedy and dismal documentary.
BBC4 Highbrow stuff, including fine documentaries and dramas.
BBC News Rolling news.
BBC Parliament Live debates.
Discovery Channel Science and nature documentaries.
E4, More4, Film4 Channel 4's entertainment and movie channels.

Five US US drama and docs.
ITV3, ITV4 US shows on 2, British reruns on 3 and 4.
Sky News Rolling news.
Sky One Sky's version of ITV.
Sky Sports Three channels.

MONEY

Britain's currency is the pound sterling (£). One pound equals 100 pence (p). Coins are copper (1p, 2p), silver (round: 5p, 10p; seven-sided: 20p, 50p), yellowy-gold (£1) or silver in the centre with a yellowy-gold edge (£2). Paper notes are blue (£5), orange (£10), purple (£20) or red (£50). You can exchange foreign currency at banks, bureaux de change and post offices; there's no commission charge at the last of these (for addresses of the most central, *see pp373-374*). Many large stores also accept euros (€).

Western Union *0800 833833, www.westernunion.co.uk.*
The old standby. Chequepoint (*see right*) also offers this service.

Banks & ATMs

ATMs can be found inside and outside banks, in some shops and in larger stations. Machines in many commercial premises levy a charge for each withdrawal, usually £1.50. If you're visiting from outside the UK, your card should work via one of the debit networks, but check charges in advance. ATMs also allow you to make withdrawals on your credit card if you know your PIN; you'll be charged interest plus, usually, a currency exchange fee. Generally, getting cash with a card is the cheapest form of currency exchange but there are hidden charges, so do your research.

Credit cards, especially Visa and MasterCard, are accepted in most shops (except small corner shops) and restaurants (except caffs). However, American Express and Diners Club tend to be accepted only at more expensive outlets. You will usually not be allowed to make a purchase with your card without your PIN. For more, see www.chipandpin.co.uk.

No commission is charged for cashing sterling travellers' cheques if you go to one of the banks affiliated with the issuing company. You do have to pay to cash travellers' cheques in foreign currencies, and to change cash. You will always need to produce ID to cash travellers' cheques.

Bureaux de change

You'll be charged for cashing travellers' cheques or buying and selling foreign currency at bureaux de change. The commission varies. Major stations have bureaux, and there are many in tourist areas and on major shopping streets. Most open 8am-10pm.

Chequepoint *550 Oxford Street, Marlyebone, W1C 1LY (7724 6127, www.chequepoint.com). Marble Arch tube.* **Open** 8am-11pm daily. **Map** p398 G6. **Other locations** throughout the city.
Garden Bureau *30A Jubilee Market Hall, Covent Garden, WC2E 8BE (7240 9921). Covent Garden tube.* **Open** 9.30am-6pm daily. **Map** p407 Z3.
Thomas Exchange *13 Maddox Street, Mayfair, W1S 2QG (7493 1300, www.thomasexchange.co.uk). Oxford Circus tube.* **Open** 8.45am-5.30pm Mon-Fri. **Map** p406 U3

Lost/stolen credit cards

Report lost or stolen credit cards both to the police and the 24 hour phone lines listed below. Inform your bank by phone and in writing.

American Express *01273 696933, www.americanexpress.com.*
Diners Club *0870 190 0011, www.dinersclub.co.uk.*
MasterCard *0800 964767, www.mastercard.com.*
Visa *0800 891725, www.visa.com.*

Tax

With the exception of food, books, newspapers and a few other items, purchases in the UK are subject to Value Added Tax (VAT), aka sales tax. The rate stood at 15% during 2009, but looks likely to rise to 17.5% in 2010. Either way, VAT is included in all prices quoted by mainstream shops, although it may not be included in hotel rates.

Foreign visitors may be able to claim back the VAT paid on most goods that are taken out of the EC (European Community) as part of a scheme generally called 'Tax Free Shopping'. To be able to claim a refund, you must be a non-EC visitor to the UK, or a UK resident emigrating from the EC. When you buy the goods, the retailer will ask to see your passport, and will then ask you to fill in a simple refund form. You need to have one of these forms to make your claim; till receipts alone will not do. If you're

leaving the UK direct for outside the EC, you must show your goods and refund form to UK customs at the airport/port from which you're leaving. If you're leaving the EC via another EC country, you must show your goods and refund form to customs staff of that country.

After customs have certified your form, get your refund by posting the form to the retailer from which you bought the goods, posting the form to a commercial refund company or handing your form at a refund booth to get immediate payment. Customs are not responsible for making the refund: when you buy the goods, ask the retailer how the refund is paid.

OPENING HOURS

Government offices close on bank (public) holidays (*see p376*), but big shops often remain open, with only Christmas Day sacrosanct. Most attractions remain open on the other public holidays.

Banks 9am-4.30pm (some close at 3.30pm, some 5.30pm) Mon-Fri; some also Sat mornings.
Businesses 9am-5pm Mon-Fri.
Post offices 9am-5.30pm Mon-Fri; 9am-noon Sun.
Pubs & bars 11am-11pm Mon-Sat; noon-10.30pm Sun.
Shops 10am-6pm Mon-Sat, some to 8pm. Many also open on Sun, usually 11am-5pm or noon-6pm.

POLICE

London's police are used to helping visitors. If you've been robbed, assaulted or involved in a crime, go to your nearest police station. (We've listed a handful in central London; look under 'Police' in Directory Enquiries or call 118 118, 118 500 or 118 888 for more.)

If you have a complaint, ensure that you take the offending officer's identifying number (it should be displayed on his or her epaulette). You can then register a complaint with the **Independent Police Complaints Commission** (90 High Holborn, WC1V 6BH, 0845 300 2002, www.ipcc.gov.uk). In non-emergencies, call 0300 123 1212; for emergencies, *see p368*.

Belgravia Police Station *202-206 Buckingham Palace Road, Pimlico, SW1W 9SX (7730 1212). Victoria tube/rail.* **Map** p400 H10.
Camden Police Station *60 Albany Street, Fitzrovia, NW1 4EE (7404 1212). Great Portland Street tube.* **Map** p398 H4.

Charing Cross Police Station *Agar Street, Covent Garden, WC2N 4JP (7240 1212). Charing Cross tube/rail.* **Map** p407 Y4.
Chelsea Police Station *2 Lucan Place, Chelsea, SW3 3PB (7589 1212). South Kensington tube.* **Map** p397 E10.
Islington Police Station *2 Tolpuddle Street, Islington, N1 0YY (7704 1212). Angel tube.* **Map** p402 N2.
Kensington Police Station *72 Earl's Court Road, Kensington, W8 6EQ (7376 1212). Earl's Court tube.* **Map** p396 B11.
Marylebone Police Station *1-9 Seymour Street, Marylebone, W1H 7BA (7486 1212). Marble Arch tube.* **Map** p395 F6.
West End Central Police Station *27 Savile Row, Mayfair, W1S 2EX (7437 1212). Piccadilly Circus tube.* **Map** p406 U3.

POSTAL SERVICES

The UK has a fairly reliable postal service. If you have a query, contact Customer Services on 08457 740740. For business enquiries, call 08457 950950.

Post offices are usually open 9am-5.30pm during the week and 9am-noon on Saturdays, although some post offices shut for lunch and smaller offices may close for one or more afternoons each week. Three central post offices, two in the New Town and one in the Old Town are listed below; for others, call the **Royal Mail** on 08457 223344 or check online at www.royalmail.com.

You can buy individual stamps at post offices, and books of four or 12 first- or second-class stamps at newsagents and supermarkets that display the appropriate red sign. A first-class stamp for a regular letter costs 39p; second-class stamps are 30p. It costs 62p to send a postcard abroad. For details of other rates, see www.royalmail.com.

See also p367 **Business: Couriers & shippers**.

Post offices

Post offices are usually open 9am-6pm Mon-Fri and 9am-noon Sat, with the exception of Trafalgar Square Post Office (24-28 William IV Street, WC2N 4DL, 0845 722 3344), which opens 8.30am-6.30pm Mon-Fri and 9am-5.30pm Sat. Listed below are the other main central London offices. For general enquiries, call 0845 722 3344 or consult www.postoffice.co.uk.

DIRECTORY

Albemarle Street *nos.43-44, Mayfair, W1S 4DS. Green Park tube.* **Map** p406 U5.
Baker Street *no.111, Marylebone, W1U 6SG. Baker Street tube.* **Map** p398 G5.
Great Portland Street *nos.54-56, Fitzrovia, W1W 7NE. Oxford Circus tube.* **Map** p398 H4.
High Holborn *no.181, Holborn, WC1V 7RL. Holborn tube.* **Map** p407 Y1.

Poste restante

If you want to receive mail while you're away, you can have it sent to Trafalgar Square Post Office (*see p373*), where it will be kept for a month. Your name and 'Poste Restante' must be clearly marked on the letter. You'll need ID to collect it.

RELIGION

Times may vary; phone to check.

Anglican & Baptist

Bloomsbury Central Baptist Church *235 Shaftesbury Avenue, Covent Garden, WC2H 8EP (7240 0544, www.bloomsbury.org.uk). Tottenham Court Road tube.* **Services & meetings** 11am, 6.30pm Sun. **Map** p399 Y1.
St Paul's Cathedral *For listings, see p63.* **Services** 7.30am, 8am, 12.30pm, 5pm Mon-Sat; 8am, 10.15am, 11.30am, 3.15pm, 6pm Sun. **Map** p404 O6.
Westminster Abbey *For listings, see p115.* **Services** 7.30am, 8am, 12.30pm, 5pm Mon-Fri; 8am, 9am, 12.30pm, 3pm Sat; 8am, 10am, 11.15am, 3pm, 5.45pm, 6.30pm Sun. **Map** p401 K9.

Buddhist

Buddhapadipa Thai Temple *14 Calonne Road, Wimbledon, SW19 5HJ (8946 1357, www.buddhapadipa.org). Wimbledon tube/rail then 93 bus.* **Open** *Temple* 9-6pm Sat, Sun. *Meditation retreat* 7-9pm Tue, Thur; 4-6pm Sat, Sun.
London Buddhist Centre *51 Roman Road, Bethnal Green, E2 0HU (0845 458 4716, www.lbc.org. uk). Bethnal Green tube.* **Open** see website.

Catholic

Brompton Oratory *For listings, see p123.* **Services** 7am, 8am (Latin mass), 10am, 12.30am, 6pm Mon-Fri; 7am, 8.30am, 10am, 6pm Sat;

7am, 8.30am, 9am (tridentine), 10am, 11am (sung Latin), 12.30pm, 4.30pm, 7pm Sun. **Map** p397 E10.
Westminster Cathedral *For listings, see p117.* **Services** 7am, 8am, 10.30am, 12.30pm, 1.05pm, 5pm Mon-Fri; 8am, 9am, 12.30pm, 6pm Sat; 8am, 9am, 10.30am, noon, 5.30pm, 7pm Sun. **Map** p400 J10.

Islamic

East London Mosque *82-92 Whitechapel Road, Whitechapel, E1 1JQ (7650 3000, www.eastlondon mosque.org.uk). Aldgate East tube.* **Services** *Friday prayer* 1.30pm (1.15pm in winter). **Map** p405 S6.
Islamic Cultural Centre & London Central Mosque *146 Park Road, Marylebone, NW8 7RG (7724 3363, www.iccuk.org). Baker Street tube or bus 74.* **Services** vary; phone 7725 2213 for details.

Jewish

Liberal Jewish Synagogue *28 St John's Wood Road, St John's Wood, NW8 7HA (7286 5181, www.ljs.org). St John's Wood tube.* **Services** 6.45pm Fri; 11am Sat.
West Central Liberal Synagogue *21 Maple Street, Fitzrovia, W1T 4BE (7636 7627, www.wcls.org.uk). Warren Street tube.* **Services** 3pm Sat. **Map** p398 J4.

Methodist & Quaker

Methodist Central Hall *Central Hall, Storey's Gate, Westminster, SW1H 9NH (7222 8010, www. c-h-w.co.uk). St James's Park tube.* **Services** 12.45pm Wed; 11am, 6.30pm Sun. **Map** p401 K9.
Religious Society of Friends (Quakers) *173-177 Euston Road, Bloomsbury, NW1 2BJ (7663 1000, www.quaker.org.uk). Euston tube/ rail.* **Meetings** 6.30pm Mon; 11am Sun. **Map** p399 K3.

SAFETY & SECURITY

There are no real 'no-go' areas in London, and despite endless media coverage of teenage stabbings, you're much more likely to get hurt in a car accident than as a result of criminal activity, but thieves haunt busy shopping areas and transport nodes as they do in all cities.

Use common sense and follow some basic rules. Keep wallets and purses out of sight, and handbags securely closed. Never leave bags or coats unattended, beside, under or on the back of a chair – even if they

aren't stolen, they're likely to trigger a bomb alert. Don't put bags on the floor near the door of a public toilet. Don't take short cuts through dark alleys and car parks. Keep your passport, cash, and credit cards in separate places. Don't carry a wallet in your back pocket. Always be aware of your surroundings.

SMOKING

July 2007 saw the introduction of a ban on smoking in all enclosed public spaces, including pubs, bars, clubs, restaurants, hotel foyers and shops, as well as on public transport. Smokers now face a penalty fee of £50 or a maximum fee of £200 if they are prosecuted for smoking in a smoke-free area. Many bars and clubs offer smoking gardens or terraces.

TELEPHONES

Dialling & codes

London's dialling code is 020; standard landlines have eight digits after that. You don't need to dial the 020 from within the area, so we have not given it in this book.

If you're calling from outside the UK, dial your international access code, then the UK code, 44, then the full London number, omitting the first 0 from the code. For example, to make a call to 020 7813 3000 from the US, dial 011 44 20 7813 3000. To dial abroad from the UK, first dial 00, then the relevant country code from the list below. For more international dialling codes, check the phone book or see www.kropla.com/dialcode.htm.

Australia 61
Canada 1
New Zealand 64
Republic of Ireland 353
South Africa 27
USA 1

Mobile phones

Mobile phones in the UK operate on the 900 MHz and 1800 MHz GSM frequencies common throughout most of Europe. If you're travelling to the UK from Europe, your phone should be compatible; if you're travelling from the US, you'll need a tri-band handset. Either way, you should check that your phone is enabled for international roaming, and that your service provider at home has a reciprocal arrangement with a UK provider.

The simplest option may be to buy a 'pay-as-you-go' phone (about £50-£200); there's no monthly fee, you top up talk time using a card. Check before buying whether it can make and receive international calls. **Phones4u** (www.phones4u. co.uk) and **Carphone Warehouse** (www.carphonewarehouse.com), which both have stores throughout the city, offer options. For phone rental, *see also p249*.

Operator services

Call 100 for the operator if you have difficulty in dialling; for an alarm call; to make a credit card call; for information about the cost of a call; and for help with international person-to-person calls. Dial 155 for the international operator if you need to reverse the charges (call collect) or if you can't dial direct, but be warned that this service is very expensive.

Directory enquiries

This service is now provided by various six-digit 118 numbers. They're pretty pricey to call: dial (free) 0800 953 0720 for a rundown of options and prices. The best known is 118 118, which charges 49p per call, then 14p per minute thereafter; 118 888 charges 49p per call, then 9p per minute; 118 180 charges 25p per call, then 30p per minute. Online, use the free www.ukphonebook.com.

Yellow Pages This 24-hour service lists the phone numbers of thousands of businesses in the UK. Dial 118 247 (49p/min) and identify the type of business you require, and in which area of London.

Public phones

Public payphones take coins or credit cards (sometimes both). The minimum cost is 40p, which buys a 110-second local call. Some payphones, such as the counter-top ones found in pubs, require more. International calling cards, offering bargain minutes via a freephone number, are widely available.

Telephone directories

There are several telephone directories for London, divided by area, which contain private and commercial numbers. Available at post offices and libraries, these hefty tomes are also issued free to all residents, as is the invaluable

Yellow Pages directory (also online at www.yell.com), which lists businesses and services.

TIME

London operates on Greenwich Mean Time (GMT), five hours ahead of the US's Eastern Standard time. In spring (28 March 2010) the UK puts its clocks forward by one hour to British Summer Time. In autumn (31 October 2010), the clocks go back to GMT.

TIPPING

In Britain it's accepted that you tip in taxis, minicabs, restaurants (some waiting staff rely heavily on tips), hotels, hairdressers and some bars (not pubs). Around 10% is normal, but some restaurants add as much as 15%. Always check whether service has been included in your bill: some restaurants include an automatic service charge, but also leave space for a gratuity on your credit card slip.

TOILETS

Pubs and restaurants generally reserve the use of their toilets for customers. However, all mainline rail stations and a few tube stations – Piccadilly Circus, for one – have public toilets (you may charge a small fee). Department stores usually have loos that you can use free of charge, and museums (most of which no longer charge an entry fee) generally have good facilities. At night, options are worse. The scattering of coin-operated toilet booths around the city may be your only option.

TOURIST INFORMATION

In addition to the tourist offices below, there is a brand-new centre by St Paul's (*see p63*).

Britain & London Visitor Centre *1 Regent Street, Piccadilly Circus, SW1Y 4XT (7808 3800, www.visit britain.com). Piccadilly Circus tube.* **Open** 9.30am-6.30pm Mon; 9am-6.30pm Tue-Fri; 9am-5pm Sat, 10am-4pm Sun. **Map** p406 W4.
Greenwich Tourist Information Centre *46 Greenwich Church Street, SE10 9BL (0870 608 2000, www. greenwich.gov.uk/tourism). Cutty Sark DLR.* **Open** 10am-5pm daily.
London Information Centre *Leicester Square, WC2H 7BP (7292 2333, www.londontown. com). Leicester Square tube.* **Open**

8am-10pm daily. *Helpline* 8am-10pm Mon-Fri; 9am-8pm Sat, Sun.
Richmond Tourist Information Centre *Old Town Hall, Whittaker Avenue, Richmond, Surrey TW9 1TP (8940 9125, www.visit richmond.co.uk). Richmond tube/rail.* **Open** 10am-5pm Mon-Sat.

VISAS & IMMIGRATION

EU citizens do not require a visa to visit the UK; citizens of the USA, Canada, Australia, South Africa and New Zealand can also enter with only a passport for tourist visits of up to six months as long as they can show they can support themselves during their visit and plan to return. Go online to www.ukvisas.gov.uk to check your visa status well before you travel, or contact the British embassy, consulate or high commission in your own country. You can arrange visas online at www.fco.gov.uk. For work permits, *see below*.

Home Office Immigration & Nationality Bureau *Lunar House, 40 Wellesley Road, Croydon, CR9 1AT (0870 606 7766 enquiries, 0870 241 0645 applications, www.homeoffice.gov.uk).*

WEIGHTS & MEASURES

It has taken a considerable amount of time, and the intervention of the European authorities, but the UK is moving towards full metrication. Distances are still measured in miles but all goods are officially sold in metric quantities, with no legal requirement for the imperial equivalent to be given. We've used the still more common imperial measurements in this guide.

Below are listed some useful conversions, first into metric figures and then from metric back to imperial:

1 inch (in) = 2.54 centimetres (cm)
1 yard (yd) = 0.91 metres (m)
1 mile = 1.6 kilometres (km)
1 ounce (oz) = 28.35 grammes (g)
1 pound (lb) = 0.45 kilogrammes (kg)
1 UK pint = 0.57 litres (l)
1 US pint = 0.8 UK pints or 0.46 litres

1 centimetre (cm) = 0.39 inches (in)
1 metre (m) = 1.094 yards (yd)
1 kilometre (km) = 0.62 miles
1 gramme (g) = 0.035 ounces (oz)
1 kilogramme (kg) = 2.2 pounds (lb)
1 litre (l) = 1.76 UK pints or 2.2 US pints

DIRECTORY

WHEN TO GO

Climate

The British climate is famously unpredictable, but Weathercall on 0906 850 0401 (60p/min) can offer some guidance. *See also below* **The Local Climate**. The best websites for weather news and features include www.metoffice. gov.uk, www.weather.com and www.bbc.co.uk/london/weather, which all offer good detailed long-term forecasts and are easily searchable.

Spring extends from March to May, though frosts can last into April. March winds and April showers may be a month early or a month late, but May is often very pleasant.

Summer (June, July and August) can be very unpredictable, with searing heat one day followed by sultry greyness and violent thunderstorms the next. There are usually pleasant sunny days, though they vary greatly in number from year to year. High temperatures, humidity and pollution can create problems for those with hay fever or breathing difficulties, and temperatures down in the tube can be uncomfortably hot in rush hour. Do as the locals do and carry a bottle of water.

Autumn starts in September, although the weather can still have a mild, summery feel. Real autumn comes with October, when the leaves start to fall; on sunny days, the red and gold leaves can be breathtaking. When the November cold, grey and wet set in, though, you'll be reminded that London is situated on a northerly latitude.

Winter can have some delightful crisp, cold days, but don't bank on them. The usual scenario is for a disappointingly grey, wet Christmas, followed by a cold snap in January and February, when London may even see a sprinkling of snow, and immediate public transport chaos.

Public holidays

On public holidays (bank holidays), many shops remain open, but public transport services generally run to a Sunday timetable. On Christmas Day, almost everything, including public transport, closes down.

All dates below are for 2010.

Good Friday Fri 2 Apr
Easter Monday Mon 5 Apr

May Day Holiday Mon 3 May
Spring Bank Holiday Mon 31 May
Summer Bank Holiday Mon 30 Aug
Christmas Day Mon 27 Dec (holiday in lieu of Sat 25 Dec)
Boxing Day Tue 28 Dec (holiday in lieu of Sun 26 Dec)
New Year's Day Mon 3 Jan 2011 (holiday in lieu of Sat 1 Jan 2011)

WOMEN

London is home to dozens of women's groups and networks; www.gn.apc.org and www.wrc.org. uk provide information and many links. It also has Europe's largest women's studies archive, the Women's Library (*see p371*).

For helplines, *see p369*; for health issues, *see pp368-369*.

WORK

Finding short-term work in London can be a full-time job. Temporary jobs are posted on the Jobs section of Gumtree (www.gumtree.com). It's also worth trying recruitment agencies such as Reed (www.reed. co.uk) or Tate (www.tate.co.uk), or the various London markets for work manning the stalls.

Work permits

With few exceptions, citizens of non-European Economic Area (EEA) countries have to have a work permit before they can legally work in the United Kingdom. Permits are issued only for high-level jobs.

Au Pair Scheme Citizens aged 17 to 27 from the following non-EEA countries (along, of course, with EEA nationals) are permitted to make an application to become au

pairs: Andorra, Bosnia-Herzegovina, Bulgaria, Croatia, the Faroe Islands, Greenland, Macedonia, Monaco, Romania, San Marino, Turkey. See the various pages of www.workingin theuk.gov.uk for details, or contact the **Border & Immigration Agency** (*see below* **Home Office**).

Working holidaymakers Citizens of Commonwealth countries aged from 17 to 27 are allowed to apply to come to the UK as a working holidaymaker. Start by contacting your nearest British diplomatic post in advance. You are then allowed to take part-time work without a DfEE permit. Contact the **Border & Immigration Agency** (*see below* **Home Office**) for more information.

Useful addresses

BUNAC *16 Bowling Green Lane, Clerkenwell, EC1R 0QH (7251 3472, www.bunac.org.uk).* *Farringdon tube/rail.* **Open** 9.30am-5.30pm Mon-Thur; 9.30am-5pm Fri. **Map** p402 N4.
Council on International Educational Exchange *300 Fore Street, Portland, ME 04101, USA (+1-207 553 4000, www.ciee.org).* **Open** 9am-5pm Mon-Fri. BUNAC and the CIEE help young people to study, work and travel abroad.
Home Office *Border & Immigration Agency, Lunar House, 40 Wellesley Road, Croydon, Surrey CR9 2BY (0870 606 7766, www.ind.home office.gov.uk).* **Open** *Phone enquiries* 9am-4.45pm Mon-Fri; 9am-4.30pm Fri. Advice on whether or not a work permit is required. If it is, application forms can be downloaded from the website.

THE LOCAL CLIMATE

Average temperatures and monthly rainfall in London.

	High (°C/°F)	Low (°C/°F)	Rainfall (mm/in)
Jan	6 / 43	2 / 36	54 / 2.1
Feb	7 / 44	2 / 36	40 / 1.6
Mar	10 / 50	3 / 37	37 / 1.5
Apr	13 / 55	6 / 43	37 / 1.5
May	17 / 63	8 / 46	46 / 1.8
June	20 / 68	12 / 54	45 / 1.8
July	22 / 72	14 / 57	57 / 2.2
Aug	21 / 70	13 / 55	59 / 2.3
Sept	19 / 66	11 / 52	49 / 1.9
Oct	14 / 57	8 / 46	57 / 2.2
Nov	10 / 50	5 / 41	64 / 2.5
Dec	7 / 44	4 / 39	48 / 1.9

Further Reference

BOOKS

Fiction & poetry

Peter Ackroyd *Hawksmoor; The House of Doctor Dee; The Great Fire of London*
Intricate studies of arcane London.
Monica Ali *Brick Lane*
Arranged marriage in East London.
Martin Amis *London Fields*
Darts and drinking way out east.
Anthony Burgess
Dead Man in Deptford
A fictionalised life of Marlowe.
Tom Chivers *How to Build a City*
A promising young poet.
Norman Collins
London Belongs to Me
A witty saga of 1930s Kennington.
Sir Arthur Conan Doyle
The Complete Sherlock Holmes
Reassuring sleuthing shenanigans.
Joseph Conrad *The Secret Agent*
Anarchism in seedy Soho.
Charles Dickens *Oliver Twist; David Copperfield; Bleak House*
Three of the Victorian master's most London-centric novels.
Jane Draycott *The Night Tree*
Poems inspired by conversations with Thames watermen.
Anthony Frewin *London Blues*
Kubrick assistant explores the 1960s Soho porn movie industry.
Graham Greene
The End of the Affair
Adultery and Catholicism during the Blitz.
Patrick Hamilton *Twenty Thousand Streets Under the Sky*
Dashed dreams at the bar of the Midnight Bell in Fitzrovia.
Neil Hanson
The Dreadful Judgement
The embers of the Great Fire.
Alan Hollinghurst *The Swimming Pool Library; The Line of Beauty*
Gay life around Russell Square;
metropolitan debauchery.
BS Johnson *Christie Malry's Own Double Entry*
A London clerk plots revenge on… everybody.
Doris Lessing *The Golden Notebook; The Good Terrorist*
Nobel winner's best London books.
Colin MacInnes *City of Spades; Absolute Beginners*
Coffee 'n' jazz, Soho 'n' Notting Hill.
Michael Moorcock
Mother London
A roomful of psychiatric patients live a love letter to London.

Alan Moore *From Hell*
Dark graphic novel on the Ripper.
Derek Raymond
I Was Dora Suarez
The blackest London noir.
Nicholas Royle *The Matter of the Heart; The Director's Cut*
Abandoned buildings and secrets.
Iain Sinclair *Downriver; White Chappell/Scarlet Tracings*
The Thames's *Heart of Darkness*;
the Ripper and book dealers.
Sarah Waters *The Night Watch*
World War II Home Front.
HG Wells *War of the Worlds*
SF classic with Primrose Hill finale.
Robert Westerby
Wide Boys Never Work
Reissued 1930s noir.
Virginia Woolf *Mrs Dalloway*
A kind of London *Ulysses*.

Non-fiction

Peter Ackroyd *London: The Biography; Thames. Sacred River*
Loving and obscurantist histories of the city and its river.
Richard Anderson *Bespoke: Savile Row Ripped and Smoothed*
Inside story of a Savile Row tailor.
Nicholas Barton
The Lost Rivers of London
Classic studies of old watercourses.
James Boswell *Boswell's London Journal 1762-1763*
Rich account of a ribald literary life.
Paul Du Noyer *In The City*
London in song.
Ed Glinert *A Literary Guide to London; The London Compendium*
Essential London minutiae.
Sarah Hartley *Mrs P's Journey*
Biography of Phyllis Pearsall, the woman who created the *A–Z*.
Edward Jones & Christopher Woodward *A Guide to the Architecture of London*
A brilliant exploration of the subject, updated for 2009.
Jenny Linford
The London Cookbook
Unsung producers and chefs share their food secrets.
Jack London
The People of the Abyss
Poverty in the East End.
HV Morton *In Search of London*
A tour of London from 1951.
George Orwell *Down and Out in Paris and London*
Waitering, begging and starving.
Samuel Pepys *Diaries*
Plagues, fires and bordellos.

Roy Porter
London: A Social History
An all-encompassing work.
Steen Eller Rasmussen
London: The Unique City
London buildings through a visitor's eyes.
Sukhdev Sandhu *Night Haunts*
London at night.
Iain Sinclair *Lights Out for the Territory; London Orbital*
Time-warp visionary crosses and then circles London.
Adrian Tinniswood
His Invention So Fertile
Biography of Sir Christopher Wren.
Richard Trench & Ellis Hillman *London under London: A Subterranean Guide*
Tunnels, lost rivers, disused tube stations, military bunkers.
Ben Weinreb & Christopher Hibbert (eds)
The London Encyclopaedia
Indispensable reference guide.
Jerry White *London in the 19th Century; London in the 20th Century*
How London became a global city.
Patrick Wright *Journey through Ruins: The Last Days of London*
Thatcherite urban blight and redevelopment in east London.

FILMS

A Clockwork Orange
dir Stanley Kubrick, 1971
Kubrick's vision still shocks – but so does Thamesmead, location for many scenes.
Alfie *dir Lewis Gilbert, 1966*
What's it all about, Michael?
Bigga than Ben
dir Suzie Halewood, 2008
Draft-dodging Muscovites in streetsmart, non-PC and very funny immigrants-in-London comedy.
Blow-Up *dir Michelangelo Antonioni, 1966*
Swinging London caught in unintentionally hysterical fashion.
Bourne Ultimatum
dir Paul Greengrass, 2007
Pacy thriller with brilliantly staged CCTV scene in Waterloo Station.
The Da Vinci Code
dir Ron Howard, 2006
Film version of Dan Brown's blockbuster novel, partly filmed in London (including Inner Temple).
Death Line
dir Gary Sherman, 1972
The last of a Victorian cannibal race is found in a lost tube station.

Derek *dir Isaac Julien, 2008*
Shorts by and memories of director
Derek Jarman.
Dirty Pretty Things
dir Stephen Frears, 2002
Body organ smuggling.
Fires Were Started
dir Humphrey Jennings, 1943
Drama-doc war propaganda about
the London Fire Brigade.
Fish Tank *dir Andrea
Arnold, 2009*
Humour, sadness, love and hope
on a ragged housing estate.
**Harry Potter & the Order of the
Phoenix** *dir David Yates, 2007*
Overlong, but with stunning aerial
shots of London.
Jump London
dir Mike Christie, 2003
Insane free-runners hop all over the
city's landmarks.
The Krays *dir Peter Medak, 1990*
The life and times of the most
notorious of East End gangsters.
The Ladykillers *dir Alexander
Mackendrick, 1951*
Classic Ealing comedy.
**Life is Sweet; Naked; Secrets
& Lies; Vera Drake; Happy-Go-
Lucky** *dir Mike Leigh, 1990-2008*
Metroland; urban misanthropy;
familial tensions; sympathy for
post-war abortionist; day and night
with a North London optimist.
**Lock, Stock & Two Smoking
Barrels; Snatch; RocknRolla**
dir Guy Ritchie, 1998-2008
Former Mr Madonna's cheeky
London faux-gangster flicks.
London; Robinson in Space
dir Patrick Keiller, 1994-1997
Arthouse documentary fiction.
The Long Good Friday
dir John MacKenzie, 1989
Bob Hoskins in the classic London
gangster flick.
Oliver! *dir Carol Reed, 1968*
Fun musical Dickens adaptation.
Peeping Tom
dir Michael Powell, 1960
Powell's creepy murder flick.
Performance *dir Nicolas Roeg
& Donald Cammell, 1970*
Cult movie to end all cult movies.
Somers Town *dir Shane
Meadows, 2008*
Sweet, slight tale of unlikely friends
in love with the same girl.
28 Days Later
dir Danny Boyle, 2002
Post-apocalyptic London, with
bravura opening sequence.
We Are the Lambeth Boys
dir Karel Reisz, 1959
'Free cinema' classic doc on
Teddy Boy culture.
Withnail & I
dir Bruce Robinson, 1987
Classic Camden lowlife comedy.

Wonderland *dir Michael
Winterbottom, 1999*
Love, loss and deprivation in Soho.

MUSIC

Lily Allen *Alright, Still*
Feisty, urban reggae-pop.
Blur *Modern Life is Rubbish;
Parklife*
Modern classics by Essex exiles.
Billy Bragg *Must I Paint You a
Picture? The Essential Billy Bragg*
The bard of Barking's greatest hits.
Burial *Untrue*
Beautiful, menacing dubstep ode to
the brooding city.
Chas & Dave
Don't Give a Monkey's
Cockney singalong revivalists.
The Clash *London Calling*
Era-defining punk classic.
Dizzee Rascal *Boy in Da Corner*
Rough-cut sounds and street-smart
lyrics from east London.
Ian Dury *New Boots & Panties!!*
Cheekily essential listening from
the Essex pub maestro.
Hot Chip *The Warning*
Wonky electro-pop.
The Jam *This is the Modern World*
Weller at his splenetic finest.
Jamie T *Kings & Queens*
Wimbledon's Mockney beats
troubadour comes good.
The Kinks *Something Else*
'Waterloo Sunset' and all.
Linton Kwesi Johnson
*Dread, Beat an' Blood; Forces of
Victory; Bass Culture*
Angry reggae from the man Brixton
calls 'the Poet'.
Madness *The Liberty of
Nolton Folgate*
Nutty Boys' psychogeographical
concept album.
Micachu *Jewellery*
Weird sounds make songs on a
precocious debut.
Saint Etienne *Tales from
Turnpike House*
Kitchen-sink opera by London-
loving indie dance band.
Speech Debelle *Speech Therapy*
Jazzy, folky British hip hop on a
Mercury Prize-winning debut LP.
Squeeze *Greatest Hits*
Lovable south London geezer pop.
The Streets *Original
Pirate Material*
Pirate radio urban meets Madness
on Mike Skinner's first and best.

WEBSITES

www.bbc.co.uk/london
News, travel, weather, sport.
www.britishpathe.com
Newsreels, from spaghetti-eating
contests to pre-war Soho scenes.

http://thecabbiescapital.co.uk
London's best blogging cabbie.
www.classiccafes.co.uk
The city's finest '50s and '60s caffs.
**http://diamondgeezer.
blogspot.com**
Fascinating, creative blogger on
all things London.
www.filmlondon.org.uk
London cinema.
**http://foodsnobblog.
wordpress.com**
Funny tales of fine dining.
**www.getlondonreading.co.uk/
books-in-london**
Map of London books by district.
www.hidden-london.com
Undiscovered gems.
www.london-footprints.co.uk
Free walks.
www.london.gov.uk
The Greater London Assembly.
http://londonist.com
News, culture and things to do.
**http://london.randomness.
org.uk**
Want to find Finnish food near a
music shop? Brilliant review site-
cum-wiki for interesting places.
**http://londonreconnections.
blogspot.com**
Transport projects.
www.londonremembers.com
Plaques and statues.
**http://londonreviewof
breakfasts.blogspot.com**
Start the day in style.
www.london2012.com
Plot the progress here.
**http://london-underground.
blogspot.com**
Daily tube blog.
www.londoneater.com
Passionate food reviews.
www.nickelinthemachine.com
Brilliant blog on history, culture
and music of 20th-century London.
http://onabus.com
Enter a bus number and its route is
mapped.
www.pubs.com
Traditional boozers.
www.seety.co.uk
Navigable photos of pretty much
every London street.
**www.3ammagazine.com/3am/
buzzwords**
Literary blog.
www.theworldin202meals.com
Discovering if it's possible to eat
around the world without leaving.
www.timeout.com
A vital source: eating and drinking
reviews, features and events listings,
and the brilliant Big Smoke blog.
www.tfl.gov.uk/tfl
Transport for London journey
planners and maps.
http://wildweb.london.gov.uk
Wildlife in the city.

Index

Note: Page numbers in **bold** indicate section(s) giving key information on a topic; *italics* indicate photographs.

A

Abney Park Cemetery 134
abortion 369
accessories shops 255
accident & emergency 368-369
accommodation *see* hotels
Ackroyd, Peter 85, *85*
addresses 367
Aegon Championships 329
age restrictions 367
AIDS & HIV 369
airports 362
Albert Bridge 152
Albert Memorial 39, **124**
Alexander Fleming Laboratory Museum 103-104
Alfie's Antique Market 103, 266
All England Lawn Tennis Club 156
All Hallows by the Tower 72, 73
All Saints 83
All Souls Church 98
Almeida 345
Alternative Fashion Week 272
American football 330
Anchor Bankside 53
antiques shops 266
apartment rental 195
Apsley House 108
aquariums *see* zoos & aquariums
Architecture 34-41
architecture galleries 300
art deco 39
Baroque spires 36
City skyscrapers 40
Tudor windows 35
Arsenal Museum 134
art deco buildings 39
art-squat movement 43-44
athletics 330
ATMs 372

B

bag shops 257-258
bakeries 258-259
Bank of England 67

Bank of England Museum 67, **68**, 278
banks 372
Bankside 53-55
Bankside Gallery 54
Banqueting House 35, 112, 113, 114, 137
barbers 264
Barbican Centre 40, **65-67**, 282, 287, 291, 308, 339
Barbican Conservatory 65
Barnes 153
basketball 331
Battersea 152
Battersea Arts Centre (BAC) 345, *345*
Battersea Bridge 152
Battersea Park 152
Battersea Park Children's Zoo 281
Battersea Power Station 152, *152*
BBC Electric Proms 313
BBC Television Centre 161
Beating the Retreat 276
Beatles, The 102, 131, 317
beauty shops & salons 265-266
Bedford Square 78
beer festivals & breweries 163, 238, 275
Belgravia 117, 123
Benjamin Franklin House 89
Bernie Spain Garden 53
Bethnal Green 139-140
Bevis Marks Synagogue 73
BFI IMAX 53, 292
BFI Southbank 51, 290, **292**
Big Ben 115
Big Dance 289
Big Draw 276
bike hire 333
bikes *see* cycling
Billingsgate Market 71
Birds Eye View 293
Black Death of 1348 and 1349 18
Black Pride 304
Blackheath 147
Blair, Tony 28
Blitz, the *25*, 27
Bloomsbury & Fitzrovia 78-82
Bloomsbury 78
Fitzrovia 83
hotels 171-175
King's Cross & St Pancras 82-83

pubs & bars 229
restaurants & cafés 203-204
Blue Elephant Theatre 144, 289
Bluebell Railway 355
boat race *see* Oxford & Cambridge Boat Race
Bonfire Night 276
Bonnington Square 151
books & literature 377
Children's Book Week 282
Jewish Book Week 271
London Literature Festival 274
Borough 55-57
Borough Market *259*, 261
Boundary Project 186, *186*
boutiques 251
Bowie, David 105
bowling 336
breakdown services 365
Breakin' Convention 289
Brick Lane 136, *138*
Brick Lane Festival 275
Brick Lane Takeover 273
Brighton 348, 351-352
Brit Oval 143, 331
British Library 82
British Museum 40, **79**, 81, 290
British Music Experience 147
Brixton 152
Brixton Academy *see* O2 Academy Brixton
Brixton Riots 28
Broadcasting House 39, **99**
Broadwalk Ballroom 274
Broadway Market 142
Brockwell Park 151
Brompton Cemetery 122, *160*, 161
Brompton Oratory 123-124
Brunel Museum 146-147
Brunswick Centre 78
BT Tower 83
Buckingham Palace 35, **117-118**, *117*
Buddhapadipa Temple 156
Bunhill Fields 65
bureaux de change 373
Burgh House 132
Burlington Arcade 108, 245
buses 364

Bush Theatre 161, 345
business services 367
Butler's Wharf 57

C

Cabbages & Frocks market 99
Cabinet War Rooms 113
cabs 365
Cadogan Hall 308, 311
cafés *see* restaurants & cafés
Calendar 270-277
Camber Sands 356
Camberwell 145
Camberwell Arts Festival 144
Camberwell College of Art 144, 145
Cambridge 348, *358*, 359-360
Cambridge University Botanic Gardens 359
Camden 128-131, *129*
Camden Arts Centre 132
Camden Crawl 273, 313
Camden Fringe 344
Camden Market 128, 129
Camden Passage 134
Camley Street Nature Park *281*, 282-283
camping & caravanning 195-196
Cannizaro Park 156
Canterbury 348, 352-356, 355
Canterbury Cathedral 352, 355
Canterbury Tales 352, 355
car hire 365
Carling Cup Final
Carlyle's House 122
Carnival del Pueblo 274
Cartoon Museum 79, **81**, 279
CD & record shops 267
cellphones 374-375
Celts 15
Cenotaph 113
Central Criminal Court *see* Old Bailey
Ceremony of the Keys 270
Challenge Cup Final 330
Changing of the Guard 117, 276, 278
Chap Olympiad 274
Charing Cross Station 89
Charles Dickens Museum 78, 81
Charles I 21
Charles, Prince 34
Charterhouse 77

Chelsea 120-122
Cheyne Walk & Chelsea
Embankment 121-122
hotels 187-189
restaurants & cafés 219
Sloane Square & King's
Road 120-121
Chelsea Arts Festival 310
Chelsea Barracks 120
Chelsea Centenary
Museum 122
Chelsea Embankment
Gardens 121
Chelsea Flower Show 121,
273
Chelsea Old Church 122
Chelsea Physic Garden
120, 121, 122
chemists 265, 369
Cheyne Walk 121
Children 278-283
eating & drinking 280-
281
entertainment 281-283
spaces to play 283
toy shops 249
where to go 278
Children's Book Week 282
Children's Film Festival
282
Chinatown **95-96**, 207
Chinese New Year
Festival 271, *271*
Chistlehurst 150
Chiswick 163-164
Chiswick House 163
Chiswick Mall 163
Christ Church Spitalfields
135-136
Christchurch Gardens 117
Christie's 119
Christmas celebrations
276
Church of St Mary
Magdalene 155
churches & cathedrals 56,
60, 61, 63, 64, 65, 67, 68,
72, 73, 74, 76, 81, 83,
112, 114, 115, 117, 122,
123, 135, 310, 374
Churchill Museum 113
Churchill, Winston 27, 56-
57, 113
cider 353
cinemas *see* film
Cinéphilia 290
City, The 59-74
Bank & Around 67-71
Fleet Street 59-60
hotels 169-170
Monument & Around
71-72
North of London Wall
65-67
North to Smithfield 64-
65
pubs & bars 227-228
restaurants & cafés 200
Temple 60-64
Tower of London 72-74

city farms 140-141, 281
City Hall 40, **57**, 278
City of London Festival
310
City of London
Information Centre 59
Clapham 152-153
Clapham Common 153
Clarence House 119
classical music venues
308-311
Cleopatra's Needle 89
Clerkenwell 76-77
climate 376
Clink Prison Museum **53**,
278
Clissold Park 134
Clockmakers' Museum &
Library 68
clothing hire 255
coaches 350, 362
cobblers 255
Coin Street Festival 274
Coliseum 88, 311
Collect 298
College of Arms 63
Columbia Road flower
market 139, 245
Comedy 284-286
Comedy Café 285, *285*
Comedy Store 284
complementary medicine
264, 369
Concrete & Glass festival
273, 313
conferences 367
congestion charge 365
Conigliaro, Tony 237, *237*
consulates 368
consumer advice 367
contraception 369
conventions 367
Coram's Fields 79, 279,
283
County Hall 46
couriers 367
**Covent Garden & the
Strand** 84-90
Aldwych, The 90-91
Covent Garden 84-89
hotels 175
pubs & bars 230-231
restaurants & cafés 204-
207
Strand & Embankment,
The 90
Covent Garden May Fayre
& Puppet Festival 272
Covent Garden Piazza 84-
88
Craven Cottage 161, **331**
Credit Crunch Culture
42-44
cricket 329, 331
Cromwell, Oliver 21
Crystal Palace 145
Crystal Palace National
Sports Centre 330-331
currency 372

customs 367
Cutlers' Hall 63
Cutty Sark **147**, 280
cycling 333, 350, 366
bike hire scheme 334-
335

D

Daily Express building
39, *39*, 60
Daily Telegraph building
60
Dali Universe 46
Dalston 134, 321
Dance 287-289
events 270
Dance Umbrella 289
darts 330
Dennis Severs' House 135,
136
dentists 369
department stores 242-245
Deptford Art Map 299
design galleries 300
Design Museum 57
designer clothes shops
251-253
dialling codes 374
Diana, Princess of Wales
Memorial Playground
126, 283
Dickens, Charles 19, 23,
78, 81, 121
disabled travellers 367-
368
Discount clothes shops
253
Discover 283
Discovering Latin
American Film Festival
293
Diwali 276
DLR *see* Docklands Light
Railway
Docklands 140-141
Docklands Light Railway
(DLR) 140, 364
doctors 368-369
Donmar Warehouse 88,
345
Dover Street Market 253
Downing Street 22, **113**
Dr Johnson's House 60
drink shops 259-261
driving 365
drugs 368
dry-cleaners 255
Duke of York column 117
Duke of York Square 120
Dulwich 145
Dulwich Picture Gallery
145
Dungeness 348, 356-358,
357

E

E Pellicci 139, **224**
Ealing Jazz Festival 319

Earl's Court 159-161
Earl's Court Exhibition
Centre 158
East Dulwich 145
East End Film Festival
293
East London 135-142
Bethnal Green 139-140
Brick Lane 136, *138*
Docklands 140-141
Hackney 141-142
pubs & bars 239-240
restaurants & cafés 223-
226
Shoreditch & Hoxton
138
Spitalfields 135-136
Three Mills & Stratford
142
Walthamstow 142
Whitechapel 136-137
East London Mosque 137
Edgware Road 103
Electric Avenue 152
electricity 368
electronics shops 249
Elephant & Castle 143
Eltham 150
Eltham Palace 150
embassies 368
emergencies 368
Emirates Stadium 134,
331
employment 376
English Heritage Picnic
Concerts 310
English National Opera,
Coliseum 311
Epsom Derby 329, 332
Eros 105
Escapes & Excursions
348-360
Estorick Collection of
Modern Italian Art 134
etiquette 367
Exhibition Road Music
Day 274
Exmouth Market *76*, 77

F

FA Cup Final 329, 331
Fabric 77, 323
Fan Museum 147-148
Faraday Museum 107
farms *see* city farms
Farringdon 76-77
Fashion & Textile
Museum 57
fashion shops 251-258
Fashion Week 275
Fenton House 131, 132
Festival of Britain 28
Festival Square 51
festivals 270-277
art & design 298
children 282
dance 289
film 293
gay & lesbian 304

INDEX

music, classical 310
music, jazz 319
music, rock, pop & roots 313
theatre 344
Field Day 313
F-IRE Collection 319
Film 290-293
festivals 293
film clubbing 291
films set in London 377-378
IMAX 292
first-run cinemas 291-292
repertory cinemas 292
Firepower 149-150
Fireworks Nights 276
fitness clubs 334-335
Fitzrovia 83
Fitzwilliam Museum, Cambridge 359. 360
Flamenco Festival 289
Fleet Street 59
Florence Nightingdale Museum 47
food & drink shops 258-263
see also restaurants & cafés
football teams & museums 331-332, *333*
Fortnum & Mason 108, 242
Foster, Lord Norman 40, 79
Foundling Museum 79, **81**, 279
Free Range 298
Free Time Festival 282
Free Word Centre 77
Freemasons' Hall 39, **88**
Freightliners City Farm 281
Freud Museum 132
Frieze Art Fair 298
Fulham 159-161
Fulham Palace & Museum 161
Fuller's Brewery 163
Further Reference 377-378

G

Gabriel's Wharf 51
Gay & Lesbian 301-307
festivals 304
nightclubs 302-305
organisations 368
pubs & bars 305-307
restaurants & cafés 302
salons 305
sex clubs & saunas 307
Soho 93
Galleries 294-295
architecture & design 300
Deptford Art Map 299
festivals 298
fine art 294

photography 300
Time Out First Thursdays 297
Garden Museum 46, 47, *47*
Gate Theatre 345
Gatwick Airport 362
Geffrye Museum 138
Get Loaded festival 313
Getting Around 362-366
Gibson Hall 73
gift shops 263-264
Golden Hinde **54**, 278
Golf 333
Grant Museum 82
Grays Antique Market 106, 107
Great British Beer Festival 275
Great Exhibition of 1851 24
Great Fire of London 21-22
Great Gorilla Run 276
Great River Race 275
Green Chain Walk 150
Green Line buses 364
Green Park 108
Greenwich & Docklands International Festival 272, 344
Greenwich 147-149
Greenwich Market 147
Greenwich Park 147
Greenwich Peninsula Ecology Park 147, 283
Gresham College 68, 75
greyhound racing 332
Grosvenor Square 106
Guards Museum 117, 118
guided tours 366
Guildhall 37, 68, **69**
Guildhall Art Gallery 68, 71
Gun Salutes 270
Gunpowder Plot 21
Gurdwara Sri Guru Singh Sabha Southall 164
gyms 334-335

H

Hackney 141-142
Hackney City Farm 281
Hackney Empire 141
Hackney Museum 142
hairdressers 264
Ham House 156
Hammersmith 161-163
Hammersmith Apollo *see* HMV Hammersmith Apollo
Hampstead 131-133
Hampstead Heath 131
Hampstead Scientific Society Observatory 131
Hampton Court Palace 19, 156, *156*, **157**

Hampton Court Palace Festival 310
Handel House Museum 106-107
Handel, George Frideric 107
Hard Rock Calling 313
Harrods 123, 242
Harrow 164
Harvey Nichols 123, 244
hat shops 255
Hatton Gardens 76
Hay's Galleria 57
Hayes 164
Hayward Gallery 40, **51**, **53**, 54, *54*
health services 368
Heathrow Airport 362
helplines 369
Hen & Chickens 285
Henley Royal Regatta 330
Henry VIII 18-19
Herne Hill 145
Herne Hill Velodrome 333
Heron Tower 73
Highgate 133-134
Highgate Cemetery 133-134
Highgate Woods 133
Hill Garden & Pergola 132
Himalaya Palace 164
Hindu temples 164
History 14-29
Blitz, the 25, 27
Celts 15
key events timeline 29
medieval era 17-18
Norman rule 17
present era 28
Romans 15
Saxons 15
Swinging '60s 28
Thatcher era 28
Tudor period 21
Victorian period 23-24
HIV & AIDS 369
HMS Belfast **57**, 278
HMV Forum 312
HMV Hammersmith Apollo 163, **313**
Hogarth's House 163
Holborn & Clerkenwell 75-77
Clerkenwell & Farringdon 77
Holborn 75-76
hotels 170-171
pubs & bars 228-229
restaurants & cafés 201-203
Smithfield 77
Holland House 158
Holland Park 158-159
home shops 266-267
Honor Oak 145
Horniman Museum 145-146, *146*
Horse Guards 112
horse racing 330, 332
horse riding 336

hospitals 368-369
Hotels 166-196
by price:
budget: 174-175, 177, 182-183, 187, 192-193
deluxe: 169-170, 171-173, 175-177, 179, 183-185, 185-186, 189-190
expensive: 170, 170-171, 173, 177, 177-178, 179, 185, 186-187, 187-189, 190, 191, 193, 193-194
moderate: 167-169, 170, 171, 173-174, 178-179, 181-182, 187, 190-191, 193, 194-195
apartment rental 195
best bargain beds 173
best high-class hotels 179
Boundary Project 186, *186*
university residences 196
youth hostels 196
see also p386 Hotels index
Hounslow 164
house prices 31
Household Cavalry Museum 117, 118
Houses of Parliament 35, **113-114**, *115*
Hoxton 138-139
Human Rights Watch International Film Festival 293
Hunterian Museum 75, 76
Hyde Park *125*, 126

I

ICA (Institute of Contemporary Arts) 117, 118, 291
ice skating 335-336
ID 369
IMAX cinema 53, 292
immigration 375
Imperial War Museum 143-145, *145*, 290
IndigO2 313
Inner Temple 60
Institute of Contemporary Arts *see* ICA
insurance 369-371
internet access 371
Island Gardens 141
Islington *132-133*, 134
Islington Museum 77

J

Jamme Masjid Mosque 136

INDEX

jazz music venues 319-320
Jewel Tower 113, 114
jewellery shops 257
Jewish Book Week 271
Jewish Museum 129, 130
jobs 376
John Wesley's House & Museum of Methodism 67
John Wesley's House 65, 67
Johnson, Boris 28, *30*, 31, 33, 34
Joseph Grimaldi Memorial Service 271

K

Keats House *130*, 132
Kelmscott House 163
Kennington 143
Kensal Green Cemetery 104
Kensington 158-159
Kensington Gardens 126
Kensington Palace 126
Kentish Town City Farm 281
Kenwood House 37, **132-133**
concerts 131
Kettle's Yard, Cambridge 359, 360
Kew 153-155
Kew Bridge Steam Museum 163
Kew Gardens *see* Royal Botanic Gardens
Kew Spring Festival 272
King's Cross 82-83, 321
King's Head Theatre 345-346
Kings Place 41, 308, **309**, *309*
Kinoteca 293
Knightsbridge & South Kensington 123-127
hotels 189
Hyde Park & Kensington Gardens 126
Knightsbridge 123-124
pubs & bars 235-236
restaurants & cafés 219-220
South Kensington 124-126
Koko *312*, 313

L

La Linea festival 313
Laban Centre 289
Lamb's Conduit Street 79
Lambeth Bridge 46
Lambeth Palace 46
Land of Kings 273
Langham Place 98

Latin American Film Festival 293
Lauderdale House 133
Leadenhall Market 71
Leather Lane 76
left luggage 371
legal help 371
Leicester Square 95-96, *96*
Leighton House 158
leisure centres 334-335
Liberty 39, 106, *106*, **244**
libraries 41, 82, 119, 371
LIFT (London International Festival of Theatre) 344
Lincoln's Inn Fields 75
lingerie shops 257
Linley Sambourne House 158
Little Angel Theatre 282
Little Portugal 151
Little Venice 129
Livingstone, Ken 28
Lloyd's of London 40, 71
London African Music Festival 313
London album covers 317
London Aquatics Centre 41
London Bridge Experience 56
London Canal Museum 82-83
London Central Mosque 102
London City Airport 3
London Design Festival 298
London Dungeon 55, **56**, 278
London Eye 46, **47**, 50, *50*, 278
London Fashion Week 275
London Festival of Architecture 41, 298
London Film Festival 293
London International Animation Festival 293
London International Mime Festival 270, 344
London International Tango Festival 289
London Jazz Festival 319
London Lesbian & Gay Film Festival 293, 304
London Literature Festival **274**, 304
London Marathon 272, 329
London Mela *272*, 275
London Short Film Festival 293
London Silver Vaults 75
London Stone 68
London to Brighton Veteran Car Run 276
London Today 30-33

London Transport Museum 84, **87**, 161, 279
London Underground 363-364
London Zoo 39, **102**, *102*, 129, 281
Loop Collective 319
Lord Mayor's Show 276
Lord's cricket ground 41, 131, **331**
Lord's Tour & MCC Museum 131
lost property 371
Lovebox Weekender 313
LSO St Luke's 310
luggage shops 257-258
Luton Airport 362
Lyric Hammersmith 346

M

Madame Tussauds 99
magazines 371-372
Magna Carta 17
Mansion House 67
marathon 272, 329
Marble Hill House 156, 157
markets 245-247
food 261
Marx Memorial Library 77
Marylebone 99-101
Maureen Paley gallery 139, 299
Mayfair 106
Mayor's Thames Festival 275
media 371-372
medical services 368-369
medieval era 17-18
Meltdown 313
memorial for the 2005 bombings 109, *109*
Metropolitan Police Museum 161, 162, *162*
Middle Ages 17-18
Middle Farm 353, *353*
Middle Temple 60
Middlesex Sevens 330
Millbank 115-116
Millennium Bridge 53, 63
mime festival 270
minicabs 365
mobile phones 374-375
money 372
Monument 35, *69*, 71, **72**
mosques 102, 136, 137, 374
motorsport 332
Moviceum 46, **49**, 278
Mr C 327
Mudchute Park & Farm 140-141, 281
Museum & Library of the Order of St John 76, 77
Museum of Brands, Packaging & Advertising 104

Museum of Childhood *see* V&A Museum of Childhood
Museum of London 65, 66, *66*, **67**, 278
Museum of London Docklands 140, 141, *141*
Museum of Richmond 155
Museum of St Bartholomew's Hospital 65
Museums & galleries
Advertising Museum of Brands, Packaging & Advertising 104
Art (Fine) Bankside Gallery 54; Barbican Art Gallery 65; Courtauld Gallery 89-90; Dulwich Picture Gallery 145; Guildhall Art Gallery 71; Estorick Collection of Modern Italian Art 134; Hayward Gallery 53; ICA (Institute of Contemporary Arts) 118; National Gallery 110; Orleans House Gallery 157; Queen's House 148; Rivington Place 139; Royal Academy of Arts 108; Saatchi Gallery 121; Serpentine Gallery 126; Tate Britain 116; Tate Modern 55; Whitechapel Gallery 138
Art (Applied) Design Museum 57; Fan Museum 147; Fashion & Textile Museum 57; Fenton House 132; Geffrye Museum 138; Ranger's House 148; William Morris Gallery 142
Art (design/graphic) Cartoon Museum 81
Archaeology & Antiquities British Museum 79; Petrie Museum of Egyptian Archaeology 81
Childhood/toys Pollock's Toy Museum 83; V&A Museum of Childhood 140
Film Moviceum 49
History Bank of England Museum 68; Clockmakers' Museum & Library 68; Foundling Museum 81; Fulham Palace & Museum 161; Guards Museum 118; Islington

Museum 77; London
Bridge Experience 56;
London Canal
Museum 82; Museum
& Library of the
Order of St John 77;
Museum of London
Docklands 141;
Ragged School
Museum 139; Tower
Bridge Exhibition 74
Horticulture Garden
Museum 47
House-museums
Benjamin Franklin
House 89; Carlyle's
House 122; Charles
Dickens Museum 81;
Dr Johnson's House
60; Freud Museum
132; Keats House 132;
John Wesley's House
& Museum of
Methodism 67;
Hogarth's House 163;
Sir John Soane's
Museum 76; Sutton
House 142
Military/Law & Order
Cabinet War Rooms
& Churchill Museum
113; Firepower 149-
150; Household
Cavalry Museum 118;
Imperial War
Museum 143;
Metropolitan Police
Museum 161;
National Army
Museum 122;
National Maritime
Museum 148;
Winston Churchill's
Britain at War
Experience 56
Music British Music
Experience 147;
Musical Museum 163
Natural History
Horniman Museum
145; Natural History
Museum 124
Science (General)
Science Museum 125
Science (Engineering)
Brunel Museum 146-
147; Kew Bridge
Steam Museum 163
Science (Medicine)
Alexander Fleming
Laboratory Museum
103-104; Florence
Nightingdale
Museum 47;
Hunterian Museum
76; Museum of St
Bartholomew's
Hospital 65; Old
Operating Theatre,
Museum & Herb

Garret 56; Wellcome
Collection 82
Sport Arsenal Museum
134; Lord's Tour &
MCC Museum 131;
Wimbledon Lawn
Tennis Museum 156;
World Rugby
Museum 157
Music 308-320
Classical & Opera 308-
311
Jazz 319-320
London albums 378
Rock, Pop & Roots
311-319
shops 267-268
Music Village 274
Musical Museum 163
musicals 340-345

N

Nash, John 37
National Archives 153
National Army Museum
121, 122
National Express coaches
362
National Gallery **110-
111**, *111*, 279, 290
National Maritime
Museum **148**, 280
National Portrait Gallery
111-112, 279
National Science &
Engineering Week 271
National Sports Centre
145, 330
National Theatre 51,
339-340
Natural History Museum
39, **124-125**, *124*,
279-280
Neasden 164
Nelson's Column 110
New Forest 350
New London Architecture
41, 300
New Scotland Yard 117
New Year's Eve
celebrations 276
Newburgh Quarter 255
newspapers 372
night buses 364
Nightlife 302-328
central 323-324
clubbing gear 303
club nights in pubs 324
east 325-328
gay & lesbian 302-305
north 324-325
south 328
19 Princelet Street 135
No.1 Poultry 67
Norman rule 17
North London 128-134
Camden 128-131
Dalston 134
Hampstead 131-133

Highgate 133-134
Islington 134
pubs & bars 236-239
restaurants & cafés
222-223
St John's Wood 131
Stoke Newington 134
Norwegian Church &
Seaman's Mission 146
Norwich Union London
Grand Prix 330
Notting Hill 104
Notting Hill Carnival
274, 275

O

O2 Academy Brixton 313
O2 Arena 147, **314**, *314*,
330
O2 Shepherd's Bush
Empire 161, **314**
office services 367
Old Bailey (Central
Criminal Court) 63, 64
Old Curiosity Shop 75
Old Operating Theatre,
Museum & Herb Garret
55, 56
Old Truman Brewery 136
Old Vic Theatre 53, 340
Olympic Park 330, *330*
Olympics in 1948 28
Olympics in 2012 28, 31,
33, 41, 142
One Canada Square 40,
73, **140**
Open Air Theatre 340
Open Garden Squares
Weekend 274
Open House London 41,
275
opening hours 373
Opera Holland Park 310
opera music venues
308-311
opticians 265
Order of St John 76
Orleans House Gallery
156, 157
Oxford & Cambridge Boat
Race 153, 272, 329
**Oxford Street &
Marylebone** 97-102
hotels 177-179
Marylebone 99-101
Oxford Street 97-99
pubs & bars 232
Regent's Park 101-102
restaurants & cafés
211-213
Oxo Tower Wharf 51
oyster cards 363

P

**Paddington & Notting
Hill** 103-104
Edgware Road &
Paddington 103-104

hotels 179-183
Notting Hill 104
pubs & bars 233
restaurants & cafés
220-222
Paddington Central 103
Pall Mall 119
Pancake Day Races 271
parking 365-366
parks & gardens 101, 117,
122, 126, 131, 147, 155
Parliament Square 113
Paternoster Square 61
PDC World
Championship (darts)
330
Pearly Kings & Queens
Harvest Festival 276
Peasants' Revolt of 1381
18
Peckham 145
Peckham Library 41
Peckham Rye 145
Peckham Space 144
Petersham 156
Petersham Nurseries 156
Petrie Museum of
Egyptian Archaelogy
81, 82
Petticoat Lane Market
135
pharmacies 265, 369
photography galleries 300
photography shops 249
**Piccadilly Circus &
Mayfair** 105-109
hotels 183-185
Mayfair 106-108
pubs & bars 233-234
Piccadilly Circus &
Regent Street 105-106
Piccadilly & Green Park
108-109
restaurants & cafés
213-216
pilates classes 336
Pimlico 117
Place 288
Place Prize 289
plague, the 21
Planetarium *see* Royal
Observatory
plaques on London
houses 19
playgrounds 283
police 373
Pollock's Toy Museum
83, 279, *279*
Port of London HQ 72
Portobello Film Festival
293
Portobello Road market
104, *104*, 245
postal services 373-374
Postman's Park 64-65
Pride London 304
Primrose Hill 129, 131
Princess Diana Memorial
Fountain 126
Proms, the 310

INDEX

INDEX

public holidays 376
public transport 363-364
Pubs & Bars 227-241
  Best cocktail bars 236
  best pub interiors 235
  Conigliaro, Tony 237,
  237
  historic pubs 228
  pop-up bars 240
  Sambrook's Brewery
  238, *238*
  see also p387 Pubs
  & Bars index
puppet shows 272, 282
Puppet Theatre Barge 282
Putney 153

Q

Queen's House 35, **148**
Queens Park Rangers 161,
  331

R

radio stations 372
Ragged School Museum
  139
rail services 348, 364
Raindance Festival 293
Rambert Dance Company
  287
Ranger's House 148
recession 30-31, 33, 43-44
record shops 267
Red House 150
Redchurch Street 262,
  262
Regent's Canal 129
Regent's Park 101-102
religion 374
Remembrance Sunday
  Ceremony 276
repairs shops 255
Resolution! 289
Restaurants & Cafés
  197-226
  best British food 201
  best curry houses 224
  best late-night eats 211
  best summer dining 199
  best winter dining 198
  child-friendly places
  280-281
  gallery/museum
  eateries 217
  gay & lesbian 302
  tipping 375
  underground restaurant
  scene/supper clubs
  212
  see also p386
  Restaurants & Cafés
  index
Reuters building 60
Richmond 153-155
Richmond Park 155
Ripley's Believe It or Not!
  105, 106
Ritz, the 24, **108**, 185

Riverfront Jazz Festival
  319
Riverside Studios arts
  centre **163**, 290, **292**
Rivington Place 41, 139
rock music venues 311-
  319
Rogers, Richard 34, 40
Roman Museum,
  Canterbury 352, 355
Romans 15
Romney Marsh 348, 356-
  358
Romney, Hythe &
  Dymchurch Railway
  356
Ronnie Scott's 91, 320
Rotherhithe 146
Rough Trade East *267*,
  268
Roundhouse 128, 314
Routemaster buses 112
rowing 330
Royal Academy of Arts
  108-109
Royal Academy of Music
  99, 308
Royal Albert Hall 124,
  310
Royal Artillery Barracks
  149
Royal Ascot 330, 332
Royal Botanic Gardens
  (Kew Gardens) 153, 155,
  155
Royal College of Art 124,
  298
Royal College of Music
  124, 308
Royal Court Theatre 120,
  340
Royal Courts of Justice 39,
  60, *61*, 89, 90
Royal Exchange 67
Royal Festival Hall 40, **51**
Royal Hospital Chelsea
  121, 122
Royal Institute of British
  Architects 99
Royal Institution 107,
  107
Royal London Hospital
  Archives & Museum
  137-138
Royal Mews 117-118
Royal Naval College 147,
  148
Royal Observatory &
  Planetarium 147, **148-
  149**, *149*, 280
Royal Opera House 87, *88*,
  288, **311**
Royal Pavilion, Brighton
  351
Royal Shakespeare
  Company 340
Royal Vauxhall Tavern
  (RVT) 151, 305
rugby 330, 332
Rugby Union 329

Rushes Soho Shorts 293
Russell Square 78
Rye 348, 356-358
Rye Castle Museum &
  Ypres Tower 356

S

Saatchi Gallery 120, 121,
  121
Sadler's Wells 288
safety & security 374
St Alban tower 68
St Andrew Undershaft 67
St Anne & St Agnes 68
St Bartholomew's
  Hospital 65
St Bartholomew-the-Great
  35, 65
St Botolph's-without-
  Aldgate 72, 73-74
St Bride Foundation
  Institute 60
St Bride's Church 59, 60
St Clement 68
St Clement Danes 89
St Dunstan-in-the-West 60
St Edmund the Kind 68
St Ethelburga Centre for
  Reconciliation & Peace
  74
St Etheldreda 76
St George's Bloomsbury
  35, 79, **81**
St George's Church 107
St George's Wharf 151
St Giles Cripplegate 65
St Helen's Bishopsgate 73,
  74
St James Garlickhythe 63
St James's 119
St James's Palace 117, 119
St James's Park 117, *118*
St James's Piccadilly 108,
  310
St John's Wood 131
St John's, Smith Square
  116, 310
St John-at-Hampstead
  Church 131
St Katharine Cree 72
St Katharine's Docks 72
St Lawrence Jewry 68
St Magnus the Martyr 71,
  72
St Margaret Lothbury 68
St Margaret Pattens 71
St Margaret's Church 114
St Martin-in-the-Fields 35,
  89, 110, **112**, 279, 310-
  311
St Mary Abbots 158
St Mary Abchurch 68
St Mary Aldermary 63
St Mary Woolnoth 68
St Mary's Battersea 152
St Mary's Rotherhithe 146
St Marylebone Church 99
St Mary-le-Bow 63
St Mary-le-Strand 35, **89**

St Michael Cornhill 68
St Michael Paternoster
  Royal 68
St Nicolas Cole Abbey 63
St Olave 72
St Pancras Gardens 83
St Pancras International
  39, 82, *82*, **83**, **362**
St Pancras Old Church
  83
St Patrick's Day Parade
  & Festival 271
St Paul's Cathedral 22, 36,
  53, **61**, **63-64**, *64*, 89
St Paul's Covent Garden
  36, 84, 85, **87**, 279
St Peter-upon-Cornhill 68
St Stephen Walbrook 67
St Vedast-alias-Foster 64
Sambrook's Brewery 238,
  238
sample sales 257
Savile Row 107
Savoy Hotel 89
Saxons 15
Scala 314-315
Science Museum 124,
  125, 279
Sea Life London
  Aquarium 46, **49**, *49*,
  278
Sea-Life Centre, Brighton
  351
Selfridges 244-245
Senate House 79, *79*
Serpentine Gallery **126**,
  290
Shaftesbury Memorial 105
Shakespeare, William 21,
  137, *137*, 272
Shakespeare's Birthday
  272
Shakespeare's Globe 53,
  54, *55*, 340
Shepherd Market 108
Shepherd's Bush 161
Shepherd's Bush Empire
  see O2 Shepherd's Bush
  Empire
Sherlock Holmes Museum
  102
shippers 367
shoe shops 258
shopping centres &
  arcades 245
Shops & Services 242-
  268
  department stores 242-
  245
  markets 245-247
  shopping centres &
  arcades 245
  specialist 247-267
  Topshop 252
  where to shop 243
Shoreditch 138-139
Shri Swaminarayan
  Mandir 164
Siobhan Davies Dance
  Studios 288-289

Sir John Soane's Museum 37, 75, **76**, *77*
skateparks 336
Skyride 275, *276*
skyscrapers 40
Sloane Square 120
Smithfield Market 77
Smithfield Nocturne cycling event 330
smoking 374
Soane, John 37, 76
Soho & Leicester Square 91-96
Chinatown & Leicester Square 95-96
hotels 175-177
Old Compton Street & Around 91-92
pubs & bars 231-232
restaurants & cafés 207-211
Soho Square 91, *92*
Wardour Street & Around 92-95
West Soho 95
Soho Pride 304
Soho Square 91, *92*
Soho Theatre 92, 285, 346
Somerset House & the Embankment Galleries 89, **90**, *90*, 279, *280*
Somerset House Summer Series 290, 313
South Downs 351
South Kensington 124-126
South London Gallery 144, *144*, 145, 300
Southall 164
Southall Market 164
South Bank & Bankside, The 46-57
Bankside 53-55
Borough 55-57
hotels 167-169
London Bridge to Tower Bridge 57-57
pubs & bars 227
restaurants & cafés 197-199
South Bank, The 46-53
Southbank Centre 51, 282, **289, 311**
South-east London 144-151
Camberwell & Peckham 145
Dulwich & Crystal Palace 145-146
Further South-east 150
Greenwich 147-149
Kennington & the Elephant 143-145
pubs & bars 240
restaurants & cafés 226
Rotherhithe 146-147
Woolwich Arsenal & the Thames Barrier 149-150

Southwark Cathedral 55, **56**, 278
Southwark Park 146
South-west London 152-158
Battersea 152
Clapham & Wandsworth 152-153
Further South-west 156-157
Kew & Richmond 153-155
pubs & bars 240
Putney & Barnes 153
restaurants & cafés 226
Vauxhall, Stockwell & Brixton 151-152
Wimbledon 155-156
souvenir shops 263-264, 265
spas 266
Speakers' Corner 126
Spencer House 119
Spitalfields 135-136
Spitalfields Festival 310
Spitalfields Market 135, *136*, 245, 247
Sport & Fitness 329-336
participation & fitness 333-336
shops 268
spectator sports 329-332
Spring Dance 289
squatting 43
Stag & Dagger festival 273, 313
Stamford Bridge 122, 161, **331**
Stan James Christmas Festival 330, 332
Stansted Airport 362
State Opening of Parliament 276
STD clinics 369
Stockwell 151-152
Story of London 273
Stratford 142
Strawberry Hill 156
street sports 336
Sunday (Up)Market 245
supper clubs 212
Supreme Court 113
surf bus 336
Sutton House 142
SW4 festival 313
swimming pools 336
Swinging '60s 28
synagogues 73, 374
Syon House 37, **164**
tailors 253-254

T

Tate Britain 115, **116**, *116*, 278
Tate Modern 41, 53, **55**, *56*, 63, 278, 290
tax 373
taxis 365

telephones 374
television stations 372
Temple 60-61
Temple Bar 60, 63
Temple Church 61
Temple of Mithras 67
tennis 332-333, 336
ten-pin bowling 336
Thames Barrier 141, 149, 150, *150*
Thames Barrier Information & Learning Centre 150
Thames Barrier Park 141
Thames Clippers 140, 147, 314, 364
Thatcher, Margaret 28
Theatre 337-346
cheap seats 339
children's 283
festivals 344
fringe venues 346
off-West End 345-346
West End 339
Theatre Royal 85, 88
Theatre Royal Stratford East 285, 346
theme parks 283
30 St Mary Axe 40, 73
Three Mills 142
Three Mills Island 142
thrift stores 254-255
tickets 268, 311, 339
time 375
Time Out First Thursdays 297
tipping 375
Tkts 339
toilets 375
Topolski Century 49-51, *51*
Topshop 252, *252*
Tour of Britain cycling event 330
tourist information 375
tours 366
Tower 42 73
Tower Bridge 24, 39, 57, **72**, *73*, 74, 278
Tower Bridge Exhibition 57, 74
Tower House 137
Tower of London 35, 72, **74**, 278
toy shops 249
Trafalgar Square **110-112**, 275
trains 348, 362-364
Tramlink 364
transport 362-366
travel shops 268
travelcards 363
Trellick Tower 104
Tricycle 346
Trinity Buoy Wharf 140
Trinity House 72
Trinity Square Gardens 72
Trocadero 105
Trooping the Colour 276

Tropical Forest animal sanctuary 163
Tube, the 363-364
Tudor period 21
Twickenham 156
Twickenham Stadium 156, 157, 332
2 Willow Road 132

U

Underage Festival 282, 313
underwear shops 257
unemployment 31, 44
University of London 78
university residences 196

V

V&A Museum of Childhood 139, **140**, 280
V&A *see* Victoria & Albert Museum
VAT 373
Vauxhall 151-152, 321, 301
Vauxhall Cross 116
Victoria & Albert Museum 124, 126, 127, *127*, 280
Victoria 116-117
Victoria Coach Station 350, 362
Victoria Tower Gardens 116
Victorian period 23-24
Vinopolis 54, 55
vintage clothes shops 254-255
visas 375
Vortex Jazz Club *318*, 320

W

walking 366
suggested walks:
Bloomsbury 80
City, the 70-71
Oxford Street's side streets 98-99
Chiswick 163-164
Earl's Court & Fulham 159-161
Hammersmith 161-163
Kensington & Holland Park 158-159
Shepherd's Bush 161
Southall 164
Walthamstow 142
Wandsworth 152-153
Watch this Space 282, *282*, 344
water transport 364
Waterloo Bridge 51
Watermans Arts Centre 153
WaterWorks Nature Reserve 142

INDEX

weather 376
websites 378
weights & measures 375
Wellcome Collection 82
Wellington Arch 108, 109
Wembley 40, **164**, 331
Wembley Arena **315**, 330
Wembley Stadium 331
West London 158-164
 pubs & bars 241
 restaurants & cafés 226
Westbourne Grove 104
Western Union 372
Westfield London 161,
 245
**Westminster & St
 James's** 110-119
 Around St James's Park
 117-118
 hotels 185-187
 Millbank 115-116
 pubs & bars 234-235
 restaurants & cafés
 216-219
 St James's 119
 Trafalgar Square
 110-112
 Victoria 116-117
 Whitehall to Parliament
 Square 112-115
Westminster Abbey
 17, 35, 113, **115**
Westminster Bridge 46
Westminster Cathedral
 117
Westminster Hall 113
when to go 376
White Cube 138, 297
White Lodge Museum
 287
Whitechapel 136-137
Whitechapel Art Gallery
 40, 136-137, **138**
Whitechapel Bell Foundry
 115, **137**
Whitehall 112-113
Whitehall, Jack 286
Whitstable 355
Who Do You Think You
 Are? Live 271
Wigmore Hall 311
William Morris Gallery
 142
Wilton's Music Hall 342-
 343, *342-343*, 346
Wimbledon 155-156
Wimbledon
 Championships 330
Wimbledon Lawn Tennis
 Museum 156
Wimbledon Park 156
Winchelsea 356
Winston Churchill's
 Britain at War
 Experience 56-57
Wireless Festival 313
Wolseley 108, 216
women 376
Woolwich Arsenal
 141, 149

Woolwich Ferry 149
Woolwich Foot Tunnel
 149
work 376
World Rugby Museum
 157
World War II 27, 113
Wren, Sir Christopher
 22, 34, 35
WWT Wetland Centre
 153

Y

yoga classes 336
Young Vic 53, 346
youth hostels 196
Yvon Lambert 138, 300

Z

Zoo 298
zoos, aquariums & farms
 49, 102, 163, 281

Hotels index

Academy Hotel 173
All Season London
 Southwark Rose 167
Andaz Liverpool Street
 169
Apex City of London
 Hotel 170
Arosfa 174
Aster House 190
B+B Belgravia 187
Base2Stay 194
Bermondsey Square Hotel
 167, 169
Bingham 193
Blakes 189
Boundary 193
Brown's 183
Charlotte Street Hotel 171
Church Street Hotel 193
City Inn Westminster 186
Claridge's 183
Clink Hostel 174
Colonnade 191
Connaught *182*, 183
Covent Garden Hotel
 175
Cumberland 177
Dean Street Townhouse
 & Dining Room 177
Dorchester 183
40 Winks *192*, 193
Fox & Anchor 171, *171*
Garden Court Hotel 182
Garret 194, *195*
Gore 189
Guesthouse West 181
Halkin 189
Hampstead Village
 Guesthouse 192
Harlingford Hotel 173
Haymarket Hotel 185
Hazlitt's 177
Hempel 179

High Road House 194
Hotel Indigo 181, *181*
Hoxton Hotel 193
Jenkins Hotel 175
Lanesborough 189
Lux Pod 190
Malmaison 170
Mayflower Hotel 194
Metropolitan 185
Milestone Hotel &
 Apartments 190
Miller's Residence 179
Montagu Place 178
Morgan 173
Morgan House 187
Myhotel Chelsea 187
New Linden 181
No.5 Maddox Street 185
Number Sixteen 190
One Aldwych 175
Park Plaza County Hall
 169
Pavilion 182
Piccadilly Backpakers 177
Portobello Hotel 179
Premier Inn London
 County Hall 169
Ritz 185
Rockwell 194
Rookery 170
Rose & Crown 191
Rough Luxe 173, *174*
Royal Horseguards 185
San Domenico House 189
Sanctum Soho 177, *178*
Sanderson 173
66 Camden Square 192
Sherlock Holmes Hotel
 178
Soho Hotel 175
St Martins Lane Hotel 175
Stylotel 182
Sumner 178
Threadneedles 170
Trafalgar 187
Twenty Nevern Square
 195
22 York Street 179
26 Hillgate Place 182
Vancouver Studios 182
Vicarage Hotel 191
Windermere Hotel 187
York & Albany *190*, 191
Zetter 171

**Restaurants
& Cafés index**

Albion 223
Amaya 219
Anchor & Hope 197
Arbutus 207
Assaggi 220
Atelier de Joël Robuchon,
 L' 205
Autre Pied, L' 211
Ba Shan 208
Balans 302
Baltic 198
Baozi Inn 207, *207*

Bar Shu 208
Bentley's Oyster Bar &
 Grill 213
Bob Bob Ricard 208
Bocca di Lupo 208
Bodean's 200
Botanist 219
Brick Lane Beigel Bake
 223
Bull & Last *221*, 222
Busaba Eathai 211
Café Anglais, Le 220
Canteen 198
Cha Cha Moon 209
Chaat 224
Chez Bruce 226
Chisou 213
Chutney Mary 219
Cinnamon Club 216
Clarke's 226
Clerkenwell Kitchen 201
Comptoir Gascon, Le 201
Corrigan's Mayfair 213
Dehesa 209
Duke of Cambridge 222
E Pellicci 224
Eagle 201
Eastside Inn 201
Eyre Brothers 224
Fairuz 211
Fernandez & Wells 209
First Out 302
Fish Central 200
Food for Thought 205
Franco Manca *225*, 226
Frizzante@Hackney City
 Farm 279
Fromagerie, La 211
Gallery Mess *217*, 219
Galvin Bistrot de Luxe
 211
Gate 226
Gaucho Piccadilly 215
Geales 221
Giaconda Dining Room
 200, 203
Giraffe 279
Golden Hind 213
Great Queen Street 205
Haché 222
Hereford Road 221
Hibiscus 215
Hix Oyster & Chop House
 201
Hummus Bros 209
Inn the Park 216
Inside 226
J Sheekey 205
Kiasu 221
Ledbury 221
M Manze 198
Madsen 219
Magdalen 198
Maison Bertaux 209
Manna 222
Market 222
Maze 215
Modern Pantry 201
Momo 215
More 199

Mudchute Kitchen 280
Nahm 220
National Dining Rooms 216
Nosh Bar 209
Olivomare 220
Ottolenghi 223
Parlour 215
Pavillion Tea House 226
Petite Maison, La 215
Princi *208*, 209
Providores & Tapa Room 213
Racine 220
Rainforest Café 281
Randall & Aubin 302
Red Fort 209
Restaurant at St Paul's 200
Rhodes W1 213
River Café 226
Roast 199
Rock & Sole Plaice 205
Rosa's 224
Royal China Club 213
S&M Café 223
Saké No Hana 219
Scoop 205, *205*
Scott's 215
Serpentine Bar & Kitchen 220
Sketch: The Parlour 215
Sông Quê 224
Sweetings 200
Taqueria 222
Tate Modern Café: Level 2 281
Tayyabs *222*, 225
Tea Smith 225
TGI Friday's 281
That Place on the Corner 281
Tibits 216
Tom's Kitchen 219
Trois Garçons, Les 225
Tsuru 199
Wahaca 207
Wapping Food 225
Whitechapel Gallery Dining Room 225
Wild Honey 216
Wagamama 223
Wolseley 216
Yauatcha 211
Zuma 220

Pubs & Bars index

Albannach 234
All Star Lanes 229
Amuse Bouche 231
Anglesea Arms 234
Artesian 232
Barcode Vauxhall 305
Blue Bar 234
Boisdale of Belgravia 234
Botanist on the Green 241
Box 305
Bradley's Spanish Bar 229
Cadogan Arms 234
Café Kick 228
Callooh Callay 239
Carpenter's Arms 239
Castle 227
Champagne Bar at St Pancras 229
Commercial Tavern 239
Connaught Bar 233, *234*
Crown & Goose 236
Dalston Superstore 305
Dartmouth Arms 240
Dog & Duck 231
Driver 236
Duke of Wellington 232
Dukes Hotel 234
Effra 240
Fox & Anchor 228
Freedom Bar 306
French House 231
Galvin at Windows 234
G-A-Y Bar 306
George & Dragon 306
Gilgamesh 236
Gipsy Moth 240
Gladstone Arms 227
Gordon's 230
Grapes 239
Green & Red 239
Green Carnation 306
Greenwich Union 240
Hoist 307
Holly Bush 236
Kensington Wine Rooms 233, *233*
KW4 307
LAB 231
Ladbroke Arms 241
Lamb & Flag 230, *231*
Lamb *229*, 230
Loft 240
Lonsdale 233
Lost Angel 240, *241*
Loungelover 239
Lucky Voice 232
Milk & Honey 232
190 Queensgate 236
Only Running Footman 234
Pendulum 307
Portobello Star 233
Princess Louise 230, *232*
Retro Bar 307
Seven Stars 228
1707 234
Shadow Lounge 307
Shochu Lounge 230, *230*
69 Colebrooke Row 236
Skylon 227
St Stephen's Tavern 234
Terroirs 231
Three Kings of Clerkenwell 228
Tini 234
Vertigo 42 Champagne Bar 228
Vinoteca 229
Wenlock Arms 239
White Horse 241
Wine Wharf 227
Yard 307

INDEX

Advertisers' Index

Please refer to the relevant pages for contact details.

Lion King	**IFC**

In Context

Oliver!	**12**
National Maritime Museum	**16**
Royal Observatory	**16**
The Queen's House	**16**
Friendly Rentals	**20**
HMS Belfast	**26**
British Museum	**26**
HMS Belfast	**26**
Imperial War Museum London	**26**
Churchill Museum and Cabinet War Rooms	**26**
Cut Shop	**32**
Lincoln House Hotel	**32**
Strand Palace Hotel	**32**

Sights

London Sea Life Aquarium	**48**
Chelsea Physic Garden	**52**
Ragged School Museum	**52**
London Eye	**52**
Museum of London	**58**
Houses of Parliament	**58**
Museum of London Docklands	**62**
Horniman Museum	**62**
Charles Dickens Museum	**62**
Chiltern Railways	**86**
Freud Museum London	**94**
Thames Rib Experience	**94**
Wallace Collection	**94**
Spencer House	**100**
Geffrye Museum	**100**
Museum of the Order of St John	**100**
Keats House	**100**
V&A	**154**
London Canal Museum	**154**

Consume

Hotels

londontown.com	**168**
Falcon Hotel	**172**
Garden Court Hotel	**172**
Clink Hostel	**172**
Ashlee House	**172**
Hart House Hotel	**176**
University of Westminster	**176**
Stylotel London	**176**
Cardiff Hotel	**180**
Vandon House	**184**
Hampstead Village Guesthouse	**184**
LSE	**184**
Smart Backpackers	**188**

Restaurants & Cafés

Hard Rock Cafe	**202**
The Rock & Sole Plaice	**206**
Bistro 1	**206**
Sagar	**206**
Sông Quê Café	**206**
Puji Puji	**210**
Delhi Brasserie	**210**
Wagamama	**210**
City Spice	**214**
North China	**214**
Signor Sassi	**214**
Maharaja	**214**
Garlic & Shots	**218**
Wok 2 Walk	**218**

Shops

Cass Art	**246**
Natural Shoe Store	**250**
Milroy's of Soho	**250**
Beatles Store	**250**
It's Only Rock 'n' Roll	**250**
The Store Rooms	**256**
Hampstead Antiques & Craft Emporium	**256**
Intoxica!	**260**
Revival Records	**260**
Haggle Vinyl	**260**

Arts & Entertainment

Nightlife

Late Night London	**322**

Theatre

Dirty Dancing	**338**

Escapes & Excursions

Roald Dahl Museum and Story Centre	**354**

Directory

Resources

New York & Co	**370**
londontown.com	**IBC**

INDEX

Maps

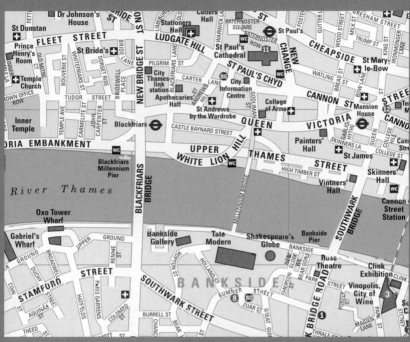

Major sight or landmark	■
Railway or coach station	■
Underground station	⊖
Park	■
Hospital or place of learning	■
Casualty unit	✚
Church	✚
Synagogue	✿
Congestion-charge zone	⊙
District . . . . MAYFAIR	
Theatre	●

Overview Maps   **390**
London Overview   390
Central London by Area   392

Street Maps   **394**
Central London   394
West End   406
Street Index   408

Transport Maps   **416**
London Underground   416

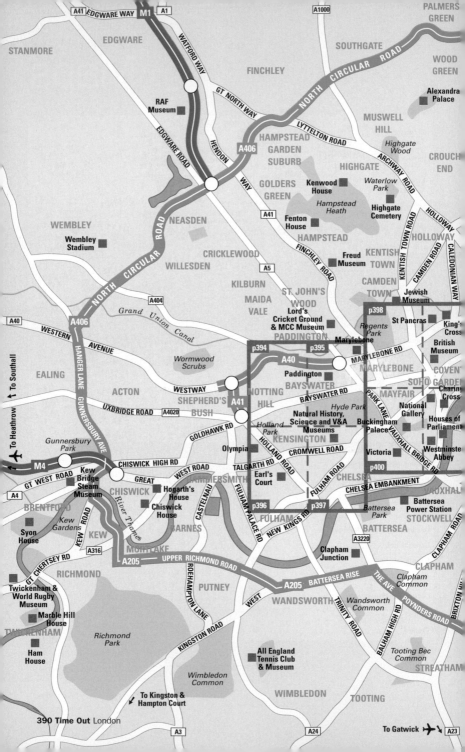

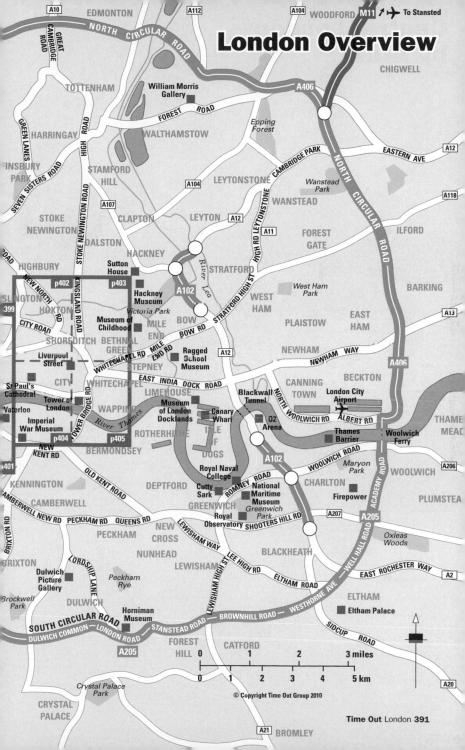

London Overview

© Copyright Time Out Group 2010

Central London
by Area

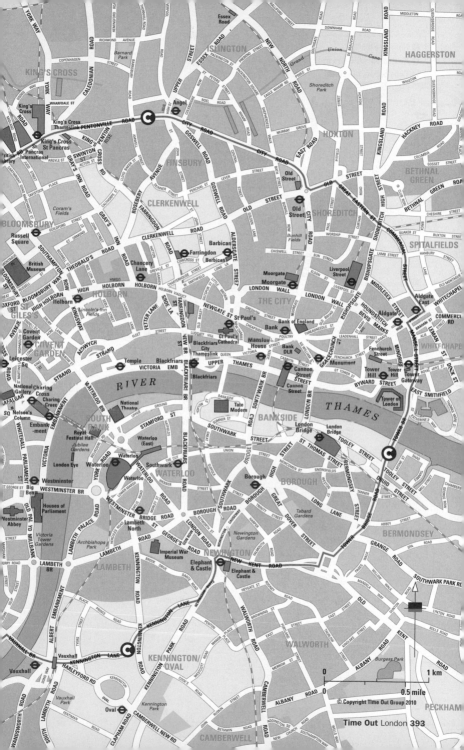

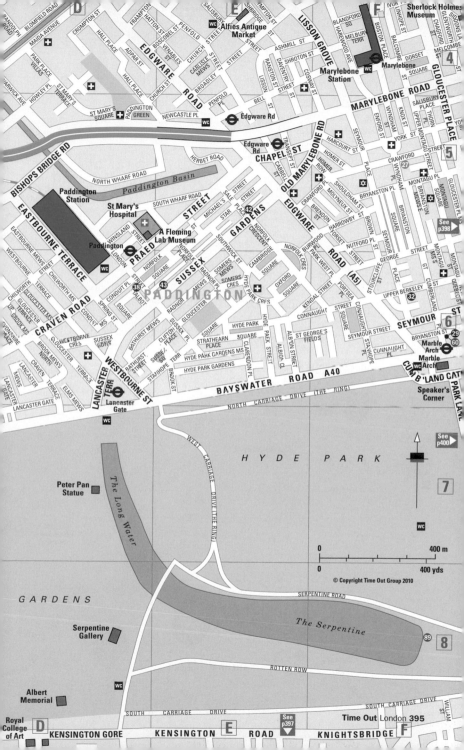

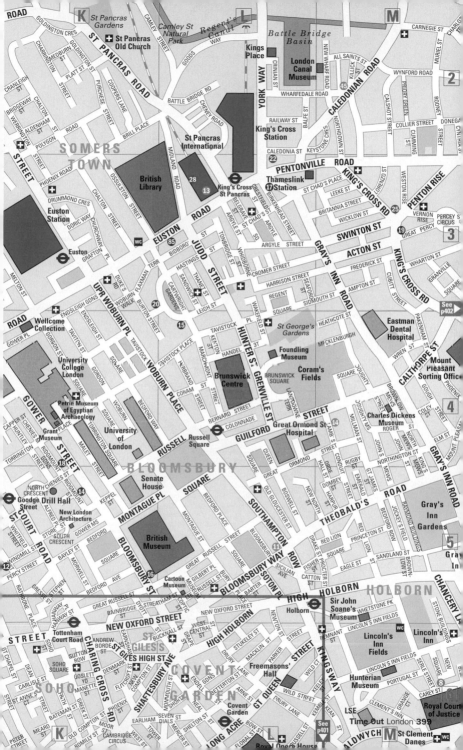

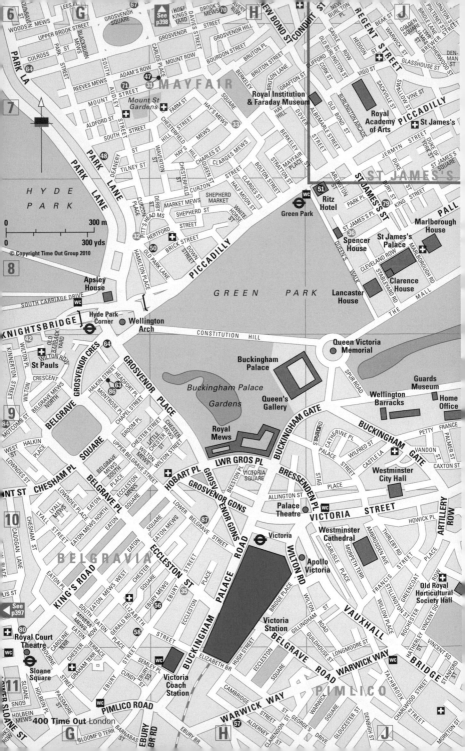

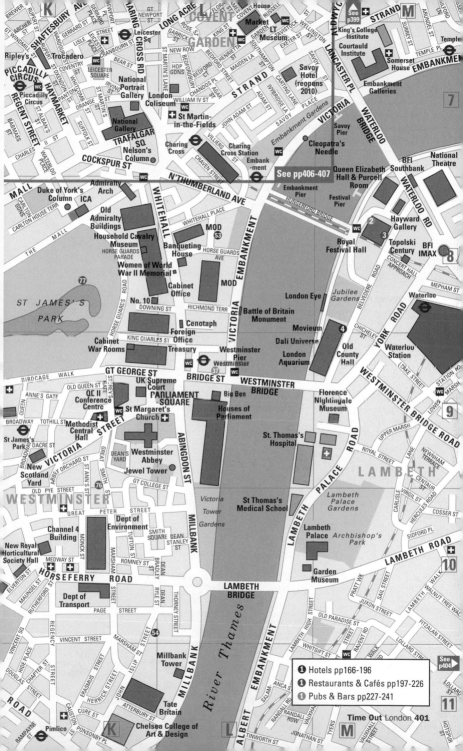

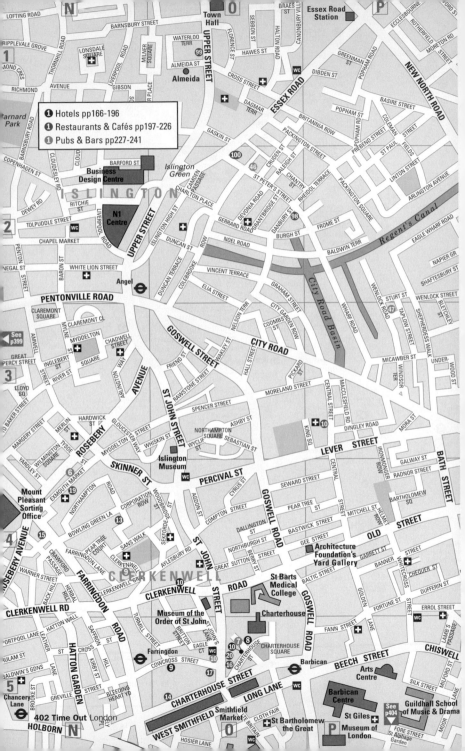

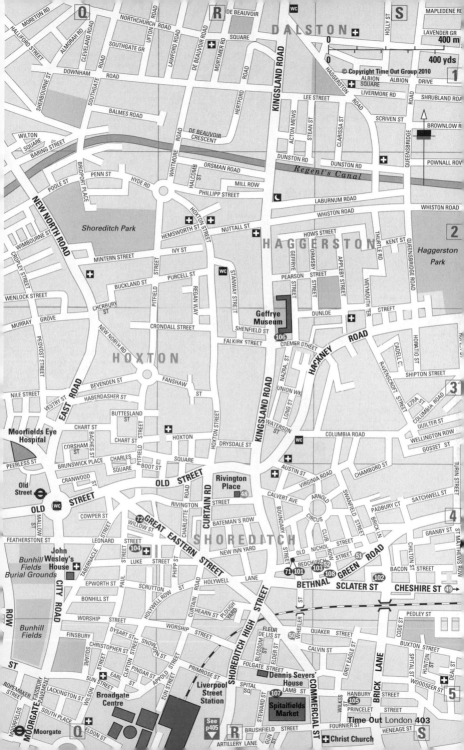

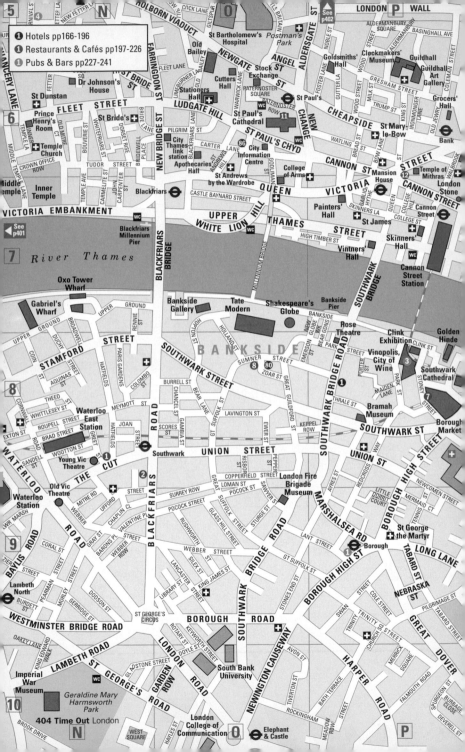

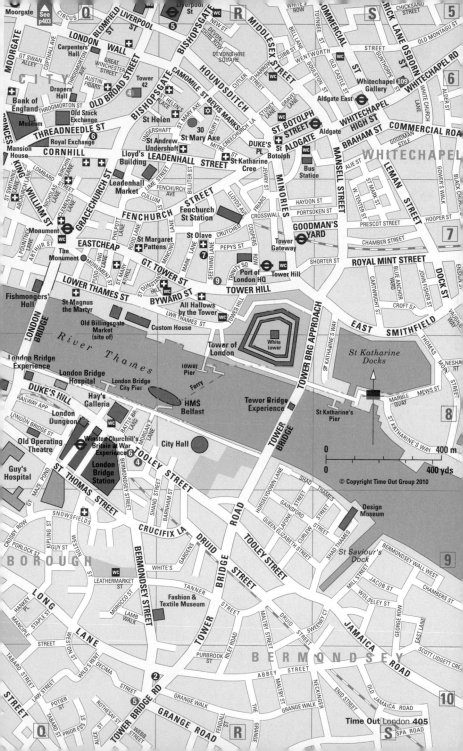

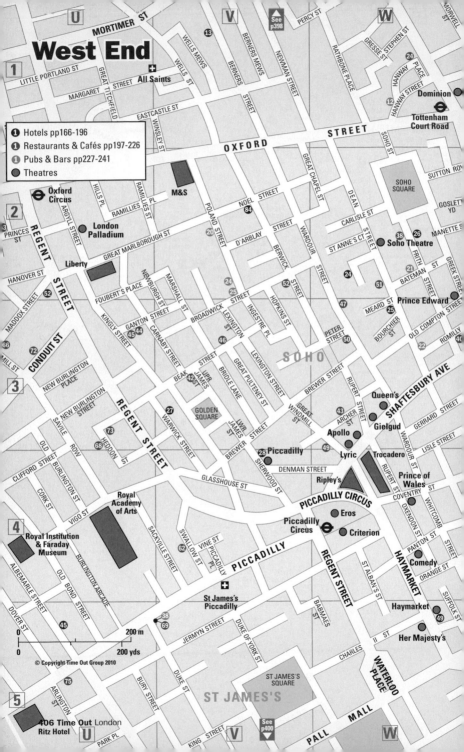

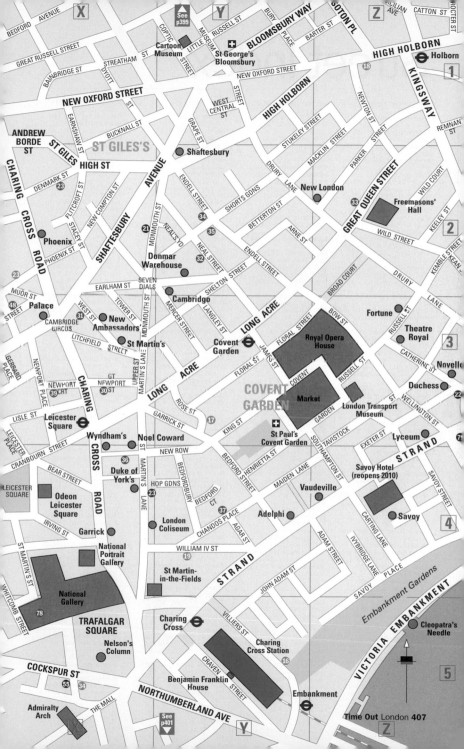

Street Index

Abbey Orchard Street - p401 K9
Abbey Street - p405 R10/S10
Abchurch Lane - p405 Q7
Abingdon Road - p396 A9/B10
Abingdon Street - p401 L9
Abingdon Villas - p396 A9/B9
Acton Mews - p403 R1
Acton Street - p399 M3
Adam & Eve Mews - p396 B9
Adam Street - p401 L7, p407 Z4
Adam's Row - p400 G7
Agar Street - p401 L7, p407 Y4
Agdon Street - p402 O4
Aisgill Avenue - p396 A11/12
Albany Street - p398 H2/3
Albemarle Street - p400 H7/J7, p406 U4/5
Albert Bridge - p397 E13
Albert Bridge Road - p397 E13
Albert Court - p397 D9
Albert Embankment - p401 L10/11
Albert Street - p398 J2
Albion Close - p395 E6
Albion Drive - p403 S1
Albion Square - p403 S1
Albion Street - p395 E6
Aldenham Street - p399 K2
Alder Street - p405 S6
Aldermanbury - p404 P6
Aldermanbury Square - p404 P6
Alderney Street - p400 H11
Aldersgate Street - p404 O6/P5/6
Aldford Street - p400 G7
Aldgate - p405 R6
Aldridge Road Villas - p394 A5
Aldwych - p399 M6
Alexander Square - p397 E10
Alexander Street - p394 B5
Alfred Place - p399 K5
Alfred Road - p394 B4
Alice Street - p405 Q10
Alie Street - p405 S6
All Saints Street - p399 M2
Allen Street - p396 B9/10
Allington Street - p400 H10
Almeida Street - p402 O1
Almorah Road - p403 Q1
Amberley Road - p394 B4
Ambrosden Avenue - p400 J10
Ampton Street - p399 M3
Amwell Street - p402 N3
Andrew Borde Street - p399 K6, p407 X1/2
Angel Street - p404 O6
Anhalt Road - p397 E13
Ann Lane - p397 D13
Ansdell Street - p396 B9
Anselm Road - p396 A12
Appleby Street - p403 S2
Appold Street - p403 Q5/R5
Aquinas Street - p404 N8
Archer Street - p401 K7, p406 W3
Argyle Square - p399 L3
Argyle Street - p399 L3
Argyll Road - p394 A9, p396 A9/B9
Arlington Avenue - p402 P2
Arlington Road - p398 J2
Arlington Street - p400 J8, p406 U5
Armstong Road - p396 A12
Arne Street - p399 L6, p407 Y2
Arnold Circus - p403 R4/S4
Artesian Road - p394 A6
Arthur Street - p405 Q7
Artillery Lane - p403 R5
Artington Way - p402 N3
Arundel Street - p401 M6/7
Aryll Street - p398 J6

Ashbridge Street - p395 E4
Ashburn Gardens - p396 C10
Ashburn Place - p396 C10
Ashburnham Road - p396 C13, p397 D13
Ashby Street - p402 O3
Ashmill Street - p395 E4
Ashwood Mews - p396 C10
Astell Street - p397 E11
Atterbury Street - p401 K11
Aubrey Road - p394 A7/8
Aubrey Walk - p394 A7/8
Augustus Street - p398 J2/3
Austin Friars - p405 Q6
Avery Row - p400 H6
Aybrook Street - p398 G5
Ayers Street - p404 P8/9
Aylesbury Road - p402 O4

Babmaes Street - p401 K7, p406 W5
Baches Street - p403 Q3
Back Church Lane - p405 S6/7
Back Hill - p402 N4
Bacon Street - p403 S4
Bainbridge Street - p399 K5, p407 X1
Baker Street - p398 G4/5
Balcombe Street - p395 F4
Balderton Street - p398 G6
Baldwin Terrace - p402 P2
Baldwin's Gardens - p402 N5
Balfe Street - p399 L2
Balmes Road - p403 Q1
Baltic Street - p402 P4
Bankside - p404 P7
Banner Street - p402 P4
Barclay Close - p396 A13
Barclay Road - p396 A13
Barford Street - p402 N2
Baring Street - p403 Q1/2
Bark Place - p394 B6/7
Barkston Gardens - p396 B11
Barnabas Street - p400 G11
Barnby Street - p398 J3
Barnham Street - p405 Q9
Barnsbury Road - p402 N1/2
Barnsbury Street - p402 N1/O1
Baron Street - p402 N2
Barons Place - p404 N9
Barter Street - p399 L5, p407 Y1/Z1
Bartholomew Square - p402 P4
Basil Street - p397 F9
Basinghall Avenue - p404 P6
Basinghall Street - p404 P6
Basire Street - p402 P1
Bastwick Street - p402 O4/4
Bateman Street - p399 K6, p406 W2
Bateman's Row - p403 R4
Bath Street - p402 P3/4
Bath Terrace - p404 P10
Bathurst Mews - p395 D6
Bathurst Street - p395 D6
Battersea Bridge - p397 E13
Battersea Bridge Road - p397 E13
Battersea Church Road - p397 E13
Battle Bridge Lane - p405 Q8
Battle Bridge Road - p399 L2
Bayley Street - p399 K5
Baylis Road - p404 N9
Bayswater Road - p394 B7/C7, p395 E6/F6
Beak Street - p400 J6, p406 V3
Bear Gardens - p404 P7/8
Bear Lane - p404 O8
Bear Street - p401 K7, p407 X4
Beauchamp Place - p397 F9/10
Beaufort Street - p397 D12
Beaumont Mews - p398 G5
Beaumont Place - p398 J4

Beaumont Street - p398 G5
Bedford Avenue - p399 K5, p407 X1
Bedford Court - p401 L7, p407 Y4
Bedford Gardens - p394 A8/B8
Bedford Place - p399 L5
Bedford Row - p399 M5
Bedford Square - p399 K5
Bedford Street - p401 L7, p407 Y4
Bedford Way - p399 K4
Bedfordbury - p401 L7, p407 Y4
Beech Street - p402 P5
Beeston Place - p400 H9
Belgrave Mews North - p400 G9
Belgrave Mews South - p400 G9
Belgrave Place - p400 G10
Belgrave Road - p400 H10/J11
Belgrave Square - p400 G9
Belgrave Street - p399 L3
Bell Lane - p405 R6
Bell Street - p395 E4/5
Bell Yard - p399 M6
Belvedere Road - p401 M8/9
Bentinck Street - p398 H5
Berkeley Square - p400 H7
Berkeley Street - p400 H7
Bermondsey Street - p405 Q8/9/10
Bermondsey Wall West - p405 S9
Bernard Street - p399 L4
Berners Mews - p398 J5, p406 V1
Berners Street - p398 J5/6, p406 V1
Berry Street - p402 O4
Berwick Street - p398 J6, p399 K6, p406 V2
Bethnal Green Road - p403 R4/S4
Betterton Street - p399 L6, p407 Y2
Bevenden Street - p403 Q3
Bevis Marks - p405 R6
Bickenhall Street - p395 F5
Bidborough Street - p399 L3
Billiter Street - p405 R6/7
Bina Gardens - p396 C11
Bingham Place - p398 G4
Binney Street - p398 G6
Birchin Lane - p405 Q6
Birdcage Walk - p401 K9
Birkenhead Street - p399 L3
Bishops Bridge Road - p394 C5, p395 D5
Bishops Road - p396 A13
Bishopsgate - p405 Q6/R5/6
Black Prince Street - p401 L11/M11
Blackburn Mews - p400 G7
Blackfriars Bridge - p404 O7
Blackfriars Lane - p404 O6
Blackfriars Road - p404 N8, p405 O8
Blackland Terrace - p397 F11
Blandford Square - p395 F4
Blandford Street - p398 G5
Blantyre Street - p397 D13
Bleeding Heart Yard - p402 N5
Bletchley Street - p402 P3
Blithfield Street - p396 B10
Blomfield Road - p394 C4, p395 D4
Blomfield Street - p405 Q5/6
Blomfield Villas - p394 C5
Bloomfield Terrace - p400 G11
Bloomsbury Square - p399 L5
Bloomsbury Street - p399 K5

Bloomsbury Way - p399 L5, p407 Y1
Blossom Street - p403 R5
Blue Anchor Yard - p405 S7
Bolsover Street - p398 H4/J5
Bolton Gardens - p396 B11/C11
Bolton Street - p400 H7/8
Bonhill Street - p403 Q4
Borough High Street - p404 P8/9
Borough Road - p404 O9
Boscobel Street - p395 E4
Boston Place - p395 F4
Boswell Street - p399 L5
Boundary Street - p403 R4
Bourchier Street - p399 K6, p406 W3
Bourdon Street - p400 H7
Bourne Street - p400 G11
Bourne Terrace - p394 B5/C5
Bouverie Street - p404 N6
Bow Lane - p404 P6
Bow Street - p399 L6, p407 Z3
Bowling Green Lane - p402 N4
Brad Street - p404 N8
Braes Street - p402 O1
Braham Street - p405 S6
Bramber Road - p396 A12
Bramerton Street - p397 E12
Bramham Gardens - p396 B11
Bray Place - p397 F11
Bread Street - p404 P6
Bream's Building - p404 N6
Brendon Street - p395 F5
Bressenden Place - p400 H9/J10
Brewer Street - p400 J7, p401 K6, p406 V3/4
Brick Lane - p403 S4/5, p405 S5/6
Brick Street - p400 H8
Bride Lane - p404 N6
Bridewell Place - p404 N6
Bridge Place - p400 H11
Bridge Street - p401 L9
Bridgeway Street - p399 K2
Bridle Lane - p400 J6/7, p406 V3
Bridstow Place - p394 B5
Brill Place - p399 K2
Bristol Gardens - p394 C4
Britannia Road - p396 B13
Britannia Row - p402 P1
Britannia Street - p399 M3
Britten Street - p397 E11
Britton Street - p402 O4/5
Broad Street - p395 E4
Broad Walk - p398 H2/3
Broadley Street - p395 E4
Broadstone Place - p398 G5
Broadway - p401 K9
Broadwell - p404 N7/8
Broadwick Street - p398 J6, p406 V2/3
Brompton Gardens - p397 F9
Brompton Park Crescent - p396 B12
Brompton Place - p397 F9
Brompton Road - p397 E9/10/F9
Brompton Square - p397 E9
Brook Drive - p404 N10
Brook Mews North - p395 D6
Brook Street W1 - p398 H6, p400 H6
Brook Street W2 - p395 E6
Brooke Street - p402 N5
Brook's Mews - p400 H6
Brown Hart Gardens - p398 G6
Brown Street - p395 F5
Brownlow Mews - p399 M4
Brownlow Road - p403 S1
Brownlow Street - p399 M5
Brunswick Gardens - p394 B7/8

STREET INDEX

Brunswick Place - p403 Q3/4
Brunswick Square - p399 L4
Brushfield Street - p403 R5
Bruton Lane - p400 H7
Bruton Place - p400 H7
Bruton Street - p400 H7
Bryanston Mews East - p395 F5
Bryanston Place - p395 F5
Bryanston Square - p395 F5
Bryanston Street - p395 F6
Buckingham Gate - p400 H9/J9
Buckingham Palace Road - p400 H10
Buckland Street - p403 Q2
Bucknall Street - p399 K6/L6, p407 X1
Bulmer Place - p394 A7
Bunhill Row - p402 P4, p403 Q4
Burbage Close - p404 P10
Burdett Street - p404 N9
Burgh Street - p402 O2
Burlington Arcade - p400 J7, p406 U4/5
Burnaby Street - p396 C13
Burnthwaite Road - p396 A13
Burrell Street - p404 O8
Burton Street - p399 K3/4
Burwood Place - p395 E5
Bury Place - p399 L5, p407 Y1
Bury Street EC3 - p405 R6
Bury Street SW1 - p400 J7/8, p406 U5/V5
Bury Walk - p397 E11
Bute Street - p397 D10
Butteslאnd Street - p403 Q3
Buxton Street - p403 S5
Byward Street - p405 Q7/R7
Bywater Street - p397 F11

Cabbell Street - p395 E5
Cadell Close - p403 S3
Cadogan Gardens - p397 F10/11
Cadogan Lane - p400 G10
Cadogan Place - p400 G10
Cadogan Square - p397 F10
Cadogan Street - p397 F10/11
Cale Street - p397 E11
Caledonia Street - p399 L2
Caledonian Road - p399 L2/M2
Callendar Road - p397 D9
Callow Street - p397 D12
Calshot Street - p399 M2
Calthorpe Street - p399 M4
Calvert Avenue - p403 R4
Calvin Street - p403 R5/S5
Cambria Road - p396 C13
Cambridge Circus - p399 K6, p407 X3
Cambridge Street - p400 H11
Camden Passage - p402 O2
Camley Street - p399 K2/L2
Camomile Street - p405 R6
Campden Grove - p394 B8
Campden Hill Gardens - p394 A7
Campden Hill Road - p394 A8/B9
Campden Hill Square - p394 A7
Campden Street - p394 A8/B7
Canning Place - p396 C9
Cannon Street - p404 P6/7
Canonbury Villas - p402 O1
Capper Street - p398 J4, p399 K4
Carburton Street - p398 H4/J4
Cardington Street - p398 J3
Carey Street - p399 M6
Carlisle Lane - p401 M9/10
Carlisle Mews - p395 E4
Carlisle Place - p400 J10
Carlisle Street - p399 K6, p406 W2
Carlton Gardens - p401 K8
Carlton House Terrace - p401 K8
Carlyle Square - p397 E12
Carmelite Street - p404 N7
Carnaby Street - p398 J6, p406 U3/V3
Carnegie Street - p399 M2
Caroline Terrace - p400 G10

Carriage Drive North - p397 F13
Carriage Drive West - p397 F13
Carter Lane - p404 O6
Carting Lane - p401 L7, p407 Z4
Carton Street - p398 G5
Cartwright Gardens - p399 L3
Cartwright Street - p405 S7
Castle Baynard Street - p404 O7
Castle Lane - p400 J9
Cathcart Road - p396 C12
Catherine Place - p400 J9
Catherine Street - p401 M6, p407 Z3
Catton Street - p399 L5/M5, p407 Z1
Causton Street - p401 K11
Cavendish Square - p398 H5/6
Caversham Street - p397 F12
Caxton Street - p400 J9, p401 K9
Cedarne Road - p396 B13
Centaur Street - p401 M9
Central Avenue - p397 F13
Central Street - p402 P3/4
Chadwell Street - p402 N3
Chagford Street - p395 F4
Chalton Street - p399 K2/3
Chamber Street - p405 S7
Chambers Street - p405 S9
Chancel Street - p404 O8
Chancery Lane - p399 M5, p404 N6
Chandos Place - p401 L7, p407 Y4
Chandos Street - p398 H5
Chantry Street - p402 O2
Chapel Market - p402 N2
Chapel Side - p394 B6/7
Chapel Street NW1 - p395 E5
Chapel Street SW1 - p400 G9
Chaplin Close - p404 N9
Chapter Street - p401 K11
Charing Cross Road - p399 K6, p401 K7, p407 X2/3/4
Charles II Street - p401 K7, p406 W5
Charles Square - p403 Q3/4
Charles Street - p400 H7
Charlotte Road - p403 R4
Charlotte Street - p398 J5, p399 K5
Charlotte Terrace - p399 M2
Charlton Place - p402 O2
Charlwood Street - p400 J11
Charrington Street - p399 K2
Chart Street - p403 Q3
Charterhouse Square - p402 O5
Charterhouse Street - p402 O5
Cheapside - p404 P6
Chelsea Embankment - p397 F12
Chelsea Manor Street - p397 E11/12
Chelsea Park Gardens - p397 D12
Chelsea Square - p397 D11/E11
Cheltenham Terrace - p397 F11
Cheney Road - p399 L2
Chenies Mews - p399 K4
Chenies Street - p399 K5
Chepstow Crescent - p394 A6
Chepstow Place - p394 B6
Chepstow Road - p394 A5/B6
Chepstow Villas - p394 A6
Chequer Street - p402 P4
Cherbury Street - p403 Q2
Chesham Place - p400 G9
Chesham Street - p400 G10
Cheshire Street - p403 S4
Chesson Road - p396 A12
Chester Gate - p398 H3
Chester Mews - p400 H9
Chester Road - p398 H3
Chester Row - p400 G10/11
Chester Square - p400 G10
Chester Street - p400 G9/H9
Chester Terrace - p398 H3
Chesterfield Hill - p400 H7
Chesterfield Street - p400 H7/8

Cheval Place - p397 E9
Cheyne Mews - p397 E12
Cheyne Row - p397 E12
Cheyne Walk - p397 D13/E12/13
Chicheley Street - p401 M8
Chichester Road - p394 B5
Chicksand Street - p405 S5
Chiltern Street - p398 G5
Chilton Street - p403 S4
Chilworth Mews - p395 D6
Chilworth Street - p395 D6
Chippenham Mews - p394 A4/5
Chiswell Street - p402 P5, p403 Q5
Chitty Street - p398 J5
Christchurch Street - p397 F12
Christopher Street - p403 Q5
Church Square - p404 P9
Church Street - p395 D5/E4
Churchway - p399 K3
Cirencester Street - p394 B4
City Garden Row - p402 O3
City Road - p402 O3/3, p403 Q4/5
Clabon Mews - p397 F10
Clanricarde Gardens - p394 B7
Claremont Square - p402 N3
Clarence Gardens - p398 H3/J3
Clarendon Place - p395 E6
Clarendon Street - p400 H11
Clareville Grove - p397 D10
Clareville Street - p397 D10
Clarges Mews - p400 H7/8
Clarges Street - p400 H7/8
Clarissa Street - p403 S1
Clement's Inn - p399 M6
Clements Lane - p405 Q7
Clerkenwell Close - p402 N4
Clerkenwell Green - p402 N4
Clerkenwell Road - p402 N4/O4
Cleveland Road - p403 Q1
Cleveland Row - p400 J8
Cleveland Square - p394 C6
Cleveland Street - p398 J4/5
Cleveland Terrace - p394 C5/6, p395 D5
Clifford Street - p400 J7, p406 U4
Clifton Gardens - p394 C4
Clifton Place - p395 E6
Clifton Street - p403 Q5
Clifton Villas - p394 C4
Clink Street - p404 P8
Clipstone Mews - p398 J4
Clipstone Street - p398 J5
Cloth Fair - p402 O5
Cloudesley Road - p402 N1/2
Cloudesley Square - p402 N1/2
Cloudesley Street - p402 N1/2
Club Row - p403 S4
Cobb Street - p405 R6
Cobourg Street - p398 J3
Cock Lane - p404 O5
Cockspur Street - p401 K7, p407 X5
Code Street - p403 S4/5
Coin Street - p404 N8
Cole Street - p404 P9
Colebrook Row - p402 O2
Coleherne Mews - p396 B11/12
Coleherne Road - p396 B11/12
Coleman Fields - p402 P1/2
Coleman Street - p404 P6
College Hill - p404 P7
College Street - p404 P7
Collier Street - p399 M2
Collingham Mews - p396 C10
Collingham Place - p396 B10
Collingham Road - p396 C10/11
Colombo Street - p404 N8
Colonnade - p399 L4
Columbia Road - p403 S3
Colville Road - p394 A6
Colville Terrace - p394 A6
Commercial Road - p405 S6
Commercial Street - p403 R5/S5, p405 S5/6
Compton Street - p402 O4
Concert Hall Approach - p401 M8
Conduit Mews - p395 D6

Conduit Place - p395 D6
Conduit Street - p400 H7/J6, p406 U3
Connaught Place - p395 F6
Connaught Square - p395 F6
Connaught Street - p395 E6/F6
Constitution Hill - p400 H8/9
Conway Street - p398 J4
Coombs Street - p402 O3
Coomer Place - p396 A12
Coopers Lane - p399 K2
Coopers Row - p405 R7
Cope Place - p396 A9
Copenhagen Street - p402 N2
Copperfield Street - p404 O8
Copthall Avenue - p405 Q6
Coptic Street - p399 L5, p407 Y1
Coral Street - p404 N9
Coram Street - p399 L4
Cork Street - p400 J7, p406 U4
Cornhill - p405 Q6
Cornwall Gardens - p396 C10
Cornwall Road - p404 N8
Corporation Row - p402 N4
Corsham Street - p403 Q3
Cosser Street - p401 M10
Cosway Street - p395 E4/F5
Cottesmore Gardens - p396 C9
Coulson Street - p397 F11
Courtfield Gardens - p396 B10/11
Courtfield Road - p396 C10
Courtnell Street - p394 A5/6
Covent Garden - p401 L6/7, p407 Y3/Z3
Coventry Street - p401 K7, p406 W4
Cowcross Street - p402 O5
Cowper Street - p403 Q4
Cramer Street - p398 G5
Cranbourn Street - p401 K7, p407 X3/4
Cranleigh Street - p398 J2
Cranley Gardens - p397 D11
Cranley Mews - p397 D11
Cranley Place - p397 D11
Cranwood Street - p403 Q4
Craven Hill - p394 C6
Craven Hill Gardens - p394 C6
Craven Road - p395 D6
Craven Street - p401 L7, p407 Y5
Craven Terrace - p395 D6
Crawford Passage - p402 N4
Crawford Place - p395 E5/F5
Crawford Street - p395 F5
Creechurch Lane - p405 R6
Cremer Street - p403 R3
Cremorne Road - p396 C13, p397 D13
Cresswell Place - p396 C11
Crestfield Street - p399 L3
Crinian Street - p399 L2
Croft Street - p405 S7
Cromer Street - p399 L3
Crompton Street - p395 D4
Cromwell Mews - p397 D10
Cromwell Place - p397 D10
Cromwell Road - p396 B10/C10/D10
Crondall Street - p403 Q3/R3
Cropley Street - p403 Q2
Crosby Row - p405 Q9
Cross Street - p402 O1
Crosswall - p405 R7
Crown Office Row - p404 N6
Crowndale Road - p398 J2, p399 K2
Crucifix Lane - p405 Q9/R9
Cruden Street - p402 O1/2
Crutched Friars - p405 R7
Cubbit Street - p399 M3
Culford Gardens - p397 F11
Cullum Street - p405 Q7/R7
Culross Street - p400 G7
Cumberland Gate - p395 F6
Cumberland Market - p398 H3/J3
Cumberland Terrace - p398 H2/3
Cumming Street - p399 M2

STREET INDEX

STREET INDEX

Cundy Street - p400 G11
Cure Street - p401 K11
Curlew Street - p405 R9/S9
Cursitor Street - p404 N6
Curtain Road - p403 R4
Curzon Place - p400 G8
Curzon Street - p400 H7/8
Cutler Street - p405 R6
Cynthia Street - p399 M2
Cyrus Street - p402 O4

Dacre Street - p401 K9
Dagmar Terrace - p402 O1
Dallington Street - p402 O4
Danbury Street - p402 O2
Danube Street - p397 E11
Danvers Street - p397 D12/E12
D'Arblay Street - p398 J6, p406 V2
Darlan Road - p396 A13
Dartmouth Close - p394 A5
Daventry Street - p395 E4/5
Davies Mews - p398 H6
Davies Street - p398 H6, p400 H6/7
Dawes Road - p396 A13
Dawson Place - p394 B6
De Beauvoir Crescent - p403 Q1
De Beauvoir Road - p403 R1
De Beauvoir Square - p403 R1
De Vere Gardens - p394 C9, p396 C9
Deal Street - p403 S5
Dean Bradley Street - p401 K10/L10
Dean Ryle Street - p401 K10/L10
Dean Stanley Street - p401 L10
Dean Street - p399 K6, p406 W2/3
Deanery Street - p400 G7
Dean's Yard - p401 K9
Decima Street - p405 Q10
Delamere Terrace - p394 C4
Denbigh Road - p394 A6
Denbigh Street - p400 J11
Denbigh Terrace - p394 A6
Denman Street - p400 J7, p406 V4/W4
Denmark Street - p399 K6, p407 X2
Denyer Street - p397 F10
Derby Street - p400 H8
Dering Street - p398 H6
Derry Street - p396 B9
Deverell Street - p404 P10
Devonia Road - p402 O2
Devonshire Close - p398 H4/5
Devonshire Mews South - p398 H5
Devonshire Mews West - p398 H4
Devonshire Place - p398 G4/H4
Devonshire Place Mews - p398 G4
Devonshire Row - p405 R6
Devonshire Square - p405 R6
Devonshire Street - p398 H4
Devonshire Terrace - p395 D6
Dewey Road - p402 N2
Dibden Street - p402 P1
Dilke Street - p397 F12
Dingley Road - p402 P3
Dock Street - p405 S7
Dodson Street - p404 N9
Dombey Street - p399 M5
Donegal Street - p399 M2, p402 N2
Doric Way - p399 K3
Dorset Rise - p404 N6
Dorset Square - p395 F4
Dorset Street - p398 G5
Doughty Mews - p399 M4
Doughty Street - p399 M4
Douglas Street - p401 K11
Douro Street - p396 C9
Dove Mews - p396 C11
Dovehouse Street - p397 E11/12
Dover Street - p400 H7/J7, p406 U5

Down Street - p400 G8/H8
Downham Road - p403 Q1
Downing Street - p401 K8/L8
Doyle Street - p404 O10
Drake Street - p399 M5
Draycott Avenue - p397 E10/F12
Draycott Place - p397 F11
Draycott Terrace - p397 F10
Drayton Gardens - p396 C11, p397 D11/12
Drayton Mews - p394 B8
Druid Street - p405 R9/S10
Drummond Crescent - p399 K3
Drummond Street - p398 J3/4
Drury Lane - p399 L6/M6, p407 Y2/Z2/3
Drysdale Street - p403 R3
Duchess of Bedford's Walk - p394 A8
Duchess Street - p398 H5
Duchy Street - p404 N8
Dufferin Street - p402 P4
Duke of York Street - p400 J7, p406 V5
Duke Street - p398 G6
Duke Street, St James's - p400 J7/8, p406 V5
Duke's Hill - p405 Q8
Dukes Lane - p394 B8
Duke's Place - p405 R6
Duke's Road - p399 K3
Duncan Street - p402 O2
Duncan Terrace - p402 O2
Dunloe Street - p403 S3
Dunraven Street - p400 G6
Dunston Road - p403 R2/S2
Durham Terrace - p394 B5
Dyott Street - p399 L6, p407 X1
Dysart Street - p403 Q5

Eagle Court - p402 O4/5
Eagle Street - p399 M5
Eagle Wharf Road - p402 P2, p403 Q2
Eardley Crescent - p396 B11
Earl Street - p403 Q5
Earlham Street - p399 K6/L6, p407 X2
Earl's Court Square - p396 B11
Earl's Court Gardens - p396 B10
Earl's Court Road - p396 A9/10/B10/11
Earls Walk - p396 E10
Earnshaw Street - p399 K6, p407 X1/2
East Lane - p405 S9
East Road - p403 Q3
East Smithfield - p405 S7
Eastbourne Mews - p395 D5/6
Eastbourne Terrace - p395 D5/6
Eastcastle Street - p398 J5/6, p406 U1/V1
Eastcheap - p405 Q7
Eaton Mews - p400 H10
Eaton Place - p400 G9/10
Eaton Square - p400 G10/H10
Eaton Terrace - p400 G10/12
Ebury Bridge - p400 H11
Ebury Bridge Road - p400 G11
Ebury Mews - p400 H10
Ebury Square - p400 G11
Ebury Street - p400 G10/11/H10
Ecclesbourne Road - p402 P1
Eccleston Mews - p400 G9
Eccleston Place - p400 H10
Eccleston Square - p400 H11
Eccleston Street - p400 G10/H10
Edge Street - p394 A7
Edgware Road - p395 D4/E4/5
Edith Grove - p396 C12/13
Edith Terrace - p396 C13
Edward Mews - p398 G6
Edwardes Square - p396 A9/10
Effie Road - p396 A13/B13
Egerton Crescent - p397 E10
Egerton Gardens - p397 E10
Egerton Terrace - p397 E10
Elcho Street - p397 E13

Elder Street - p403 R5
Eldon Road - p396 C9
Eldon Street - p403 Q5
Elia Street - p402 O2
Elizabeth Avenue - p402 P1, p403 Q1
Elizabeth Bridge - p400 H11
Elizabeth Street - p400 G10/H10
Elkstone Road - p394 A4
Elliot's Row - p404 O10
Elm Park Gardens - p397 D11/12
Elm Park Lane - p397 D12
Elm Park Road - p397 D12
Elm Place - p397 D11
Elm Street - p399 M4
Elms Mews - p395 D6
Elvaston Place - p396 C9, p397 D9
Elverton Street - p401 K10
Ely Place - p402 N5
Elystan Place - p397 F11
Elystan Street - p397 E11
Emerald Street - p399 M5
Emerson Street - p404 O8
Emperor's Gate - p396 C10
Endell Street - p399 L6, p407 Y2
Endsleigh Gardens - p399 K3/4
Endsleigh Street - p399 K4
Enford Street - p395 F5
Enid Street - p405 S10
Ennismore Gardens - p397 E9
Ennismore Mews - p397 E9
Ensign Street - p405 S7
Epirus Road - p396 A13
Epworth Street - p403 Q4
Erasmus Street - p401 K11
Errol Street - p402 P4
Essex Road - p402 O1/P1
Essex Street - p401 M6
Essex Villas - p396 A9
Eustace Road - p396 A13
Euston Road - p398 J4, p399 K3/4/L3/4
Euston Street - p398 J3
Evelyn Gardens - p397 D11
Eversholt Street - p398 J2, p399 K3
Ewer Street - p404 O8
Exeter Street - p401 L7, p407 Z3
Exhibition Road - p397 D9/10
Exmouth Market - p402 N4
Exton Street - p404 N8

Fabian Road - p396 A13
Falkirk Street - p403 R3
Falmouth Road - p404 P10
Fann Street - p402 P5
Fanshaw Street - p403 R3
Farm Lane - p396 A13/B13
Farm Street - p400 H7
Farringdon Lane - p402 N4
Farringdon Road - p402 N4/5
Farringdon Street - p404 N6/O6
Fashion Street - p405 S5
Fawcett Street - p396 C12
Featherstone Street - p403 Q4
Fenchurch Avenue - p405 R7
Fenchurch Street - p405 Q7/R7
Fendall Street - p405 R10
Fenelon Place - p396 A10
Fernshaw Road - p396 C12/13
Fetter Lane - p404 N6
Finborough Road - p396 B12/C12
Finsbury Circus - p403 Q5, p405 Q5
Finsbury Pavement - p403 Q5
Finsbury Square - p403 Q5
First Street - p397 E10
Fisher Street - p399 L5
Fitzalan Street - p401 M10
Fitzhardinge Street - p398 G6
Fitzroy Square - p398 J4
Fitzroy Street - p398 J4
Flaxman Terrace - p399 K3
Fleet Lane - p404 O6
Fleet Street - p404 N6
Fleur de Lis Street - p403 R5

Flitcroft Street - p399 K6, p407 X2
Flood Street - p397 E12/F12
Flood Walk - p397 E12
Floral Street - p399 L6, p401 L6, p407 Y3
Florence Street - p402 O1
Foley Street - p398 J5
Folgate Street - p403 R5
Fore Street - p402 P5
Formosa Street - p394 C4
Forset Street - p395 F5/6
Fortune Street - p402 P4
Foster Lane - p404 P6
Foubert's Place - p398 J6, p406 U2
Foulis Terrace - p397 D11
Fournier Street - p403 S5
Frampton Street - p395 D4
Francis Street - p400 J10
Franklin's Row - p397 F11
Frazier Street - p404 N9
Frederick Street - p399 M3
Friend Street - p402 O3
Frith Street - p399 K6, p406 W2/3
Frome Street - p402 P2
Fulham Broadway - p396 A13/B13
Fulham Road - p396 A13/B13/C12/13/D12, p397 D11/12/E11
Furnival Street - p404 N5

Gainsford Street - p405 R9/S9
Galway Street - p402 P3/4
Gambia Street - p404 O8
Garden Row - p404 O10
Garlichythe - p404 P7
Garrick Street - p401 L7
Garway Road - p394 B6
Gaskin Street - p402 O1
Gate Place - p397 D10
Gaunt Street - p404 O10
Gee Street - p402 O4/4
Geffrye Street - p403 R2
George Row - p405 S9
George Street - p395 F5/6, p398 G5
Gerald Road - p400 G10
Gerrard Road - p402 O2
Gerrard Street - p401 K6/7, p406 W3
Gerridge Street - p404 N9
Gertrude Street - p397 D12
Gibson Road - p401 M11
Gibson Square - p402 N1
Gilbert Place - p399 L5
Gilbert Street - p398 H6
Gillingham Street - p400 H10/J10
Gilston Road - p396 C12
Giltspur Street - p404 O5
Gladstone Street - p404 N10/O10
Glasshill Street - p404 O9
Glasshouse Street - p400 J7, p406 V4
Glebe Place - p397 E12
Gledhow Gardens - p396 C11
Glendower Place - p397 D10
Glentworth Street - p395 F4
Gloucester Gate - p398 H2
Gloucester Mews - p395 D6
Gloucester Place - p395 F5, p398 G5/6
Gloucester Place Mews - p395 F5
Gloucester Road - p396 C9/10
Gloucester Square - p395 E6
Gloucester Street - p400 J11
Gloucester Terrace - p394 C5, p395 D6
Gloucester Walk - p394 B8
Gloucester Way - p402 N3
Godfrey Street - p397 E11
Godliman Street - p404 O6
Golden Lane - p402 P4/5
Golden Square - p400 J7, p406 V3
Goldington Crescent - p399 K2
Goldington Street - p399 K2